The Jewish World
in Modern Times

About the Book and Authors

The momentous events of modern Jewish history have led
to a proliferation of books and articles on Jewish life over
the last 350 years. Placing modern Jewish history into both
universal and local contexts, this selected, annotated
bibliography organizes and categorizes the best of this vast
array of written material. The authors have included all
English-language books of major importance on world Jewry
and on individual Jewish communities, plus books most
readily available to researchers and readers, and a select
number of pamphlets and articles. The resulting bibliography is also a guide to recent Jewish historiography and
research methods.

The authors begin with an essay that introduces the
reader to the broad scope of Jewish history, describing
briefly the key events, personalities, and movements that
have shaped it since the mid-seventeenth century. Part I
is a treatment of the Jewish world as a whole. Part II,
organized geographically, deals with individual Jewish
communities. After citing regional surveys, the authors
treat each country separately in alphabetical order. Entries
are extensively cross-referenced, and author, title, and
subject indexes are included.

Abraham J. Edelheit, an instructor in history at Touro
College, New York City, holds degrees from Yeshiva and
Brandeis Universities in modern Jewish history. Hershel
Edelheit is a student, researcher, and speaker on the
Holocaust.

The Jewish World in Modern Times

A Selected, Annotated Bibliography

Abraham J. Edelheit
and Hershel Edelheit

Westview Press
BOULDER, COLORADO

Mansell Publishing Limited
LONDON, ENGLAND

Published in 1988 in the United States of America by Westview Press, Inc.;
Frederick A. Praeger, Publisher; 5500 Central Avenue, Boulder, Colorado 80301

Published in 1988 in Great Britain by Mansell Publishing Limited, 6 All Saints
Street, London N1 9RL

Library of Congress Cataloging-in-Publication Data
Edelheit, Abraham J.
    The Jewish world in modern times: a selected, annotated
bibliography/by Abraham J. Edelheit and Hershel Edelheit.
        p.   cm.
    Includes indexes.
    ISBN 0-8133-0572-1
    1. Jews--History--Bibliography.   I. Edelheit, Hershel.
II. Title.
Z6372.E25   1988
[DS117]
016.909'04924--dc19   87-35200
                                                               CIP
British Library Cataloguing in Publication Data
The Jewish World in modern times: a
  selected, annotated bibliography.
  1. Jewish civilization, 1600-1988.
  Bibliographies
I. Edelheit, Abraham J.   II. Edelheit,
Hershel
016.909'04924
ISBN 0-7201-1988-X

Printed and bound in the United States of America

6   5   4   3   2   1

Dedicated to

Rabbi and Mrs. Amos Edelheit

Contents

17 The Land of Israel   415

18 Africa, Asia, and the Pacific   445

19 Bibliographies and Guides   458

Preface

For the Jewish world the twentieth century has been truly momentous. From the depths of Gehenna to which the Jewish world was plunged by Nazi Germany, to the rebirth of Israel, the march of Jewish events has been a rapid and often bewildering one. Teachers, students, and interested laypersons need access to a wide range of sources in a number of languages that would offer them a proper understanding of historical developments and their context. This fact became obvious to us while working on our BIBLIOGRAPHY ON HOLOCAUST LITERATURE [1986]. To fill this gap, we decided to author a selective bibliography covering modern Jewish history. The most important books on world Jewry and on individual Jewish communities would be cited, categorized, and annotated. When no "best" book was available, then we would annotate the books most readily accessible to both the general public and those with specific interest in Judaica. In addition, we decided to include pamphlets and articles selected from a small number of scholarly periodicals. That, in brief, constitutes the present bibliography.

The authors make no claim about the comprehensiveness of the bibliography. Citations are limited only to books, articles, and pamphlets that we actually saw. We have restricted ourselves to works in English, despite the existence of important materials in Hebrew, Yiddish, and all European languages. Although many important books have been published on Jewish history in almost every modern language, most such books and periodicals are accessible only to a small part of the American Jewish reading public.

In general, the annotations cover the book, its contents, and the methodology used by the author. Where appropriate, we have not refrained from offering criticism of glaring problems, whether methodological or factual, of some of the

works. Foreign terms quoted in the annotations have been
cited in the original language and transliterated. Definitions for all such terms will be found in the glossary.
Edited books have been cited and, in all cases, annotated.
Multi-authored anthologies of independent essays have their
contents listed as part of the annotation. Such essays are
not cross-referenced, nor do they appear in the index. The
contents of anthologies, whether of one author or of collec-
tions of primary sources, are not so listed. Finally,
materials that were not actually published, i.e., mimeo-
graphed or other limited-circulation materials, were not
cited at all, since their availability outside of major
research libraries was doubtful.

Part I deals with the Jewish world as a whole. Books and
a limited number of pamphlets and articles are cited in this
section, which is organized thematically. It will be noted
that a few books dealing with pre-modern Jewry are also
included. These provide necessary background and are of
special historiographical or methodological importance. Of
necessity some of the chapters in Part I are only introductory. In particular, the chapter on the Holocaust offers a
very abbreviated selection. Readers wishing more material on
that subject are referred to the authors' BIBLIOGRAPHY ON
HOLOCAUST LITERATURE [Boulder, CO: Westview Press, 1986].
Books and articles belonging in more than one section are
cross-referenced to the extent possible, although full citations and annotations are not repeated. Obviously, cross-
referenced books could not be cited in every place where
they might belong. In particular, most of the surveys cited
in the first chapter contain sections relating to almost
every chapter in the book.

Part II deals with individual Jewish communities. We have
organized this part of the book by geographical regions,
beginning with Central Europe. Each chapter follows the same
basic order: After the citation of surveys covering the
region as a whole, the countries are arranged in alphabetical order. We have tried to include as many communities as
possible; unfortunately, some communities still lack a
historian or a chronicler. Here again, materials will be
cross-referenced when necessary.

We have subdivided national sections into appropriate
thematic categories when the amount of material warranted
additional rubrics, but we have not used the same categories
for every country. The emphases of historians obviously
differ in light of specific events in each country.

Three indexes - an author, a title, and a subject index -
have been included and should help interested readers find

books and articles on related topics.

The appended introductory essay serves to complement the book citations and is an attempt to portray the broad scope of modern Jewish history. We have sought to describe briefly the key events, personalities, and movements that have shaped Jewish history since the mid-seventeenth century. The essay suggests one way to reconstruct the past 350 years of Jewish history. Other approaches, equally valid, are suggested by the cited books and articles. To paraphrase Hillel - the rest is commentary, go and study it.

This project could not have come to fruition if not for the kind assistance rendered to the authors by the following individuals and institutions.

The librarians and staff of the Brooklyn and New York Public libraries. Although we cannot list their names individually we owe each of them a debt of gratitude. Dr. Robert M. Seltzer of Hunter College made valuable suggestions about the citations included. Allen Wollman and Marc Rose helped with the proofreading. To Mrs. Ann Edelheit, mother and wife, for her patience and encouragement. Finally, we also thank Ms. Susan L. McEachern, the editors, and staff of Westview Press who helped turn this project into reality.

Nonetheless, all mistakes are ours and do not reflect upon the aforementioned individuals.

A.J.E.
H.E.

Index of Periodicals
and Abbreviations

* in bibliography indicates pamphlet
\> in bibliography indicates cross-reference

Introduction: The Outline
of Modern Jewish History

The historian attempting to study the Jewish community in modern times faces a complex task. Until the mid-seventeenth century, Jews were a fairly homogeneous group that could be studied with relative ease, but this homogenity no longer prevailed after the 1650s. Even the periodization of modern Jewish history presents difficulties of definition and analysis. A precise periodization that would lay bare the inner structure of modern Jewish history requires one to trace the stages of overall development while allowing for regional differences. It is the necessity of keeping local conditions in mind that creates a distinct problem for historians and students. In a word, in the modern era, different parts of the Jewish world developed in separate ways. Moreover, it must be noted that trends in Jewish history do not always coincide conceptually or chronologically with their European counterparts.

At least with regard to European Jewry, the modern period can be divided into five sub-eras, each reflecting a different stage in the Jewish accommodation with modernity. Each sub-era represents a step in the continuing redefinition of Judaism and Jewishness, a process affected by contemporaneous ideologies, mores, and sociopolitical conditions. These five periods are [1] 1650-1750, a transitional period from medieval to modern life; [2] 1750-1789, an era of greater Jewish receptivity to the modern age – an acceptance that, however, was not reciprocated by the outside world during the period in question; [3] 1789-1881, the era of Jewish emancipation and entry into the mainstream of European civilization; [4] 1881-1948, a period of Jewish readjustment to new internal and external realities; [5] 1948 to the present, the post-modern period wherein Jews adjust to the advent of national sovereignty and independence.

1

In general this periodization also applies to Jews living
outside of the European sphere of influence, particularly in
the Muslim world. It must, however, be noted that Jews in
modern times never really entered the mainstream of Muslim
civilization; even when they acculturated, the balance
struck between the host society and the Jewish community was
the result of conditions that arose in a much earlier
period. When dealing with Muslim-Jewish relations in modern
times, one must realize that the accommodation between
Muslims and Jews dates to the early medieval era. In the
eyes of the Islamic faithful, the place of the Jewish
dhimmis and their role in society remains constant even
though world perceptions, and subjective Jewish viewpoints,
may change. The future of relations between Jews and Arabs
cannot be charted at this time; yet it is clear that the
Arab desire to return Jews to their pre-State condition is
neither possible nor desirable, irrespective of the desire
of certain elements in the Arab world to turn back the
clock.

The years 1650-1750 represent a period of transition
during which the Jewish world suffered both internal and
external crises and found itself in a state of flux. The
disasters that accompanied the Cossack uprising [1648-1649]
and subsequent events in Poland as well as the Shabbatean
heresy [1660s] and its Frankist offshoot in eastern Europe
were external symbols of crisis. They also attested deep
internal divisions, which can be traced back to the Marrano
problem of the late fifteenth century. The expulsion of the
Jews from Spain and the continuing and problematic existence
of crypto-Jews [Marranos] in and out of Spain created divi-
siveness, dissatisfaction, and tension within the Jewish
world. These divisions played themselves out during the late
seventeenth and early eighteenth centuries. Although the
divisions were primarily social or economic and had political overtones, disunity was also expressed in intellectual
terms.

The culmination of these tensions was the false messianism of Shabbetai Zevi. The subsequent conversion of the
"messiah" to Islam nearly rent the Jewish world. His death
[1676] did not completely heal the wounds, and for the first
time the Jewish community had to contend and coexist with a
largely disaffected, clandestine sub-culture. Although we
will never know how many secret Shabbateans remained, it
appears that some of them influenced Jewish life by encouraging the creation of a religiously neutral, secular
society. Like the Marranos before them, they no longer lived
as Jews, but the Shabbateans also found Christianity and

Islam unacceptable; they therefore sought some other state of being.

Arising out of similar dissatisfaction with the state of affairs in the Jewish community at the time, but unrelated to Shabbateanism, was Baruch [Benedict] Spinoza. The scion of a Marrano family, Spinoza found much to criticize, even in the relative security of tolerant Amsterdam. Spinoza, in his writings, took the Marrano crisis to its [in his eyes] logical conclusion. Unable to accept ancient conventions, he sought the complete dissolution of Judaism, since he believed Judaism was no longer viable in light of modern social and political realities.

Equally divisive, but in a different way, was hasidism, which arose in eastern Europe in the mid-eighteenth century. Hasidism absorbed the messianic fervor of Lurianic kabbalism, while neutralizing its messianic activism. Stressing the cosmic importance of halakhah and the need to preserve the morale of the Jewish everyman, hasidism, nevertheless, fostered disunity within East European Jewry.

The important contribution of hasidism was the reorientation of Jewish mystical thought away from metaphysical contemplations and toward a more humanistic mysticism dealing with human problems and frailties. The emphasis on hallowing the profane and the notion of perfectibility through the zaddik made hasidism an appealing movement for poor and uneducated Jews. The movement begun by Israel ben Eliezer, the Ba´al-Shem-Tov, soon spread from Podolia northward and westward, entrenching itself in Jewish communities that needed both psychological and moral rejuvenation. Hasidism did not, by and large, gain adherents in Lithuania. There the yeshivot, with their emphasis on intellectual accomplishment, continued to hold sway. In the meritocracy of the yeshivah world, such hasidic concepts as devekut and hitlahavut played only a secondary role, if even that.

Significantly, the period between 1650 and 1750 also saw a shift in the center of gravity of European and world Jewry. Jews who had moved to eastern Europe as a result of expulsions and persecutions now returned westward. Edicts expelling Jews during the thirteenth and fourteenth centuries were rescinded when Jews were permitted to reside in England [1665] and France [1723], while a new Jewry was founded by the landing of twenty-three Sephardim in New Amsterdam in September 1654. Economically, socially, and intellectually, the Jews of western Europe once again came to the fore.

Symbolizing this new shift was the emphasis of western European Jews on efforts to reach an accommodation with

European society while retaining Jewish identity. Thus the
second era in modern Jewish history, 1750-1789, saw the rise
of a Jewish enlightenment primarily, though not exclusively,
based in Germany. While no single event can be seen as
representing the period of the Haskalah, it is possible to
describe it by reference to Moses Mendelssohn.

Mendelssohn, like Spinoza, reacted to the challenge
facing Jews who sought integration into an enlightened society. Mendelssohn sought entrance into European society while
at the same time justifying continued Jewish identity and
survival. Mendelssohn´s ideal society, as presented in
JERUSALEM [1783], would be free of religious coercion and
would in general remain religiously neutral. All religious
groups would be permitted to develop to the fullest in this
pluralistic society. Thus, Jews could survive with a double
identity - as citizens and Jews. Although at first glance
this modus vivendi might seem problematic because it had not
been attempted before, in reality, Jews would receive
nothing more than any other religious group living in a
secular [neutral] society.

The major difference between this period and those preceding and following it stems, not from Jewish considerations, but rather from the change in attitude of the European nation-states toward the Jews. By the mid-eighteenth
century people friendly to the Jews throughout western and
central Europe were calling for an "improvement" of Jewish
status, in other words, emancipation. To be sure, this call
for civic equality for Jews had as much to do with the
exigencies of the modern state as with any particular Jewish
need. The modern nation-state could no longer tolerate
autonomous political and cultural entities in its midst.
Either one was a part of the organic national entity or one
was not; if not, then one was automatically an alien, and
perhaps an enemy of the nation. However, the debate for and
against emancipation accomplished nothing in the half-
century under review. Nevertheless, the attitudinal change
was indicative of broader trends in both Jewish and non-
Jewish society in western and central Europe.

The third period, 1789-1881, represented the accommodation of Jewish society to modernity and the Jewish entry
into European society. Ushered in by the French Revolution,
we can date this period with the emancipation of French
Jewry in 1791, although American independence [1776] also
offers a convenient date. Over the next century Jews were
emancipated in England [1858], Italy [1867], and Germany
[1871]. In turn, new social realities as well as new ideas
became important throughout world Jewry.

The tension between trying to be a good Jew and trying to be a good citizen had almost immediate consequences, which were felt in every Jewish community. On the most basic level there was a need to reorganize the Jewish community on religious, as opposed to national, lines. This reorganization occurred most notably in post-emancipation Germany and France, although American Jewry and even the unemancipated Jews of eastern Europe also found their communities largely, if not completely, transformed. As a result of the transformation of Jewish communal life, and the external pressure upon Jews to "change" in order to be worthy of emancipation, a process of religious reform also began, again primarily in western Europe. Living as they did in a less developed environment, Jews in eastern Europe tended to lag behind those in the west in this regard. In fact, the process of religious reform was to a large extent ignored by secular Jews in Russia and Poland. Reform Judaism was also ignored by large numbers of Jews in western Europe who sought entry into modern society through assimilation or the complete surrender of all individual Jewish characteristics.

Over time, the three formulas – denationalization, religious reform, and assimilation – played themselves out differently among various communities. As has already been noted, religious reform did not take root in eastern Europe, though rampant secularization did. Jews in England, Germany, and America experienced both religious reform and secularization, with the former taking on the characteristics of an almost mass movement. French Jewry also experienced large-scale assimilation and secularization, yet never really experienced a major reform movement. Even while their traditional communities were collapsing, French and English Jewry were reorganized as governmentally recognized religious minorities via the Consistory and the Chief Rabbinate, respectively. The Jewish community as an organized body never existed per se in the United States, where a voluntary community structure emerged. A similarly anarchic situation of local communities – the gemeinde – lacking any national center, existed in Germany until the 1890s.

The different nuances of modernization can also be discerned on an individual level. All Jewish thinkers and communal leaders were aware of the problems facing organized Judaism and all proposed solutions. Differences arose primarily on the question of the extent to which they hoped to maintain Jewish law and tradition. Thus Samson Raphael Hirsch's neo-Orthodoxy differed from Abraham Geiger's Reform Judaism with regard to the status of halakhah and not on the definition of Judaism as a religious entity. The same may be said about other movements, particularly for the "Positive-Historical" [Conservative] branch of Judaism and its leading thinker Zechariah Frankel.

As the drama of the emancipation unfolded, newer ideologies emerged and in turn influenced the Jewish community. Perhaps the two most important were romanticism and historicism.

Romanticism was a nineteenth-century reaction to the Enlightenment and would be most influential later in Jewish history and historiography. The romanticist idea that the group is more than merely the sum of its parts and that the group as a whole possesses some form of organic life would influence a younger generation of Jewish thinkers who flourished at a later date. Romanticism was also a major influence on the growing nationalism of the early nineteenth century and would later feed into the antisemitic crusade that culminated in nazism.

During the early part of the nineteenth century, historicism, or Wissenschaft des Judentums, as it was more commonly known, was more influential than romanticism, especially in Germany. The Wissenschaft was at once an idea, a method, and an organization, that sought to apply modern historical methods to the history of the Jews. This was not, however, mere academicism, since the Wissenschaftlichers also had a clear religious and political agenda. The latter was a response to the continuing crisis created by emancipation. By showing Judaism to be a "great" religion, Jews were proved to be "worthy" of civil rights. Similarly, by proving the existence of a multiplicity of Judaisms in the past, one could prove the permissibility of modern heterodoxy. These ideological angles notwithstanding, the Wissenschaft also opened an entirely new method for the understanding of Judaism and broadened the types of sources and methods used to understand Jewish history. More fundamentally, the Wissenschaft established a new focal point: Jewish history was no longer only the history of Judaism but also the story of the Jews.

The fourth period in modern Jewish history, 1881-1948, was, once again, a period of crisis and ferment. Jews sought a new accommodation with social, political, economic, and historical realities; some of these were internal, others external. Significantly, the focus of Jewish history again shifted - to eastern Europe, Palestine, and the United States. Depressed economic conditions, the failure of emancipation and assimilation, and the outbursts of violence in Russia in 1881-1882 led to a renewed ferment within the Jewish community as well as a major migratory movement wherein approximately five million Jews left eastern Europe.

Jews were now obliged to formulate new approaches to Jewish survival and to reevaluate the previous century of Jewish history. As the crisis of the so-called Jewish problem spread to western Europe, the Americas, and the Middle East, new ideologies emerged. The primary Jewish response to the crisis was to turn inward. The prevalence of nationalism and its application to the Jewish case brought three nationalist ideologies to the fore. Folkism, as propounded by Simon Dubnow, accepted the idea of Jewish nationalism and posited that Jews are a political entity. The Folkists, however, saw no need for a specific Jewish territory nor any utility in emigration. Rather, they believed that a renewed kehillah on a nationwide basis and guarantees for Jewish cultural autonomy would suffice to permit Jews the cultural and political expression they sought. The second emerging ideology was Bundism, or Jewish socialist nationalism. The Bundists adopted a form of Dubnow's diaspora nationalism and combined it with an intense revolutionary fervor that presumed that Jews would find peace only with the establishment of a truly just and egalitarian socialist society.

Thus, diaspora nationalism saw no ultimate utility in emigration, whereas zionism, and its schismatic offshoot of territorialism, saw no long-term ability for Jews to survive in Europe. Zionism sought the solution to the Jewish problem through the creation of a Jewish state in Palestine and the subsequent normalization of Jewish-gentile relations. For Zionists the problem was not that society at large no longer accepted Jewish membership nor that social inequalities caused considerable suffering for individual Jews. Rather, the Zionists saw these problems as symptoms of a worse malady - Jews suffered primarily because they were homeless. Thus, Jewish dispersion was the cause of antisemitism, and palliatives such as a renewed kehillah or social justice could not, in the Zionist view, solve the fundamental problem of Jewish powerlessness. Only a Jewish homeland would.

It must be emphasized that not all Zionists subscribed to the Herzlian concept of mass evacuation. Ahad Ha'am, for example, presumed the continued existence of diaspora Jewry. Zion, in his view, need not be an independent, sovereign state, but a cultural and social entity that would solve the more pressing problems of Jewish identity.

External factors settled the internal Jewish debates, which, by the 1920s, had become even more fractious. The rise of the Nazis, the free world's abandonment of the Jews,

and the Final Solution settled the problem once and for all.
The Holocaust proved to be the worst phase in the history of
Jewish powerlessness. The Jewish people, having descended
past the seventh level of Gehenna, concluded that only one
option remained - to fight for survival with all means
available. The death of the six million might thus be seen
as the denouement of the previous two centuries. The Nazis
had repudiated the emancipation; Jews now repudiated assimilation and, on 5 Iyyar 5708 [May 14, 1948], the Jewish
state was born.

The forty years since the establishment of the State of
Israel, representing the fifth era in modern Jewish history,
have brought about a new social and political reality.
Although it is impossible to describe in full the changes
that have occurred in the Jewish world since that time, it
is clear that the development of the last three hundred
years has not yet come to an end and, it is hoped, never
will.

PART 1

The Jewish World

1

Surveys of Jewish History

OVERVIEWS

1. Alpher, Joseph [ed.]: ENCYCLOPEDIA OF JEWISH HISTORY: EVENTS AND ERAS OF THE JEWISH PEOPLE. New York: Facts on File, 1986. 288 pp., apps., chron., gloss., index.

Chronologically organized, encyclopedic review of Jewish history. Each entry covers a period or topic in an extensive way. Illustrations are integrated into, and form a major part of, each entry. The entries themselves are short summaries of topics or periods of importance in Jewish history and each entry is written by an expert in the field. All the entries are cross-referenced, thus bringing together all related subjects. The book includes a general introduction by Shmuel Ettinger, "Major Themes in the History of the Jewish People," as well as 19 appendixes covering a variety of topics not discussed in the main text.

2. Baron, Salo W.: THE JEWISH COMMUNITY: ITS HISTORY AND STRUCTURE TO THE AMERICAN REVOLUTION. 3 vols. Philadelphia: JPS, 1942. 1,312 pp., notes, bibliog., index.

The first systematic study of the history, ideology, and organization of the Jewish community as it developed over the course of history. Baron begins with communal organization during the First Commonwealth. Also important as a contribution to the study of Jewish political and social history. Part I is a chronological study of Jewish communal organization. Part II deals with communal life in a thematic way. In addition to deepening the reader´s understanding of the Jewish community, the book is a superior example of a comparative history of Jews in various lands and periods.

9

3. ___ : A SOCIAL AND RELIGIOUS HISTORY OF THE JEWS. 2nd
Edition. Philadelphia: JPS / New York: Columbia Univ. Press,
1952-1983. 8,106 pp. + 163 pp. index volume, notes.

A masterful and authoritative review of Jewish history
from ancient times to the early modern period [ca. 1650].
The original edition, [1937] comprised three volumes which
analyzed the main themes in Jewish history. The most
important contribution of the first edition was Baron's
emphasis on the positive elements in Jewish life and his
opposition to the so-called lachrymose conception of Jewish
history, which reduced Jewish history to a story of scholars
and martyrs. In his emphasis on social, political, and
intellectual elements, Baron, virtually created a revolution
in Jewish historiography. The second edition [1952] is
greatly enlarged, being more synthetic and based on a wider
range of sources. In the most recently published, and in
future volumes of this work in progress, the histories of
lesser known Jewish communities broaden and complete Baron's
analysis.

Published Volumes: 1. TO THE BEGINNING OF THE CHRISTIAN ERA
(1952): 415 pp. / 2. CHRISTIAN ERA: THE FIRST FIVE CENTURIES
(1952): 436 pp. / 3. HEIRS OF ROME AND PERSIA (1957): 340
pp. / 4. MEETING OF EAST AND WEST (1957): 352 pp. / 5. RE-
LIGIOUS CONTROLS AND DISSENSIONS (1957): 416 pp. / 6. LAWS,
HOMILIES, AND THE BIBLE (1958): 486 pp. / 7. HEBREW LANGUAGE
AND LETTERS (1958): 321 pp. / 8. PHILOSOPHY AND SCIENCE
(1958): 405 pp. / 9. UNDER CHURCH AND EMPIRE (1965): 350
pp. / 10. ON THE EMPIRE'S PERIPHERY (1965): 432 pp. / 11.
CITIZEN OR ALIEN CONJURER (1967): 422 pp. / 12. ECONOMIC
CATALYST (1967): 359 pp. / 13. INQUISITION, RENAISSANCE, AND
REFORMATION (1969): 463 pp. / 14. CATHOLIC RESTORATION AND
WARS OF RELIGION (1969): 412 pp. / 15. RESETTLEMENT AND EX-
PLORATION (1973): 550 pp. / 16. POLAND-LITHUANIA, 1500-1650
(1976): 460 pp. / 17. BYZANTINES, MAMELUKES, AND MAGHRIBIANS
(1980): 434 pp. / 18. THE OTTOMAN EMPIRE, PERSIA, ETHIOPIA,
INDIA, AND CHINA (1983): 620 pp.

4. Ben-Sasson, Haim Hillel [ed.]: A HISTORY OF THE JEWISH
PEOPLE. Trans. from the Hebrew by Weidenfeld and Nicolson.
Cambridge, MA: Harvard Univ. Press, 1976. 1,170 pp., maps,
illus., bibliog., index.

Authoritative survey of Jewish history from the period
before the Israelite conquest of Canaan until the 1970s.
Written by six Israeli historians, each an expert in his own

field. Not especially important for its methodological nov-
elties, the book is significant as a synthetic work. A wide
number of topics is dealt with in each era, with emphasis
on the development of Jewish society and religion. Comprehensive in scope, the book is extremely useful as a study
and teaching guide.

CONTENTS: A. Malamat: Origins and the Formative Period / H.
Tadmor: The Period of the First Temple, The Babylonian Exile
and the Restoration / M. Stern: The Period of the Second
Temple / S. Safrai: The Era of the Mishnah and Talmud / H.
H. Ben-Sasson: The Middle Ages / S. Ettinger: The Modern
Period.

   5. ___ and Shmuel Ettinger [eds.]: JEWISH SOCIETY THROUGH
THE AGES. New York: Schocken Books, 1971. 352 pp., notes,
bibliog., index.

Anthology reviewing Jewish history. Originally prepared
under the auspices of UNESCO and published in the Journal of
World History. Most of the essays are defined geographically
and chronologically, though some are thematic. Each is written by a recognized scholar, and all are noteworthy. Especially outstanding are Dinur´s essay "Jewish History - Its
Uniqueness and Continuity" and Werblowsky´s "Messianism in
Jewish History." Dinur´s essay is important as a systematic effort at a historiographical interpretation of Jewish history.

CONTENTS: B. Z. Dinur: Jewish History - its Uniqueness and
Continuity / R. J. Z. Werblowsky: Messianism in Jewish
History / Hayim Tadmor: "The People" and the Kingship in
Ancient Israel: the Role of Political Institutions in the
Biblical Period / Y. F. Baer: Social Ideals of the Second
Jewish Commonwealth / M. Stern: The Hasmonean Revolt and its
Place in the History of Jewish Society and Religion / D. G.
Flusser: The Social Message from Qumran / E. E. Urbach: The
Talmudic Sage - Character and Authority / Shmuel Safrai:
Elementary Education, its Religious and Social Significance
in the Talmudic Period / S. D. Goitein: Jewish Society and
Institutions under Islam / I. Twersky: Aspects of the Social
and Cultural History of Provencal Jewry / H. H. Ben-Sasson:
The "Northern" European Jewish Community and its Ideals / H.
Beinart: Hispano-Jewish Society / C. Roth: Jewish Society in
the Renaissance Environment / Shmuel Ettinger: The Hasidic
Movement - Reality and Ideals / J. Katz: The Jewish National
Movement: a Sociological Analysis / Moshe Mishkinsky: The

Jewish Labor Movement and European Socialism / Lloyd P.
Gartner: Immigration and the Formation of American Jewry,
1840-1925 / S. N. Eisenstadt: Israeli Society Major Features
and Problems / H. H. Ben-Sasson: Dynamic Trends in Modern
Jewish Thought and Society.

6. de Lange, Nicholas: ATLAS OF THE JEWISH WORLD. New
York: Facts on File, 1984.   240 pp., maps, illus., chron.,
charts, gloss., bibliog., index.

Cartographic study of Jewish history, culture, and life.
Primary emphasis is on the modern era, though de Lange's
coverage of the ancient and medieval periods is adequate.
Maps supplement de Lange's text, and both are nicely complemented by the book's profuse illustrations. The book may
be broadly divided into three parts: the first section is a
survey of Jewish history; the second is a survey of Jewish
culture, identity, and religion; and the third offers a
review of the state of world Jewry today. Fifteen special
features offer insight into specific topics and shed even
more light on Jewish beliefs and practices.

7. Dubnow, Simon: HISTORY OF THE JEWS. Trans. from the
Russian by M. Spiegel. South Brunswick, NJ: Thomas Yoseloff,
1967-1973. 4,323 pp., apps., bibliog.

Massive synthetic history of the Jews by the dean of East
European Jewish historians. Covers the broad sweep of Jewish
history from the First Commonwealth to the rise of Hitler,
with special emphasis on social and sociological history.
The English translation is based on the definitive Russian
edition which was published in Riga in 1938. An interesting
sidelight to the book and its author is provided by the
sense of foreboding in Dubnow's foreword; the author was
murdered by the Nazis in Riga in 1941.
    Long considered a masterful reconstruction of Jewish his-
tory, much of Dubnow's analysis has been superseded. In particular Dubnow's acceptance of the veracity of the so-called
lachrymose concept of Jewish history [see #3 and #11] has
been largely, though not completely overturned. Nevertheless, the book retains historiographical and methodological
interest. Also noteworthy are the supplementary studies
appended to each volume, which add insight to significant
events, concepts, and individuals from the Jewish past.

Published Volumes: 1. FROM THE BEGINNING TO EARLY CHRISTIAN-
ITY (1967): 904 pp. / 2. FROM THE ROMAN EMPIRE TO THE EARLY

MEDIEVAL PERIOD (1968): 853 pp. / 3. FROM THE LATER MIDDLE
AGES TO THE RENAISSANCE (1969): 862 pp. / 4. FROM CROMWELL´S
COMMONWEALTH TO THE NAPOLEONIC ERA (1971): 789 pp. / 5. FROM
THE CONGRESS OF VIENNA TO THE EMERGENCE OF HITLER (1973):
915 pp.

8. Eban, Abba: HERITAGE: CIVILIZATION AND THE JEWS. New
York: Summit Books, 1984. 354 pp., illus., index.

Profusely illustrated popular history of the Jews, based
on Eban´s twelve-part PBS-TV series in 1984. Eban explores
the 5,000-year evolution of Jewish civilization and the
connections between Jews and the cultures of the world.
Breaking no new ground, the book is most important for its
interpretations.

9. ___: MY PEOPLE: THE STORY OF THE JEWS. New York:
Behrman / Random House, 1968. 534 pp., illus., index.

General survey of Jewish history by an eminent Israeli
statesman. Primarily aimed at explaining the Jewish people
to non-Jews, friend and foe alike. The book is organized
chronologically. Modern Jewish history, and especially the
twentieth century, is the central focus. The book is not a
scholarly history, but rather a popular synthetic volume; it
is profusely illustrated. A two-volume adaptation, designed
for younger readers, has been published for use as a school
text. In addition, workbooks and a teachers´ guide make Eban
the most accessible textbook on Jewish history for elementary and high schools.

10. Finkelstein, L. [ed.]: THE JEWS: THEIR HISTORY; THEIR
RELIGION AND CULTURE; THEIR ROLE IN CIVILIZATION. 3 vols.
New York: Schocken Books, 1970 [Rep. of 1949 Ed.]. 1,552
pp., maps, notes, bibliog., index.

Three-volume anthology on Judaism, Jews, and Jewish history. Offers a review of nearly every aspect of Jewish life
over the last 5,000 years. Divided thematically and chronologically, with each era and topic surveyed by a noted
historian. In addition to the narrow confines of Jewish
history, the authors attempt to place Jewish civilization
into its global context. Primarily important as a synthetic
work, the books lend themselves to use in introductory
college level courses on Judaic studies.

CONTENTS: Volume I. THE JEWS: THEIR HISTORY. W. F. Albright:

The Biblical Period / Elias J. Bickerman: The Historical
Foundations of Postbiblical Judaism / J. Goldin: The Period
of the Talmud / Cecil Roth: The European Age in Jewish History; The Jews of Western Europe / Israel Halpern: The Jews
in Eastern Europe / B. D. Weinryb: East European Jewry /
Izhak Ben-Zvi: Eretz Yisrael under Ottoman Rule / Anita L.
Lebeson: The American Jewish Chronicle.

* For contents of vols. 2 and 3 see > chaps. 4 and 5.

11. Graetz, Heinrich: POPULAR HISTORY OF THE JEWS. Edited
by Alexander Harkavy; Trans. from the German by A. B. Rhine.
Revised Edition. New York: Hebrew Pub. Co., 1949. 2,444 pp.,
illus., app., index.

English translation of the multivolume survey of Jewish
history by the most important Jewish historian of the nineteenth century. A number of different editions in German,
English, and Hebrew exist, but all are basically the same.
Some of the original chapters have been rearranged and a
supplemental volume was added to the Rhine edition. Written
by Max Raisin, the supplement took up where Graetz left off
and corrected some of Graetz´s more controversial viewpoints
[see #34]. The text itself has been largely superseded, but
still retains some historiographical interest.
 Graetz was the proponent of the so-called lachrymose conception of Jewish history. This posited a tragic and heroic
nature to the Jews´ past and portrayed Jewish history as the
story of scholars and martyrs. Unfortunately, such a concept
ignored the development of Jewish society. Graetz also
tended to view key personalities of the past through Jewish
eyes. He thus lionized those non-Jews who were friendly
toward Jews, and excoriated those who, like Martin Luther,
attacked Jews. Graetz´s orientation led some historians to
view him as a precursor of Jewish nationalism, especially of
zionism.

Published Volumes: 1. FROM THE FORMATION OF THE NATION TO
THE DEATH OF ANTIGONUS THE ASMONEAN: 499 pp. / 2. FROM THE
REIGN OF HEROD I TO THE DEATH OF MOHAMMED: 526 pp. / 3. FROM
THE COMING OF THE JEWS UNDER THE DOMINATION OF THE ISLAM TO
THEIR FIRST EXPULSION FROM FRANCE: 420 pp. / 4. FROM THE
FIRST EXPULSION OF THE JEWS FROM FRANCE TO THE SETTLEMENT OF
DON JOSEPH NASSI IN TURKEY: 453 pp. / 5. FROM THE REIGN OF
STEPHEN BATORY OF POLAND TO THE PRESENT TIME [1873]: 546 pp.

12. Grayzel, Solomon: A HISTORY OF THE JEWS: FROM THE
BABYLONIAN EXILE TO THE PRESENT, 5728-1968. Philadelphia:
JPS, 1968. 768 pp., maps, bibliog., index.

Survey of Jewish history, especially useful in high-
school courses. Begins with the reconstruction of Jewish
life during the Babylonian Exile. The survey is divided into
chapters, which are subdivided into paragraph-length sections. Coverage is thus extensive, but sometimes super-
ficial. While most of the sections are chronological in
their development, a few are topical. The most recent edition covers contemporary events through the Six-Day War.

13. Kedourie, Elie [ed.]: THE JEWISH WORLD: HISTORY AND
CULTURE OF THE JEWISH PEOPLE. New York: Harry N. Abrams
Pub., 1979. 328 pp., illus., chron., bibliog., index.

Collection of essays which, together, form a general
survey of Jewish history. The book aims at answering three
questions: why have Jews survived? how are Jews unique? what
constitutes Jewishness? Each author is an expert in his own
field and attempts to answer the questions as they relate to
the specific period or topic covered. Purely historical
chapters alternate with chapters on the internal history of
world Jewry and on Jewish literature and philosophy.

CONTENTS: H. W. F. Saggs: Pre-Exilic Jewry / H. Maccoby:
The Bible / Zvi Yavetz: The Jews and the Great Powers of the
Ancient World / Jacob Neusner: The Talmud / A. Shiloah: The
Ritual and Music of the Synagogue / Haim Beinart: The Jews
in Spain / A. Grossman: The Jews in Byzantium and Medieval
Europe / Shlomo D. Goiten: The Jews under Islam 6th-16th
Centuries / A. Cohen: The Jews under Islam c.1500-Today /
A. Hyman: Jewish Philosophy / R. J. Zvi Werblowsky: Jewish
Mysticism / S. Ettinger: The Jews and the Enlightenment /
Ezra Spicehandler: Jewish Literature: Fiction / T. Carmi:
Poetry / L. Kochan: European Jewry in the 19th and 20th
Centuries / Oscar Handlin: American Jewry / A. Hertzberg:
Judaism and Modernity / David Vital: Zionism and Israel.

14. Keller, Werner: DIASPORA: THE POST-BIBLICAL HISTORY
OF THE JEWS. Trans. from the German by R. and C. Winston.
New York: Harcourt, Brace and World, 1969. 522 pp., illus.,
bibliog., index.

Survey of Jewish history from Roman times to the establishment of Israel. Keller was trained as a lawyer, worked

as a journalist, and is a historian by avocation. The key
events and personalities of Jewish history are synthesized
in each of the chapters. Nothing new is uncovered, but the
book is a useful review. Included is a chapter "A History of
the Jews in America" by Ronald Sanders.

15. Margolis, Max L. and A. Marx: A HISTORY OF THE JEWISH
PEOPLE. New York: Meridian, 1959. 803 pp., bibliog., index.

Possibly the best one-volume survey of Jewish history
from the biblical period to the 1920s. Covers the subject
chronologically and quite in-depth, considering the size of
the volume and the amount of material to be covered. Heavi-
est emphasis is on the First [21 chapters] and the Second
[14 chapters] Temple periods. Coverage of social, political,
and intellectual history is fairly balanced. A useful study
aid is the placement of dates at the top of most pages, so
that chapters and sections can be placed in chronological
context. Unfortunately, the text ends with 1925 and the book
lacks the crucial events of the last sixty years.

16. Mazar, Benjamin and M. Davis [eds.]: THE ILLUSTRATED
HISTORY OF THE JEWS. New York: Israeli Publishing Institute,
1963. 414 pp., illus., index.

Concise illustrated history of the Jews, written by a
group of Israeli historians. Some of the chapters are
broader, especially those on the Middle Ages, while others
are very narrowly constructed, e.g., the chapter on Bar
Kokhba. This leads to certain imbalance, only partly compen-
sated for by the copious illustrations. Greatest emphasis is
on the modern era, especially on the twentieth century. The
text is written in simple style and is good for laymen and
students.

CONTENTS: S. Yeivin: From Fathers to Saul / Ch. Tadmor: The
House of David / J. Liver: Exile and Return / Menachem
Stern: Hellenistic and Roman Periods / S. Safrai: Bar-
Kochba and Crisis in the Old East / H. H. Ben-Sasson: The
Jews in the Middle Ages / Shmuel Ettinger: The Renaissance
and Modern Times / Jack Cohen: The Jews in America / I.
Goldstein: Two World Wars / Shaul Esh: The Holocaust / N.
Lorch: The War of Independence / Moshe Perlman: The Rise of
Israel / R. Backi: World Jewish Population.

17. Parkes, James: A HISTORY OF THE JEWISH PEOPLE. New
York: Penguin Books, 1964. 254 pp., bibliog., index.

Brief history of the Jews by an eminent Christian
historian and expert on antisemitism. Interweaves religious
and social history to provide a broad picture of Jewish
civilization. The emphasis is on the medieval and modern
periods. The book is particularly useful for those with
little or no background in Jewish history.

18. Potok, Chaim: WANDERINGS. New York: Alfred A. Knopf,
1978. 431 pp., illus., maps, bibliog., index.

Profusely illustrated history of the Jews by the well-
known Jewish novelist. The book is based on Potok´s rumina-
tions about Jewish history and Jewish life. Places Jews into
the social context of the world at large in each period
reviewed. Although popular in style, the scholarly content
is unmistakable, proving that proper scholarship does not
have to be boring. The book is organized around a series of
wanderings experienced by the Jews in the last 4,000 years.

19. Roth, Cecil: HISTORY OF THE JEWS. New York: Schocken
Books, 1961. 452 pp., bibliog., index.

Surveys Jewish history from the Patriarchal period to the
Six-Day War. Follows a mostly chronological pattern, though
the division of the various periods is not the one commonly used by historians. Some chapters, for example, on the
development of the Talmud, are thematic. Each chapter is
subdivided into sections which are numbered rather than
named. This inner organization makes the book easier for
classroom use but can be confusing for a layman.

20. Sachar, Abram L.: A HISTORY OF THE JEWS. New York: A.
A. Knopf, 1948. 478 pp., maps, bibliog., index.

Often reprinted history of the Jews from the biblical
period to the establishment of the State of Israel. Divided
into three sections. Part I deals with the First and Second
Commonwealths, Part II with the Middle Ages, and Part III
with the modern era. The latter has the lion´s share of
material [14 chapters of 33]. Main emphasis is on social
and political history, and the interaction of Jews and non-
Jews throughout the ages is a subtheme. The sections on
specific Jewish communities are especially interesting.

21. Schwarz, Leo W. [ed.]: GREAT AGES AND IDEAS OF THE
JEWISH PEOPLE. New York: The Modern Library, 1956. 515 pp.,
bibliog., index.

Exploration of Jewish history by six eminent Jewish historians. Each age is set out in compelling detail, and Jewish life and thought are placed into the social and political contexts of the surrounding world. Primarily useful for self-study, the book was originally published for The National Education Advisory Committee of Hadassah.

CONTENTS: Y. Kaufman: The Biblical Age / Ralph Marcus: The Hellenistic Age / G. D. Cohen: The Talmudic Age / Abraham S. Halkin: The Judeo-Islamic Age / C. Roth: The European Age / S. W. Baron: The Modern Age.

22. Schweitzer, Frederick M.: A HISTORY OF THE JEWS SINCE THE FIRST CENTURY A. D.. New York: Macmillan, 1971. 319 pp., notes, app., bibliog., index.

Survey of Jewish history by a Catholic historian writing under the impact of Vatican II. Primary emphasis is on correcting Christian misrepresentations and distortions of Jewish history. Schweitzer undertakes his task with sensitivity and dispassion, though he is somewhat apologetic on the issue of antisemitism. The most important contribution of the book is Schweitzer's effort to describe the important role Jews have played in Western civilization. The book is more significant for what its perspective represents than for its contents.

23. Seltzer, Robert M.: JEWISH PEOPLE, JEWISH THOUGHT: THE JEWISH EXPERIENCE IN HISTORY. New York: Macmillan, 1980. 874 pp., illus., maps, chron., notes, bibliog., index.

Synthetic survey, with emphasis on intellectual history. Places each era's intellectual currents into their sociopolitical contexts, while comparing them to similar currents among other peoples. As such Seltzer attempts, and largely succeeds, in viewing Jewish history as an ever-changing dynamic of Jewish self-definition. In light of Seltzer's emphasis on Jewish thought, the book is as much a history of Judaism as of Jews; all types of Jewish religious thought and major religious thinkers are analyzed. In addition, Seltzer reviews the development of secular Jewish thought in modern times, including an analysis of Jewish nationalism. The book is illustrated with maps and photographs.

24. Wagner, Stanley M. and Allen D. Breck [eds.]: GREAT CONFRONTATIONS IN JEWISH HISTORY. Denver, CO: The Univ. of Denver Dept. of History, 1977. 135 pp.

Collection of six essays all delivered as part of the
Goodstein Lectures in Judaic Studies at the University of
Denver. The essays cover some of the key turning points in
Jewish history. The book is organized around a series of
"confrontations" between the Jews and their sociocultural
environment in the diaspora. Each essay also offers an
interpretation and overview of the period in question, thus
providing a context for the selected "confrontation." The
essays make for interesting comparisons, even though not
all are of equal quality. Unfortunately, the essays are
reproduced without footnotes and it is thus difficult to
gauge the veracity of some of the assertions.

CONTENTS: Nahum N. Sarna: Paganism and Biblical Judaism / S.
Sandmel: Hellenism and Judaism / Morton Smith: Early
Christianity and Judaism / A. I. Katsh: Islam and Judaism /
I. Agus: Medieval European Christendom and Judaism / Arthur
Hertzberg: Modernity and Judaism.

THE MODERN PERIOD

25. Ackerman, Walter: OUT OF OUR PEOPLE´S PAST: SOURCES
FOR THE STUDY OF JEWISH HISTORY. New York: United Synagogue
Commission on Jewish Education, 1977. 719 pp., bibliog.

Anthology on Jewish history from the expulsion from Spain
to the twentieth century. The sections are presented
thematically and in chronological order. Each section is an
entity unto itself, with introductions for each selection.
Most of the documents were published before, but many were
not previously available in English. Wisely, Ackerman has
not taken any selections from secondary sources, but has
permitted the primary sources to speak for themselves. On
the other hand, Ackerman does not include references or
explanatory notes for the documents. This occasionally diminishes the usefulness of a document, especially those
containing obscure data. Nevertheless the book is a useful
documentary covering rich and important eras in Jewish
history.

26. Chazan, Robert and Marc Lee Raphael [eds.]: MODERN
JEWISH HISTORY: A SOURCE READER. New York: Schocken Books,
1974. 381 pp., bibliog., index.

Anthology of documents on modern Jewish history. Deals
thematically and chronologically with the issues raised by

the Jewish experience of the last 200 years. Each document
cited is prefaced by an introduction dealing with authorship
and context. Designed from the start to provide a reader for
college courses dealing with modern Jewry. Chazan and
Raphael have collected a wide variety of sources into a book
that is useful in both school and home.

27. Cohen, Israel: CONTEMPORARY JEWRY. London: Methuen,
1950. 410 pp., charts, bibliog., indexes.

Authoritative but now dated history of the Jews in the
first half of the twentieth century. Arranged thematically,
Cohen primarily analyzes the shifts that this dynamic period
wrought upon the Jewish world. Especially interesting are
Cohen´s chapters on the Holocaust, the Yishuv, and the rise
of the State of Israel. Still useful for many details and
for several novel interpretations, Cohen´s book, nevertheless, emphasizes the need for an up-to-date synthetic history of the Jews.

28. Ehrman, Eliezer [ed.]: READINGS IN JEWISH HISTORY:
FROM THE AMERICAN REVOLUTION TO THE PRESENT. New York: Ktav,
1981. 491 pp., bibliog., index.

Anthology of sources on modern Jewish history, primarily
organized for high-school history and social studies
teachers. As a teaching book it has many merits and few
problems. The chapters are organized thematically with extensive introductions, and each selection is placed into
context. The chapters include questions for discussion and
bibliographies for students and teachers. On the negative
side are the dearth of explanatory footnotes and the
author´s idiosyncratic organization. Most of the documents
were published previously. Since Ehrman is not aiming at
scholarship, but at providing a useful anthology for
teachers, students, and laymen, these problems are minor.

29. Elbogen, Ismar: A CENTURY OF JEWISH LIFE. Trans. from
the German by Moses Hadas. Philadelphia: JPS, 1944. 823 pp.,
notes, bibliog., index.

Follow-up historical survey supplemental to Graetz´s HIS-
TORY OF THE JEWS [see #11]. Published posthumously, with a
preface by Solomon Grayzel. Covers the period from 1840 to
World War II. Each chapter represents a methodical examination of the major trends, both internal and external, in
world Jewry during the period examined. The book is

especially important for its nearly global review of Jewish
life. Elbogen´s review thus represents one of only a few
synthetic histories of contemporary Jewry.

* 30. Frankel, Wm. [ed.]: HOPES AND REALITIES 1945-1985.
London: Institute of Jewish Affairs, 1986. 77 pp.

31. Goldscheider, Calvin and A. S. Zuckerman: THE TRANS-
FORMATION OF THE JEWS. Chicago: The Univ. of Chicago Press,
1984. 279 pp., notes, bibliog., index.

Important and innovative inquiry into Jewish society and
politics. Goldscheider is a sociologist, Zuckerman a political scientist; the integration of the two methodologies provides an interesting methodological background to their
study of the transformation of Jewish communities. The
authors focus most of their attention on the subject of
modernization and on the Jewish confrontation with the concept of modernity. In their eyes, new ideologies, economic
and social realities, and communal organizations have led to
a fundamental reorientation of Jewish society. This, in
turn, has led to the collapse of traditional patterns of
Jewish identity and their replacement with newer forms of
identification. A major subtheme is the analysis of why some
communities modernized faster, sooner, or with less compli-
cations than others. A broad comparative approach is thus
central to the book. Unfortunately, some of the chapters are
based on loose generalizations, that do not always support
the conclusions offered.

32. Mahler, Raphael: A HISTORY OF MODERN JEWRY 1780-1815.
New York: Schocken Books, 1971. 742 pp., bibliog., index.

Synthetic history emphasizing social and economic factors.
The book was to be part of a series, and the present volume
is an abridgement of Mahler´s four-volume Hebrew edition.
Unfortunately, Mahler´s death left the Hebrew edition incom-
plete and no further volumes have appeared in English.
Although following Dubnow in his sociocultural analysis,
Mahler differed from Dubnow in two important ways. First,
Mahler showed a keen interest in economic history, which
Dubnow ignored. Second, he attempted to shed light on the
inner dynamics of modern Jewry, and was especially inter-
ested in what Jews thought and felt about the key issues of
their time. Mahler´s chapters are divided by country.
Slightly less than half of the book deals with eastern
Europe. Other Jewish centers which receive significant

attention are France, Germany, the United States, and
Palestine. Deeply committed to Socialist zionism, Mahler
nevertheless maintains his objectivity throughout.

33. Mendes-Flohr, Paul R. and J. Reinharz [eds.]: THE JEW
IN THE MODERN WORLD: A DOCUMENTARY HISTORY. New York: Oxford
Univ. Press, 1980. 556 pp., demographic tables, index.

Authoritative but flawed documentary collection on modern
Jewish history. Though the documents provide an important
glimpse into aspects of Jewish life, the introductory
material does not adequately place the documents into context. Clear emphasis is on social and intellectual history,
with political history a major subtopic. The editors´ main
theme appears to be the complexity of life for the Jew
caught between modernity and Jewish mores. Most of the documents have appeared before, but many were not previously
available in English.

34. Raisin, Max: A HISTORY OF THE JEWS IN MODERN TIMES.
New York: Hebrew Pub. Co., 1949. 508 pp., illus., bibliog.,
index.

Survey appended to some of the English editions of
Graetz´s POPULAR HISTORY OF THE JEWS [see #11]. Deals with
the subject geographically. Some sections, especially on the
period after World War I, are dealt with in a cursory and
facile way. Raisin also attempts to correct what he sees as
some of Graetz´s ideologically motivated conclusions, particularly as regards Reform Judaism and East European Jewry.

35. Ruppin, Arthur: THE JEWISH FATE AND FUTURE. London:
Macmillan, 1940. 386 pp., notes, index.

Sociological study of the Jewish world, the culmination of
Ruppin´s previous works. Written under the impact of nazism,
Ruppin examined the decline of diaspora Jewry. He also,
however, attempted to explain the reasons for Jewish
survival throughout the years. Most significant are Ruppin´s
statistical and demographic studies. Given the period in
which he wrote, Ruppin´s coverage of the Nazi peril and the
rise of zionism are outdated. Nevertheless, the book retains
much of its methodological importance despite its age.

36. ___ : THE JEWS IN THE MODERN WORLD. New York: Arno
Press, 1977 [Rep. of 1934 Ed.]. 423 pp., notes, index.

Extensive sociological study dealing with Jews, an expansion of the author´s JEWS OF TODAY [see #37]. Although outdated and overtaken by events which Ruppin could not have foreseen, the book still contains a good deal of useful information concerning Jewish life. Ruppin opens with a consideration of who or what is a Jew, concluding that Jews are a race. It must, however, be noted that Ruppin used the terms race and nation interchangeably; here he emphasizes the racial aspect. The purely sociological chapters - for example, on demography, birth rate, and mortality - are still of interest. The book contains a large number of charts. Ruppin´s trailblazing work in Jewish sociology still stands as a methodological model and is unparalleled in more recent works.

37. ___: THE JEWS OF TODAY. Trans. from the German by M. Bentwich. New York: Henry Holt, 1913. 310 pp., notes, index.

Important but outdated sociological survey of Jewish history and life. Nevertheless, Ruppin was an innovator in the application of sociology to Jewish history. The book thus contains many valuable methodological insights. The book is organized into two sections, which may be viewed in opposition to each other. Part I deals with assimilation. Part II reviews the rise and ideology of Jewish nationalism, which Ruppin sees as opposing assimilation. These two movements are, according to Ruppin, the basis for any understanding of the needs and possibilities of Jewish survival.

38. Sachar, Abram L.: SUFFERANCE IS THE BADGE. New York: Alfred A. Knopf, 1939. 585 pp., bibliog., index.

Country by country survey of the Jewish condition in the late 1930s. Begins with a discussion of World War I and its impact on Jewish life. Sachar then turns to Germany, central, and eastern Europe, and the Balkans. In all those countries Jews suffered a greater or lesser degree of persecution, which Sachar describes carefully and without overstatement. Turning to Italy, Sachar offers an interesting analysis of Mussolini´s flirtation with Hitler and with antisemitism. Sachar is also blunt when it comes to Jews in western Europe, the Arab world, and the Americas. However, Sachar saves his best chapter for an analysis of the Yishuv. Without being melodramatic, Sachar discusses the rise and decline of the Yishuv up to the May 1939 White Paper, by which the British repudiated the Mandate. Yet, Sachar still saw the Yishuv as the most vibrant source of Jewish survival in the long run. The book is outdated and was, tragically, overtaken by events. Nevertheless, it is a good example of what can be done by a careful and patient scholar.

39. Sachar, H. M.: THE COURSE OF MODERN JEWISH HISTORY. Updated and Expanded Edition. New York: Dell, 1977. 669 pp., maps, notes, bibliog., index.

One-volume survey of modern Jewish history. The book opens with the French Revolution. Sachar covers both eastern and western European Jewry, but emphasis is on the latter. The book's main focus is social history, although political and intellectual history are also covered. Each chapter has a conclusion which inserts the subject discussed into the broader pattern of modern Jewish history. While some of Sachar's interpretations are not widely accepted, his synthesis is very useful for both school and home study.

40. ___: DIASPORA: AN INQUIRY INTO THE CONTEMPORARY JEW-ISH WORLD. New York: Harper and Row, 1985. 539 pp., map, bibliog., index.

Inquiry into the development and condition of world Jewry, outside of Israel and America, since World War II. Organized by country and region. Each chapter gives both historical data as well as individual glimpses of post-Holocaust Jewry. Since many of the events are too recent to describe on the basis of formal historical sources, Sachar relies heavily on anecdotal material. His choice of anecdotes, however, is occasionally questionable. Nevertheless, the book represents the only up-to-date synthesis of post-Holocaust Jewish history presently available.

HISTORIOGRAPHY

41. Agus, J. B.: THE MEANING OF JEWISH HISTORY. 2 vols. New York: Abelard Schuman, 1963. 509 pp., notes, bibliog., index.

Inquiry into, and an effort at establishing, a philosophy of Jewish history. Agus seeks the answers for three ques-tions: First, what is the nature of Jewish history? Second, of what importance is Jewish history for the understanding of contemporary events? Third, what are the parameters of relations between Jews and non-Jews? To answer these ques-tions, Agus adopts a broad survey approach. Many issues of

the Jewish past are thus dealt with as they relate to these
three questions. The preponderance of material is on the ancient period, which Agus sees as the formative era of Jewish
history. The chapters are organized as separate but interconnected essays. Altogether, the book is a thought provoking, insightful, and stimulating review. Foreword by Salo W.
Baron.

42. Baer, Yitzhak: GALUT. New York: Schocken Books, 1947.
123 pp.

Brief inquiry into the Jewish historical and historiographical position on golah and galut. Baer is especially
interested in how Jews viewed their condition. As Baer sees
the issue, a distinction must be made between golah, which
is an objective condition, and galut, the feeling of which
is subjective. It is thus possible to be in galut even while
living in Eretz-Israel.
Unfortunately, Baer´s analysis shows a clear ideological
orientation. Baer, a Zionist, wrote the book originally as
an epistle to strengthen the morale of German Jewish youth.
As a result of his orientation, he was forced to adopt some
rather curious positions. Most vexing are Baer´s polemic
against nonspiritual messianism and his explanation of
Maimonides. When one considers that zionism may also be seen
as a form of secular messianism, the paradox becomes even
more interesting, but completely unanswerable.

43. Baron, S. W.: "American Jewish Scholarship and World
Jewry." AJHQ, v.52 #4 (June, 1963): 274-282.

44. ___ : "Emphases in Jewish History." JSS, v.1 #1 (Jan.,
1939): 15-38.

45. ___ : HISTORY AND JEWISH HISTORIANS: ESSAYS AND AD-
DRESSES. Philadelphia: JPS, 1964. 504 pp., notes, index.

Collection of essays dealing with the underpinnings of
Jewish history and historiography. Compiled with a foreword
by Arthur Hertzberg and Leon A. Feldman. Divided into three
distinct parts. Part I deals with significant theoretical
and methodological issues; Part II with the historical
outlook of Maimonides; Part III with the viewpoints and
methodologies of five early Jewish historians. An important
essay deals with placing Jewish history into its proper
global context. Baron particularly emphasizes the need to
study Jewish history as the development of a total society,

and he completely rejects the so-called lachrymose concept of Jewish history [see #3 and #11].

46. ___: "Newer Emphases in Jewish History." JSS, v.25 #4 (Oct., 1963): 235-248.

47. ___: "World Dimensions of Jewish History." LBML #5 (1962): 5-26.

48. Biale, D.: "The Kabbala in Nachman Krochmal´s Philosophy of History." JJS, v.32 #1 (Spr., 1981): 85-97.

49. Cohen, Morris R.: "Philosophies of Jewish History." JSS, v.1 #1 (Jan., 1939): 39-72.

50. Dinur, B. Z.: ISRAEL AND THE DIASPORA. Philadelphia: JPS, 1969. 206 pp., notes.

Anthology of three explanatory essays providing a historiographical overview of Jewish history. Emphasis is on the modern period. Dinur attempts to synthesize the events of Jewish history and the interpretations of other historians to provide an integrated approach. Dinur´s method is to let the sources speak for themselves. While not all of Dinur´s positions are accepted by a majority of scholars, they are still thought-provoking and intensely interesting. Introduction by Yizhak F. Baer.

51. Dubnow, Simon: NATIONALISM AND HISTORY: ESSAYS ON OLD AND NEW JUDAISM. Edited with introduction by K. S. Pinson. Philadelphia: JPS, 1958. 385 pp., notes, index.

Anthology of the writings of Simon Dubnow, one of the greatest modern Jewish historians and political activists. Includes some essays on methodological issues, although most deal with political matters. Especially important are Dubnow´s thirteen "Letters on Old and New Judaism," which encapsulate his political philosophy, known as "Autonomism." The main purpose of the methodological essays is to define the warp and woof of Jewish history, and to justify Dubnow´s chronological division thereof. Whether one agrees or disagrees with Dubnow, his essays are, provocative and extremely interesting for both student and scholar.

52. Friedman, P.: "Polish Jewish Historiography between the Two Wars 1918-1939." JSS, v.11 #4 (Oct., 1949): 373-408.

53. Graetz, Heinrich: THE STRUCTURE OF JEWISH HISTORY AND
OTHER ESSAYS. Trans. from the German, edited, and introduced
by Ismar Schorsch. New York: The Jewish Theological Seminary
of America, 1975. 325 pp., notes, bibliog., index.

Collection of historiographical essays by Heinrich
Graetz. Includes an extensive study of his orientations and
methods by Ismar Schorsch. Attempts to place Graetz into
context, seeing in him the most highly developed form of the
Wissenschaft des Judentums. Although not directly dealing
with methodological issues, the book does provide an interesting case study in the thought and method of a major
Jewish historian.

54. Gruenwald, Max: "Theology and History." LBML #3
(1960): 5-13.

55. Kochan, Lionel: THE JEW AND HIS HISTORY. New York:
Schocken Books, 1977. 164 pp., notes, bibliog., index.

Thought-provoking inquiry into Jewish historiography. The
purpose of the study is to explain why Jews were so slow to
develop a historiographical sense. Kochan postulates that
historical inquiry was considered in the exclusive context
of messianic speculation by Jewish authorities. According to
this hypothesis, history always served a didactic purpose as
a guide to past, present, and future behavior. Historical
understanding for its own sake was not valued, since this
world was viewed as merely a preparation for the world to
come. As a result, Kochan argues, Jews studied the past only
insofar as it prefigured the future. A historiographical
sense developed in periods when this messianic expectation
was weakened by external influences, for example, during the
Renaissance or in post-emancipation Germany. Kochan is at a
loss to explain historical writing that did not conform to
his hypothesis, for example, medieval martyrologies. Ultimately, Kochan does not satisfactorily explain why Jews were
slow to develop a historiographical orientation.

56. ___ : "A Model for Jewish Historiography." MJ, v.1 #3
(Dec., 1981): 263-278.

57. Meyer, Michael A. [ed.]: IDEAS OF JEWISH HISTORY. New
York: Behrman House, 1974. 360 pp., notes, bibliog., index.

Anthology of Jewish historical writing and historiography. Most of the selections have never appeared before in

English. Covers the topic broadly, citing documents that exemplify the Jewish attitude toward history. Unfortunately, some of Meyer´s choices seem arbitrary. For example, why is MEGILLAT TA´ANIT ignored, while Rashi´s explanation of a verse in Genesis is included? The former at least claimed to be a historical source; Rashi never claimed to be a source for history, Jewish or otherwise. Meyer´s introduction provides a good synthetic review of Jewish historiography, but the subject is still in need of a systematic study.

58. Rivkin, E.: THE SHAPING OF JEWISH HISTORY: A RADICAL NEW INTERPRETATION. New York: Charles Scribner´s Sons, 1971. 256 pp., bibliog., index.

Controversial attempt at a unified philosophy of Jewish history, based on a review of the key epochs of both the Western and Jewish past. Rivkin attempts to integrate both histories and to revise numerous misconceptions about Jews. As an effort at integration it is somewhat useful, but the book suffers on a number of accounts. First, Rivkin´s emphasis, especially in the later chapters, on the economic functions of society is excessive. Similarly, Rivkin´s account of nationalism is weak - he mentions zionism but once - and his thoughts on the "demise" of nationalism in the post-World War II era are naive at best. Finally, the book is not documented, and Rivkin´s most controversial sections - on the emergence of Pharisaism and on the Jewish schism with Christianity - cannot be decisively proved.

59. Yerushalmi, Y. H.: ZAKHOR: JEWISH HISTORY AND JEWISH MEMORY. Seattle: Univ. of Washington Press, 1982. 144 pp., notes, index.

A series of connected lectures on Jewish historiography and historical memory. Provocatively, Yerushalmi argues that the latter did not necessarily express itself in the former, i.e., memory of historical events did not imply an historiographical understanding of these events. By way of example, the commandment that each Jew "remember" the exodus as though he/she had personally left Egypt, was fulfiled on emotional and active levels, but was not studied as an historical phenomenon. The last chapter is both a review of the origins of modern historiography and a confession of the problems of being a Jew and a Jewish historian. This chapter, however, is the weakest in the book. The other chapters are eloquent and well documented. Despite some reservations the book is, nevertheless, very useful and interesting.

2

Social History

SOCIOLOGY

60. Bubis, Gerald B. [ed.]: SERVING THE JEWISH FAMILY.
New York: Ktav, 1977. 367 pp., gloss., bibliog., index.

Anthology of studies on the sociology of the Jewish
family, with primary emphasis on American Jewry. Most of the
essays are, however, written in a general way and can thus
be applied to almost any Jewish community. The book is
divided into five sections: "The Family," "The Synagogue,"
"Centers and Camps," "Family Service," and "Outreach
Services." Although not a main focus, most of the contributors do use a historical viewpoint. The key issue addressed
in the essays is the survival of the Jewish family and
the strengthening of American Jewry's foundations. Most of
the essays were previously published elsewhere, and they are
brought together here for the first time. The multiplicity
of approaches and viewpoints makes for interesting reading,
both for scholars and interested laypersons.

CONTENTS: V. D. Sanua: The Contemporary Jewish Family: a
Review of Social Science Literature / N. Lamm: Family Values
and Family Breakdown: Analysis and Prescription / Manheim S.
Shapiro: In My Footsteps: Some Dilemmas of Jewish Parents /
H. M. Schulweis: Reconstructing the Synagogue / G. B. Bubis:
Facing New Times: a Response to Changing Needs / Edwin H.
Friedman: Family Systems Thinking and a New View of Man / B.
Braun: Havurah as a New Dimension in Congregational Life /
G. B. Bubis: The Jewish Community Center's Responsibility
for the Needs of the Jewish Family / M. Bienstock: Designing
Center Programs for Families / B. Reisman: Serving Jewish
Families in Camp Settings / Ruth Silver: Family Camping: To-

getherness Two Hours a Day / J. Dauber and F. Katleman: The
Los Angeles Jewish Centers Association Jewish Family Living
Program / M. Bienstock: Single-parent Families in the Jewish
Community / M. S. Shapiro: Survival and Service: Who? What?
Why? How? / P. D. Goldberg: Jewish Values in the Clinical
Casework Process / F. Carmelly: A Family Life Education
Program / S. M. Brownstein: The Contemporary Jewish Family:
Innovative Programming by Local Service Agencies - the Role
of the Jewish Family Agency / A. F. Weinberg: The Response
of Jewish Family Service to the Issue of Conversion and
Intermarriage / Marcia W. Levine: New Family Structures:
Challenges to Family Casework / Th. R. Isenstadt: Toward
Enriching the Quality of Jewish Life: the Role of the Jewish
Family and Children's Agency / E. L. Herman et al: Outreach
Programs to Jewish Families: The Union of American Hebrew
Congregation's Response to the Synagogue's Crisis.

   61. Cohen, S. M.: AMERICAN MODERNITY AND JEWISH IDENTITY.
New York: Tavistock, 1983. 210 pp., charts, notes, bibliog.,
indexes.

   Sociological inquiry into Jewish identity in the American
environment. Based almost exclusively on first-hand research, with special emphasis being laid on the use of questionnaires, surveys, and polls. Using these tools, Cohen has
made important contributions to the study of Jewish sociology, and the use of computers to collate findings constitutes a major technological breakthrough. As a result, Cohen
is able to revise some of the most widely held beliefs about
American Jewry. First, that the generational pattern for
declining religiosity, which held that each generation is
less pious than its predecessor, is not completely accurate;
some practices decline generationally but others actually
increase. Second, the widely held view which correlated
religious orthodoxy with political conservatism is proven
false; completely secular Jews are shown, as a group, to be
as politically conservative as the Orthodox, while all Jews
are shown to be more liberal than any other American ethnic
group. Third, while colleges have been seen as a "disaster
area" for Jewish identity, Cohen's results suggest that
Jewish college students and faculty members have a higher
degree of Jewish identity than members of other professions
with similar educational and religious backgrounds. On the
negative side, Cohen does not deal with such issues as
antisemitism and Jewish self-perceptions. His chapter on
recent family trends is adequate as a beginning but requires
further elucidation. Overall Cohen provides a new and

important insight into American Jewry in the last quarter of the twentieth century.

62. ___ and P. E. Hyman [eds.]: THE JEWISH FAMILY: MYTHS AND REALITY. New York: Holmes & Meier, 1986. 242 pp., notes, index.

Anthology of studies on the family, based on a colloquium held at Queens College. The essays could be divided into three broad categories: historical, literary, and sociological studies. The literary studies explore the image of the Jewish family in both Jewish and secular literature. The main purpose of the book is to offer a new perspective on the family with a view to correcting the romantic, but unrealistic, view of the Jewish family as a perfect model for a warm, caring, and nurturing environment. Paula Hyman´s introduction offers a useful survey of both the myth and current literature on the Jewish family, emphasizing historical studies. Her afterword stresses literary aspects, although in both Hyman touches on methodological issues.

CONTENTS: P.E. Hyman: Perspectives on the Evolving Jewish Family / Gershon D. Hundert: Approaches to the History of the Jewish Family in Early Modern Poland-Lithuania / S. Deshen: The Jewish Family in Traditional Morocco / D. Biale: Childhood, Marriage, and the Family in the Eastern European Jewish Enlightenment / M. A. Kaplan: Priestess and Hausfrau: Women and Tradition in the German-Jewish Family / M. Shokeid: The Impact of Migration on the Moroccan Jewish Family in Israel / A. Norich: Jewish Family Images in the English Novel / S. A. Slotnick: Charmed and Vicious Circles: the Study of the Yiddish Family Saga Novel/ G. Rothbell: The Jewish Mother: Social Construction of a Popular Image / C. Goldscheider: Family Change and Variation Among Israeli Ethnic Groups / S. Della Pergola: Contemporary Jewish Family Patterns in France: a Comparative Perspective / F. K. Goldscheider: Family Patterns Among the U. S. Yiddish-Mother-Tongue Subpopulation 1970 / W. Shaffir: Persistence and Change in the Hasidic Family / C. Weissler: Coming of Age in the Havurah Movement: Bar Mitzvah in the Havurah Family / S. M. Cohen: Vitality and Resilience in the American Jewish Family / P. E. Hyman: Afterword.

* 63. Davis, M.: JEWISH COMMUNITIES IN WORLD PERSPECTIVE. New York: Council of Jewish Federations, 1964. 27 pp.

* 64. Elias, Joseph: SOCIAL ORDER, THE JEWISH VIEW. New York: Jewish Pocket Books, 1947. 76 pp.

65. Geismar, Ludwig L.: "Ideology and the Adjustment of Immigrants." JSS, v.21 #3 (July, 1959): 155-164.

66. ___: "A Scale for the Measurement of Ethnic Identification." JSS, v.16 #1 (Jan., 1954): 33-60.

67. Gould, Julius: JEWISH COMMITMENT: A STUDY IN LONDON. London: Institute of Jewish Affairs, 1984. 113 pp., notes, apps.

Sociological study of Jewish religious commitment in the greater London area. The Book is based on a two-generational study undertaken by the Institute of Jewish Affairs of the World Jewish Congress. The core of the study comprises ten case studies, selected from more than 200 interviews. A majority of the respondents, 80 percent of them in fact, were synagogue members. Three-quarters of those belonged to Orthodox synagogues. Gould includes a full statistical analysis of all the respondents. The study suggests a slow but clear decline in Jewish religious practice, though not necessarily in commitment to some form of Jewish identity. The study also includes two methodological appendixes. Irrespective of its exact conclusions, the book has possible applications for similar studies in any Jewish community.

68. Greenberg, Meyer: "The Jewish Student at Yale: His Attitude Toward Judaism." Y/A, v.1 (1946): 217-240.

69. Koenig, Samuel: "Methods of Studying Jewish Life in America." Y/A, v.2/3 (1947/48): 282-294.

70. Lehrer, L.: "The Jewish Elements in the Psychology of the Jewish Child in America." Y/A, v.1 (1946): 195-216.

71. Lennard, Henry L.: "Jewish Youth Appraising Jews and Jewishness." Y/A, v.2/3 (1947/48): 262-281.

72. Levinson, Boris M.: "The Socioeconomic Status, Intelligence and Personality Traits of Jewish Homeless Men." Y/A, v.11 (1956/57): 122-141.

73. Oppenheim, Michael: "A ´Fieldguide´ to the Study of Modern Jewish Identity." JSS, v.46 #3/4 (Sum./Fall, 1984): 215-230.

74. Patai, Raphael: ON JEWISH FOLKLORE. Detroit: Wayne
State Univ. Press, 1983. 511 pp., notes, index.

Collection of Patai´s studies into Jewish folklore, folk-
culture, and ethnography. Spanning fifty years of research,
the essays cover a wide range of topics, from biblical mythology to sixteenth-century Kabbalah. Many of the essays are
published in English for the first time. Patai has grouped
the essays into thematic categories, of which the first,
"Introductory and Programmatic," is most important. The four
essays in this section cover methodological issues. Patai´s
other sections are divided as follows: Sephardi folklore,
folklore of the Meshedi crypto-Jews, Jewish customs relating
to childbirth, and peripheral Jewries. Each essay is an important contribution in its own right, offering insights
into the folkways of different Jewish communities around the
world.

75. ___ and Jenifer P. Wing: THE MYTH OF THE JEWISH RACE.
New York: Charles Scribner´s Sons, 1975. 350 pp., illus.,
tables, notes, gloss., index.

Attempt to assess whether or not Jews constitute one
distinct race. Divided into three sections: historical,
psychological, and genetic. Each one is, in turn, subdivided
thematically. Some of the sections cover the issues quite
extensively. The chapter dealing with historical views on
the Jewish race is especially interesting. Less so is the
chapter on physiognomy, which serves a dubious purpose. It
is clear that Patai and Wing do not believe that Jews
constitute one race. Unfortunately, their argument is marred
by the absence of an encompassing conclusion and the difficulty in fitting together the various pieces of evidence.

76. Pipe, Samuel Z.: "Napoleon in Jewish Folklore." Y/A,
v.1 (1946): 294-304.

77. Rotenberg, M.: DIALOGUE WITH DEVIANCE: THE HASIDIC
ETHIC AND THE THEORY OF SOCIAL CONTRACTION. Philadelphia:
ISHI, 1983. 214 pp., notes, bibliog., index.

Sociological study of hasidism and hasidic ethics. Rotenberg views hasidism as an optimistic form of prospective
therapy, which orients man toward a better future and helps
him cope with the present. Much of Rotenberg´s study is
based on the concept of the "I-Thou" relationship, as
developed by hasidim. Although used here in a sociological

sense, the same idea has also been used by philosophers such as Abraham J. Heschel and Martin Buber. Hasidism is thus given an existentialist flavor which aligns it with the theory of social contraction. Rotenberg can thus offer a reasonably accurate explanation for many hasidic beliefs and practices. In particular his explanations of "tikkun" and of the role of the zaddik are greatly enhanced by the "I-Thou" approach and heighten the interest of the work. Unfortunately, some of Rotenberg´s sections are difficult for the layperson to follow. The sections on sociological theory are very rough going. Nevertheless, the book contains important insights into hasidic life and into Jewish sociology as well.

> #35. Ruppin, Arthur: THE JEWISH FATE AND FUTURE.

> #36. ___ : THE JEWS IN THE MODERN WORLD.

> #37. ___ : THE JEWS OF TODAY.

78. Sachar, Howard M.: "Objectivity and Jewish Social Science." AJHQ, v.55 #4 (June, 1966): 434-450.

79. Segalman, Ralph: "Jewish Identity Scales: a Report." JSS, v.29 #2 (Apr., 1967): 92-111.

80. Sharot, Stephen: JUDAISM: A SOCIOLOGY. London: David and Charles, 1976. 224 pp., app., notes, index.

Attempts to integrate a sociological and historical analysis of Jews and Judaism in modern times. Begins with the pre-emancipation period and then elucidates the transformations that have occurred since the eighteenth century. Sharot divides modern Jewish history into three periods: from the French Revolution to 1881; from 1881 to World War I; and from World War I to the present. Although his first chapter adopts a global viewpoint, the succeeding chapters focus almost exclusively on Europe and North America. Thus the book actually details much less than might be expected. On the other hand, Sharot does offer some interesting insights and a few novel interpretations. In particular his use of statistics is careful and shows how sociological data can be used by historians. The book has further interest as a comparative study. Other authors have adopted a similar approach [see #31] with a considerably larger database and therefore more success.

81. Sklare, Marshall and J. Greenbaum: JEWISH IDENTITY ON THE SUBURBAN FRONTIER. 2nd Edition. Chicago: The Univ. of Chicago Press, 1979. 437 pp., notes, index.

Path-breaking sociological study of Jewish communal life in the suburban environment. This is the first of Sklare´s "Lakeville" studies. Although based on a real community, all names [including the town´s name] have been altered. In addition to his analysis of the internal organization and operation of Lakeville, Sklare makes comparisons to other Jewish communities. Basic demographic and social data are integrated into the views and attitudes of Lakeville Jews on a wide range of topics, including religion, Israel, and the relationship between Jews and non-Jews. An especially interesting chapter discusses "The Image of a Good Jew in Lakeville." The second edition supplements the study and reviews major changes that have occurred in Lakeville since 1967. In particular the influx of a relatively large body of younger Jews has modified the suburb´s character. Sklare´s study is still a model for Jewish sociology and, irrespective of the actual community studied, contains important methodological insight. Foreword by John Slowlson.

82. Tartakower, Arieh: "New Trends in Jewish Sociology." JSS, v.12 #2 (Apr., 1950): 113-118.

* 83. Waterman, Stanley and B. Kosmin: BRITISH JEWRY IN THE EIGHTIES: A STATISTICAL AND GEOGRAPHICAL STUDY. London: Research Unit, Board of Deputies of British Jews, 1986. 56 pp.

84. Weller, Leonard: SOCIOLOGY IN ISRAEL. Westport, CT: Greenwood Press, 1974. 315 pp., tables, notes, bibliog., index.

Synthetic sociological survey of the State of Israel. Weller attempts to review and integrate the relevant sociological research, which has mushroomed since the establishment of the state. Weller also surveys the ongoing research at Israel´s universities. Comments on special methodologies are kept to a minimum, and Weller also includes historical background to provide a proper context for the studies and their findings. The book is divided into two sections. The first deals with immigration and group interactions. The second covers interpersonal issues, such as family, criminality, and religion. A separate chapter deals with the kibbutz, which Weller sees as a unique sociological workshop. In light of the ongoing nature of much of the re-

search, Weller offers only tentative conclusions instead of
attempting to tie the research together in a larger - but
not necessarily accurate - theoretical framework.

MIGRATION

   85. Berger, David [ed]: THE LEGACY OF JEWISH MIGRATION:
1881 AND ITS IMPACT. New York: Brooklyn College Press, 1983.
185 pp., notes.

   Inquiry into the significance of 1881 as a watershed in
Jewish history. Based on a colloquium at Brooklyn College in
March 1981. Primary emphasis is on social history, with
intellectual history a major subtheme. Political history receives less attention, but is also reviewed. The essays are
grouped into three sections: "The Old World Context," Ideology and Culture," and "New Modes of Jewish Community." The
three essays forming the first part, by Stanislawski,
Frankel, and Zipperstein, are important contributions to
East European Jewish history. In his essay Frankel makes a
strong case for viewing 1881 as a watershed in Jewish history, since it sowed the seeds for the momentous events of
the twentieth century. Endelman's study on London provides a
counterpoint to the America-centered view of nineteenth-
century Jewish migration, and also provides the basis for a
comparison of Jewish experiences in different countries.
Rounding out the collection are Seltzer's review of East
European Jewish historiography and Cohen's investigation of
the relations between German and Russian Jews. Both essays
provide important historical and methodological insight, in
Cohen's case into an issue that is still somewhat controversial. The legacy of 1881 is comprehensively described in
this book, which offers an assessment of both Jewish and
world history.

CONTENTS: J. Frankel: The Crisis of 1881-82 as a Turning
Point in Modern Jewish History / M. Stanislawski: The Trans-
formation of Traditional Authority in Russian Jewry: the
First stage / S. J. Zipperstein: Russian Maskilim and the
City / R. Seltzer: From Graetz to Dubnow: the Impact of the
East European Milieu on the Writing of Jewish history / B.
Avishai: The Conquest of Labor: Gordon and the Idea of the
Kvutzah / M. Rischin: Abraham Cahan: Guide Across the
American Chasm / F. Burko: The American Yiddish Theater and
its Audience Before World War I / Robert Alter: The Inner
Immigration of Hebrew Prose / Todd M. Endelman: Native Jews

and Foreign Jews in London, 1870-1914 / Naomi W. Cohen: The
Ethnic Catalyst: the Impact of the East European Immigration
on the American Jewish Establishment / I. Howe: Pluralism in
the Immigrant World / Paula E. Hyman: Culture and Gender:
Women in the Immigrant Jewish Community / Thomas Kessner:
The Selective Filter of Ethnicity: a Half Century of Immigrant Mobility.

* 86. Marcus, Jacob R.: MASS MIGRATIONS OF JEWS AND THEIR
EFFECTS ON JEWISH LIFE. Cincinnati: Central Conference of
American Rabbis, 1940. 23 pp.

87. Shulvass, Moses A.: FROM EAST TO WEST: THE WESTWARD
MIGRATION OF JEWS FROM EASTERN EUROPE DURING THE SEVENTEENTH
AND EIGHTEENTH CENTURIES. Detroit: Wayne State Univ. Press,
1971. 161 pp., notes, index.

Study into the westward migration of Jews, both within
and from Europe, from 1648 to the end of the eighteenth century. Until 1648 the primary Jewish migration trend had been
eastward. The reversal of Jewish migratory trends was to
have a major impact on Jewish life in Europe for the next
two hundred years, as Shulvass amply documents. An important
thematic study for early modern Jewish history.

88. Szajkowski, Zosa: "How the Mass Migration to America
Began." JSS, v.4 #4 (Oct., 1942): 291-310.

89. Tartakower, A.: "The Jewish Refugees: a Sociological
Survey." JSS, v.4 #4 (Oct., 1942): 311-348.

90. Wischnitzer, Mark: TO DWELL IN SAFETY: THE STORY OF
JEWISH MIGRATION SINCE 1800. Philadelphia, JPS, 1948. 368
pp., maps, illus., notes, index.

Surveys the trends of Jewish migration since 1800.
Wischnitzer divides migration into eight phases, but does
not distinguish between transcontinental migration and
migration within Europe: [1] 1800-1880, Jewish migration
from central and eastern Europe; [2] 1881-1890, the first
wave of emigration from Russia; [3] 1891-1900, the second
wave of emigration from Russia and southeastern Europe; [4]
1900-1914, the peak of East European Jewish migration; [5]
1914-1932, the nadir of Jewish migration; [6] 1933-1939,
migration under Nazi pressure; [7] 1939-1945, migration
during the war; [8] 1945-1948, post-Holocaust emigration.
Each of the periods is charted clearly, and the causes and

effects of each wave of migration are also reviewed. Migration is very correctly dealt with in two stages: emigration from, and immigration to. Causes for wanting to leave must, therefore, also be integrated with reasons for selecting a particular country of immigration. Special emphasis is placed on Jewish and international organizations dealing with emigration, colonization, and immigrant aid. For obvious reasons the last two chapters, dealing with the Holocaust and immediate postwar condition, are not complete and have been superseded. Nevertheless, the book still has much to offer, including some very useful statistical appendixes. Preface by James G. McDonald.

ECONOMIC ACTIVITY

91. Aris, Stephen: THE JEWS IN BUSINESS. London: Jonathan Cape, 1971. 255 pp., illus., bibliog., index.

Inquiry into Jewish economic activity in England from the 1880s onward. Aris is keenly interested in assessing the extent of Jewish influence on the English economy so as to answer the antisemitic canard of Jewish "domination" and economic treachery. Most of the chapters are topical, except two which deal with distinct individuals - Sir Isaac Wolfson, the mail-order magnate, and Sir John Cohen, known for his popular retail chain. Aris also explores economic antisemitism and business prejudice against hiring Jews. Although written in a journalistic style, Aris obviously did painstaking research to prepare the book. He offers interesting conclusions about the Jewish role in the English economy, and compares the English economic community to that of other diaspora communities.

92. Arkin, Marcus: ASPECTS OF JEWISH ECONOMIC HISTORY. Philadelphia: JPS, 1975. 271 pp., illus., bibliog., index.

Collection of Arkin's studies on the Jewish role in the economic development of the Western world. The book is not a comprehensive study of the subject, but provides the groundwork for a possible future synthetic history. The chapters are arranged thematically, with most covering the modern age. All of the essays are interesting and provide new insights into a number of themes in Jewish history. Especially noteworthy are Arkin's essays on "The Economic Background to the Expulsion of Spanish Jewry," "Sombart, Modern Capitalism, and Jewish Enterprise," and "Marx's Writings and Jewish

Enterprise." All the essays appeared previously in a number
of scholarly and popular journals, but are here brought
together for the first time.

93. Engelman, U. Z.: THE RISE OF THE JEW IN THE WESTERN
WORLD: A SOCIAL AND ECONOMIC HISTORY OF THE JEWISH PEOPLE OF
EUROPE. New York: Behrman House, 1944. 238 pp.

Inquiry into the role Jews have played in European history. Engelman has adopted a socioeconomic approach to the
question, integrating demographic, political, and cultural
trends as well. Engelman´s methodological underpinning is
significant. Beginning with the oft-stated conundrum that
Jews have been an agent of ferment in European life, for
better or worse, Engelman attempts to test the validity of
this hypothesis. Also put to the test are theories about
Jews propounded by Werner Sombart [see #99], Houston
Stewart Chamberlain, and Karl Marx, among others; all are
found sorely lacking in their scholarship and intellectual
honesty. A clearer understanding of antisemitism is a by-
product of Engelman´s research and his analysis of Jew-
hatred has much merit. Although most of the data are now
obsolete, the book remains a methodological classic.

94. Fischel, Walter: JEWS IN THE ECONOMIC AND POLITICAL
LIFE OF MEDIEVAL ISLAM. Revised Edition. New York: Ktav,
1969. 139 pp., notes, app., index.

Investigation of the sociopolitical role that Jews played
in the Muslim world through the thirteenth century. Fischel
adopts a new approach, viewing the lives of what he terms
"court Jews" in the Muslim world. This raises two questions:
First, how typical were the individuals selected; for if
they were not typical Jews, they tell us nothing of the
Jewish community. Second, can the term "court Jews" properly be applied to these individuals, or to any other Jewish
community outside of German Jewry in the absolutist era?
Fischel answers the latter question affirmatively, and the
introduction to the Ktav edition explains why. Nevertheless, as conditions in the early Muslim world differed
significantly, especially in political ideology, from those
of absolutist Europe, the question is by no means defini-
tively answered. The first question is not addressed
directly; in light of the Jews´ "dhimmi" status as protected
second-class citizens, the first question gains relevance
only if one agrees with Fischel that court Jews did exist
in the Muslim world. On the other hand, Fischel has a large

number of sources under review, many consulted for the first
time. The book is a useful, but methodologically limited,
study on an important and little known subject.

* 95. Goldberg, Nathan: OCCUPATIONAL PATTERNS OF AMERICAN
JEWRY. New York: JTSP Univ. Press, 1947.   85 pp., notes,
index.

96. Levine, Aaron: FREE ENTERPRISE IN JEWISH LAW: ASPECTS
OF JEWISH BUSINESS ETHICS. New York: Ktav for Yeshiva Univ.
Press, 1980. 224 pp., notes, gloss., indexes.

Study of Jewish law and business ethics. Reviews the
halakhic implications of free enterprise, competition, and
"hazakah." Natural monopolies, and government regulation are
also discussed. Levine is able to use rabbinic sources to
explicate the Jewish attitude regarding issues of prime public concern. As a result the book can be useful for those
interested in history, economics, Talmud, law, and Jewish
public affairs. To his credit, Levine conducts his study
with little use of jargon. His careful use of rabbinic
materials stands in contrast with the distorted views of
Sombart [see #99] and others who, unable to read Hebrew
sources, nevertheless presumed to explain what Jews believe
and practice. Levine´s book shows the way for a fundamentally different and more accurate approach. Introduction by
Norman Lamm.

97. Poliakov, Leon: JEWISH BANKERS AND THE HOLY SEE FROM
THE THIRTEENTH TO THE SEVENTEENTH CENTURY. Trans. from the
French by Miriam Kochan. London: Routledge and Kegan, 1978.
275 pp., app., notes, index.

Studies the rise, decline, and fall of Jewish money
traders in Italy from the thirteenth to the seventeenth
centuries. Jewish money trade at the time was usually
carried out as a form of pawnbroking. Although this was not
actually usury, often the two types of banking have been
confused. In fact, Jews were encouraged to enter the pawnbroking business, and the bankers were protected by the
Vatican. Poliakov views the process, as well as the economic
importance of Jewish banking activities, while also charting
the changes in Jewish and papal attitudes. Fluctuations in
attitude are primarily ascribed to changes in economic
conditions; Poliakov does not lightly use the accusation of
antisemitism. The end of papal support for the Jewish pawn-
brokers, which ultimately ended this type of Jewish economic

activity, is placed in ideological and economic context. The counter-Reformation swept away the final vestiges of papal-sponsored "usury"; yet this was also brought about by changed economic circumstances. Poliakov´s conclusions about the role of pawnbroking in Jewish survival and his rumina-tions about Jewish historiography must, however, be taken as tentative.

* 98. Radan, G. T.: THE SONS OF ZEBULON: JEWISH MARITIME HISTORY. Chicago: Spertus College Press, 1978. 85 pp.

99. Sombart, Werner: THE JEWS AND MODERN CAPITALISM. Trans. from the German by M. Epstein. Glencoe, IL: The Free Press, 1951. 402 pp., notes, references.

Trailblazing study of the Jewish role in building modern capitalism. Sombart´s analysis, reduced to its simplest for-mula, can be divided into two parts. First, Sombart sought to define the historical role of Jews in founding the capi-talist system. Second, he also sought to view the social and psychological forces that led Jews to adapt more easily to capitalism than their non-Jewish neighbors. Methodologically Sombart adopted Max Weber´s conclusion on the so-called Protestant ethic as a source for capitalism but, unlike Weber, he attributed those elements to a Jewish work ethic.
Sombart´s thesis has proved controversial. While out-right accusations of antisemitism seem out of place, much of the criticism is appropriate. First, and foremost, Sombart completely misunderstood Jewish law. Since he did not have access to the primary sources, his use of talmudic and rabbinic materials is extremely suspect. Similarly, Sombart viewed Judaism as a materialistic religion and completely ignored its spiritual aspects. Finally, Sombart´s account often lapsed into improbable fictions, for lack of hard evidence forced Sombart to use a more impressionistic approach. Sometimes Sombart´s impressions are masterful expositions; more often they are puzzling guesses that have no basis in fact. These criticisms notwithstanding, Sombart is still a basic source on Jewish economic history, and the argument on the accuracy of his thesis will continue for years to come.

100. Straus, Raphael: "The Jews in the Economic Evolution of Central Europe." JSS, v.3 #1 (Jan., 1941): 15-40.

DEMOGRAPHY

101. Engelman, Uriah Zvi: "Intermarriage Among Jews in Germany, USSR, and Switzerland." JSS, v.2 #2 (Apr., 1940): 157-178.

102. Schmelz, Uriel O. and P. Glickson: JEWISH POPULATION STUDIES, 1961-1968. Jerusalem/London: The Institute for Contemporary Jewry, Hebrew Univ./IJA, 1970. 174 pp., bibliog.

Guide and research into Jewish demography in the 1960s. Divided into three parts. Part I is a methodological guide which includes a modern questionnaire for Jewish-population studies. Part II comprises eleven research reports on Jewish population trends in the Americas, Europe, and Australia. Part III is a seven-year bibliography listing studies of Jewish population, demography, and sociology. Interestingly, the authors maintain that Jewish population research has come to a virtual standstill since World War II, despite the evermore pressing need for accurate statistical information on Jews throughout the world. The book is a useful contribution to a most important subject of concern to all Jews.

CONTENTS: Uriel O. Schmeltz: A Guide to Jewish Population Studies / S. Goldstein: U.S.A. / L. Rosenberg: Canada / Haim Avni: Latin America / M. Schmool: United Kingdom / W. Bok: Belgium / D. Bensimon-Donath: France / S. Della Pergola and F. Sabatello: Italy / U. O. Schmelz: Germany [Federal Republic] and Austria / Jan Herman: Czechoslovakia / P. Glikson: Poland / W. M. Lippmann: Australia / Paul Glikson: Selected Bibliography.

* 103. Shapiro, Harry L.: THE JEWISH PEOPLE: A BIOLOGICAL HISTORY. Paris: UNESCO, 1960. 84 pp.

104. Vago, B. [ed.]: JEWISH ASSIMILATION IN MODERN TIMES. Boulder, CO: Westview Press, 1981. 220 pp., notes, index.

Anthology of studies on Jewish assimilation, with emphasis on the late nineteenth and early twentieth centuries. All but two of the essays deal with aspects of assimilation in Europe. Many of the essays deal with assimilationist ideology, primarily expressed by the Jewish left, for example, in France during the 1930s. Leni Yahil´s essay is an important contribution to the study of pre-Nazi German Jewry and offers an explanation for the confusion and disunity of German Jews in 1933. The five essays dealing with Hungary and Rumania cover a much debated subject extensively. Roi´s and Altshuler´s essays represent two significant contributions on the assimilation and national reawakening of Soviet Jewry. In all, the book offers historical perspectives on issues that are of contemporary importance to Jews and Jewish communities everywhere.

CONTENTS: M. R. Marrus: European Jewry and the Politics of Assimilation: Assessment and Reassessment / D. Weinberg: Left-wing Jews and the Question of Assimilation: Immigrant Jewish Communists in Paris During the 1930s / Leni Yahil: Jewish Assimilation vis-a-vis German Nationalism in the Weimar Republic / Nathanel Katzburg: Assimilation in Hungary During the Nineteenth Century: Orthodox Positions / Asher Cohen: The Attitude of the Intelligentsia in Hungary Toward Jewish Assimilation between the Two World Wars / George Schoepflin: Jewish Assimilation in Hungary: a Moot Point / S. Fischer-Galati: The Radical Left and Assimilation: the Case of Romania / Bela Vago: Communist Pragmatism Toward Jewish Assimilation in Romania and Hungary / Wm. O. McCagg: The Assimilation of Jews in Austria / E. Mendelsohn: A Note on Jewish Assimilation in Poland / M. Altschuler: Factors in the Process of Assimilation within Soviet Jewry, 1917-1947 / Y. Ro´i: The Dilemma of Soviet Jewry´s Assimilation After 1948 / L. P. Gartner: Assimilation and American Jews / S. Della Pergola: Quantitative Aspects of Jewish Assimilation.

3

The Emancipation and Transformation of European Jewry

JEWRY ON THE EVE OF EMANCIPATION

105. Abrahams, Israel: JEWISH LIFE IN THE MIDDLE AGES. New York: Atheneum, 1969. 452 pp., notes, indexes.

Social history of the medieval Jewish community. Every possible topic is dealt with, to the extent that sources will allow. Details Jewish life thematically. No single community is dealt with, although most of the information is on Ashkenazic Jewry. Unfortunately, no sense of historical development is present, nor are regional variations on similar customs detailed in a systematic way. A case in point is the discussion of Jewish accommodation to general culture. While some lifestyles were incorporated into Jewish custom, there were fundamentally different approaches to acculturation among Ashkenazic, Sephardic, and other Jewries. In general Sephardim were more open to outside influences while Ashkenazim less so. Yet, this difference is not clear from Abraham's account.

106. Barzilay, I. E.: "Manasseh of Ilya 1767-1831 and the European Enlightenment." JSS, v.46 #1 (Wint., 1984): 1-8.

107. Carmilly-Weinberger, Moshe: CENSORSHIP AND FREEDOM OF EXPRESSION IN JEWISH HISTORY. New York: Sepher Hermon Press for Yeshiva University, 1977. 295 pp., notes, index.

Inquiry into the history of censorship and the role it has played in Jewish communal life. Deals with the issue both chronologically and by type of book censored. Notes that censorship never played the same role in Jewish communal life as it did among European nations, primarily because

Jews lacked a single central authority. Also discusses the arguments, pro and con, which raged around the censorship of individual books and particular genres.

108. Israel, Jonathan I.: EUROPEAN JEWRY IN THE AGE OF MERCANTILISM, 1550-1750. Oxford: Clarendon Press, 1985. 293 pp., notes, bibliog., index.

Synthetic history of early modern European Jewry. Opens with the removal of Jews from western Europe, which culminated in the expulsion from Spain in 1492. Unlike other historians, Israel views the period as a distinct whole, rather than as an interregnum between the Middle Ages and modern times. In turn, Israel divides the era into three periods. First, 1570 to 1650, a period of consolidation and reintegration. During this period world Jewry recovered from the persecutions of the previous two centuries and was able once again to consolidate its social and economic role. Second, 1650 to 1713, the high point, during which Jewish economic and political activity came to the fore. This became possible as a result of Jewish neutrality in the Catholic-Protestant schism. More directly the new Jewish role in European public affairs resulted from the devastation and deadlock that followed the Thirty Years´ War. Third, 1713 to 1750, which Israel sees as an era of decline, caused by internal crisis and the reorientation associated with the rise of nation states. Then too, changes in the economic life of Europe and the demographic lag within Jewish communities in western Europe also helped to reduce the importance of the Jews in European society. Israel argues forcefully that the eighteenth century should be viewed as a period of decline.

109. Katz, David S.: "Menasseh ben Israel´s Mission to Queen Christina of Sweden, 1651-1655." JSS, v.45 #1 (Wint., 1983): 57-72.

110. Katz, Jacob: EXCLUSIVENESS AND TOLERANCE: STUDIES IN JEWISH-GENTILE RELATIONS IN MEDIEVAL AND MODERN TIMES. New York: Schocken Books, 1962. 200 pp., bibliog., notes, index.

Studies Jewish-Gentile relations in medieval and early-modern times from the Jewish perspective. While dealing with antisemitism, Katz´s primary focus is on the way Jews viewed non-Jews. His most important contribution is the systematic use of rabbinic sources, many of which were never used before. Katz notes that Jews were not always ideologically oriented to toleration, viewing Christians as pagans, except

when necessary. Even then, most halakhists spoke only in an
ad hoc way. This perspective must be viewed in context. All
monotheistic religions consider their teaching to be true;
for Jews this necessitated a degree of religious competition
with Christians. Further, as Jewish law attempts to guide
all aspects of daily life, the Jewish view of the Christian
had important implications for Jewish social and economic
activity, as well as for communal survival. Paradoxically,
as Jews were ghettoized and suffered intolerance in the
early modern period, they became more tolerant of Christians. Coincidentally, the non-Jewish world also became more
tolerant of Jews during this period, leading to a new era in
Jewish history.

111. ___: TRADITION AND CRISIS: JEWISH SOCIETY AT THE END
OF THE MIDDLE AGES. New York: Schocken Books, 1971. 280 pp.,
bibliog., index.

Intensive study of Jewish society in early modern times.
Divided into three sections: the first deals with the
foundations of early modern Jewry; the second deals with
communal institutions; the third with the disintegration of
the Jewish community. The section on institutions and
structures covers both local, regional, and supranational
organizations and is among the best reviews available on the
subject. In particular, Katz´s survey of the Va´ad Arba
Arazot is unsurpassed in English sources. Unfortunately, the
footnotes and references were deleted in the English edition. The lack of documentation makes the book less useful
for the serious researcher, though as a school text the book
is still extremely important.

112. Marcus, J. R. [ed.]: THE JEW IN THE MEDIEVAL WORLD
A SOURCE BOOK, 315-1791. New York: Atheneum, 1969. 504 pp.,
bibliog., references to sources, index.

Thematically organized anthology. Primary emphasis is on
Jews of Christian lands, and relatively little on the Jews
of the Muslim world is included. Both external and internal
history are charted, with greater stress on the latter. Relations between Jews and non-Jews are covered well. Marcus
concentrates on the social, intellectual, and religious life
of the Jew as well as the place of the individual in the
community. The documents selected come from a wide variety
of sources. The book is consciously designed for classroom
use in college or high school. Marcus introduces each
chapter, explaining the source and context of the cited

documents. Each section also contains a short bibliography,
keyed to three of the most widely used textbooks in Jewish
history.

113. Netanyahu, Benzion: THE MARRANOS OF SPAIN. New York:
American Academy for Jewish Research, 1966. 254 pp., apps.,
notes, index.

Revisionist history of the Marrano experience, based on
an in-depth study of rabbinic material. Written to correct
the overly romantic view that all Marranos were Jews who
showed not only heroism but deep personal committment by
continuing the practice of Judaism in secret. Netanyahu´s
reevaluation is based on his careful reconstruction of the
rabbinic opinions and attitudes expressed in the responsa
literature dealing with Marranos. Five appendixes citing key
proof-texts reinforce Netanyahu´s thesis.
Netanyahu´s hypothesis has not, however, been universally
accepted. Most critics have emphasized the necessity to distinguish between behavioral manifestations that can be considered Jewish by historical standards and those that would
be deemed Jewish by rabbinic authorities. The Marranos, in
other words, may have felt subjectively Jewish - and must
therefore be treated as such by historians - even if they
were not objectively considered Jews by rabbinic authorities. Nevertheless, Netanyahu´s book serves as a useful
corrective to the over-romanticization of the Marranos and
the exaggeration of their practical Jewish commitment.

114. Popper, William: THE CENSORSHIP OF HEBREW BOOKS.
New York: Ktav, 1969. 156 pp., illus., notes, app., index.

Study of the censorship of Hebrew books during the Middle
Ages and early modern times. First published in 1899, this
edition contains an introduction by M. Carmilly-Weinberger
explaining the historical and historiographical contexts of
Popper´s work. Deals exclusively with censorship of books by
non-Jewish authorities in Europe, though mention is made of
compulsory Jewish self-censorship. Although outdated, the
book still contains some useful insights and data.

115. Roth, Cecil: A HISTORY OF THE MARRANOS. New York:
Meridian Books / Philadelphia: JPS, 1959. [Rep. of 1932 Ed.]
424 pp., notes, bibliog., index.

Study of the origins, development, and fate of the secret
Jews of Spain and Portugal, commonly known as Marranos.

Covers all aspects of marranism, with primary focus on the period of the Inquisition. Also deals with the spread of the Marrano diaspora. A glaring lacuna is that Roth does not explore the spiritual extent of marranic Judaism, nor does he define what was Jewish about the Marranos´ Judaism. The book is, nevertheless, well written and quite dramatic in its presentation.

116. Stern, Selma: THE COURT JEW: A CONTRIBUTION TO THE HISTORY OF THE PERIOD OF ABSOLUTISM IN CENTRAL EUROPE. Trans. from the German by Ralph Weiman. Philadelphia: JPS, 1950. 312 pp., notes, index.

A classic account of the role, personality, and fate of the Hofjuden in Germany and Austria during the age of absolutism. Places the rise of the court Jews into both Jewish and European contexts. Stern´s primary focus is on the economic role of the court Jews and the roles they played in their respective communities. A major subtheme is the changes in both European and Jewish society that led to the rise of the Hofjuden, which also eventually led to the emancipation of European Jewry.

THE PROCESS OF EMANCIPATION

117. Avineri, Shlomo: "A Note on Hegel´s Views on Jewish Emancipation." JSS, v.25 #2 (Apr., 1963): 145-151.

118. Baron, Salo W.: "Aspects of the Jewish Communal Crisis in 1848." JSS, v.14 #2 (Apr., 1952): 99-144.

119. ___ : "The Impact of the Revolution of 1848 on Jewish Emancipation." JSS, v.11 #3 (July, 1949): 195-248.

120. Katz, Jacob: JEWS AND FREEMASONS IN EUROPE, 1723-1939. Trans. From the Hebrew by Leonard Oschry. Cambridge, MA: Harvard Univ. Press, 1970. 293 pp., notes, index.

Sociohistorical investigation of the relations between Jews and Freemasons. Katz attempts to cut through the propaganda, especially the antisemitic myth of a Judaeo-masonic world conspiracy, in order to chart the actual contacts between the groups and the results of their interaction. Katz also traces the origins and implications of the myth. On the basis of his research, Katz concludes that Jews were drawn to Freemasonry as a method of gaining entry into European

society before the Emancipation. At no time did Jewish Freemasonry become a mass movement. Furthermore, becoming a
mason implied neither complete assimilation nor automatic
acceptance by other masons. Many masonic lodges, especially
in Germany, refused membership, or at least full membership,
to Jews. When the Emancipation actually occurred, Jews no
longer felt impelled to join lodges, and many founded their
own associations, such as B´nai B´rith, to foster self-
awareness, friendship, and inter-Jewish contact.

Yet in the minds of European antisemites, Jews and Freemasons were viewed as allies in a universal conspiracy to
rule the world. Although tangential to Katz´s social study,
he also charts the growts and impact of this myth. In time,
the conspiracy became an important element of antisemitic
propaganda, culminating in THE PROTOCOLS OF THE ELDERS OF
ZION. The myth ultimately provided a justification for the
Nazis and has been used in Soviet and Arab anti-Israel propaganda. The contrast between the alleged and actual relationship of Jews to Freemasonry emerges clearly from Katz´s
imprtant contribution to Jewish historiography.

121. ___: OUT OF THE GHETTO: THE SOCIAL BACKGROUND OF
JEWISH EMANCIPATION, 1770-1870. New York: Schocken Books,
1978. 271 pp., notes, index.

Effort at a social history of the emancipation between
1770-1870. Places the emancipation into ideological and
social context, within the framework of a comparison of conditions in Germany and France. The book is less than satis-
fying in its treatment of social and sociological elements,
being essentially an intellectual and political study. Outside of Germany and France, Katz gives only fleeting coverage of the emancipation. Specifically, Italy is completely
ignored and England is dealt with only briefly. More interesting is Katz´s chapter on post-emancipation European
Jewry.

* 122. Mahler, Raphael: JEWISH EMANCIPATION: A SELECTION OF
DOCUMENTS. New York: American Jewish Committee, 1941. 72 pp.

123. ___: "The Social and Political Aspects of the
Haskalah in Galicia." Y/A, v.1 (1946): 64-85.

124. Mayer, Gustav: "Early German Socialism and Jewish
Emancipation." JSS, v.1 #4 (Oct., 1939): 409-422.

125. Meyer, Michael A.: THE ORIGINS OF THE MODERN JEW: JEWISH IDENTITY AND EUROPEAN CULTURE IN GERMANY, 1749-1824. Detroit, MI: Wayne State Univ. Press, 1979. 249 pp., notes, bibliog., index.

Intellectual history focusing on the attempts of German Jews, from Moses Mendelssohn to Leopold Zunz, to redefine Judaism in light of the Haskalah, emancipation, and assimilation. Meyer concentrates on the ways in which major Jewish figures redefined Jewish identity. Also included are an analysis of the role that conversion played among German Jews at the time and the rise and purpose of early Reform Judaism. The book is strong on the description of distinct individuals, but is weaker on the social and societal background that led to the modern redefinition of Jewish identity.

126. Morgenstern, Friedrich: "Hardenberg and the Emancipation of Franconian Jewry." JSS, v.15 #3/4 (July/Oct., 1953): 253-274.

127. Ratcliffe, Barrie M.: "Crisis and Identity: Gustave d´ Eichthal and Judaism in the Emancipation Period." JSS, v.37 #2 (Spr., 1975): 122-140.

128. Rinott, Moshe: "Gabriel Riesser - Fighter for Jewish Emancipation." LBIYB, v.7 (1962): 11-38.

129. Rotenstreich, Nathan: "For and Against Emancipation: The Bruno Bauer Controversy." LBIYB, v.4 (1959): 3-36.

* 130. Sacher, H.: JEWISH EMANCIPATION: THE CONTRACT MYTH. London: English Zionist Federation, 1917. 24 pp.

131. Scult, M.: "English Missions to the Jews: Conversion in the Age of Emancipation." JSS, v.35 #1 (Jan., 1973): 3-17.

* 132. Weinryb, B. D.: JEWISH EMANCIPATION UNDER ATTACK. New York: American Jewish Committee, 1942. 95 pp.

THE RESULTS OF EMANCIPATION

133. Arendt, H.: "The Jew as Pariah: a Hidden Tradition." JSS, v.6 #2 (Apr., 1944): 99-122.

134. ___: "Priviledged Jews." JSS, v.8 #1 (Jan., 1946): 3-30.

135. Duker, Abraham G. and Meir Ben-Horin [eds.]: EMANCI-PATION AND COUNTER-EMANCIPATION. New York: Ktav, 1974. 413 pp., notes, bibliog., index to bibliog.

Anthology of scholarly essays on emancipation culled from Jewish Social Studies, with an introduction by S. W. Baron. Primary focus is political history, with social and intel-lectual history duly represented. The subjects covered are defined broadly, and include antisemitism and Jewish nation-alism, as well as emancipation. All of the essays are important contributions in their own right, and the book offers a good resource for college courses on modern Jewish history. The bibliography provides a useful selection of relevant literature in English and is a good starting point for students and serious researchers. It was originally intended to publish further thematic anthologies on related subjects, but none have appeared to date.

CONTENTS: Salo W. Baron: The Journal and the Conference of Jewish Social Studies / M. R. Cohen: Philosophies of Jewish History / H. Arendt: Privileged Jews / Isaac E. Barzilay: The Jew in the Literature of the Enlightenment / Abraham G. Duker: The Polish Democratic Society and the Jewish Problem, 1832-1846 / Salo W. Baron: The Impact of the Revolution of 1848 on Jewish Emancipation / Mario Rossi: Emancipation of the Jews of Italy / E. Silberner: Friedrich Engels and the Jews / R. F. Byrnes: Antisemitism in France before the Dreyfus Affair / Koppel Pinson: Arkady Kremer, Vladimir Medem, and the Ideology of the Jewish "Bund" / O. Karbach: The Founder of Modern Political Antisemitism: Georg von Schoenerer / A. G. Duker: Selected Bibliography on Jewish Emancipation and Counter-Emancipation.

136. Glatzer, N. N. [ed.]: THE DYNAMICS OF EMANCIPATION: THE JEW IN THE MODERN AGE. Boston: Beacon Press, 1965. 320 pp., notes, bibliog., index.

Anthology studying the dilemma of Jews and Judaism in the modern age. The tension forming the basis of the anthology involves the Jew's desire to retain his Jewish identity while fully participating in secular society. Glatzer has taken selections from a wide variety of Jewish thinkers, activists, and leaders. The selections are grouped themati-cally and divided into seven sections: "In the Perspective

of Emancipation;" "Rethinking Jewish Faith;" "Religious
Movements in Modern Judaism;" "The Dark Years;" "Zionism and
the Land of Israel;" "The American Scene;" and "Allowing the
Heart to Speak." Some of the sections are subdivided chronologically, but others are not, leading to possible confusion. Nevertheless the selections offer an insight into the
problems Jews have faced in the modern world.

137. Graff, Gil: SEPARATION OF CHURCH AND STATE: DINA DE-
MALKHUTA DINA IN JEWISH LAW, 1750-1848. University: Univ. of
Alabama Press, 1985. 223 pp., notes, bibliog., index.

Inquiry into the status of Jewish law and legal ideology
in modern times. Graff studies the development of the principle that stipulated "the law of the kingdom is the law"
that regulated Jewish communal relations with the non-Jewish
environment. In ancient and medieval times, the concept was
limited in its import because of Jewish communal autonomy.
Thus, although the law of the kingdom was considered authoritative, its applicability to Jewish life was limited to
taxation and regulating Jewish relations with the local
ruler. Only in modern times did the concept begin to take on
broader meanings for the separation of church and state.
Graff focuses on the attitude of Jews from the Enlightenment
onward. Moses Mendelssohn and his followers attempted to
develop a viable system of religious freedom in a neutral
society where Jews and Christians would enjoy equal rights,
even while maintaining different modes of worship and separate religious identities. In Graff´s view the redefinition
of "dina de-malkhuta dina" culminated in the Paris Sanhedrin, which legalized and systematized the concept of Judaism
as an exclusively religious community, a "church" completely
separated from any tinge of Jewish nationalism.

138. Hertzberg, Arthur: "The Emancipation: a Reassessment
After Two Centuries." MJ, v.1 #1 (May, 1981): 46-53.

139. Jehouda, Josue: THE FIVE STAGES OF JEWISH EMANCIPA-
TION. Trans. from the French with an introduction by Eva
Jackson; Revised by Robert Lilienfeld. South Brunswick, NJ:
Thomas Yoseloff, 1966. 119 pp., notes.

Philosophical and historical inquiry into the emancipation of European Jewry. Jehouda´s main effort is an attempt
to explain the broader purpose of modern Jewry and of Jewish
history. Jehouda places his ruminations into five phases,
each one based on a forty year generation beginning with

Moses Mendelssohn. The fifth phase has not, according to
Jehouda, dawned yet; this era is the long-awaited messianic
period that will develop out of the reconciliation of the
three great monotheistic faiths. This latter assertion may
be a bit controversial; it is certainly unprovable. Albeit,
Jehouda offers a thought provoking theological analysis of
modern Jewish history.

140. Kallen, Horace M.: "The Bearing of Emancipation on
Jewish Survival." Y/A, v.12 (1958/59): 9-35.

141. Katz, Jacob: EMANCIPATION AND ASSIMILATION: STUDIES
IN MODERN JEWISH HISTORY. Farnborough, UK: Gregg, 1972. 293
pp., notes.

Collection of essays on modern Jewish history. Katz deals
with the topics of emancipation, assimilation, antisemitism,
and nationalism as interwoven themes. His method has often
been called sociological history, because Katz emphasizes
the societal aspects of the historical process. In this
work, one theme, that of Jewish integration into European
society as a result of the Emancipation, leads Katz to view
events as they relate to the aforementioned sociohistorical
conception of history. Unfortunately, the doctoral dissertation in which Katz first proposed this type of study is reproduced in this volume in German and was not translated.
Another essay, also in German, is included, and both are unavailable to non-German readers. The essays cover a variety
of subtopics related to the concepts and themes Katz set
out. Of special interest is "The Concept of Social History
and its Possible Use in Jewish Historical Research," where
Katz delineates his methodology. Also interesting is Katz´s
sociological analysis of zionism and his inquiry into the
antisemitic slogan of a "state within a state."

142. ___ [ed.]: TOWARD MODERNITY: THE EUROPEAN JEWISH
MODEL. New Brunswick, NJ: Transaction Books, 1987. 279 pp.,
notes, index.

Anthology of Jewish social and intellectual history,
based on a symposium held in the spring of 1983 at Haifa
University. The theme of the anthology is the modernization
of European Jewry during the eighteenth and nineteenth
centuries. Identified with modernization is the haskalah
movement, which argued that Jews had to catch up with the
scientific advances and new ideologies of modern Europe. The
anthology is most important for the comparative analysis

offered by the essays: each author deals with one specific
country. The reader thus gains a broad overview of issues,
personalities, and organizations responsible for the modernization of European Jewry, while also gaining specific insights into national developments.

CONTENTS: E. Etkes: Immanent Factors and External Influences
in the Development of the Haskalah Movement in Russia / I.
Bartel: 'The Heavenly City of Germany' and Absolutism a la
Mode d´Autriche: the Rise of the Haskalah in Galicia / R. S.
Wistrich: The Modernization of Viennese Jewry: the Impact of
German Culture in a Multi-Ethnic State / Hillel J. Kieval:
Caution´s Progress: the Modernization of Jewish Life in
Prague, 1780-1830 / M. Silber: The Historical Experience of
German Jewry and its Impact on the Haskalah and Reform in
Hungary / M. Graetz: The History of an Estrangement between
Two Jewish Communities: German and French Jewry During the
Nineteenth Century / J. Michman: The Impact of German-Jewish
Modernization on Dutch Jewry / Lois C. Dubin: Trieste and
Berlin: the Italian Role in the Cultural Politics of the
Haskalah / Todd M. Endelman: The Englishness of Jewish Mo-
dernity in England / M. A. Meyer: German-Jewish Identity in
Nineteenth-Century America.

143. Pelli, Moshe: THE AGE OF HASKALAH: STUDIES IN HEBREW
LITERATURE OF THE ENLIGHTENMENT IN GERMANY. Leiden: E. J.
Brill, 1979. 255 pp., notes, bibliog., index.

Collection of studies on Haskalah literature, divided
into two parts. Part I offers a broad analytical approach to
literary styles and issues raised by the Haskalah. Part II
deals with specific authors and their contributions to Jewish literature. Pelli´s approach is a combination of literary criticism and intellectual history, with emphasis on the
latter. Pelli´s motivation is to reevaluate the German
Haskalah and its contributions. In some of the essays, Pelli
attempts to revise generally accepted positions. This is
especially true of "An Outlook to the Past, the Sacred Literature: Did the Hebrew Maskilim Hate the Talmud?" which
also happens to be one of the book´s most interesting essays. Other essays are less revisionist in their position,
but they are all important contributions to the study of the
Haskalah and of German Jewry as a whole.

144. Wolf, Immanuel: "On the Concepts of a Science of
Judaism." LBIYB, v.2 (1957): 194-204.

4

Religious Trends

SURVEYS

145. Blau, Joseph L.: MODERN VARIETIES OF JUDAISM. New
York: Columbia Univ. Press, 1966. 217 pp., notes, index.

Survey of modern Jewish religious thought, based on a
series of lectures given at Northwestern University. Blau´s
main theme is the emancipation and the subsequent need to
accommodate Judaism to modern realities. In all cases of
Reform, Conservative, and Orthodox Judaism, Blau adopts a
universal approach, dealing with both European and American
trends. An important chapter is on the role of zionism as a
secularized, humanistic Jewish national religion. Blau sees
the emancipation as unleashing a great deal of Jewish creative energy, while also destroying the communal foundations
of world Jewry. Ultimately, Blau concludes, the creativeness
of modern Jewry will prevail, despite the immediate negative
consequences of the emancipation.

146. __: THE STORY OF JEWISH PHILOSOPHY. New York: Random
House, 1962. 322 pp., bibliog., notes, index.

History of Jewish philosophy from the Bible to modern
times. The book is written as a primer in Jewish philosophy,
adopting an intellectual-historical approach. Blau defines
the highlights of each philosopher´s work, explaining their
formulations, and buttressing his explanations with important quotes. Blau is fair in his treatment of differing
philosophies; he does not limit his inquiry only to the
rationalist philosophers. The book is well suited as an
introductory survey, especially if used with other textbooks
in Jewish history.

147. Epstein, Isidore: THE FAITH OF JUDAISM: AN INTERPRE-
TATION FOR OUR TIME. London: The Soncino Press, 1968. 418
pp., notes, excurses, indexes.

Systematic restatement of Orthodox Judaism by a leading
Anglo-Jewish scholar. The book may be seen as a statement of
the faith of a modern Orthodox Jew, who accepts both the
scientific and the traditional interpretations of religion.
Based on an appreciation of traditional sources, Epstein
also gives his own, sometimes novel, interpretations. He is
best at explaining the interrelationship between God and
man, as well as God and history. Willing to keep an open
mind, Epstein has no qualms about citing non-Jewish and
heterodox Jewish sources.

148. __: JUDAISM: A HISTORICAL PRESENTATION. Baltimore,
MD: Penguin Books, 1959. 349 pp., notes, bibliog., index.

Brief but comprehensive history of Judaism. Shows the
developments, internal and external, that constituted the
Jewish experience during 4,000 years. Spiritual, political,
and social movements of note are explored. The book is
fairly balanced between the factual and the interpretive.
The focus is clearly on the biblical and talmudic eras, with
seventeen chapters out of twenty-two covering the First and
Second Commonwealth periods. Later eras are reviewed more
briefly, since the basic religious premises had already been
established in the earlier, formative phases of Jewish
history.

> #10. Finkelstein, Louis [ed.]: THE JEWS.

CONTENTS: Volume II. THE JEWS: THEIR RELIGION AND CULTURE.
R. Gordis: The Bible as a Cultural Monument / Ralph Marcus:
Hellenistic Jewish Literature / Shalom Spiegel: On Medieval
Hebrew Poetry / A. S. Halkin: Judeo-Arabic Literature / A.
J. Heschel: The Mystical Element in Judaism / Abraham Menes:
Patterns of Jewish Scholarship in Eastern Europe / H. Bavli:
The Modern Renaissance of Hebrew Literature / Moshe Davis:
Jewish Religious Life and Institutions in America / Simon
Greenberg: Jewish Educational Institutions / Yudel Mark:
Yiddish Literature / Louis Finkelstein: The Jewish Religion:
its Beliefs and Practices.

149. Friedlander, Michael: THE JEWISH RELIGION. New York:
Pardes Pub. House, 1946. 530 pp., notes, apps., bibliog.,
indexes.

Survey of Jewish religious doctrine. Friedlander cites most of the classical Jewish thinkers and every important issue. Attempts to answer a deceptively simple question: What is Judaism? His answer, more complex than the question, is quite successful. The book is divided into two parts. At the core of Part I, "Our Creed," Friedlander places Maimonides' Thirteen Principles, grouping them into general categories and extending them to deal with important theocentric issues. By way of example, Friedlander uses the First Principle, that there is a God who is creator and ruler of the world, to distinguish Judaism from other theologies both ancient and modern - naturalism, polytheism, pantheism, atheism, and deism. Part II, "Our Duties," uses the Ten Commandments as a starting point for a full analysis of Jewish practice. Significantly, Friedlander does not argue for any branch of modern Judaism, although himself Orthodox, he refused to recognize any such distinction. The book is about Judaism, which Friedlander saw as eternal, and eternally true. Interpretations of Judaism might change from generation to generation but, in his opinion, these were all manifestations of one truth. Foreword by Theodore Gaster; preface by Joshua Bloch.

150. Glatzer, Nachum N. [ed.]: MODERN JEWISH THOUGHT: A SOURCE READER. New York: Schocken Books, 1977. 240 pp., notes, bibliog., index.

Anthology of modern Jewish philosophy. Includes both religious and political philosophers. The selections are grouped in chronological order. This organization may leave the reader puzzled, however, as the table of contents deals with authors, not issues. Thus, for example, Ahad Ha'am, Judah L. Magnes, Simon Dubnow, and Yehezkel Kaufmann are grouped together for no apparent reason save their chronological proximity. Glatzer gives a brief introduction for each selection, while the appended notes identify sources and individuals referred to by the authors. Most of the texts have never appeared before in English, but the anthology is not definitive.

151. Guttmann, Julius: PHILOSOPHIES OF JUDAISM: THE HISTORY OF JEWISH PHILOSOPHY FROM BIBLICAL TIMES TO FRANZ ROSENZWEIG. Trans. from the Hebrew by David W. Silverman. 464 pp., bibliog., notes, index.

Survey of Jewish philosophy. The book is not an effort at philosophical inquiry, but rather an exercize in intellec-

tual history. Guttmann carefully charts the development of
Jewish philosophy and places Jewish thought into the broader
philosophical systems of each era. According to Guttmann,
despite the existence of a very clear pattern of biblical
thought, philosophy per se did not begin among Jews until
the confrontation with Hellenism. Jewish philosophy is thus
the absorption and adaptation of philosophical ideas, and
their transformation for Jewish needs. Guttmann sees three
eras of philosophical activity: the Hellenistic period,
based on Plato and Aristotle; the Middle Ages, when Jews
were confronted with Muslim philosophy; and the modern age,
which confronted Jews with a multiplicity of philosophical
models. His emphasis on individual thinkers makes Guttmann´s
work an important contribution to Jewish intellectual
history.

152. Herzog, I.: JUDAISM: LAW AND ETHICS. London: Soncino
Press, 1974. 227 pp., notes.

Collection of essays written by the first Ashkenazi Chief
Rabbi of Israel, Rav Isaac Halevy Herzog. The collection was
edited by his son Chaim, president of the State of Israel.
Herzog was a giant in the Torah world but was equally comfortable in the secular world of scholarship. Included in
this anthology are his doctoral dissertation, "The Dyeing of
Purple in Ancient Israel," and two dozen of his other essays. Of special interest is his three-part essay "The
Talmud as a Source for the History of Ancient Science" and
his four-part "The Administration of Justice in Ancient
Israel." These essays show a depth of understanding as well
as a clear acceptance of scientific methodology. Herzog
argues forcefully that Jewish law and tradition must be
understood in historic and social context, and claims that
such an understanding in no way undermines the authority of
the Torah or of halakhah.

153. Horowitz, George: THE SPIRIT OF JEWISH LAW: A BRIEF
ACCOUNT OF BIBLICAL AND RABBINICAL JURISPRUDENCE WITH A SPE-
CIAL NOTE ON JEWISH LAW AND THE STATE OF ISRAEL. New York:
Central Book Company, 1963. 812 pp., chron., notes, apps.,
gloss., bibliog., indexes.

Guidebook to Jewish law, with emphasis on civil law. In
addition to being one of the first English-language compen-
diums on halakhah, the book contains a special note on the
status of halakhah in Israel. An introductory chapter explains the method and spirit of halakhah, but is only a

brief review of that complex topic. Then too, the actual authority of halakhah is not debated, but rather assumed. Very usefully the author places halakhah into historical context. Horowitz also offers short summaries of important halakhic literature and sketches the governmental forms that have prevailed in Jewish communities at various times. The book has special usefulness as an introduction to Jewish jurisprudence for both students and interested laymen.

154. Husik, I.: A HISTORY OF MEDIAEVAL JEWISH PHILOSOPHY. New York: Atheneum, 1973. 464 pp., notes, bibliog., indexes.

Survey organized around the philosophers, presented in chronological order. In his introduction Husik deals with the broad issues which animated medieval Jewish philosophy, and in subsequent chapters he shows how the individual philosophers dealt with those issues. Both the well-known philosophers, and those considerably less known are reviewed. Husik's largest chapter is dedicated to an extensive study of the philosophical activity of Moses Maimonides. Unfortunately, Husik limits himself only to rationalist philosophers and does not deal with the Kabbalah. He does, however, attempt to explain each philosopher in terms of both internal logic as well as external influences, both Jewish and non-Jewish.

155. Katz, Jacob [ed.]: THE ROLE OF RELIGION IN MODERN JEWISH HISTORY. Cambridge, MA.: Assn. for Jewish Studies, 1975. 171 pp., notes, conference program.

Anthology based on two conferences held in March and April, 1974, at the Universities of Pennsylvania and Toronto, on the subject of religion in modern Jewish history. While their emphasis is on movements, Orthodox and modern heterodox groups are included. Although historical analysis is the primary methodology, many essays also issue from a sociological premise. Originating as conference papers, many of the essays have a response, which adds another perspective to complex and, at times, controversial issues. Katz's second essay, "Sources of Orthodox Trends," includes an appendix containing nine Hebrew sources documenting the development of traditional Jewish positions in western and central Europe during the mid-nineteenth century.

CONTENTS: J. Katz: Religion as a Uniting and Dividing Force in Modern Jewish History / L. S. Feuer and L. Silberstein: Responses / J. Katz: Sources of Orthodox Trends / M. Fox:

Philosophy and Religious Values in Modern Jewish Thought /
W. Harvey: Response / Michael A. Meyer: Universalism and
Jewish Unity in the Thought of Abraham Geiger / S. Poppel:
Response / Zosa Szajkowski: Secular Versus Religious Jewish
Life in France / I. Friedman: Dissensions over Jewish Iden-
tity in West European Jewry / M. Scult: Response / Marshall
Sklare: Religion and Ethnicity in the American Jewish Com-
munity: Changing Aspects of Reform, and Orthodox Judaism /
F. Talmage: Perspectives on a Conference.

156. Lewittes, Mendell: THE NATURE AND HISTORY OF JEWISH
LAW. New York: Yeshiva Univ. Dept. of Special Publ., 1966.
81 pp., notes.

Brief review of the history of halakhah. Primarily useful
as an introductory guide to Jewish law, the book deals with
each of the key concepts and issues in halakhic history.
Lewittes does not even try to give a chronological sketch of
the subject, which could easily fill volumes. Each concept
is dealt with in context of both the Written and Oral Law.
Some sections of the book are polemical, especially the last
section dealing with the modern period, a chapter that is
totally inadequate. Foreword by Leon D. Stitskin.

157. Montagu, L. H.: "Spiritual Possibilities of Judaism
Today." JQR, v.11 #2 (Jan., 1899): 216-231.

158. Montefiore, Claude G.: "Some Notes on the Effect of
Biblical Criticism upon the Jewish Religion." JQR, v.4 #2
(Jan., 1892): 293-306.

159. Newman, Louis I.: THE JEWISH PEOPLE, FAITH AND LIFE:
A MANUAL AND GUIDEBOOK OF INFORMATION CONCERNING JEWRY AND
JUDAISM. New York: Bloch, 1965. 277 pp., bibliog.

Lexicon and guidebook to Judaism, Jewry, and Jewish culture. The book is divided into three parts. Part I, "The
Jewish People," is a broad survey of Jewish history and contemporary affairs. Part II, "The Jewish Faith," is a survey
of different religious movements and summaries of key religious concepts. This section also contains four credos representing the Orthodox, Conservative, Reform, and Reconstructionist positions on religion and faith. Part III, "The
Jewish Life," offers an explanation for important Jewish
ceremonies, customs, and holidays. Though the bibliography
is a bit outdated, the book is still useful for those with
little or no background who wish to get a basic idea about

Jews and Judaism.

160. Rosenbloom, Joseph R.: CONVERSION TO JUDAISM: FROM
THE BIBLICAL PERIOD TO THE PRESENT. Cincinnati, OH: Hebrew
Union College Press, 1978. 178 pp., notes, bibliog., index.

Chronological study of conversion to Judaism. Emphasis is
on the rabbinic and medieval periods. The biblical foundation for proselytizing is, however, also covered. A separate
section is dedicated to the problem of group conversion, including the conversion of the Falashas. Most interesting is
Rosenbloom's chapter on contemporary problems of conversion
and intermarriage. Rosenbloom implies strongly that one way
to bolster the faltering Jewish demographic picture is to
return to a policy of seeking converts, although he by no
means argues for active mass proselytization. Rosenbloom
adopts a broad approach, sacrificing much detail in order to
cover every base. This weakens some sections, while others
could easily be enlarged. Nevertheless, this is an interesting and provocative study.

161. Rosenthal, Gilbert: FOUR PATHS TO ONE GOD: TODAY'S
JEW AND HIS RELIGION. New York: Bloch Pub., 1973. 323 pp.,
notes, bibliog., index.

Comparative study of American Judaism. After a brief introductory chapter reviewing general historical developments, Rosenthal gets to the main section of his work. In
eight chapters he reviews the history and ideology of Orthodox, Reform, Conservative and Reconstructionist Judaism as
they have developed over the nineteenth and twentieth
centuries. The book is based largely, but not completely, on
secondary sources. In particular Rosenthal has consulted
the writings of key thinkers in order to form a general
picture of what each branch believes. Rosenthal's last
chapter offers his critique and prognosis for each of the
four branches. Although himself a Conservative, Rosenthal's
approach is objective and his critique is neither unfair nor
outlandish. His basic prognosis is that American Judaism
will continue to be creative in its pursuit of the Divine.

162. Rudavsky, David: MODERN JEWISH RELIGIOUS MOVEMENTS:
A HISTORY OF EMANCIPATION AND ADJUSTMENT. 3rd Edition. New
York: Behrman House, 1979. 460 pp., notes, bibliog., index.

Social and intellectual study of Judaism and Jewish
thought in the last 200 years. Attempts to assess the effect

of emancipation and the continuing efforts at adjusting the
Jewish religion to contemporary realities. The book is divided into three sections. Part I, "Backgounds," deals with
pre-emancipation Jewry and with the emancipation and its
impact; Part II, "European Roots," deals with the results of
the emancipation in Europe and the redefiniton of Judaism by
European Jewish thinkers; Part III, "American Shoots," deals
with the mainstream American Jewish religious thought.
Rudavsky integrates individual thinkers within the context
of their movements, while also comparing them with leaders
of other movements. Most important are Rudavsky´s comparison
of different varieties of Judaism and his discussion of
Jewish religious thought under the impact of modernity.

163. Schechter, Solomon: "The Dogmas of Judaism." JQR,
v.1 #1 (Oct., 1888): 48-61; #2 (Jan., 1889): 115-127.

164. Simon, Oswald J.: "Authority and Dogma in Judaism."
JQR, v.5 #2 (Jan., 1893): 231-243.

165. Wiener, Max: "The Conception of Mission in Traditional and Modern Judaism." Y/A, v.2/3 (1947/48): 9-24.

HASIDISM, MYSTICISM, AND MESSIANISM

166. Buber, Martin: HASIDISM AND MODERN MAN. Trans. from
the Hebrew by M. Friedman. New York: Horizon, 1958. 256 pp.

Philosophical restatement of Buber´s views on hasidism.
Basically an attempt to interpret hasidism in light of and
as a form of existentialist philosophy. Buber also explains
key hasidic concepts, such as hitlahavut, avodah, kavanah,
and shiflut. Much of Buber´s philosophy is based on his interpretation of hasidic tales, especially those on Israel
Ba´al Shem Tov. Though also published in a separate volume,
a selection of tales about the founder of hasidism is included in this book. Friedman´s introduction is a succint
summary of Buber´s philosophy.

It is important to note that Buber´s interpretation of
hasidism is not accepted by the majority of scholars. They
felt he was in a way distorting hasidism by ignoring its
revivalist and fundamentalist religious elements, rendering
hasidism into a modern, secularized philosophy that would
appeal to those seeking spiritual sustenance.

167. ___: THE ORIGIN AND MEANING OF HASIDISM. Edited with Introduction and Trans. from the German by M. Friedman. New York: Harper & Row, 1966. 254 pp.

Attempt to interpret hasidism in light of Buber´s other works. Especially important to Buber´s interpretation are the hasidic tales, which Buber published in three volumes. Primarily, Buber is interested in pointing to a hasidic way of life, rather than defining hasidic concepts. As a result, Buber´s work is by no means accepted by a majority of scholars. His particularly idiosyncratic attempt to place hasidism in the broader context of the history of religion is interesting but weak, as it fails to place hasidism into a specifically Jewish religious context. This same weakness holds true for Buber´s supplementary chapter, "A Response to Rudolf Pannwitz," which compares hasidism, gnosis, and Christianity.

168. Dresner, Samuel H.: THE ZADDIK: THE DOCTRINE OF THE ZADDIK ACCORDING TO THE WRITINGS OF RABBI YAAKOV YOSEF OF POLNOY. New York: Schocken Books, 1974. 312 pp., notes.

Hallmark study based on the writings of Rabbi Yaakov Yosef of Polnoy, who was one of the keenest theorists of the role of the "zaddik" in the hasidic community. The book is divided into two distinct parts: Part I offers the historical background to Rabbi Yaakov and his writings. This section also deals with the questions that Rabbi Yaakov attempted to answer. Part II covers Rabbi Yaakov´s answers, comprising his theory about the role of the zaddik. According to Rabbi Yaakov, the zaddik had to be both a true spiritualist, capable of oneness with the Divine, and a compassionate activist involved in the Jewish community. Even without the analysis of Rabbi Yaakov´s work, Dressner has made an important contribution to the study of hasidism. Preface by Abraham J. Heschel.

169. Minkin, Jacob S.: THE ROMANCE OF HASIDISM. New York: Macmillan, 1935. 398 pp., notes, bibliog., index.

Survey of hasidism, with emphasis on its intellectual and social elements. Interwoven with the story of hasidism are the biographies of key zaddikim, including the Ba´al Shem Tov, Shneur Zalman of Lyadi, and Nachman of Bratslav. In the chapters on these zaddikim, Minkin carefully charts the patterns of thought that characterize them. Unlike other historians of hasidism, Minkin does not gloss over negative or unpleasant details, for example the regal and self-seeking behavior of some of the zaddikim. Even so, Minkin concludes that hasidism was a historically significant movement which contributed considerably to Jewish survival. Minkin also discusses the split with the "mitnagdim" in similar fashion. He ends with a discussion of the decline of hasidism since the mid-nineteenth century. Of course, he could neither foresee the virtual destruction of European hasidism during the Holocaust, nor could he predict the transplanting of some hasidic sects to America and Israel.

170. Newman, Louis I. with S. Spitz [eds.]: THE HASIDIC ANTHOLOGY: TALES AND TEACHINGS OF THE HASIDIM. Trans. from the Hebrew, Yiddish, and German by the editors. New York: Schocken Books, 1963. 556 pp., notes, bibliog., indexes.

Anthology of tales displaying the wisdom of the zaddikim. The primary purpose of the collection is to provide a guide to hasidic doctrine and belief. Unlike other, more literary or philosophical anthologies, Newman attempts to be more analytical. The anthology is organized topically; selections are arranged alphabetically. Within each chapter citations from the masters are organized chronologically. Newman offers a broad introduction that places hasidic theology into context. The message of the anthology is hasidism´s affirmation of life, and the masters´ deeper appreciation of the importance of communal and personal life.

171. Rabinowicz, Harry: THE WORLD OF HASSIDISM. London: Vallentine, Mitchell, 1970. 271 pp., illus., notes, gloss., bibliog., index.

History of the hasidic movement, from its origins to the 1970s. Views hasidism in its most pristine form as a type of religious revivalism. Hasidism is also placed into the specific cultural context of East European Jewry. An incisive chapter deals with Jewish mysticism. Rabinowicz does not break any new ground methodologically, but is trying to provide a synthetic history, and as such the book is very useful. Rabinowicz details the split between hasidim and mitnagdim, and the reactions of both to the Haskalah, fairly and in an objective way. Of particular interest are Rabinowicz´s chapters on the Holocaust and the State of Israel. Although the Holocaust caused a massive loss of Jewish life, losses that were especially felt among East European Orthodox and hasidic Jews, the destruction did not signal the end of hasidism. To the contrary, Rabinowicz ends with a survey of how hasidic communities have been rebuilt in Israel, England, and the United States.

> #77. Rotenberg, M.: DIALOGUE WITH DEVIANCE.

172. Scholem, G.: MAJOR TRENDS IN JEWISH MYSTICISM. New York: Schocken Books, 1961. 460 pp., notes, bibliog., index.

Review of the development of Kabbalah by one of the deans of the modern study of Jewish mysticism. After dealing with general and methodological issues, Scholem reviews Kabbalah in all its forms and permutations. Scholem's presentation synthesizes both extensive interpretation with intensive analytical study. The chapters are actually separate but interconnected lectures. Most important is his analysis of Lurianic Kabbalah, Shabbateanism, and hasidism. Unlike previous forms of Jewish mysticism, Lurianic Kabbalah was both exoteric and activist in seeking the Messiah. The resulting false messianic movement of Shabbetai Zevi nearly rent Judaism asunder. Scholem sees hasidism as a deactivated form of Lurianic Kabbalah, which thus avoided the pitfalls of the Shabbatean heresy.

173. ___: THE MESSIANIC IDEA IN JUDAISM AND OTHER ESSAYS ON JEWISH SPIRITUALITY. New York: Schocken Books, 1971. 376 pp., notes, index.

Anthology of essays representing an effort at synthesizing Scholem's research on Kabbalah. Primary emphasis in this case is on the relationship between Kabbalah and messianic speculation. Two-thirds of the essays are narrowly focused studies on aspects of mystical and messianic ideology. Especially important in this group of essays is "Redemption Through Sin," which is an intensive inquiry into the ideology of the Shabbatean movement and its leader Shabbetai Zevi. The remaining third of the book might be termed historiographical, discussing how scholars have dealt with Kabbalah in the past and present. Arguing forcefully for his own methodology, Scholem scrutinizes and criticizes the position of the nineteenth-century Science of Judaism, Martin Buber, and also Franz Rosenzweig. Whether in agreement or disagreement, the essays are a thought-provoking compelling analysis of the forms of Jewish mysticism.

174. ___: "The Neutralisation of the Messianic Element in Early Hasidism." JJS, v.20 #1/4 (1969): 25-55.

175. Silver, Abba H.: A HISTORY OF MESSIANIC SPECULATION IN ISRAEL: FROM THE FIRST THROUGH THE SEVENTEENTH CENTURIES. Boston: Beacon Press, 1959. 268 pp., notes, index.

Traces the messianic idea from its earliest expressions to the seventeenth century. Shows the logic and sources behind a variety of messianic calculations. In addition to these calculations, the false messiahs of each age are enumerated, as are the various opponents to messianic speculation. The book ends before the rise of the Shabbatean heresy, which is unfortunate since Silver´s account is lucid, well documented, and very perceptive. The Beacon edition contains a new introduction, where Silver brings the story of the Jews´ messianic expectation up to date, including his thoughts on the creation of the State of Israel and its role in Jewish messianism.

176. Weiss, J. G.: "A Circle of Pre-Hasidic Pneumatics." JJS, v.8 #3/4 (1957): 199-213.

177. ___: "Contemplative Mysticism and ´Faith´ in Hasidic Piety." JJS, v4 #1 (1953): 19-29.

178. ___: "The Kavvanoth of Prayer in Early Hasidism." JJS, v.9 #3/4 (1958): 163-192.

179. ___: STUDIES IN EASTERN EUROPEAN JEWISH MYSTICISM. Edited by D. Goldstein. Oxford: Oxford Univ. Press for the Littman Library, 1985. 272 pp., notes, index.

Collection of studies on hasidism. Two-thirds of the essays were previously published. All of Weiss´s essays are meticulously documented and cover two themes: the origin and social context of hasidism, and aspects of hasidic ideology. The latter essays are narrowly focused and carefully defined. Important to Weiss´s understanding of hasidism is the total mobilization of the hasid´s emotions. Weiss also offers an intriguing revision on the origins of hasidism. Rather than attribute hasidism to one single charismatic leader, Weiss identifies five other charismatic preachers who were contemporaries of, or even preceded, Israel Ba´al Shem Tov. Weiss also has some insights revising the general views on the zaddik and on the Habad movement. The present book is an important contribution to the study of hasidism.

180. ___: "Via Passiva in Early Hasidism." JJS, v.11 #3/4 (1960): 137-155.

REFORM JUDAISM

181. Blau, Joseph L. [ed.]: REFORM JUDAISM: A HISTORICAL
PERSPECTIVE. New York: Ktav, 1973. 529 pp., notes.

Anthology offering a historical perspective on American
Reform Judaism. The essays were selected from THE CENTRAL
CONFERENCE OF AMERICAN RABBIS YEARBOOK and are divided by
topic. A general introduction ties the essays together while
also providing a context for the understanding of Reform in
America. An especially interesting section deals with ritual; another deals with zionism, an issue that sparked a
debate within the Reform movement during the 1930s. Each
section has a brief introduction which annotates the essays.
The dynamic nature of Reform positions emerges clearly from
the essays, and as a result the anthology is useful for
understanding American Reform Judaism.

CONTENTS: Emil G. Hirsch: The Philosophy of the Reform Move-
ment in American Judaism / Julian Morgenstern: Were Isaac M.
Wise Alive Today: a Program for Judaism in America / Bernard
J. Bamberger: The Developing Philosophy of Reform Judaism /
Levi A. Olan: From the Point of View of Philosophy / Wm. G.
Braude: From the Point of View of History / K. Kohler: The
Mission of Israel and its Application to Modern Times / Lou
H. Silberman: The Theologian's Task / E. B. Borowitz: The
Idea of God / R. B. Gittelsohn: No Retreat from Reason! / K.
Kohler: The Origin and Function of Ceremonies in Judaism /
W. G. Plaut: The Sabbath in the Reform Movement / Samuel S.
Cohon: The Theology of the Union Prayer Book / I. Bettan:
The Function of the Prayer Book / E. Rivkin: Some Historical
Aspects of Authority in Judaism / S. B. Freehof: Reform
Judaism and the Halacha / A. Guttmann: The Moral Law as
Halacha in Reform Judaism / Jacob Z. Lauterbach: Talmudic-
Rabbinic View on Birth Control / H. Berkowitz: Why I am not
a Zionist / C. Levias: The Justification of Zionism / S.
Schulman: Israel / A. H. Silver: Israel / J. L. Liebman: God
and the World Crisis - Can We Still Believe in Providence? /
Emil L. Fackenheim: Two Types of Reform: Reflections Occa-
sioned by Hasidism / S. Atlas: The Contemporary Relevance of
the Philosophy of Maimonides.

182. Borowitz, E. B.: LIBERAL JUDAISM. New York: Union of
American Hebrew Congregations, 1984. 468 pp.

Thematic restatement of Reform Jewish ideology. Written
for the interested layperson, Borowitz attempts to answer

one question: what makes a good Jew? The book is nicely
written in a clear nontechnical style. Borowitz reviews
philosophical and practical aspects of Jewish life from the
prism of Reform Judaism. To do so he divides his work into
four parts: "The Jewish People," "The God We Affirm," "The
Bible and Tradition," and "Living as a Jew." In each case
Borowitz provides a historical overview and explains the
evolution of Reform thought. He is not afraid to discuss
controversial topics, and his positions are stated forthrightly. One may not agree with everything Borowitz says,
but his book is both interesting and thought-provoking.

183. Meyer, Michael A.: "Alienated Intellectuals in the
Camp of Religious Reform: the Frankfurt Reformfreunde, 1842-
1845." AJS Review, v.6 (1981): 61-86.

184. Montefiore, C. G.: "Liberal Judaism." JQR, v.20 #3
(Apr., 1908): 363-390.

185. Philipson, David: "The Beginnings of the Reform
Movement in Judaism." JQR, v.15 #3 (Apr., 1903): 475-521;
v.16 #1 (Oct., 1903): 30-72; #3 (Apr., 1904): 485-524; v.17
#2 (Jan., 1905): 307-353.

186. ___: "The Progress of the Jewish Reform Movement in
the United States." JQR, v.10 #1 (Oct., 1897): 52-99.

187. ___: THE REFORM MOVEMENT IN JUDAISM. New York: Ktav,
1967. Revised Ed. 503 pp., notes, index.

Classic history of Reform Judaism. Based on the second
edition, the Ktav reprint includes an extensive introduction
by Solomon B. Freehof. The text covers the Reform movement
from its origins to the early 1930s. Most of the book deals
with Reform in Germany; relatively less attention is paid to
the course of Reform in England and the United States.
Philipson also studies the European Reform rabbinical conferences, but does not detail their American counterparts.
    Although the book is the standard account of the rise of
Reform Judaism, Philipson's account is not without flaws.
His positions on pre-Emancipation Jewry and on the Orthodox
and Conservative movements are one-sided and highly polemical. His position on the question of zionism was probably
obsolete even before it was written and does not take American Reform zionism - as represented by Abba Hillel Silver
and Stephen S. Wise - into account. Finally, the book is incomplete and in clear need of an update.

188. Plaut, W. Gunther: THE GROWTH OF REFORM JUDAISM. New York: World Union for Progressive Judaism, 1965. 383 pp., bibliog., index.

Continuation of Plaut´s THE RISE OF REFORM JUDAISM [see #189]. Again the approach is that of an anthology of sources unified by Plaut´s prefatory remarks and his introductory essay. The emphasis is on Reform as a movement, although individual voices are also heard. The main thrust of the present volume is the development of Reform Judaism in the United States, although European Reform is brought to its majority as well. Key issues - such as the Reform attitude toward zionism - are covered extensively. Theology is given a separate chapter. Although by no means authoritative, Plaut´s review is more than adequate. An epilogue charts the development of Reform Judaism since 1948.

189. ___: THE RISE OF REFORM JUDAISM: A SOURCEBOOK OF ITS EUROPEAN ORIGINS. New York: World Union for Progressive Judaism, 1963. 288 pp., bibliog., index.

Anthology of sources offering a history of the develop-ment of Reform Judaism in the nineteenth century. Almost ex-clusively focused on Reform in Europe, the book is limited to a discussion of the Reform movement. Plaut deals with issues of religion separately, underscoring the early Reform movement´s attitude toward halakhah. Some selections from non-Reform sources are included to provide the context for nineteenth-century Reform. Each entry includes an introduc-tion, and Plaut provides an overview of the growth of modern Jewish ideologies in his introductory essay.

190. Simon, Oswald J.: "Reformed Judaism." JQR, v.6 #2 (Jan., 1894): 262-277.

191. Weil, G.: "A Copenhagen Report Concerning ´Reform´ Addressed to Rabbi Meir Simha Weil." JJS, v.8 #1/2 (1957): 91-101.

CONSERVATIVE JUDAISM

192. Davis, Moshe: THE EMERGENCE OF CONSERVATIVE JUDAISM: THE HISTORICAL SCHOOL IN NINETEENTH-CENTURY AMERICA. Phila-delphia: JPS, 1965. 527 pp., illus., apps., notes, bibliog., index.

Historical study of the context and ideology of the Positive Historical or, more popularly, the Conservative, branch of Judaism. Primarily focused on American Conservative Judaism. Stress is on ideology, although social conditions are also discussed. Details the early relations between Conservative and Reform leadership in the United States, both positive and negative. The issues that separated Conservative and Orthodox Jews are reviewed objectively. Davis carries the story to 1902, by which time Conservative Judaism had fully emerged as a distinct movement.

193. Gordis, Robert: UNDERSTANDING CONSERVATIVE JUDAISM. Edited by Max Gelb. New York: The Rabbinical Assembly, 1978. 235 pp., notes, bibliog., indexes.

Collection of Gordis´s writings on the ideology and meaning of Conservative Judaism. The essays provide excellent insight into the orientation of traditional Conservative Judaism and its views on Jewish law and life. The book is divided into four sections, of which the first is introductory and serves as a framework for the rest. Part II covers the Conservative attitude toward halakhah and the Jewish tradition. While accepting change as necessary, Gordis rejects the idea of change for its own sake and does not advocate the dismanteling of Judaism merely to keep it "relevant." Part III looks, in a similar vein, at contemporary problems, such as education, religion in Israel, and the role of women in Judaism. Part IV argues for the continued vitality of Judaism and the continued viability of conservatism as a movement and an approach. Gordis´s "Seven Principles of Conservative Judaism" are the most succint summary of the movement and its ideology. The seventh of these principles, that the unity of the Jewish people is more important than ideological or religious orientation, bears repeating by all Jews throughout the world.

194. Parzen, Herbert: ARCHITECTS OF CONSERVATIVE JUDAISM. New York: Jonathan David, 1964. 240 pp., notes, index.

Inquiry into the development of American Conservative Judaism, using a biohistorical approach. Parzen seeks to portray those thinkers who, by their original contributions, led Conservative Judaism to develop into the premier American religious movement. Secondarily, Parzen also seeks to examine the social, cultural, and intellectual environment in which they operated. The social context of American Conservative Judaism is, unfortunately, not clearly delineated, nor is the ideological background of Positive-Historical Judaism, as espoused in Europe by the followers of Zecharia Fraenkel, elaborated. Most significantly, the concept of Masorati Judaism, advocated by most of the early Conservative leadership, is never mentioned. Yet, for the first half of the nineteenth century the concepts of Conservative and Orthodox had no separate religious meaning in the United States. Only after 1880 did a difference between these groups develop, and only in this century have the two schools of thought branched out in separate ways. These issues are dealt with only in a cursory and ideologically motivated way. This is especially true in Parzen's highly polemical last chapter, where he attempts to paint the scenario for the future of Conservative Judaism, but actually wages war against two of traditional Conservatism's great scholars - Abraham J. Heschel and Saul Lieberman.

195. ___ : "Conservative Judaism and Zionism, 1896-1922." JSS, v.23 #4 (Oct., 1961): 235-264.

196. Rosenblum, Herbert: CONSERVATIVE JUDAISM: A CONTEMPORARY HISTORY. New York: United Synagogue of America, 1983. 144 pp., illus., notes, index.

Surveys Conservative Judaism in the United States in its historical and contemporary manifestations. The book could be divided into two parts. The first is historical in nature and surveys the development of the movement from the 1840s through the early 1980s. Interspersed with the history of the movement are the biographies of some of the most important leaders and ideologues of conservatism in the United States. The second section is more thematic, dealing with ideological, theological, and religious issues. An especially important chapter summarizes the position of the Conservative movement on halakhah. Rosenblum is very careful in the way he summarizes positions and avoids oversimplification. Although not as detailed as other studies on Conservative Judaism, the book offers a good introductory survey.

197. Siegel, Seymour and E. Gertel [eds.]: CONSERVATIVE JUDAISM AND JEWISH LAW. New York: The Rabbinical Assembly of America, 1977. 337 pp., notes, gloss., index.

Anthology attempting to explain the role halakhah plays in the Conservative movement. The essays had all been previously published, most in Conservative Judaism. Part I, which comprises two-thirds of the book, includes essays

covering the general approach of Conservative thinkers to
the status and significance of halakhah. The shorter, second
part includes five recent case studies, essentially Conservative responsa on important halakhic issues. Coincidentally
four of the five responsa deal with women's issues and are a
useful summary of Conservative thought on the role of women
in Judaism through the early 1970s. Siegel's introduction
reinforces the overall trend of the book and is itself a
superb summary of what American Conservative thinkers have
formulated as "The Conservative Program" for integrating
both observance and, when needed, change of halakhah.

CONTENTS: S. Siegel: The Meaning of Jewish Law in Conserva-
tive Judaism: an Overview and Summary / L. Ginzberg: Jewish
Law as an Expression of the People of Israel's Religious
Consciousness / M. M. Kaplan: Jewish Law as an Expression of
Jewish Civilization / J. B. Agus: Jewish Law as Standards /
R. Gordis: Jewish Law and Catholic Israel / B. Cohen: Jewish
Law: the Traditionalist Standpoint / L. Jacobs: Jewish Law:
a Synthesis / S. Siegel: Jewish Law and Jewish Ethics / A.
J. Heschel: Jewish Law as Response / W. Herberg: Jewish Law
and the Existentialist Viewpoint / S. Greenberg: Torah Mi
Sinai: the Divine Origin of Jewish Law / Louis Finkelstein:
Jewish Law as a Symbolic System / Max Kadushin: Jewish Law
Concretizing Jewish Value Concepts / E. Simon: Jewish Law:
an Expression of the Jewish World View / I. Klein: Teshuvah
on Abortion / A. H. Blumenthal: An Aliyah for Women / P.
Sigal: Women in a Prayer Quorum / D. M. Feldman: Women's
Role and Jewish Law / I. Silverman: Are all Wines Kosher?

 * 198. Stern, N.: THE JEWISH HISTORICO-CRITICAL SCHOOL OF
THE NINETEENTH CENTURY. New York: Arno Press, 1973. 82 pp.

   199. Waxman, Mordecai [ed.]: TRADITION AND CHANGE: THE
DEVELOPMENT OF CONSERVATIVE JUDAISM. New York: The Burning
Bush Press, 1958. 477 pp.

   Anthology covering American Conservative Judaism in
theory and practice. The book may be divided into three
sections. The first covers the history of the Conservative
movement in the United States. Including Waxman's very informative survey, this section is an authoritative review of
the development of Conservative Judaism to the 1950s. Missing is an in-depth analysis of the relations between American Conservative and European Positive-Historical Judaism.
The second deals with philosophy and shows both the unity
and diversity of Conservative Jewish thought. The third

deals with practical issues, including prayer, Sabbath
observance, education, and zionism. Again, the unity and
diversity of Conservative Jews is shown - from the Masorati
on the right to the Reconstructionists on the left. The result is a collection that provides a clear overview helping
to define Conservative Judaism.

CONTENTS: M. Waxman: Conservative Judaism - a Survey / Z.
Frankel: On Changes in Judaism / Excerpts from the Addresses
of Rabbi Isaac Leeser / Sabatto Morais: Can We Change the
Ritual? / A. Kohut: Which is Right: a Talmudical Disputa-
tion / I. Friedlander: The Problem of Judaism in America /
S. Schechter: Historical Judaism: Excerpts from the Seminary
Addresses of Solomon Schechter / H. Szold: Catholic Israel /
L. Ginzberg: Our Standpoint - an Address / M. Arzt: Conser-
vative Judaism as a Unifying Force / S. Morais: A Jewish
Theological Seminary - an Address / S. Schechter: The Work
of Heaven - an Address / Preamble to the United Synagogue
Constitution / C. Adler: The Standpoint of the Seminary / L.
Finkelstein: Tradition in the Making / S. Goldman: Towards a
National Synagogue - an Address / M. M. Kaplan: Unity in
Diversity in the Conservative Movement / Robert Gordis: A
Program for American Judaism / M. Steinberg: Reconstruction-
ism: a Creative Program / S. Greenberg: Standards for the
Conservative Movement in Judaism / M. Adler: New Goals for
Conservative Judaism - an Address / M. M. Kaplan: Toward the
Formulation of Guiding Principles for the Conservative Move-
ment / Louis Finkelstein: The Things That Unite Us - an
Address / Prayer and the Prayerbook / M. Adler, J. Agus and
Th. Friedman: A Responsum on the Sabbath / Robert Gordis: A
Modern Approach to a Living Halachah / Ben Zion Bokser: The
Halachah on Travel on the Sabbath / A. H. Neulander: The Use
of Electricity on the Sabbath / S. Greenberg: Basic Premises
of Jewish Education in America / Moshe Davis: The Ladder of
Jewish Education / Ira Eisenstein: The Need for Legislation
in Jewish Law - a Community Philosophy / Solomon Schechter:
Zionism: a Statement / M. Davis: Our Share in Eretz Israel /
A Resolution of the United Synagogue / Mordechai M. Kaplan:
A New Zionism.

RECONSTRUCTIONISM

 * 200. Goldberg, H. L.: INTRODUCTION TO RECONSRTUCTIONISM.
New York: Jewish Reconstructionist Foundation, 1957. 16 pp.

201. Kaplan, Mordechai M.: JUDAISM AS A CIVILIZATION: TOWARD A RECONSTRUCTION OF AMERICAN-JEWISH LIFE. New York: Thomas Yoseloff, 1957. 600 pp., notes, index.

Classic statement of Reconstructionist Judaism by the founder of the Society for the Advancement of Judaism. Kaplan is quite correctly viewed as the father of reconstructionism. The movement arose out of American Conservative Judaism, and saw itself as a force for the creation of a positive Jewish identity based on social rather than theological needs.

Kaplan began his study with a statement concerning what was generally seen as a crisis of Judaism. He then elucidated the factors causing the crisis and the programs offered by the different branches of American Jewry. What was needed, Kaplan argued, was a new program, since neither traditional Judaism nor any of its modern competitors addressed the problem properly. His proposed solution was to view Judaism as a civilization, not as a religious cult. It therefore followed that Jewish tradition had to be viewed in terms of objective and subjective needs. According to Kaplan, a sociological view would clarify these needs, which religious leaders would then have to answer through the creative use of Jewish practice. When necessary, new rituals would have to be introduced to fill voids not filled by tradition.

Although the book was written during the 1930s, reconstructionism came to the fore only after World War II. While many of Kaplan's criticisms were appropriate, and many were accepted even by traditionally oriented Jews, reconstructionism never managed to become the major force in Judaism that Kaplan thought it would be. In part, this is because Kaplan established the parameters for a dynamic and constantly changing religion, rooted in nothing save the needs of the moment.

* 202. ___: JUDAISM AS A MODERN RELIGIOUS CIVILIZATION. New York: Jewish Reconstructionist Foundation, 1958. 19 pp.

203. ___: QUESTIONS JEWS ASK: RECONSTRUCTIONIST ANSWERS. New York: Reconstructionist Press, 1956. 532 pp., index.

Authoritative statement of Reconstructionist ideology by the father of reconstructionism. Based on Kaplan's articles and his "Know to Answer" columns in Reconstructionist. He completely rejects the notion that Judaism is a stale, fossilized, or outdated religion. To the contrary, Kaplan

saw reconstructionism as the means to revitalize Jewish
creativity. Especially important is Kaplan's statement of
"The Principles of Reconstructionism," which help explain
the movement and its orientations. Kaplan's innovation was
to view Judaism as a historically developed, but ever
dynamic, religious civilization. One need not be a Reconstructionist to accept the gist of Kaplan's principles.
Since they are generalizations, they would likely be acceptable to most Jews, including the Orthodox. Kaplan, however,
does not specify the practical goals of the principles he
formulates, and this vagueness has led to conflicting interpretations of his beliefs and their implications.

* 204. Kohn, Eugene: WHAT IS JEWISH RELIGION. New York:
Jewish Reconstructionist Foundation, 1958. 25 pp.

ORTHODOX JUDAISM

205. Bernstein, Louis: CHALLENGE AND MISSION: THE EMER-
GENCE OF THE ENGLISH SPEAKING ORTHODOX RABBINATE. New York:
Shengold, 1982. 269 pp., notes, index.

Thematically organized history of the Rabbinical Council
of America [RCA], the primary vehicle for the development of
modern Orthodoxy in the United States. Although a chapter
deals with the RCA from its founding in 1926 to 1945, the
bulk of the book covers the postwar era to the 1960s. Key
issues and personalities are interwoven into a readable and
reasonably well-documented text. Nevertheless, as Bernstein
notes, documentation is, and will continue to be, a major
obstacle to studying the development of American Orthodoxy.
Stated simply, Orthodox organizations and leadership did not
preserve documents in a systematic way before World War II.
This is true of the RCA and, to a great extent, of other
Jewish religious organizations. Bernstein's book fills in a
number of missing links in the history of the RCA and the
development of American Orthodox Judaism.

206. Bulka, R. P. [ed.]: DIMENSIONS OF ORTHODOX JUDAISM.
New York: Ktav, 1983. 471 pp., chap. notes, bibliog., gloss.

Collection of previously published essays covering the
post-Holocaust development of American Orthodox Judaism. The
volume also attempts to place Orthodoxy within the overall
communal context of American Jewry. The book is divided into
two broad sections, one dealing with "The Reality" and the

other covering "The Challenge." As a whole the essays have
both merits and flaws. Most glaringly, those issues affecting all Jews, regardless of denomination - e.g., religion in
the State of Israel - are not treated in separate essays.
Nor is there any discussion of historical development per
se. On the positive side Bulka has included a wide range of
Orthodox sources and a few non-Orthodox as well. The book
contains an extensive bibliography and is a very useful introduction to the state of Orthodox Jews and Judaism today.

CONTENTS: / R. P. Bulka: Orthodoxy Today: an Overview of the
Achievements and the Problems / Ch. S. Liebman: Orthodoxy in
American Jewish Life; Orthodox Judaism Today / G. Kranzler:
The Changing Orthodox Jewish Community / B. Mandelbaum: The
Right to Be Different / S. Spero: A Rejoinder to Bernard
Mandelbaum's The Right to Be Different / J. J. Petuchowski:
Plural Models Within the Halakhah / W. S. Wurzburger: Plural
Models and the Authority of Halakhah / J. H. Lookstein: The
View from the Right: a Critique and a Plea / D. S. Shapiro:
Amicus Plato, Amicior Veritas / Marvin Schick: Borough Park:
a Jewish Settlement / S. Poll: The Impact of Hasidism on
American Judaism / Marc D. Angel: Religious Life of American
Sephardim / Jerome R. Mintz: Ethnic Activism: the Hasidic
Example / L. Kaplan: The Ambiguous Modern Orthodox Jew / Ch.
D. Keller: Modern Orthodoxy: an Analysis and a Response / N.
Lamm: Pluralism and Unity in the Orthodox Jewish Community /
Irving Greenberg: Jewish Values and the Changing American
Ethic / D. Singer: The Case for an Irrelevant Orthodoxy: an
Open Letter to Yitzchak Greenberg / O. S. Fasman: Trends in
the American Yeshiva Today / E. Feldman: Trends in the
American Yeshivot: a Rejoinder / E. Berkovits: Orthodox
Judaism in a World of Revolutionary Transformations / G.
Kranzler: The Changing Orthodox Jewish Family / Ch. K.
Poupko and D. L. Wohlgelernter: Women's Liberation - an
Orthodox Response / I. N. Levitz: Crisis in Orthodoxy: the
Ethical Paradox / E. Mayer and Ch. I. Waxman: Modern Jewish
Orthodoxy in America: Toward the year 2000 / S. Riskin:
Where Modern Orthodoxy Is At - and Where It Is Going / J.
Hochbaum: American Orthodoxy: Some Guidelines for its
Community Development and Organization / Epilogue.

207. Heilman, Samuel C.: "The Many Faces of Orthodoxy."
MJ, v.2 #1 (Feb., 1982): 23-51; #2 (May, 1982): 171-198.

* 208. Homa, Bernard: ORTHODOXY IN ANGLO-JEWRY, 1880-1940.
London: Jewish Historical Society of England, 1969. 52 pp.

209. Liberles, Robert: RELIGIOUS CONFLICT IN SOCIAL CON-
TEXT: THE RESURGENCE OF ORTHODOX JUDAISM IN FRANKFURT AM
MAIN, 1838-1877. Westport, CT: Greenwood Press, 1985. 295
pp., illus., notes, bibliog., index.

Studies Orthodox Jewry in the German context during the
mid-nineteenth century. Sees neo-Orthodoxy as a response to
the challenge of the Reform movement, i.e., as an attempt to
make Judaism more acceptable to modern sensibilities. The
author also sets out to revise some of the more glaring misconceptions about nineteenth-century German neo-Orthodoxy.
In particular, he does not view Samson Raphael Hirsch as the
first, or even the most systematic, advocate of a more modern orientation within the traditional context. By studying
one community, Liberles hopes to chart the social and intellectual aspects of the confrontation between Reform and
Orthodoxy. In this he is largely successful. In the epilogue
Liberles makes some important comparative notes, relating to
England and France; these definitely deserve further investigation. Foreword by Henry Boden.

210. Ury, Zalman: THE MUSAR MOVEMENT. New York: Yeshiva
Univ. Press, 1969. 81 pp., notes, bibliog.

Survey of the movement for moderate modernization in the
Lithuanian yeshivot during the nineteenth century. The Musar
movement represented an effort by East European rabbis to
integrate the best qualities of the yeshivot, their high
intellectual capacity, with the emotional and ethical
qualities of hasidism. Since the term "musar" means ethics,
Ury views the Musar movement primarily in its psychological
and religious contexts. His discussion of the theoretical
underpinnings of the Musar movement is very important and
explains many of its characteristics. Ury notes that although opposed to the Haskalah movement, the rabbis who formulated the Musar movement recognized the need for Jews to
attain a broad secular education. Thus, in a way Musar
represented not only the synthesis of the yeshivot with
hasidism, but also of Orthodoxy with a form of Haskalah.
Significantly, the Lithuanian yeshivot thus became not only
a source for modern orthodoxy, but also for modern Judaic
studies. Introduction by Leon D. Stitskin.

5

Cultural Trends

CIVILIZATIONS

211. Benardete, Mair J.: HISPANIC CULTURE AND THE CHAR-
ACTER OF THE SEPHARDI JEWS. 2nd Edition. Edited by Marc D.
Angel. New York: Sepher-Hermon Press, 1982. 226 pp., notes,
apps., bibliog., index.

History of Sephardi culture after the expulsion from
Spain. Benardete attempts to place Sephardi Jewry into the
broad patterns of Spanish culture. Within this analysis he
also includes Marrano literature. The book is both a monument to, and analysis of, Sephardi culture. As a contribution to intellectual history, the book has much to offer,
especially since Sephardim have been ignored by many recent
Jewish historians. Laymen may find some of the chapters hard
to follow without a deeper background in Sephardi lifestyles. Benardete does not deal with Sephardi religious life
in a systematic way. Such an analysis might have provided an
interesting comparison to Ashkenazi Jewry in the modern era.

212. Cooperman, Bernard D. [ed.]: JEWISH THOUGHT IN THE
SIXTEENTH CENTURY. Cambridge, MA: Harvard Univ. Press, 1983.
492 pp., notes, bibliog.

Anthology of studies based on a Harvard University colloquium on sixteenth-century Jewish thought. The book's purpose
is to establish the limits of scholarship presently possible
on the sixteenth century. Within this context essays on both
individuals and communities are included. Five Jewish centers predominated during the sixteenth-century: the Jewish
community of Spain, then in its death throes; Italy; Poland;
Turkey; and the community of Eretz-Israel. All receive due

attention, although Italian Jewry during the renaissance gets the lion´s share.

The editor and the authors appear to share a common belief that the sixteenth century was pivotal for the development of Jewish history. The expulsion from Spain had ended one era; a new one would soon emerge. In many ways the sixteenth century, which saw the development of Jewish historiography as well as the refinement of Kabbalah and the establishment of one single authoritative halakhah, proved a watershed of the old and the new.

CONTENTS: A. Altmann: Ars Rhetorica as Reflected in Some Jewish Figures of the Italian Renaissance / R. Bonfil: Some Reflections on the Place of Azariah de Rossi´s MEOR ENAYIM in the Cultural Milieu of Italian Renaissance Jewry / M. Breuer: Modernism and Traditionalism in Sixteenth-Century Jewish Historiography: a Study of David Gans´ TZEMAH DAVID / B. D. Cooperman: Some Recent Research / J. Dan: "No Evil Descends from Heaven" - Sixteenth-Century Jewish Concepts of Evil / H. Davidson: Medieval Jewish Philosophy in the Sixteenth Century / J. Elbaum: Aspects of Hebrew Ethical Literature in Sixteenth-Century Poland / M. Fox: The Moral Philosophy of MaHaRal / M. Idel: The Magical and Neoplatonic Interpretations of the Kabbalah in the Renaissance / A. Ivry: Remnants of Jewish Averroism in the Renaissance / L. Kaplan: Rabbi Mordekhai Jaffe and the Evolution of Jewish Culture in Poland in the Sixteenth Century / J. Katz: Post-Zoharic Relations between Halakhah and Kabbalah / J. Kugel: The Influence of Moses ibn Habib´s DARKHEI NO´AM / H. A. Oberman: Three Sixteenth-Century Attitudes to Judaism: Reuchlin, Erasmus and Luther / Sh. Pines: Medieval Doctrines in Renaissance Garb? Some Jewish and Arabic Sources of Leone Ebreo´s Doctrines / Sh. Rosenberg: Exile and Redemption in Jewish Thought in the Sixteenth Century: Contending Conceptions / Isidor Twersky: Talmudists, Philosophers, Kabbalists: the Quest for Spirituality in the Sixteenth Century / Y. H. Yerushalmi: Messianic Impulses in Joseph ha-Kohen.

213. Faur, Jose: "Introducing the Materials of Sephardic Culture to Contemporary Jewish Studies." AJHQ, v.63 #4 (June, 1974): 340-349.

214. Gaster, Theodor H.: THE HOLY AND THE PROFANE: EVOLUTION OF JEWISH FOLKWAYS. New York: William Morrow, 1980. 256 pp., notes, index.

Interesting reconstruction of Jewish folkways and popular

customs. The book is organized around the cycles of Jewish
life. Adopting a comparative approach, the author tries to
fathom the origins of many Jewish customs as well as the
comparable customs of other peoples. Primarily, Gaster compares Jewish customs to those of ancient Near Eastern nations, though some customs are compared to those of European
nations also. Not all of Gaster's comparisons are convincing and his identification of some customs as bearing a
non-Jewish influence is not always on the mark. Obviously,
many similarities arose among peoples living in similar
conditions; it is not necessary to always prove a causal or
influential relationship between such customs. Nevertheless,
the book contains interesting information and not a few
novel interpretations.

215. Handlin, O.: "Jews in the Culture of Middle Europe."
LBML, #7 (1964): 5-20.

216. Hubmann, Franz: THE JEWISH FAMILY ALBUM: YESTERDAY'S
WORLD IN OLD PICTURES. Edited by Miriam and Lionel Kochan.
London: Routledge & Kegan Paul, 1975. 318 pp., illus.

Photographic kaleidoscope of Jewry from the 1890s to the
early 1930s. The photos are grouped geographically; beginning with eastern Europe, Hubmann's lens turns to western
Europe, America, and finally the Yishuv. The photographs are
a stunning reminder of a bygone world. The introduction, by
Miriam and Lionel Kochan, imparts a flavor of the wide
range of Jewish life, but provides only cursory background
to the communities, without explaining the photos in any
specific way. Yet nothing more is really needed from the
essay - the pictures more than speak for themselves.

217. Patai, Raphael: THE VANISHED WORLDS OF JEWRY. Picture research by Eugene Rosow with Vivian Kleiman. New York:
Macmillan, 1980. 194 pp., illus., index.

Memorial volume eulogizing the Jewish communities of the
world which no longer exist. Attempts to reconstruct the
lives of the Jews of these communities in words, and as much
as possible, in pictures. Each country is dealt with separately. The demise of each community is also reviewed,
albeit briefly. The text with the accompanying photographs,
taken together, provide an interesting comparative survey of
Jewish life in the first half of the twentieth century.

218. Ross, Dan: ACTS OF FAITH: A JOURNEY TO THE FRINGES
OF JEWISH IDENTITY. New York: St. Martin's Press, 1982. 244
pp., illus., notes, bibliog., index.

Popular account of the history and lives of Jewish, or
quasi-Jewish, sects across three continents. In all of the
cases Ross cites, the residual memory of having been Jewish
in the past qualifies the "Jewishness" of the members more
than, or as much as, religious practice. Consequently, in
half the cases the sect eventually moved away from Judaism.
This is clearest with the Donmeh - the remnants of the
Shabbatean movement - who converted to Islam while awaiting
the return of their messiah, Shabbetai Zevi. The other sects
cited have had a more complicated history. Of them the Bene
Israel of India most clearly remained within the Jewish
mainstream. The definition of Samaritans, Karaites, and
Falashas as Jews has proved problematic, although few would
deny their Jewish origins. In the case of the Portuguese
Marranos, the Jewish concept is present, but is devoid of
Jewish content. Ultimately, Ross accurately concludes that
the importance of these groups is to define the outer limits
of Jewishness, thereby also defining what constitutes
normative Judaism.

219. Rubens, Alfred: A HISTORY OF JEWISH COSTUME. New
York: Crown, 1973 [Rep. of 1967 Ed.]. 220 pp., 264 illus.,
notes, bibliog., index.

History of how Jews dressed from biblical times to the
eighteenth century. Rubens shows that, except for ritual
differences, Jews usually dressed in the style of the surrounding society. Moreover, Rubens argues that recent ar-
chaeological discoveries show parallels to some of the
ritual aspects of Jewish dress among other nations of the
ancient Near East. Rubens notes that the words costume and
custom have almost the same meaning. In matters of dress,
halakhah allowed a great deal of latitude for "minhag." This
is amply proven by the photos, prints, and other illustrations Rubens uses to substantiate his hypothesis. Since the
sixteenth century, most Jews have adopted the popular styles
of dress, and the more traditionally minded have adapted
them to conform with halakhah.

220. Straus, Raphael: "The 'Jewish Hat' as an Aspect of
Social History." JSS, v.4 #1 (Jan., 1942): 59-72.

221. Zimmels, H. J.: ASHKENAZIM AND SEPHARDIM: THEIR
RELATIONS, DIFFERENCES, AND PROBLEMS AS REFLECTED IN THE
RABBINIC RESPONSA. London: Oxford Univ. Press, 1958. 347
pp., notes, index.

Comparative history of northern and southern Jewry over
the course of ten centuries. The book is divided into three
parts. Part I is purely historical, dealing with the relations between northern and southern Jews, who were separated
from each other as a result of the world division into
Christian and Muslim empires. Although Sephardim, strictly
speaking, are Jews from Spain, Zimmels uses the term more
loosely as it relates to events after-1492. Part II is a
discussion of the differences between Ashkenazim and
Sephardim in terms of attitudes and practices. Part III is a
compilation of halakhic material, primarily taken from
responsa literature, regarding the practical differences
elucidated in Part II. In order to explain the differences,
Zimmels advances three hypotheses: [1] anthropology, i.e.,
there are different types [tribes or races] of Jews. Although the weakest of the hypotheses, Zimmels does not
reject this altogether; [2] divergent traditions, i.e., differences between Ashkenazim and Sephardim reflect the differences between the halakhic traditions of Eretz-Israel and
Babylonia; [3] different external conditions led to different orientations and attitudes. The last two hypotheses form
the basis for Zimmels´s work. Zimmels was a trailblazer in
the use of rabbinic material in this comparative way, and
his work therefore offers important methodological insight.

LANGUAGES

222. Chomsky, Wm: HEBREW THE ETERNAL LANGUAGE. Philadelphia: JPS, 1957. 321 pp., illus., notes, bibliog., index.

Surveys the history of the Hebrew language and its literature, from antiquity to modern times. The book is also an
inquiry into Jewish and world culture. The book is divided
into four parts, each covering a broad theme. The chapters
review more specific questions in the development of Hebrew
and its use. Part IV, "How the Language Meets Modern Needs,"
reviews modern Hebrew. Although scholarly in approach,
Chomsky writes for the layperson, offering a good introduction to Hebrew and to the historical study of linguistics
as well.

223. Crews, C. M.: "The Vulgar Pronunciation of Hebrew in the Judaeo-Spanish of Salonica." JJS, v.13 #1/4 (1962): 83-95.

224. Doroshkin, Milton: YIDDISH IN AMERICA: SOCIAL AND CULTURAL FOUNDATIONS. Rutherford, NJ: Fairleigh Dickinson Univ. Press, 1969. 281 pp., notes, apps., bibliog., index.

Sociological inquiry into the Yiddish language in the United States. The role Yiddish played in Americanizing immigrants is Doroshkin´s main focus. Furthermore, according to the author, Yiddish helped integrate the new immigrants into the already existing community. This, in turn, allowed East European Jews to maintain a much higher degree of communal cohesion than did the previous Sephardic and German Jewish communities. Thus, though the use of Yiddish has declined, the Jewish values represented by the language have not. To prove his thesis, Doroshkin studies the Yiddish press and the "Landsmanschaften" in detail. Chapters 2-4 contain background material which is primarily designed for laymen; these can be ignored by those interested in Doroshkin´s more detailed sections.

225. Fishman, Joshua A.: "Language Maintenance and Language Shift: Yiddish and Other Immigrant Languages in the United States." Y/A, v.14 (1969): 12-26.

226. ___ [ed.]: READINGS IN THE SOCIOLOGY OF JEWISH LANGUAGES. Leiden: E. J. Brill, 1985. 298 pp., illus., bibliog.

Sociological investigation into Jewish linguistics. The anthology is designed as an introduction to a series of monographs on Jewish linguistics and also offers a brief overview of the subject. The book is divided into five parts, organized by language, with sections specifically dedicated to Hebrew, Yiddish, and Judezmo. Another section deals with "Other Jewish Languages." The essays are of uneven quality, some being too narrowly constructed to offer any insight for non-specialists. On the other hand some of the essays, for example, Katz´s on the Hebrew-Aramic component in Yiddish, contain useful methodological and sociohistorical insights.

CONTENTS: J. A. Fishman: The Sociology of Jewish Languages from a General Sociolinguistic Point of View / Uzzi Ornan: Hebrew is not a Jewish Language / Jack Fellman: A Sociolinguistic Perspective on the History of Hebrew / Bernard Spolsky: Jewish Multilingualism in the First Century: an Essay in Historical Sociolinguistics / J. E. Hofman: The Commitment to Modern Hebrew: Value or Instrument / Robert L. Cooper: Language and Social Stratification among the Jewish Population of Israel / Dovid Katz: Hebrew, Aramaic and the Rise of Yiddish / Arye L. Pilowski: Yiddish alongside the Revival of Hebrew: Public Polemics on the Status of Yiddish in Eretz Israel, 1907-1929 / R. Peltz: The Dehebraization Controversy in Soviet Yiddish Language Planning: Standard or Symbol? / Harold Hearmann: Yiddish and the Other Jewish Languages in the Soviet Union / H. V. Sephiha: "Christianisms" in Judeo-Spanish / Tracy K. Harris: The Decline of Judezmo: Problems and Prospects / Arlene Malinowski: Judezmo in the U.S.A. Today: Attitudes and Institutions / Paul Wexler: Recovering the Dialects and Sociology of Judeo-Greek in Non-Hellenic Europe / G. Jochnowitz: Had Gadya in Judeo-Italian and Shuadit / David Cohen: Some Historical and Sociolinguistic Observations on the Arabic dialects Spoken by North African Jews / J. Chetrit: Judeo-Arabic and Judeo-Spanish in Morocco and their Sociolinguistic Interaction / David L. Gold: Jewish English.

227. Goldsmith, Emanuel S.: ARCHITECTS OF YIDDISHISM AT THE BEGINNING OF THE TWENTIETH CENTURY. Rutherford, NJ: Fairleigh Dickinson Univ. Press, 1976. 308 pp., illus., notes, bibliog., index.

Goldsmith studies the Yiddish-language movement of the pre-Holocaust era. In the secularized society of pre-World War II eastern Europe, a linguistic schism erupted among Jews, one that had political, social, and cultural perspectives. Essentially, assimilationists opted for Slavic [Russian or Polish], Zionists for Hebrew, and diaspora nationalists for Yiddish. It must, however, be emphasized that these were not solid breakdowns. Most Socialist-Zionists were pro-Yiddish, whereas all Zionists [and many assimilationists] recognized the need to use Yiddish in convincing the Jewish masses of their ideology. Goldsmith views the issues from the Yiddishist perspective, including literary and artistic aspects. After a general chapter on the history of Yiddish, Goldsmith points out the literary and ideological catalysts for the creation of the Yiddishist movement. The culmination of this movement is descibed in the chapter on "The Czernowitz Conference." The other chapters review significant individuals and explain the growth and decline of Yiddishism through World War II.

228. Mark, Yudel: "The Yiddish Language: its Cultural Impact." AJHQ, v.59 #2 (Dec., 1969): 201-209.

229. Neubauer, Adolf: "On Non-Hebrew Languages Used by Jews." JQR, v.4 #1 (Oct., 1891): 9-19.

230. Spiegel, Shalom: HEBREW REBORN. New York: Meridian, 1962 [Rep. of 1930 Ed.]. 479 pp., notes, gloss., index.

Investigates the rebirth of the Hebrew language since the Haskalah. Primary emphasis is on literature, and the book is arranged as a series of biographical sketches of important contributors to Hebrew belles lettres. Stress is evenly divided between the usage of Hebrew by the maskilim, in both Germany and eastern Europe, and the association of Hebrew with the national rebirth as advocated by the Zionist movement. Since the book is primarily a literary review, this division works well and traces some of the continuing themes in the development of modern Hebrew and its literature. However, Spiegel makes his best comments in the prelude: he notes that it is misleading to say Hebrew was "reborn," since the language was never, in fact, really dead. Jews in modern times have found a new, secular role for their ancient language. Thus, the rebirth of Hebrew is actually a revitalization and, in the final analysis, a reorientation of an ancient language.

231. Weinreich. Max: HISTORY OF THE YIDDISH LANGUAGE. Trans. from the Yiddish with a Foreword by Shlomo Noble and Joshua A. Fishman. Chicago: Univ. of Chicago Press, 1980. 833 pp., charts, index.

A sociolinguistic study of Yiddish, the book is also a study of the culture of Ashkenazic Jewry before World War II. Chapters are organized thematically. Weinreich, in describing the development of Yiddish, also describes the Jewish worldview. He presents Yiddish as a total system that cannot be understood as a patchwork of separate components. By way of example, though one might find Latin, German, and Slavic loan-words in Yiddish, it is not possible to describe the relation between Yiddish and European languages without also understanding the relation of Yiddish to Hebrew. Although the style is simple, few nonlinguists will be able to follow most of Weinreich's account.

LITERATURE AND THE ARTS

232. Altmann, Alexander: ESSAYS IN JEWISH INTELLECTUAL
HISTORY. Waltham, MA: Brandeis University Press, 1981. 324
pp., notes, indexes.

Collection of essays on a wide variety of topics related
to Jewish thought and themes in Jewish intellectual history.
Just over half deal with the modern period. If there is one
consistent theme, it is Altmann´s effort to uncover the
motifs behind Jewish thought patterns, and to place these
patterns into chronological context. Four essays deal with
aspects of Moses Mendelssohn´s thought and are very useful
summaries of Mendelssohn´s philosophical premises. All of
Altmann´s essays are thought-provoking, well argued, and
well documented.

233. ___ [ed.]: STUDIES IN NINETEENTH-CENTURY JEWISH
INTELLECTUAL HISTORY. Cambridge, MA: Harvard Univ. Press,
1964. 215 pp., notes, indexes.

Anthology based on colloquia in modern Jewish history
held at Brandeis University during 1961-1962. Primary focus
is on Germany and especially on charting the results of the
Emancipation. Jewish attitudes are carefully studied on such
issues as poetry, philosophy, religion, and politics. Within
these contexts the impact of the civil emancipation of German Jewry is charted. The term Emancipation is placed under
close scrutiny in Katz´s essay; he discovers that the term
implied different results to different people and was used
with different meanings in various contexts. Glatzer´s essay
on the Wissenschaft des Judentums sheds new light on both
the organization and its goals. The methodologies of the
leading personalities of the Wissenschaft are described;
Glatzer both explains and criticizes, offering more than
historical insight. Although limited in focus, the book is
an important contribution to the understanding of Jewish
intellectual history.

CONTENTS: J. Katz: The Term "Jewish Emancipation": Its Origin and Historical Impact / N. N. Glatzer: The Beginnings of
Modern Jewish Studies / J. J. Petuchowski: Manuals and Cate-
chisms of the Jewish Religion in the Early Period of Emancipation / A. Altmann: The New Style of Preaching in Nineteenth-Century German Jewry / E. Silberschlag: Parapoetic
Attitudes and Values in Early Nineteenth-Century Hebrew
Poetry / H. Liebeschuetz: German Radicalism and the Forma-

tion of Jewish Political Attitudes During the Early Part of
the Nineteenth Century / E. C. Fackenheim: Samuel Hirsch and
Hegel.

234. Bialer, Yehuda L.: JEWISH LIFE IN ART AND TRADITION.
New York: G. P. Putnam´s, 1976. 189 pp., illus., gloss.

Thematically organized survey of Jewish life, based on
the Wolfson art collection at Heikhal Shelomo in Jerusalem.
Bialer begins and ends with the life cycle: marriage, birth,
and death, interspersing these chapters with others covering
Jewish holiday customs and art. The multiplicity of styles
in which ceremonial and ritual objects were made testifies
to the diversity of Jewish culture, but also proves the
basic unity of Jewish civilization. Although lacking a clear
sense of historical development, Bialer´s comparative
viewpoint offers an inside view of the life of both the
wealthy and the simple Jews before the twentieth century.

* 235. Fiedler, Leslie A.: THE JEW IN THE AMERICAN NOVEL.
New York: Herzl Press, 1966. 64 pp.

236. Gutmann, Joseph [ed.]: BEAUTY IN HOLINESS: STUDIES
IN JEWISH CUSTOMS AND CEREMONIAL ART. New York: Ktav, 1970.
513 pp., illus., notes.

Anthology on Jewish art, artisanry, and folkways. The
theme of the book is the diversity within Jewish practice
and the dynamic nature of ethnic Jewish customs as they
developed and adapted to changes in the outside world. To
develop this hypothesis further, Gutmann collected a large
number of essays from a wide variety of sources that he
divides into six sections. The first deals with art and
artisanry in general. The next four deal with specific types
of Jewish ceremonial art: Torah decorations, Sabbath,
Hanukkah, and nuptial art. The last section deals with an
assortment of traditions from the Ashkenazi and Sephardi
communities. Not all the essays are of equal quality and
some are quite polemical. Taken as a whole, however, the
book is an important contribution to the study of Jewish
traditions and ceremonial art.

CONTENTS: S. B. Finesinger: The Custom of Looking at the
Fingernails at the Outgoing of the Sabbath / S. B. Freehof:
Ceremonial Creativity among the Ashkenazim; Home Rituals and
the Spanish Synagogue / J. Gutmann: The Second Commandment
and the Image of Judaism; Priestly Vestments, Torah Orna-

ments and the King James Bible; Wedding Customs and Cere-
monies in Art; How Traditional are our Traditions? / Samuel
Krauss: The Jewish Rite of Covering the head / Moses Kremer:
Jewish Artisans and Guilds in Former Poland, 16th-18th
Centuries / F. Landsberger: The Origin of European Torah
Decorations; A German Torah Ornamentation; Old-Time Torah-
Curtains; The Origin of the Ritual Implements for the
Sabbath; Old Hanukkah Lamps; Illuminated Marriage Contracts;
The Origin of the Decorated Mezuzah / J. Z. Lauterbach: The
Origin and Development of Two Sabbath Ceremonies; The Cere-
mony of Breaking a Glass at Weddings / G. Schoenberger: The
Ritual Silver Made by Myer Myers / Alfred Werner: Contem-
porary Ritual Art / Mark Wischnitzer: Notes to a History of
the Jewish Guilds.

237. Halkin, Simon: MODERN HEBREW LITERATURE FROM THE EN-
LIGHTENMENT TO THE BIRTH OF THE STATE OF ISRAEL: TRENDS AND
VALUES. 2nd Edition. New York: Schocken Books, 1970. 238
pp., notes, guide to authors, index.

Guide to the development and literary importance of Hebrew literature since the Haskalah. The chapters are divided
thematically and deal with the typologies of Hebrew literature. Two interesting chapters, for example, deal with "Pre-
monitions and Disaster" and "The Meaning of Disaster" among
Hebrew writers. These two chapters review the impact of outside events on Hebrew literary figures, including the effect
of the Holocaust on Israeli writers. Halkin distinguishes
between Hebrew writers who lived in or migrated to Palestine
and native Israelis who began writing after the establishment of the state; in both categories, considerable attention is paid to poetry. Halkin also attempts to assess the
place of Hebrew literature in the broader category of Jewish
belle lettres. Halkin's most important contribution is his
exploration of the theme of Jewishness in modern Hebrew
literature.

238. Landsberger, Franz: A HISTORY OF JEWISH ART. Cincinnati: UAHC, 1946. 369 pp., illus., notes, bibliog., index.

Inquiry into the history of Jewish art. Landsberger attempts to answer two basic questions. Is there a Jewish art,
and if there is, what is Jewish about it? The book is divided into two sections. Part I covers the aforementioned
issues involved and also reviews the relations of art to
Jewish life and customs. Landsberger concludes from his
sources that although the second commandment may have ham-

pered certain art styles, especially sculpture, it did not ban the plastic arts altogether. Looking at both the cycle of the Jewish year and of a Jew's life in general, one can see numerous examples of ritual and nonritual artwork, ranging from finely decorated ritual objects to illuminated manuscripts and letters. All of these art forms are placed into the context of Jewish culture. Part II reviews the chronological development of Jewish art. Architecture is included in this section, since the decoration of a building with friezes or other objects is a form of artistic endeavor. It proves that Jews - even the most religious ones - always appreciated beauty and sought to enhance their environment. The last chapter covers the rise of Jewish themes in the plastic arts of the modern era, with special emphasis on painting and sculpture. The book may be considered an authoritative review that will be a source of interest to both scholars and laypersons.

239. Levy, S.: "Is There a Jewish Literature." JQR, v.15 #4 (July, 1903): 583-603.

240. Liptzin, S.: A HISTORY OF YIDDISH LITERATURE. Middle Village, NY: J. David, 1972. 521 pp., bibliog., index.

Survey of Yiddish literature. Although the earliest examples of Yiddish literature are reviewed, Liptzin concentrates on the modern period. The chapters primarily deal with the authors, their works, and related stylistic issues. Liptzin includes little in the way of historical background, and a sense of a dynamic literary life, outside of changing literary vogues, is lacking. An especially interesting chapter deals with Soviet Yiddish literature. Yiddish literature as it developed in many other climes - the United States, South America, and Israel - is also given due consideration.

241. Mazor, Y.: "The Poetics of Composition of the Hebrew Short Story in the Haskalah Period." AJS Review, v.10 #1 (Spr., 1985): 89-110.

242. Miron, Dan: "The Discovery of Mendele Mokher-Sforim and the Beginnings of Modern Jewish Literature." Y/A, v.15 (1974): 66-81.

243. Neubauer, A.: "The Literature of the Jews in Yemen." JQR, v.3 #4 (July, 1891): 604-621.

244. Opatoshu, Joseph: "Fifty Years of Yiddish Literature in the United States." Y/A, v.9 (1954): 72-82.

* 245. Patterson, David: THE FOUNDATIONS OF MODERN HEBREW LITERATURE. London: Liberal Jewish Synagogue, 1961. 59 pp.

246. ___: "Modern Hebrew Literature Goes on Aliyah." JJS, v.29 #1 (Spr., 1978): 75-84.

247. Pelli, Moshe: "The Impact of Deism of the Hebrew Literature of the Enlightenment in Germany." JJS, v.24 #2 (Aut., 1973): 127-146.

248. ___: "Isaac Euchel: Tradition and Change in the First Generation of Haskalah Literature in Germany." JJS, v.26 #1/2 (Spr./Aut., 1975): 151-167; v.27 #1 (Spr., 1976): 54-70.

> #141. Pelli, M.: THE AGE OF HASKALAH.

* 249. Rosenau, H.: A SHORT HISTORY OF JEWISH ART. London: James Clarke, 1948. 78 pp., illus.

250. Silberschlag, Eisig: "Recent Trends in Hebrew Literature." JSS, v.2 #1 (Jan., 1940): 3-22.

251. Solomon, Solomon J.: "Art and Judaism." JQR, v.13 #4 (July, 1901): 553-566.

252. Urzidil, Johannes: "The Living Contribution of Jewish Prague to Modern German Literature." LBML #11 (1968): 3-26.

253. Waxman, Meyer: A HISTORY OF JEWISH LITERATURE. 5 vols. South Brunswick, NJ: Thomas Yoseloff, 1960. 3,691 pp., maps, notes, bibliog., index.

Extensive survey of Jewish literature from the rabbinic period to the twentieth century. Jewish literature is divided by typology and theme. Within each chapter individual authors, books, and literary styles are reviewed. Much of the book covers the medieval and modern periods, with the fifth volume covering Jewish literature from 1935 to 1960. Waxman's commentaries are written lucidly and the breadth of his knowledge is encyclopedic. Each of Waxman's chapters contains an introduction, followed by Waxman's reviews. These introductions provide a useful context for the rest

of the chapter. In his broad definition of literature Waxman
does not limit himself to belle lettres, fiction, or to the
traditional realms of literature. To the contrary, Waxman
places much of his emphasis on Jewish scholarship. The
sections on trends in Judaica research are among Waxman's
best, and his keen perceptions into Jewish historiography
are enlightening.

254. Wischnitzer, Mark: A HISTORY OF JEWISH CRAFTS AND
GUILDS. New York: Jonathan David, 1965. 342 pp. apps.,
notes, index.

History of Jewish artisanry from ancient times to the
nineteenth century. Wischnitzer's approach is social, with
secondary attention given to economics. His primary goal is
to chart the role Jewish artisans and artisan guilds played
in Jewish and non-Jewish societies. Insofar as an individual's socioeconomic standing affected Jewish communal life,
the issues of class, income, and status are also reviewed.
Wischnitzer does not, however, write from a Marxist perspective, nor does he follow Max Weber's interpretation that
Jews naturally preferred the money trade over craftsmanship.
In general Wischnitzer eschews ideologically motivated generalizations, preferring to document his assertions carefully and without polemic. Although organized chronologically, some of the chapters deal with craft guilds in specific countries. Six appendixes cite Jewish guild charters
from different countries and periods. In all periods, Jewish
guilds are compared to non-Jewish ones. Wischnitzer's study
ends with the first glimmerings of the Industrial Revolution, before the almost complete collapse of the guild
system. Foreword by Salo W. Baron; introduction by Werner J.
Cahnman.

255. Zinberg, Israel: A HISTORY OF JEWISH LITERATURE. 12
vols. Trans. from the Yiddish by Bernard Martin. Cleveland:
The Press of Case Western Univ., 1972 / Cincinnati: Hebrew
Union College / New York: Ktav, 1974-1978. 3,247 pp., notes,
gloss., index.

Authoritative history of Jewish literature from the tenth
through the nineteenth centuries. Chapters are thematic or
biographical. All types of literature are included, although
philosophical, religious, and scholarly works receive the
most attention. In every generation Jewish literature is
placed into a general context. In addition to judging works
for their literary merit, Zinberg explains their social and

cultural importance. Medieval and modern debates on the religious implications of literary issues, for example, during the Haskalah, are explained in detail. All of Zinberg's statements are well documented and his work offers a fascinating and important insight into Jewish creativity. Bernard Martin's introduction to Volume I includes a biography of the author.

Published Volumes: 1. THE ARABIC-SPANISH PERIOD (1972): 231 pp. / 2. FRENCH AND GERMAN JEWRY IN THE EARLY MIDDLE AGES; THE JEWISH COMMUNITY OF MEDIEVAL ITALY (1972): 257 pp. / 3. THE STRUGGLE OF MYSTICISM AND TRADITION AGAINST PHILOSOPHICAL RATIONALISM (1973): 323 pp. / 4. ITALIAN JEWRY IN THE RENAISSANCE ERA (1974): 214 pp. / 5. THE JEWISH CENTER OF CULTURE IN THE OTTOMAN EMPIRE (1974): 204 pp. / 6. THE GERMAN-POLISH CULTURAL CENTER (1975): 324 pp. / 7. OLD YIDDISH LITERATURE FROM ITS ORIGINS TO THE HASKALAH PERIOD (1975): 403 pp. / 8. THE BERLIN HASKALAH (1976): 256 pp. / 9. HASIDISM AND ENLIGHTENMENT 1780-1820 (1976): 298 pp. / 10. THE SCIENCE OF JUDAISM AND GALICIAN HASKALAH (1977): 249 pp. / 11. THE HASKALAH MOVEMENT IN RUSSIA (1978): 227 pp. / 12. HASKALAH AT ITS ZENITH (1978): 261 pp.

EDUCATION

   256. Bomzer, Herbert W.: THE KOLEL IN AMERICA. New York: Shengold Press, 1985. 182 pp., notes, bibliog., index.

   Sociological and educational survey of the kolel in America. Traces the rise of the kolel in the East European yeshivot and the transference of the idea to the United States. The study is based on first-hand observations as well as interviews with both students and administrators. Although all kolelim concentrate on teaching Talmud, Bomzer notes that few share the same approach and characteristics. His study of the fourteen most famous, and coincidentally largest, kolelim in America divides them into four types: Lithuanian, hasidic, new, and community. It should be noted that the kolel is a postgraduate religious institution and should not be confused with a strictly rabbinic school that confers ordination. The typology reflects the institution's orientation and not its physical or educational status. Thus, by way of example, Bomzer describes the Yeshiva University Kolel as a "new" one, although he notes that it was founded in 1960; in this case, the "newness" of the kolel refers to its generally more modern orientation and to the secular entrance requirements demanded of the kolel fellows and their teachers.

* 257. Brown, Sheldon: GUIDANCE AND COUNSELING FOR JEWISH EDUCATION. New York: Bloch, 1964. 88 pp., bibliog., apps., index.

258. Dushkin, A. M. with N. Greenbaum: COMPARATIVE STUDY OF THE JEWISH TEACHER TRAINING SCHOOLS IN THE DIASPORA. Jerusalem: Institute of Contemporary Jewry, Hebrew Univ., 1970. 128 pp., app.

Sociological inquiry into the preparation of teachers for Jewish schools outside Israel. Primary emphasis is on the differing approaches of the various teacher training programs. The different requirements for admission and graduation as well as courses of study are investigated in detail. The problems and needs of teacher training programs are also reviewed. Not surprisingly, these are similar in many different countries, despite differences in approach and emphasis. The most commonly noted problem relates to teachers' salaries; this has been and continues to be one of the inhibiting factors in the development of Jewish education. In turn, the communal implications of teacher education are also noted. The authors provide interesting insight into the subject of teacher training on a global scale and review important issues related to Jewish education in the diaspora.

259. Goldman, Israel M.: LIFELONG LEARNING AMONG JEWS: ADULT EDUCATION IN JUDAISM FROM BIBLICAL TIMES TO THE TWENTIETH CENTURY. New York: Ktav, 1975. 364 pp., illus., notes, bibliog., index.

Survey of adult education with special emphasis on the development of the Bet Midrash, the Jewish house of study. The interrelationship between prayer and learning forms the basis for Goldman's study; for Jews, prayer was study and study was a form of prayer. Each period and its system of adult education is reviewed by Goldman - from the "yarhei kallah" of the Babylonian yeshivot [first through tenth centuries] to the "Hevrutot" of eastern, western, and southern Europe in the early modern period, including adult education in contemporary America and Israel. The breadth and depth of Goldman's review is amazing. In effect Goldman has written a brief history of Jewish education in its various forms and climates. Introduction by Louis Finkelstein.

260. Gordis, R.: "Jewish Learning and Jewish Existence: Retrospect and Prospect." LBML, #6 (1963): 5-34.

261. Henriques, Alfred G.: "Religious Education." JQR, v.3 #1 (Oct., 1890): 85-105.

262. Joseph, Morris: "Jewish Religious Education." JQR, v.9 #4 (July, 1897): 631-668.

263. Kronish, Ronald: "John Dewey and Horace M. Kallen on Cultural Pluralism: Their Impact on Jewish Education." JSS, v.44 #2 (Spr., 1982): 135-148.

264. Lucas, Alice: "Jewish Religious Education." JQR, v.2 #3 (Apr., 1890): 270-290.

* 265. Neusner, J.: JUDAIC STUDIES IN UNIVERSITIES: TOWARD THE SECOND QUARTER-CENTURY. Durham, NC: Center for Judaic Studies, Duke Univ., 1984. 18 pp.

* 266. ___: PROFESSORS OR CURATORS UNIVERSITIES OR MUSEUMS: THE CASE OF JEWISH STUDIES. Columbus: Melton center for Jewish Studies, The Ohio State Univ., 1983. 14 pp.

267. ___: "Two Settings for Jewish Studies." Y/A, v.15 (1974): 204-224.

* 268. Pate, Glenn S.: THE TREATMENT OF THE HOLOCAUST IN UNITED STATES HISTORY TEXTBOOKS. New York: ADL, 1980. 25 pp.

269. Pilch, J.: "Changing Patterns in Jewish Education." JSS, v.21 #2 (Apr., 1959): 91-117.

270. Rosenbloom, N. H.: "Religious and Secular Coequality in S. R. Hirsch's Educational Theory." JSS, v.24 #4 (Oct., 1962): 223-247.

271. Roskies, Diane: "Alphabet Instruction in the East European Heder: Some Comparative and Historical Notes." Y/A, v.17 (1978): 21-53.

272. Rudavsky, David: "Jewish Education and the Religious Revival." Y/A, v.13 (1965): 95-124.

273. Shumsky, Abraham: THE CLASH OF CULTURES IN ISRAEL: A PROBLEM FOR EDUCATION. New York: Teachers College Columbia Univ., 1955. 170 pp., bibliog.

Investigates ethnic and social problems in Israel.
Shumsky also offers suggestions for a solution to the clash
of cultures through greater educational and employment opor-
tunities. The Ashkenazi and Oriental communities are surveyed in a comparative way. On the basis of research
available in the mid-1950s, Shumsky also proposes areas for
further study. The book is now outdated, since many of the
etnic problems Shumsky discusses have been largely, though
not completely, resolved. It is interesting to note that the
general solution suggested by Shumsky was, coincidentally,
followed by Israel.

THE SYNAGOGUE

274. de Breffny, B.: THE SYNAGOGUE. New York: Macmillan,
1978. 215 pp., illus., notes, gloss., bibliog., index.

History of the synagogue from its earliest manifestations
until modern times. Stylistic and religious concerns are
interwoven. Breffny begins by charting the origins of the
synagogue during the Babylonian exile. Synagogue styles are
compared to contemporary secular and religious architecture.
Social and communal elements of Jewish religious life are
also reviewed. The book is illustrated throughout, with examples of unique and unusual synagogues.

275. Eisenberg, Azriel: THE SYNAGOGUE THROUGH THE AGES.
New York: Bloch, 1974. 206 pp., illus., bibliog., index.

History of the synagogue from the First Temple until
recent times. Eisenberg begins by explaining man´s religious
impulse and sees the origin of the synagogue in the biblical
command to seek the divine. One method of doing so culminated in Solomon´s Temple. However, with the destruction of
the First Temple a new form of holy place came into being,
which is now known as the synagogue. In addition to tracing
the idea of the synagogue, Eisenberg also gives concrete
examples of synagogue art and architecture from a number of
different eras and communities. Synagogue functionaries and
furnishings are also covered, although only briefly. The
changing role of the synagogue is one of Eisenberg´s main
themes, and he amply fulfills that goal.

276. Heilman, Samuel C.: SYNAGOGUE LIFE: A STUDY IN SYM-
BOLIC INTERACTION. Chicago: The Univ. of Chicago Press,
1976. 306 pp., notes, gloss., bibliog., index.

Sociological inquiry into the inner life of an Orthodox synagogue. Unlike other sociological studies, which rely on statistics, Heilman operates on the individual level, having gathered his information on the basis of several years as a participant observer in the described setting. Each of the locales of synagogue activity and the personalities active in shul life are described. The interaction of distinct individuals in the shul is placed into social and symbolic context. Heilman also studies synagogue conversation – which is usually overlooked, except by rabbis who complain about the noise – and shows that it is more than just gossip. The social interaction within a typical shul offers an insight into the sociology of religion and into ethnology. Written without jargon, the narrative is readily accessible and will be of interest to the layperson as well as the scholar.

277. Kaufmann, D.: "Art in the Synagogue." JQR, v.9 #2 (Jan., 1897): 254-269.

278. Krinsky, C. H.: SYNAGOGUES OF EUROPE: ARCHITECTURE, HISTORY, MEANING. New York: The Architectural History Foundation, 1985. 457 pp., illus., apps., gloss., notes, bibliog., index.

Architectual inquiry into the European synagogue. The book is divided into two parts. Part I deals with the synagogue and its history up to the modern period. Ritual arrangements are reviewed, as are the changes in style over the course of time. An interesting section draws a comparison between synagogues, churches, and mosques in terms of architecture and style. Part II is a detailed study of selected examples of synagogue architecture. Although this section is divided geographically, Krinsky has attempted to find synagogues representing all of the different styles she mentions in Part I. Most of the synagogues studied are traditional [Orthodox], but a number of Reform centers are also cited. Krinsky´s comments are closely coordinated with the illustrations, many of which are stunning, and with floor plans where available.

279. Levy, Isaac: THE SYNAGOGUE: ITS HISTORY AND FUNCTION London: Vallentine Mitchell, 1963. 152 pp., notes, index.

Guidebook and history of the synagogue from earliest times. Organized around the functional aspects, although the first chapter deals with how the synagogue came into being. After this introduction, the concrete issues concerning

the synagogue building, its decoration, and lay and religious officials are discussed. Developments over the years,
from the simplest Pharisaic synagogues to the more complex
models of today, are reviewed, albeit briefly. Levy ends
with a discussion of proper decorum in the synagogue and the
various postures of prayer. Reform practice is not dealt
with systematically – Levy primarily deals with the organization and practice of a traditional [Orthodox] synagogue.

280. Milgram, Abraham A.: JEWISH WORSHIP. Philadelphia:
JPS, 1971. 673 pp., notes, bibliog., index.

History and guide to Jewish liturgy. Millgram explains
both the development of the "siddur" and its meaning. The
book also offers a "how to" guide to Jewish prayer. Millgram
divides Jewish prayer into its three bases: the Shema´, the
Shemoneh Esreh, and teaching the Torah. Millgram surveys the
historical development and ultimate crystallization of the
siddur as we know it today. Although Milgram´s work primarily deals with the traditional orthodox prayer book, the
issue of Reform and variant heterodox siddurim is also reviewed. An especially interesting chapter deals with the
theology of the siddur, and many other interesting topics
are covered in subsections. Millgram keeps his sections
brief and to the point. In simple but flowing style, he explains the prayers, their meanings, and proper procedure.
Those well versed in the prayers and those eager to learn
more about them will find much of interest in this useful
summary.

281. Posner, Raphael, Uri Kaploun and Sh. Cohen [eds.]:
JEWISH LITURGY: PRAYER AND SYNAGOGUE SERVICE THROUGH THE
AGES. Jerusalem: Keter, 1975. 278 pp., illus., index.

Encyclopedic review of Jewish prayer in its various manifestations. In addition to surveying the various types of
prayers, the book also discusses modes of prayer in everyday, Shabbat, and holiday contexts. An interesting chapter
investigates the concept of prayer as it developed from the
biblical period until the modern era. The different variants
on the Jewish rite are reviewed in detail, with special
attention given to the influence of Kabbalah on the liturgy
particularly in the East European nusha´ot. The book is
richly illustrated and is a good introduction to the subject
of prayer, liturgy, and the synagogue.

282. Rankin, O. S.: "The Extent of the Influence of the Synagogue Service upon Christian Worship." JJS, v.1 #1 (1948/49): 27-32.

283. Reisman, Bernard: THE CHAVURAH: A CONTEMPORARY JEW-ISH EXPERIENCE. New York: Union of American Hebrew Congregations, 1977. 234 pp., notes, apps., tables, bibliog.

Sociological investigation of the development of the Chavurah in American Jewry. The Chavurah began to develop in the early 1970s and can best be described as a small fellowship of mutually interested individuals. Emphasis within the Chavurah movement is on fostering a sense of community, which most members feel has been lost in contemporary America. Reisman surveys both the historical and contemporary manifestations of the Chavurah idea. Relations between Chavurot and synagogues are charted in detail. Reisman offers an interim evaluation of the Chavurah experience, noting that the phenomenon is still in a state of development. The book could also be used as a guide to the establishment of a Chavurah, with two chapters covering the "how-to" aspect. Rounding out the book are five appendixes dealing with methodological procedures.

284. Wischnitzer, R.: THE ARCHITECTURE OF THE EUROPEAN SYNAGOGUE. Philadelphia: JPS, 1964. 312 pp., illus., notes, bibliog., gloss., index.

Inquiry into the architecture and art history of the synagogue since Roman times. Differences in synagogue style are clearly shown to reflect changes in Jewish orientation. Wischnitzer also investigates the history of Jewish artisanry, although Jews have been permitted to work as architects only since the emancipation. As an introduction Wischnitzer provides a chapter on Jewish synagogues of Roman times. Her chapters are organized chronologically, each period and locale exemplifying style or stress in the building of synagogues.

285. ___: "Mutual Influences between Eastern and Western Europe in Synagogue Architecture from the 12th to the 18th Century." Y/A, v.2/3 (1947/48): 25-68.

THE SCIENCES

286. Friedenwald, Harry: THE JEWS AND MEDICINE: ESSAYS. 2 vols. Baltimore, MD: The John Hopkins Press, 1944. 817 pp., illus., notes, bibliog., index.

Collection of essays on the Jewish role in the history of medicine, based on Friedenwald's previously published articles. Chronological stress is on the medieval period, though some essays also discuss ancient Jewish medicine and two deal with modern issues. The subjects covered are quite varied. Friedenwald divides the book into eight sections: "On the Practice of Medicine Among the Jews," which also includes three satires on Jewish doctors; "Ancient and Medieval Jewish Physicians"; "Jews and the Early Universities"; "Biographical Sketches"; "Jewish Hospitals"; "Concerning Diseases of the Jews"; "Opthamological Notes of Jewish Interest"; and "Chronicles." Not all the essays are placed in the appropriate section: thus Friedenwald's essay on the life of Maimonides is included in "Ancient and Medieval Jewish Physicians" and not among the biographies.

287. Gershenfeld, L.: THE JEW IN SCIENCE. Philadelphia: JPS, 1934. 224 pp., index.

Historical inquiry into Jewish interest and participation in scientific research. The book is arranged in chronological order, beginning with the Greek period. Brief reviews of Jewish history and of scientific inquiry are appended. The chapters relating to the modern era are lists of Jews active in the sciences; although these are of interest, they are of little use historically. The book has a clear apologetic undertone, and the attempt to prove positive Jewish contributions to society is stated explicitly in Gershenfeld's preface.

288. Goldberg, Jacob A.: "Jews in the Medical Profession: a National Survey." JSS, v.1 #3 (July, 1939): 327-336.

289. Jakobovits, I.: "The Medical Treatment of Animals in Jewish Law." JJS, v.7 #3/4 (1956): 207-220.

290. Kagan, Solomon R.: JEWISH CONTRIBUTIONS TO MEDICINE IN AMERICA. Boston, MA: Boston Medical Pub., 1934. 549 pp., illus., notes, bibliog., apps., chron., indexes.

Historical inquiry into American Jewish doctors and their

contributions. The book is organized by specialization. Each chapter contains a list of important American Jewish doctors in each field, arranged in chronological order by birth. Each entry then details the contribution of each doctor and his important publications, if any. The tone of the book is somewhat apologetic, as if trying to prove how - in one area at least - Jews have contributed greatly to America. The antisemitic canard that Jews are parasites is never stated explicitly, but is certainly implied in Kagan´s response. The book is unlikely to have more than passing interest for anyone except those interested in the specific subject at hand.

291. Ostow, Mortimer [ed.]: JUDAISM AND PSYCHOANALYSIS. New York: Ktav, 1982. 305 pp., bibliog.

Anthology dealing with the interaction of Judaism and psychiatry. The ten essays seek to answer three questions: is psychiatry a "Jewish" science?; alternatively, is psychiatry opposed to Judaism?; and what can a psychiatric approach teach us about the Jewish past? In their responses to these questions, the authors operate from different perspectives, seeking general answers from specific case studies. Most of the studies, however, are too broad to allow specific conclusions; they show what could be done by combining psychological methodology with research in Judaic studies. Each essay is prefaced by an abstract which briefly summarizes the subject. Most of the authors avoid excessive technicality and thus the majority of essays are readable by laymen as well as specialists.

CONTENTS: J. A. Arlow: The Consecration of the Prophet; A Psychoanalytic Study of a Religious Initiation Rite: Bar Mitzvah; Unconscious Fantasy and Political Movements / M. S. Bergmann: Moses and the Evolution of Freud´s Jewish Identity / M. Ostow: Judaism and Psychoanalysis; The Psychologic Determinants of Jewish Identity; The Hypomanic Personality; The Jewish Response to Crisis / M. Ostow and R. J. Lifton: Discussion / R. L. Rubenstein: The Meaning of Anxiety in Rabbinic Judaism / R. L. Sillman: Monotheism and the Sense of Reality.

JEWS AND WORLD CULTURE

> #10. Finkelstein, Louis [ed.]: THE JEWS.

CONTENTS: Volume III. THE JEWS: THEIR ROLE IN CIVILIZATION.
J. J. Rabinowitz: The Influence of Jewish Law on the Devel-
opment of the Common Law / M. M. Kaplan: A Philosophy of
Jewish Ethics / A. Altmann: Judaism and World Philosophy:
from Philo to Spinoza / E. Werner: The Jewish Contribution
to Music / R. Wischnitzer: Judaism and Art / A. Castiglioni:
The Contribution of the Jews to Medicine / Charles Singer:
Science and Judaism / O. I. Janowsky: The Rise of the State
of Israel / Milton R. Konvitz: Judaism and the Democratic
Ideal / D. Daiches: The Influence of the Bible on English
Literature / F. Lehner: The Influence of the Bible on Euro-
pean Literature.

292. Lehrman, Charles C.: JEWISH INFLUENCE ON EUROPEAN
THOUGHT. Trans. from the French by G. Klin; from the German
by V. Capenter. Rutherford, NJ: Fairleigh Dickinson Univ.
Press, 1976. 323 pp., index.

Inquiry into the Jewish role in world civilization from
the Judeo-Arabic culture of the tenth century to the
twentieth century. The book is written as a series of
related essays dealing with Jewish culture, the Jewish role
in European culture, and the image of the Jew in European
literature. Some of Lehrman´s essays are descriptive, but
most are analytical. His essays include quite a few novel
interpretations, some of which might seem a bit controversial. In particular, Lehrman´s assertion that Shakespeare
was not an antisemite, but was in fact a pioneer of the idea
of toleration of Jews, will not convince everyone. Other
essays, however, contain useful insights; for example,
Lehrman distinguishes between "Jews in Literature and Jewish
Literature." Another important essay covers "The Disintegration of the German-Jewish Symbiosis." The book thus has
much to offer for both students and interested laymen.

293. Roth, C.: THE JEWISH CONTRIBUTION TO CIVILIZATION.
Cincinnati: Hebrew Union College, 1940. 295 pp., notes, bibliog., index.

Survey of Jewish contributions to Western civilization,
with special emphasis on the modern era. In addition to
ethical and moral values, Roth concludes that Jews have contributed greatly to all forms of culture. Written specifically to counter antisemitic propaganda, which identified
Jews as parasites who contributed nothing positive to European life or culture. Despite this orientation, Roth is
never apologetic in his review. He covers a broad sweep of

subjects, but understandably could not deal with every area
to which Jews contributed or with every Jewish contribution.
Nevertheless, his survey is a useful and interesting contribution to the historiography on the subject.

294.___: THE JEWS IN THE RENAISSANCE. Philadelphia: JPS,
1959. 378 pp., illus., notes, bibliog., index.

Investigation of the impact of the renaissance on Italian
Jewry. Primarily an exercise in intellectual history, the
book also explores the social background of the Italian
Jewish renaissance. Roth attempts to analyze the mutual cultural influences, Italian and Jewish, during a period of
social and intellectual openness. An especially interesting
chapter deals with "Manners and Morals." Here again, Roth
tries to portray the specific character of Renaissance-era
Italian Jewry. Roth´s text is written in a simple but
flowing style. All manners of Jewish cultural activity are
reviewed, providing an important contribution to Italian and
Jewish history.

295. Runes, Dagobert [ed.]: THE HEBREW IMPACT ON WESTERN
CIVILIZATION. New York: Philosophical Library, 1951. 922
pp., notes, bibliog., index.

Polemical anthology on the Jewish role in modern civilization. Although scholarly in approach, the book primarily
is oriented toward a denial of all the negative stereotypes
which reduce Jews to cultural parasites, cowards, and money-
hungry "philistines." Once the polemical and apologetic
premise is understood, the essays provide a source of interesting information. Especially enlightening are Katsh´s
and Roth´s essays. Both deal with the role Jews have played
as transmitters of broad ideas about culture, the arts, and
proper government.

CONTENTS: L. L. Bernard: Jewish Sociologists and Political
Scientists / H. Bieber: Jews in Public Office; The Jewish
Contribution to the Exploration of the Globe / V. Ferm: The
Fountainhead of Western Religion / S. R. Kagan: The Influ-
ence of the Jew on Modern Medicine / M. J. Karpf: Jewish
Social Service and its Impact upon Western Civilization / A.
I. Katsh: Hebraic Foundations of American Democracy / Rudolf
Kayser: The Jew in Literature / K. F. Leidecker: Jewish
Philosophers / C. Lubinski: The Jew in Drama, Theatre, and
Film / P. Nettl: Judaism and Music / A. A. Roback: The Jew
in Modern Science / Cecil Roth: Jewish Cultural Influence in

the Middle Ages / K. Schwarz: The Hebrew Impact on Western
Art / W. Sorell: Israel and the Dance / R. Van Dyck: The
Jewish Influence on Journalism / M. L. Wolf: The Jew and the
Law / W. B. Ziff: The Jew as Soldier, Strategist and
Military Adviser.

296. Shulvass, Moses A.: THE JEWS IN THE WORLD OF THE
RENAISSANCE. Trans. from the Hebrew by E. Kose. Leiden: E.
J. Brill, 1973. 367 pp., notes, index.

Social history of Italian Jewry during the Renaissance,
organized thematically. Shulvass adopts a dual approach by
charting both the communal and intellectual aspects of Renaissance Jewry. An especially important section deals with
"The Community" and another with "Family and Social Life."
Typologies of Jewish Renaissance activity are charted in detail, with emphasis on literature and the sciences. The fine
arts receive less attention, since Jewish activity in this
field was more tentative. Jews adopted many of the mores of
Renaissance society, including some of its vices. Thus a
unique form of Italo-Jewish culture was created, which prefigured some of the problems experienced by Jews in northern
Europe during the Emancipation.

297. Sterling, Ada: THE JEW AND CIVILIZATION. New York:
Aetco Publishing Co., 1924. 330 pp., bibliog., index.

Apologetic review of the Jewish role in modern culture.
Primary emphasis is to prove the positive contributions Jews
made, thereby disproving the antisemitic contention that
Jews are power-hungry, money-worshipping parasites. The subject is treated thematically. While the book must be viewed
in the context of the period in which it was written, it
does contain some interesting bits of information, despite
Sterling's apologetic undertone.

6

Antisemitism

SURVEYS

298. Baron, Salo W.: "Changing Patterns of Antisemitism." JSS, v.38 #1 (Wint., 1976): 5-38.

299. Bergman, Shlomo: "Some Methodological Errors in the Study of Antisemitism." JSS, v.5 #1 (Jan., 1943): 43-60.

300. Eckardt, A. Roy: "Theological Approaches to Anti-semitism." JSS, v.33 #4 (Oct., 1971): 272-284.

301. Flannery, E. H.: THE ANGUISH OF THE JEWS: TWENTY-THREE CENTURIES OF ANTISEMITISM. New York: Macmillan, 1965. 332 pp., notes, bibliog.

Synthetic history of antisemitism, the first written by a Catholic historian. Flannery is passionate in his condemnation of Jew-hatred, but is quite apologetic in his explanation of the phenomenon. In particular, Flannery has three problematic interpretations. He sees Christian antisemitism as developing from pagan Jew-hatred; he accepts accounts of Jewish persecution of early Christianity; and he denies any connection between Christian and Nazi antisemitism. None of the three can be fully supported by available evidence, although the third point is his weakest. The book also has some merit. Flannery´s broad synthetic approach allows the reader to grasp the continuity of ideas, themes, and motifs in antisemitic propaganda. All forms of Jew-hatred are included in Flannery´s analysis, although he places most of his emphasis on mass, rather than individual, prejudice.

302. Glassman, Samuel: EPIC OF SURVIVAL: TWENTY-FIVE CEN-
TURIES OF ANTISEMITISM. New York: Bloch Pub., 1980. 438 pp.,
app., notes, bibliog., index.

Idiosyncratic history of antisemitism. Glassman also
presents an overview of Jewish history as background to the
anti-Jewish movements and groups surveyed. Glassman follows
the sociohistorical method developed by Yehezkel Kaufman,
although in a substantially modified form. This allows a
rather simple but profound conclusion about antisemitism and
its causes: antisemitism exists because Jews exist. All
other causes - religious, economic, social, or psychological - explain the manifestations of antisemitism, but do
not get at its roots.

As with any synthetic work, there may be some quibbles on
details. Some of the chapters are better documented than
others. Altogether, the book offers a good summary of the
history of antisemitism as well as some Jewish responses to
it. Glassman's chapters are kept short and easily readable,
making the book attractive for schools and lay readership.

303. Grosser, Paul E. and Edwin Halperin: ANTISEMITISM:
THE CAUSES AND EFFECTS OF A PREJUDICE. Secaucus, NJ: Citadel
Press, 1979. 408 pp., charts, graphs, notes, bibliog.

Encyclopedic survey of the history of antisemitism. The
book's divisions are somewhat confusing, but can be reduced
to three major sections: [1], a catalogue of Christian antisemitism from 70 CE to the present; [2], an explanatory
section which seeks the causes of antisemitism. Primary
emphasis in this section is on psychological explanations,
although other factors are also included; and [3], a further
catalogue of Islamic antisemitism from 600 CE to present
times. The authors define antisemitism somewhat vaguely, in
a very general way. Specialists might argue with this, but
it does provide the book with a common denominator that can
be helpful in the discussion of antisemitism and its
results. The book is a useful sourcebook on antisemitism and
can easily be adapted to school use. Foreword by Robert St.
John; preface by Franklin H. Littell.

304. Halpern, Ben: "What is Antisemitism?" MJ, v.1 #3
(Dec., 1981): 251-262.

305. Hay, Malcolm: THY BROTHER'S BLOOD: THE ROOTS OF
CHRISTIAN ANTISEMITISM. New York: Hart, 1975. 356 pp., app.,
bibliog., notes, index.

History of antisemitism, with special emphasis on Christian policy in regard to the Jewish question. Also published
as THE FOOT OF PRIDE [1950] and EUROPE AND THE JEWS [1960].
Hay made his life's study the history of the Catholic
Church. His conclusion was that the Church's conscious
policy was to hound the Jews, degrade them, and ground them
to dust. The general parameters of this policy were copied
by all modern Jew-haters, culminating with Nazi Germany.

306. Katz, J. FROM PREJUDICE TO DESTRUCTION: ANTISEMITISM
1700-1933. Cambridge, MA: Harvard Univ. Press, 1980. 392
pp., notes, index.

Surveys the development of modern antisemitism from 1700
to the Holocaust. Attempts to place individual antisemitic
ideologues into social and intellectual context, while also
analyzing the development of the modern Jewish problem. Unfortunately, the question of direct influence from one
generation to the next, which seems implied in the book's
simple chronological organization, is never clarified.
Significantly, Katz notes that modern antisemitism sprang
simultaneously from a number of different sources, all
culminating in Nazi antisemitism. A useful synthesis, the
book is nevertheless disappointing for those seeking a more
in-depth analysis.

307. Littell, Franklin H.: THE CRUCIFICTION OF THE JEWS:
THE FAILURE OF CHRISTIANS TO UNDERSTAND THE JEWISH EXPERI-
ENCE. Macon, GA: Mercer Univ. Press/Rose, 1986 [Rep. of 1975
Ed.]. 153 pp., notes, apps.

Surveys the failure of Christians to understand Jewish
history. Littell's point of departure is the historical
development of antisemitism and the results of Jew-hatred
during the Holocaust. Littell also argues forcefully that
Christians must come to grips with the State of Israel.
Littell suggests that twentieth century Jewish history is,
ironically, the fulfillment of Christian symbolology - the
Holocaust and the rise of Israel are, for him, crucifiction
and resurrection. Controversial at every point, Littell is
thought-provoking and the book is a must read for all
believing Christians and Jews.

308. Pinson, K. S.: "Antisemitism in the Post-War World."
JSS, v.7 #2 (Apr., 1945): 99-118.

309. Poliakov, Leon: THE HISTORY OF ANTISEMITISM. 4 vols. New York: Vanguard Press, 1965-1986. apps., notes, indexes.

Thorough and detailed history of antisemitism from Roman times unto the Holocaust. Although Poliakov aims at a synthetic history, his depth of analysis makes the book a classic study. The scope of Poliakov´s survey is impressive; all forms of antisemitism are reviewed and all are related to the continuum of Jew-hatred that culminated in the Holocaust. In each period antisemitism is placed into social, economic, and political context. The life of the Jewish community is also reviewed, providing the necessary background for an understanding of antisemitism´s impact. The Jewish responses to antisemitism are included. Appendixes in each volume add additional information on related topics. Translated from the French by Richard Howard, Natalie Gerardi, and Miriam Kochan.

Published Volumes: 1. FROM THE TIME OF CHRIST TO THE COURT JEWS (1965): 340 pp. / 2. FROM MOHAMMED TO THE MARRANOS (1973): 399 pp. / 3. FROM VOLTAIRE TO WAGNER (1975): 582 pp. / 4. SUICIDAL EUROPE, 1870-1933 (1986): 528 pp.

THEMATIC STUDIES

310. Byrnes, Robert F.: "Edouard Drumont and La France Juive." JSS, v.10 #2 (Apr., 1948): 165-184.

311. Cohn, Norman: WARRANT FOR GENOCIDE: THE MYTH OF THE JEWISH WORLD-CONSPIRACY AND THE PROTOCOLS OF THE ELDERS OF ZION. New York: Harper & Row, 1966. 303 pp., illus., notes, apps., bibliog., index.

Studies the myth of a Jewish world conspiracy in its literary and political ramifications. Primarily organized around the literary history of THE PROTOCOLS OF THE ELDERS OF ZION, from the early nineteenth-century version to current Arab and neo-Nazi versions. Cohn proves that the origins of the myth had nothing to do with Jews, having originated in a book condemning Napoleon III. Soon, the myth was reoriented by adding the Jewish component and ascribing to Jews a will to dominate and rule the world. Finally, the weapons that the Jews allegedly use, freemasonry, liberalism, and bolshevism, were also added to the myth. In 1910 the Tsarist secret police published what has become the most developed form of this myth, as described by Cohn. Beside

literary aspects Cohn also shows interest in the psycho-
pathology of demonological antisemitism.

312. Curtis, Michael [ed.]: ANTISEMITISM IN THE CONTEMPO-
RARY WORLD. Boulder, CO.: Westview Press, 1986. 333 pp.,
notes, index.

Anthology addressing the issue of postwar antisemitism
and its manifestations in the contemporary world. Based on a
conference on antisemitism held at Rutgers University in
November 1983. The essays cover virtually every aspect of
antisemitism since World War II from political, social, and
philosophical perspectives. The book is divided into five
parts: "Philosophy and Ideology," "Religion and Politics,"
"Israel and Zionism," "Discrimination: Action and Expression," and "Contemporary Perceptions." All of the essays
offer insight into the subjects discussed, but the contributions of Fackenheim, Johnson, and Wistrich stand out. It is
especially important to note that Fackenheim's quote of Raul
Hilberg "The German Nazis at last decreed: 'You have no
right to live' [p. 25]" is most appropriate for both neo-
antisemitism and its very weak cover, antizionism. The essays on Muslim antisemitism should be read by all who believe concessions by Israel will automatically bring peace
to the Middle East. Likewise, Dinnerstein's essay on self-
defense is a masterful study and has implications beyond its
limited scope. The entire anthology is pulled together by
Curtis's introductory essay, which places antisemitism into
its past and present contexts.

CONTENTS: M. Curtis: Antisemitism - the Baffling Obsession /
Emil L. Fackenheim: Philosophical Reflections on Antisemi-
tism / Paul Johnson: Marxism Versus the Jews / R. Wistrich:
The "Jewish Question": Left-wing Antizionism in Western
Societies / E. Sivan: Radical Islam and the Arab-Israeli
Conflict / N. A. Stillman: Antisemitism in the Contemporary
Arab World / R. Yadlin: Arab Antisemitism in Peacetime: the
Egyptian Case / R. L. Nettler: Past Trials and Present
Tribulations: a Muslim Fundamentalist Speaks on the Jews /
J. T. Pawlikowski: New Testament Antisemitism: Fact or
Fable? / J. S. Conway: The German Churches and the Jewish
People Since 1945 / D. V. Segre: Is Antizionism a New Form
of Antisemitism? / Nathan Glazer: Antizionism - a Global
Phenomenon / Arthur Hertzberg: Zionism as Racism: a Semantic
Analysis / M. R. Marrus: Is There a New Antisemitism? / Z.
Gitelman: Soviet Antisemitism and its Perception by Soviet
Jews / T. Prittie: Economic Boycott and Discrimination / S.

J. Roth: Antisemitism and the Law: Effects and Options for
Action / E. Alexander: Stealing the Holocaust / Wendy S.
Flory: The Psychology of Antisemitism: Conscience-Proof
Rationalization and the Deferring of Moral Choice / J. L.
Goldstein: Antisemitism, Sexism, and the Death of the
Goddess: Some Problems with New Readings of Old Texts / D.
Schnapper: Perceptions of Antisemitism in France / William
Safran: Problems of Perceiving and Reacting to Antisemitism:
Reflections of a "Survivor" / Earl Raab: Attitudes Toward
Israel and Attitudes Toward Jews: the Relationship / Leonard
Dinnerstein: American Jewish Organizational Efforts to Com-
bat Antisemitism in the United States Since 1945.

313. Epstein, Simon: CRY OF CASSANDRA: THE RESURGENCE OF
EUROPEAN ANTISEMITISM. Trans. from the French by Norman S.
Posel. Bethesda, MD: Zenith Edition, 1985. 221 pp., notes.

Clarion call urging Jews to awaken to the current threat
of antisemitism and the potentiality of a new Holocaust.
Based on extensive research into the past - into antisemitism in France, Russia, and Germany and the rise of the
Nazis and the Holocaust. In addition to the historical
information, Epstein juxtaposes the rise of neo-antisemitism
in France in the 1970s and 1980s. While one might quibble
with some of Epstein's reconstructions, especially as relating to the Holocaust in France, his conclusions are sound
and very frightening. The book should be read and digested
by every concerned Jew, in France, America, and throughout
the world.

314. Gelber, Mark H.: "What is Literary Antisemitism?"
JSS, v.47 #1 (Wint., 1985): 1-20.

315. Lestschinsky, J.: "The Anti-Jewish Program: Tsarist
Russia, the Third Reich and Independent Poland." JSS, v.3 #2
(Apr., 1941): 141-158.

316. Oberman, Heiko: THE ROOTS OF ANTISEMITISM IN THE AGE
OF THE RENAISSANCE AND REFORMATION. Trans. from the German
by James I. Porter. Philadelphia: Fortress Press, 1984. 163
pp., notes, app., indexes.

Investigation into the origins of modern antisemitism.
Oberman has no qualms about the Christian origins of modern
Jew-hatred. Nevertheless, he feels that the sixteenth century was a watershed for future developments. He tests his
hypothesis by viewing the attitudes toward Jews of key

figures from the Renaissance and the Reformation. An especially interesting section deals with Martin Luther. His
analysis leads Oberman to a clear conclusion: The religious
fervor of the sixteenth century transformed antisemitism
from a mere vice into a virulent and potentially genocidal
ideology which has not yet been fully uprooted from the core
of Christianity. Oberman's style is simple and straight-
forward, making the book easily accessible to scholars and
laymen alike.

317. Parkes, James: THE CONFLICT OF THE CHURCH AND THE
SYNAGOGUE: A STUDY IN THE ORIGINS OF ANTISEMITISM. New York:
Atheneum, 1969. 430 pp., bibliog., notes, apps., index.

Competent study of antisemitism by an eminent Christian
scholar. After a general introduction detailing the Jews'
status in the Roman empire, Parkes deals with Jewish-Christian relations in depth. He sees Christian antisemitism as
sui generis, in other words, as distinct from pagan antisemitism. Parkes posits the origins of Jew-hatred to the
Christian denial of Judaism and the subsequent coopting of
the Old Testament for Christian purposes. Parkes also
debunks the claims of Jewish cooperation in Roman persecution of early Christianity and denies any role played by
Jews in the deaths of Christian martyrs.

318. Pollak, Oliver B.: "Antisemitism, the Harvard Plan,
and the Roots of Reverse Discrimination." JSS, v.45 #2
(Spr., 1983): 113-122.

319. Roth, Cecil: "Marranos and Racial Antisemitism: a
Study in Parallels." JSS, v.2 #3 (July, 1940): 239-248.

320. Ruether, Rosemary R.: FAITH AND FRATRICIDE: THE
THEOLOGICAL ROOTS OF ANTISEMITISM. New York: Seabury Press,
1974. 294 pp., notes, indexes.

Controversial study of the origins of antisemitism. The
author argues that antisemitism is a key component in Christian theology and is not an accidental result of Jewish-
Christian competition in the first century CE. After
rejecting all notions of antisemitism that she considers
apologetic, Ruether turns to the theological roots of Jew-
hatred. Ruether sees Christian antisemitism as a major
feature of modern anti-Judaism and claims that the Nazis
justified their Jew-hatred on the basis of Christian antisemitism. She views the removal of christological antisemi-

tism as vital not only to atone for past injustices but also to insure Christianity's future. Her analysis is well documented, making use of numerous New Testament and patristic sources. Introduction by Gregory Baum.

321. Silberner, Edmund: "The Attitude of the Fourierist School Towards the Jews." JSS, v.9 #4 (Oct., 1947): 339-362.

322. Synan, E. A.: THE POPES AND THE JEWS IN THE MIDDLE AGES. New York: Macmillan, 1965. 246 pp., notes, apps., index.

Studies the relations between the popes and the Jewish community from the fifth to the fifteenth centuries. While papal policy is charted in general, the attitudes of Gregory I and Innocent III are studied in detail. Synan, a Catholic historian, reviews the subject dispassionately and wisely avoids being polemical. An important subtheme is the development of the Church's Jewry-law and its overall relation to papal and Roman law. Especially interesting is Synan's chapter "Reflections," which is an insightful, if incomplete, review of Jewish-Christian relations.

323. Trachtenberg, Joshua: THE DEVIL AND THE JEWS: THE MEDIEVAL CONCEPTION OF THE JEW AND ITS RELATION TO MODERN ANTISEMITISM. Philadelphia: JPS, 1983. 278 pp., notes, bibliog., index.

Studies the medieval conception of the Jew and its influence on modern antisemitism. Primary focus is on demonological antisemitism. Trachtenberg surveys the popular identification of the Jew with the Devil and the Antichrist. Although never official Church dogma, this mythological concept took root in northern Europe during the twelfth century. Aspects of the myth which Trachtenberg analyzes in detail include the ritual-murder accusation, the blood libel, and the desecration of the Host libel. All of these canards, and the entire myth, are based on the assumption of Jewish perversity. In the popular mind, the truth of Christianity was so clear that it was naturally presumed everyone, Jews included, knew it. How then could one explain the Jews' rejection of salvation? Ultimately, therefore, the Jews became identified as agents of the Devil on Earth, if not as evil incarnate.
Trachtenberg's analysis offers an important insight for the understanding of the modern diabolization of Jews through racism and conspiracy theories. As is well known,

modern antisemites of all ideological orientations have made
use of similar accusations, mythologizing Jews and turning
them into lepers who had to be eradicated for the sake of
humanity. The multidimensional process of diabolization, and
its results, are fully documented by Trachtenberg in all
their ramifications. Foreword by Mark Saperstein.

324. Vishniak, Mark: "New Studies on the Elders of Zion."
Y/A, v.2/3 (1947/48): 140-145.

AREA STUDIES

325. Belth, Nathan C.: A PROMISE TO KEEP: A NARRATIVE OF
THE AMERICAN ENCOUNTER WITH ANTISEMITISM. New York: Shocken
Books, 1979. 305 pp., illus., notes, bibliog., index.

Journalistic history of American antisemitism. Primary
emphasis is on the development of antisemitism after the
1880s and into the twentieth century. Belth attempts to adjust the perceptions about American antisemitism to the realities of Judaeophobia in the United States. Admitting that
American antisemitism has been more muted than antisemitism
in Europe, he nevertheless notes that some form of Judaeophobia has been present in America for as long as there have
been Jews. All forms of antisemitism are reviewed, although
Belth focuses on its social, political, and literary forms.
Jewish responses to antisemitism are reviewed as well. American Jews are warned to take antisemitism seriously, but
also not to exaggerate its import. In an afterword to the
Schocken edition, Belth brings his analysis up to date. Although not documented in the scholarly sense, Belth has undertaken serious and well thought out research.

326. Byrnes, Robert F.: "Antisemitism in France before
the Dreyfus Affair." JSS, v.11 #1 (Jan., 1949): 49-68.

327. ___: ANTISEMITISM IN MODERN FRANCE: THE PROLOGUE TO
THE DREYFUS AFFAIR. New Brunswick, NJ: Rutgers Univ. Press,
1950. 348 pp., notes, index.

Inquiry into French antisemitism, the first volume of a
projected series that was never completed. This volume
covers French antisemitism from the 1880s to the Dreyfus
Affair. Byrnes attempts to place antisemitism into social
context, but his exclusively political and ideological orientation limits his social viewpoint. Although recognizing

that antisemitism has had a long history in France, he
begins his study with Eduard Drumont and LA FRANCE JUIVE. To
his credit, Byrnes also analyzes left-wing manifestations of
Judaeophobia. Byrnes attempts to correlate antisemitic incidents with the actual demography of French Jewry; although
not fully successful, he did show the way for later historians [see #355]. Byrnes attempts to ascertain the reception
of antisemitism by different social classes; this too is not
fully developed but does offer a good beginning for further
elaboration.

328. Dobkowski, M. N.: THE TARNISHED DREAM: THE BASIS OF
AMERICAN ANTISEMITISM. Westport, CT: Greenwood Press, 1979.
291 pp., notes, bibliog., index.

Revisionist history of American antisemitism. Unlike more
traditional scholars who see antisemitism as a relatively
late American development, Dobkowski traces the origins of
American Judaeophobia to the decades before 1890. Moreover,
where other historians view antisemitism as an exaggerated
response to social and economic tensions, Dobkowski views it
as a consistent and fully developed ideology which originated in the religious revivalism of the 1870s and 1880s.
Dobkowski does not ignore other factors but merely emphasizes the fact that antisemitism is more deeply rooted in
the American psyche than is generally realized.
Dobkowski makes some very important points. In particular
his analysis of the attitude toward Jews and Judaism in late
nineteenth-century American literature exposes the distinct
antisemitic bias of many American writers. As a corrective
of the overly optimistic view that Judaeophobia is an import
from Europe and has no American roots, Dobkowski´s work is
crucial, although it does not intrinsically prove the early
origin of American antisemitism. Dobkowski does prove that
the antisemitism of America´s gilded age originated a decade
before most analysts thought it began. Yet ten years is not
a major revision of historic chronology. In fact, one might
still argue that antisemitism developed more slowly in the
United States, since by 1880 a fully ramified "Jewish
Question" had existed in Europe for more than a decade.

329. Duker, A. G.: "Polish Emigre Christian Socialists on
the Jewish Problem." JSS, v.14 #4 (Oct., 1952): 317-342.

330. Feingold, Henry L.: "Finding a Conceptual Framework
for the Study of American Antisemitism." JSS, v.47 #3/4
(Sum./Fall, 1985): 313-326.

331. Freedman, Theodore [ed.]: ANTISEMITISM IN THE SOVIET
UNION: ITS ROOTS AND CONSEQUENCES. New York: Freedom Library
Press of the Anti-Defamation League of B'nai B'rith, 1984.
664 pp., illus., notes, index.

Collection of articles and documents on Soviet neo-antisemitism, based on international conferences on the subject
held in Jerusalem and Paris. A wide range of factors in
Soviet antisemitism are charted in detail. Special emphasis
is placed on the almost psychopathic mythology of zionism
equals nazism, used by Soviet authorities in almost every
medium to justify both their anti-Israel positions and their
attack on the reborn Soviet Jewish culture. Emigration as an
issue is dealt with only tangentially. The book also
includes excerpts of writings emanating from official Soviet
sources, from the samizdat, and from the Jewish samizdat. A
massive bibliography of Soviet antisemitic books is included. Viewed within the context of the Holocaust, the book is
a chilling reminder of how insecure Jewish life still is.

CONTENTS: Sh. Ettinger: The Historical Roots of Antisemitism
in the USSR / R. Nudelman: Contemporary Soviet Antisemitism:
Form and Content / G. Ilin: The Character of Soviet Anti-
semitism / Y. Tsigelman: Antisemitism in Soviet Publica-
tions / D. Tiktina [Shturman]: The Reception of Antisemitic
Propaganda in the USSR / A. Voronel: The Reasons for Anti-
semitism in the USSR / E. Sotnikova: The Jewish Problem in
Samizdat and the Emigration Press / L. Dimerski-Tsigelman:
The Attitude Toward Jews in the USSR / Sh. Hirsh: State and
Popular Antisemitism in Soviet Lithuania / M. Azbel: Aspects
of Antisemitism and the Fight Against It / Leon Dulzin: The
Status of Jews in Soviet Society / Ch. Abramsky: The Soviet
Attitude Toward Jews: Ideology and Practice / W. Korey: The
Soviet Protocols of the Elders of Zion / S. J. Roth: Anti-
zionism and Antisemitism in the USSR / Umberto Terracini:
Israel as a Factor in Soviet Antisemitism / Shmuel Ettinger:
Historical and Internal Political Factors in Soviet Anti-
semitism / Laurent Schwartz: Soviet Antisemitism and Jewish
Scientists / E. Litvinoff: The Slavophile Revival and its
Attitude to Jews / Sofia Tartakovsky: Antisemitism in Daily
Life / G. Freiman: I Am a Jew, It Turns Out / Ruth Okuneva:
Antisemitic Notions: Strange Analogies / Yaacov Tsigelman:
The Universal Jewish Conspiracy in Soviet Antisemitic Propa-
ganda / R. Okuneva: Jews in the Soviet School Syllabus / M.
Kaganskaya: Intellectual Fascism in Soviet-Russian Estab-
lishment Culture / J. Vogt: When Nazism Became Zionism: an
Analysis of Political Cartoons / Excerpts from Soviet

Publications and Samizdat / N. Bibichkova: Antisemitic and Anti-Israeli Publications in the USSR 1960-1981.

332. Gerber, David A. [ed.]: ANTISEMITISM IN AMERICAN HISTORY. Urbana: The Univ. of Illinois Press, 1986. 428 pp., notes, index.

Anthology investigating the history and historiography of American antisemitism. Gerber begins by defining antisemitism. The essayists elucidate their subjects as they see fit, but their essays share a common frame of reference. A number of different methodologies are brought to bear. American antisemitism is viewed historically within its political, social, economic, and psychological dimensions. One essay deals directly with Jewish self-defense, although most make reference to the subject. None of the essays was previously published, and they represent the state of the art on the subject. Of special interest is the essay by Breitman and Kraut, which is part of a larger study on American diplomacy and strategy affecting Jews during the 1930s and 1940s. Another important contribution is Liebman's essay on leftist antisemitism.

CONTENTS: David A. Gerber: Antisemitism and Jewish-Gentile Relations in American Historiography and the American Past / J. D. Sarna: The "Mythical Jew" and the "Jew Next Door" in Nineteenth-Century America / E. Schiff: Shylock's Mishpoheh: Antisemitism on the American Stage / R. Singerman: The Jew as Racial Alien: the Genetic Component of American Anti-semitism / E. S. Shapiro: Antisemitism Mississippi Style / G. Jeansonne: Combating Antisemitism: the Case of Gerald L. K. Smith / R. D. Breitman and A. M. Kraut: Antisemitism in the State Department, 1933-44: Four Case Studies / David A. Gerber: Cutting out Shylock: Elite Antisemitism and the Quest for Moral Order in the Mid-Nineteenth-Century American Marketplace / Marcia G. Synnott: Antisemitism and American Universities: Did Quotas Follow the Jews? / L. Dinnerstein: The Funeral of Rabbi Jacob Joseph / E. Lerner: American Feminism and the Jewish Question, 1890-1940 / A. Liebman: Antisemitism in the Left? / E. Feldman: American Protestant Theologians on the Frontiers of Jewish-Christian Relations, 1922-82 / David G. Singer: From St. Paul's Abrogation of the Old Covenant to Hitler's War Against the Jews: the Response of American Catholic Thinkers to the Holocaust, 1945-76.

333. Hirshfield, Claire: "The British Left and the Jewish Conspiracy: a Case Study of Modern Antisemitism." JSS, v.43 #2 (Spr., 1981): 95-112.

334. Holmes, Colin: ANTISEMITISM IN BRITISH SOCIETY 1876-1939. New York: Holmes & Meier, 1979. 320 pp., illus., notes, bibliog., index.

History of British antisemitism in all its manifestations. Primary emphasis is on the social and societal effects of antisemitism, and on the political implications of Judaeophobia. Holmes does not review political antisemitism per se. According to Holmes, modern British antisemitism must be divided into three periods. The first, from 1876 to 1914, manifested itself primarily in literary antisemitism and intense social discrimination against Jews. Antisemitic public policy was primarily oriented toward limiting Jewish immigration, if not stopping it altogether. The second era was coterminous with World War I. Jews were identified with the Germans and their loyalty was publicly suspect. The third era, from 1919 to 1939, was the period of overt antisemitic agitation against Jews in all sectors of British society and of all social strata. Leonard Mosley and the British Union of Fascists [BUF] led this agitation, but they were by no means the only rabble-rousers. Holmes also traces Jewish methods of defense, primarily during the 1930s. This chapter is a good model of a systematic study of Jewish defense tactics, in England and elsewhere. For the period covered, Holmes may be considered an authoritative source. Unfortunately, English antisemitism during and after World War II has yet to be studied in a systematic way.

* 335. Kingston, Paul J.: ANTISEMITISM IN FRANCE DURING THE 1930s: ORGANISATION, PERSONALITIES, AND PROPAGANDA. North Humberside, Eng.: The Univ. of Hull Press, 1983. 52 pp.

336. Korey, William: THE SOVIET CAGE: ANTISEMITISM IN RUSSIA. New York: Viking Press, 1973. 369 pp., notes, index.

Studies the parameters, causes, and results of Soviet antisemitism. The book contains fourteen interconnected but separate essays covering Korey's research on the subject. All of the essays are carefully documented from Soviet sources. Especially important are the chapters on Soviet distortion of the Holocaust and the grotesque Russian equation of zionism and nazism. The issue of Jewish emigration, which aroused the entire world to protest the condition of Soviet Jewry, is also reviewed as part of the book's main topic. Soviet antisemitism is placed into the broader contexts of postwar Jew-hatred and pre-Soviet antisemitism.

337. Lebzelter, G. G.: POLITICAL ANTISEMITISM IN ENGLAND, 1918-1939. New York: Holmes & Meier, 1978. 222 pp., illus., notes, bibliog., index.

Inquiry into the rise of political antisemitism in England during the interbellum period. Lebzelter's review serves three purposes. First, to document the development of English antisemitism; second, to chart the organized anti-semitic movement and its vicissitudes; third, to assess the impact of antisemitism on English social and political life. After an intensive but selective review, Lebzelter also deals with the reactions of English Jews, a cross-section of philosemitic groups, and the forces of law and order. Her definition of antisemitism is both unique and useful, empha-sizing the totality of the antisemitic program rather than any one of its manifestations. Lebzelter's conclusions are sound and offer an alternative model for the study of anti-semitism in modern times. She notes that despite massive support for antisemitism in England, the movement was never able to translate support into electoral success.

338. Ledeen, Michael A.: "The Evolution of Italian Fas-cist Antisemitism." JSS, v.37 #1 (Jan., 1975): 3-17.

339. Lendvai, Paul: ANTISEMITISM WITHOUT JEWS: COMMUNIST EASTERN EUROPE. Garden City, NY: Doubleday, 1971. 393 pp., notes, index.

Studies the continuing role antisemitism has played in the Communist bloc since World War II. Especially important is Lendvai's identification of antizionism as a pretext for antisemitism of the most obscene variety. After a general introduction Lendvai looks into two specific cases - Poland and Czechoslovakia - where antizionism was used to justify purges of Jewish Communists. This usage also provided a means of weakening anti-Communist opposition, since all opponents of the regime could be easily identified with re-actionary Zionist-imperialist agents. It might be added that recent events in the Soviet Union and the United Nation's "Zionism is Racism" resolution once again prove Lendvai's thesis and make it more ominous.

* 340. Ma´oz, Moshe: THE IMAGE OF THE JEW IN OFFICIAL ARAB
LITERATURE AND COMMUNICATIONS MEDIA. Jerusalem: Institute of
Contemporary Jewry, 1976. 33 pp., notes.

341. Massing, Paul W.: REHEARSAL FOR DESTRUCTION: A STUDY
OF POLITICAL ANTISEMITISM IN IMPERIAL GERMANY. New York:
Harper & Row, 1949. 341 pp., notes, documents, index.

Surveys the growth of the "Jewish Question" in Germany
from 1870 to 1914. Antisemitism is reviewed in all its ramifications, from the radical right to the Marxist left. The
book is arranged thematically, but follows the chronological
development of antisemitism in Germany. Much emphasis is
placed on the politicization of antisemitism by demagogues
and opportunistic politicians. Racial antisemitism is given
special attention. Massing seeks to provide the background
to explain Nazi antisemitism. How was it possible, he asks,
for the Nazis to subvert the concept of socialism and ex-
ploit racial theories to exterminate six million Jews? His
answer is that German antisemitism had legitimated the idea
that a Jewish threat had to be eliminated for the good of
all mankind. While this concept most clearly originated with
the reactionary right, even the progressive left in Germany
was ambivalent toward Jews. Some theoreticians of class
struggle - Marx and Engels, for example - were overtly hostile. Jews thus found themselves under intense attack, be-
reft of allies or protectors; ultimately powerless to affect
their own fate.

342. Mehlman, J.: LEGACIES OF ANTISEMITISM IN FRANCE.
Minneapolis: Univ. of Minnesota Press, 1983. 141 pp., apps.,
notes, index.

Surveys the literary legacy of French antisemitism before
and since World War II. Mehlman argues that Hitler destroyed
French antisemitism, but that Jew-hatred has, nevertheless,
had a residual survival among some literary figures. Organized into four essays, each analyzing a different person.
Mehlman does not, however, provide the reader with enough
background information to evaluate his thesis, nor does he
offer a general portrait of postwar French antisemitism.

343. Niewyk, Donald L.: SOCIALIST, ANTISEMITE, AND JEW:
GERMAN SOCIAL DEMOCRACY CONFRONTS THE PROBLEM OF ANTI-
SEMITISM. Baton Rouge: Louisiana State Univ. Press, 1971.
254 pp., notes, bibliog., index.

Examines the Jewish question in Germany and Austria through the prism of the German Social-Democratic Party [SPD]. Emphasis is on the Weimar Republic, although SPD policy before 1918 is also reviewed. Niewyk also studies the attitude of SPD ideologues on Jewish matters, such as zionism. Notes that the SPD was active in combating antisemitism, but did so for the wrong reasons and with naive tactics. In particular Niewyk argues that the Socialists lacked a long-range assessment of antisemitism and failed to recognize the depth of antisemitic sentiments. Moreover, the SPD failed to consider antisemitism as a separate phenomenon, viewing it as merely another of the Conservatives' antidemocratic tactics. Finally, Niewyk also documents cases of antisemitism masquerading as anti-capitalism; these were popular among the less sophisticated members of the SPD.

344. Pedattella, R. Anthony: "Italian Attitudes Toward Jewry in the Twentieth Century." JSS, v.47 #1 (Wint., 1985): 51-62.

345. Pulzer, Peter G. J.: THE RISE OF POLITICAL ANTISEMITISM IN GERMANY AND AUSTRIA. New York: Wiley and Sons, 1964. 364 pp., notes, apps., bibliog., index.

Study into the rise of antisemitism in central Europe before World War I. As the environment was suffused with antisemitism, and since that environment eventually gave rise to nazism, the book offers a useful background to the Holocaust. Pulzer organizes the book both geographically and chronologically. After a general discussion of the conservative rejection of liberal ideas, Pulzer proceeds to review the development of antisemitic parties until World War I. The approach has both merits and weaknesses. By selecting a broad approach, Pulzer is able to show the appeal of antisemitism to politicians of widely divergent ideologies, including many Socialists. At the same time, this broad approach weakens Pulzer's coverage of key issues, especially racism and demonic antisemitism. Similarly, though the intertwining of Austrian and German models provides the needed background to Hitler, it also blurs the specific features of the antisemitic movements in either country. Despite these reservations, Pulzer's is still one of the best introductory surveys on the subject.

346. Samuel, Maurice: BLOOD ACCUSATION: THE STRANGE HISTORY OF THE BEILISS CASE. New York: Alfred A. Knopf, 1966. 286 pp., notes, bibliog., index.

Well documented account of the Beiliss trial of 1911.
Mendel Beiliss, a young Russian Jew, was accused of the
ritual murder of a young Christian boy near Kiev. His trial
by tsarist courts became an international cause celebre.
Samuel reconstructs the case in all its ramifications and
nuances. He presents the cases of both the prosecution and
the defense and explains the short and long-range implications of the trial. Also interesting is his inclusion of a
discussion of the world press reaction to the trial. The
book is an important contribution to the study of the modern
use of medieval antisemitic demonology.

347. Schwartz, Kessel: "Antisemitism in Modern Argentine
Fiction." JSS, v.40 #2 (Spr., 1978): 131-140.

348. Silberner, E.: "Anti-Jewish Trends in French Revolutionary Syndicalism." JSS, v.15 #3/4 (July/Oct., 1953):
195-202.

349. Smith, David Ch.: "Protestant Anti-Judaism in the
German Emancipation Era." JSS, v.36 #3/4 (July/Oct., 1974):
203-219.

350. Starr, Joshua: "Italy´s Antisemites." JSS, v.1 #1
(Jan., 1939): 105-124.

351. Szajkowski, Zosa: "Socialists and Radicals in the
Development of Antisemitism in Algeria 1884-1900." JSS, v.10
#3 (July, 1948): 257-280.

352. Tager, Alexander B.: THE DECAY OF CZARISM: THE
BEILISS TRIAL. Philadelphia: JPS, 1935. 296 pp., documents,
apps., index.

History of the trial of Mendel Beiliss, based almost
entirely on documents found after the revolution in the
Russian State Archives. Tager views the trial from the perspective of a decaying political system which used antisemitism as a last prop to maintain its existence. The Jewish
problem in Russia is shown to be an outgrowth of the crisis
of political life in Russia at the turn of the century.
Russian rightists, according to Tager, manipulated antisemitism as a way of weakening the opposition and keeping the
autocracy intact. On the basis of the archival material
Tager cites, it is clear that local police authorities knew
that Beiliss was innocent but proceeded with the trial any-
way. That Beiliss was aquitted and justice done had nothing

to do with the miscarriages of justice within the tsarist system. Tager proves the existence of fabricated and falsified evidence during the trial and points an accusing finger at the guilty parties both in and out of the government.

353. Tartakower, Arieh: "The Jewish Problem in the Soviet Union." JSS, v.33 #4 (Oct., 1971): 285-306.

354. Tillich, Paul: "The Jewish Question: Christian and German Problem." JSS, v.33 #4 (Oct., 1971): 253-271.

355. Wilson, S.: IDEOLOGY AND EXPERIENCE: ANTISEMITISM IN FRANCE AT THE TIME OF THE DREYFUS AFFAIR. Rutherford, NJ: Fairleigh Dickson Univ. Press, 1982. 812 pp., maps, notes, bibliog., index.

Analysis of fin-de-siecle French antisemitism. Wilson does not view racism, antisemitism, or social upheavals as isolated phenomena, but rather as related indicators of crisis in a society in flux. Antisemitism is reviewed in all its guises, from left to right. The role antisemitism played in French society and politics is surveyed by Wilson in two chapters, "Antisemitism as an Ideology and its General Function" and "The Aims of Antisemitism." Supporting Wilson's thesis is a study of the French antisemitic movement, with special emphasis on the Dreyfus affair. Wilson pays careful attention to French public opinion in charting the successes and failures of the various antisemitic rabble-rousers.
In addition to his historical and intellectual study, Wilson has also undertaken a complex and very useful sociological inquiry into French antisemitism. Not surprisingly, Wilson discovers no particular correlation between the existence of antisemitism and Jewish population. Only in a few districts, Paris and Alsace-Lorraine being prime examples, can antisemitism and Jewish population be correlated. Jewish responses to antisemitism are given a chapter, although it is by no means as detailed as the preceding sections on antisemitism. Ultimately, Wilson sees antisemitism as a reaction to social crisis and to events only remotely connected with Jews.

PHILOSEMITISM

356. Edelstein, Alan: AN UNACKNOWLEDGED HARMONY: PHILOSEMITISM AND THE SURVIVAL OF EUROPEAN JEWRY. Westport, CT: Greenwood Press, 1982. 235 pp., notes, bibliog., index.

Inquiry into the history of philosemitism. Sees philosemitism as the opposite of antisemitism; thus Edelstein
does not need to deny antisemitism in order to develop his
hypothesis. His sociological underpinning is especially interesting and merits further elucidation. Weaker, perhaps,
is his historical development, although this is primarily a
matter of working with a more detailed database. Edelstein´s
conclusion that Jews survived in medieval and modern times
solely because of the actions of philosemites seems a bit
extravagant. These criticisms notwithstanding, the book is a
good corrective to the lachrymose conception of Jewish
history [see #11].

357. Rappaport, S.: JEW AND GENTILE: THE PHILOSEMITIC
ASPECT. New York: Philosophical Library, 1980. 258 pp.,
notes.

Study of the philosemitic element in relations between
Jews and non-Jews. Rappaport is fully cognizant that antisemitism has been much more prevalent than philosemitism.
Nevertheless, Jews could not have survived as a people had
all gentiles been unremittingly hostile. His basic goal is
to offer a balanced concept of Jewish history. Rappaport
defines philosemitism broadly, seeing both Christian zionism
and admiration for the Bible as typologies of pro-Jewish
sentiment. The culmination of the account is the action,
during the Holocaust, of those non-Jewish saviors who have
come to be known as the "hasidei umot haolam."

JEWISH RESPONSES

358. Cohen, Naomi W.: "Antisemitism in the Gilded Age:
the Jewish View." JSS, v.41 #3/4 (Sum./Fall, 1979): 187-210.

359. Diesendruck, Z.: "Antisemitism and Ourselves." JSS,
v.1 #4 (Oct., 1939): 399-408.

360. Golomb, Abraham I.: "Jewish Self-Hatred." Y/A, v.1
(1946): 250-259.

361. Herman, S. N.: THE REACTION OF JEWS TO ANTISEMITISM.
Johannesburg: The Witwatersrand Univ. Press, 1945. 123 pp.,
notes, apps., indexes.

Pathbreaking but now outdated sociological inquiry into
Jewish responses to Judaeophobia. Herman´s specific frame of

reference is South Africa, and his study primarily focuses on Jewish students. Two questionnaires plus interviews with the respondents were Herman's main source of data. Herman's comments on methodology are interesting. He raises the issues of objectivity and potential bias when discussing the problem of Jews studying themselves for sociological purposes; his comments on this are particularly insightful. The conclusions of the study must be viewed in context, since many things have changed since 1945 - in South Africa and the rest of the world. An updated study would survey new factors, but might arrive at similar conclusions.

362. Lamberti, Marjorie: JEWISH ACTIVISM IN IMPERIAL GERMANY. New Haven, CT: Yale Univ. Press, 1978. 235 pp., notes, bibliog., index.

Studies the Jewish political response to antisemitism in Willhelmian Germany. Lamberti primarily attempts to revise the popular misconception that Jews remained passive in the face of German antisemitic propaganda and did not properly respond to the assault on Jewish rights and status. Instead of naive passivity, Lamberti found courage and political wisdom among the Jewish activists. The principal organization studied by Lamberti is the Centralverein [CV], although the attitudes of German Zionists are also reviewed. The difficulties of establishing a Jewish voting bloc is described in detail. No German party wanted to be associated in the public eye as the "Jewish" party. Jews thus found themselves giving support to parties which were, with the exception of the SPD, not completely supportive of Jewish needs. On the other hand, Jews never considered the possibility of forming their own national political party. The Zionists adopted a more radical position against antisemitism than did the CV, and they generally held a more pessimistic view of Jewish chances for success. Yet the Zionist position was in reality no more active than the CV's, since the former emphasized ideological radicalism instead of greater activity.

363. Marrus, Michael R.: THE POLITICS OF ASSIMILATION: A STUDY OF THE FRENCH JEWISH COMMUNITY AT THE TIME OF THE DREYFUS AFFAIR. New York: Oxford Univ. Press, 1971. 300 pp., illus., notes, bibliographic essays, index.

Investigation of the Jewish reaction to the Dreyfus case and to antisemitism in post-Emancipation France. Marrus sees the Jewish response to antisemitism as weak-willed. French Jews, according to Marrus, had adopted assimilation as their

public ideology; they could not, therefore, respond to antisemitism in a proper way and prefered to avoid the issue altogether. Only the Zionists did not suffer from the fear of
dual loyalties and could react properly to the canard that
one French Jewish traitor represented the lack of patriotism
of all French Jews. It should be noted that although the
Dreyfus case is Marrus´s backdrop, he wisely eschews any
attempt at dealing with the case per se, but only covers its
echoes in the Jewish community.

     Although an important addition to the study of antisemi-
tism and Jewish self-defense, Marrus´s book suffers from a
major weakness. Marrus tends to telescope events, for example, the Dreyfus affair and the Vichy experience. In light
of the survival of two-thirds of French Jewry during the
Holocaust, despite both Vichy and Nazi antisemitic policy,
such telescoping cannot be justified historiographically.

     364. Peal, D.: "Jewish Responses to German Antisemitism:
the Case of the Boeckel Movement, 1887-1894." JSS, v.48 #3/4
(Sum./Fall, 1986): 269-282.

     365. Ragins, Sanford: JEWISH RESPONSES TO ANTISEMITISM IN
GERMANY, 1870-1914: A STUDY IN THE HISTORY OF IDEAS.
Cincinnati, OH: Hebrew Union College Press, 1980.   226 pp.,
notes, bibliog., index.

     Intellectual and ideological inquiry into the different
responses to antisemitism of German Jews. Divides the Jewish
response into three typologies: that of the Centralverein
[CV], that of first-generation Zionists, and that of second-
generation Zionists. Despite the Zionist critique of the CV,
Ragins believes that the CV acted properly and used all
weapons at the disposal of German Jewry to defend Jewish
rights and honor. In Ragins´s view, the difference between
the Zionist position and that of the CV was not as substan-
tial as it appears. The Zionists also accepted the univer-
salist social orientation of German Jewish liberals. Moreover, although they clashed, both the CV and the Zionists
rejected assimilation as a viable solution to the Jewish
question. Unfortunately, Ragins´s study is limited to the
analysis of ideological statements and is based almost entirely on press reports. Despite its important insights, the
study affords an incomplete view of the inner dynamics of
German Jewry.

366. Schorsch, Ismar: JEWISH REACTIONS TO GERMAN ANTI-
SEMITISM, 1870-1914. New York / Philadelphia: Columbia Univ.
Press / JPS, 1972. 291 pp., notes, bibliog., index.

Studies the rise and development of Jewish self-defense
in Imperial Germany. Primary emphasis is on the role of the
Centralverein as an agency for both defense and the creation
of Jewish identity. Schorsch traces the response of German
Jews to antisemitism from the 1840s onward, showing that the
idea of defense, and the self-respect that such an under-
taking implied, took root only very slowly. The book also
deals with the role of liberal Germans in the fight against
antisemitism. In this case, Schorsch correctly points out
that the liberal´s struggle against prejudice did not
develop from a philosemitic feeling, but rather from a
feeling that love would lead Jews to assimilation and ultimate disappearance. This point is important because it
proves that, for their own merits, Jews had no unequivocal
allies in Imperial Germany; a fact which helps explain the
ultimate failure of the self-defense. Less well-developed,
but still of interest, is Schorsch´s analysis of the rise of
German zionism and the Centralverein´s conflict with the
Zionists in the last years before World War I.

7

Public Affairs

ANALYSES OF JEWISH POLITICAL HISTORY

367. Berlin, William S.: ON THE EDGE OF POLITICS: THE ROOTS OF JEWISH POLITICAL THOUGHT IN AMERICA. Westport, CT: Greenwood Press, 1978. 206 pp., app., bibliog., notes, index.

Investigation of the political ideology of American Jewry. Berlin operates on a narrow level to prove American Jewish noninvolvement in, and alienation from, politics. Recognizing that Jews did have a politically active past, Berlin argues that the diaspora placed the Jewish polity into limbo and, as a result of antisemitism and other external causes, alienated Jews from the political process. Jews immigrating to the United States brought this isolationist legacy and their ideas about communal autonomy with them, but in large measure found them to be inapplicable on American soil. Thus, according to Berlin, American Jews suffer a basic conflict of emotions which has animated the thought of American Jewish intellectuals, particularly those who are or have been politically active. Berlin most clearly proves his point when dealing with the role of Judaic tradition in the political thought of Justice Louis D. Brandeis. Although Brandeis accepted the premise of Jewish participation in American politics, and although he claimed that his liberalism originated with his Judaism, both the Jewish content of his Judaic-liberalism and its political efficacy are questioned by Berlin. It is not quite clear, however, how this conflict has affected American Jewry as a whole; Berlin implies that American Jews are politically naive and inactive. These implications do not square with reality: American Jewry is more active and

126

better organized for political action than any other ethnic/
minority group, and in recent years American Jews have shown
considerable political savvy.

368. Biale, David: POWER AND POWERLESSNESS IN JEWISH HIS-
TORY. New York: Schocken, 1986. 244 pp., notes, index.

Interesting revisionist history dealing with the question
of Jewish power and powerlessness. Biale attempts to under-
take a systematic revision of the lachrymose concept of Jewish history. He argues, correctly, that Jews have never in
the past been totally powerless to affect their fate, nor
are they so powerful now that they can act irresponsibly.
Biale's analysis of zionism and Israel is, however, somewhat one-sided and polemical. Biale also has an unfortunate
tendency to denounce those with whom he disagrees as
"orthodox" without offering any scholarly reasons to reject
their arguments. This notwithstanding, Biale offers a fresh
approach to an aspect of Jewish history too often ignored.

369. Elazar, D. J.: "Jewish Political Studies as a Field
of Inquiry." JSS, v.36 #3/4 (July/Oct., 1974): 220-233.

370. ___: "The Place of Jewish Political Studies on the
Campus." AJHQ, v.63 #4 (June, 1974): 334-339.

371. ___ and Stuart A. Cohen: THE JEWISH POLITY: JEWISH
POLITICAL ORGANIZATION FROM BIBLICAL TIMES TO THE PRESENT.
Bloomington: Indiana Univ. Press, 1985. 303 pp., diagrams,
bibliog.

Hallmark study of Jewish political and communal organization from biblical times to the present. Virtually an encyclopedia of Jewish communities, statesmen, key terminology,
and key issues in Jewish public affairs. After a general
introduction that details the methodological background to
the book, the authors set out the epochs of Jewish political
history in chronological order. Each section is reviewed
briefly, in the style of a lexicon. Charts and diagrams are
used extensively to illustrate relations between and within
Jewish communities. The book has only one weakness, insofar
as Jewish foreign relations are not reviewed systematically. Methodologically and factually, the book is an
extremely important contribution to Jewish historiography.

372. Finkelstein, Louis: JEWISH SELF-GOVERNMENT IN THE
MIDDLE AGES. New York: Feldheim, 1964. 390 pp., notes,
apps., index.

Classic study of rabbinic synods during the Middle Ages.
Studies the various synods in light of the evolving needs of
Judaism. The premise of Finkelstein's work is that halakhah
is the universally accepted constitution of the Jewish people, as opposed to minhag, which is locally accepted custom.
As conditions at large change, however, halakhah must be
constantly adjusted by "takkanot." Since Jews possessed communal autonomy, change via the system of local, national, or
international takkanot was built into the halakhic system.
Takkanot could only be enacted by accepted rabbinic bodies,
hence the importance of the synods during the Middle Ages.
In an in-depth study, Finkelstein divides the book into two
parts. Part I is his reconstruction of the synods and their
work; Part II reproduces texts and translations of the most
important takkanot.
    Beyond its limited scope, the book has many important
implications. The rabbinic synods not only kept halakhah
practicable, but they also were the clearest organizations
of Jewish communal autonomy. They represented the quasigovernment of the Jewish community for both internal affairs
and external relations. Moreover, Finkelstein's analysis
proves that social, economic, and political conditions must
be studied in order to fully review the history of halakhah.
Finally, Finkelstein proves beyond any doubt that Jews were
not politically inactive during the years of exile, and that
political and constitutional history is an appropriate subtopic of Jewish history.

373. Levine, Etan [ed.]: DIASPORA: EXILE AND THE JEWISH
CONDITION. New York: Jason Aronson, 1983. 368 pp., gloss.,
notes, index.

Collection of twenty-eight studies which attempt to chart
the post-1948 meanings of the concepts "galut" and "golah".
The theme of the book is the new perspective of diaspora
life since the establishment of the State of Israel.
Emphasis is on the concepts as they relate to American
Jewry. The articles have no one focus, each author using his
or her own methodology. Although the articles are of unequal
quality, all of them are nevertheless thought-provoking and
insightful.

CONTENTS: Etan Levine: The Jews in Time and Space / A. B .

Yehoshua: Exile as a Neurotic Solution / R. A. Rosenberg:
Exile, Mysticism and Reality / Etan Levine: The Land Flowing
with Milk and Honey / H. Halkin: The Ba´al Shem Tov and the
Flaming Sword / J. Heckelman: Jewish Exile and Jewish
Redemption / L. B. Gaber: The Psychological Phenomenology of
Exile / M. Grossman: Exiled and Exile: Existential Reflec-
tions / J. B. Agus: Metamyth: The Diaspora and Israel / J.
J. Cohen: Exile and Redemption in Modern Jewish Theology /
B. Berofsky: Jewish Spirituality in the Diaspora / W. P.
Zenner: The Jewish Diaspora and the Middleman Adaptation /
E. C. Wiener: The Death Taint and Uncommon Vitality / B.
Berofsky: Jewish Self-definition and Exile / A. Hertzberg:
The Lessons of Emancipation / M. Buber: The Jews in the
Soviet Union / D. Braginsky: Strangers in Paradise: the
American Experience / D. R. Hershberg: The American Jewish
Non-Community / A. Hadary: The Modern Literature of Apart-
hood / A. Kanof: Here I Am; Here I Remain / I. Leibowitz:
Religion and State in Israel / M. M. Kaplan: The Next Stop /
J. Neusner: The Jewish Condition after Galut / B. Z. Sobel:
Unease in Zion: The New Israeli Exile / Wm. Freedman:
Israel: the New Diaspora / N. Lyn: Zionism and the Legacy of
Exile / G. Meir: What We Want of the Diaspora / S. W. Baron:
A New Outlook for Israel and the Diaspora / Y. Rabin:
American Jews and Israel: Strengthening the Bonds / A.
Kaplan: Identity and Alienation: Zionism for the West / E.
Levin: Confronting the Aliyah Option.

374. Lewittes, Mendell: RELIGIOUS FOUNDATIONS OF THE JEW-
ISH STATE: THE CONCEPT AND PRACTICE OF JEWISH STATEHOOD FROM
BIBLICAL TIMES TO THE MODERN STATE OF ISRAEL. New York: Ktav
Pub. House, 1977. 271 pp., notes, indexes.

Review of Jewish political theory and practice from the
biblical period to the founding of the State of Israel.
Lewittes´s main goal is to prove the continuity of a Jewish
polity and thereby establish that Israel is a legitimate, if
imperfect, reflection of the religious ideal of a Jewish
state. As such, Lewittes is the most sophisticated of Orthodox thinkers who view Israel as "the beginning of the redemption." An especially important chapter deals with the
messianic implications of zionism and Israel. Although
Lewittes´s conclusions may be debated ad infinitum, he
offers an important insight into the historical and religious significance of modern Israel.

375. Rubinstein, W. D.: THE LEFT, THE RIGHT AND THE JEWS.
New York: Universe Books, 1982. 234 pp., notes, index.

Inquiry into the state of the Jews since World War II. Begins by charting the general patterns of Jewish history before the Holocaust. Argues that as diaspora Jews have been absorbed into political, social, and economic elites, anti-semitism has increasingly shifted from the political right to the traditionally philosemitic left. This trend has been reinforced by the enmity of would-be progressives to Israel, and by the birth of neo-antisemitism in the Soviet Union. The most interesting aspect of Rubinstein´s account is the comparative approach - using American, British, and Australian Jewry to buttress his general conclusions. This is an extremely important book which should be read by both scholars and laypersons.

376. Schorsch, Ismar: "On the History of the Political Judgment of the Jew." LBML, #20 (1976): 3-23.

377. Szajkowski, Zosa: "Jewish Diplomacy." JSS, v.22 #3 (July, 1960): 131-158.

378. Zimmer, Eric: HARMONY AND DISCORD: AN ANALYSIS OF THE DECLINE OF JEWISH SELF-GOVERNMENT IN FIFTEENTH CENTURY CENTRAL EUROPE. New York: Yeshiva Univ. Press, 1970. 264 pp., notes, bibliog., index.

In-depth analysis of the decline of Jewish self-government, and with it of the Jewish community, in central Europe during the fifteenth and sixteenth centuries. The book is focused upon the communal institutions - kehillot, batei din, and the rabbinate. Relations within the community, between communities, and between the communities and the local and national governments are major themes. Zimmer´s conclusions are that economic and social pressure from without and communal reorientation led to the decline of the institutions of self-government, especially of the kahal. On the other hand, the status and authority of the rabbi, particularly of gentile-appointed "Grand Rabbis," rose to fill the power vacuum within the community. Zimmer´s book shows what can be accomplished by the proper use of rabbinic sources by a competent scholar.

POLITICAL IDEOLOGY, BEHAVIOR, AND ORGANIZATION

379. Agar, Herbert: THE SAVING REMNANT: AN ACCOUNT OF JEWISH SURVIVAL. New York: Viking Press, 1960. 269 pp., maps, charts, bibliog., index.

Brief survey of modern Jewish history viewed from the perspective of the American Jewish Joint Distribution Committee [JDC]. Surveys JDC activities in two world wars and on numerous other occasions. The book is not judgmental and is very sympathetic to the JDC. Agar details JDC rescue efforts, and political and philanthropic activities. He particularly emphasizes JDC operations during and after the Holocaust. In light of the selflessness of JDC operatives, both in and out of Europe, the title is most appropriate. Unfortunately the book is not fully documented, a problem that is only partially rectified by more recent works.

380. Cohen, Naomi W.: NOT FREE TO DESIST: THE AMERICAN JEWISH COMMITTEE, 1906-1966. Philadelphia: JPS, 1972. 652 pp., notes, index.

Institutional history of the American Jewish Committee from 1906 to 1966. Details both the social context and the political activity of the Committee. Reviews the Committee's activities in defense of Jewish rights, at home and abroad, as well as the attitude of the members of the Committee to the burning issues of the day. The most important chapters deal with the Committee's reaction to the Nazi threat and the rise of Israel. Although critical of the Committee's outdated approach during the 1940s, Cohen is nevertheless sympathetic to their plight and fair in her evaluations. In her section on postwar activities, Cohen also elucidates the ideology of the Committee on issues of key importance to American Jewry. The book is judicious in praise and blame and is a good example of organizational history.

381. Etzioni-Halevy, E. and R. Shapira: POLITICAL CULTURE IN ISRAEL: CLEAVAGE AND INTEGRATION AMONG ISRAELI JEWS. New York: Praeger, 1977. 249 pp., illus., tables, notes, apps., bibliog., index.

Sociological study of the Israeli political system. Based on a re-analysis of empirical research done by other sociologists and political scientists. The development of the Israeli polity post-1973 is charted in historical context. The authors attempt to develop two theses. First, that despite stresses and strains, the Israeli polity is a successful example of political integration. Second, that public protest plays a decreasing role in Israeli political life. Good as generalizations, neither thesis can fully account for political developments since the Yom Kippur war. The electoral success of the Likud, the peace negotiations with

Egypt, the rise of Peace Now, and recent conflicts over religious issues seem to belie both hypotheses. At the same
time, however, the theses do represent one trend, among
many, in Israeli political life of the late 1960s and early
1970s. Obviously, new sociological research will sharpen the
focus and fill the lacunae of this study; but this is
clearly a good model from which to start such research.

382. Fuchs, Lawrence H.: THE POLITICAL BEHAVIOR OF AMERI-
CAN JEWS. Glencoe, IL: The Free Press, 1956. 220 pp., notes,
bibliog., index.

Outdated but pathbreaking study into the political history of American Jewry. Fuchs was one of the first to systematically study Jewish voting patterns. He was also one of
the first to accept and assume the existence of a "Jewish
vote" in America, something known intuitively by American
Jews but, until after World War II, hotly denied by their
leaders. Fuchs adopts an historical approach, charting the
Jewish transitions from largely democratic voters [in the
years before the Civil War] to largely Republican [from 1860
to the 1920s], and back again. Independent parties, especially the Socialists, and their relations with Jews are
also charted. Fuchs concluded that Jews tended to vote within a certain style - the party which emphasized their idea
of liberalism has always received the highest proportion of
Jewish votes. The study is in need of an update because
events since the mid-1960s have changed the current. Jews
are still largely oriented to liberalism, but a fully developed conservative trend has also arisen and offers a new
alternative for American Jewish political behavior.

383. Goldscheider C. and A. S. Zuckerman: "The Formation
of Jewish Political Movements in Europe." MJ, v.4 #1 (Feb.,
1984): 83-104.

384. Goldstein, Israel: JEWISH JUSTICE AND CONCILIATION:
HISTORY OF THE JEWISH CONCILIATION BOARD OF AMERICA. New
York: Ktav, 1981. 251 pp., illus., notes, apps.

History of the Jewish Conciliation Board of America
[JCB]. Goldstein also includes a section on Jewish judicial
autonomy in the diaspora. The JCB was, and is, America's
foremost bet din, and it is in that context that Goldstein
details the history of batei din. Although brief, this section is well written and carefully researched, providing a
good summary of the history of Jewish courts. Part II is a

history of the JCB per se, with emphasis on the types and tenor of cases adjudicated. The JCB is surveyed for a turbulent period, from 1930 to 1968. An especially interesting section covers "Cases Related to the Nazi Era." Six appendixes relate to other aspects of the JCB's history and its activities, providing an interesting view into the way American Jewry operates. Preface by Simon Agranat.

385. Golub, J.: "The JDC and Health Programs in Eastern Europe." JSS, v.5 #3 (July, 1943): 293-304.

* 386. Goodman, Paul: BNAI BRITH: THE FIRST LODGE OF LONDON 1910-1931. London: Bnai Brith, 1936. 63 pp.

387. Grusd, E. E.: B´NAI B´RITH: THE STORY OF A COVENANT. New York: Appelton-Century, 1966. 315 pp., index.

Organizational history of B´nai B´rith, the world-wide Jewish fraternal organization. Grusd covers both the internal and external history of B´nai B´rith, with emphasis on the American branch. He does not shy away from controversial issues, whether of ideology or praxis, and appears to discuss such clashes in an objective and fair manner. Although clearly based on intensive research, the sources are not cited, thus weakening the overall usefulness of the book. This weakness is especially apparent in the chapters on the Holocaust and on the rise of Israel, where serious students could have made more use of clearly cited documentation. Preface by Robert F. Kennedy.

388. Hertz, Jacob S.: "The Bund's Nationality Program and its Critics in the Russian, Polish, and Austrian Socialist Movements." Y/A, v.14 (1969): 53-67.

389. Kahana, K.: THE CASE FOR JEWISH CIVIL LAW IN THE JEWISH STATE. London: Soncino, 1960. 120 pp., notes, index.

Inquiry into Mishpat Ivri and a call for the adoption of Jewish civil law in Israel. The book is also a survey of the history and historiography of halakhah. Kahana does not view the adoption of Mishpat Ivri as a religious issue, but rather as a guarantor of the Jewish nature of the Jewish state. In order to complete his argument, Kahana undertakes a survey of the terminology and application of Jewish law. One may agree or disagree with Kahana's position on Jewish law and its applicability in Israel, but his survey is a good introduction to the subject.

390. Menes, Abraham: "The Am Oylom Movement." Y/A, v.4 (1949): 9-33.

391. Shapiro, Leon: THE HISTORY OF ORT: A JEWISH MOVEMENT FOR SOCIAL CHANGE. New York: Schocken Books, 1980. 412 pp., illus., notes, gloss., index.

Organizational biography of the Organization for Rehabilitation through Training [ORT] from 1880 to 1980. A philanthropic and educational organization, ORT´s mission is to help Jews in need by teaching them to help themselves. In particular, ORT has expressed this goal through the creation of trade and technical schools. The beginnings of ORT in tsarist Russia are covered by Shapiro in detail, as are ORT activities in various countries and periods. ORT work with the survivors of the Holocaust is described in the book´s two most poignant chapters. Although written to mark the 100th anniversary of ORT, the book is not an official history. Shapiro deals with both the positive and negative elements of ORT policies, though clearly he accentuates the positive developments in the history of ORT. ORT´s first century is viewed in historical context, and its continuing role in the Jewish world today and for the forseeable future is discussed in the final chapter.

392. Szajkowski, Z.: "Conflicts in the Alliance Israelite Universelle and the Founding of the Anglo-Jewish Association, the Vienna Allianz and the Hilfsverein." JSS, v.19 #1/2 (Jan./Apr., 1957): 29-50.

393. Vlavianos, Basil and F. Gross [eds.]: STRUGGLE FOR TOMORROW: MODERN POLITICAL IDEOLOGIES OF THE JEWISH PEOPLE. New York: Arts, 1954. 303 pp., notes, bibliog., index.

Anthology surveying the political ideologies current among Jews in the twentieth century. Each chapter is written by an expert on the ideology of the specific movement under discussion. Each section also contains a general introduction by the editors. Special emphasis is on zionism, and six of the thirteen chapters deal with different aspects of Zionist ideology. Especially important are the differing viewpoints of each party on how to insure the Jewish future and their atittudes toward broader political and ideological questions.

CONTENTS: Isaac I. Schwartzbart: General Zionism / Aryeh Tartakower: The Essence of Labor Zionism / The Editors:

Mapam / S. Federbush: Religious Zionism / J. B. Schechtman: Revisionism / E. Simon: Ihud / I. Steinberg: Territorialism: Free Israel and Freeland / E. Scherer: The Bund / I. Lewin: Agudism / R. Gotesky: Assimilationism / M. Balberyszki: Volkism and the Volksparty / G. Aronson: Communism and the Jews / H. Frank: Anarchism and the Jews.

394. Woocher, Jonathan S.: SACRED SURVIVAL: THE CIVIL RELIGION OF AMERICAN JEWS. Bloomington: Indiana Univ. Press, 1986. 244 pp., notes, bibliog., index.

Analytic investigation of the sociopolitical ideology underlying American Jewry's civil religion. Although not strictly a religious ideology, Woocher sees the symbols, myths, and rituals of American Jewry as reflecting the values of Jewish tradition. In that sense survival becomes the religion of American Jewry and the focal point for communal unity. Irrespective of their purely theological perspectives, all major American Jewish denominations agree on the basic principles and thus on the public agenda of this civil religion. In Woocher's analysis the basis for American Jewry's civil religion was established when Jews realized that their community had developed beyond the stage of a philanthropic group into a fully ramified polity. Accordingly the major organizational element is the federation of local Jewish organizations. Woocher's analysis has important implications not only for American Jewry but for most diaspora communities as well, and is thus a welcome addition to the growing literature of Jewish political ideology.

JEWS AND WORLD POLITICS

395. Aronsfeld, C. C.: "Jewish Bankers and the Tsar." JSS, v.35 #2 (Apr., 1973): 87-104.

396. Baron, Salo W. and George Wise [eds.]: VIOLENCE AND DEFENSE IN THE JEWISH EXPERIENCE. Philadelphia: JPS, 1977. 362 pp., notes, index.

Anthology based on a seminar held at Tel Aviv University, August 18 through September 4, 1974. The basic theme of the book is the role that violence and self-defense have played in Jewish life and thought. Five of the essays concentrate on ideology, with the role of violence and defense in the value systems of differnet ages and nations getting the most extensive discussion. Although all of the essays are well written and of interest, not all are directly relevant to the issue of violence and self-defense. This is particularly evident in Part II, "The Modern and Contemporary Periods." Baron´s two historical reviews, although not comprehensive, are important for the context that they provide for the analytical essays. Especially lacking in the book is a detailed exposition of the ideology of "Kiddush ha´Shem" as it developed over the past 2,000 years.

CONTENTS: S. W. Baron: Review of History / H. M. Orlinsky: The Situational Ethics of Violence in the Biblical Period / Y. Aharoni: Violence and Tranquility in Ancient Israel: an Archaelogical View / Ephraim E. Urbach: Jewish Doctrines and Practices in the Hellenistic and Talmudic Periods; Jewish Doctrines and Practices in Halakhic and Aggadaic Literature / E. Rackman: Violence and the Value of Life: the Halakhic View / J. L. Kraemer: War, Conquest, and the Treatment of Religious Minorities in Medieval Islam / S. W. Baron: The Modern and Contemporary Periods: Review of the History / S. Shamir: Muslim-Arab Attitudes Toward Jews in the Ottoman and Modern Periods / Uriel Tal: Violence and the Jew in the Nazi Ideology / Michael Confino: Soviet Policy Versus the Jewish State / D. Schers: Antisemitism in Latin America / Ben Halpern: Self-Denial and Self-Preservation: Responses to Antisemitism Among American Jews / G. Berger: The Role of Communal Workers in Jewish Self-Defense / Haim Cohn: Law and Reality in Israel Today.

397. Cohen, I.: "Jewish Interests in the Peace Treaties." JSS, v.11 #2 (Apr., 1949): 99-118.

398. Hamburger, Ernest: "Jews, Democracy, and Weimar Germany." LBML, #16 (1973): 3-31.

399. Henkin, Louis [ed.]: WORLD POLITICS AND THE JEWISH CONDITION. New York: Quadrangle Books for The American Jewish Committee, 1972. 342 pp., notes, index.

Anthology studying world politics and the implications of recent events for Jewish security and survival. Limited to the 1970s, the essays now have only historical and methodological interest; obviously the authors could not foresee the stormy decade that would follow. The basic contention of the book - that world affairs have serious implications for Jews throughout the world - is never proved, but justly assumed to be axiomatic. Most of the essays are based on the

American Jewish Committee's task force report on the world
in the 1970s. The editors are especially sensitive to issues
of human rights as they relate to Jews, and to the situation
of Israel within the Middle East. Methodologically the book
deserves to be studied and is a good model for future
research into Jewish foreign affairs.

CONTENTS: H. L. Roberts: World Politics in the 1970s / E. V.
Rostow: American Foreign Policy and the Middle East / S.
Friedlander and E. Luttwak: War and Peace in the Middle
East: an Israeli Perspective / Ch. Adler: Inside Israel / Z.
Shuster: Western Europe / Zvi Gitelman: Eastern Europe /
Haim Avni: Latin America / S. Liskofsky: Human Rights /
Implications for the American Jewish Community.

400. Janowsky, Oscar I.: THE JEWS AND MINORITY RIGHTS,
1898-1919. New York: AMS Press, 1966 [Rep. of 1933 Ed.].
419 pp., notes, bibliog., index.

Carefully documented investigation into the history of
the movement to attain recognition of Jewish minority rights
in eastern Europe until 1919. Janowsky also analyzes the
legality of the minority treaties that were negotiated by
the east European successor states after World War I. The
author primarily concentrates on the ideology of Jewish
autonomists, without focusing exclusively on them. The book
is thus an important contribution to the diplomatic history
of the Jewish question during the nineteenth and twentieth
centuries. Not directly dealt with is the question of the
success or failure of the treaties that were established.
The autonomists seemed to have succeeded when the League of
Nations accepted the premise of Jewish minority rights.
Soon, however, the minorities treaties proved to be mere
scraps of paper; goodwill alone could not guarantee Jewish
survival. Preface by Julian W. Mack.

401. ___ and M. M. Fagen: INTERNATIONAL ASPECTS OF GERMAN
RACIAL POLICIES. Oxford: Oxford Univ. Press, 1937. 266 pp.,
notes, apps., index.

Historical and documentary analysis of the free world's
response to Nazi racial policies in the early and mid-1930s.
The book is a useful contribution to the study of both Jewish history and the history of international law. The main
body of the text is James G. McDonald's lengthy analysis of
the failure of The League of Nations Commission for Refugees. This analysis formed the bulk of McDonald's letter of

resignation from the post of High Commissioner for Refugees.

402. Liskofsky, Sidney: "Human Rights: from Helsinki to Belgrade." AJYB, vol.78 (1978): 121-145.

* 403. Marcus, J. R. [ed.]: JEWS, JUDAISM, AND THE AMERICAN CONSTITUTION. Cincinnati: Am. Jewish Archives, 1982. 35 pp.

404. Morgenthau, Hans J.: "The Tragedy of German-Jewish Liberalism." LBML, #4 (1961): 5-16.

405. Robinson, Nehemiah [ed.]: EUROPEAN JEWRY TEN YEARS AFTER THE WAR. New York: Institute of Jewish Affairs of the World Jewish Congress, 1956. 293 pp.

Survey of European Jewry in the post-Holocaust era. A follow-up to the Institute of Jewish Affairs´ HITLER´S TEN YEAR WAR AGAINST THE JEWS [1943]. Deals with both destruction and reconstruction, with emphasis on Jewish reconstruction in light of postwar political realignments. Robinson also reviews cultural and religious life as well as Jewish economic activity. Each country is dealt with independently.

406. Schechtman, J. B.: "The Jabotinsky-Slavinsky Agreement: a Chapter in Ukrainian-Jewish Relations." JSS, v.17 #4 (Oct., 1955): 289-306.

407. Teller, Judd L.: SCAPEGOAT OF REVOLUTION: THE FATE OF THE JEWS IN THE POLITICAL UPHEAVALS OF THE LAST FIVE CENTURIES. New York: Scribner´s Sons, 1954. 352 pp., bibliog., index.

Important journalistic contribution to the role Jews have played in the political world of modern times. His thesis is that modern utopian/apocalyptic movements - beginning with the Lutheran reformation and culminating in nazism, fascism, and communism - are at best ambivalent towards Jews and Judaism. At their worst these movements are extremely malevolent and aim at nothing less than the extermination of Jews and Judaism. The culmination of Teller´s examination is the attitude of communism towards all positive manifestations of Judaism. Although written more than thirty years ago, the book still has much to offer in reminding Jews of their potential vulnerability.

8

The Holocaust

408. Bauer, Yehuda with Nili Keren: A HISTORY OF THE HOLOCAUST. New York: Franklin Watts, 1982. 398 pp., maps, notes, bibliog., index.

Authoritative and up-to-date survey of the Holocaust. Designed primarily for college level courses on the subject. Begins with a very brief review of pre-Holocaust Jewish history. While useful for students with little or no background in Jewish history, this chapter is too general to really offer a survey of pre-Holocaust Jewish life. Once Bauer begins to deal with the subject of the Nazi assault on European and world Jewry, the book shows its true quality. Nazi policies, Jewish responses, and the reactions of internal and external factors are all discussed. Bauer is very careful in his reconstruction of the events. His chapters on the ghettos and on resistance are especially interesting. Although the book does not contain new insights Bauer´s synthesis is very useful.

409. Dawidowicz, Lucy S.: THE WAR AGAINST THE JEWS, 1933-1945. New York: Holt, Rinehart and Winston, 1975. 460 pp., maps, apps., notes, bibliog., index.

Synthetic history of the Holocaust, designed to give prominence to the Jewish sources that Raoul Hilberg ignored in his book [see #415]. As a corrective the book is useful, but there are a number of problems with the text. For one, Dawidowicz confines the Holocaust almost exclusively to Nazi murderers and Jewish victims; neither local non-Jews nor outside powers play any role in the text. Second, the book is almost exclusively focused on events in Germany and Poland, virtually ignoring other Jewries that suffered under the Nazi heel. Dawidowicz attempts to correct this omission with an appendix covering the general fate of European Jewry under the Nazis. Third, a number of factual errors, e.g., Dawidowicz´s misreading of the role of religion in the ghettos, also mar the account. Finally, and most controversial, is Dawidowicz´s hypothesis that Nazi plans for World War II were based exclusively on the wish to murder Jews.

410. Eisenberg, Azriel: WITNESS TO THE HOLOCAUST. New York: Pilgrim Press, 1981. 649 pp., notes, bibliog., chron.

Anthology of sources and voices from the Holocaust. Most of the documents have been culled from previously published works. The book is comprehensive and the range of topics covered is impressive. Chapters are divided both thematically and chronologically. Documents illustrate both the Jewish and Nazi perspectives, though prominence is given to the former. Special sections deal with issues such as children, the "righteous gentiles," and the relation of the Holocaust to the rebirth of Israel. Two poignant chapters end the book on a note of rememberance of the victims. Each chapter includes an introduction which places the documents into context. Many of the documents also contain introductions, though these and the notes to the documents are not always as useful as they could have been. These are, however, minor problems compared to the magnitude of the book, which has many applications for teachers, students, and researchers.

411. Fein, Helen: ACCOUNTING FOR GENOCIDE: NATIONAL RESPONSES AND JEWISH VICTIMIZATION . DURING THE HOLOCAUST. New York: The Free Press/Macmillan, 1979. 468 pp., tables, maps, apps., notes, bibliog.

Important sociological inquiry into the Holocaust. Fein opens on the paradoxical note that, although two of three European Jews alive in 1939 were dead by 1945, in half of the countries occupied by the Nazis more than half of the Jewish population survived. Fein thus attempts to answer two related questions: Why did the Final Solution meet with varying degrees of success in various countries? Why were some Jews able to survive while others perished?
Her answer is based on a complex, but plausible, set of sociological formulae. The full matrix of questions and the types of data used are summarized in two methodological

appendixes. Fein´s overview is important and her conclusions are, on the whole, sound. However, a number of
errors can be detected - most notably in Fein´s evaluation
of the Soviet response to the Final Solution - but these
detract nothing from Fein´s contribution.

412. Gilbert, Martin: THE HOLOCAUST: A HISTORY OF THE
JEWS OF EUROPE DURING THE SECOND WORLD WAR. New York: Holt,
Rinehart and Winston, 1985. 959 pp., illus., notes, index.

Personalized history of the Holocaust from the Jewish
perspective. Tries to penetrate the world that was destoyed
by integrating extensive citations from survivors. The book
is chronologically organized and emphasizes the period after
the outbreak of World War II. By its stark power, the book
has an impact beyond individual historicity. As such the
book is a useful corrective to those histories which only
view the Final Solution from the perspective of the
murderers.

413. Grobman, Alex, Daniel Landes, and S. Milton [eds.]:
GENOCIDE: CRITICAL ISSUES OF THE HOLOCAUST. A COMPANION TO
THE FILM GENOCIDE. Los Angeles: The Simon Wiesenthal Center/
Chappaqua, NY: Rossel Books, 1983. 501 pp., illus., notes,
bibliog., gloss., index.

Collection of 49 essays forming an overall synthetic history of the Holocaust. Organized as a companion to the
film Genocide. Each contribution is written by a recognized
expert, although the chapters are of uneven quality.
Particularly interesting contributions are offered by
Friedlander and Browning, who deal with the system of mass
murder that the Nazis and their helpers developed. Surprisingly, the book contains no separate chapter on resistance,
even though four essays touch upon the subject. Each section
opens with a quote from the film. The book is a useful
contribution and has particular classroom applications.

CONTENTS: Alex Grobman: Approaching Genocide and the Holo-
caust / S. Milton: Sensitive Issues about Holocaust Films /
D. Landes: Modesty and Self-Dignity in Holocaust Films / S.
M. Lowenstein: Eastern European Jews Before World War II;
Western European Jews Before World War II / Jane Gerber: The
Life and Culture of Sephardic Jews Before World War II / D.
G. Roskies: And Under Every Roof They Would Sing / Z. F.
Ury: Impressions of Religious Life of the Shtetl Before
World War II / N. Polen: Aspects of Hasidic Life in Eastern

Europe Before World War II / D. Ellenson: Jewish Religious
leadership in Germany: Its Cultural and Religious Outlook /
P. M. van Buren: The Theological Roots of Antisemitism: a
Christian View / F. Sherman: Luther and the Jews / Yisrael
Gutman: Why the Jew?: Modern Antisemitism / H. Friedlander:
The Geography of the Holocaust / Y. Gutman: The History of
the Holocaust / Jane Gerber: The Fate of Sephardic and
Oriental Jews During the Holocaust / E. Zuroff: Timeline /
Ch. R. Browning: The German Bureaucracy and the Holocaust /
H. Friedlander: The SS and Police; The Perpetrators / Ch.
R. Browning: Deportations / Y. Gutman: The Ghettos / S.
Beinfeld: Life in the Ghettos of Eastern Europe / Y. Gutman:
The Battles of the Ghettos / D. Landes: Spiritual Responses
in the Ghettos / Dov Levin: Eastern European Jews in the
Partisan Ranks During World War II / H. Friedlander: The
Nazi Camps / Henry Friedlander and Sybil Milton: Surviving /
S. Robbin: Life in the Camps: the Psychological Dimension /
Alex Grobman: Attempts at Resistance in the Camps / Y.
Gutman: Rebellions in the Camps: Three Revolts in the Face
of Death / D. Landes: Spiritual Responses in the Camps / S.
Milton: The Righteous Who Helped Jews / Jan T. Pawlikowski:
The Holocaust: Failure in Christian Leadership? / Henry L.
Feingold: The Importance of Wartime Priorities in the
Failure to Rescue Jews; Could American Jews Have Done More /
A. Grobman: From the Holocaust to the Establishment of the
State of Israel / Joel S. Fishman: The European Jewish
Communities After the Holocaust / Jane Gerber: The Impact of
the Holocaust on Sephardic and Oriental Jews / D. Landes:
Renewal of Religious Life After the Holocaust / R. Krell:
Aspects of Psychological Trauma in Holocaust Survivors and
Their Children / Henry Friedlander: Nurenberg and Other
Trials / A. Cooper: Simon Wiesenthal: The Man, the Mission,
His Message / Martin Mendelsohn: World War II Nazis in the
United States / Henry L. Feingold: How Unique Is the Holo-
caust? / D. Landes: The Threefold Covenant: Jewish Belief
After the Holocaust / J. T. Pawlikowski: Implications of the
Holocaust for the Christian Churches / Daniel Landes: A
Jewish Reflection on Christian Responses; The Holocaust and
Israel / M. Hier: The Making of the Film, Genocide.

414. Guttmann, Josef: "The Fate of European Jewry in the
Light of the Nuremberg Documents." Y/A, v.2/3 (1947/48):
313-327.

415. Hilberg, Raul: THE DESTRUCTION OF THE EUROPEAN JEWS.
3 vols. Revised and Definitive Edition. New York: Holmes &
Meier, 1986. 1,300 pp., notes, apps., index.

Definitive but one-sided history of the Holocaust. The
original edition was based primarily on Nazi sources and
viewed the events from the perspective of the murderers. In
the new edition a wider variety of sources, including some
Jewish sources, are integrated into the account. A few of
the sections were expanded. In particular, Hilberg´s
analysis of the ghettos and Judenraete was enlarged, and a
section on the Allied reaction was added. Yet Hilberg´s conclusions are basically unchanged. Hilberg still belittles
the significance of Jewish resistance. By associating Jewish
passivity with the Nazi extermination and by limiting
resistance to physical combat Hilberg is almost accusing
Jews of collaborating in their own destruction. This conclusion is problematic - especially in light of recent analyses
of all forms of Jewish resistance - and was the crux of a
dispute during the 1960s.

416. Jewish Black Book Committee, The: THE BLACK BOOK:
THE NAZI CRIME AGAINST THE JEWISH PEOPLE. New York: Nexus
Press, 1981 [Rep. of 1946 Ed.]. 560 pp., illus., charts,
apps., notes, index.

Anthology covering the Nazi attempt to exterminate world
Jewry. Originally published in 1946, THE BLACK BOOK was
sponsored by the World Jewish Congress, the Jewish Anti-
Fascist Committee, the Va´ad Leumi, and the American Committee of Jewish Writers, Artists, and Scientists. Although
now superseded, the book still contains some very useful
information. Especially interesting is the chapter on "The
Law" which has no comparable equivalent in more recent
literature. As a survey, the chapter "Resistance" likewise
remains one of the best summaries on the subject. The
appendix contains numerous significant documents, in both
the German original and in English translation.

CONTENTS: M. Radin: Indictment / F. McClernan: Conspiracy /
A. L. Bloch: The Law / Gitel Poznanski: Strategy of Decima-
tion / P. L. Fox: Annihilation / F. McClernan: Resistance /
B. Z. Goldberg: Justice.

417. Katz, Steven T.: "The ´Unique´ Intentionality of the
Holocaust." MJ, v.1 #2 (Sept., 1981): 161-183.

418. Lamm, Hans: "Note on the Number of Jewish Victims of
National Socialism." JSS, v.21 #2 (Apr., 1959): 132-134.

> #269. Pate, G.: TREATMENT OF THE HOLOCAUST.

419. Poliakov, Leon: HARVEST OF HATE: THE NAZI PROGRAM
FOR THE DESTRUCTION OF THE JEWS OF EUROPE. Edited by Martin
Greenberg; Trans. from the French by A. J. George. New York:
Holocaust Library, 1979 [Rep. of 1954 Ed.]. 350 pp., maps,
notes, apps., index.

Classic survey of the Holocaust, representing one of the
earliest systematic studies on the subject. Concise but comprehensive, the book is well documented. A survivor of the
Nazi horror, Poliakov is able to be objective while empa-
thizing with the victims. Only one issue is ignored - the
reaction of the Allied powers. An interesting chapter deals
with "Nazi Plans for the ´Inferior Peoples´", where Poliakov
distinguishes between Nazi plans for the Jews - total
extermination - and for other racial groups. Another interesting section covers the euthanasia program. Despite more
recent efforts, Poliakov still gives one of the best introductions to the Holocaust. The present paperback edition
also contains two lengthy notes dealing with the number of
Jewish victims.

* 420. Rabinowitz, Dorothy: ABOUT THE HOLOCAUST: WHAT WE
KNOW AND HOW WE KNOW IT. New York: Am. Jewish Committee,
1979. 48 pp., notes.

421. Wistrich, Robert S.: HITLER´S APOCALYPSE: JEWS AND
THE NAZI LEGACY. New York: St. Martin´s Press, 1986. 309
pp., notes, index.

Important attempt at an analytical interpretation of the
Holocaust. The book can be divided into three distinct
parts. The first deals with the causes of the Holocaust; the
second attempts to place the Final Solution into the overall
context of Nazi goals; and the last part deals with the continuity of the Nazi mindset even after the collapse of the
Third Reich. Wistrich sees the Holocaust as developing from
a racially motivated "either-or" mentality which was heavily
influenced by social darwinism. In this view the two contending races, semites [Jews] and aryans, are in constant
conflict. One of the groups must emerge from this conflict
victorious; the other must perish. Racism, in turn, was combined with an apocalyptic vision of the world, according to
which Hitler was to be the messiah and the Jews, as the
epitome of pure evil, had to perish to allow the perfection
of mankind.
Wistrich´s most interesting points relate to the use of
Nazi-like ideas by the Arabs, Soviets, and others who seek

to delegitimize the existence of Israel. Lucidly, Wistrich
shows antizionism to be a poor front for antisemitism, and
he sees an ominous pattern in recent anti-Israel mythology.
The author´s conclusions must be read and digested not only
by Jews but by all those who seek to understand the present
and avert a future catastrophe.

TOPICAL STUDIES

   422. Ainsztein, Reuben: JEWISH RESISTANCE IN NAZI OCCU-
PIED EASTERN EUROPE WITH A HISTORICAL SURVEY OF THE JEW AS A
FIGHTER AND SOLDIER IN THE DIASPORA. New York: Barnes and
Noble, 1974. 970 pp., notes, bibliog., index.

   Massive, well-documented, but ultimately flawed history
of Jewish resistance to the Nazis. Ainsztein has collected
detailed information on the heroic resistance of East European Jewry during the Nazi period. In addition, the first
twelve chapters cover the subject of Jewish military prowess
and heroism from antiquity to the twentieth century. These
chapters are of interest but are wholly irrelevant to the
Holocaust. They do, however, highlight Ainsztein´s most important flaw - his lack of objectivity and apologetic and
polemical purpose. The book was written primarily to refute
accusations of passivity and fatalism leveled at the victims
of nazism by such authors as Raul Hilberg [see #415]. Yet,
this leaves Ainsztein vulnerable to criticism. To be sure,
Hilberg´s accusations are incorrect, and the extent of Jewish resistance to the Nazis was greater than many historians
realized. Even so, most Jews never had the opportunity to
resist the Nazis, owing to conditions at the time. The im-
plication that when provoked Jews have always engaged in
some form of resistance, is partly accurate, but Ainsztein
tends to minimize the powerless state of world Jewry before
and during the Nazi period. Notwithstanding a grand martial
tradition, the lack of a Jewish army and of a Jewish state
physically doomed European Jews, despite their best efforts,
as amply chronicled by Ainsztein.

   423. Apenszlak, Jacob et al [eds.]: THE BLACK BOOK OF
POLISH JEWRY: AN ACCOUNT OF THE MARTYRDOM OF POLISH JEWRY
UNDER THE NAZI OCCUPATION. New York: Roy Publishers, 1943.
343 pp., app., indexes.

   Early account of the destruction of Polish Jewry, written
under the auspices of the Institute of Jewish Affairs of the

World Jewish Congress. Divided into two parts. Part I is a
region by region survey of Nazi extermination and Jewish
resistance. Some chapters deal with specific themes, for example, Nazi legislation concerning Jews. Numerous documents
are cited throughout all the chapters, but no facsimiles of
German documents were reproduced. Part II is a kaleidoscopic
review of Polish Jewry before the Nazi onslaught. This
section is organized thematically.

In light of the documentation that has become available
since 1945, the book is less useful than it might be, but
still represents the only systematic study in English on the
global extermination of Polish Jewry; as such, it is more
encompassing than other works dealing with specific ghettos,
camps, or Holocaust themes. Note by Jacob Robinson; introduction by Ignacy Schwarzbart.

424. Arad, Yitzhak: GHETTO IN FLAMES: THE STRUGGLE AND
DESTRUCTION OF THE JEWS IN VILNA IN THE HOLOCAUST. New York:
Holocaust Library, 1982. 500 pp., illus., apps., notes, bib-
liog., list of archival material, indexes.

Definitive study of the destruction and resistance of the
Jews of Vilna. Includes information on the conditions in
Jewish Vilna during the Soviet occupation, from September
1939 to June 1942. The bulk of Arad´s account is on the era
of Nazi occupation. His reconstruction is very detailed and
is based on a wide variety of sources. The activities of
Jacob Gens, the Judenaelteste, come under close scrutiny.
Arad is at his best, however, when he details the Jewish
resistance. Himself a partisan, Arad analyzes the conditions
under which the Faraynikte Partizaner Organizacie [FPO]
operated and details the development of the resistance from
its first tentative steps. The book is an excellent model
for a history of any other ghetto and breaks new ground in
the study of the Holocaust.

425. Avni, H.: SPAIN, THE JEWS, AND FRANCO. Trans. from
the Hebrew by E. Shimoni. Philadelphia: JPS, 1982. 268 pp.,
illus., apps., notes, bibliog., index.

Well-documented study of modern Spanish-Jewish relations.
Avni opens by posing a simple question: In light of various
claims about the tragedy which faced European Jewry in World
War II, what was the attitude of Fascist Spain? Avni has
attempted to place the issue into its broad context, beginning with the emancipation of Spanish Jewry during the
nineteenth century. Meticulously, the story of Spain´s "Law

of Return" - which recognized as Spanish citizens all
Sephardim who could prove that their ancestors were expelled
in 1492 - and the direct and indirect rescue by Spanish
officials of nearly 40,000 Jews during World War II are explained and clarified. Avni notes that although in effect
philosemitic, the Spanish government´s attitude was always
ambivalent and remained so throughout.

426. Bauer, Y.: "The Death-Marches, January-May 1945."
MJ, v.3 #1 (Feb., 1983): 1-21.

* 427. ___: THEY CHOSE LIFE: JEWISH RESISTANCE IN THE HOLO-
CAUST. New York: American Jewish Committee / Jerusalem: The
Institute of Contemporary Jewry, 1973. 61 pp., illus.

428. Chary, Frederick B.: THE BULGARIAN JEWS AND THE
FINAL SOLUTION, 1940-1944. Pittsburgh: Univ. of Pittsburgh
Press, 1972. 246 pp., notes, apps., bibliog., index.

Investigation of the role that Bulgaria played in the
Holocaust. Chary´s point of departure is the fact that most
Bulgarian Jews survived World War II unharmed. He then
attempts to explain this situation. Noting that antisemitism
was not lacking in Bulgaria before the war, Chary concludes
that moral factors proved more important than Bulgaria´s relations with her partner, Germany. It is interesting to note
why some things were possible in Bulgaria and not elswhere;
accordingly Chary investigates both the internal and external pressures placed on the Bulgarian government in regard
to the Jewish question.

429. Des Pres, Terrence: THE SURVIVOR: AN ANATOMY OF LIFE
IN THE DEATH CAMPS. New York: Oxford Univ. Press, 1976. 257
pp., bibliog.

Psychological perspective on the concentration camps,
attempting to explain why some individuals were able to cope
and others were not. Des Pres uses a very interesting comparative method, taking selections from the literature of
Nazi and Soviet concentration camps. On the basis of all
concentration camp experiences, Des Pres concludes that
morality and fraternity - remaining moral and becoming part
of a group - can increase the probability of survival even
under the worst conditions. The book does have some flaws,
the most notable being Des Pres´s speculation about possible
genetic bases for survival. Without access to direct interviews with concentration camp survivors, all of Des Pres´s

conclusions are tentative.

430. Engel, David: "An Early Account of Polish Jewry under Nazi and Soviet Occupation Presented to the Polish Government-in-Exile, February 1940." JSS, v.45 #1 (Wint., 1983): 1-16.

431. ___: "The Frustrated Alliance: the Revisionist Movement and the Polish Government-in-Exile, 1939-1945." SiZ, v.7 #1 (Spr., 1986): 11-36.

432. Fackenheim, Emil: "The Spectrum of Resistance during the Holocaust: an Essay in Description and Definition." MJ, v.2 #2 (May, 1982): 113-130.

433. Feingold, Henry L.: THE POLITICS OF RESCUE: THE ROOSEVELT ADMINISTRATION AND THE HOLOCAUST, 1938-1945. New York: Holocaust Library, 1970. 416 pp., notes, bibliog., index.

Studies the response of the Roosevelt administration to the Nazi persecution of European Jewry. Begins with 1938 and the Evian Conference. Feingold's main focus is on the issue of wartime rescue. Although not a systematic study of American Jewry, Feingold also deals with the issues of communal responsibility and communal power as relating to the American Jewish response to the Holocaust. One of a growing number of similar studies, and by no means the most detailed of them, what makes Feingold's analysis compelling is his exclusively scholarly approach. Feingold neither indicts nor apologizes. Failures to rescue - the numerous individual acts which added up to the virtual abandonment of world Jewry in its hour of need - are documented and explained.

434. Finger, Seymour M. [ed.]: AMERICAN JEWRY DURING THE HOLOCAUST: A REPORT SPONSORED BY THE AMERICAN JEWISH COMMISSION ON THE HOLOCAUST. New York: Holmes & Meier, 1985. 417 pp., notes, apps.

Report of the American Jewish Commission on the response of American Jewry to the Holocaust. The book is a very controversial look at an extremely sensitive subject. On the positive side, the book is candid and based on solid research. Unfortunately, the negative aspects of the book outweigh its positive elements. First, it is clear the book was written by a committee, since the chapters are disjointed. The appendixes appear to have been chosen arbitrarily - some of those included have no direct bearing on the subject, whereas some relevant material was exluded [it is apparently "available upon request"]. Second, much of the book seems to be a polemic against Professor Yehuda Bauer of Hebrew University. While one may disagree with Bauer´s assertions, the obviously polemic nature is inappropriate in what is ostensibly a scholarly report. Finally, the authors have set up two straw men that are easily knocked down: the organized American Jewish community as a whole and the American Zionist movement. Both can be and are easily criticized, but in the report none of the critics suggests a concrete alternative policy to the one pursued by American Jewry at the time. The report is by no means the final word on the subject, but may serve as the catalyst for a more objective, analytical, and comprehensive study in the near future.

CONTENTS: Hitler, the Holocaust and Wartime Allies / The American Jewish Community / What the Jewish Leadership Knew: Tragic Misconceptions / Jewish Attitudes and Priorities in Europe and America, 1880-1945 / APPENDIXES: A. J. Goldberg and Arthur Hertzberg et al: Commentary from Commission Members on American Jewry and the Holocaust / M. N. Penkower: The Efforts of the American Jewish Congress and the World Jewish Congress in the Years of the Holocaust / D. Kranzler: The Role in Relief and Rescue During the Holocaust by the Jewish Labor Committee; Orthodox Ends, Unorthodox Means: the Role of the Vaad Hatzalah and Agudath Israel During the Holocaust / E. Pinsky: The American Jewish Committee and the Joint Distribution Committee / H. Diner: The B´nai B´rith / H. Eshkoli: The Transdnistrian Plan: an Opportunity for Rescue or a Deception / L. Rothkirchen: The Europa Plan: a Reassessment / S. Merlin: The Europa Plan: a Real Opportunity, a Fantasy or Trap / Bela Vago: The Horthy Offer: a Missed Opportunity for Rescuing Jews in 1944 / G. Riegner: The Efforts of the World Jewish Congress to Mobilize the Christian Churches Against the Final Solution / Documents and Commentaries Concerning the Emergency Committee to Save the Jewish People of Europe / S. Liskofsky: Immigration Policy of the United States / S. S. Friedman: Perspectives: the Power and/or Powerlessness of American Jews, 1939-1945.

435. Fisher, Julius: "How Many Died in Transnistria?" JSS, v.20 #2 (Apr., 1958): 95-101.

436. Fleming, Gerald: HITLER AND THE FINAL SOLUTION. Berkeley: Univ. of California Press, 1982. 219 pp., illus., notes, apps., bibliog., index.

Analytical study attempting to ascertain Hitler's role in the Final Solution. One of a number of similar efforts aimed at responding to antisemitic revisionist denials of the Holocaust. Also penetrates the veil of mystery that surrounds the issue of authority and decision-making in the Final Solution. In his Hitler-centered approach, Fleming takes issue with those historians who relegate Hitler to a secondary role or even deny that he had any role in the planning and implementation of the Final Solution. For Fleming Hitler's direct role is irrelevant, since it was Hitler who set the entire process into motion. In light of the controversy brewing on the issue, Fleming's book can by no means be considered authoritative. Introduction by Saul Friedlander.

437. Friedman, Philip: "The Jewish Ghettos of the Nazi Era." <u>JSS</u>, v.16 #1 (Jan., 1954): 61-88.

438. Ganin, Zvi: "Activism Versus Moderation: the Conflict between Abba Hillel Silver and Stephen Wise during the 1940s." <u>SiZ</u>, v.5 #1 (Spr., 1984): 71-95.

439. Gelber, Y.: "The Mission of the Jewish Parachutists from Palestine in Europe in World War II." <u>SiZ</u>, v.7 #1 (Spr., 1986): 51-76.

440. Gellman, Irwin F.: "The St. Louis Tragedy." <u>AJHQ</u>, v.61 #2 (Dec., 1971): 144-156.

441. Gordon, Sarah: HITLER, GERMANS, AND THE "JEWISH QUESTION". Princeton, NJ: Princeton Univ. Press, 1984. 412 pp., tables, notes, bibliog., index.

Interesting but ultimately unsuccessful revisionist history dealing with the reaction of the German people to the Holocaust. Based almost exclusively on the Gestapo files on Germans suspected of Judenfreundschaft. As a result the book seems to be an apologia for the Germans, despite Gordon's denial of such an intent. Correctly, Gordon notes that antisemitism was a secondary issue in the Nazi rise to power, but in her zeal to revise she has raised relatively minor incidents to the level of central historical theory.

442. Gottlieb, Moshe: "In the Shadow of War: the American Anti-Nazi Boycott Movement in 1939-1941." <u>AJHQ</u>, v.62 #2 (Dec., 1972): 146-161.

443. Gringauz, S.: "The Ghetto as an Experiment of Jewish Social Organization." JSS, v.11 #1 (Jan., 1949): 3-20.

444. Gutman, Y.: THE JEWS OF WARSAW, 1939-1943: GHETTO, UNDERGROUND, REVOLT. Bloomington, Indiana Univ. Press, 1982. 487 pp., notes, bibliog., index.

Definitive history of the Warsaw ghetto from its establishment to its destruction. Divided into three parts. Part I, "Ghetto," reviews the Nazi occupation and conditions in the ghetto until the mass deportations. Part II, "Underground," covers the history of the political undergrounds - from the Communists on the left to the Revisionist Zionists on the right - and their responses to Nazi persecutions. The reaction to the mass deportations is reviewed by Gutman and related to the creation of the Jewish Combat Organization [ZOB]. The Polish response to Nazi antisemitism is also detailed in a dispassionate but nevertheless highly condemnatory chapter. Part III, "Revolt," surveys the history of ZOB and its preparations for battle. Gutman offers a detailed day-by-day reconstruction of the twenty-eight days of the revolt, as well as its repercussions and implications. Gutman is meticulous and careful in his documentation. This is clearly the definitive account of a tragic era that ended in heroism and martyrdom.

445. Haesler, Alfred A.: THE LIFEBOAT IS FULL: SWITZERLAND AND THE REFUGEES, 1933-1945. New York: Funk & Wagnals, 1969. 366 pp., illus., index.

Journalistic account of the Swiss governmental reaction to the extermination of European Jewry. Although Switzerland was a haven for 300,000 refugees during World War II, including thousands of German army deserters, hundreds of Jews fleeing persecution were at the same time turned back to almost certain death. Haesler charts the actions of those [the majority] who sought to limit the entry of refugees, and of those who placed humanity above self-interest and tried to aid Jews in mortal danger. Swiss policy is placed into the context of the Swiss humanitarian tradition. Swiss antisemitism and the activities of the Swiss Nazi party are fully exposed in Haesler´s text. Though not written in an accusatory tone, Haesler´s book is nevertheless a strong condemnation of the apathy shown to Jewish suffering by many of the democratic, neutral states and their institutions.

446. Haft, C. J.: THE BARGAIN AND THE BRIDLE: THE GENERAL UNION OF THE ISRAELITES OF FRANCE, 1941-1944. Chicago, IL: Dialoge Press, 1983. 137 pp., notes, index.

Important contribution to the history of French Jewry during the Holocaust. Focused on the Union General des Israelites en France [UGIF], which Haft sees as a French Judenrat. Although it was not the intention of the UGIF leadership, ultimately they became unwitting collaborators in the Nazi roundup of French Jews. Intending to assist Jews, the UGIF, like any Judenrat, could not escape from the German demands - which became more strident with each passing month. It is important to note that Haft shows exemplary scholarly objectivity. Her desire is not to blame, but to understand. That UGIF members sought to alleviate Jewish suffering is beyond question. That some used their position to foster resistance and rescue Jews is also proved by the documents. But, as Haft amply proves, the UGIF as a whole and especially its top echelon found themselves caught in a bind. The purpose of the UGIF was to carry out Nazi orders; these orders were nothing short of genocidal in intent. The UGIF thus faced the same problem every other Judenrat faced: to colloborate or to act illegally. Like other Judenrats the UGIF chose the former and must be analyzed accordingly.

447. Hayes, Carlton J. H.: "Spain, and the Refugee Crisis 1942-1945." AJHQ, v.62 #2 (Dec., 1972): 99-110.

> #401. Janowsky, O. & M. M. Fagen: GERMAN RACIAL POLICIES.

448. Katz, Fred E.: "A Sociological Perspective to the Holocaust." MJ, v.2 #3 (Oct., 1982): 273-296.

449. Klein, Bernard: "The Judenrat." JSS, v.22 #1 (Jan., 1960): 27-42.

450. Krakowski, Shmuel: THE WAR OF THE DOOMED: JEWISH ARMED RESISTANCE IN POLAND, 1942-1944. New York: Holmes & Meier, 1984. 340 pp., maps, notes, bibliog., index.

Definitive history of the Jewish resistance in Poland, based on an intensive study of the pertinent documentation. Covers all the manifestations of armed active resistance of Jews by region. There are also a number of chapters that deal with specific thematic issues. Throughout, Jewish underground activities are compared to their Polish counterparts. The Warsaw ghetto uprising is covered in a broad way,

but with deep understanding. In particular, Krakowski´s
military analysis of the balance of forces in the ghetto is
very interesting. Overall Krakowski´s book offers an
excellent model of Holocaust historiography. Foreword by
Yehuda Bauer.

451. Kulka, E.: "Attempts by Jewish Escapees to Stop Mass
Extermination." JSS, v.47 #3/4 (Sum./Fall, 1985): 295-306.

452. Laqueur, Walter: THE TERRIBLE SECRET: SUPPRESSION OF
THE TRUTH ABOUT HITLER´S FINAL SOLUTION. Boston, MA: Little,
Brown and Co., 1980. 262 pp., notes, index.

Inquiry into the flow of information on the Holocaust.
Laqueur tries to answer two questions: When and to what
degree did information on the Final Solution became available to victims, bystanders, and witnesses alike? What was
the reaction of those receiving this information? Laqueur
concludes that although a large amount of information was
available, both in and out of Germany, this information was
not properly analyzed and could not, in fact, have been
properly analyzed at that time. The book contains five
appendixes, each of which is worthy of further research.

453. Latour, Anny: THE JEWISH RESISTANCE IN FRANCE, 1940-
1944. Trans. from the French by I. R. Ilton. New York: Holocaust Library, 1981. 287 pp., illus., map, chron., index.

Anecdotal but important history of Franco-Jewish resistance to nazism. Although little known, the contribution of
French Jewry to the resistance was signal. The Jews provided
some 35,000 men and women to the Maquis and struck at the
Germans whenever and wherever possible. Moreover, the Jewish
resisters also undertook quite successful rescue operations,
saving many of those who otherwise faced Nazi-sponsored
"resettlement" in the gas chambers of Auschwitz.
Within the context of Franco-Jewish resistance, the 2,000
strong Armee Juive [AJ] stands out for special attention.
Zionist in orientation, the AJ saw itself as not only a
self-defense organization but also as the vanguard of a Jewish renaissance in Palestine and Europe. Not surprisingly,
Latour pays much attention to the AJ, its leaders, militants, and operations.

454. Levin, Dov: FIGHTING BACK: LITHUANIAN JEWRY´S ARMED
RESISTANCE TO THE NAZIS 1941-1945. New York: Holmes & Meier,
1985. 298 pp., map, apps., notes, bibliog., index.

Definitive history of Lithuanian Jewish resistance to the
Nazis. A brief introduction charts the history of Lithuanian
Jews to the eve of World War II. Levin also documents underground Jewish political activity during the period of Soviet
domination. Although not out to destroy Jews, the Russians
did attempt to stifle every positive manifestation of Jewish
identity. With the Nazi invasion, however, a greater enemy
had appeared and Jews of all ideological stripes flocked to
the Russian colors. The story of Jewish heroism in the face
of Nazi terror is described in detail. Levin's research is
careful and objective. His assertions are well documented.
Correctly, Levin divides Jewish resistance into three
elements: Jews in the Red Army's Lithuanian divisions, described in eight chapters; revolts in camps and ghettos, also
in eight chapters; and partisan warfare, in five chapters.
In addition to his contribution to Holocaust history, Levin
has a keen eye for political and military history. The book
includes a selection of eyewitness testimonies [Appendix B],
many from the Yad Vashem Archives. Foreword by Y. Bauer.

455. Lifton, Robert J.: THE NAZI DOCTORS: MEDICAL KILLING
AND THE PSYCHOLOGY OF GENOCIDE. New York: Basic Books, 1986.
561 pp., notes, bibliog., index.

Important but controversial contribution to the psychological study of the Holocaust. Lifton concentrates on the
medical aspects of Nazi crimes, seeking to answer one key
question: How could doctors, who by their Hippocratic oath
were charged with preserving life and easing human suffering, willingly and knowingly participate in the Final Solution? More broadly Lifton asks, under what circumstances can
an ordinary person become involved in extraordinary evil? To
illustrate his point Lifton reviews the careers of three
Nazi doctors; his special emphasis is Josef Mengele, "the
angel of death" of Auschwitz. Lifton also includes some important observations on his methodology, a subject that
deserves the reader's careful attention. Lifton's chapters
on prisoner-doctors has aroused some controversy because
they seem to imply the guilt of prisoner-doctors in war-
crimes. The latter needs more research; Lifton, it seems, is
only suggesting one avenue of approach.

456. Lipstadt, Deborah E.: BEYOND BELIEF: THE AMERICAN
PRESS AND THE COMING OF THE HOLOCAUST, 1933-1945. New York:
The Free Press, 1986. 370 pp., notes, index.

Extensive study on the reporting of the Holocaust in the

American press. Lipstadt proves beyond doubt that much of
the American press understated the facts of the Final Solution, despite a wealth of information. This policy, in turn,
encouraged the American public to underestimate the importance of Nazi antisemitism. Unfortunately, Lipstadt's second
contention - that the press's failure to properly inform
the public further deactivated those groups who were not
sufficiently motivated for rescue - is weaker. No definite
proof of press influence on those who might have assisted
Jews is presented, although Lipstadt seems to assume that
better press coverage would inevitably have led to a more
vigorous Allied rescue policy. While better press coverage
certainly was to be desired, it is not at all clear, in
light of other determinants of Allied rescue policy, that
more coverage would have translated into more action.

457. ___: "Pious Sympathies and Sincere Regrets: the
American News Media and the Holocaust from Krystallnacht to
Bermuda, 1938-1943." MJ, v.2 #1 (Feb., 1982): 53-72.

458. Marrus, M. and R. O. Paxton: VICHY FRANCE AND THE
JEWS. New York: Schocken Books, 1983. 432 pp., notes, index.

Investigation of the role France played in the Final
Solution. The focus is on the policy of the collaborationist
Vichy government toward Jews. As such the book is not a comprehensive history of the Holocaust in France. This caveat
is very important, as the impression given by the book is
overly pessimistic. The fact is that two-thirds of French
Jewry survived, despite Vichy policy. Marrus and Paxton cite
the thought of Vichy leadership on the Jewish question in
considerable detail.

459. Morley, John F.: VATICAN DIPLOMACY AND THE JEWS
DURING THE HOLOCAUST, 1939-1943. New York: Ktav, 1980. 327
pp., apps., notes, bibliog., index.

Well-documented investigation of Vatican reactions to the
Final Solution. Morley begins by explaining the parameters
of Vatican diplomacy, with special reference to World War
II. The next chapter deals with the attempt to save Jewish
converts to Catholicism by getting them visas for Brazil.
The remaining chapters, organized by country, cover Vatican
diplomacy on Jewish affairs. The upshot of Morley's research is that the Vatican proper was interested primarily
in saving converts, and only secondarily in saving Jews per
se. However, Vatican policy notwithstanding, papal nuncios

and officials often attempted to render assistance to Jews. Morley only indirectly deals with Pope Pius XII and the issue of his response to the events. Until the Vatican archives are open to independent researchers, Morley´s book will continue to be the definitive source on the subject, despite its many lacunae.

460. Orbach, William: "Shattering the Shackles of Powerlessness: the Debate Surrounding the Anti-Nazi Boycott of 1933-41." MJ, v.2 #2 (May, 1982): 149-169.

461. Penkower, M. N.: "American Jewry and the Holocaust: from Biltmore to the American Jewish Conference." JSS, v.47 #2 (Spr., 1985): 95-114.

462. ___: THE JEWS WERE EXPENDABLE: FREE WORLD DIPLOMACY AND THE HOLOCAUST. Urbana: Univ. of Illinois Press, 1983. 429 pp., notes, bibliog., index.

Studies the rescue issue from the perspective of Allied diplomacy and strategy, while integrating free world Jewish responses. Possibly the most intensive study of the documents on the subject. The book is organized as a series of separate but connected essays. Provides new insights and offers a synthetic overview of the issues involved.

463. ___: "The World Jewish Congress Confronts the International Red Cross during the Holocaust." JSS, v.41 #3/4 (Sum./Fall, 1979): 229-256.

464. Poliakov, Leon: "Mussolini and the Extermination of the Jews." JSS, v.11 #3 (July, 1949): 249-258.

465. Sachar, Abram L.: THE REDEMPTION OF THE UNWANTED: FROM THE LIBERATION OF THE DEATH CAMPS TO THE FOUNDING OF ISRAEL. New York: St. Martin´s Press, 1983. 334 pp., maps, apps., notes, bibliog., index.

Inquiry into Allied policy in regard to Jews during the twilight of the Holocaust and the postwar era. Argues that the United States maintained a very strict and ultimately antisemitic policy towards displaced persons, fearing a massive influx of poor Jews to the United States. American policy changed only after the establishment of the State of Israel. The struggles of the Jewish settlement in pre-Israel Palestine is thus linked by Sachar with the struggle for survival by the Jewish postwar remnants. Includes some of

Sachar´s reflections on the Holocaust. Altogether Sachar has presented a very powerful and stimulating account.

466. Schleunes, Karl A.: THE TWISTED ROAD TO AUSCHWITZ: NAZI POLICY TOWARD GERMAN JEWS, 1933-1939. Urbana: Univ. of Illinois Press, 1970. 280 pp., notes, bibliog., index.

Offers a useful counterpoint to the "straight line" interpretation of the Holocaust, as developed by such authors as Lucy Dawidowicz [see #409]. Schleunes argues that far from being a straight line, the pathway leading from Nazi antisemitism to the Final Solution was convoluted and often filled with potential alternatives. Murder, according to Schleunes, was by no means the Nazis´ only option, nor, according to his reconstruction, was it necessarily their original intent. Schleunes correctly sees the period before the war as a testing stage during which the Nazis tried a number of solutions to their Jewish problem. Only when those did not work to the satisfaction of the Nazi hierarchy was a more radical, and ideologically more suitable, "Final Solution" proposed, accepted, and carried out.

467. Shapira, Anita: "The Yishuv and the Survivors of the Holocaust." SiZ, v.7 #2 (Aut., 1986): 277-301.

468. Spear, Sheldon: "The United States and the Persecution of the Jews in Germany, 1933-1939." JSS, v.30 #4 (Oct., 1968): 215-242.

469. Syrkin, Marie: BLESSED IS THE MATCH: THE STORY OF JEWISH RESISTANCE. Philadelphia: JPS, 1980. 366 pp.

Survey of Jewish resistance during World War II, based primarily on interviews conducted with survivors in the immediate postwar period. Includes reviews of Jewish resistance in the ghettos and forests of eastern and western Europe. The major sections of the work, however, deal with the mission of the thirty-two Palestinian paratroopers and with the activities of the Haganah during and after the war. The paperback edition includes a new introduction and epilogue, containing Syrkin´s reflections after nearly thirty years.

470. Szajkowski, Zosa: "Relief for German Jewry: Problems of American Involvement." AJHQ, v.62 #2 (Dec., 1972): 111-145.

471. Tec, Nechama: WHEN LIGHT PIERCED THE DARKNESS. New York: Oxford Univ. Press, 1986. 262 pp., illus., notes, bibliog., index.

Important but flawed history of Polish-Jewish relations during the Holocaust. Attempts to revise the stereotypical notion that all Poles did nothing to help save Jews. The fact is that many Poles did try to save Jews - more than 1,500 are recognized by Israel as Hasidei Umot Ha´olam. Nevertheless, despite Tec´s methodological postscript, her database is not sufficiently deep. Moreover, the book is only useful as a corrective of accepted assumptions and is not an all-encompassing study of Polish-Jewish relations.

472. Tenenbaum, Joseph: "The Einsatzgruppen." JSS, v.17 #1 (Jan., 1955): 43-64.

473. Trunk, Isaiah: JEWISH RESPONSES TO NAZI PERSECUTION: COLLECTIVE AND INDIVIDUAL BEHAVIOR IN EXTREMIS. New York: Stein and Day, 1982. 371 pp., illus., maps, notes, indexes.

Important anthology reviewing the day-to-day stand of the Jews under the impact of nazism. Basing himself on hitherto unpublished testimonies from the YIVO archive, Trunk attempts to understand the typologies of Jewish response. In particular the testimonies offer a context for the development of Jewish resistance, especially in light of the adverse conditions under which Jewish resistance groups operated. Trunk also offers a brief review of Jewish reactions to previous persecutions, again to provide a typology for Jewish response. Ultimately, Trunk concludes that although most Jews did not resist actively, few - if any - actually collaborated and none surrendered their human dignity to the Nazi moloch.

474. ___: JUDENRAT: THE JEWISH COUNCILS IN EASTERN EUROPE UNDER NAZI OCCUPATION. New York: Stein and Day, 1977. 664 pp., illus., maps, notes, index.

Authoritative study into the Nazi-sponsored Jewish Councils of eastern Europe during the Holocaust. Eschewing generalizations, Trunk prefers to survey the different councils in order to get to the facts. Nevertheless, he recognizes the need to categorize the councils. Trunk uses three typologies: positive, those councils which were willing to follow Nazi orders only until the threshold of actually handing over Jews; negative, those councils which obeyed all

Nazi orders and cooperated with the deportations; and, directionless, those councils which were unable to take decisive action in either direction.

Trunk traces the emergence of the Judenraete from the prewar kehillot. After detailing their origins, Trunk reviews the activities of the councils and covers such issues as finances, relations with the Nazis, relations between the councils, the resistance, and the Nazi-sponsored ghetto police. One of Trunk´s important observations is his clarification of the dynamic nature of the councils and the deliberately confusing, inconsistent directives the Nazis issued to keep council members and elders compliant. Trunk is correct in his conclusion that the councils must be seen from both Jewish and Nazi eyes, in light of the dual, and ultimately contradictory, function of the Judenrat: Most elders wanted to help their communities as much as possible, but also were committed to carrying out a Nazi policy whose purpose, unbeknownst to these elders was to ultimately destroy the very community the councils wished to assist. Introduction by Jacob Robinson.

* 475. THE WARSAW GHETTO UPRISING. New York: Congress for Jewish Culture, 1976. 47 pp.

476. Wasserstein, Bernard: BRITAIN AND THE JEWS OF EUROPE 1939-1945. Oxford: Clarendon Press for the Institute of Jewish Affairs, 1979. 389 pp., notes, sources, index.

Well-documented investigation of British policy toward the Jews during the Second World War. Significantly, Wasserstein looks at the Jewish problem in light of Allied [mostly British] war aims and concludes that rescue was only a secondary interest for the Allies, whereas murder was a paramount military goal for the Nazis. Wasserstein also connects Britain´s lack of a coherent rescue policy to her involvement in Palestine; in particular British fears that anything done to aid Jews would also help the Zionists and, in the long run, hurt her own imperial interests. He does not view antisemitism as the principal component in Britain´s policy, although he does note that Jew-hatred did play an important role among second-level bureaucrats.

477. Yahil, Leni: THE RESCUE OF DANISH JEWRY: TEST OF A DEMOCRACY. Trans. from the Hebrew by Morris Gradel. Philadelphia: JPS, 1969. 536 pp., apps., notes, bibliog., index.

Authoritative history of Danish heroism during World War

II. Based on an extensive study of key documents. Also contains an outline history of Danish Jewry. Seeing the Danish
rescue operation as worthy of its legendary status, Yahil
still seeks to place the events into context. Important
appendixes cover the organization of the German Foreign
Ministry, the career of Werner Best, and a survey of the
documents. Yahil´s book also has very clear methodological
insights and is an important example of Holocaust historiography.

478. Zuccotti, Susan: THE ITALIANS AND THE HOLOCAUST:
PERSECUTION, RESCUE, AND SURVIVAL. New York: Basic Books,
1987. 334 pp., illus., notes, index.

Survey of the Holocaust in Italy. Zuccotti interweaves
personal stories with a broader communal picture. Nazi policies, the positions of the Fascist party and its functionaries, and the reaction of common Italians are all surveyed.
So too are Jewish responses to persecution. Italian Jewish
resistance is given a separate chapter. Zuccotti seeks to
answer one question: Why were the Jews of Nazi Germany´s
closest ally almost completely spared the Final Solution?
She finds three answers for this question. First, the Nazi
occupation was relatively brief and late in the war. Second,
antisemitism was weak in Italy, despite Mussolini´s attempt
to introduce German-style racism into the country. Third,
there were relatively few Jews in Italy, and they were
almost completely assimilated, so that they could almost
disappear with the help of sympathetic Italians. Zuccotti is
careful in documenting both suffering and rescue; she does
not reach outlandish or rash conclusions. It can be stated,
nevertheless, that beside the Danes no other people did as
much for Jews during the Holocaust as the Italians.

9

Zionism and
Jewish Nationalism

JEWISH NATIONALISM

* 479. Adler, Felix: NATIONALISM AND ZIONISM. New York: The American Ethical Union, 1919. 15 pp.

480. Harris, Maurice H.: "Are the Jews a Nation Today?" JQR, v.2 #3 (Apr., 1890): 166-171.

481. Norman, Theodore: AN OUTSTRETCHED ARM: HISTORY OF THE JEWISH COLONIZATION ASSOCIATION. London: Routledge and Kegan Paul, 1985. 326 pp., illus., maps, tables, apps., notes, index.

Chronological history of the Jewish Colonization Association [JCA]. The JCA was a movement which sought the establishment of a Jewish national home outside of Palestine. According to Norman, however, the JCA was never opposed to the settlement of Palestine nor did JCA leaders oppose zionism per se. The JCA leadership did not believe Palestine was economically capable of absorbing all Jews. Hence, other colonies would be needed in addition to Palestine. Though primarily a history of the JCA, the book also contains biographical data on Baron Maurice de Hirsch, the founder and ideological and financial guide of the JCA.
According to Norman, the JCA was important for four reasons. First, this was a "new model" charity. Second, the JCA undertook one of the first attempts at a planned migration. Third, the JCA was constantly experimenting with new and better ways to assist Jews and make them productive. Lastly, the JCA represented, in word and deed, the best concepts of Klal Yisrael and of arevut. Foreword by L. H. L. Cohen.

161

* 482. Sherman, C. Bezalel: BUND, GALUTH NATIONALISM AND
YIDDISHISM. New York: Herzl Press, 1958. 32 pp., bibliog.

483. Vital, D.: "Zangwill and Modern Jewish Nationalism."
MJ, v.4 #3 (Oct., 1984): 243-253.

484. Weisbord, Robert: AFRICAN ZION. Philadelphia: JPS,
1968. 347 pp., notes, bibliog., index.

Investigation into Britain´s offer in 1903 to create a
Jewish national home in Uganda. Based on extensive archival
research in Israel, England, and Kenya. Zionist, British,
and colonial opinion on the proposal is carefully dissected.
The relationship between the Uganda proposal and the Balfour
Declaration is also taken up by Weisbord, although with more
speculation than actual evidence. More important is his
study of the resulting conflict within the Zionist camp, and
the schism between the "Zionists for Zion" and the territo-
rialists. Weisbord has done a good job of clarifying many of
the obscure aspects of the proposal. An interesting aside
deals with the name; although called the Uganda Plan, the
territory actually offered encompassed contemporary Kenya.
The book thus offers an interesting insight into Jewish,
British, and African history.

485. ___ : "Israel Zangwill´s Jewish Territorial Organization and the East African Zion." JSS, v.30 #2 (Apr., 1968):
89-108.

486. Wolf, Lucien: "The Zionist Peril." JQR, v.17 #1
(Oct., 1904): 1-25.

JEWISH SOCIALISM AND RADICALISM

487. Berman, Hyman: "A Cursory View of the Jewish Labor
Movement: an Historiographical Survey." AJHQ, v.52 #2 (Dec.,
1962): 79-97.

* 488. Bittelman, A.: TO SECURE JEWISH RIGHTS: THE COMMU-
NIST POSITION. New York: Century Publishers, 1948.

489. Cohen, Percy S.: JEWISH RADICALS AND RADICAL JEWS.
London: Academic Press for the Institute of Jewish Affairs,
1980. 224 pp., notes, index.

Inquiry into the origins and implications of Jewish

leftist radicalism. Cohen operates on two planes, the historical and psychological, to explain why Jews have traditionally been, or at least have appeared to be, active in left-wing radical and Socialist groups. An important element in Cohen's study is the connection between Jewishness and radicalism. He seeks the parameters of this connection by assessing the Jewish roots of the radicals and their commitment to Jewish values and Jewish survival. His chapter "Jewish Identity and Radical Commitment" fleshes out the distinction between Jewish radicals and radical Jews. The former is a radical who happens to be Jewish. His Jewishness plays little or no role in his radicalism, and his impact on the Jewish world is marginal or negative. The radical Jew, however, is a radical because of his definition of Jewishness. Although he may oppose many of the policies of the Jewish establishment, the radical Jew nevertheless retains a connection with the Jewish community. Often the radical Jew integrates both his radicalism and his Judaism, suggesting a reordering of the priorities of the Jewish community. In all, Cohen offers an important, though not definitive, insight into an interesting and still important subject.

490. Levin, Nora: WHILE MESSIAH TARRIED: JEWISH SOCIALIST MOVEMENTS, 1871-1977. New York: Schocken Books, 1977. 554 pp., illus., maps, notes, index.

History of Jewish Socialist movements across three continents. Levin begins with the earliest glimmers of a Jewish labor movement in Russia, then turns to the events of 1881-1882. The assassination of the tsar and subsequent pogroms converted the almost defunct Jewish labor movement into a vibrant and numerically significant Socialist movement. This movement, however, expressed itself in three different ways. The element which argued for work in Europe crystallized into the Socialist and nationalist revolutionary party, the Bund. Those laborites who immigrated to America surrendered revolutionary ideology for a trade union approach, which eventually developed into the American Jewish alliance with the liberals and Democrats. Finally, those who organized themselves for socialism and secular Jewish messianism crystallized into the Socialist Zionist movement. Obviously there was a strain of messianism in all three strands, but from the perspective of the nineteenth century, zionism appeared the most utopian. Unlike many other Jewish Socialists, the ones Levin describes were not alienated from Judaism. Although primarily important as a synthetic work, the book also analyzes the difference between radical Jews and Jewish radicals.

491. Mendelsohn, Ezra: "The Jewish Socialist Movement and the Second International, 1889-1914: a Struggle for Recognition." JSS, v.26 #3 (July, 1964): 131-145.

492. ___: "The Russian Roots of the American Jewish Labor Movement." Y/A, v.16 (1976): 150-177.

493. Porter, Jack Nusan and Peter Dreier [eds.]: JEWISH RADICALISM: A SELECTED ANTHOLOGY. New York: Grove Press, 1973. 389 pp., bibliog.

Anthology covering Jewish radical movements in the United States during the 1960s. Includes both right wing and left wing radical movements, with emphasis on the latter. The editors´ main focus is on campus radicalism. They define Jewish radicalism broadly, including any Jewish group, irrespective of ideology, which denounced the Jewish establishment for its supposed sins. The introduction seeks to place current Jewish radicalism into historical context, but fails to mention that the radical Jews of earlier generations did not pursue self-destructive policies quite as eagerly as their would-be American imitators. While the editors take radical Jews seriously, neither they, nor the radicals they study, fully explore the ramifications of radical ideology for American or world Jewry. One might, therefore question the efficacy of most of the Jewish radicals included in the book, especially those of the new left.

* 494. Rifkind, Lewis: ZIONISM AND SOCIALISM. London: Jewish Socialist Labour Party, 1918. 20 pp.

495. Tobias, Henry J. and C. E. Woodhouse: "Revolutionary Optimism and the Practice of Revolution: the Jewish Bund in 1905." JSS, v.47 #2 (Spr., 1985): 135-150.

496. Wistrich, Robert S.: REVOLUTIONARY JEWS FROM MARX TO TROTSKY. London: George Harrap, 1976. 254 pp., maps, notes, bibliog., index.

Biographical study of the lives and careers of ten Jewish radicals. Wistrich uses their biographies as a way of analyzing the role Jews and Judaism played in the history of socialism. His conclusion is that while Jews have often played an important role in the development of both socialism and communism, Judaism per se has played almost no

role. As often as not, Wistrich finds the revolutionary Jew
was isolated and even alienated from Judaism. In at least
two cases, Karl Marx and Rosa Luxemburg, the result was a
degree of apathy to Jewishness that turned into self-hatred
and antisemitism. Even where the results were not so extreme
an indifference to things Jewish meant that the radical Jew
was usually disinclined to see any positive element to
Jewish religious or cultural survival. The individuals
Wistrich describes were thus radicals who were Jewish, not
really Jewish radicals. Foreword by James Joll.

497. Wolkinson, Benjamin: "Labor and Jewish Tradition."
JSS, v.40 #3/4 (Sum./Fall, 1978): 231-238.

THE ZIONIST MOVEMENT

498. Adler, Joseph: "The Morgenthau Mission of 1917."
HYB, v.5 (1963): 249-281.

499. Bein, Alex: "The Origin of the Term and Concept
'Zionism'." HYB, v.2 (1959): 1-27.

500. Berlin, George L.: "The Brandeis-Weizmann Dispute."
AJHQ, v.60 #1 (Sept., 1970): 37-68.

501. Bodenheimer, Hannah: "The Statutes of the Keren
Kayemeth: a Study of Their Origin, Based on the Known as
well as hitherto Unpublished Sources." HYB, v. 6 (1964/65):
153-181.

502. Cohen, Naomi W.: AMERICAN JEWS AND THE ZIONIST IDEA.
New York: Ktav, 1975. 172 pp., notes, bibliog., index.

Synthetic history of American zionism from 1897 to the
Six-Day War. Cohen attempts to interpret the significance of
zionism for the American Jewish community. Places zionism
into both communal and political context, emphasizing the
American nature of American zionism. Cohen does survey the
interaction of zionism with U.S. foreign policy, when
relevant. Little attention is focused on ideology, particularly of the individual Zionist groups and thinkers. Although brief, the book contains many insights and is a
useful addition to the history of American zionism.

503. Eloni, Yehuda: "The Zionist Movement and the German Social Democratic Party, 1897-1918." SiZ, v.5 #2 (Aut., 1984): 181-199.

504. Epstein, Lawrence J.: ZION'S CALL: CHRISTIAN CONTRIBUTIONS TO THE ORIGINS AND DEVELOPMENT OF ISRAEL. Landham, MD: University Press of America, 1984. 165 pp., notes, bibliog., index.

History of Christian zionism. Epstein has brought together a good deal of interesting information, especially on the position of some evangelical Christians on zionism. Nevertheless, the book does not offer a cogent analysis of Christian zionism. For one thing, Epstein's account is too descriptive and insufficiently analytical. Furthermore, Epstein's definition of Christian zionism is appropriate only for post-World II America; it does not fully explain the motives of those Europeans who support the restoration of the Jews. The concept of restoration, which played an important role in modern Protestant theology, is described as a monolithic ideology, and its nuances and varying approaches are ignored. Finally, no distiction is made between those who argued for Jewish restoration on christological grounds and those who did so out of sincere commitment to Jewish rights.

505. Fraenkel, J.: "The Jewish Chronicle and the Launching of Political Zionism." HYB, v.2 (1959): 217-227.

506. Friedman, Isaiah: "The Austro-Hungarian Government and Zionism." JSS, v.27 #3 (July, 1965): 147-167; #4 (Oct., 1965): 236-249.

507. Goldman, Guido G.: ZIONISM UNDER SOVIET RULE [1917-1928]. New York: Herzl Press, 1960. 136 pp., notes.

Investigates the status of zionism and Jewish nationalism from the Bolshevik takeover until the suppression of all non-Socialist forms of Jewish culture in 1928. Zionist activity per se is outside of Goldman's purview, rather he concentrates on Zionist relations with the government and the eventual outlawing of Jewish nationalist activities. Not surprisingly the Soviet policy on zionism was largely the creation of the Jewish Communist Yevsektsias. Although Jews, the members of these bodies often put ideological purity and Socialist universalism ahead of communal concerns or interests, and they opposed positive manifestations of Jewish identity. The Yevsektsias themselves were suppresed after 1928 - they too were seen as manifestations of counter-revolutionary Jewish nationalism. Soviet policy on Jewish affairs is amply demonstrated by Goodman, albeit briefly. Not dealt with, but related to the subject, is the attempt to create a Jewish National SSR in the Birobidjan province, where Stalin hoped to coopt Jewish nationalism and use it for Communist purposes.

508. Goldston, Robert: NEXT YEAR IN JERUSALEM: A SHORT HISTORY OF ZIONISM. Boston: Little, Brown and Co., 1978. 255 pp., maps, bibliog., suggested reading, index.

Panoramic review of Jewish history. The book is organized around the central themes of "hibat Zion" and Jewish de-sires, hopes, and dreams of a return to the land. Inter-spersed among the dreamers and visionaries are the activists who, in the nineteenth and twentieth centuries, made a real-ity of the dream in the State of Israel. Each chapter is followed by a "haggadah" which uses documents to evoke the spirit of the period. The book is especially useful for pri-mary and secondary schools and for home study.

509. Gonen, Jay Y.: A PSYCHOHISTORY OF ZIONISM. New York: Mason/Charter, 1975. 374 pp., bibliog., index.

Effort at applying psychohistorical methodology to the study of Jewish nationalism, antisemitism, and the Zionist movement. The author, a psychiatrist, has made an admirable but ultimately failed effort. This is inherent in the weak nature of the methodology. Ultimately, not a single one of Gonen's contentions can be proved or disproved. Since he never interviewed any of the abstractions he is ostensibly analyzing, any conclusions are moot at best. Similarly, any effort at mass psychology, which treats the group as a monolithic whole, is by its very nature open to an either-or analysis. How can one psychoanalyze a movement com-prising millions of members, many of whom are no longer alive? At no point does Gonen offer any statistical evidence, nor could he since no such evidence exists. The net result is a good deal of psychological jargon, a few generalizations, and pitifully little history - all of which tell us more about the author than about zionism.

* 510. Goodman, P.: ZIONISM IN ENGLAND 1899-1949: A JUBILEE RECORD. London: Zionist Federation of Great Britain and Ire-land, 1949. 86 pp., illus.

511. Greenstein, Howard R.: TURNING POINT: ZIONISM AND REFORM JUDAISM. Chico, CA: Scholars Press, 1981. 186 pp., notes, bibliog., apps., index.

Incisive inquiry into the relationship and contacts between American Reform Judaism and zionism. Greenstein opens by analyzing the position of American Reform thinkers on issues of religion, nationalism, and the idea of Jewish redemption. Thereafter he proceeds to survey the contacts and controversies that raged within the Reform movement on the issue of Jewish nationalism. Focus is on the period after the Columbus Platform of 1937, which reflected increasing Zionist influence within significant elements of the American Reform movement. Greenstein´s emphasis is on the intellectual and ideological leadership of American Reform and not on rank and file Reform Jews. The important leaders - such as Isaac M. Wise, Stepen S. Wise, Abba Hillel Silver, Judah P. Magnes, and others - and their positions on the burning issues of the day are Greenstein´s main subjects. The book´s most significant contributions are the analysis of change in the Reform position on zionism and the explanation of the rise of the American Council for Judaism within the Reform movement.

* 512. Hadary, O.: ROOTS IN ZION. Jerusalem: National Union of Israeli Students, 1976. 48 pp., notes.

513. Halperin, Samuel: THE POLITICAL WORLD OF AMERICAN ZIONISM. Detroit, MI: Wayne State Univ. Press, 1961. 431 pp., tables, apps., notes, bibliog., index.

Sociopolitical study of American zionism. The book is arranged thematically and tries to place American zionism into both American and global contexts. Halperin concentrates on the way zionism elevated an ethnic political issue to one of national and international concern. Emphasis is on the tactics American Zionists employed, whether successful or not, both among Jews and non-Jews. Special focus is placed on understanding zionism´s role within the American Jewish community. Finally, Halperin also includes a discussion of the role zionism has played in American foreign policy to explain American involvement in an area previously unlinked to American interests.

514. Halpern, Ben: THE IDEA OF THE JEWISH STATE. 2nd Edition. Cambridge, MA: Harvard Univ. Press, 1969. 413 pp., apps., notes, bibliog., index.

Definitive study into the development of zionism and
Israel through 1967. Primary focus is on the evolution of
the Zionist idea in the pre-state era. The idea of Jewish
restoration in Israel is explored in both its intellectual
and social ramifications. Especially important is Halpern's
chapter on "Zionist Conceptions of Sovereignty," where he
differentiates between Jewish and other forms of nationalism. Halpern's chapters on the political history of the
Mandate and the establishment of Israel are also lucid, albeit cursory, studies.

515. Kallen, Horace M.: ZIONISM AND WORLD POLITICS: A
STUDY IN HISTORY AND SOCIAL PSYCHOLOGY. Garden City, NY:
Doubleday, Page & Co., 1921. 345 pp., index.

Interesting study of zionism, nationalism, and Jewish
status. As much an inquiry into the psychology of Jews and
non-Jews as it is a history of Zionist activity. Also offers
Kallen's insights, from a philosophical and historical perspective, into the possible future organization of Jewish
Palestine. Kallen argues forcefully for zionism as an anti-
dote to antisemitism and the "chosen people" concept, both
of which he believes are incompatible with modern, liberal
society.

* 516. Karpman, I.: GENERAL ZIONISM IN ERETZ ISRAEL. New
York: World Federation of General Zionists, 1948. 22 pp.

517. Kutscher, Carol: "From Merger to Autonomy: Hadassah
and the ZOA, 1918-1921." HYB, v.8 (1978): 61-76.

518. Laqueur, Walter Z.: A HISTORY OF ZIONISM. New York:
Holt, Rinehart and Winston, 1972. 640 pp., maps, notes, bibliog., index.

Synthetic history of the Zionist movement from nineteenth-century forerunners to 1948. Combines an intensive
analysis with a broad review of issues, personalities, and
ideologies. Laqueur also attempts to place zionism into its
broader nineteenth-and twentieth-century contexts. Although
viewing zionism as a form of European nationalism, Laqueur
sees it as a uniquely Jewish response to the national question. A major subtheme is Zionist diplomacy and politics,
both internal and external. Laqueur's conclusions are stated
in the form of "Thirteen Theses on Zionism." While not all
of his conclusions are accepted by a majority of scholars,
they do offer an easily summarized interpretation of the

movement, its goals, and its historical significance.

519. Levin, M.: BALM IN GILEAD: THE STORY OF HADASSAH. New York: Schocken Books, 1973. 274 pp., illus., app., index.

Journalistic account of Hadassah, the women´s international Zionist organization. The history of Hadassah is interwoven by Levin with the development of the Yishuv. Unfortunately Levin does not cite specific sources, although he seems to have made use of some archival material. The backbone of his research rests on 200 interviews with a cross section of Hadassah members. In turn, these interviews yielded not only historical data but also an insight into the typical Hadassah member. Indicative of Hadassah´s importance is that, seventy-five years after its founding, the organization is still growing. Rightfully, the lion´s share of the book is devoted to the life and work of Henrietta Szold, founder and first president of Hadassah. Foreword by Golda Meir.

520. Narrowe, Morton H.: "Jabotinsky and the Zionists in Stockholm [1915]." JSS, v.46 #1 (Wint., 1984): 9-20.

521. Neumann, Emanuel: "The Decline and Rise of Herzlian Zionism." HYB, v.3 (1960): 15-26.

522. Oke, Mim Kemal: "Young Turks, Freemasons, Jews and the Question of Zionism in the Ottoman Empire [1908-1913]." SiZ, v.7 #2 (Aut., 1986): 199-218.

523. Rinott, Moshe: "Religion and Education: the Cultural Question and the Zionist Movement, 1897-1913." SiZ, v.5 #1 (Spr., 1984): 1-17.

524. Rose, Norman A.: THE GENTILE ZIONISTS. London: Cass, 1973. 242 pp., illus., notes, bibliog., index.

Studies Zionist-British relations during the crisis period before World War II. Focused on British gentiles who were zionistically inclined and attempts to assess their role in both English and Zionist politics. Rose tries to sketch how Zionists attempted to mobilize their supporters in Parliament, the press, and public affairs to help defer a pro-Arab shift in Britain´s Palestine policy. Rose hypothesizes that Zionist diplomacy did not, in this case fail, as the complete repudiation of the Jewish national home was delayed for nearly a decade. However, Rose views the question on the personal level, rather than the political. His conclusions are, therefore, only tentative. He nevertheless illuminates a little-known chapter on the road toward the establishment of the State of Israel.

525. Sachar, Howard M.: A HISTORY OF ISRAEL: FROM THE RISE OF ZIONISM TO OUR TIME. New York: Alfred A. Knopf, 1976. 883 pp., maps, bibliog., index.

Synthetic history of zionism and Israel from the 1880s to 1973. Primarily focused on political history, although social, intellectual, and economic factors are also reviewed. Covers the subject chronologically. The pre-state and state periods are dealt with roughly equally, although the history of the state is given in more depth. As a synthesis the book breaks no new ground, but includes a wealth of detailed information. Eschewing purely descriptive prose, Sachar also attempts to interpret, and he contemplates what might have been in addition to what was. Zionist dealings on the international scene are reviewed forthrightly, without an accusatory or conspiratorial tone.

526. Schama, S.: TWO ROTHSCHILDS AND THE LAND OF ISRAEL. New York: Alfred A. Knopf, 1978. 399 pp., illus., notes.

Intensive study of the renowned philanthropist Baron Edmund de Rothschild, his son James, and their contributions to the cause of zionism. Although not actually Zionists, at least not at first, the French Rothschilds provided vital financial and technical assistance to the settlements of the First Aliyah [1881-1903]. This assistance, in turn, helped lay the foundation for the development of the Yishuv and placed it on a stable, if not sound, financial footing. Only later did the French Rothschilds and their English cousins become involved with Zionist political activity. Schama recounts how James de Rothschild founded the Palestine Jewish Colonization Association [PICA], which both competed and cooperated with the World Zionist Organization and the Jewish Agency. The book is based on PICA's archives and is a useful addition to Zionist historiography.

* 527. Schechtman, J. B.: ZIONISM AND ZIONISTS IN SOVIET RUSSIA: GREATNESS AND DRAMA. New York: ZOA, 1966. 94 pp., notes.

528. ___ and Y. Benari: HISTORY OF THE REVISIONIST MOVE-
MENT. Tel Aviv: Hadar Pub., 1970. 424 pp., gloss., bibliog.,
index.

Synthetic history of the New Zionist Organization and the
Revisionist movement. The central organization is charted as
are the local branches up to 1931. Also reviewed is the history of Betar, the Revisionist-sponsored youth movement. The
book was to be the first volume of a complete history, but
no subsequent volumes have appeared to date. Revisionist
ideology is elucidated, though not systematically. It must
be realized that the movement's ideology was in a state of
flux throughout the 1920s and 1930s. Much attention is paid,
rightfully, to the activities of Vladimir Jabotinsky, who
founded revisionism and led the movement until his death in
1940. As can be expected, the conflicts within the Yishuv
are viewed from the Revisionist viewpoint. Nevertheless,
that narrow point of view offers a useful corrective to much
of Zionist historiography which ignored revisionism almost
completely. Furthermore, the authors present their position
without being unnecessarily polemical. The chapters on the
national movements contain much interesting data on groups
that have received scant attention by experts on the Zionist
movement.

529. Silverberg, Robert: IF I FORGET THEE O´ JERUSALEM.
New York: Wm. Morrow, 1970. 620 pp., maps, illus., list of
Jewish organizations, bibliog., index.

Surveys the interest of American Jews in the Jewish state
from Herzl to the Six-Day War. The book is very personal,
opening with the author's reminiscence of June 1967. This
chatty style is both an advantage and disadvantage, broad-
ening the appeal of the book while narrowing its historical
depth. Primary emphases are on the communal and political
activities of American Zionists. Silverberg recounts both
the successes and failures of American zionism, especially
during the crucial years of the 1940s.

530. Sternstein, Joseph P.: "Reform Judaism and Zionism,
1895-1904." HYB, v.5 (1963): 11-31.

531. Urofsky, Melvin I.: AMERICAN ZIONISM FROM HERZL TO
THE HOLOCAUST. Garden City, NY: Doubleday, 1976. 506 pp.,
notes, bibliographic essay, index.

In-depth study of American zionism. Places American

Zionists into their American and Jewish contexts. Based on extensive use of archival material from America, England, and Israel. Main interests are the social and political activities of American Zionists. Urofsky analyzes the major events of the period, with special emphasis on the attempts by American Zionists to harmonize their Jewish nationalism with American patriotism. Especially important is Urofsky's meticulous analysis of the Weizmann-Brandeis dispute and the subsequent schism in American zionism during the 1920s. The roles of important leaders and the state of American zionism on the eve of the Holocaust round out Urofsky's text.

532. Vital, David: THE ORIGINS OF ZIONISM. Oxford: At the Clarendon Press, 1975. 396 pp., notes, bibliog., index.

First volume of a projected synthetic history of the Zionist movement from its origins to 1922. Integrates social, intellectual, and political trends, but emphasizes the last. The most important innovation in Vital's account of the early period is his interpretation of the origins of zionism, which he sees as part of an internal Jewish development and not as a reaction to antisemitism, in contradistinction to more traditional explanations. From there Vital undertakes a detailed analysis of Zionist diplomacy up to the First Zionist Congress. Unfortunately, Vital places too little emphasis on the practical achievements of zionism: the establishment of settlements in the new Yishuv before 1917 is hardly dealt with. Despite this gap the book is a useful synthesis and represents a maturing of Zionist historiography.

533. ___ : ZIONISM: THE FORMATIVE YEARS. Oxford: Clarendon Press, 1982. 514 pp., tables, app., bibliog., index.

Continuation of Vital's synthetic history of zionism [see #532]. Vital's discussion focuses primarily on political events after the first Zionist Congress, and special attention is paid to Zionist diplomatic activity. Herzl's search for a major power to offer a "Charter" for Palestine to the Jews is carefully traced. The results of Herzl's search for an immediate refuge, the Uganda controversy, is reviewed extensively. Herzl's death and the subsequent reorientation of the movement as a whole to gegenwartsarbeit and "practical zionism" form the end of the book. As with the previous volume, developments in the Yishuv per se receive less attention. It is not, at present, clear how Vital plans to proceed, although he seems to have a third volume in mind.

ZIONIST IDEOLOGY

534. Adelson, H. L.: "Ideology and Practice in American
Zionism: an Overview." HYB, v.8 (1978): 1-17.

535. Avineri, Shlomo: THE MAKING OF MODERN ZIONISM: THE
INTELLECTUAL ORIGINS OF THE JEWISH STATE. New York: Basic
Books, 1981. 244 pp., notes, bibliog., index.

Inquiry into the intellectual and ideological backgrounds
of the State of Israel. Based upon a bio-intellectual
approach, Avineri uses representative thinkers to chart the
development of zionism from an amorphous yearning to a
statist reality. Although the book provides no new or innovative interpretations, nevertheless it is a most useful
compendium and synthesis. In each case Avineri charts both
the origins and results of the thinker's ideology. Avineri
sees zionism as an authentic expression of Jewish thought
and not merely as a response to antisemitism. His own Zionist manifesto is offered in an epilogue. At times controversial, Avineri is always thought-provoking and incisive.
The chapters on Jabotinsky and Ben-Gurion are among the best
analyses of their thought.

536. Cohen, Mitchell: ZION AND STATE: NATION, CLASS, AND
THE SHAPING OF MODERN ISRAEL. New York: Basil Boswell, 1987.
322 pp., notes, bibliog., index.

Investigates the ideological origins of modern Israel.
Cohen's analysis is both provocative and highly controversial. Essentially, Cohen argues that the statist position
advocated by David Ben-Gurion during the 1930s and 1940s,
which led to the creation of the State of Israel, sowed the
seeds for the defeat of the Labor Party and consequent rise
of the Likud, led by Menachem Begin, in 1977. Cohen bases
this rather startling conclusion on a detailed analysis of
the ideological battle between the Zionist labor movement
and the Revisionist Zionists in the Yishuv. Also included is
a careful comparison of the political and ideological orientations of Ben-Gurion and revisionist leader Zeev [Vladimir]
Jabotinsky. In order to place the conflict between left and
right into historical context, Cohen analyzes the development of the Zionist idea and the Yishuv from an ideological
perspective. Although Cohen expresses a clear political
orientation of his own [pro-Labor], his analysis is objective and free from polemic. While many readers will disagree
with his conclusions, the book is still of great interest

for its in-depth comparative analysis.

* 537. Fleg, Edmond: THE LAND IN WHICH GOD DWELLS. London:
Lincolns-Prager for the World Jewish Congress, 1955. 78 pp.,
notes.

538. Gorni, Yosef: "Utopian Elements in Zionist Thought."
SiZ, v.5 #1 (Spr., 1984): 19-27.

539. Hertzberg, Arthur [ed.]: THE ZIONIST IDEA: A HISTOR-
ICAL ANALYSIS AND READER. New York: Atheneum, 1976. 638 pp.,
notes, sources.

Definitive anthology of Zionist writings with an historical analysis by Hertzberg. Although one might quibble with
some of the selections, they are representative of the varieties of Zionist thought. Each selection is introduced,
providing a context for each ideologist. Notes to each
selection explain arcane references. Hertzberg's extensive
introduction represents a synthetic analysis of Zionist
thought. Hertzberg sees zionism as sui generis, holding that
it cannot fully be compared to European nationalism of the
last century. Foreword by Emanuel Newman.

540. Kahn, Lothar: "The Zionist Attitudes of Some European Writers." HYB, v.6 (1964/65): 109-132.

541. O'Brien, Conor C.: "Some Reflections on Religion and
Nationalism." SiZ, v.6 #2 (Aut., 1985): 161-169.

542. Penkower, M. N.: THE EMERGENCE OF ZIONIST THOUGHT.
New York: Associated Faculty Press, 1986. 159 pp., bibliog.,
index.

Collection of essays on the diverse forms of zionism.
Initially presented as a series of radio lectures on the
history of Zionist thought. Although the main thrust of the
book is on individual ideologues, movements within zionism -
e.g. religious zionism - are also covered, even when no
single thinker of major proportions could be identified.
Penkower's is primarily a synthesis and little new information is uncovered. Nevertheless, his interpretations often
differ from the standard approach and are based on careful
reading of key documents. Deals with organizational history
only to a limited degree where relevant, although ideology
is the main focus of the essays. The goal of the book is to
offer an evaluation of zionism as it developed during the

years before the creation of Israel.

543. Schweid, Eliezer: THE LAND OF ISRAEL: NATIONAL HOME
OR LAND OF DESTINY. Trans. from the Hebrew by D. Greniman.
New York: Herzl Press, 1985. 225 pp., notes, index.

Erudite philosophical inquiry into the place of Eretz
Israel in Jewish thought, life, and history. Schweid analyzes all forms of Jewish attachment to the land from biblical times to the twentieth century. On the basis of this
analysis, he concludes that the Jews´ claim to Eretz Israel
is still sound. Schweid also discusses the concepts of "a
national home" and "the land of destiny." Paradoxically,
these concepts have led to a crisis of identity among secular Israelis in recent years. Schweid, however, concludes
that the paradox can be solved by molding a more authenti-
cally Jewish, though not necessarily religious, society in
Israel. Only thus can Israel survive its crisis of identity
and continue to thrive as both the national home and land of
destiny for the Jewish people.

544. ___ : "The Rejection of the Diaspora in Zionist
Thought: Two Approaches." SiZ, v.5 #1 (Spr., 1984): 43-70.

545. Shavit, Yakov: "Politics and Messianism: the Zionist
Revisionist Movement and Polish Political Culture." SiZ, v.6
#2 (Aut., 1985): 229-246.

546. Simon, L.: STUDIES IN JEWISH NATIONALISM. Westport,
CT: Hyperion Press, 1976 [Rep. of 1920 Ed.]. 177 pp.

Series of essays attempting to define Jewish nationalism
in general, and zionism in particular. Simon bases himself
on the spiritual zionism of Ahad Ha´am. Broadly speaking,
Simon therefore sees zionism as a solution to the problem of
Judaism, and not as a refuge for Jews. This can be seen from
the first few essays, where Simon follows Ahad Ha´am in
general position: Judaism was able to survive because, over
the years of the diaspora, it inculcated in Jews a hope for
collective redemption. The emancipation, however, offered
individual salvation in exchange for the surrender of the
Jews´ collective identity. Although Jews wished to remain
Jewish, Judaism no longer played a relevant role in their
daily lives. Only by returning to the idea of a Jewish
nation could Judaism, secularized and modernized, return to
its previous position of relevance. Palestine, in this
schema, was important as a spiritual and cultural center.

The small Yishuv would represent the vanguard of a Hebrew
renaissance, but would not necessarily be a refuge for
masses of Jews. Nor would this entity necessarily crystal-
lize into a state in the political sense of the term. Ahad
Ha'am was an influential force in post-Herzlian zionism,
while Simon played a parallel role in the English Zionist
Federation; their position - by no means universally
accepted - is summarized succinctly in this book.

> #393. Vlavianos, B. and F. Gross: STRUGGLE FOR TOMORROW.

ZIONISM AND THE RISE OF ISRAEL

547. Adler, Selig: "The Roosevelt Administration and
Zionism: the Pre-War Years, 1933-1939." HYB, v.8 (1978):
132-148.

* 548. American Zionist Council: AFTER THE VICTORY: A BLUE-
PRINT FOR THE REHABILITATION OF EUROPEAN JEWRY. New York:
The American Zionist Emergency Council, 1943. 20 pp.

* 549. ___ : THE JEWISH CASE: THE PLACE OF PALESTINE IN THE
SOLUTION OF THE JEWISH QUESTION. New York: The American
Zionist Emergency Council, 1945. 30 pp., illus., map.

550. Bauer, Yehuda: FROM DIPLOMACY TO RESISTANCE: A HIS-
TORY OF JEWISH PALESTINE, 1939-1945. Trans. from the Hebrew
by A. M. Winters. New York: Atheneum, 1973. 432 pp., apps.,
notes, bibliog., index.

Contribution to the history of the Yishuv during World
War II. Seeing the period as a crucial one, Bauer deals with
the major issues of Yishuv history: the British repudiation
of the Mandate, the transformation of Zionist policy and
goals, relations between the Jewish underground movements,
and the frantic efforts by the Yishuv to rescue at least a
remnant of European Jewry. Primary focus is political
history, placed in social context. Bauer is not afraid to
deal with controversial issues, for example, the fragile relations between the Haganah, Irgun [IZL], and LEHI groups.
His evaluation of the so-called hunting season, which was
virtually a civil war between the groups, is generally fair
and well balanced. Bauer is critical of official Zionist
policy on this issue, as he sees the in-fighting between the
undergrounds as wasteful and unnecessary. The book deepens
one's understanding of both Jewish fate in an era of power-

lessness and of the ultimate Jewish emergence from powerlessness.

> #431. Engel, David: "The Frustrated Alliance."

551. Friedman, Isaiah: THE QUESTION OF PALESTINE. New
York: Schocken Books, 1973. 433 pp., notes, bibliog., index.

Political study of the Balfour Declaration, organized as
a supplement to Leonard Stein´s book THE BALFOUR DECLARATION
[see #570]. Friedman had access to the files in the Public
Record Office unavailable to Stein. Concludes that Britain´s
strategic interests, and not some amorphous philosemitism,
was the primary reason for the British diplomacy in the
Middle East which culminated in the declaration. In fact,
antisemitism may have played more of a role in the declaration than philosemitism. Many of those connected with the
British Foreign Office appear to have taken the myth of a
Jewish world government to heart, and they hoped to use
Palestine as a bait to rally Jewish support for the Allies
in both Russia and the United States. Friedman also carefully reconstructs the literary history of the declaration.

552. Gal, Allon: "Zionist Foreign Policy and Ben-Gurion´s
Visit to the United States in 1939." SiZ, v.7 #1 (Spr.,
1986): 37-50.

> #438. Ganin, Zvi: "Activism Versus Moderation."

553. Ganin, Zvi: "The Limits of American Jewish Political
Power: America´s Retreat from Partition, November 1947-March
1949." JSS, v.39 #1/2 (Wint./Spr., 1977): 1-36.

554. ___: TRUMAN, AMERICAN JEWRY, AND ISRAEL 1945-1948.
New York: Holmes & Meier, 1979. 238 pp., illus., notes, bibliog., index.

Insightful study into the political activity of American
Zionists after World War II. Ganin focuses on two
interrelated themes: the organizational dynamics of American
zionism, and the interplay between American Zionists and the
Truman administration. Ganin begins his study by charting
developments during World War II, widely and correctly seen
as a watershed in Zionist history. He then demonstrates the
remarkable rallying of American Jewry around the Zionist
cause as a result of the Holocaust. On this basis he then
evaluates Zionist diplomacy in the United States, citing

both success and failures; on the whole the former out-
numbered the latter. Even so, Ganin notes that American
Jewry had only limited political power and had not yet
learned how to use that power for national and international
goals. The role the United States played in the creation of
the State of Israel, despite opposition in some circles, is
also discussed. Ganin argues that although domestic politics
played a role in President Truman´s decision to recognize
Israel, humanitarian and other altruistic concerns also
played their part.

555. Gilbert, Martin: EXILE AND RETURN: THE STRUGGLE FOR
A JEWISH HOMELAND. Philadelphia: J. B. Lippincott, 1978. 364
pp., illus., maps, archival sources, bibliog., index.

History of the modern Jewish efforts to secure a national
home. Really two books in one: Part I is a broad synthetic
review of Jewish history from the dispersion to World War I,
Part II is an intensive, and more interesting, review of the
British Mandate, from the Balfour Declaration to 1948.
Despite the intensive research and use of numerous documents, the lack of adequate documentation through reference
notes considerably diminishes the book´s usefulness. This
weakness is not offset by the chronological list of documents used, although the list has considerable intrinsic
merit. Special emphasis is placed on Zionist, British, and
international diplomacy on the Palestine issue during the
years of the Mandate.

556. Grose, P.: ISRAEL IN THE MIND OF AMERICA. New York:
Schocken Books, 1984. 360 pp., illus., bibliog., index.

Study of the role zionism has played in American public
life in the last 150 years. Most of the book covers the
twentieth century. Unfortunately, the journalistic style at
times obscures the intensive research of the book and
Grose´s many novel interpretations. Especially important are
his analyses of the attitudes of Presidents Roosevelt and
Truman toward Jews, Jewish issues, and zionism during the
crucial period from 1933 to 1948. Here Grose offers an
interesting and important revisionist hypothesis. Barring
discussion of the rescue issue, Grose believes that
President Roosevelt actually was more receptive to zionism
than Truman. Remarkably, the standard approach offers the
opposite analysis. Although not yet definitely proved, Grose
has challenged historians to take a fresh and more careful
look at the events leading up to the creation of Israel.

557. Haim, Yehoyada: "Zionist Attitudes Toward Partition, 1937-1938." JSS, v.40 #3/4 (Sum./Fall, 1978): 303-320.

558. Hurewitz, J. C.: THE STRUGGLE FOR PALESTINE. New York: W. W. Norton, 1950. 404 pp., notes, bibliog., index.

Authoritative review of the impact of World War II on the Yishuv. Begins with the situation in Mandatory Palestine on the eve of World War II. Deals with Jewish, British, and Arab positions. Hurewitz's main focus is on the institutions of Palestine. Especially important for the emergence of Israel, according to Hurewitz, was the existence of a Jewish quasigovernment, in the form of the Jewish Agency and the Vaad Le'umi. Charts the changes that the war wrought on Palestine, in particular from the political and economic perspective. The book is considered a classic example of historiography in zionism and Israel, and is unsurpassed.

559. Kaufman, Menahem: "The American Jewish Committee and Jewish Statehood, 1947-1948." SiZ, v.7 #2 (Aut., 1986): 259-275.

560. ___: "From Neutrality to Involvement: Zionists, Non-Zionists and the Struggle for a Jewish State, 1945." HYB, v.8 (1978): 263-283.

561. Knee, Stuart E.: "Jewish Non-Zionism in America and Palestine Commitment 1917-1941." JSS, v.39 #3 (Sum., 1977): 209-226.

562. Koestler, Arthur: PROMISE AND FULFILLMENT. New York: Macmillan, 1949. 335 pp., map, notes.

History and investigation of Israel, divided into three parts. Part I, "Background," covers the bulk of the book and offers a broad review of the events leading to the creation of Israel. Koestler's investigation of the history of Palestine emphasizes the period of the Mandate. Part II, "Close-Up," focuses on Israel's War of Independence and the efforts at consolidating governmental authority in the new state. Part III, "Perspectives," offers a brief summary of the culture and social patterns of Israel.

Clearly the historical review is the most interesting and important part of the book. Koestler's text is well written and offers a detailed review of events and their implications. Some sections, however, are a bit one-sided and given to broad generalizations. This imbalance may reflect the sources Koestler used, which are limited to memoirs, press reports, and the few histories available in 1949. Nevertheless the conclusions that Koestler draws from the British experience in Palestine are interesting and probably correct. Koestler lays much of the blame for the Arab-Israeli conflict on the British administration, which continually wavered between extreme forms of the goals it set for itself: creation of a Jewish national home and protection of the Arabs. As a result, according to Koestler, only partition could satisfy both parties.

563. Neustadt-Noy, Isaac: "Toward Unity: Zionist and Non-Zionist Cooperation, 1941-1942." HYB, v.8 (1978): 149-165.

564. Peters, Joan: FROM TIME IMMEMORIAL: THE ORIGINS OF THE ARAB-JEWISH CONFLICT OVER PALESTINE. New York: Harper & Row, 1984. 601 pp., apps., notes, bibliog., index.

Somewhat controversial history of pre-state Palestine. Primarily focused on Jewish and Arab population trends and the claim of Jewish displacement of Arab fellahin. Peters also looks at the propaganda over refugees and discerns some hypocrisy in the commonly held view that only Palestinian Arabs were uprooted as a result of the creation of Israel. As a corrective, Peters notes that twice as many Jews became refugees as a result of genocidal hatred in Arab lands, as compared to the number of Arabs who were forced, or cajoled by their Arab leaders, to leave Palestine. Controversy has swirled around Peters´ use of demographic data, the accuracy of her statistics, and her blanket assertion that Arabs in all cases benefited from the Jewish presence in Palestine. Notwithstanding these differences, Peters offers an important contribution to the history of the Arab-Israeli conflict. The book is especially useful as a corrective to Arab propaganda, and the continuing apathy of many so-called liberals to the Jewish fate.

565. Robinson, Jacob: PALESTINE AND THE UNITED NATIONS. Westport, CT: Greenwood Press, 1971 [Rep. of 1947 Ed.]. 269 pp., notes, index.

Chronicle of the Palestine issue at the United Nations from 1945 to the debates on partition in mid-1947. Although written before the UN decision to establish the State of Israel, the volume is a useful compendium of the issues, arguments, and opinions raised on the Palestine problem. Especially useful is Robinson´s analysis of the UNSCOP, the

United Nations Special Committee on Palestine. The cases of
both Jews and Arabs are presented objectively, although
Robinson clearly sees more justice in the Jewish case. As a
whole, the book is a useful primary source and can help considerably in understanding the events that led to the rise
of Israel.

566. Sanders, Ronald: THE HIGH WALLS OF JERUSALEM: A HIS-
TORY OF THE BALFOUR DECLARATION AND THE BIRTH OF THE BRITISH
MANDATE FOR PALESTINE. New York: Holt, Rinehart and Winston,
1983. 746 pp., maps, bibliographic notes, index.

Inquiry into the origins of the Balfour Declaration.
Briefly reviews British interest in the Middle East before
World War I. The war years are dealt with chronologically;
in each year Zionist and English contacts, plans, and negotiations are elucidated. An epilogue spans the years of the
Mandate in an unfortunately facile fashion. The book is useful as an explanation of the complexities of English policy
toward Jews and Jewish nationalism, but is by no means a
definitive account.

567. Schechtman, J. B.: THE UNITED STATES AND THE JEWISH
STATE MOVEMENT: THE CRUCIAL DECADE, 1939-1949. New York:
Herzl Press / Thomas Yoseloff, 1966. 474 pp., illus., notes,
bibliog., index.

Political and diplomatic history reviewing America's role
in the creation of Israel. Although superseded in some respects by more recent works [see #554 and #556], his synthesis is still of interest. Schechtman's theme is the interplay of events and personalities during the ten years
between the outbreak of World War II and the establishment
of Israel. America's role is placed into the broader context
of American interests in the Middle East. Also reviewed are
Zionist diplomatic and political activities in the United
States. Schechtman eschews partisanship in his analysis of
Zionist diplomatic activities during and after the war. Although himself a leading Revisionist Zionist, Schechtman
sees no justification in denigrating reputations. He prefers
a careful judgment of events, based on meticulous documentation. Containing many novel interpretations, the book
still has use for students and scholars of that key period
in Jewish history.

568. Shafir, Shlomo: "Taylor and McDonald: Two Diverging Views on Zionism and the Emerging Jewish State." JSS, v.39 #4 (Fall, 1977): 323-346.

> #467. Shapira, Anita: "Yishuv and the Survivors."

569. Shpiro, David H.: "The Political Background of the 1942 Biltmore Resolution." HYB, v.8 (1978): 166-177.

570. Stein, Leonard: THE BALFOUR DECLARATION. New York: Simon and Schuster, 1961. 681 pp., app., sources, index.

Authoritative study into the political and historical context of the British declaration of sympathy with zionism. Stein begins by charting the development of Great Britain's interests in the Middle East from the 1830s to World War I. As a result of these interests Britain became a protector of Jewish rights in Palestine and, in the twentieth century, was seen by Englishmen and Zionists alike as a possible sponsor of a Jewish national home.

The outbreak of World War I strengthened the commonality of interests between the Zionists and Britain, leading to numerous contacts and, eventually, to negotiations for a declaration of support for Jewish/Zionist goals. The reasons for British interest are set out quite clearly by Stein: although some British leaders were sympathetic to zionism, most were motivated by their assessment of Great Britain's strategic interests in the area. Some were even indirectly motivated by antisemitism, thinking that they could manipulate the governments of Russia and America by aiding the Jews; this is probably the only case of the philosemitic use of the ideas expressed by THE PROTOCOLS OF THE ELDERS OF ZION. Stein's analysis is still authoritative, although much of the documentary evidence became available only after the book was written [see #551].

571. Syrkin, Marie: THE STATE OF THE JEWS. Washington, DC: New Republic Books, 1980. 368 pp.

Historical reflections on postwar conditions in the Jewish world, mostly reprints of Syrkin's essays originally published from 1947 to 1980. The three main themes of the book are the Displaced Persons camps, Israel, and American Jewry. Although not scholarly, the essays contain a wealth of information and some very provocative ideas. Syrkin's Zionist spirit and her keen interest in all things Jewish make the collection quite interesting, even for the general reader.

572. Urofsky, Melvin I.: "Ha Ma´avek: American Zionists,
Partition and Recognition, 1947-1948." HYB, v.8 (1978):
284-309.

573. ___: "Rifts in the Movement: Zionist Fissures, 1942-
1945." HYB, v.8 (1978): 195-211.

574. Wilson, H.: THE CHARIOT OF ISRAEL: BRITAIN, AMERICA,
AND THE STATE OF ISRAEL. New York: W. W. Norton, 1981. 406
pp., illus., maps, notes, index.

Apologetic political history of zionism by England´s
former Prime Minister. After a very brief review of Jewish
yearnings for their homeland, Wilson charts the rise of
zionism. Six chapters cover the period of the Mandate in
some detail. It is precisely on the issue of Britain´s
involvement in Palestine that the author is weakest. The
apologetic tone is particularly evident in Wilson´s chapter
on the Holocaust, which is inadequate. Nevertheless, the
book does offer an insider´s view, from the perspective of a
leader of the Labour Party. Moreover, Sir Harold´s position
especially allows him to detail some anecdotal evidence that
would otherwise be unknown.

The Jewish Community

10

Central Europe
and Scandinavia

SURVEYS

575. Elazar, Daniel J., A. Weiss Liberles, and S. Werner: THE JEWISH COMMUNITIES OF SCANDINAVIA: SWEDEN, DENMARK, NORWAY AND FINLAND. Lanham, MD: Univ. Press of America, 1984. 171 pp., gloss., notes.

Surveys the communal life and structure of the Jewish communities in Scandinavia since World War II. Primarily organized as a series of "communal maps" to Jewish political and communal organization. The volume is intimately connected with THE BALKAN JEWISH COMMUNITIES [see #827] and THE JEWISH POLITY [see #371], providing a useful comparison of Jewish political life and public affairs.

CONTENTS: D. J. Elazar: The Jewries of Scandinavia / Adina Weiss Liberles: The Jewish Community of Sweden; The Jewish Community of Denmark; The Jewish Community of Finland / A. W. Liberles and S. Werner: The Jewish Community of Norway.

> #215. Handlin, O.: "Jews in the Culture of Middle Europe."

> #343. Niewyk, D.: SOCIALIST, ANTISEMITE AND JEW.

> #345. Pulzer, P. G.: RISE OF POLITICAL ANTISEMITISM.

576. Sichrovsky, P.: STRANGERS IN THEIR OWN LAND: YOUNG JEWS IN GERMANY AND AUSTRIA TODAY. Trans. from the German by Jean Steinberg. New York: Basic Books, 1986. 165 pp.

Details Jewish life in postwar Central Europe. The author, himself an Austrian Jew, interviewed thirteen young

187

German and Austrian Jews. Some of the material in the book
is interesting, but given the small number of individuals
involved and the journalistic, overly melodramatic style,
the book is not as illuminating as it might be. For example,
while the lack of formal antisemitism is discussed, informal
Judaeophobia in the social or economic spheres is not mentioned. Similarly, Sichrovsky does not clearly distinguish
between conscious Jewish identity and the simple fact of
being born Jewish, nor does he weigh the value attached by
these young Jews to their own Jewishness.

> #116. Stern, Selma: THE COURT JEW.

> #100. Straus, H.: "Jews in the Economic Evolution."

577. Wilhelm, K.: "The Influence of German Jewry on Jewish Communities in Scandinavia." LBIYB, v.3 (1958): 313-332.

> #378. Zimmer, E.: HARMONY AND DISCORD.

AUSTRIA

578. Boyer, John W.: "Karl Lueger and the Viennese Jews."
LBIYB, v.26 (1981): 125-141.

579. Bross, Jacob: "The Beginning of the Jewish Labor
Movement in Galicia." Y/A, v.5 (1950): 55-84.

580. Fraenkel, Josef [ed.]: THE JEWS OF AUSTRIA: ESSAYS
ON THEIR LIFE, HISTORY AND DESTRUCTION. London: Valentine
Mitchell, 1967. 585 pp., notes, index.

Anthology on the history of Austrian Jewry in modern
times. Most of the essays are in English, but the book also
contains contributions in German and French. The main focus
of the essays is social history, although political history
is also reviewed. Fraenkel grouped the essays into four
parts, by subject: Life; Biography and Memoirs; History; and
Destruction. The essays display both the deep attachment of
Jews to Austria as well as their isolation from the mainstream of Austrian society. The reader can thus find essays
on art, music, literature, and journalism, juxtaposed with
others on antisemitism, the Anschluss, and the virtual destruction of Austrian Jewry. Vienna plays a special role in
the book, although the Viennese community is not the exclusive focus. Fraenkel´s introduction is adequate in tying

together the divergent focal points of the essays, but does not offer an overview of Austrian Jewish history.

CONTENTS: W. Pillich: Jewish Artists in the 16th, 17th and 18th Centuries / P. Gradenwitz: Jews in Austrian Music / F. Kobler: The Contribution of Austrian Jews to Jurisprudence / Harry Zohn: Three Austrian Jews in German Literature: Schnitzler, Zweig, Herzl / R. Grunberger: Jews in Austrian Journalism / Hilde Spiel: Jewish Women in Austrian Culture / Josef Fraenkel: The Chief Rabbi and the Visionary / S. A. Birnbaum: Nathan Birnbaum and National Autonomy / Leon Kolb: The Vienna Jewish Museum / E. Juhn: The Jewish Sports Movement in Austria / O. Dutch: Seeds of a Noble Inheritance / Martin Freud: Who was Freud? / Sol Liptzin: Richard Beer-Hofmann / E. Mandell: Salomon Sulzer 1804-90 / J. Leftwich: Thinking of Vienna / A. Tartakower: Jewish Migratory Movements in Austria in Recent Generations / N. H. Tur-Sinai: Viennese Jewry / A. Willman: Famous Rabbis of Vienna / M. Papo: The Sephardi Community of Vienna / J. Heshel: The History of Hasidism in Austria / M. Henisch: Galician Jews in Vienna / E. S. Rimalt: The Jews of Tyrol / S. S. Stoessl: The Jews of Carinthia / M. K. Schwarz: The Jews of Styria / P. G. J. Pulzer: The Development of Political Antisemitism in Austria / Robert Schwarz: Antisemitism and Socialism in Austria 1918-62 / N. Bentwich: The Destruction of the Jewish Community in Austria 1938-42 / H. Rosenkranz: The Anschluss and the Tragedy of Austrian Jewry, 1934-45 / Ilse R. Wolff: Bibliography.

> #506. Friedman, I.: "Austria-Hungary and Zionism."

581. Gelber, N. M.: "The Sephardic Community in Vienna." JSS, v.10 #4 (Oct., 1948): 359-396.

582. Goldhammer, Leo: "Jewish Emigration from Austria-Hungary in 1848-1849." Y/A, v.9 (1954): 332-362.

583. Grunwald, Max: VIENNA. Philadelphia: JPS, 1936. 557 pp., illus., apps., bibliog., index.

History of Viennese Jewry, part of the Jewish Publication Society [JPS] communities series. The book has, to a degree, been superseded by more recent scholarship. Grunwald follows a chronological organization and defines each era by its great men. The history of the Jewish community is intertwined in every era with Jewish-Gentile relations and with the government's Jewish policy. Considerable attention is given to the modern era, especially on the eighteenth and early nineteenth centuries. As with many of the other volumes in the series, events overtook the Jewries described and ended their long and productive histories.

> #388. Hertz, J. S.: "The Bund's Nationality Program."

584. Jenks, William A.: "The Jews in the Habsburg Empire, 1879-1918." LBIYB, v.16 (1971): 155-162.

585. Kann, Robert: "German-Speaking Jewry during Austria-Hungary's Constitutional Era [1867-1918]." JSS, v.10 #3 (July, 1948): 239-256.

586. Karbach, Oskar: "The Liquidation of the Jewish Community of Vienna." JSS, v.2 #3 (July, 1940): 255-278.

> #142. Katz, J.: TOWARD MODERNITY.

> #123. Mahler, R.: "Aspects of the Haskalah in Galicia."

587. Mahler, Raphael: "The Austrian Government and the Hasidim during the Period of Reaction." JSS, v.1 #2 (Apr., 1939): 195-240.

588. Not Used.

589. Oxaal, Ivar and Walter R. Weitzmann: "The Jews of Pre-1914 Vienna: an Exploration of Basic Sociological Dimensions." LBIYB, v.30 (1985): 395-432.

590. Rosensaft, M. Z.: "Jews and Antisemites in Austria at the End of the Nineteenth Century." LBIYB, v.21 (1976): 57-86.

591. Rozenblit, Marsha L.: " The Assertion of Identity: Jewish Student Nationalism at the University of Vienna before the First World War." LBIYB, v.27 (1982): 171-186.

592. ___: THE JEWS OF VIENNA, 1867-1914: ASSIMILATION AND IDENTITY. Albany: State Univ. of New York Press, 1983. 284 pp., tables, maps, notes, bibliog., index.

Social history of Viennese Jewry at the turn of the century. The book may be divided into two roughly equal sections. In the first, Rozenblit describes the condition of Viennese Jewry and the transformations that occurred within

Jewish society. Especially interesting is the process of internal migration of Jews to Vienna from all parts of the Austro-Hungarian empire. The second section of the book encompasses Rozenblit´s analysis of the tension between the forces promoting Jewish identity and those encouraging assimilation in post-Emancipation Vienna. Considerable attention is focused on Austrian zionism and its position on the issues of modernity and Jewish identity. Rozenblit wisely adopts a thematic approach, which lends itself to comparison with other Jewish communities.

> #102. Schmelz, U.: JEWISH POPULATION STUDIES.

593. Schoeps, Julius H.: "Modern Heirs of the Maccabees: the Beginning of the Vienna Kadimah, 1882-1897." LBIYB, v.27 (1982): 155-170.

594. Simon, Walter B.: "The Jewish Vote in Austria." LBIYB, v.16 (1971): 97-121.

595. ___ : "The Jewish Vote in Vienna." JSS, v.23 #1 (Jan., 1961): 38-48.

> #392. Szajkowski, Z.: "Conflicts in the A.I.U."

596. Toury, J.: "Jewish Townships in the German-Speaking Parts of the Austrian Empire - Before and After the Revolution of 1848-1849." LBIYB, v.26 (1981): 55-72.

597. ___ : "Troubled Beginnings: the Emergence of the Oesterreichisch-Israelitische Union." LBIYB, v.30 (1985): 457-475.

> #104. Vago, B.: JEWISH ASSIMILATION IN MODERN TIMES.

598. Wank, Solomon: "A Case of Aristocratic Antisemitism in Austria: Count Aehrenthal and the Jews 1878-1907." LBIYB, v.30 (1985): 435-456.

599. Wistrich, Robert S.: "Austrian Social Democracy and the Problem of Galician Jewry, 1890-1914." LBIYB, v.26 (1981): 89-124.

600. ___ : "Socialism and Antisemitism in Austria before 1914." JSS, v.37 #3/4 (July/Oct., 1975): 323-332.

DENMARK

601. Bamberger, Ib Nathan: THE VIKING JEWS. New York: Shengold, 1983. 158 pp., illus., notes, apps., bibliog.

Synthetic history of Denmark´s Jews from their settlement to the Holocaust. A minuscule community in one of Europe´s smallest countries, Danish Jewry existed on the periphery of Jewish history until World War II. The actions of the Danes in October 1943, has become synonymous with selfless and altruistic heroism. Nevertheless, Danish Jewish history cannot be reduced solely to the Holocaust. Bamberger´s effort is more remarkable precisely because he deals with the previous Jewish experience in Denmark and views the Danish response during the Nazi era as part of a continuum. An interesting chapter deals with the Jewish community and its institutions. Assimilation, intermarriage, and religious reform are covered forthrightly and without polemic. Some issues might have been covered in greater detail, but the book is still a useful history of a little-known community.

> #575. Elazar, D.: THE JEWISH COMMUNITIES OF SCANDINAVIA.

* 602. KINGS AND CITIZENS: THE HISTORY OF THE JEWS IN DENMARK, 1622-1983. New York: The Jewish Museum, 1983. 128 pp.

> #191. Weil, G.: "A Copenahgen Report Concerning Reform."

> #477. Yahil, Leni: RESCUE OF DANISH JEWRY.

FINLAND

> #575. Elazar, D.: THE JEWISH COMMUNITIES OF SCANDINAVIA.

GERMANY/FRG/GDR

Overviews

603. Adler, Helmut G.: THE JEWS IN GERMANY: FROM THE ENLIGHTENMENT TO NATIONAL SOCIALISM. South Bend, IN: Univ. of Notre Dame Press, 1969. 152 pp., bibliog., index.

Synthetic history of modern German Jewry. Adler first gives a brief account of Jews in Germany during the Middle Ages, beginning his synthesis with the Enlightenment. Adler

has organized the book so as to provide a guide to major
historical and historiographical issues, rather than a
straight history. Jewish status and antisemitism are Adler´s
main themes. An additional subtheme is the search by German
Jews for a modus vivendi that would balance two conflicting
aims: the desire to assimilate and to remain Jewish. Where
appropriate, Adler integrates religious, economic, and
political issues into the main theme of his work. Zionism is
also reviewed within this framework. An interesting chapter,
"Germany and World Jewry," reviews the impact, positive and
negative, of German antisemitism and German culture on Jews
and Judaism during the nineteenth century. Adler´s work contains important insights into the development of German
Jewry up to the Holocaust.

604. Cahnman, Werner J.: "Village and Small-Town Jews in
Germany: a Typological Study." LBIYB, v.19 (1974): 107-130.

605. Cecil, Lamar: "Jew and Junker in Imperial Berlin."
LBIYB, v.20 (1975): 47-58.

606. Graupe, Heinz Moshe: THE RISE OF MODERN JUDAISM: AN
INTELLECTUAL HISTORY OF GERMAN JEWRY 1650-1942. Trans. from
the German by J. Robinson. Huntington, NY: Robert E. Krieger
Pub., 1978. 329 pp., illus., notes, bibliog., index.

Intellectual history of German Jewry in modern times.
Graupe also incorporates social, economic, and political
history in his analysis. Emphasis is placed on Judaism
rather than on Jews per se. Graupe´s theme is the development of new forms of Jewish thought and their impact on
Jewish identity and existence. He sees German Jewry as an
innovator of ideas and an experimentor with new forms of
Jewish identity. In turn, German Jewry passed these innova-
tions on to other Jewish communities, particularly in
eastern Europe. Graupe proves this in an in-depth analysis
of German Haskalah, of the "Science of Judaism," and of the
spread of both Reform and neo-Orthodox religious ideologies.
Graupe offers many novel interpretations, but it is his synthesis of the different strands of German Jewish creativity
that is most important.

607. Jochmann, Werner: "The Jews and German Society in
the Imperial era." LBIYB, v.20 (1975): 5-11.

608. Jospe, Alfred: "The Study of Judaism in German Universities before 1933." LBIYB, v.27 (1982): 295-319.

609. Kaplan, Marion A.: "For Love or Money: the Marriage Strategies of Jews in Imperial Germany." LBIYB, v.28 (1983): 263-300.

610. ___: "German-Jewish Feminism in the Twentieth Century." JSS, v.38 #1 (Wint., 1976): 39-53.

611. Kisch, Guido: THE JEWS IN MEDIEVAL GERMANY: A STUDY OF THEIR LEGAL AND SOCIAL STATUS. New York: Ktav, 1970 [Rep. 1949 Ed.]. 655 pp., notes, bibliog., indexes.

Intensive study of the social and legal status of Jews in medieval Germany. The book is a definitive inquiry into German Jewry-law of the Middle Ages. Begins with important methodological concerns, then deals with the sources. Thereafter, the sections and chapters cover a wide variety of specific issues in medieval Jewry-law. Although his main sources were the German law codes, Kisch also reviewed Jewish sources. Significant changes in Jewry-law that occurred during the thirteenth century are carefully reconstructed. In particular, Kisch studies the changes in law as a symptom of the decline in Jewish status - from urban freemen to Servi Camarae. In all Kisch has provided a meticulous, careful and extremely important study.

612. Kober, Adolf: "Jewish Communities in Germany from the Age of Enlightenment to Their Destruction by the Nazis." JSS, v.9 #3 (July, 1947): 195-238.

613. Lowenstein, S. M.: "Jewish Residential Concentration in Post-Emancipation Germany." LBIYB, v.28 (1983): 471-495.

614. Lowenthal, E. G.: "The Ahlem Experiment: a Brief Survey of the ´Juedische Gartenbauschule´." LBIYB, v.14 (1969): 165-181.

615. Marcus, Jacob R.: THE RISE AND DESTINY OF THE GERMAN JEW: WITH A POSTMORTEM. New York: Ktav, 1973 [Rep. of 1934 Ed.]. 365 pp., apps., bibliog., index.

Thematic history of Jews in Germany from ancient times to the Nazi era. Primary focus is on Jewish political life and on the interaction of Jews and Germans up to and including the early years of the Nazi regime. Jewish social, economic, cultural, and communal history are all reviewed, though less extensively than the political aspects of the modern German-Jewish experience. Marcus´s analysis of the

Nazi regime and the fate of German Jewry makes for
interesting reading, though he obviously could not predict
which way Nazi policy would develop.

616. Mayer, Paul Y.: "Equality - Egality: Jews and Sport
in Germany." LBIYB, v.25 (1980): 221-241.

617. Niewyk, Donald L.: THE JEWS IN WEIMAR GERMANY. Baton
Rouge: Louisiana State Univ. Press, 1980. 229 pp., notes,
bibliog., index.

Important social and political study of German Jewry
during the brief existence of the Weimar Republic. Niewyk
focuses on both internal and external relations of the Jewish community. Antisemitism, Jewish responses to the antisemitic threat, and the deep ideological divisions within
the community are major subthemes. Niewyk also assesses the
role Jews played in the cultural, political, and economic
life of Weimar, which was widely condemned by its conservative opponents as the "Jew-republic." Three interesting
chapters deal with different Jewish perceptions of
Jewishness and Germanness, while also charting the quest for
a Jewish identity in the new liberal Germany. Niewyk
concludes that the Weimar era was one of Jewish love for
Germany, an affection which was not, however, reciprocal.
Despite German Jewry's unequivocal pro-German attitude,
Niewyk does not believe that criticism of Jewish communal
behavior is warranted. Unlike other historians, Niewyk does
not believe Jewish self-defense efforts were naive. To the
contrary, he argues that the Jewish liberal trend in Germany
represented a rational and careful assessment of Jewish
needs and of the best way to attain the maximum for Germany
and German Jews.

618. Ottenheimer, Hilde: "The Disappearance of Jewish
Communities in Germany 1900-1938." JSS, v.3 #2 (Apr., 1941):
189-206.

619. Philipsborn, Alexander: "The Jewish Hospitals in
Germany." LBIYB, v.4 (1959): 220-234.

620. Preston, David L.: "The German Jews in Secular Education, University Teaching, and Science: a Preliminary Inquiry." JSS, v.38 #2 (Spr., 1976): 99-116.

621. Richarz, Monika: "Jews in Today's Germanies." LBIYB,
v.30 (1985): 265-274.

622. Rosenthal, Erich: "Trends of the Jewish Population in Germany, 1910-39." JSS, v.6 #3 (July, 1944): 233-274.

623. Sandler, Ahron: "The Struggle for Unification." LBIYB, v.2 (1957): 76-84.

> #102. Schmelz, U.: JEWISH POPULATION STUDIES.

624. Schwab, Hermann: A WORLD IN RUINS: HISTORY, LIFE AND WORK OF GERMAN JEWRY. Trans. from the German by C. Fullman. London: E. Goldston, 1946. 316 pp., illus., notes, bibliog., index.

Survey of the history of German Jewry, with primary emphasis on modern times. The first section, History, is a straight review of key events and personalities. This section proves once again how difficult it can be to survey 1,000 years of history in less than one hundred pages. Part II, Life, is the lion's share of the book. Unfortunately, this section is the least useful, since most of Schwab's discussion relates to north European Jewry in general and does not specifically deal with issues unique to German Jewry. Part III, Work, is a survey of Jewish contributions in a variety of fields and contains a considerable amount of interesting information. Schwab's emphasis on German Jews, rather than on German Jewry, makes the book less useful than it might be. But as one of the few synthetic histories of German Jewry, the book can be of some use to students and scholars.

625. Stern-Taubler, Selma: "The German Jew in a Changing World." LBIYB, v.7 (1962): 3-10.

626. Strauss, Herbert: "The ´Jugendverband´: a Social and Intellectual History." LBIYB, v.6 (1961): 206-235.

627. Wertheimer, Jack: "The ´Auslaenderfrage´ at Institutions of Higher Learning: a Controversy Over Russian-Jewish Students in Imperial Germany." LBIYB, v.27 (1982): 187-215.

Historiography

628. Cahnman, Werner J.: "A Regional Approach to German Jewish History." JSS, v.5 #3 (July, 1943): 211-224.

629. Kulka, Otto D.: "Major Trends and Tendencies in German Historiography on National Socialism and the ´Jewish Question´ [1924-1984]." LBIYB, v.30 (1985): 215-242.

630. Kwiet, Konrad: "Historians of the German Democratic Republic on Antisemitism and Persecution." LBIYB, v.21 (1976): 173-198.

631. Liebeschuetz, Hans: "Past, Present and Future of German-Jewish Historiography." LBIYB, v.23 (1978): 3-21.

632.   : "Problems of Diaspora History in XIXth-Century Germany." JJS, v.8 #1/2 (1957): 103-111.

633. Lowenthal, E. G.: "In the Shadow of Doom: Post-War Publications on Jewish Communal History in Germany." LBIYB, v.11 (1966): 306-335; v.15 (1970): 223-242; v.23 (1978): 283-308; v.29 (1984): 419-468.

634. Schorsch, Ismar: "German Antisemitism in the Light of Post-War Historiography." LBIYB, v.19 (1974): 257-271.

635. Wassermann, Henry: "The ´Fliegende Blaetter´ as a Source for the Social History of German Jewry." LBIYB, v.28 (1983): 93-138.

Emancipation and Assimilation

> #1333. Barzilay, I. E.: "The Italian and Berlin Haskalah."

636. Carsten, F. L.: "The Court Jews: a Prelude to Emancipation." LBIYB, v.3 (1958): 140-156.

> #101. Engelman, U. Z.: "Intermarriage Among Jews."

637. Freimark, Peter: "Language Behaviour and Assimilation: the Situation of the Jews in Northern Germany in the First Half of the Nineteenth Century." LBIYB, v.24 (1979): 157-177.

638. Hamburger, Ernest: "One Hundred Years of Emancipation." LBIYB, v.14 (1969): 3-66.

> #1096. Helfand J. I.: "The Symbiotic Relationship."

639. Kaplan, M. A.: "Tradition and Transition: the Acculturation, Assimilation, and Integration of Jews in Imperial Germany, a Gender Analysis." LBIYB, v.27 (1982): 3-35.

640. Katz, Jacob: "The Fight for Admission to Masonic Lodges." LBIYB, v.11 (1966): 171-209.

> #120. ___: OUT OF THE GHETTO.

> #142. ___: TOWARD MODERNITY.

641. Kober, Adolf: "Emancipation´s Impact on the Education and Vocational Training of German Jewry." JSS, v.16 #1 (Jan., 1954): 3-32; #2 (Apr., 1954): 151-176.

642. ___: "The French Revolution and the Jews in Germany." JSS, v.7 #4 (Oct., 1945): 291-322.

643. Lowenstein, Steven M.: "The Pace of Modernisation of German Jewry in the Nineteenth Century." LBIYB, v.21 (1976): 41-56.

> #124. Mayer, G.: "Early German Socialism."

> #125. Meyer, M. A.: ORIGINS OF THE MODERN JEW.

> #126. Morgenstern, F.: "Hardenberg and the Emancipation."

644. Mork, G. R.: "German Nationalism and Jewish Assimilation: the Bismarck Period." LBIYB, v.22 (1977): 81-90.

645. Mosse, George L.: GERMAN JEWS BEYOND JUDAISM. Bloomington: Indiana Univ. Press / Cincinnati: Hebrew Union College, 1985. 98 pp., notes, index.

Five connected essays reviewing the reorientation of German Jewish identity in the period between the Enlightenment and the Holocaust. Mosse emphasizes the isolation of German Jews from the general trends of German culture. This held true despite the fact that Jews saw themselves as an integral part of the bildungsbuergertum; the way Jews perceived German culture differed widely from German perceptions of both German and German-Jewish culture. Nevertheless, according to Mosse, German Jewry´s efforts to humanize and moderate German nationalism was an important, if unsuccessful, legacy.

646. Oelsner, Toni: "Three Jewish Families in Modern Germany: a Study of the Process of Emancipation." JSS, v.4 #3 (July, 1942): 241-268; #4 (Oct., 1942): 349-398.

647. Pelli, Moshe: "The Attitude of the First Maskilim in Germany towards the Talmud." LBIYB, v.27 (1982): 243-260.

648. Richarz, Monika: "Jewish Social Mobility in Germany during the Time of Emancipation [1790-1871]." LBIYB, v.20 (1975): 69-77.

649. Riff, Michael A.: "The Anti-Jewish Aspect of the Revolutionary Unrest of 1848 in Baden and its Impact on Emancipation." LBIYB, v.21 (1976): 27-40.

650. Ruerup, Reinhard: "Emancipation and Crisis: the Jewish Question in Germany, 1850-1890." LBIYB, v.20 (1975): 13-25.

651. ___: "German Liberalism and the Emancipation of the Jews." LBIYB, v.20 (1975): 59-68.

652. ___: "Jewish Emancipation and Bourgeois Society." LBIYB, v.14 (1969): 67-91.

653. Schmidt, H. D.: "The Terms of Emancipation 1781-1812: the Public Debate in Germany and its Effect on the Mentality and Ideas of German Jewry." LBIYB, v.1 (1956): 28-47.

654. Stern-Taeubler, S.: "The First Generation of Emancipated Jews." LBIYB, v.15 (1970): 3-40.

655. ___: "Principles of German Policy Towards the Jews at the Beginning of the Modern Era." LBIYB, v.1 (1956): 15-27.

656. Toury, Jacob: "Types of Jewish Municipal Rights in German Townships: the Problem of Local Emancipation." LBIYB, v.22 (1977): 55-80.

> #104. Vago, B.: JEWISH ASSIMILATION IN MODERN TIMES.

657. Wilhelm, Kurt: "The Jewish Community in the Post-Emancipation Period." LBIYB, v.2 (1957): 47-75.

Religion and Culture

> #233. Altmann, A.: STUDIES

658. Altmann, Alexander: "Theology in Twentieth-Century German Jewry." LBIYB, v.1 (1956): 193-216.

659. Bach, Hans: THE GERMAN JEW: A SYNTHESIS OF JUDAISM AND WESTERN CIVILIZATION, 1730-1930. New York: Oxford Univ. Press, 1984. 255 pp., index.

Study of the synthesis of German and Jewish cultures from the Emancipation until National Socialism. The chapters are organized chronologically, although about half are thematic in nature. Central to Bach´s account are the results of German-Jewish intellectual activity, which are viewed from both the German and Jewish perspectives. Bach´s primary methodology is intellectual history, although social history is not completely ignored. The book covers a major slice of German Jewish history. It is not, however, documented and thus is of more use to the interested layperson than to students or scholars. Nevertheless, Bach does offer some insights as well as a useful interpretation of German Jewish history.

> #62. Cohen, S. M. and P. Hyman: THE JEWISH FAMILY.

660. Gay, Peter: "The Berlin-Jewish Spirit: a Dogma in Search of Some Doubts." LBML, #15 (1972): 3-19.

661. Greive, Hermann: "On Jewish Self-Identification: Religion and Political Orientation." LBIYB, v.20 (1975): 35-46.

662. Kober, Adolf: "150 Years of Religious Instruction." LBIYB, v.2 (1957): 98-118.

> #209. Liberles, R.: RELIGIOUS CONFLICT IN SOCIAL CONTEXT.

> #183. Meyer, M. A.: "Alienated Intellectuals."

663. Meyer, M. A.: "The Orthodox and the Enlightened: an Unpublished Contemporary Analysis of Berlin Jewry´s Spiritual Condition in the Early Nineteenth Century." LBIYB, v.25 (1980): 101-130

> #143. Pelli, M.: THE AGE OF HASKALAH.

> #247. Pelli, M.: "The Impact of Deism."

> #248. Pelli, M.: "Isaac Euchel."

> #187. Philipson, D.: THE REFORM MOVEMENT IN JUDAISM.

664. Pollack, Herman: JEWISH FOLKWAYS IN GERMANIC LANDS, 1648-1806: STUDIES IN ASPECTS OF DAILY LIFE. Cambridge, MA: MIT Press, 1971. 410 pp., illus., notes, bibliog., indexes.

Anthropological study focusing on the daily life of German Jewry in the premodern era. Opens with a description of the physical surroundings of the "Jewish street." Thereafter the elements of day-to-day living - family, dress, education, holidays, diet, and life cycles - are detailed. Of course, some of the data overlap. Based on extensive use of both communal and rabbinic sources. The book has both scholarly and popular value for anyone interested in Jewish folk life.

665. Poppel, Stephen M.: "Rabbinical Status and Religious Authority in Imperial Germany: the German Rabbinical Association." AJS Review, v.9 #2 (Fall, 1984): 185-213.

666. Reinharz, J. and W. Schatzberg [eds.]: THE JEWISH RESPONSE TO GERMAN CULTURE: FROM THE ENLIGHTENMENT TO THE SECOND WORLD WAR. Hanover, NH: Univ. Press of New England for Clark Univ., 1985. 362 pp., notes, index.

Anthology of studies on German Jewry's cultural role. Based on a symposium held at Clark University in October 1983. The theme of the essays is the interaction between Jewish and German culture. The main emphasis is on intellectual history, with philosophy and literary history providing major subthemes. On the basis of new materials or novel interpretations, many of the essays show an original approach, rejecting widely held stereotypes. Germany is defined broadly so as to include the "German cultural zone" and especially Vienna. The preface offers summaries of the essays, but does not place them into historical context. In general, the anthology lacks a historical framework and thus loses its usefulness for those not specializing in German history. Nevertheless, the individual contributions are of interest and present a unique insight into the heart of pre-Nazi German Jewry.

CONTENTS: G. L. Mosse: Jewish Emancipation: Between Bildung

and Respectability / A. Altmann: Moses Mendelssohn as the Archetypal German Jew / W. Roell: The Kassel "Ha-Meassef" of 1799: an Unknown Contribution to the Haskalah / Nathan Rotenstreich: Hermann Cohen: Judaism in the Context of German Philosophy / M. A. Meyer: Reform Jewish Thinkers and Their German Intellectual Context / J. Katz: German Culture and the Jews / D. Sorkin: The Invisible Community: Emancipation, Secular Culture, and Jewish Identity in the Writings of Berthold Auerbach / Lothar Kahn: Heine´s Jewish Writer Friends: Dilemmas of a Generation 1817-33 / H. Zohn: Fin-de-Siecle Vienna: the Jewish Contribution / G. Stern: German-Jewish and German-Christian Writers: Cooperation in Exile / W. E. Mosse: Wilhelm II and the Kaiserjuden: a Problematical Encounter / S. Volkov: The Dynamics of Dissimilation: Ost-juden and German Jews / S. E. Aschheim: The Jew Within: the Myth of Judaization in Germany / M. Kaplan: Sisterhood under Siege: Feminism and Antisemitism in Germany 1904-38 / Jehuda Reinharz: The Zionist Response to Antisemitism in the Weimar Republic / Kurt Duewell: Jewish Cultural Centers in Nazi Germany: Expectations and Accomplishments / S. H. Milton: Lost, Stolen, and Strayed: the Archival Heritage of Modern German-Jewish History.

667. Rosenau, Helen: "German Synagogues in the Early Period of Emancipation." LBIYB, v.8 (1963): 214-225.

> #271. Rosenbloom, N.: "S. R. Hirsch´s Educational Theory."

668. Schwab, Hermann: THE HISTORY OF ORTHODOX JEWRY IN GERMANY. Trans. from the German by I. R. Birnbaum. London: Mitre Press, 1950. 159 pp., illus., notes, bibliog., index.

Survey of German Orthodox Judaism from the eighteenth to the twentieth centuries. Schwab adopts a chronological survey, dividing German Orthodoxy into three eras: the rise of Orthodox Judaism, from roughly the mid-eighteenth to the mid-nineteenth centuries; the zenith of Orthodox Judaism, from the mid-nineteenth century to World War I; and the eclipse of German Judaism, from World War I to 1945. The book also offers a glimpse, if limited in scope, of German Jewry in general. Schwab opens by explaining the state of affairs in German Jewry before the advent of Samson Raphael Hirsch, whom he sees as the spiritual father of German Orthodoxy. Unfortunately, Schwab is too one-sided in his approach to Hirsch. He concentrates on the traditional aspects of Hirsch´s thought, while mentioning only briefly, and without elucidation, Hirsch´s modernism. Schwab´s account

has its villains, Reform Jews, and heroes, the Torah-true
Jews, but it fails to provide more than a cursory glance at
German Jewish religious life in modern times.

669. ___: JEWISH RURAL COMMUNITIES IN GERMANY. London:
Cooper Books, 1957. 93 pp., notes, bibliog., index.

Survey history of German Jewry in the rural setting.
Schwab is trying to correct the view that German Jewry was
exclusively urban by elucidating the life of nonurban Jewish
communities. Unfortunately, the book uses a large degree of
anecdotal material and does not consistently remain on the
subject. Thus eight of the nine chapters in Part I are accurate portrayals of Jewish rural life in any European locality over the last 250 years. Nothing specifically identifies
these localities as German, much less as south west German,
which they ostensibly were. Parts II and III are better organized, but are so brief as to be virtually lost when compared to Part I. An epilogue of one page attempts to cover
the destruction of German Jewry at the hands of the Nazis,
but again fails to convey more than a thumbnail sketch.

670. Walk, Joseph: "The ´Torah va´Avodah´ Movement in
Germany." LBIYB, v.6 (1961): 236-256.

671. Wolfsberg, Yeshayahu: "Popular Orthodoxy." LBIYB,
v.1 (1956): 237-254.

Migration

672. Adler-Rudel, S.: "East-European Jewish Workers in
Germany." LBIYB, v.2 (1957): 136-165.

673. Aschheim, Steven E.: BROTHERS AND STRANGERS: THE
EAST EUROPEAN JEW IN GERMAN AND GERMAN JEWISH CONSCIOUSNESS,
1800-1923. Madison: The Univ. of Wisconsin Press, 1982. 331
pp., illus., notes, bibliog., index.

Cultural history of the relations between immigrant and
native Jews in Germany during the nineteenth century.
Aschheim´s theme is the influence of the Ostjude on German
Jewish identity. In point of fact, as Aschheim amply proves,
the concept of Ostjuden was a mythical creation of the German environment, Jewish and non-Jewish. In particular assimilationist Jews felt a need to dissociate themselves from
the Ostjuden in order not to compromise their integration

into German society. The assimilationists, of course, held a
very low opinion of Ostjuden and hoped merely to expose them
to proper culture, or be rid of them through migration.
After 1880 another view of Ostjuden gained currency. This
view, often associated with the Zionists, though Aschheim
shows they were not its only proponents, was a counter-myth
that turned Ostjuden into cultural heroes and the embodiment
of a more pristine form of Jewish identity. The supporters
of this position felt that, far from needing to be educated
by German Jews, German Jewry could learn much from the Ostjuden. As a cultural analysis, Aschheim´s work offers an
important supplement to recent social and political studies
on Jewish immigration to Germany.

674. ___ : "The East European Jew and German Jewish Identity." SCJ, v.1 (1984): 3-25.

675. ___ : "Eastern Jews, German Jews and Germany´s Ost-
politik in the First World War." LBIYB, v.28 (1983): 351-
365.

676. Barkai, Avraham: "German-Jewish Migrations in the
Nineteenth Century, 1830-1910." LBIYB, v.30 (1985): 301-318.

677. Lowenstein, Steven M.: "The Yiddish Written Word in
Nineteenth-Century Germany." LBIYB, v.24 (1979): 179-192.

678. Wertheimer, Jack: "Between Tsar and Kaiser: the
Radicalisation of Russian-Jewish University Students in
Germany." LBIYB, v.28 (1983): 329-349.

679. ___ : "The ´Unwanted Element´: East European Jews in
Imperial Germany." LBIYB, v.26 (1981): 23-46.

> #90. Wischnitzer, M.: TO DWELL IN SAFETY.

Public Affairs

680. Bristow, Edward: "The German-Jewish Fight Against
White Slavery." LBIYB, v.28 (1983): 301-328.

681. Caron, Vicki and Paula Hyman: "The Failed Alliance:
Jewish-Catholic Relations in Alsace-Lorraine, 1871-1914."
LBIYB, v.26 (1981): 3-21.

682. Eckstein, G. G.: "The Freie Deutsch-Juedische Jugend [FDJJ]: 1932-1933." LBIYB, v.26 (1981): 231-239.

683. Edelheim-Muehsam, Margaret T.: "The Jewish Press in Germany." LBIYB, v.1 (1956): 163-176.

684. Gelber, N. M.: "The Intervention of German Jews at the Berlin Congress 1878." LBIYB, v.5 (1960): 221-248.

685. Goldstein, Moritz: "German Jewry's Dilemma before 1914." LBIYB, v.2 (1957): 236-254.

> #660. Grieve, H.: "On Jewish Self-Identification."

> #398. Hamburger, E.: "Jews, Democracy and Weimar Germany."

686. Hamburger, Ernest: "Jews in Public Service under the German Monarchy." LBIYB, v.9 (1964): 206-238.

687. ___: and Peter Pulzer: "Jews as Voters in the Weimar Republic." LBIYB, v.30 (1985): 3-66.

688. Holeczek, Heinz: "The Jews and the German Liberals." LBIYB, v.28 (1983): 77-91.

689. Kober, Adolf: "Jews in the Revolution of 1848 in Germany." JSS, v.10 #2 (Apr., 1948): 135-164.

690. Kohler, Max J.: "Jewish Rights at the Congress of Vienna and Aix-la-Chapelle." PAJHS, #26 (1918): 33-125.

> #362. Lamberti, M.: JEWISH ACTIVISM IN IMPERIAL GERMANY.

691. Lamberti, Marjorie: "The Jewish Struggle for the Legal Equality of Religions in Imperial Germany." LBIYB, v.23 (1978): 101-116.

692. Lotan, Giora: "The Zentralwohlfahrtsstelle." LBIYB, v.4 (1959): 185-207.

693. Marcus, Jacob R.: COMMUNAL SICK-CARE IN THE GERMAN GHETTO. Cincinnati, OH: Hebrew Union College Press, 1947. 335 pp., notes, apps., bibliog., index.

Study of the Jewish societies dealing with care of the sick and invalids in Germany during the medieval and early modern periods. Marcus's main focus is on the Hevrah

Kaddisha, which started out as a burial society and then developed into a more encompassing communal organization. Other communal organs covered in Marcus's review include the hekdesh; medical personnel, who were all kahal functionaries; and youth societies. Marcus believes that he discovered the existence of an eighteenth-century Jewish youth movement. The evidence he provides seems to prove his contentions, although this conclusion is not as extreme as it seems at first glance. Unlike European youth groups during the eighteenth and nineteenth centuries, which were hotbeds for radical politics the Jewish groups cited by Marcus also dealt with sick-care or other philanthropic services. As an inquiry into Jewish communal life and behavior, the book is of some interest, although few are going to be interested in the specific data Marcus presents.

694. Maurer, Trude: "The East European Jew in the Weimar Press: Stereotype and Attempted Rebuttal." SCJ, v.1 (1984): 176-198.

695. Mendes-Flohr, Paul: "Fin-de-Siecle Orientalism, the Ostjuden and the Aesthetics of Jewish Self-Affirmation." SCJ, v.1 (1984): 96-139.

696. Moldenhauer, R.: "Jewish Petitions to the German National Assembly in Frankfurt, 1848/1949." LBIYB, v.16 (1971): 185-223.

> #404. Morgenthau, H. J.: "German-Jewish Liberalism."

697. Mosse, George L.: "German Socialists and the Jewish Question in the Weimar Republic." LBIYB, v.16 (1971): 123-151.

698. Niewyk, Donald L.: "Jews and the Courts in Weimar Germany." JSS, v.37 #2 (Apr., 1975): 99-113.

> #364. Peal, D.: "Jewish Responses to German Antisemitism."

699. Pierson, Ruth: "Embattled Veterans: the ´Reichsbund juedischer Frontsoldaten´." LBIYB, v.19 (1974): 139-154.

> #365. Ragins, S.: JEWISH RESPONSES TO ANTISEMITISM.

700. Reinharz, J.: "Deutschtum and Judentum in the Ideology of the Centralverein Deutscher Staatsbuerger Juedischen Glaubens 1893-1914." JSS, v.36 #1 (Jan., 1974): 19-39.

701. Rheins, C. J.: "The Verband nationaldeutscher Juden, 1921-1933." LBIYB, v.25 (1980): 243-268.

702. Rinott, Chanoch: "Major Trends in Jewish Youth Movements in Germany." LBIYB, v.19 (1974): 77-95.

> #366. Schorsch, I.: JEWISH REACTIONS TO GER. ANTISEMITISM.

703. Sterling, Eleonore: "Jewish Reaction to Jew-Hatred in the First Half of the Nineteenth Century." LBIYB, v.3 (1958): 103-121.

704. Suchy, Barbara: "The Verein zur Abwehr des Antisemitismus: from its Beginnings to the First World War." LBIYB, v.28 (1983): 205-239.

705. ___ : "The Verein zur Abwehr des Antisemitismus: from the First World War to its Dissolution in 1933." LBIYB, v.30 (1985): 67-103.

> #392. Szajkowski, Z.: "Conflicts in the A.I.U."

706. Szajkowski, Zosa: "Jewish Relief in Eastern Europe, 1914-1917." LBIYB, v.10 (1965): 24-56.

707. Toury, Jacob: "Organizational Problems of German Jewry: Steps towards the Establishment of a Central Organization [1893-1920]." LBIYB, v.13 (1968): 57-90.

708. Wertheimer, Jack: "Jewish Lobbyists and the German Citizenship Law of 1914: a Documentary Account." SCJ, v.1 (1984): 140-162.

Labor and Economics

709. Auerbach, S. M.: "Jews in the German Metal Trade." LBIYB, v.10 (1965): 188-203.

710. Grunwald, Kurt: "Europe's Railways and Jewish Enterprise: German Jews as Pioneers of Railway Promotion." LBIYB, v.12 (1967): 163-209.

711. ___ : "Three Chapters of German-Jewish Banking History." LBIYB, v.22 (1977): 191-208.

712. Heid, Ludger: "East European Jewish Workers in the Ruhr, 1915-1922." LBIYB, v.30 (1985): 141-168.

713. Landes, David S.: "The Jewish Merchant: Typology and Stereotypology in Germany." LBIYB, v.19 (1974): 11-23.

714. Marcus, A.: "Jews as Entrepreneurs in Weimar Germany." Y/A, v.7 (1952): 175-203.

715. Niewyk, Donald L.: "The Economic and Cultural Role of the Jews in the Weimar Republic." LBIYB, v.16 (1971): 163-173.

716. ___ : "The Impact of Inflation and Depression on the German Jews." LBIYB, v.28 (1983): 19-36.

717. Rosenbaum, Eduard: "Some Reflections on the Jewish Participation in German Economic Life." LBIYB, v.1 (1956): 307-314.

718. Rosenthal, Heinz: "Jews in the Solingen Steel Industry." LBIYB, v.17 (1972): 205-223.

719. Stern-Taeubler, S.: "The Jews in the Economic Policy of Frederick the Great." JSS, v.11 #2 (Apr., 1949): 129-152.

720. Toury, Jacob: "Jewish Manual Labor and Emigration: Records from some Bavarian Districts [1830-1857]." LBIYB, v.16 (1971): 45-62.

721. Weinryb, Bernard D.: "Prolegomena to an Economic History of the Jews in Germany in Modern Times." LBIYB, v.1 (1956): 279-306.

Antisemitism

722. Angress, W. T.: "The German Army´s ´Judenzaehlung´ of 1916: Genesis - Consequences - Significance." LBIYB, v.23 (1978): 117-137.

723. ___ : "The Impact of the ´Judenwahlen´ of 1912 on the Jewish Question: a Synthesis." LBIYB, v.28 (1983): 367-410.

724. ___ : "Prussia´s Army and the Jewish Reserve Officer Controversy before World War I." LBIYB, v.17 (1972): 19-42.

725. Asch, Adolph and Johanna Philippson: "Self-Defence at the Turn of the Century: the Emergence of the K. C.." LBIYB, v.3 (1958): 122-139.

726. Bachrach, Walter Zvi: "Jews in Confrontation with Racist Antisemitism 1879-1933." LBIYB, v.25 (1980): 197-219.

727. Bieber, Hugo: "Antisemitism in the First Years of the German Republic." Y/A, v.4 (1949): 123-145.

728. Frye, Bruce B.: "The German Democratic Party and the Jewish Problem in the Weimar Republic." LBIYB, v.21 (1976): 143-172.

729. Herzig, Arno: "The Role of Antisemitism in the Early Years of the German Workers´ Movement." LBIYB, v.26 (1981): 243-259.

730. Kampe, Norbert: "Jews and Antisemites at Universities in Imperial Germany. Jewish Students: Social History and Social Conflict." LBIYB, v.30 (1985): 357-394.

731. Kann, Robert A.: "Assimilation and Antisemitism in the German and French Orbit in the Nineteenth and Early Twentieth Century." LBIYB, v.14 (1969): 92-115.

732. Lamberti, Marjorie: "Liberals, Socialists and the Defence against Antisemitism in the Wilhelminian Period." LBIYB, v.25 (1980): 147-162.

733. Laqueur, Walter: "The German Youth Movement and the ´Jewish Question´." LBIYB, v.6 (1961): 193-205.

> #315. Lestchinsky, J.: "The Anti-Jewish Program."

734. Liebeschuetz, Hans: "German Politics and Jewish Existence." LBIYB, v.20 (1975): 27- 33.

735. Lowenstein, S. M.: "Governmental Jewish Policies in Early Nineteenth Century Germany and Russia: a Comparison." JSS, v.46 #3/4 (Sum./Fall, 1984): 303-320.

> #341. Massing, P.: REHEARSAL FOR DESTRUCTION.

736. Meyer, Michael A.: "Great Debate on Antisemitism: Jewish Reaction to New Hostility in Germany, 1879-1881." LBIYB, v.11 (1966): 137-170.

737. Mosse, Werner E.: "The Conflict of Liberalism and Nationalism and its Effect on German Jewry." LBIYB, v.15 (1970): 125-139.

738. Pulzer, Peter: "Religion and Judicial Appointments in Germany, 1869-1918." LBIYB, v.28 (1983): 185-204.

739. ___: "Why Was there a Jewish Question in Imperial Germany?" LBIYB, v.25 (1980): 133-146.

740. Rabinbach, Anson and J. D. Zipes [eds.]: GERMANS AND JEWS SINCE THE HOLOCAUST: THE CHANGING SITUATION IN WEST GERMANY. New York: Holmes & Meier, 1986. 365 pp., notes, bibliog.

Investigation of relations between Germans and Jews in the post-Holocaust era. The focus of the anthology is on the changes in mutual relations over the years since 1945. The essays are arranged by subject and are grouped into four sections: "Historical Background," Jewish Responses," "Holocaust," and "Antisemitism: A Reassessment." The third section deals with the reception of the TV miniseries Holocaust in West Germany. In general the essays underscore the need to reconsider the tenor of the German-Jewish relationship. Although German society now reflects many of the liberal ideas that Jews had struggled for in the nineteenth century, neither antisemitism nor hypernationalism have been eliminated. Thus, despite some change for the better, recent German-Jewish relations remain as complex as they were before the Nazis.

CONTENTS: Anson Rabinbach: Reflections on Germans and Jews since Auschwitz / J. Zipes: The Vicissitudes of being Jewish in West Germany / D. Claussen: In the House of the Hangman / M. Sperber: My Jewishness / J. Amery: On the Necessity and Impossibility of being a Jew / T. Oelsner: Dreams of a Better Life: Interview with Toni Oelsner / Dan Diner: Fragments of an Uncompleted Journey: on Jewish Socialization and Political Identity in West Germany / J. Yago-Jung: Growing up in Germany: After the War – After Hitler – ´Afterwards´ / P. Breines: Germans, Journals, and Jews / Madison, Men, Marxism and Mosse: a Tale of Jewish-Leftist Identity Confusion in America / A. Grossmann: Questions of Jewish Identity: a Letter from New York / J-P. Bier: The Holocaust, West Germany, and Strategies of Oblivion, 1947-1979 / J. Herf: The "Holocaust" Reception in West Germany: Right, Center, and Left / A. S. Markovits and R. S. Hayden: "Holocaust" before and

After the Event: Reactions in West Germany and Austria / S.
Zielinski: History as Entertainment and Provocation: the TV
Series "Holocaust" in West Germany / M. Jay: The Jews and
the Frankfurt School: Critical Theory's Analysis of Anti-
semitism / M. Postone: Antisemitism and National Socialism /
F. Feher: The Jewish Question Reconsidered: Notes on Istvan
Bibo's Classic Essay.

741. Ringer, Fritz K.: "Inflation, Antisemitism and the
German Academic Community of the Weimar Period." LBIYB, v.28
(1983): 3-9.

> #349. Smith, D. Ch.: "Protestant Anti-Judaism."

742. Tal, U.: "Liberal Protestanism and the Jews in the
Second Reich, 1870-1914." JSS, v.26 #1 (Jan., 1964): 23-41.

> #354. Tillich, P.: "The Jewish Question."

743. Volkov, Shulamit: "Antisemitism as a Cultural Code:
Reflections on the History and Historiography of Antisemitism in Imperial Germany." LBIYB, v.23 (1978): 25-46.

Zionism

744. Baldwin, Peter M.: "Zionist and Non-Zionist Jews in
the Last Years before the Nazi Regime." LBIYB, vol.27
(1982): 87-108.

745. Eisen, George: "Zionism, Nationalism and the Emergence of the 'Juedische Turnerschaft'." LBIYB, v.28 (1983):
247-262.

746. Eloni, Yehuda: "German Zionism and the Rise of Power
of National Socialism." SiZ, v.6 #2 (Aut., 1985): 247-262.

> #503. ___: "Zionist Movement and the German SPD."

747. Friedman, Isaiah: "The 'Hilfsverein der deutschen
Juden', the German Foreign Ministry and the Controversy with
the Zionists, 1901-1918." LBIYB, v.24 (1979): 291-319.

748. Greive, Hermann: "Zionism and Jewish Orthodoxy."
LBIYB, v.25 (1980): 173-195; v.28 (1983): 241-246.

749. Gross, Walter: "The Zionist Students´ Movement." LBIYB, v.4 (1959): 143-164.

750. Lamberti, Marjorie: "From Coexistence to Conflict: Zionism and the Jewish Community in Germany, 1877-1914." LBIYB, v.27 (1982): 53-86.

751. Poppel, Stephen M.: "German Zionism and Jewish Identity." JJoS, v.18 #2 (Dec., 1976): 115-122.

752. ___: ZIONISM IN GERMANY, 1897-1933: THE SHAPING OF A JEWISH IDENTITY. Philadelphia: JPS, 1977. 234 pp., illus., notes, bibliog., index.

Social history of German zionism. Poppel´s subject is the role zionism played in the shaping of a new Jewish identity in post-Emancipation Germany. Also deals, to a lesser degree, with the political aspects of German zionism. Portrays the specifically German elements in German Zionist thought, seeing them as paradoxical. The very elements that made zionism attractive to young German Jews, in particular the "German" way of zionism, made German Zionists more comfortable in German society and less likely to opt for aliyah. Poppel´s placing of German zionism into its cultural context is thus important and the book contains a number of novel interpretations.

753. Reinharz, Jehuda: "East European Jews in the ´Weltanschauung´ of German Zionists, 1882-1914." SCJ, v.1 (1984): 55-95.

754. ___: FATHERLAND OR PROMISED LAND: DILEMMA OF THE GERMAN JEW, 1893-1914. Ann Arbor: Univ. of Michigan Press, 1975. 328 pp., notes, bibliog., index.

Surveys the dynamics of emancipation and counteremancipation among fin-de-siecle German Jews. Primarily focused on the organizational history of German Jewry and on the dynamics of the ideological struggle between the Centralverein and the Zionists. The theme of the book is the balance struck, by all German Jews, between Deutschtum and Judentum. For its insights into the problem of defining Jewishness in the modern context, the book is useful, but its narrow approach reduces the book´s overall significance.

* 755. ___: THE GERMAN ZIONIST CHALLENGE TO THE FAITH IN EMANCIPATION, 1897-1914. Tel Aviv: Tel Aviv Univ. Press, 1982. 32 pp., notes.

756. ___: "Ideology and Structure in German Zionism 1882-1933." JSS, v.42 #2 (Spr., 1980): 119-146.

757. ___: "The Zionist Response to Antisemitism in Germany." LBIYB, v.30 (1985): 105-140.

758. Rinott, Moshe: "The Zionist Organisation and the Hilfsverein: Cooperation and Conflict [1901-1914]." LBIYB, v.21 (1976): 261-278.

759. Walk, Joseph: "Profile of a Local Zionist Association, 1903-1904: on the Social History of German Zionism." LBIYB, v.24 (1979): 369-374.

760. Wertheimer, J.: "The Duisburg Affair: a Test Case in the Struggle for ´Conquest of the Communities´." AJS Review, v.6 (1981): 185-206.

761. Wistrich, Robert S.: "German Social Democracy and the Problem of Jewish Nationalism, 1897-1917." LBIYB, v.21 (1976): 109-142.

762. Zimmerman, Moshe: "Jewish Nationalism and Zionism in German-Jewish Student´s Organizations." LBIYB, v.27 (1982): 129-153.

The Destruction of German Jewry

763. Adam, Uwe D.: "Persecution of the Jews, Bureacracy and Authority in the Totalitarian State." LBIYB, v.23 (1978): 139-148.

> #396. Baron, S. W. and G. Wise: VIOLENCE AND DEFENSE.

764. Blau, Bruno: "The Jewish Population of Germany 1939-1945." JSS, v.12 #2 (Apr., 1950): 161-172.

765. Boas, Jacob: "German-Jewish Internal Politics under Hitler: 1933-1938." LBIYB, v.29 (1984): 3-25.

766. ___: "Germany or Diaspora? German Jewry´s Shifting Perceptions in the Nazi Era." LBIYB, v.27 (1982): 109-126.

767. Drutmann, D.: "The Displaced Jews in the American Zone in Germany." JJoS, v.3 #2 (Dec., 1961): 261-263.

768. Ebert, Hans: "The Expulsion of the Jews from the Berlin-Charlottenburg ´Technische Hochschule´." LBIYB, v.19 (1974): 155-171.

769. Edelheim-Muehsam, M. T.: "Reactions of the Jewish Press to the Nazi Challenge." LBIYB, v.5 (1960): 308-329.

770. Eschwege, Helmut: "Resistance of German Jews against the Nazi Regime." LBIYB, v.15 (1970): 143-180.

> #436. Fleming, G.: HITLER AND THE FINAL SOLUTION.

771. Freeden, Herbert: "A Jewish Theatre under the Swastika." LBIYB, v.1 (1956): 142-162.

772. Friedlander, Fritz: "Trials and Tribulations of Jewish Education in Nazi Germany." LBIYB, v.3 (1958): 187-201.

773. Friedlander, Henry: "The Deportation of the German Jews: Post-War German Trials of Nazi Criminals." LBIYB, v.29 (1984): 201-226.

774. Gaertner, H.: "Problems of Jewish Schools in Germany during the Hitler Regime." LBIYB, v.1 (1956): 123-141.

> #441. Gordon, S.: HITLER, GERMANS AND THE JEWISH QUESTION.

775. Grossman, Kurt R.: "Zionists and Non-Zionists under Nazi Rule in the 1930s." HYB, v.4 (1961/62): 329-344.

776. Gruenwald, Max: "The Beginning of the ´Reichsvertretung´." LBIYB, v.1 (1956): 57-67.

> #401. Janowski, O. and M. M. Fagen: INTERNATIONAL ASPECTS.

777. Kershaw, I.: "The Persecution of the Jews and German Popular Opinion in the Third Reich." LBIYB, v.26 (1981): 261-289.

778. Kwiet, K.: "The Ultimate Refuge: Suicide in the Jewish Community under the Nazis." LBIYB, v.29 (1984): 135-167.

779. Mathieu, G. B.: "The Secret Anti-Juden-Sondernummer of 21st May 1943." LBIYB, v.26 (1981): 291-300.

780. Milton, Sybil: "The Expulsion of Polish Jews from Germany October 1938 to July 1939: a Documentation." LBIYB, v.29 (1984): 169-199.

> #1325. Moore, B.: "Jewish Refugees in The Netherlands."

781. Pinson, K. S.: "Jewish Life in Liberated Germany." JSS, v.9 #2 (Apr., 1947): 101-126.

782. Rheins, Carl J.: "´Deutscher Vortrupp, Gefolgschaft deutscher Juden´: 1933-1935." LBIYB, v.26 (1981): 207-229.

783. ___ : "The ´Schwarzes Faehnlein, Jugenschaft´, 1932-1934." LBIYB, v.23 (1978): 173-197.

784. Rosenstock, Werner: "Exodus 1933-1939: a Survey of Jewish Emigration from Germany." LBIYB, v.1 (1956): 373-390.

785. Schiratzki, S.: "The ´Rykestrasse´ School in Berlin: a Jewish Elementary School during the Hitler Period." LBIYB, v.5 (1960): 299-307.

> #466. Schleunes, K. A.: THE TWISTED ROAD TO AUSCHWITZ.

786. Simon, E.: "Jewish Adult Education in Nazi Germany as Spiritual Resistance." LBIYB, v.1 (1956): 68-104.

787. Stahl, Rudolph: "Vocational Retraining of Jews in Nazi Germany 1933-1938." JSS, v.1 #2 (Apr., 1939): 169-194.

788. Strauss, Herbert: "Jewish Emigration from Germany: Nazi Policies and Jewish Responses." LBIYB, v.25 (1980): 313-361; v.26 (1981): 343-409.

789. Szanto, A.: "Economic Aid in the Nazi Era: the Work of the Berlin Wirtschafshilfe." LBIYB, v.4 (1959): 208-219.

790. Wischnitzer, Mark: "Jewish Emigration from Germany, 1933-1938." JSS, v.2 #1 (Jan., 1940): 23-44.

Communal Histories

791. Adler, Leo: "´Israelitische Religionsgemeinschaft´ of Wurttemberg: Its Development and Changes." LBIYB, v.5 (1960): 287-298.

792. Altmann, Berthold: "The Autonomous Federation of Jewish Communities in Paderborn." JSS, v.3 #2 (Apr., 1941): 159-188.

793. ___: "Jews and the Rise of Capitalism: Economic Theory and Practice in a Westphalian Community." JSS, v.5 #2 (Apr., 1943): 163-186.

794. Angress, W. T.: "Auswandererlehrgut Gross-Breesen." LBIYB, v.10 (1965): 168-187.

795. Bartys, Julian: "Grand Duchy of Poznan under Prussian Rule: Changes in the Economic Position of the Jewish Population 1815-1848." LBIYB, v.17 (1972): 191-204.

796. Barzilay, I. E.: "National and Anti-National Trends in the Berlin Haskalah." JSS, v.21 #3 (July, 1959): 165-192.

797. Birnbaum, Max P.: "On the Jewish Struggle for Religious Equality in Prussia, 1897-1914." LBIYB, v.25 (1980): 163-171.

798. Breslauer, Walter: "Jews of the City of Posen One Hundred Years Ago." LBIYB, v.8 (1963): 229-237.

799. Brilling, B.: "Jews in Breslau in the Sixteenth Century." JJS, v.3 #3 (1952): 119-126.

800. ___: "The Struggle of the ´Vaad Arba Arazot´ for the Jewish Right of Religious Worship in Breslau in the Seventeenth Century." Y/A, v.11 (1956/57): 163-187.

801. Cahnman, Werner J.: "The Decline of the Munich Jewish Community, 1933-38." JSS, v.3 #3 (July, 1941): 285-300.

802. Caron, Vicki: "The Social and Religious Transformation of Alsace-Lorraine Jewry, 1871-1914." LBIYB, v.30 (1985): 319-356.

803. Dicker, H.: CREATIVITY, HOLOCAUST, RECONSTRUCTION: JEWISH LIFE IN WUERTTEMBERG, PAST AND PRESENT. New York: Sepher-Hermon Press, 1984. 234 pp., illus., notes, app., gloss., bibliog., index.

Communal biography of the Jews in Wurttemberg, in western Germany during the nineteenth and twentieth centuries. Primary emphasis is on social history, and Dicker places the

community into the broad German Jewish context. As a result
of its isolated geographic position, Wurttemberg Jewry did
not experience the crisis of Jewish identity to the extent
that other, larger Jewish communities did in nineteenth-
century Germany. Traditional observances were maintained
until the Nazi era. Dicker describes the daily life of
Wurttemberg Jewry in Part I of his book, which is organized
thematically. This part also includes a chapter on the
Holocaust and a most interesting one on reconstruction after
the trauma. Part II deals with distinct individuals,
offering literary or scholarly selections from five famous
Wurttemberg Jews. These documents offer an insight into the
psyche of Wurttemberg Jews and also supplement Dicker's
text.

804. Galliner, A.: "The Philanthropin in Frankfurt: It's
Educational and Cultural Significance for German Jewry."
LBIYB, v.3 (1958): 169-186.

805. Halff, Sylvain: "The Jews of Alsace-Lorraine [1870-
1920]." AJYB, v.22 (1920/21): 53-79.

806. Harmelin, W.: "Jews in the Leipzig Fur Industry."
LBIYB, v.9 (1964): 239-266.

807. Jersch-Wenzel, S.: "The Jews as a Classic Minority
in Eighteenth and Nineteenth-Century Prussia." LBIYB, v.27
(1982): 37-49.

808. Kober, Adolf: "Documents Selected from the Pinkas of
Freidberg, a former Free City in Western Germany." PAAJR,
v.17 (1947/48): 19-59.

809. ___: COLOGNE. Trans. from the German by S. Grayzel.
Philadelphia: JPS, 1940. 412 pp., illus., apps., notes, bibliog., index.

History of Cologne Jewry from Roman to modern times; part
of the Jewish Publication Society communal history series.
About half the book deals with the medieval period, an equal
section covering the community in modern times. Organization is basically chronological, though many chapters deal
with specific themes. Although the book is supposed to cover
Cologne Jewry until the 1930s, the Nazis are never mentioned. In general, Kober's text is weakest when dealing
with the most recent events. As a result the book is outdated, but has not yet been superseded. The old communities

series still has much to offer, especially in methodological terms.

810. Lamberti, M.: "The Prussian Government and the Jews: Official Behaviour and Policy-Making in the Wilhelminian Era." LBIYB, v.17 (1972): 5-17.

811. Menes, A.: "The Conversion Movement in Prussia during the First Half of the Nineteenth Century." Y/A, v.6 (1951): 187-205.

812. Petuchowski, Jakob J.: "Frankfurt Jewry: a Model of Transition to Modernity." LBIYB, v.29 (1984): 405-417.

813. Poppel, S. M.: "The Politics of Religious Leadership: the Rabbinate in Nineteenth-Century Hamburg." LBIYB, v.28 (1983): 439-470.

814. Seeliger, Herbert: "Origin and Growth of the Berlin Jewish Community." LBIYB, v.3 (1958): 159-168.

815. Stein, Nathan: "Oberrat der Israeliten Badens, 1922-1937." LBIYB, v.1 (1956): 177-190.

816. Straus, Raphael: REGENSBURG AND AUGSBURG. Trans. from the German by Felix N. Gerson. Philadelphia: JPS, 1939. 261 pp., illus., map, notes, index.

Historical biography of two important Bavarian Jewish centers, part of the JPS community history series. Straus´s work is more analytical than the other volumes in the series and is based on extensive research into documentary sources. Deals primarily with the medieval period, although Straus concludes with the end of the nineteenth century. There is some usefulness to the comparative approach, especially for the inner life of the communities. Straus correctly distinguishes between the legal and actual situation of Bavarian Jewry and includes economic, religious, and political developments.

817. Strauss, H.: "Pre-Emancipation Prussian Policies towards the Jews 1815-1847." LBIYB, v.11 (1966): 107-136.

818. Strauss, Max: "The Jewish Community of Aachen Half a Century Ago." Y/A, v.4 (1949): 115-122.

NORWAY

819. Abrahamsen, Samuel: "The Exclusion Clause of Jews in the Norwegian Constitution of May 17, 1814." JSS, v.30 #2 (Apr., 1968): 67-88.

> #575. Elazar, D. J.: JEWISH COMMUNITIES OF SCANDINAVIA.

SWEDEN

> #575. Elazar, D. J.: JEWISH COMMUNITIES OF SCANDINAVIA.

820. Herz, Livia: "A Note on Identificational Assimilation Among Forty Jews in Malmo." JJoS, v.11 #2 (Dec., 1969): 165-173.

> #109. Katz, D.: "Menashe ben Israel´s Mission."

SWITZERLAND

> #101. Engelman, U. Z.: "Intermarriage among Jews."

> #445. Haesler, A. A.: THE LIFE BOAT IS FULL.

821. Kaufmann, Uri Robert: "Swiss Jewry: From the Jewish Village to the City 1780-1930." LBIYB, v.30 (1985): 283-299.

822. Stroock, Sol M.: "Switzerland and American Jews." PAJHS, #11 (1903): 7-52.

11

Eastern Europe and the Balkans

SURVEYS

823. Andreski, Stanislav: "An Economic Interpretation of Antisemitism in Eastern Europe." JJoS, v.5 #2 (Dec., 1963): 201-213.

824. "The Balkan Wars and the Jews." AJYB, v.15 (1913/14): 188-206.

> #62. Cohen, S. and P. Hyman: THE JEWISH FAMILY.

825. Dawidowicz, Lucy S. [ed.]: THE GOLDEN TRADITION: JEWISH LIFE AND THOUGHT IN EASTERN EUROPE. Boston: Beacon Press, 1967. 502 pp., maps, notes, index.

Anthology sketching East European Jewish life in all its variations. Includes an extensive introductory essay covering the broad lifestyle of East European Jewry. Primarily focused on the internal life of the Jewish community and on the role modern ideologies - hasidism, haskalah, zionism, and bundism - played in that life. Social and political history are both documented, with emphasis on the former. Many of the documents appear in English for the first time. All are introduced with brief data about the author and context.

826. Dubnow, Simon: HISTORY OF THE JEWS IN RUSSIA AND POLAND. Trans. from the Russian by I. Friedlaender. New York: Ktav, 1973 [Rep. of 1916/20 Ed.]. 1,253 pp., notes, bibliog., index.

Classic history of East-European Jewry from earliest times until 1920. Dubnow's emphasis is social history, and his main theme is the interaction of the Jewish community with the various governments. Chronological stress is on the nineteenth century. The breadth of Dubnow´s review is astounding, and covers virtually every aspect of Jewish life in that period. The best chapters deal with the inner life of East European Jewry, for example, the development of hasidism, the Haskalah in Russia, and the rise of Jewish nationalism. Although Dubnow expressed his own political orientation quite forcefully, he shows scholarly dispassion when dealing with controversial issues. The book is weakest on the subject of the twentieth century and is almost completely lacking in events after 1911. Unfortunately, Dubnow´s synthesis has not been replaced by a more recent overview and it appears likely that the book will continue to be the standard source for years to come.

> #135. Duker, A. and M. Ben-Horin: EMANCIPATION.

827. Elazar, Daniel J., H. P. Friedenreich, B. Hazzan and A. Weiss Liberles: THE BALKAN JEWISH COMMUNITIES: YUGO-SLAVIA, BULGARIA, GREECE AND TURKEY. Lanham, MD: University Press of America, 1983. 191 pp., notes.

Survey of the situation of the Jewish communities in the Balkans after World War II. Primary focus is on communal structures and organizations in the post-Holocaust period. Some important background information is provided to place the communities into context. Each country is surveyed separately by an expert on that Jewry. As part of a series on Jewish communal life and organization, all edited by Elazar, the essays present a very useful comparative study on Jewish life, organization, and community throughout the world.

CONTENTS: D. J. Elazar: The Sunset of Balkan Jewry / H. P. Friedenreich: The Jewish Community of Yugoslavia / Baruch Hazzan: The Jewish Community of Bulgaria / A. W. Liberles: The Jewish Community of Greece; The Jewish Community of Turkey.

828. Friedberg, Maurice: "Antisemitism as a Policy Tool in the Soviet Bloc." AJYB, v.71 (1970): 123-140.

> #385. Golub, J.: "JDC Health Programs in Eastern Europe."

829. Halevi, H. S.: "The Demography of Jewish Communities in Eastern Europe." JJoS, v.2 #1 (June, 1960): 103-109.

> #399. Henkin, L.: WORLD POLITICS AND THE JEWISH CONDITION.

> #388. Hertz, J. S.: "The Bund's Nationality Program."

830. Heschel, Abraham J.: "The Eastern European Era in Jewish History." Y/A, v.1 (1946): 86-106.

831. Hindus, Milton: A WORLD AT TWILIGHT: A PORTRAIT OF THE JEWISH COMMUNITIES OF EAST EUROPE BEFORE THE HOLOCAUST. New York: Jewish Book of the Month Club, 1973. 174 pp., bibliog.

Popular inquiry into East European Jewry before the Holo-caust. In some cases the text is an explanation for Lionel Reiss's artwork, which is itself a stunning memorial to a world that once was. Emphasis is on the day-to-day manifes-tations of Jewish life, with special reference to religion. The text is well written and is especially useful as an in-troduction to East European Jewry. Not a work of scholar-ship, the book can be seen as a memorial to the Jews who perished during the Holocaust.

832. Hundert, Gershon D. and Gershon C. Bacon: THE JEWS IN POLAND AND RUSSIA: BIBLIOGRAPHICAL ESSAYS. Bloomington: Indiana Univ. Press, 1984. 276 pp., bibliog.

Bibliographic survey covering almost 1,000 years of eastern European Jewish history. Divided into two parts: Part I, by Gershon D. Hundert, covers the period from 1100 to 1795 and divides the topic thematically. Part II, by Gershon C. Bacon, covers the period from 1795 to the present. Divided thematically, this section is also sub-divided by territory [Russia, Poland, and Russian-Poland]. In addition to the bibliographic material, the authors have written two bibliographic essays which review the literature and provide general background to the history of eastern European Jewry. The essays and the bibliographic citations complement each other, providing a good guide to the sources on East European Jewish history, although the lack of numbered citations and absence of an index may cause some difficulty in finding specific items.

> #400. Janowski, O.: JEWS AND MINORITY RIGHTS.

833. Kalish, Ita: "Life in a Hassidic Court in Russian Poland Toward the End of the 19th and the Early 20th Centu-ries." Y/A, v.13 (1965): 264-278.

834. Kohler, Max J. and S. Wolf: "Jewish Disabilities in the Balkan States: American Contributions toward their Removal, with particular Reference to the Congress of Berlin." PAJHS, #24 (1916): 1-153.

835. Laserson, Max M.: "The Jewish Minorities in the Baltic Countries." JSS, v.3 #3 (July, 1941): 273-284.

> #339. Lendvai, P.: ANTISEMITISM WITHOUT JEWS.

> #490. Levin, N.: WHILE MESSIAH TARRIED.

836. Loker, Zvi: "Balkan Jewish Volunteers in the Spanish Civil War." SJA, v.6 #2 (1976): 71-82.

837. Meltzer, Milton: WORLD OF OUR FATHERS: THE JEWS OF EASTERN EUROPE. New York: Farrar, Straus and Giroux, 1974. 274 pp., gloss., bibliog., index.

Synthetic history of East European Jewry from the eighteenth century to the years before World War I. The text is written in simple style and is particularly good for school use. Meltzer quotes extensively from primary and secondary sources, culled from both historical and fictional literature. The chapters are organized thematically, dealing with both internal and external history. Meltzer´s emphasis is on social and religious history. Events of the twentieth century after 1914 are covered in a brief afterword.

838. Mendelsohn, Ezra: THE JEWS OF EAST CENTRAL EUROPE BETWEEN THE WORLD WARS. Bloomington: Indiana Univ. Press, 1983. 300 pp., maps, notes, bibliographic essay, index.

Synthetic history of interbellum East European Jewry. Primary emphasis is on social and political history. Major subthemes include antisemitism, Jewish responses to persecution, zionism, internal political changes in the Jewish community, and the economic transformation of Jews in the post-World War I successor states. The problems of Jewish minority status, minority politics in states aspiring to single nationality, and the purpose and usefulness of the minority treaties are also presented from both Jewish and general perspectives. The book is organized by country, although Mendelsohn often makes cross-references to problems or issues that were common to all the Jewish communities. The chapter on Poland may be considered as the state of the art and is an authoritative synthesis. The other chapters are equally authoritative, if not quite as definitive. The comparative nature of Mendelsohn´s work makes it especially useful for serious students and scholars.

839. ___: "Recent Work on the Jews in Inter-war East-Central Europe: a Survey." SCJ, v.1 (1984): 316-337.

840. Meyer, Peter et al: THE JEWS IN THE SOVIET SATEL-LITES. Syracuse, NY: Syracuse Univ. Press, 1953. 637 pp., notes, tables, index.

Country-by-country survey of postwar East European Jewry. Designed as a supplement to Solomon Schwarz´s THE JEWS IN THE SOVIET UNION [see #1035]. The book contains a wealth of information on the state of East European Jewry under communism. The authors and editors have, wisely, also included information on prewar conditions. It is interesting to note that at the time of writing, it seemed that some form of Jewish life was possible in the Soviet-controlled People´s Republics. Events in Poland and Czechoslovakia have proved otherwise. Although overtaken by these more recent events, the book is still an important contribution to the study of post-Holocaust Jewish affairs.

CONTENTS: P. Meyer: Czechoslovakia / B. D. Weinryb: Poland; Polish Jews under Soviet Rule / E. Duschinsky: Hungary / N. Sylvain: Rumania / P. Meyer: Bulgaria.

841. Polonsky, A.: "Jews in Eastern Europe after World War II: Documents from the British Foreign Office." SJA, v.10 #1 (Feb., 1980): 52-70.

> #272. Roskies, D. K.: "Alphabet Instruction in the Heder."

842. Roskies, Diane K. and David G. Roskies: THE SHTETL BOOK. 2nd Edition. New York: Ktav, 1979. 327 pp., illus., maps, gloss., sources, indexes.

Survey of Jewish life in eastern Europe before World War I. Concentrates on the small Jewish communities of eastern Europe, the shtetls. The Roskies provide both a broad over-view and an intensive thematic study of shtetl lifestyles. Includes citations from a myriad of sources, with emphasis on the everyday life of ordinary Jews. Social history is the book´s primary emphasis; the controversial issues that cre-ated storms in the larger centers of Jewish life had almost no impact on shtetl life and are not cited.

843. Shulvass, M. A.: JEWISH CULTURE IN EASTERN EUROPE: THE CLASSICAL PERIOD. New York: Ktav, 1975. 180 pp., index.

Comprehensive survey of Jewish culture and scholarship in eastern Europe. Surveys the subject chronologically. Though centered on Torah study, a chapter also deals with Jewish interest in secular studies. The two great luminaries of the seventeenth century, Rabbi Solomon Luria [Maharshal] and Rabbi Moses Isserles [Rema], are seen as creators, though not the exclusive creators, of a massive efflorescence of Jewish culture. This culture was most strongly represented in the creativity of the Yeshivot - those in Lithuania as well as the Grand Yeshivah in Lublin - where hundreds of students daily pored over talmudic and rabbinic tomes. The seventeenth century is seen by Shulvass as a golden age. Throughout, the social and communal backdrop to Jewish culture is reviewed. Unfortunately, the book is not documented and contains no references to sources.

844. Strom, Yale and Brian Blue: THE LAST JEWS OF EASTERN EUROPE. New York: Philosophical Library, 1986. 51 pp. Text; 148 pp. of Photographs.

Illustrated documentary written as an elegy for East European Jewry. Strom and Blue remind readers of what was lost during the Holocaust by describing for us the remnants of 28 Jewish communities in Poland, Czechoslovakia, Russia, Hungary, Rumania, Bulgaria, and Yugoslavia. The once brilliant centers of a vibrant Jewish life are now empty shells. Nevertheless, the remaining Jews continue to live and, to an extent, practice as Jews. In light of that fact, the book is also a celebration of Jewish life in locales steeped in Jewish history. Foreword by George Schwab.

845. Szajkowski, Zosa: "The Alliance Israelite Univer-selle and East-European Jewry in the '60s." JSS, v.4 #2 (Apr., 1942): 139-160.

> #472. Tenenbaum, J.: "The Einsatzgruppen."

> #474. Trunk, Isaiah: JUDENRAT.

846. Vago, Bela and George L. Mosse [eds.]: JEWS AND NON-JEWS IN EASTERN EUROPE, 1918-1945. Jerusalem: Israel Univ. Press / New York: John Wiley and Sons, 1974. 334 pp., notes.

Collection of essays on twentieth-century East European

Jewry. Based on a University of Haifa colloquium held in May
1972. The main focus of the book is on the relations between
Jews and non-Jews. Each author approached the subject from
his own perspective, but political and social history are
the main methodologies. The essays are important contributions to the study of the above relations and Jewish foreign
affairs. More significantly, they provide the clear basis
for a comparative history dealing with the Jewish problem in
the post-World War I successor states of eastern Europe.

CONTENTS: S. Ettinger: Jews and Non-Jews in Eastern and
Central Europe between the Wars: an Outline / B. Vago: The
Attitude toward the Jews as a Criterion of the Left-Right
Concept / G. Barany: "Magyar Jew or Jewish Magyar?" Reflec-
tions on the Question of Assimilation / H. Seton-Watson: Two
Contrasting Policies toward Jews: Russia and Hungary / N.
Katzburg: The Jewish Question in Hungary during the Inter-
war Period - Jewish Attitudes / C. A. Macartney: Hungarian
Foreign Policy during the Interwar Period, with Special
Reference to the Jewish Question / Randolph L. Braham: The
Rightist, Horthy, and the Germans: Factors Underlying the
Destruction of Hungarian Jewry / S. Fischer-Galati: Fascism,
Communism, and the Jewish Question in Romania / Th. Lavi:
The Background to the Rescue of Romanian Jewry during the
Period of the Holocaust / G. Castellan: Remarks on the
Social Structure of the Jewish Community in Poland between
the Two World Wars / E. Mendelsohn: The Dilemma of Jewish
Politics in Poland: Four Responses / Yeshayahu Jelinek: The
Vatican, the Catholic Church, the Catholics and the Persecu-
tion of the Jews during World War II: the Case of Slovakia /
A. A. Greenbaum: Soviet Nationality Policy and the Problem
of the "Fluid" Nationalities / Y. Bauer: The Relations
between the American Jewish Joint Distribution Committee and
the Soviet Government, 1924-1938 / L. Schapiro: The Jewish
Anti-Fascist Committee and Phases of Soviet Antisemitic
Policy during and after World War II / A. Schochat: Jews,
Lithuanians and Russians, 1939-1941 / L. Yahil: Madagascar -
Phantom of a Solution for the Jewish Question.

> #179. Weiss, J.: STUDIES / EAST EUROPEAN JEWISH MYSTICISM.

> #90. Wischnitzer, M.: TO DWELL IN SAFETY.

847. Yaari, Abraham: "´Ner Tamid´ Societies in Poland and
Lithuania." JSS, v.21 #2 (Apr., 1959): 118-131.

848. Zborowski, Mark and Elizabeth Herzog: LIFE IS WITH PEOPLE: THE CULTURE OF THE SHTETL. New York: Schocken Books, 1952. 452 pp., bibliog., gloss., index.

Anthropological study of shtetl life before the Holocaust. Organized around the cycle of life in the shtetl. The book, however, is not a history, and the developmental aspects of East European Jewish culture are not discussed. This is not to imply that the book is of no use; rather the book must be viewed in its broader context. The book is especially useful for the source material gathered, which included nearly 200 interviews and oral histories; literary sources, including Yiddish literature of the nineteenth and twentieth centuries; and historical research.

BULGARIA

> #428. Chary, F. B.: BULGARIAN JEWS AND THE FINAL SOLUTION.

> #827. Elazar, D. J. et al: BALKAN JEWISH COMMUNITIES.

849. Gelber, N. M.: "Jewish Life in Bulgaria." JSS, v.8 #2 (Apr., 1946): 103-126.

> #840. Meyer, P. et al: THE JEWS IN THE SOVIET SATELLITES.

850. Oschlies, Wolf: "The Jews in Bulgaria since 1944." SJA, v.14 #2 (May, 1984): 41-54.

> #844. Strom, Y. and B. Blue: LAST JEWS OF EASTERN EUROPE.

851. Tamir, Vicki: BULGARIA AND HER JEWS: THE HISTORY OF A DUBIOUS SYMBIOSIS. New York: Sepher-Hermon for Yeshiva Univ. Press, 1979. 313 pp., illus., notes, apps., index.

Survey of Bulgarian Jewish history. Primary emphasis is on the modern period, and her main focus is on Bulgarian-Jewish relations. Tamir´s "Dubious Symbiosis" relates to the less virulent eruption of antisemitism in post-World War I Bulgaria. But Tamir sees this distinction as insignificant. That Bulgaria was unwilling to cooperate with the Nazi Final Solution did not, in Tamir´s estimation, derive from love of Jews but from fear of possible retaliation for obviously criminal behavior. The government is shown by Tamir to have been quite antisemitic, reflecting a clear current in Bulgarian society at the time. Tamir´s analysis of Bulgarian zionism is interesting, especially her discussion of zionism under the Communist regime. The mass aliyah of Bulgaria's Jews seems to bear out Tamir's contentions. Less convincing is Tamir's analysis of the Bulgarian psyche as relating to Jews. Her effort at psychoanalyzing the entire Bulgarian people does, however, highlight the difficulties inherent in psychohistory.

CZECHOSLOVAKIA

852. Baum, Karl: "Nazi Anti-Jewish Legislation in the Czech Protectorate: a Documentary Note." SJA, v.2 #1 (May, 1972): 116-128.

853. Cervinka, Frantisek: "The Hilsner Affair." LBIYB, v.13 (1968): 142-157.

854. Goldstuecker, Eduard: "Jews between Czechs and Germans around 1848." LBIYB, v.17 (1972): 61-71.

855. Jelinek, Yeshayahu: "The Jews in Slovakia, 1945-1949." SJA, v.8 #2 (1978): 45-56.

> #142. Katz, J.: TOWARD MODERNITY.

856. Kestenberg-Gladstein, Ruth: "Differences of Estates within Pre-Emancipation Jewry: a Study in the Social Structure of Bohemian Provincial Jewry." JJS, v.5 #4 (1954): 156-166; v.6 #1 (1955): 35-49.

857. Kieval, Hillel: "In the Image of Hus: Refashioning Czech Judaism in Post-Emancipatory Prague." MJ, v.5 #2 (May, 1985): 141-157.

858. Lion, Jindrich: THE PRAGUE GHETTO. Photographs by J. Lukas; Trans. from the Czech by J. Layton. London: Spring Books, 1959. 96 + 36 pp. of illustrations.

Illustrated history of the Prague ghetto, with emphasis on the folk history of Prague Jewry. The book is primarily a description, with very little analysis. Prague Jewry is evoked sympathetically. Lion graphically describes the quality of Jewish life in pre-Holocaust Prague, details the destruction of Czech Jewry, and ends with the efforts to rebuild after the trauma. Although Jewish communal life has, for all intents and purposes, ended in Czechoslovakia since

1968, the sites of the old ghetto remain; some have been
converted into museums, others are commemorated by monu-
ments. Lion's book is a fitting eulogy to the life and death
of Prague Jewry.

859. Meissner, Frank: "German Jews of Prague: a Quest for
Self-Realization." PAJHS, v.50 #2 (Dec., 1960): 98-120.

> #838. Mendelsohn, E.: JEWS OF EAST CENTRAL EUROPE.

> #840. Meyer, P. et al: THE JEWS IN THE SOVIET SATELLITES.

> #459. Morley, J. F.: VATICAN DIPLOMACY AND THE JEWS.

860. Moskowitz, Moses: "The Jewish Situation in the Protectorate of Bohemia-Moravia." JSS, v.4 #1 (Jan., 1942):
17-44.

861. Newman, A.: "The Expulsion of the Jews from Prague
in 1745 and British Foreign Policy." TJHSE, v.22 (1968/69):
30-41.

862. Riff, Michael A.: "Assimilation and Conversion in
Bohemia: Secession from the Jewish Community in Prague 1868-
1917." LBIYB, v.26 (1981): 73-88.

> #102. Schmelz, U.: JEWISH POPULATION STUDIES.

863. Society for the History of Czechoslovak Jews, The:
THE JEWS OF CZECHOSLOVAKIA: HISTORICAL STUDIES AND SURVEYS.
3 vols. Philadelphia: JPS, [1968]: 583 pp., [1971]: 705 pp.,
[1983]: 700 pp., illus., notes, indexes.

Anthology of historical essays covering the Jewish experience in modern Czechoslovakia. Every aspect of Jewish
life and Jewish participation in Czech society is covered.
Special emphasis is on social and communal history, but
intellectual and political history are also reviewed. The
first two volumes cover independent Czechoslovakia. Volume
III deals with the Nazi era, the Holocaust, and postwar efforts at reconstruction. As with any anthology of this
scope, the essays are not all uniformly interesting, although the vast majority are of high scholarly caliber.

CONTENTS: [Volume I]. Guido Kisch: Jewish Historiography in
Bohemia, Moravia, Silesia / H. Kohn: Before 1918 in the
Historic Lands / R. Kestenberg-Gladstein: The Jews between

Czechs and Germans in the Historic Lands, 1848-1918 / Livia
Rothkirchen: Slovakia: 1848-1938 / Aryeh Sole: Subcarpathian
Ruthenia: 1918-1938/ A. M. Rabinowicz: The Jewish Minority /
G. Fleischmann: The Religious Congregation, 1918-1938 / H.
Stransky: The Religious Life in the Historic Lands / J. C.
Pick: The Economy / Egon Hostovsky: Participation in Modern
Czech Literature / Petr Den: A Note on Egon Hostovsky / A.
Dagan: Jewish Themes in Czech Literature / H. Zohn: Partici-
pation in German Literature / A. Dagan: The Press / Meir
Faerber: Publishing Houses / Paul Nettl: Music.
[Volume II]. C. Roth: My Friendship with O. K. Rabinowicz /
Th. K. Rabb: The Oeuvre of Dr. Oscar K. Rabinowicz / O. K.
Rabinowicz: Czechoslovak Zionism: Analecta to a History / I.
Polak: The Zionist Women's Movement / E. Hostovsky: The
Czech-Jewish Movement / G. Hirschler: The History of Agudath
Israel in Slovakia, 1918-1939 / S. Goshen: Zionist Students'
Organizations / J. C. Pick: Sports / Meir Faerber: Jewish
Lodges and Fraternal Orders Prior to World War II / J. W.
Bruegel: Jews in Political Life / A. M. K. Rabinowicz: The
Jewish Party / H. Stransky: The Religious Life in Slovakia
and Subcarpathian Ruthenia / Ch. Yahil: Social Work in the
Historic Lands / A. Sole: Modern Hebrew Education in Sub-
carpathian Ruthenia / F. Weltsch: Realism and Romanticism:
Observations on the Jewish Intelligentsia of Bohemia and
Moravia / Jan Ehrenwald: On the So-called Jewish Spirit /
Hana Volavkova: Jewish Artists in the Historic Lands / Frank
Reichenthal: Jewish Art in Slovakia: a Personal Recollec-
tion / Z. Muenzer: The Old-New Synagogue in Prague: Its
Architectual History / R. Teltscher: The Altschul Synagogue
in Mikulov / S. J. Harendorf: The Yiddish Theater in
Czechoslovakia / E. Barkany: Jewish Cemeteries in Slovakia /
Kurt R. Grossman: Refugees to and from Czechoslovakia / M.
George: Refugees in Prague, 1933-1938 / F. Brada: Emigration
to Palestine / A. Zwergbaum: From Internment in Bratislava
and Detention in Mauritius to Freedom.
[Volume III]. From the Munich Agreement to the Communist
Takeover in Czechoslovakia: Chronology of Events 1938-1948 /
Livia Rothkirchen: The Jews of Bohemia and Moravia: 1938-
1945 / J. G. Lexa: Anti-Jewish Laws and Regulations in the
Protectorate of Bohemia and Moravia / Z. Lederer: Terezin /
L. Lipscher: The Jews of Slovakia: 1939-1945 / E. Kulka: The
Annihilation of Chechoslovak Jewry; Jews in the Czechoslovak
Armed Forces during World War II / A. Dagan: The Czecho-
slovak Government-in-Exile and the Jews / Kurt Wehle: The
Jews in Bohemia and Moravia: 1945-1948 / Y. Jelinek: The
Jews in Slovakia: 1945-1949 / Ehud Avriel: Prague and
Jerusalem: the Era of Friendship / Hana Volavkova: The

Jewish Museum of Prague / J. C. Pick: The story of the Czech scrolls.

864. Steiner, Max: "The Rise and Fall of a Jewish Community in Bohemia." Y/A, v.12 (1958/59): 247-258.

> #844. Strom, Y. and B. Blue: LAST JEWS OF EASTERN EUROPE.

> #252. Urzidil, J.: "Living Contribution of Jewish Prague."

865. Wischnitzer, Mark: "Origins of the Jewish Artisan Class in Bohemia and Moravia 1500-1648." JSS, v.16 #4 (Oct., 1954): 335-350.

866. Zwergbaum, Aaron: "Czechoslovak Jewry in 1979." SJA, v.10 #3 (Nov., 1980): 29-46.

GREECE

867. Benaroya, Abraham: "A Note on ´The Socialist Federation of Saloniki´." JSS, v.11 #1 (Jan., 1949): 69-72.

> #223. Crews, C. M.: "The Vulgar Pronunciation of Hebrew."

> #827. Elazar, D. J.: BALKAN JEWISH COMMUNITIES.

868. Gelber, Nathan M.: "An Attempt to Internationalize Salonika." JSS, v.17 #2 (Apr., 1955): 105-120.

869. Rodrigue, Aron: "Jewish Society and Schooling in a Thracian town: the Alliance Israelite Universelle in Dmotica 1897-1924." JSS, v.45 #3/4 (Sum./Fall, 1983): 263-286.

870. Starr, J.: "The Socialist Federation of Saloniki." JSS, v.7 #4 (Oct., 1945): 323-336.

HUNGARY

Overviews

871. Benoschofsky, I.: "The Position of Hungarian Jewry After the Liberation." HJS, v.1 (1966): 237-260.

> #584. Jenks, W. A.: "Jews in the Habsburg Empire."

> #585. Kann, R. A.: "German-Speaking Jewry."

872. Kann, Robert A.: "Hungarian Jewry during Austria-Hungary´s Constitutional Period [1867-1918]." JSS, v.7 #4 (Oct., 1945): 357-386.

873. Katzburg, N.: "Hungarian Jewry in Modern Times: Political and Social Aspects." HJS, v.1 (1966): 137-170.

874. ___: "The Jewish Congress of Hungary, 1868-1869." HJS, v.2 (1969): 1-33.

875. Marton, Erno: "The Family Tree of Hungarian Jewry: Outline of the History of the Jewish Settlement in Hungary." HJS, v.1 (1966): 1-59.

> #838. Mendelsohn, E.: JEWS OF EAST CENTRAL EUROPE.

> #840. Meyer, P. et al: THE JEWS IN THE SOVIET SATELLITES.

> #844. Strom, Y. and B. Blue: LAST JEWS OF EASTERN EUROPE.

> #846. Vago, B. an G. Mosse: JEWS AND NON-JEWS.

Education and Culture

876. Adler, P. J.: "The Introduction of Public Schooling for the Jews of Hungary [1849-1860]." JSS, v.36 #2 (Apr., 1974): 118-133.

877. Balla, Erzsebet: "The Jews of Hungary: a Cultural Overview." HJS, v.2 (1969): 85-136.

878. Handler, A.: FROM THE GHETTO TO THE GAMES: JEWISH ATHLETES IN HUNGARY. Boulder, CO: East European Monographs, 1985. 140 pp., bibliog., index.

Revisionist history of Jewish participation and contribution to the world of sport. The book contains no reference notes, but is obviously well documented. Handler gives a basically chronological exposition. The subject of sports can also be seen as a barometer of Jewish accommodation to the local culture. Hence, Hungarian-Jewish athletes were both Magyars and Jews - a dual identity, but one that downplayed Jewishness as the overriding category. A most interesting section is on Hungarian Jewish participation in the

1936 Berlin Olympics; another deals with Jewish athletes in postwar Hungary. Overall the book is an interesting effort and makes a contribution to a little-known field of Jewish history. Unfortunately, the focus is a bit too narrow to provide any broad conclusions about Jews and sports in general.

879. Heller, Imre and Zsigmond Vajda: THE SYNAGOGUES OF HUNGARY: AN ALBUM. Edited by Randolph L. Braham and Ervin Farkas. New York: Diplomatic Press for World Federation of Hungarian Jews, 1968. 197 pp., illus., geographical list of illus., index, bibliog.

Memorial album for the synagogues of Hungary and, by ex- tension, for Hungarian Jewry as a whole. The text is in English, Hebrew, and Magyar. Synagogues are classified by architectural style; these are arranged chronologically. Most of the illustrations show only the synagogue exteriors, though some interiors are included. A historical review ties the various styles together and also deals with the aesthetics of synagogue decoration. A geographic list, broken down by style and era, allows relatively easy access to those seeking specific synagogues or styles.

880. Karady, V.: "Jewish Enrollment Patterns in Classical Secondary Education in old Regime and Inter-war Hungary." SCJ, v.1 (1984): 225-252.

> #142. Katz, J.: TOWARD MODERNITY.

881. McCagg, William O.: JEWISH NOBLES AND GENIUSES IN MODERN HUNGARY. New York: Columbia Univ. Press, 1973. 254 pp., tables, notes, bibliographic essays, index.

Historical and sociological study of the Jewish nobles of Hungary during the nineteenth and twentieth centuries. Attempts to see the Jewish notables in three contexts: their Jewish role, the reasons behind their will to become nobles, and their role in Hungarian culture. The book pinpoints a very interesting phenomenon among late nineteenth-century Hungarian Jews - intensive assimilation, as represented by the nobles, coexisting with a fundamentalist religious orientation, e.g., Hungarian hasidism. McCagg surveys the relations between Jews and Hungary's old regime; he tends to deemphasize the role fascism and antisemitism played in Hungarian history. The Magyarization of Hungarian Jewry is very clearly spelled out in McCagg's text, although the result of this process requires further elucidation in light of post-World War I conditions.

Sociology and Demography

882. Don, Yehuda and George Magos: "The Demographic Development of Hungarian Jewry." JSS, v.45 #3/4 (Sum./Fall, (1983):189-216.

883. Laszlo, Erno: "Hungarian Jewry: Settlement and Demography 1735-38 to 1910." HJS, v.1 (1966): 61-136.

884. ___: "Hungary´s Jewry: a Demographic Overview, 1918-1945." HJS, v.2 (1969): 137-182.

> #104. Vago, B.: JEWISH ASSIMILATION IN MODERN TIMES.

885. Veghazi, Istvan: "The Role of Jewry in the Economic Life of Hungary." HJS, v.2 (1969): 35-84.

The Jewish Question

886. Braham, Randolph L.: "The Jewish Question in German-Hungarian relations during the Kallay Era." JSS, v.39 #3 (Sum. 1977): 183-208.

887. Garai, George: "Hungary´s Liberal Policy and the Jewish Question, with a Note on Rakosi." SJA, v.1 #1 (June, 1971): 101-107.

888. Katzburg, Nathaniel: HUNGARY AND THE JEWS: POLICY AND LEGISLATION 1920-1943. Ramat-Gan, Israel: Bar-Ilan Univ. Press, 1981. 299 pp., notes, bibliog., index.

Surveys the relation of the Jewish community with the Hungarian government during the Fascist era. Primary focus is on Hungarian law dealing with Jews. Jewish responses and foreign reactions to Hungarian antisemitism are also reviewed. Katzburg concludes that Hungarian Jewry-policy must be divided into four periods: first, 1919-1921, an era of counterrevolution; second, the Bethlen era of 1921-1931; third, the premiership of Gombos from 1932 to 1938; and fourth, 1938-1943, when Hungarian Jewry was effectively disenfranchised. In each era the situation of Hungarian Jewry deteriorated as the government increasingly legislated the

Jewish community out of existence. The book is especially useful in providing background for understanding the Holocaust experience in Hungary. A number of documents are appended, which provide the sources for the views analyzed in the text.

889. Klein, Bernard: "Anti-Jewish Demonstrations in Hungarian Universities, 1932-1936: Istvan Bethlen vs. Gyula Gombos." JSS, v.44 #2 (Spr., 1982): 113-124.

890. ___: "Hungarian Politics and the Jewish Question in the Interwar Period." JSS, v.28 #2 (Apr., 1966): 79-98.

891. Kovacs, Janos: "Neo-Antisemitism in Hungary." JSS, v.8 #3 (July, 1946): 147-160.

The Holocaust

892. Braham, Randolph L.: "The Destruction of the Jews of Carpatho-Ruthenia." HJS, v.1 (1966): 223-235.

893. Cohen, Asher: "Continuity in the Change: Hungary, 19 March 1944." JSS, v.46 #2 (Spr., 1984): 131-144.

894. Vago, Bela: "The Destruction of the Jews of Transylvania." HJS, v.1 (1966): 171-221.

Communal Histories

895. Dicker, Herman: PIETY AND PERSEVERANCE: JEWS FROM THE CARPATHIAN MOUNTAINS. New York: Sepher-Hermon Press, 1981. 226 pp., illus., notes, app., bibliog., index.

Journalistic but documented history of the Jews of the Hungarian Carpathians. The book is divided into two parts. Part I, "History," is a chronological review of the story of the Jewish communities in the Hungarian Carpathians. Part II, "The People," contains reminiscences, documents, and snapshots of life in the region. The book is pervaded by a sense of nostalgia, which weakens the author's objectivity. The historical section is the best part of the book, containing many interesting bits of information. Though he has written an interesting book, Dicker nevertheless proves the dearth of serious scholarship on some aspects of modern Jewish history. Foreword by Elie Wiesel.

LATVIA

> #1019. Aronson, G.: RUSSIAN JEWRY, 1917-1967.

896. Levin, D.: "The Jews and the Sovietisation of Latvia 1940-41." SJA, v.5 #1 (1975): 39-56.

> #838. Mendelsohn, E.: JEWS OF EAST CENTRAL EUROPE.

LITHUANIA

> #424. Arad, Yitzhak: GHETTO IN FLAMES.

> #1019. Aronson, G.: RUSSIAN JEWRY, 1917-1967.

897. Cohen, Israel: VILNA. Philadelphia: JPS, 1943. 571 pp., Illus., notes, bibliog., index.

Communal biography of the "Jerusalem of Lithuania," part of the Jewish Publication Society community history series. The book is also a contribution to the history of the Jews in Lithuania in general, from the mid-fourteenth century to the Nazi period. Arranged chronologically, although some of the chapters are thematic in nature. Social and religious issues get the most systematic coverage, with economics, politics, and intellectual history given fair treatment as well. The book may be divided into three parts. First, the era of Lithuanian independence [to 1793]; second, Russian Vilna [1793-1914]; third, post-World War I Vilna [1914-1943]. A separate chapter is devoted to the history of Lithuanian karaism and the relations between Karaites and Rabbinites. The Holocaust in Vilna, so far as it was known in 1943, is reviewed in an epilogue by the author.

898. Friedman, Mark: "The Kehillah in Lithuania, 1912-1926: a Study Based on Panevezys and Ukmerge [Vilkomir]." SJA, v.6 #2 (1976): 83-103.

899. Gringauz, S.: "Jewish National Autonomy in Lithuania [1918-1925]." JSS, v.14 #3 (July, 1952): 225-246.

900. Lestchinsky, Jacob: "The Economic Struggle of the Jews in Independent Lithuania." JSS, v.8 #4 (Oct., 1946): 267-296.

> #454. Levin, Dov: FIGHTING BACK.

901. Levin, Dov: "The Jews and the Election Campaigns in Lithuania, 1940-41." SJA, v.10 #1 (Feb., 1980): 39-51.

902. ___: "Jews in the Soviet Lithuanian Forces in World War II: the Nationality Factor." SJA, v.3 #1 (1973): 57-64.

903. ___: "The Jews in the Soviet Lithuanian Establishment, 1940-41." SJA, v.10 #2 (May, 1980): 21-37.

> #838. Mendelsohn, E.: JEWS OF EAST CENTRAL EUROPE.

904. Rabinowitsch, Wolf: "Karlin Hasidism." Y/A, v.5 (1950): 123-151.

905. ___: LITHUANIAN HASIDISM FROM ITS BEGINNINGS TO THE PRESENT DAY. Trans. from the Hebrew by M. B. Dagut. New York: Schocken Books, 1971. 263 pp., illus., notes, app., gloss., index.

Study of the development of hasidism in Lithuania, based on original documentation from the genizah of the Karliner hasidim. Rabinowitsch's focus is on the struggles of the zaddikim to establish themselves in Lithuania and on the relations between hasidim and mitnagdim. The book is organized around the two main branches of Lithuanian hasidism: the Karliner and the Amdurer. Four smaller hasidic dynasties in Polesia, Libeshei, Berezna, and Horodek are also reviewed. The book charts the growth, successes, and failures of the dynasties from their founding through the nineteenth century and to their destruction by the Nazis. In light of the loss of most of the primary sources on which this study is based, the magnitude of Rabinowitsch's scholarly contribution is even more significant. Foreword by Simon Dubnow.

906. Salmon, Yosef: "The Yeshiva of Lida: a Unique Institution of Higher Learning." Y/A, v.15 (1974): 106-125.

907. Trunk, Isaiah: "The Council of the Province of White Russia." Y/A, v.11 (1956/57): 188-210.

> #210. Ury, Zalman: THE MUSAR MOVEMENT.

> #846. Vago, B. and G. Mosse: JEWS AND NON-JEWS.

> #847. Yaari, A.: "Ner Tamid Societies."

POLAND

Overviews

908. Abramsky, Chimen et al [eds.]: THE JEWS IN POLAND.
New York: B. Blackwell, 1986. 264 pp., maps, notes, index.

Anthology based on a conference on Polish-Jewish studies
held at Oxford University in September 1984. The essays
cover the gamut of Polish Jewish history, from the earliest
settlements to Communist Poland. Each essay was prepared by
a reputable scholar and expert in the field of Polish-Jewish
history. Noteworthy are the essays by Ezra Mendelsohn and
Yisrael Gutman, both of which deal with historiography as
well as history. Some of the essays, particularly that of
Wladyslaw Bartoszewski, contain an apologetic undertone in
trying to exculpate Poles from the onus of antisemitism and
partial responsibility for the Holocaust. As a whole, the
book is an important and interesting contribution to the
study of Polish Jewish history.

CONTENTS: A. Gieysztor: The beginnings of Jewish settlement
in the Polish lands / D. Tollet: Merchants and businessmen
in Poznan and Cracow, 1588-1668 / J. Goldberg: The privi-
leges granted to Jewish communities of the Polish Commonwealth as a stabilizing factor in Jewish support / Gershon
Hundert: The implications of Jewish economic activities for
Christian-Jewish relations in the Polish Commonwealth / A.
Ciechanowiecki: A footnote to the history of the integration
of converts into the ranks of the szlachta in the Polish-
Lithuanian Commonwealth / S. Kieniewicz: Polish society and
the Jewish problem in the nineteenth century / D. Beauvois:
Polish-Jewish relations in the territories annexed by the
Russian Empire in the first half of the nineteenth century /
R. Bender: Jews in the Lublin region prior to the January
uprising, 1861-1862 / F. Golczewski: Rural antisemitism in
Galicia before World War I / Joseph Lichten: Notes on the
assimilation and acculturation of Jews in Poland 1863-1943 /
E. Mendelsohn: Interwar Poland: good for the Jews or bad for
the Jews? / J. Holzer: Relations between Polish and Jewish
left wing groups in interwar Poland / W. Bartoszewski:
Polish-Jewish relations in occupied Poland, 1939-1945 / T.
Prekerowa: The Relief Council for Jews in Poland 1942-1945 /
Y. Gutman: Polish and Jewish historiography on the question
of Polish-Jewish relations during World War II / M. Borwicz:
Polish-Jewish relations, 1944-1947 / Lukasz Hirszowicz: The
Jewish issue in post-war Polish Communist politics.

909. Fishman, Joshua [ed.]: STUDIES ON POLISH JEWRY 1919-1939. New York: YIVO Institute for Jewish Research, 1974. English Section: 294 pp., notes; Yiddish Section: 537 pp., documents, notes, bibliog.

Collection of essays on pre-Holocaust Polish Jewry. Primary emphasis is on the social life of the Jewish community and the interplay between Jews and Poles. The book is bilingual; half the essays are in English and half in Yiddish. Of the English essays, Pawel Korzec´s on antisemitism is almost a book in itself, representing the single most intensive but brief analysis on the subject published to date, while Leonard Rowe´s on Jewish self-defense breaks new ground in a little-known field of Jewish history. The same holds true for Shimshon Tapuach´s Yiddish essay on Jewish farming. Unfortunately the book lack summaries of the Yiddish essays, which limits the audience to those who are able to read Yiddish. Then too, the idiosyncratic pagination [separate for the English and Yiddish sections] can make citation confusing. These minor problems detract nothing from the significant contributions to Jewish history collected here.

CONTENTS: J. A. Fishman: Minority Resistance: Some Comparisons between Interwar Poland and Postwar U.S.A. / P. Korzec: Antisemitism in Poland as an Intellectual, Social and Political Movement / L. Rowe: Jewish Self-Defense: a Response to Violence / Zosa Szajkowski: Western Jewish Aid and Intercession for Polish Jewry, 1919-1939 / C. S. Heller: Poles of Jewish Background: the Case of Assimilation without Integration in Interwar Poland / E. Lifschutz: Selected Documents Pertaining to Jewish Life in Poland, 1919-1939.

> #832. Hundert, G. and G. Bacon: JEWS OF RUSSIA AND POLAND.

910. Lewin, Isaac: THE JEWISH COMMUNITY IN POLAND: HISTORICAL ESSAYS. New York: Philosophical Library, 1985. 247 pp., notes, index, map.

A valuable collection of essays on the history of the Jews of Poland. The thousand-year history is reviewed in a very simple and often picturesque style. Some of the essays are broad reviews dealing with communities and institutions; others deal with individual Jews, their communities, and the government. Most of the essays involve social history. Lewin has insights into almost every era of Polish-Jewish history before the Holocaust. Although his analysis of events in the twentieth century presents the particular viewpoint

of Agudas Israel, Lewin is not apologetic and is willing to
discuss modern Polish-Jewish relations in a forthright
manner. His essay "The Political Orientation of Agudas
Israel" is a good summary of the Orthodox political position
during the interwar era and places the party's position into
context.

911. Marcus, Joseph: SOCIAL AND POLITICAL HISTORY OF THE
JEWS IN POLAND, 1919-1939. New York: Mouton Pub., 1983. 569
pp., tables, app., notes, bibliog., index.

Important contribution to the historiography of Polish
Jewry. Marcus concentrates on social and political history,
with emphasis on the former. Social structure, institutions,
demography, and the social policy of Polish Jewry are all
elucidated, as are the social and economic standing of Jews
within Polish society. The section on political history is a
straight chronological survey of the Jewish question in independent Poland. An especially interesting chapter reviews
the ideology and history of the major Jewish parties active
in Poland. Special attention in this chapter is focused on
the Zionist parties, although all parties are discussed.
Polish antisemitism and Jewish responses are a major subtheme of Marcus's study. In particular he discusses economic
features of antisemitism and its political manifestations.
Marcus's chapter dealing with the political situation on the
eve of the Second World War is interesting, but runs counter
to the generally accepted interpretation. Whether Marcus's
revisions will be accepted remains to be seen, but the
entire work is carefully documented and is a useful contribution to Polish-Jewish history.

> #838. Mendelsohn, E.: JEWS OF EAST CENTRAL EUROPE.

912. Rabinowicz, Harry M.: THE LEGACY OF POLISH JEWRY: A
HISTORY OF POLISH JEWS IN THE INTERWAR YEARS, 1919-1939. New
York: Thomas Yoseloff, 1965. 256 pp., illus., notes, gloss.,
bibliog., index.

Elegy and historical review of interbellum Polish Jewry.
Covers both political and social history. The author writes
from an Orthodox and Zionist perspective. Despite this
orientation, Rabinowicz is objective in his analysis of the
variety of Jewish parties. Polish Jewry is described with a
sense of nostalgia, but without filial pietism. Rabinowicz
sees Polish governmental policies as exclusively, consistently, and consciously antisemitic. This thesis has some

merits, but is considerably overstated. True, the government was largely oriented toward establishing "Poland for the Poles." But Polish governmental antisemitism was never a consistently applied policy and was often distorted to suit the needs of the moment. Also posits that the ease with which the Nazis destroyed Polish Jewry is indicative of a long-standing Polish antisemitic tradition, a thesis which is probably true.

913. Vishniac, Roman: A VANISHED WORLD. New York: Farrar, Strauss and Giroux, 1983. 179 pp.

Photographic kaleidoscope of pre-Holocaust Polish Jewry. Aptly titled, the book portrays the manifestations of Jewish life in Poland that were destroyed by Nazi Germany. The book is not a work of scholarship, but is nevertheless compelling evidence that a picture is truly worth a thousand words. Most of the photos are annotated to explain both subject and context. Foreword by Elie Wiesel.

Jews in the Polish Commonwealth

914. Balaban, Majer: "Jews in Cracow at the Time of the Confederacy of Bar 1768-72." Y/A, v.5 (1950): 9-30.

915. Duker, Abraham G.: "Polish Frankism's Duration: From Cabbalistic Judaism to Roman Catholicism and from Jewishness to Polishness. a Preliminary Investigation." JSS, v.25 #4 (Oct., 1963): 287-233.

916. Hundert, Gershon: "An Advantage to Peculiarity?: the Case of the Polish Commonwealth." AJS Review, v.6 (1981): 21-38.

917. ___: "Jewish Urban Residence in the Polish Commonwealth in the Early Modern Period." JJoS, v.26 #1 (June, 1984): 25-34.

918. ___: "Jews, Money and Society in the Seventeenth-Century Polish Commonwealth: the Case of Krakow." JSS, v.43 #3/4 (Sum./Fall, 1981): 261-274.

919. Kremer, Moses: "Jewish Artisans and Guilds in Former Poland, 16th-18th Centuries." Y/A, v.11 (1956/57): 211-242.

920. Ruderman, David: "Three Contemporary Perceptions of a Polish Wunderkind of the Seventeenth Century." AJS Review, v.4 (1979): 143-163.

921. Shatzky, Jacob: "An Attempt at Jewish Colonization in the Kingdom of Poland." Y/A, v.1 (1946): 44-63.

922. Stanley, John: "The Politics of the Jewish Question in the Duchy of Warsaw, 1807-1813." JSS, v.44 #1 (Wint., 1982): 47-62.

923. Weinryb, Bernard D.: THE JEWS OF POLAND: A SOCIAL AND ECONOMIC HISTORY OF THE JEWISH COMMUNITY IN POLAND FROM 1100 TO 1800. Philadelphia: JPS, 1972. 424 pp., tables, apps., notes, bibliog., index.

Broad history of Polish Jewry from its origins through the eighteenth century. Primarily focused on social and economic history, but intellectual, religious, and political currents are also discussed. The best chapters deal with social trends, legal status, and economics. The chapter on the Shabbatean heresy is probably the weakest. Weinryb's discussion of the Cossack massacres, known as "Gezerot tah vetat," is interesting and contains important methodological insight. The book is well documented and remains a useful survey.

Public Affairs

924. Bacon, Gershon: "The Politics of Tradition: Agudat Israel in Polish Politics, 1916-1939." SCJ, v.2 (1985): 144-163.

925. Cohen, I.: "Documents: My Mission to Poland [1918-1919]." JSS, v.13 #2 (Apr., 1951): 149-172.

> #135. Duker, A. and M. Ben-Horin: EMANCIPATION.

926. Gelber, N. M.: "A Jewess' Memoirs of the Polish Uprising of 1863." Y/A, v.13 (1965): 243-263.

927. Glicksman, Wm. M.: "The Halutz Ideology and Experience as Reflected in the Yiddish Novel in Poland 1919-1939." Y/A, v.14 (1969): 270-284.

928. ___: JEWISH SOCIAL WELFARE INSTITUTIONS IN POLAND AS DESCRIBED IN THE MEMORIAL [YIZKOR] BOOKS. Philadelphia: M. E. Kalish Folkshul, 1976. 177 pp., bibliog., notes, indexes.

Investigation of Jewish social and communal activity in interwar Poland. Social welfare institutions are charted in light of the role they played in Jewish life. Relations between these institutions and the kehillah are also reviewed [see #929]. Glicksman draws upon unusual sources. Instead of relying on archival material, almost all of which was destroyed by the Nazis and is thus no longer available, Glicksman relied on the 34 Yizkor Bicher dealing with Polish Jewry that were available in the mid-1970s. Yizkor Bicher are memorial volumes written by or for the organization of survivors or emigrants from a given locality, primarily in eastern Europe. Although containing much dross and a considerable amount of unsubstantiated material, the Yizkor Bicher also convey vital information on the genesis of the communities, how Jews lived before the Nazi onslaught, their hardships, tribulations, and sufferings under Nazi rule, and finally, how they and their communities were ground to dust. Glicksman's introduction, "Yizkor Books as a Source for Historical Studies," could thus be the most important part of the book. The kind of information Glicksman uncovered clearly shows the potentially fruitful results of his approach. Foreword by Solomon Grayzel.

929. ___: A KEHILLAH IN POLAND DURING THE INTERWAR YEARS: STUDIES IN JEWISH COMMUNITY ORGANIZATION. Philadelphia: M. E. Kalish Folkshul, 1969. 155 pp., notes, index, gloss.

Studies the history and organization of the kehillah in interwar Poland. Based on the minute book, or pinkas, of the Czestochowa kehillah, part of which was saved from the Nazis by Glicksman. As with his other work [see #928], the specific information gleaned is less important than the use to which it is put. In this case the pinkas is used as a source of information on social, political, and economic conditions, or as reference material to explain the organization and operations of a typical Polish kehillah. The kehillot functioned as autonomous Jewish communities, filling all Jewish needs in social, educational, and welfare services. The kehillot were legally recognized, albeit begrudgingly, by the Polish government, and their right to exist was guaranteed by the Polish constitution and the Minority Treaties Poland signed with the League of Nations. In light of the historical importance of the kehillah and his analysis of rare and little-known sources, Glicksman has made a notable and important contribution.

930. Heller, Celia S.: "´Anti-Zionism´ and the Political Struggle within the Elite of Poland." JJoS, v.11 #2 (Dec., 1969): 133-150.

931. ___: "Assimilation: a Deviant Pattern among the Jews of Interwar Poland." JJoS, v.15 #2 (Dec., 1973): 221-237.

932. Johnpoll, Bernard K.: THE POLITICS OF FUTILITY: THE GENERAL JEWISH WORKERS BUND OF POLAND 1917-1943. Ithaca, NY: Cornell Univ. Press, 1967. 298 pp., notes, bibliog., index.

Political study of the bund, the Jewish Marxist national-ist labor party. Johnpoll attempts to explore the workings of the party within its historical, cultural, and political context. His approach is to review key doctrinal issues that arose from 1897 to 1945. Issues such as Jewish nationalism, zionism, emigration, antisemitism, and communism are viewed from the perspective of Bundist ideology. Although sympa-thetic to the Bund, Johnpoll is critical of some aspects of Bund policy, especially as they relate to communism. Even so, the book is an objective and well-organized investiga-tion of Bundist ideology and practice. Johnpoll´s chapter on the Holocaust is interesting although extremely one-sided. The futility of Bundist politics, according to Johnpoll, was that this fundamentally powerless party concentrated on issues of ideological purity rather than on the attainment of power; for lack of any practical political activity the Bund, in essence, reduced itself to a Socialist debating society.

933. Mendelsohn, Ezra: "The Politics of Agudas Yisroel in Interwar Poland." SJA, v.2 #2 (1972): 47-60.

934. ___: ZIONISM IN POLAND: THE FORMATIVE YEARS, 1915-1926. New Haven, CT: Yale Univ. Press, 1981. 373 pp., map, notes, gloss., bibliog., index.

Comprehensive study of Polish zionism. This volume is part of a more encompassing review of zionism in interwar Poland. Concentrates primarily on social and political his-tory, although the ideological orientation of the various Zionist parties is also discussed. Special emphasis is placed on the role of aliyah in both the ideology and praxis of Polish zionism. Mendelsohn attempts to place Polish

Zionist activity into its specifically Polish and Jewish contexts, including Polish politics during the 1920s. An introductory chapter places Polish zionism into its broader sociopolitical context and also traces the rise of other forms of Jewish nationalism. Two appendixes deal with the interaction of Polish nationalism with zionism, and with the Polish-Zionist view of the Arab problem.

* 935. ___: ZIONISM IN THE JEWISH COMMUNITY OF POLAND DURING THE TWENTIES. Tel-Aviv: Tel Aviv Univ. Press, 1982. 23 pp., notes.

> #545. Shavit, Y.: "Politics and Messianism."

936. Szajkowski, Zosa: "The German Ordinance of November 1916 on the Organization of Jewish Communities in Poland." PAAJR, v.34 (1966): 111-139.

> #846. Vago, B. and G. Mosse: JEWS AND NON-JEWS.

Sociology

937. Bronsztejn, S.: "The Jewish Population of Poland in 1931." JJoS, v.6 #1 (July, 1964): 3-29.

938. Czekanowski, Jan: "Anthropological Structure of the Jewish People in the Light of Polish Analyses." JJoS, v.2 #2 (Nov., 1960): 236-243.

939. Lestchinsky, Jacob: "Aspects of the Sociology of Polish Jewry." JSS, v.28 #4 (Oct., 1966): 195-211.

940. ___: "Economic Aspects of Jewish Community Organization in Poland." JSS, v.9 #4 (Oct., 1947): 319-338.

941. ___: "The Industrial and Social Structure of the Jewish Population of Interbellum Poland." Y/A, v.11 (1956/1957): 243-269.

942. ___: "The Jews in the Cities of the Republic of Poland." Y/A, v.1 (1946): 156-177.

943. Mahler, Raphael: "Jews in Public Service and the Liberal Professions in Poland, 1918-39." JSS, v.6 #4 (Oct., 1944): 291-350.

> #102. Schmelz, U.: JEWISH POPULATION STUDIES.

944. Shatzky, Jacob: "Institutional Aspects of Jewish Life in Warsaw in the Second Half of the 19th Century." Y/A, v.10 (1955): 9-44.

945. ___: "Warsaw Jews in the Polish Cultural Life of the Early 19th Century." Y/A, v.5 (1950): 41-54.

> #104. Vago, B.: JEWISH ASSIMILATION IN MODERN TIMES.

946. Weinryb, Bernard D.: "Studies in the Communal History of Polish Jewry." PAAJR, v.12 (1942): 121-140; v.15 (1945): 93-129.

947. ___: "Texts and Studies in the Communal History of Polish Jewry." PAAJR, v.19 (1950): 1-110.

948. Zelkovitch, Joseph: "A Picture of the Communal Life in a Jewish Town in Poland in the Second Half of the Nineteenth Century: the Association Ose Hesed in Lutomiersk." Y/A, v.6 (1951): 253-266.

The Jewish Question in Poland

949. Blejwas, Stanislaus A.: "Polish Positivism and the Jews." JSS, v.46 #1 (Wint., 1984): 21-36.

950. Cang, Joel: "The Opposition Parties in Poland and Their Attitude Towards the Jews and the Jewish Problem." JSS, v.1 #2 (Apr., 1939): 241-256.

> #329. Duker, A. G.: "Emigre Christian Socialists."

951. Duker, Abraham G.: "The Polish Democratic Society and the Jewish Problem, 1832-1846." JSS, v.19 #3/4 (July/ Oct., 1958): 99-112.

952. ___: "The Polish Insurrection's Missed Opportunity: Mochnacki's Views on the Failure to Involve the Jews in the Uprising of 1830-31." JSS, v.28 #4 (Oct., 1966): 212-232.

953. Heller, Celia S.: ON THE EDGE OF DESTRUCTION: JEWS OF POLAND BETWEEN THE TWO WORLD WARS. New York: Schocken Books, 1980. 369 pp., illus., notes, index.

Interesting but flawed study of Polish Jewry in the crisis years before World War II. Quite useful for her review of Polish antisemitism and Jewish responses, Heller represents one of only a few books dealing seriously with the history of Polish Jewry. Heller's sociological viewpoint, however, leads to several problematic interpretations. Most significantly, Heller sees Polish Jewry as a caste - the pariah or untouchable - in Polish society, which she identifies as a distinctly stratified society. To a degree Poland can be seen this way; however, the social hierarchy in Poland differed from the Hindu caste system. In Poland Jews represented a clear national minority within the body if a nation seeking to define itself. As a result of internal conditions and of economic realignments produced by the loss of Russian and German markets after 1919, Poles became more narrowly ethnocentric. The results of the aforementioned crises led Polish nationalists to attempt to eliminate Jews from Polish life during the twentieth century. This process had begun before World War I, but was accelerated and intensified during the interwar era. Jews, as a relatively powerless national minority, were unable to influence the broad Polish population; in general they lacked reliable allies and could not create a coalition that would accede to their needs. But any attempt to create a parallel to conditions in India does not fully explain the depth of the crisis and misses the point.

> #315. Lestschinsky, J.: "The Anti-Jewish Program."

954. Rothenberg, Joshua: "The Przytyk Pogrom." SJA, v.16 #2 (May, 1986): 29-46.

Culture and Education

> #212. Cooperman, B.: JEWISH THOUGHT IN THE 16TH CENTURY.

955. Eck, Nathan: "The Educational Institutions of Polish Jewry [1921-1934]." JSS, v.9 #1 (Jan., 1947): 3-32.

956. Eisenstein, Miriam: JEWISH SCHOOLS IN POLAND, 1919-39: THEIR PHILOSOPHY AND DEVELOPMENT. New York: King's Crown Press, 1950. 112 pp., map, notes, tables, bibliog., index.

Investigation of Jewish schools in interwar Poland, attempting to place them into political and social context. The two main school systems, the Bundist Central Yiddish

School Organization [CYSHO] and the Zionist Tarbut, are
studied in detail. In both cases ideological orientations,
curriculums, and teacher qualifications are elucidated. The
Orthodox school system and the small number of bilingual
schools [Hebrew-Yiddish and Hebrew-Polish] are also studied,
but in less detail than the other schools. The Jewish school
systems are also placed in the context of Polish minority
policies and Polish law. The Polish education law in 1932
and its effect in reforming Jewish education is briefly
covered, as is fundraising. Eisenstein's conclusion places
the Jewish school system into communal and social context.

957. Mahler, Raphael: HASIDISM AND THE JEWISH ENLIGHTEN-
MENT: THEIR CONFRONTATION IN GALICIA AND POLAND IN THE FIRST
HALF OF THE NINETEENTH CENTURY. Trans. from the Yiddish by
E. Orenstein, and from the Hebrew [Part II] by A. and J. M.
Klein. Philadelphia: JPS, 1985. 411 pp., notes, index.

Social, economic, and intellectual study of the clash between hasidim and maskilim in nineteenth-century Galicia and
Congress Poland. Relations between the two groups are viewed
from both a social and political perspective [e.g., their
relations with the governments - Austrian or Russian]. Dealing with social and intellectual movements, Mahler lays his
greatest stress on the socioeconomic factors that led to the
transformation of East European Jewry. Part of a broader
organic series of works - most of which have not yet appeared in English translation - dealing with the socioeconomic bases of modern Jewry. Unfortunately contains no
bibliography, although the notes detail the extensive documentation on which the book is based.

958. Shtern, Yehiel: "A Kheyder in Tyszowce [Tishevits]."
Y/A, v.5 (1950): 152-171.

> #847. Yaari, A.: "Ner Tamid Societies."

The Holocaust

> #423. Apenzslak, J. et al: THE BLACK BOOK OF POLISH JEWRY.

* 959. Bernfes, A. B.: THE WARSAW GHETTO NO LONGER EXISTS.
London: Orbis Pub., 1973. 64 pp., illus.

> #430. Engel, D.: "An Early Account of Polish Jewry."

960. Fass, Moshe: "Theatrical Activities in the Polish Ghettos during the Years 1939-1942." JSS, v.38 #1 (Wint., 1976): 54-72.

> #444. Gutman, Y.: THE JEWS OF WARSAW.

> #450. Krakowski, S.: THE WAR OF THE DOOMED.

> #780. Milton, S.: "The Expulsion of Polish Jews."

> ##459. Morley, J. F.: VATICAN DIPLOMACY AND THE JEWS.

> #471. Tec, N.: WHEN LIGHT PIERCED THE DARKNESS.

> #475. WARSAW GHETTO UPRISING.

The Polish People's Republic

961. Banas, Josef: THE SCAPEGOATS: THE EXODUS OF THE REM-NANTS OF POLISH JEWRY. Trans. from the Polish by T. Szafar; Edited by L. Kochan. New York: Holmes & Meier, 1979. 271 pp., illus., notes, index.

Important inquiry into the purge of Polish Jewry that occurred after the Six-Day War. Antisemitism was used by the Polish government, according to Banas, as a way to divert attention from the real problems facing the country. Banas also relates the antisemitic campaign in Poland to similar abuses of power, e.g., the victimization of Jews in the Soviet Union. Placing the Jewish question into the broad context of totalitarian power politics, Banas offers a new and disturbing insight into the continuing threats to Jewish survival after the Holocaust.

962. Bronsztejn, Szyja: "A Questionnaire Inquiry into the Jewish Population of Wroclaw." JJoS, v.7 #2 (Dec., 1965): 246-275.

963. Checinski, M.: "The Kielce Pogrom: Some Unanswered Questions." SJA, v.5 #1 (1975): 57-72.

964. ___: POLAND, COMMUNISM, NATIONALISM, ANTISEMITISM. New York: Karz-Cohl, 1982. 289 pp., notes, apps., index.

Convincing revisionist history of Polish Jewry after the Holocaust. Intertwines the fate of Polish Jewry, the rise of

the Polish Communists, and the development of the Polish
police state. Checinski also charts the use of nationalism
and the distortion of nationalist symbols by the Communist
regime. Most interesting from the Jewish perspective is
Checinski´s hypothesis that the postwar antisemitic campaign, which culminated in the Kielce pogrom, has been in-
correctly blamed on the Armja Krajowa [the anti-Communist
Polish underground]. Actually, according to Checinski, the
pogroms were coordinated by the Communist secret police. The
purpose of this cynical use of antisemitism was to discredit
the non-Communists and pave the way for the Communist takeover. The success of this campaign convinced the leaders
that antisemitism could be used as a lever to regulate the
tensions in Polish society. The government exploited these
nationalist and antisemitic sentiments during the crises of
both 1956 and 1968. One might add that events surrounding
the suppression of the Solidarity movement in late 1981,
though not part of Checinski´s account, are the clearest
proof for the plausibility of his thesis.

965. Dobroszycki, Lucjan: "Restoring Jewish Life in Postwar Poland." SJA, v.3 #2 (1973): 58-72.

966. Hirszowicz, L.: "Antisemitism in Today´s Poland."
SJA, v.12 #1 (Feb., 1982): 55-65.

> #840. Meyer, P. et al: THE JEWS IN THE SOVIET SATELLITES.

967. Niezabitowska, Malgorzata: REMNANTS: THE LAST JEWS
OF POLAND. Trans. from the Polish by Wm. Brand and Hanna
Dobosiewicz; Photographs by Tomasz Tomaszewski. New York:
Friendly Press, 1986. 272 pp., illus., chron.

Journalistic eulogy of Polish Jewry, written by a Polish
journalist. The accompanying photographs were taken by her
husband, Tomasz Tomaszewski. Both were involved with the
Solidarity movement and became interested in the state of
current Polish Jewry as a result of the government´s use of
antisemitism to discredit the independent trade union movement. The book can be summed up in one quote: "There are no
young Jews in Poland anymore." Much of the book comprises
interviews with the few Polish Jews that remain, and here
and there a snippet of direct historical information comes
out. By no means scholarly, the book is a eulogy for what
once was, and a look at what is now, Polish Jewry.

> #Strom, Y. and B. Blue: LAST JEWS OF EASTERN EUROPE.

968. Szafar, Tadeusz: "´Endecized´ Marxism: Polish Communist Historians on Recent Polish Jewish History." SJA, v.8 #1 (1978): 57-71.

Communal Histories

969. Shneiderman, S. L.: THE RIVER REMEMBERS. New York: Horizon Press, 1978. 192 pp., illus., bibliog.

Memoir-history of Jewish life in prewar Poland. The book is written as a memorial to the destroyed Jewish communities of central Poland and places the shtetl of Kazimierz at its center. Shneiderman adopts a journalistic approach, interspersing his own story with that of the shtetl and of Polish Jewry as a whole. As such, Shneiderman provides both his own personal heritage and a worthy epitath for Polish Jewry.

970. Twersky, Isadore [ed.]: DANZIG, BETWEEN EAST AND WEST: ASPECTS OF MODERN JEWISH HISTORY. Cambridge: Harvard Univ. Press, 1985. 172 pp., illus., notes.

Anthology of scholarly papers on the importance of Danzig for Jewish history. The essays were taken from a continuing symposium held at Harvard University in conjunction with the Jewish Museum´s Danzig exhibit. Danzig is viewed as both a small and almost peripheral Jewish community, and as a connecting point between East and West European Jewry. As the latter, Danzig was something of a melting pot for developments of Jewish art, literature, and ideology. Thus it was at Danzig that Russian Jews first came into contact with Reform Judaism and Western Jews first came into contact with their more narrowly "Jewish" cousins. Danzig also was a conduit for Zionist ideology, spreading ideas in eastern and western Europe. Unfortunately, none of the essays provides a history of Danzig Jewry per se, although all are important contributions to such a history.

CONTENTS: I. Bartal: The Image of German Jewry in East European Jewish Society during the 19th Century / Y. Cohen: Problems of Western European Jews in the 20th Century: a Comparative Study of Danzig and Paris / Jacob Katz: From Ghetto to Zionism, Mutual Influences of East and West / Sid Z. Leiman: R. Israel Lipschutz and the Portrait of Moses Controversy / M. A. Meyer: The German Model of Religious Reform and Russian Jewry / S. Prawer: The Death of Sigismund Markus: the Jews of Danzig in the Fiction of Guenter Grass /

M. J. Rosman: Polish Jews in the Gdansk Trade in the Late
17th and Early 18th Centuries / Joseph Salmon: The Rise of
Jewish Nationalism on the Border of Eastern and Western
Europe: Rabbi Z. H. Kalischer, David Gordon, Peretz
Smolenskin / I. Schorsch: Art as Social History: Moritz
Oppenheim and the German Jewish Vision of Emancipation.

RUMANIA

971. Eskenasy, Victor: "A Note on Recent Romanian Historiography on the Jews." SJA, v.15 #3 (Nov., 1985): 55-60.

> #435. Fisher, J. S.: "How Many Died in Transnistria."

972. Gelber, N. M.: "The Problem of the Rumanian Jews at
the Bucharest Peace Conference, 1918." JSS, v.12 #3 (July,
1950): 223-246.

973. Lachower, Abraham: "Jewish Burial Associations in
Moldavia in the Eighteenth and the Beginning of the Nineteenth Centuries." Y/A, v.10 (1955): 300-319.

974. Lavi, Theodor: "Jews in Rumanian Historiography of
World War II." SJA, v.4 #1 (1974): 45-52.

975. Levin, Dov: "The Jews and the Inception of Soviet
Rule in Bukovina." SJA, v.6 #2 (1976): 52-70.

> #838. Mendelsohn, E.: JEWS OF EAST CENTRAL EUROPE.

> #840. Meyer, P. et al: THE JEWS IN THE SOVIET SATELLITES.

976. Millman, Ivor: "Romanian Jewry: a Note on the 1966
Census." SJA, v.2 #1 (May, 1972): 105-110.

> #459. Morley, J. F.: VATICAN DIPLOMACY AND THE JEWS.

977. Schwarzfeld, E.: "The Jews of Moldavia at the Beginning of the Eighteenth Century." JQR, v.16 #1 (Oct., 1903):
113-134.

978. ___: "The Jews of Roumania: From the Earliest Times
to the Present Day." AJYB, v.3 (1901/02): 25-62.

979. ___: "The Situation of the Jews in Roumania Since
the Treaty of Berlin, 1878." AJYB, v.3 (1901/02): 63-87.

980. Starr, Joshua: "Jewish Citizenship in Rumania: 1878-1940." <u>JSS</u>, v.3 #1 (Jan., 1941): 57-80.

981. ___: ROMANIA: THE JEWRIES OF THE LEVANT AFTER THE FOURTH CRUSADE. Paris: Editions du Centre, 1949. 123 pp., bibliographic note, app., notes, plates, index.

Inquiry into the history of the Jews of the Levant after the thirteenth century. Reviews both internal and external affairs. The book is organized by territory, and an attempt to place Jews into a broader historical context is made. Starr saw the thirteenth century as a turning point in the history of the Jews in the Near East and the Balkans. Before the Ottoman Empire extended its rule over these areas, Jews lived under the heel of less than friendly Christian governments. When the Byzantine Empire reached the point of disintegration as a result of the Crusades, Jews had to cope with new social and economic conditions, a process that Starr documents within the constraints of available documentary evidence.

> #844. Strom, Y. and B. Blue: LAST JEWS OF EASTERN EUROPE.

> #104. JEWISH ASSIMILATION IN MODERN TIMES.

982. Vago, Bela: "The Jewish Vote in Romania between the Two World Wars." <u>JJoS</u>, v.14 #2 (Dec., 1972): 229-244.

> #846. ___ and G. Mosse: JEWS AND NON-JEWS.

YUGOSLAVIA

983. Alcalay, I.: "The Jews of Serbia." <u>AJYB</u>, v.20 (1918/19): 75-87.

> #827. Elazar, D. J.: THE BALKAN JEWISH COMMUNITIES.

984. Friedenreich, Harriet P.: THE JEWS OF YUGOSLAVIA: A QUEST FOR COMMUNITY. Philadelphia: JPS, 1979. 323 pp., maps, illus., apps., notes, bibliog., index.

Social history of interwar Yugoslav Jewry. Friedenreich's primary interest is the Jewish quest to create a viable identity, a minority wedged between the two competing majority groups in Yugoslav society. The problem of establishing the parameters of Jewish existence was complicated by the unique and divided nature of the country. The Serb and Croat pluralities had little in common; disliked and distrusted each other; and distrusted the Jewish minority even more. Jews were almost always isolated and continually accused of dual loyalty by both sides. During the war Nazi Germany was able to enlist many local volunteers for the task of murder, who accomplished their goal with grisly efficiency.

Friedenreich attempts to place these currents into a communal context. First she reviews the major Jewish communities of Sarajevo, Belgrade, and Zagreb. Thereafter, community structure is detailed. Finally the relations between Jews and the government are charted. Foreign-policy concerns and their influence on the rise of Yugoslav anti-semitism in the 1930s are also reviewed. The Nazi extermination of Yugoslav Jewry is covered in an epilogue, which also details the immigration of a majority of the survivors to Israel and the United States.

985. ___: "Sephardim and Ashkenazim in Interwar Yugoslavia: Attitudes toward Jewish Nationalism." PAAJR, v.44 (1977): 53-80.

> #459. Morley, J. F.: VATICAN DIPLOMACY AND THE JEWS.

> #844. Strom, Y. and B. Blue: LAST JEWS OF EASTERN EUROPE.

12

The Union of Soviet
Socialist Republics/Russia

SURVEYS

986. Baron, Salo W.: THE RUSSIAN JEW UNDER TSARS AND
SOVIETS. 2nd Edition. New York: Macmillan, 1976. 468 pp.,
notes, index.

Surveys Russian Jewry's crises and achievements over 200
years. Internal and external factors are integrated, as are
political, social, and intellectual trends. The approach is
basically chronological. The sources are quite varied and
some are analyzed in-depth. Baron's basic theme is the ability of Russian Jews to survive - as Jews - despite the apathetic position of both Tsarist and Communist bureauc-
racies and the virtual destruction of Jewish institutions.
Baron's chapter on the Holocaust is one of few systematic
studies on the subject available in English. The revival of
Russian Jewry after World War II and the apparent vitality
of a national minority lacking national institutions leads
Baron to a guardedly optimistic conclusion about the
possible future of these "new Marranos."

987. Israel, Gerald: THE JEWS IN RUSSIA. Trans. from the
Russian by S. L. Chernoff. New York: St. Martin's Press,
1974. 329 pp., notes, chron.

Brief survey of the Jewish problem in Russia, with primary emphasis on the Communist period. The book attempts to
survey the political, social, and economic history, but is
too narrowly focused to represent a full history of Russian
Jewry. Israel's focus is on antisemitism and oppression, and
on Jewish efforts to counteract both of them. Most impor-
tantly Israel had access to files of the Alliance Israelite

255

Universelle and to testimonies by Jewish emigrants from Russia, which give his book a unique and somewhat useful viewpoint.

> #373. Levine, D.: DIASPORA.

TSARIST RUSSIA

Overviews

> #908. Abramsky, Ch.: THE JEWS OF POLAND.

> #85. Berger, D.: THE LEGACY OF JEWISH MIGRATION.

> #826. Dubnow, S.: HISTORY OF THE JEWS / RUSSIA AND POLAND.

 * 988. Feldman, E.: THE RUSSIAN JEWS IN 1905 THROUGH THE EYES AND CAMERA OF A BRITISH DIPLOMAT. Tel Aviv: Tel Aviv Univ. Press, 1986. 55 pp., Hebrew summary, illus., notes.

989. Frumkin, Jacob et al [eds.]: RUSSIAN JEWRY: 1860-1917. New York: Th. Yoseloff, 1966. 492 pp., notes, index.

Anthology surveying Russian Jewish history from the great reforms of Tsar Alexander II to the Russian revolutions of 1917. Some of the essays are purely historical, others cover specific themes. Unfortunately, Russian antisemitism of this era is not given separate treatment. On the other hand the essays on the inner life of Russian Jewry break new ground. Dijur´s discussion of Jewish economic life and Trunk´s essay on Jewish historiography are especially important contributions to their respective fields. The importance of Russian Jewry for the development of world Jewry, for example, in the zionist context, is a major subtheme. A further volume surveyed Russian Jewish history to the mid-1960s [see #1019].

CONTENTS: M. Aldanov: Russian Jews of 1870s and 1880s / J. G. Frumkin: Pages from the History of Russian Jewry / A. Goldenweiser: Legal Status of Jews in Russia / I. M. Dijur: Jews in the Russian Economy / G. Aronson: Ideological Trends Among Russian Jews / G. Swet: Russian Jews in Zionism and in the Building of Palestine / Itzhak Ben-Zvi: Labor Zionism in Russia / S. Kucherov: Jews in the Russian Bar / Gregor Aronson: Jews in Russian Literary and Political Life / G. Swet: Russian Jews in Music / R. Wischnitzer: The Russian

Jew in Art / Judel Mark: Yiddish Literature in Russia / I.
M. Klausner: Literature in Hebrew in Russia / N. Menes:
Yeshivas in Russia / I. Trotzky: Jews in Russian Schools;
Jewish Institutions of Welfare, Education, and Mutual Assis-
tance / M. Osherovich: Russian Jews in the United States /
I. Trunk: Historians of Russian Jewry / Mark Wischnitzer:
Reminiscences of a Jewish Historian.

990. Greenberg, Louis: THE JEWS IN RUSSIA: THE STRUGGLE
FOR EMANCIPATION. New York: Schocken Books, 1976. 423 pp.,
notes, bibliog., indexes.

History of the Jewish problem in Russia from the eighteenth century to the rise of communism. Surveys the basic
elements of the problem, as well as its underlying causes,
from both Jewish and Russian perspectives. Primary focus is
on the failure of the Haskalah in Russia to effect any
fundamental changes in Jewish status, and on the subsequent
channeling of Jewish activism into the quest for salvation
through assimilation, emigration, revolution, and zionism.
The various Jewish parties and their ideologies are fairly
presented, and Greenberg remains neutral throughout. The
book actually comprises two volumes, bound as one. Volume I
covers the years between 1772 and 1880, and volume II covers
1881 through 1917. The original editions were published by
Yale University Press, in 1944 and 1951 respectively. Edited
by Mark Wischnitzer with a foreword by Alfred Levin.

991. Korzec, Pawel: "Three Documents of 1903-1906 on the
Russian Jewish Situation." SJA, v.2 #2 (1972): 75-86.

992. Levitats, Isaac: THE JEWISH COMMUNITY IN RUSSIA,
1772-1844. New York: Octagon Books, 1970 [Rep. of 1943 Ed.].
300 pp., illus., tables, notes, bibliog., index.

Documentary study of Jewish autonomy in Russia during the
late eighteenth and early nineteenth centuries. Autonomy is
studied through the agency of the kahal and its associated
hevrot. The book is divided into three sections. First,
kahal relations with the government; second, kahal organization; and third, kahal functions. The chapters in these sections are organized thematically. Levitats ended his study
with 1844, since that was the year when the tsarist government ordered the disbanding of all autonomous Jewish structures. Although they officially disbanded, the kehillot
continued to function in the guise of voluntary social
welfare agencies, but this is not reviewed by Levitats. His

review of Russian legislation on Jewish affairs in the
period offers the necessary background for an understanding
of Russian antisemitism in the tsarist period. Also significant is Levitats´s contribution to the study of Jewish
autonomy on the communal level in modern times.

> #678. Wertheimer, J.: "Between Tsar and Kaiser."

> #90. Wischnitzer, M.: TO DWELL IN SAFETY.

Public Affairs

> #395. Aronsfeld, C. C.: "Jewish Bankers and the Tsar."

 * 993. Frankel, J.: JEWISH POLITICS AND THE RUSSIAN REVOLU-
TION OF 1905. Tel-Aviv: Tel Aviv Univ. Press, 1982. 21 pp.

 994. ___: PROPHECY AND POLITICS. New York: Cambridge
Univ. Press, 1981. 686 pp., illus., notes, bibliog., index.

Social and political study of the influence of both nationalism and socialism on the political parties of Russian
Jewry that developed after 1881-1882. Frankel opens by explaining the roots of the Russian Jewish ideological crisis
engendered by the pogroms. Although all factions knew that
emancipation was impossible under the status quo, they differed fundamentally on the question of how best to achieve
self-emancipation. Their divergent views on the matter led
to the rise of two political ideologies. As they crystallized, the positions became mutually exclusive. One trend
emerged as the Algemeyner Yidisher Arbeter Bund in Lite,
Poyln un Rusland, the other as zionism. However, as Frankel
points out, zionism too developed a Socialist trend, as
represented by Ber Borochov and Nachman Syrkin. Frankel´s
study centers on the ways that politics modified ideology as
a result of changed circumstances between 1907 and 1917. The
Revolution of 1905 had led to an unsuccessful emancipation
in Russia, while the reaction after 1907 led to a reordering of Jewish priorities. The Bolshevik takeover and
the Balfour Declaration further polarized Jewish Socialists,
forcing them to choose between nationalism and assimilation
in the name of internationalism.

 995. Goldstein, Joseph: "Some Sociological Aspects of the
Russian Zionist Movement at its Inception." JSS, v.47 #2
(Spr., 1985): 167-178.

996. Lambroza, Shlomo: "Jewish Self-Defence During the Russian Pogroms of 1903-1906." JJoS, v.23 #2 (Dec., 1981): 123-134.

997. Mendelsohn, Ezra: CLASS STRUGGLE IN THE PALE: THE FORMATIVE YEARS OF THE JEWISH WORKERS´ MOVEMENT IN TSARIST RUSSIA. New York: Cambridge Univ. Press, 1970. 180 pp., notes, bibliog., index.

Social and political study of the formative years of the Bund in Russia. Focused primarily, though not exclusively, on the Socialist Jewish intelligentsia and their role in creating a mass Jewish Socialist movement. Mendelsohn is careful to chart the shift from propaganda to agitation in both ideology and praxis. A separate chapter is devoted to the strike movement and to Jewish workers´ aims and tactics. Relations with other groups, Socialist and non-Socialist, Jewish and non-Jewish, are also detailed. Mendelsohn ends his account with 1905, by which time the Bund had crystallized into the General Jewish Workers´ Union of East European Jewry. In brief but astute chapters, without polemic and with careful documentation, Mendelsohn reviews inner dissension among the Bund´s factions as well as the Bund´s opposition to zionism and its position in relation to the Russian Socialists.

998. ___: "Jewish and Christian Workers in the Russian Pale of Settlement." JSS, v.30 #4 (Oct., 1968): 243-251.

999. ___: "The Russian Jewish Labor Movement and Others." Y/A, v.14 (1969): 87-98.

1000. Mishkinski, Moshe: "Regional Factors in the Formation of the Jewish Labor Movement in Czarist Russia." Y/A, v.14 (1969): 27-52.

1001. Schwartz, P.: "Revolutionary Activities of the Jewish Labor Bund in the Czarist Army." Y/A, v.13 (1965): 227-242.

1002. Tobias, Henry J.: THE JEWISH BUND IN RUSSIA FROM ITS ORIGINS TO 1905. Stanford, CA: Stanford Univ. Press, 1972. 409 pp., notes, bibliog., index.

Studies the Jewish Socialist Nationalist Party from 1897 to 1905. Most of Tobias´s attention is given to the Bund´s relations with other Socialist and non-Socialist parties,

both Jewish and general. A second theme is the understanding
of the Bund in its specifically Jewish context. In light of
these two themes, ideological issues tend to be discussed
more extensively than social or economic ones. Little is
said about the interactions between the Bund and Polish
Socialist Nationalists, and the discussion of Lenin´s rejection of Bundist claims for Jewish national autonomy and
the withdrawal of the Bund from the larger Russian Social-
Democratic Party, is sketchy. On the other hand, the Bund
polemic against zionism, and the Zionist counter-polemic, is
extensively treated.

> #495. ___ and C. E. Woodhouse: "The Jewish Bund in 1905."

The Jewish Question

1003. Berk, S. M.: "The Russian Revolutionary Movement and
the Pogroms of 1881-1882." SJA, v.7 #2 (1977): 22-39.

1004. ___ : YEAR OF CRISIS, YEAR OF HOPE: RUSSIAN JEWRY AND
THE POGROMS OF 1881-1882. Westport, CT: Greenwood Press,
1985. 231 pp., notes, bibliog., index.

Social and political study of the causes and results of
the Russian pogroms of 1881-1882. The events are viewed as a
watershed in Russian and Jewish history, with repercussions
in and out of Russia. The pogroms resulted from a widely
repeated rumor that Jews had been implicated in the assassination of Tsar Alexander II. Although there is no evidence
of government complicity in the pogroms, it is clear that
some elements within the autocracy viewed them with favor.
The attacks, it should be noted, began in the Ukraine and
spread north. The core of the book is an analysis of the
responses of Russian Jewry, the government, and the Russian
intelligentsia to the pogroms. More significant in the long-
run was the disillusionment caused by the pogroms. Jews knew
the government would support the pogromchiks, but the
Maskilim had expected to find an ally in the intelligentsia.
This hope was deeply disappointed when the Russian intelligentsia also supported the pogroms; as a result, Jews were
forced to turn elsewhere in their hopes for the future. Jews
gradually turned inward, which led to pronouncements on the
need for Jewish self-emancipation. Emigration became the
immediate solution chosen by a majority of Russian Jews, who
left for the United States, western Europe, or Palestine. A
study of two decisive years in Jewish history, Berk´s work

contains an important and insightful analysis.

> #1142. Cowan, A. and R. Cowan: VICTORIAN JEWS.

1005. Glouberman, Emanuel: "Vasilii Rozanov: the Antisemitism of a Russian Judeophile." JSS, v.38 #2 (Spr., 1976): 117-144.

1006. Harcave, Sidney: "The Jewish Question in the First Russian Duma." JSS, v.6 #2 (Apr., 1944): 155-176.

> #315. Lestschinsky, J.: "The Anti-Jewish Program."

1007. Pipes, Richard: "Catherine II and the Jews: the Origins of the Pale of Settlement." SJA, v.5 #2 (1975): 3-20.

1008. Rogger, H.: JEWISH POLICIES AND RIGHT-WING POLITICS IN IMPERIAL RUSSIA. Berkeley, CA: Univ. of California Press, 1986. 287 pp., notes, bibliog., index.

Important reappraisal of Russian antisemitism. Also deals with the role of the Russian right in the radicalization of antisemitism in late Imperial Russia. Rogger dismisses the idea that blind hatred was the cause of Russian antisemitism, especially in light of the otherwise moderate positions of some of the most vehement Jew-baiters. Rather, he argues, Russian antisemitism must be viewed as a movement reflecting a calculated and officially sanctioned policy of antisemitism. Much of the text was previously published as a series of articles scattered widely in scholarly publications, and they are brought together here for the first time. Rogger's erudition brings the study of Russian Jewry in the decaying years of tsarism to a new height and represents an important contribution to the history of Russian Jewry, Russian politics, and antisemitism.

1009. ___: "Tsarist Policy on Jewish Emigration." SJA, v.3 #1 (1973): 26-36.

> #346. Samuel, M.: BLOOD ACCUSATION.

> #352. Tager, A.: THE DECAY OF CZARISM.

Society and Culture

> #142. Katz, J.: TOWARD MODERNITY.

1010. Perlmann, M.: "Razsvet 1860-1861: the Origins of the Russian Jewish Press." JSS, v.24 #3 (July, 1962): 162-182.

1011. Raisin, Jacob S.: THE HASKALAH MOVEMENT IN RUSSIA. Philadelphia: JPS, 1913. 355 pp., notes, bibliog., index.

Study of the emergence of the Haskalah in Russia. Primarily focused on the social and intellectual elements of the Haskalah. The different trends and tendencies of the Russian maskilim are charted for such issues as nationalism vs. assimilation, emigration vs. integration, and the question of which language Jews should adopt. Insofar as outside events played a role in the development of the Haskalah, Russian political history is also covered. As a first systematic study, the book has some usefulness, but there are many loose ends that still are in need of intensive study: for example, the different modes of haskalah in Lithuania, Congress Poland, and the Pale of Settlement.

1012. Silber, Jacques: "Some Demographic Characteristics of the Jewish Population in Russia at the End of the Nineteenth Century." JSS, v.42 #3/4 (Sum./Fall, 1980): 269-280.

1013. Stanislawski, Michael: TSAR NICHOLAS I AND THE JEWS: THE TRANSFORMATION OF JEWISH SOCIETY IN RUSSIA, 1825-1855. Philadelphia: JPS, 1983. 246 pp., illus., tables, notes, bibliog., index.

Study of a key era in the history of Russian Jewry: 1825 to 1855, the era of Tsar Nicholas I. This period represented the only systematic effort by the government to incorporate and assimilate Russian Jewry, and was also the heyday of the Russian Haskalah. Combines religious, political, and social history. As a result the book has methodological and factual importance, and may be seen as a further extension of the Baronian school of Jewish historiography. In addition to charting the development of Russian policies, the consequences of those policies from the Jewish perspective are also reviewed. Jewish communal activities, whether by the Russian maskilim or by their opponents, are surveyed. Stanislawski concludes that although Nicholas´s Jewish policy was a failure, that policy provided the impetus for the virtual transformation of Russian Jewry at a later date.

1014. Zipperstein, S. J.: "Haskalah, Cultural Change, and Nineteenth-Century Russian Jewry: A Reassessment." JJS v.34 #2 (Aut., 1983): 191-207.

1015. ___: "Jewish Enlightenment in Odessa: Cultural Characteristics, 1794-1871." JSS, v.44 #1 (Wint., 1982): 19-36.

1016. ___: THE JEWS OF ODESSA: A CULTURAL HISTORY, 1794-
1881. Stanford, CA: Stanford Univ. Press, 1986. 212 pp.,
map, notes, bibliog., index.

Social and cultural history of Odessa Jewry from its
founding in the 1790s until 1881. The book focuses on how
Odessa Jews accommodated themselves to many of the modernizing tendencies that developed in the city during its glory
days. Zipperstein charts the spread of haskalah in Odessa in
order to explain how cultural patterns unique to the city
led to similarly unparalleled social patterns. Especially
important is the potential comparative method that his analysis permits - Odessa can be compared to any other frontier
town in any other country. In turn, this comparison permits
broader generalizations to be fleshed out with specific
details.

THE SOVIET UNION

The Soviet Regime and the Jews

* 1017. Abramsky, Chimen: 1917 - LENIN AND THE JEWS. London:
World Jewish Congress British Section, 1969. 22 pp.

1018. Altshuler, M.: "The Attitude of the Communist Party
of Russia to Jewish National Survival, 1918-1930." Y/A, v.14
(1969): 68-86.

1019. Aronson, Gregor et al [eds.]: RUSSIAN JEWRY: 1917-
1967. Trans. from the Russian by Joel Carmichael. Cranbury,
NJ: Th. Yoseloff, 1969. 613 pp., notes, index.

Anthology of studies on Soviet Jewry since 1917. Includes
the Jewish communities of the Baltic Republics, even though
they were independent until 1940. A wide variety of topics
are covered. The main focus is on social and cultural
aspects of Soviet Jewish history until the mid-1960s. This
volume is a follow-up to RUSSIAN JEWRY: 1860-1917 [see
#989]. The essays on the Holocaust are of particular
interest. Unfortunately Russian antisemitism is not detailed
in a separate essay.

CONTENTS: G. Aronson: Jewish Communal Life in 1917-1918 / J.

Schechtman: Jewish Community Life in the Ukraine 1917-1919 / Samuel Gringauz: The Jewish National Autonomy in Lithuania, Latvia, and Estonia / Ilya Trotzky: Jewish Pogroms in the Ukraine and in Byelorussia [1918-1920] / A. Goldstein: The Fate of the Jews in German-occupied Soviet Russia / J. Gar: Jews in the Baltic Countries under German occupation / S. Gringauz: The Death of Jewish Kaunas [Kovno] / G. Aronson: The Jewish Question during the Stalin era / G. Swet: Jewish Religion in Soviet Russia / Judel Mark: Yiddish Literature in Soviet Russia; Jewish Schools in Soviet Russia / G. Swet: Jews in Musical Life in Soviet Russia; The Jewish Theater in Soviet Russia / V. Alexandrova: Jews in Soviet Literature / Jewish Scientists in Soviet Russia / Solomon Schwarz: Birobidzhan: an Experiment in Jewish Colonization / J. Slutzki: The Fate of Hebrew in Soviet Russia / Joseph B. Schechtman: Soviet Russia, Zionism and Israel / Leon Shapiro: Russian Jewry after Stalin / S. Gepstein: Russian Zionists in the Struggle for Palestine / Ilya Trotzky: New Russian-Jewish Immigration in the United States / Julius Margolin: Russian-Jewish Immigration into Israel / Andrei Sedych: Russian Jews in Emigre Literature.

> #396. Baron, S. W. and G. Wise: VIOLENCE AND DEFENSE.

1020. Cang, J.: THE SILENT MILLIONS: A HISTORY OF THE JEWS IN THE SOVIET UNION. New York: Talpinger, 1970. 246 pp., notes, bibliog., index.

Somewhat outdated history of Russian Jewry from the Bolshevik revolution to the 1960s. Cang begins by providing background on the state of pre-Communist Russian Jewry and on the attitudes of Lenin and Stalin to the Jewish question. The bulk of the book is an analysis of the policies pursued in regard to Jews by Stalin and Khruschev. Although Cang concentrates on internal policy, Russian relations with Israel are also reviewed in a brief postscript.

1021. Freedman, Robert [ed.]: SOVIET JEWRY IN THE DECISIVE DECADE, 1971-1980. Durham, NC: Duke Univ. Press, 1984. 167 pp., notes, bibliog., index.

Anthology assessing the development of Soviet Jewry during the 1970s. Primary focus is on the movement for Jewish emigration from the Soviet Union. Secondary themes include Russian antisemitism, the influence of public opinion on Soviet policy making, and the resettlement of Soviet Jewish emigrants in Israel and the United States. The problem of neshirah is keenly felt throughout the anthology, but is only reviewed in depth in Kolker´s essay. The book is an insightful contribution on the current state of Soviet Jewry.

CONTENTS: J. M. Gilison: Soviet-Jewish Emigration, 1971-80: an Overview / J. Goodman: The Jews in the Soviet Union: Emigration and its Difficulties / Wm. Korey: Brezhnev and Soviet Antisemitism / R. Freedman: Soviet Jewry and Soviet-American Relations: a Historical Analysis / Th. Friedgut: The Welcome Home: Absorption of Soviet Jews in Israel / F. Kolker: A New Soviet Jewry Plan / Z. Gitelman: Soviet-Jewish immigrants to the United States: Profile, Problems, Prospects / Stephen C. Feinstein: Aspects of Integrating Soviet-Jewish immigrants in America: attitudes of American Jewry Toward the Recent Immigration / I. I. Levkov: Adaptation and Acculturation of Soviet Jews in the United States: a Preliminary Analysis.

> #331. Freedman, Th.: ANTISEMITISM IN THE SOVIET UNION.

1022. Friedgut, Theodore H.: "Soviet Jewry: the Silent Majority." SJA, v.10 #2 (May, 1980): 3-19.

1023. Gilboa, Y. A.: THE BLACK YEARS OF SOVIET JEWRY 1939-1953. Trans. from the Russian by Y. Schachter and Dov Ben-Abba. Boston: Little, Brown, 1971. 418 pp., notes, index.

Inquiry into the state of Soviet Jewry for the years 1939-1953. Beginning with World War II Gilboa charts the systematic and premeditated destruction of all positive elements of Jewish culture in Russia, including the tolerated Socialist Jewish culture. An important subtheme for Gilboa is the recurrence of antisemitism in the Soviet Union, despite Communist efforts to uproot this form of "bourgeois contradiction." Although the decision to begin with 1939 has considerable justification, it is clear that Gilboa could also have pushed his study back and opened with an analysis of the Jewish condition from Lenin´s siezure of power onward. Gilboa ends with the "doctor´s plot" and Stalin´s death. Important for its analysis of the rise of official antisemitism in Russia, the book is not a complete analysis of Russian Jewish history under the impact of communism.

1024. Gitelman, Zvi Y.: JEWISH NATIONALITY AND SOVIET POL-ITICS: THE JEWISH SECTION OF THE CPSU, 1917-1930. Princeton: Princeton Univ. Press, 1972. 573 pp., illus., tables, notes, bibliog., index.

Important study of the history of the Yevsektsias from 1917 to 1930. Gitelman begins with Communist ideology regarding the Jewish question in the final days of the tsarist regime. He then focuses on the efforts of the Yevsektsias to bolshevize the Jews of Russia after the revolutions of 1917. The Jewish sections, representing an autonomous national entity, coupled Jewish form and a socialist content to bring the Jewish community closer to communism. The Bolshevik leadership realized that any other approach to the Jewish community would fail on both linguistic and emotional grounds. Emphasis is on political history, although social and religious issues are also dealt with. The positive results of Yevsektsia activity in modernizing Russian Jewish culture are given a prominent role in Gitelman's account. So too are the results of the purges which effectively destroyed the Jewish sections and spelled the almost complete uprooting of any positive manifestations of Jewish identity.

> #507. Goldman, G.: ZIONISM UNDER SOVIET RULE.

1025. Hirszowicz, Lukasz: "Birobidzhan After Forty Years." SJA, v.4 #2 (1974): 38-45.

1026. ___: "Soviet Perceptions of Zionism." SJA, v.9 #1 (1979): 53-65.

1027. Kochan, Lionel [ed.]: JEWS IN SOVIET RUSSIA SINCE 1917. London: Oxford Univ. Press, 1978. 431 pp., notes, bibliog., index.

Collection of scholarly studies on the history of Soviet Jewry. Virtually every aspect of Soviet Jewish life is covered, both historically and in light of more recent developments. Presents both Soviet theory and practice concerning Jewish affairs as well as social and intellectual trends among Russian Jews. The underlying theme of the essays is the continued existence of a Jewish problem in Russia, after half a century of communism. Despite the utopian promise of the Bolsheviks to create a workers' heaven without "bourgeois contradictions" and racial discrimination, both still exist in Russia and Jews are still the alienated minority tenaciously fighting to remain different. That Soviet policy in regard to Jews has changed is amply demonstrated by a number of the essays, most particularly by Korey, Miller, and Weinryb. Foreign-policy considerations that have affected Soviet policy toward Jews are discussed by Schechtman and Katz. The collection is important and useful for specialists and interested laypersons.

CONTENTS: S. Ettinger: The Jews in Russia at the Outbreak of the Revolution / S. Levenberg: Soviet Jewry: Some Problems and Perspectives / J. Miller: Soviet Theory on the Jews / C. Abramsky: The Biro-Bidzhan Project, 1927-1959 / W. Korey: The Legal Position of Soviet Jewry: a Historical Enquiry / J. B. Schechtman: The USSR, Zionism, and Israel / A. Nove and J. A. Newth: The Jewish Population: Demographic Trends and Occupational Patterns / J. Rothenberg: Jewish Religion in the Soviet Union / M. Friedberg: Jewish Themes in Soviet Russian Literature; Jewish Contributions to Soviet Literature / Y. A. Gilboa: Hebrew Literature in the USSR / Ch. Shmeruk: Yiddish Literature in the USSR / Reuben Ainsztein: Soviet Jewry in the Second World War / B. D. Weinryb: Antisemitism in Soviet Russia / Zev Katz: After the Six-Day War / P. Lewis: The Jewish Question in the Open: 1968-71 / L. Hirszowicz: The Soviet-Jewish Problem: Internal and International Developments, 1972-1976.

> #336. Korey, Wm.: THE SOVIET CAGE.

1028. London, Isaac: "Days of Anxiety: a Chapter in the History of Soviet Jewry." JSS, v.15 #3/4 (July/Oct., 1953): 275-292.

1029. Nove, Alec: "Jews in the Soviet Union." JJoS, v.3 #1 (June, 1961): 108-120.

1030. Orbach, William: "A Periodization of Soviet Policy Towards the Jews." SJA, v.12 #3 (Nov., 1982): 45-62.

1031. Redlich, Shimon: "Khrushchev and the Jews." JSS, v.34 #4 (Oct., 1972): 343-353.

1032. Rubin, Ronald I.: "The Soviet Jewish problem at the United Nations." AJYB, v.71 (1970): 141-159.

1033. ___: "Soviet Jewry and the United Nations: the Politics of Non-governmental Organizations." JSS, v.29 #3 (July, 1967): 139-154.

1034. Sawyer, Thomas E.: THE JEWISH MINORITY IN THE SOVIET UNION. Boulder, CO: Westview Press, 1979. 353 pp., notes, apps., bibliog., index.

Surveys the treatment accorded to Jews in Soviet theory

and practice. Not specifically focused on antisemitism, Sawyer´s primary interest is the civic status of Jews in Soviet Russia. Begins with an analysis of the role Jews played in theoretical Communist writings, from Marx to Stalin. Demographic data are also analyzed, leading to Sawyer´s comparison of the legal status of Jews to their actual status. Russian Jewry´s ethnic identity is also charted, and the book culminates with an analysis of the emigration issue through 1978.

> #527. Schechtman, J. B.: ZIONISM IN SOVIET RUSSIA.

1035. Schwarz, Solomon M.: THE JEWS IN THE SOVIET UNION. Syracuse, NY: Syracuse Univ. Press, 1951. 380 pp., notes, index.

Political study of the treatment of Jews by the Soviet government. In light of changes in the Soviet Union´s Jewish policy, especially since the Six-Day War, the book is somewhat outdated, but is still a standard source. The sad fact is that aside from the oral testimony of recent Soviet emigrants, little documentation on the era covered by Schwarz has become available since the late 1950s. Schwarz analyzes Soviet policy toward Jews and explains why antisemitism is still a feature of Russian life despite Soviet efforts to uproot racial hatred. Russian government policy is shown to permit Jewish identity in name only, while strongly emphasizing the desirability of Jewish assimilation. Consequently, although Jews were formerly allowed to form their own cultural groups, they were prohibited from studying or perpetuating their Jewish culture. Schwarz´s chapter on the Holocaust merits careful study; his conclusion that the Russians did nothing systematic to aid Jews in danger is probably correct. In his analysis, the evacuation of Jews from eastern Poland between 1939-1941 was not designed to save their lives, but was a political act to quell potential opposition by removing its leadership.

1036. Shapiro, Leon: "Soviet Jewry Since the Death of Stalin: a Twenty-five Year Perspective." AJYB, v.79 (1979): 77-103.

> #844. Strom, Y. and B. Blue: LAST JEWS OF EASTERN EUROPE.

> #353. Tartakower, A.: "The Jewish Problem."

* 1037. Teller, Judd L.: IDEOLOGY AND HISTORY OF SOVIET JEW-
ISH POLICY. New York: The Farband, 1964. 32 pp.

> #846. Vago, B. and G. Mosse: JEWS AND NON-JEWS.

1038. Wiesel, Elie: THE JEWS OF SILENCE: A PERSONAL REPORT
ON SOVIET JEWRY. New York: Holt, Rinehart and Winston, 1966.
143 pp.

Journalistic account of the state of Soviet Jewry, based
on Wiesel´s impressions of a trip to Russia in September
1965. Although not a work of scholarship, the book did much
to publicize the plight of Jews in the Soviet Union and to
galvanize the Soviet-Jewry movement in the United States.
Well-known for his Holocaust fiction, Wiesel´s prose is mov-
ing. Contains an afterword by Neal Kozodoy, who presents an
historical survey in order to supplement Wiesel´s text. The
two parts of the book complement each other well and provide
a good insight into Russian Jewry during the 1960s.

The Holocaust

1039. Ainsztein, Reuben: "The War Record of Soviet Jewry."
JSS, v.28 #1 (Jan., 1966): 3-24.

1040. Altshuler, Mordecai: "The Jewish Anti-Fascist Committee in the USSR in Light of New Documentation." SCJ, v.1
(1984): 253-291.

1041. Green, Warren: "The Fate of the Crimean Jewish Communities: Ashkenazim, Krimchaks, and Karaites." JSS, v.46 #2
(Spr., 1984): 169-176.

1042. Pinchuk, Ben-Cion: "Jewish Refugees in Soviet Poland
1939-1941." JSS, v.40 #2 (Spr., 1978): 141-158.

1043. Redlich, Shimon: "The Jewish Antifascist Committee
in the Soviet Union." JSS, v.31 #1 (Jan., 1969): 25-39.

1044. ___ : "The Jews in the Soviet Annexed Territories,
1939-41." SJA, v.1 #1 (June, 1971): 81-90.

> #472. Tenenbaum, J.: "The Einsatzgruppen."

Emigration

1045. Altman, Y. and G. Mars: "The Emigration of Soviet Georgian Jews to Israel." <u>JJoS</u>, v.26 #1 (June, 1984): 35-45.

1046. Gilbert, Martin: THE JEWS OF HOPE. New York: Viking/ Penguin, 1985. 237 pp., illus., index.

Personalized history of Jewish refuseniks in the Soviet Union. Interspersed with the interviews and individual sketches are reflections on the past and future of Soviet Jewry. Included in Gilbert´s review are his analysis of the causes and purposes of Soviet neo-antisemitism and a frank discussion of the Soviet distortion of Jewish history - especially the history of the Holocaust.

1047. Jaffe, Daniel M.: "Refusenik Life." <u>SJA</u>, v.8 #2 (1978): 24-35.

1048. Rothchild, Sylvia: A SPECIAL LEGACY: AN ORAL HISTORY OF SOVIET JEWISH EMIGRES IN NEW YORK. New York: Simon and Schuster, 1985. 336 pp., map, index.

History of the contemporary Jewish emigration movement, primarily focused on the emigres. The book is based on 176 oral histories which were deposited at the William E. Wiener Oral History Library of the American Jewish Committee. Covers the topic thematically, interspersing historical insights with the interview material. In effect the book covers three generations - Jews who grew up during the Revolution, Jews who matured during the Stalin era, and Russian Jews of the post-Stalin era. Unfortunately, the issue of neshirah - the "dropout" of Russian Jews who leave the Soviet Union via Israel, with the intention of settling in the United States - is not dealt with adequately. Nevertheless, the book is an important introduction to the current condition of Soviet Jewry.

Religious and Social History

1049. Altshuler, Mordechai: "Jewish Studies in the Ukraine in the Early Soviet Period." <u>SJA</u>, v.7 #1 (1977): 19-30.

1050. ___ : "Some Statistical Data on the Jews among the Scientific Elite of the Soviet Union." <u>JJoS</u>, v.15 #1 (June, 1973): 45-55.

1051. Brumberg, A.: "Sovyetish Heymland and the Dilemmas of Jewish Life in the USSR." SJA, v.2 #1 (May, 1972): 27-41.

1052. Checinski, Michael: "Soviet Jews and Higher Education." SJA, v.3 #2 (1973): 3-16.

1053. Gitelman, Zvi.: "What Future for Jewish Culture in the Soviet Union?" SJA, v.9 #1 (1979): 20-28.

1054. Greenbaum, Alfred A.: "Hebrew Literature in Soviet Russia." JSS, v.30 #3 (July, 1968): 135-148.

1055. ___: "Jewish Historiography in Soviet Russia." PAAJR, v.28 (1959): 57-76.

1056. ___: "Nationalism as a Problem in Soviet Jewish Scholarship." PAAJR, v.30 (1962): 61-77.

1057. Halevy, Zvi: "Jewish Students in Soviet Universities in the 1920s." SJA, v.6 #1 (1976): 56-70.

1058. Hirszowicz, Lukasz: "Jewish Cultural Life in the USSR - a Survey." SJA, v.7 #2 (1977): 3-21.

1059. Lvavi, Jacob: "Jewish Agricultural Settlement in the USSR." SJA, v.1#1 (June, 1971): 91-100.

1060. Miller, Jack [ed.]: JEWS IN SOVIET CULTURE. New Brunswick, NJ: Transaction Books/Rutgers University, 1984. 331 pp., notes, tables, index.

Anthology on the place of Jews in Soviet culture. Special emphasis is on the period before 1967. By and large the essays are attempts to define the field, rather than analyze it in depth. No effort is made to review Jewish culture in Soviet Russia, although the essay on Babel argues strongly that his Judaism influenced his literature. The idea that Jewish culture is not the same as contributions of Jews to general culture, is discussed in the essay on Ehrenburg, whom the author sees as a Russian writer who happened to be Jewish. Obviously the book is only the introduction to a new and interesting aspect of Jewish history.

CONTENTS: Shmuel Ettinger: The Position of Jews in Soviet Culture: a Historical Survey / I. Golomstock: Jews in Soviet Art / J. Braun: Jews in Soviet Music / Benzion Munitz: A Structural Study of Jews in Russian Literary Criticism / E.

Sicher: The Jewishness of Babel / Anatol Goldberg: Ilya Ehrenburg / Y. Yakhot: Jews in Soviet Philosophy / Inessa A. Rubin: The Jewish Contribution to the Development of Oriental Studies in the USSR.

1061. Millman, Ivor I.: "Major Centers of Jewish Population in the USSR and a Note on the 1970 Census." SJA, v.1 #1 (June, 1971): 13-18.

1062. Pinkus, Benjamin: "Yiddish-Language Courts and Nationalities Policy in the Soviet Union." SJA, v.1 #2 (Nov., 1971): 40-60.

1063. Ro´i, Yaacov: "Jewish Religious Life in the USSR: Some Impressions." SJA, v.10 #2 (May, 1980): 39-50.

1064. Rothenberg, Joshua: "How Many Jews Are There in the Soviet Union?" JSS, v.29 #4 (Oct., 1967): 234-240.

1065. ___: JEWISH RELIGION IN THE SOVIET UNION. New York: Ktav, 1971. 242 pp., notes, apps., index.

Inquiry into the state of Judaism, and therefore also of Jews, in the Soviet Union. Deals with both legal theory and public practice, proving that the Soviets often do not permit in practice what they permit in theory. In this regard it is important to note that Judaism is not always treated on a par with other religious groups, especially the various Christian groups. Primary focus is on the late 1960s, when religion became a rallying point for the nascent Soviet-Jewish national consciousness. The book begins with a broad general survey, then turns to a series of case studies on related topics. In addition to his analysis of Judaism´s relative position in the USSR [as a religion], Rothenberg also offers a broad look into the Soviet Union´s policy toward Jews in general, e.g., in issues of Jewish education.

1066. Schmelz, U. O.: "New Evidence on Basic Issues in the Demography of Soviet Jews." JJoS, v.16 #2 (Dec., 1974): 209-223.

1067. Sonntag, Jacob: "Yiddish Writers and Jewish Culture in the USSR: Twenty Years After." SJA, v.2 #2 (1972): 31-38.

> #104. Vago, B.: JEWISH ASSIMILATION IN MODERN TIMES.

1068. Voronel, Alexander: "The Search for Jewish Identity in Russia." SJA, v.5 #2 (1975): 69-74.

1069. Yodfat, Aryeh Y.: "The Closure of Synagogues in the Soviet Union." SJA, v.3 #1 (1973): 48-56.

1070. ___ : "Jewish Religious Communities in the USSR." SJA, v.1 #2 (Nov., 1971): 61-67.

Communal Histories

1071. Altshuler, Mordechai: "Georgian Jewish Culture under the Soviet Regime." SJA, v.5 #2 (1975): 21-39.

1072. Brutzkus, J.: "The Jewish Mountaineers in Caucasia." Y/A, v.6 (1951): 267-286.

1073. Fischel, Walter J.: "Azarbaijan in Jewish History." PAAJR, v.22 (1953): 1-21.

1074. Gergel, N.: "The Pogroms in the Ukraine in 1918-21." Y/A, v.6 (1951): 237-252.

1075. Hunczak, Taras: "A Reappraisal of Symon Petliura and Ukrainian-Jewish Relations, 1917-1921." JSS, v.31 #3 (July, 1969): 163-183.

1076. Kolack, Shirley: "A Note on the Georgian Jews of Tbilisi." JJoS, v.26 #1 (June, 1984): 47-52.

1077. Salgaller, Emanuel: "Anthropology in Miniature - a Note on the Jews of Soviet Georgia [Gruzia]." JSS, v.26 #4 (Oct., 1964): 195-202.

> #406. Schechtman, J. B.: "Jabotinsky-Slavinsky Agreement."

1078. Szajkowski, Zosa: "A Reappraisal of Symon Petliura and Ukrainian-Jewish Relations, 1917-1921: a Rebuttal." JSS, v.31 #3 (July, 1969): 184-213.

1079. Zand, Mikhail: "Bukharan Jewish Culture Under Soviet rule." SJA, v.9 #2 (1979): 15-23.

1080. ___ : "The Literature of the Mountain Jews of the Caucasus." SJA, v.15 #2 (May, 1985): 3-22; v.16 #1 (Feb., 1986): 35-51.

13

Western Europe

SURVEYS

> #399. Henkin, L.: WORLD POLITICS AND THE JEWISH CONDITION.

1081. Mandel, Arnold: "The Jews in Western Europe Today." AJYB, v.68 (1967): 3-28.

1082. Szajkowski, Zosa: "The Impact of the Beilis Case on Central and Western Europe." PAAJR, v.31 (1963): 197-218.

BELGIUM

1083. Gutwirth, Jacques: "Antwerp Jewry Today." JJoS, v.10 #1 (June, 1968): 121-137.

> #102. Schmelz, U.: JEWISH POPULATION STUDIES.

FRANCE

Overviews

1084. Debre, S.: "The Jews of France." JQR, v.3 #3 (Apr., 1891): 367-435.

1085. Hyman, Paula: FROM DREYFUS TO VICHY: THE REMAKING OF FRENCH JEWRY, 1906-1939. New York: Columbia Univ. Press, 1979. 338 pp., illus., notes, bibliog., index.

Surveys the transformation of French Jewry under the impact of immigration from eastern Europe. Explores the social process of the transformation, placing it also into the contexts of French immigration policy and the increasing antisemitism of the 1930s. Covers both social and political issues. Deals with fascism only indirectly, and then only as related to the general topic. In general, Hyman focuses on the confrontation between "native" Jews and immigrants, comparing it to parallels in England and America. Hyman argues forcefully that specifically French factors exacerbated the confrontation in the community, and that the Francification of immigrant Jews was less successful than the integration of Jews in America and England.

1086. Levitte, Georges: "Impressions of French Jewry Today." JJoS, v.2 #2 (Nov., 1960): 172-184.

1087. Malino, Frances and Bernard Wasserstein: THE JEWS IN MODERN FRANCE. Hanover, NH: Univ. Press of New England for the Tauber Inst. at Brandeis Univ., 1985. 354 pp., notes, index.

Anthology of eighteen studies based on a conference held at Brandeis University in 1982. The essays are arranged around a basic theme: the attempt to understand the points of contact between French and Jewish history. Each contributor brings his or her own approach to the subject. There are some organizational anomalies - two essays on antisemitism are contained in the section "Left and Right," as is an essay on Vichy. Why this is so is not clear; nor is it clear why the Emancipation is treated near the end of the volume. Eugen Weber's essay provides a good overview of Franco-Jewish history and historiography. Michael Marrus tackles the difficult issues of postwar antisemitism in his contribution, which also contains a good comparison of pre-and post-Holocaust French antisemitism. Despite a few organizational problems, the book is an important contribution to Franco-Jewish history and represents a maturation of Franco-Jewish historiography.

CONTENTS: E. Weber: Reflections on the Jews in France / M. Abitbol: The Encounter between French Jewry and the Jews of North Africa: Analysis of a Discourse [1830-1914] / Nancy L. Green: The Contradictions of Acculturation: Immigrant Oratories and Yiddish Union Sections in Paris before World War I / W. B. Cohen and I. Wall: French Communism and the Jews / Z. Sternhell: The Roots of Popular Antisemitism in the Third Republic / S. A. Schuker: Origins of the "Jewish Problem" in the Later Third Republic / Y. Cohen: The Jewish Community of

France in the Face of Vichy-German Persecution: 1940-44 / P. Higonnet: On the Extent of Antisemitism in Modern France / P. Birnbaum: Antisemitism and Anticapitalism in Modern France / M. R. Marrus: Are the French Antisemitic? Evidence in the 1980s / Shmuel Trigano: From Individual to Collectivity: The Rebirth of the "Jewish Nation" in France / S. Hoffmann: Remarks on Trigano / D. S. Landes: Two Cheers for Emancipation / G. Weill: French Jewish Historiography: 1789-1870 / P. E. Hyman: French Jewish Historiography Since 1870.

1088. Memmi, Albert et al: "Differences and Perception of Differences Among Jews in France." JJoS, v.12 #1 (June, 1970): 7-19.

1089. Posener, S.: "The Social Life of the Jewish Communities in France in the Eighteenth Century." JSS, v.7 #3 (July, 1945): 195-232.

1090. Rabinowitz, Louis: THE SOCIAL LIFE OF THE JEWS OF NORTHERN FRANCE IN THE XII-XIV CENTURIES AS REFLECTED IN THE RABBINICAL LITERATURE OF THE PERIOD. New York: Hermon Press, 1972. 268 pp., notes, bibliog., apps., index.

Study of late-medieval Jewry in northern France. Based primarily on rabbinic sources. Rabinowitz is interested in how the rabbis of northern France attempted to adjust halakhah to accord with contemporary needs. The book is organized around the important questions of the day and the answers given by halakhic scholars. In turn, the questions are grouped into broader themes: internal relations, external relations, family life, religion and morals, and education and leisure. The book is a classic study and is of special interest methodologically.

1091. Szajkowski, Z.: "The Growth of the Jewish Population of France: the Political Aspects of a Demographic Problem." JSS, v.8 #3 (July, 1946): 179-186; #4 (Oct., 1946): 297-318.

1092. ___: "Population Problems of Marranos and Sephardim in France from the 16th to the 20th Centuries." PAAJR, v.27 (1958): 83-105.

1093. ___: "Relations Among Sephardim, Ashkenazim and Avignonese Jews in France from the 16th to the 20th Centuries." Y/A, v.10 (1955): 165-196.

> #1179. ___: "Sources for Anglo-Jewish History."

Emancipation

* 1094. Albert, P. C.: THE JEWISH OATH IN NINETEENTH-CENTURY
FRANCE. Tel-Aviv: Tel Aviv Univ. Press, 1982. 43 pp., notes.

1095. ___: THE MODERNIZATION OF FRENCH JEWRY: CONSISTORY
AND COMMUNITY IN THE NINETEENTH CENTURY. Hanover, NH: Univ.
Press of New England for Brandeis Univ. Press, 1977. 450
pp., maps, tables, apps., notes, bibliog., index.

Extensive social and institutional history of nineteenth-
century French Jewry. Primarily focused on the Consistory
and its role in modernizing the Jewish community. Other issues covered are the demographic, economic, and intellectual
trends of French Jewry in the mid-nineteenth century. Albert
begins with the legislation of Jewish affairs in the post-
Napoleonic period. The Consistory was a governmentally sponsored Jewish religious agency, composed of both rabbinic and
lay members. The ideological patterns reflected in it may be
seen as typical of French Jewry as a whole. Similarly, conflicts within the Consistory, whether between the central
and local consistories or between Rabbis and laymen, reflected stresses among the French community. These stresses,
in turn, exemplified the need to adapt to new realities
and a modern outlook, while still maintaining some form of
Jewish identity. A compelling, detailed, and useful account.

1096. Helfand, Jonathan I.: "The Symbiotic Relationship
between French and German Jewry in the Age of Emancipation."
LBIYB, v.29 (1984): 331-350.

1097. Hersch, I. H.: "The French Revolution and the Emancipation of the Jews." JQR, v.19 #3 (Apr., 1907): 540-565.

1098. Hertzberg, Arthur: THE FRENCH ENLIGHTENMENT AND THE
JEWS. New York: Columbia Univ. Press / Philadelphia: JPS,
1968. 420 pp., notes, bibliog., index.

Revisionist history of the emancipation of French Jewry
and the origins of modern racism and antisemitism. Actually
the book contains three distinct elements: an analysis of
French Jewry in the late eighteenth century; an analysis of
the emancipation of French Jewry; and a survey of the
position of the philosophes on the Jewish question. Emphasis
in the first two sections is on social history. The third
segment is most controversial, since Hertzberg links the
antisemitism of the French Enlightenment with a form of neo-

paganism that ultimately culminated in nazism. Many of the philosophes followed Voltaire in his analysis of Jewish history and the influences of Jewry on the world. Voltaire held the Jews responsible for foisting Christianity, and hence Jewish morality, on the unsuspecting pagans. This neo-paganism was to become a recurring theme in antisemitic propaganda. The section on Enlightenment Judaeophobia is of great interest, but also raises a number of questions. First, Hertzberg almost completely ignores the long-term role of demonology in modern antisemitism. Second, although he claims that the views of the philosophes culminated in nazism, he does not explain how this process occurred; nor does he resolve the paradox of their liberalism and advocacy of a secular, liberal state and the ultimate use of their doctrines for antisemitic purposes.

> #120. Katz, J.: OUT OF THE GHETTO.

> #142. ___ : TOWARD MODERNITY.

1099. Posener, S.: "The Immediate Economic and Social Effects of the Emancipation of the Jews in France." JSS, v.1 #3 (July, 1939): 271-326.

1100. Schwarzfuchs, Simon: NAPOLEON, THE JEWS AND THE SANHEDRIN. London: Routledge & Kegan Paul, 1979. 218 pp., bibliog., notes, index.

Social and political study of the relations between Napoleon and the Jews. Seeks to study the impact of Napoleonic policy on the Jewish community´s structure and on Jewish identity. In particular, Schwarzfuchs charts the division between the public and private lives of Jews, i.e., the tension between being a loyal citizen of a secular state while also remaining Jewish. Napoleon is seen as the culmination of the Emancipation, which demanded that Jews redefine themselves in light of contemporary realities. Nevertheless, Schwarzfuchs is not uncritical in his evaluation of Napoleon. He sees Napoleon as having a personal aversion to Jews, although in a muted form. The Jewish Consistory is viewed as an attempt to reorganize Franco-Jewish religious life, reducing Judaism to a "church." Although initially designed to encourage Jewish assimilation, the Consistory became a major source of Jewish identity in post-Napoleonic France. As such, it was the vehicle through which Jews attempted to solve the crisis of Jewish identity in the modern world. Foreword by Lionel Kochan.

1101. Szajkowski, Zosa: "Jewish Religious Observance During the French Revolution of 1789." Y/A, v.12 (1958/59): 211-234.

1102. ___ : JEWS AND THE FRENCH REVOLUTIONS OF 1789, 1830 AND 1848. New York: Ktav, 1970. 1,161 pp., notes, apps.

Collection of essays on the role Jews played in revolutionary France. Szajkowski tried to broaden the historical focus by studying the Jewish demography and the economic, social, and intellectual history of the era. Main emphasis is on the revolution of 1789 and the background to the Emancipation. Even together, the essays do not form a complete history, but provide the groundwork for such a survey. His introduction is a polemical but thought-provoking analysis of Jewish historiography on the revolutions and the Emancipation. Szajkowski particularly argues against those who link the Enlightenment and the revolutions with the rise of modern antisemitism [see #1098]. Clearly, much has yet to be said about this key era in Jewish history; Szajkowski´s studies are important stepping stones in the understanding of these events and their impact.

An especially interesting essay deals with the interaction between Sephardim and Ashkenazim in France from the sixteenth to the twentieth centuries. Others attempt to analyze the Jews in their relation to the revolution. Jews, Szajkowski shows, did not react as a community to the revolution. Some supported the revolution, others were apathetic to it, while still others - to be sure, a minority - opposed it. The revolutionaries are also shown to have had mixed feelings about Jews. Basing himself on careful documentation, Szajkowski argues forcefully for an objective analysis of Franco-Jewish history during a period of uprisings and near constant political change.

1103. ___ : "Protestants and Jews of France in Fight for Emancipation, 1789-1791." PAAJR, v.25 (1956): 119-135.

1104. ___ : "Religious Propaganda Against Jews during the French Revolution of 1789." PAAJR, v.28 (1959): 103-113.

1105. ___ : "The Sephardic Jews of France during the Revolution of 1789." PAAJR, v.24 (1955): 137-164.

1106. ___ : "Synagogues during the French Revolution of 1789-1800." JSS, v.20 #4 (Oct., 1958): 215-231.

Sociology

1107. Benguigni, Georges et al: ASPECTS OF FRENCH JEWRY. London: Vallentine Mitchell, 1969. 142 pp., notes, tables.

Essays on the sociology of French Jewry since the Holocaust. Includes a methodological essay by Otto Klinberg, which points to the difficulties of studying "the Jews" as a single distinct entity. The data presented by the studies proper provide   interesting   information and raise the possibility of comparison to other communities. In fact, one of the conclusions of the study was that it is necessary to compare differing elements, Ashkenazi and Sephardi, within French Jewry itself. The essays are not difficult to follow, although they include a large amount of statistical data. One might have liked to see more in the way of documentation, but as most of the studies were based on surveys and polls, this is not a major criticism.

CONTENTS: G. Benguigni: First-Year Jewish Students at the University of Paris / O. Klinberg: Towards a Sociology of the Jews / Georges Levitte: A Changing Community / Prefatory Note: Some Aspects of the Integration of North African Jews.

> #62. Cohen, S. and P. Hyman: THE JEWISH FAMILY.

1108. Green, Nancy L.: THE PLETZL OF PARIS: JEWISH IMMIGRANT WORKERS IN THE BELLE EPOQUE. New York: Holmes & Meier, 1985. 270 pp., tables, maps, apps., notes, bibliog., index.

Social history dealing with the Jewish immigrant experience in France. Main focus is on immigrant workers and on the relations between class and community before World War I. Green sees the Pletzl, one of Paris´s main East European Jewish neighborhoods, as a microcosm for the study of migration, Jewish migrant experience, and living conditions for French laborers at the turn of the century. Thus, she places the immigrant Jewish laborers at the crossroad of Jewish, French, labor, and migration history. With such a variety of subjects, one would think the book would be facile. In some instances it is; Green is at times more concerned with immigrant-labor themes than with specifically Jewish ones. Then too, her epilogue, covering the plight of immigrant laborers in France in the late 1970s, is thoroughly anachronistic and of no relevance to the study of Jewish history. These flaws do not detract from the importance of the main contents, however. Especially interesting is Green's reconstruction of the rise of the Jewish labor movement, and its relations with the overall French labor movement. The book is thus not definitive, but quite useful.

> #102. Schmelz, U.: JEWISH POPULATION STUDIES.

1109. Schnapper, Dominique: JEWISH IDENTITIES IN FRANCE: AN ANALYSIS OF CONTEMPORARY FRENCH JEWRY. Trans. from the French by A. Goldhammer. Chicago: Univ. of Chicago Press, 1983. 181 pp., apps., notes, index.

Sociological analysis of French Jewry. Based on a series of ninety interviews with members of all strata of Franco-Jewry. Main focus is on Franco-Jewish identity. Schnapper divides French Jewry into three broad categories: practicing, those who keep Shabbat, kashrut, or both; militants, either Zionists or non-Zionists; and assimilated, those whose Jewish identity is almost completely lost. There are, nonetheless, some rather surprising conclusions drawn from Schnapper's formulation and from the responses to her questions. For example, consciousness of antisemitism is strongest among the neo-assimilated, but almost negligible among Zionists. This is hardly what would be expected and raises some doubts about the size of Schnapper's database. When one looks more closely at her schema, other questions arise. Why does Schnapper place anti-Zionists in the militant category with Zionists, and not with the assimilated? Similarly, why are merchants placed among the assimilated? Finally, why is no specific distinction drawn between Sephardim and Ashkenazim in terms of religious practice? These lacunae notwithstanding, the book does offer an interesting sociological insight into conditions of Jewish identity.

> #104. Vago, B.: JEWISH ASSIMILATION IN MODERN TIMES.

Antisemitism

1110. Arendt, Hannah: "From the Dreyfus Affair to France Today." JSS, v.4 #3 (July, 1942): 195-240.

1111. Bredin, Jean-Denis: THE AFFAIR: THE CASE OF ALFRED DREYFUS. Trans. from the French by J. Mehlman. New York: G. Braziller, 1986. 628 pp., notes, bibliog., index.

Extensive and well written history of the Dreyfus affair. Unlike most other books on the subject Bredin includes a

profile of Dreyfus as background to the affair. Also included are a detailed analysis of the political forces in the
Second Republic, a study of the rise of French antisemitism,
and a discussion of the intelligence war waged between
France and Germany in the mid-1890s. Piece by piece Bredin
uncovers the particulars of the case, which reads almost
like a spy novel. A lawyer by profession, Bredin deals objectively with all the sordid details of the affair as well
as its implications, both in the short and long terms. The
importance of the affair in French and Jewish history is
carefully calculated with an appreciation of the significance of the affair for the development of both zionism and
French antisemitism. Dreyfus´s biography is recounted to its
conclusion, as are the stories of the key Dreyfusards and
anti-Dreyfusards.

> #326. Byrnes, R. F.: "Antisemitism in France."

> #327. ___: ANTIESMITISM IN MODERN FRANCE.

> #310. ___: "Edouard Drumont and La France Juive."

> #135. Duker, A. and M. Ben-Horin: EMANCIPATION.

> #313. Epstein, S.: CRY OF CASSANDRA.

1112. Glasberg, Victor M.: "Intent and Consequences: the
Jewish Question in the French Socialist Movement in the Late
Nineteenth Century." JSS, v.36 #1 (Jan., 1974): 61-71.

> #731. Kann, R. A.: "Assimilation and Antisemitism."

> #335. Kingston, P. J.: ANTISEMITISM IN FRANCE.

> #342. Mehlman, J.: LEGACIES OF ANTISEMITISM IN FRANCE.

> #348. Silberner, E.: "Anti-Jewish Trends."

> #321 ___: "The Attitude of the Fourierist School."

1113. Szajkowski, Zosa: "The Jewish Saint-Simonians and
Socialist Antisemites in France." JSS, v.9 #1 (Jan., 1947):
33-60.

> #355. Wilson, S.: IDEOLOGY AND EXPERIENCE.

Public Affairs

1114. Caron, Vicki: "Patriotism or Profit?: the Emigration of Alsace-Lorraine Jews to France, 1871-1872." LBIYB, v.28 (1983): 139-168.

> #681. ___ and P. Hyman: "The Failed Alliance."

1115. Frydman, Szajko [Z. Szajkowski]: "Internal Conflicts in French Jewry at the Time of the Revolution of 1848." Y/A, v.2/3 (1947/48): 100-117.

1116. Greilsammer, Ilan: "The Democratization of a Community: French Jewry and the Fonds Social Juif Unifie." JJoS, v.21 #2 (Dec., 1979): 109-124.

1117. Halff, Sylvain: "The Participation of the Jews of France in the Great War." AJYB, v.21 (1919/20): 31-97.

1118. Hyman, P.: "Challenge to Assimilation: French Jewish Youth Movements between the Wars." JJoS, v.18 #2 (Dec., 1976): 105-114.

1119. ___: "From Paternalism to Cooptation: the French Jewish Consistory and the Immigrants, 1906- 1939." Y/A, v.17 (1978): 217-237.

1120. Kobler, Franz: NAPOLEON AND THE JEWS. New York: Schocken Books, 1975. 220 pp., notes.

Studies the relations between Bonaparte, the French Jews, and other Jewish communities. The central theme in Kobler´s review is Napoleon´s 1799 proclamation for the restoration of the Jewish people to the land of Israel. Also deals with the Napoleonic Sanhedrin. Sees Napoleon as the first European statesman to deal with the Jewish problem in a systematic way. Kobler´s unequivocal admiration of Napoleon, however, seems a bit problematic, and the emphasis on his acceptance of Jewish nationhood is overstated. At best one can say that Napoleon, while ambivalent towards Jews, was never an outright enemy. Like many statesmen before and since the nineteenth century, he hoped to use Jews and Jewish support for his ends. But since his policy accorded with Jewish needs at the time, he could be seen as a philosemite. Nevertheless, when his interests differed from those of the Jews, Napoleon could be, and was, a difficult foe who was guided solely by self-interest.

> #363. Marrus, M.: THE POLITICS OF ASSIMILATION.

1121. Szajkowski, Zosa: "Jewish Emigres during the French revolution." JSS, v.16 #4 (Oct., 1954): 319-334.

The Holocaust

> #446. Haft, C. J.: THE BARGAIN AND THE BRIDLE.

1122. Kaplan, Jacob: "French Jewry under Nazi occupation." AJYB, v.47 (1945/46): 71-118.

> #453. Latour, A.: JEWISH RESISTANCE IN FRANCE.

> #458. Marrus, M. and R. O. Paxton: VICHY FRANCE.

> #459. Morley, J. F.: VATICAN DIPLOMACY AND THE JEWS.

1123. Sinder, Henri: "Lights and Shades of Jewish Life in France, 1940-42." JSS, v.5 #4 (Oct., 1943): 367-382.

1124. Szajkowski, Zosa: "The Organization of the ´UGIF´ in Nazi-Occupied France." JSS, v.9 #3 (July, 1947): 239-256.

Communal Histories

1125. Anchel, Robert: "The Early History of the Jewish Quarters in Paris." JSS, v.2 #1 (Jan., 1940): 45-60.

> #802. Caron, V.: "Alsace-Lorraine Jewry."

> #805. Halff, S.: "The Jews of Alsace-Lorraine."

1126. Kober, Adolf: "Jewish Converts in Provence from the Sixteenth to the Eighteenth Century." JSS, v.6 #4 (Oct., 1944): 351-374.

1127. Malino, F.: THE SEPHARDIC JEWS OF BORDEAUX: ASSIMI-LATION AND EMANCIPATION IN REVOLUTIONARY AND NAPOLEONIC FRANCE. University: The Univ. of Alabama Press, 1978. 166 pp., notes, bibliog., index.

Analytical study of the history of the Sephardic commu-nity in southern France during the period of the Emancipa-tion. Primarily written as a social study of the accommoda-

tion of Jews to modernity. Malino´s central focus is on the
efforts of French Sephardim to maintain their Jewish identity while also becoming Frenchmen. As the first community
in France to become interested in citizenship, the Sephardim
played a major role in the Emancipation and in the debates
surrounding the issue of Jewish civil status. Sephardi
efforts to synthesize Frenchness and Jewishness thus prefigured the concerns of all of French Jewry, and much of
West European Jewry, during the nineteenth century.

1128. Singer, Barnett: "A Remnant: the Jews of Vaucluse in
the Nineteenth Century." JSS, v.40 #2 (Spr., 1978): 159-176.

1129. Szajkowski, Zosa: "The Decline and Fall of Provencal
Jewry." JSS, v.6 #1 (Jan., 1944): 31-54.

1130. ___: "Jewish Emigration from Bordeaux during the
Eighteenth and Nineteenth Centuries." JSS, v.18 #2 (Apr.,
1956): 118-124.

> #1093. ___: "Reactions Among / Jews in France."

1131. Tapia, Clauede: "North African Jews in Belleville."
JJoS, v.16 #1 (June, 1974): 5-23.

> #970. Twersky, I.: DANZIG.

1132. Weinberg, David H.: A COMMUNITY ON TRIAL: THE JEWS
OF PARIS IN THE 1930s. Chicago: The Univ. of Chicago Press,
1977. 239 pp., notes, bibliog., index.

Important contribution to the social history of European
Jewry on the brink of the Holocaust. Weinberg´s main focus
is on communal tensions between native and immigrant French
Jews and the resulting disunity within the Paris Jewish community. By studying one community, Weinberg offers insight
into communal operation; by studying Paris in particular, he
offers insight into a microcosm of French and European
Jewry. It is clear from his study that the natives and the
immigrants differed in their perceptions of the Jewish question. Moreover, neither community truly grasped the implications of the Nazi threat. Neither community realized how
dependent each was on the other, despite the half-hearted
attempt at a unified front in the late 1930s. Weinberg is
very careful with documentation and eschews vilification. As
a result, his book is a model of judicious historical investigation and offers a sober analysis of a somber era in

Jewish history.

1133. ___: "´Heureux comme Dieu en France´: Jewish Immigrants in Paris, 1881-1914." SCJ, v.1 (1984): 26-54.

GIBRALTAR

1134. Benady, Mesod: "The Settlement of Jews in Gibraltar, 1704-1783." TJHSE, v.26 (1974/78): 87-110.

GREAT BRITAIN

Overviews

1135. Aronsfeld, Caesar C.: "German Jews in Victorian England." LBIYB, v.7 (1962): 312-329.

1136. Barnett, R. D.: "The Correspondence of the Mahamad of the Spanish and Portuguese Congregation of London during the Seventeenth and Eighteenth Centuries." TJHSE, v.20 (1959/61): 1-50.

1137. Bentwich, N.: "The Social Transformation of Anglo-Jewry 1883-1960." JJoS, v.2 #1 (June, 1960): 16-24.

> #85. Berger, D.: THE LEGACY OF JEWISH IMMIGRATION.

1138. Berghahn, M.: GERMAN-JEWISH REFUGEES IN ENGLAND. New York: St. Martin´s Press, 1984. 194 pp., notes, bibliog., index.

Comprehensive social study of the integration of German and Austrian Jewish refugees into English society. In fact, their assimilation was actually a process of reassimilation, although into a different milieu. Berghahn notes that the sociological data seem to run counter to the commonly accepted notion of German Jews being fully assimilated into German society. Her study is based on extensive interviews and proves a remarkably strong Jewish ethnic identity. In addition, Berghahn attempts to view Jewish assimilation within the broad sociological context of relations between minorities and majorities. An especially interesting chapter deals with "Life Under the Threat of Nazism," which charts the reorientation of German Jews as a result of Nazi policy.

1139. Bermant, Chaim: THE COUSINHOOD: THE ANGLO-JEWISH
GENTRY. London: Eyre & Spottiswoode, 1971. 466 pp., illus.,
notes, index.

Biographical history of the grand monied Anglo-Jewish
families, the Rothschilds, Montefiores, Sassoons, Goldsmids,
Cohens, and Samuels. Bermant describes their rise to gran-
deur and the role they played in the development of Anglo-
Jewry. The roles that each member played in British history
are also described. It should be noted that Bermant is not
filial pietistic - the "cousins" are shown with all their
faults and flaws. As great as they may have been, the men
and women Bermant describes are treated as human beings. The
book is thus a fascinating look into the Anglo-Jewish
aristocracy and their place in Anglo-Jewish history.

1140. ___: TROUBLED EDEN: AN ANATOMY OF BRITISH JEWRY. New
York: Basic Books, 1970. 274 pp., notes, index.

Journalistic account of Anglo-Jewry in the late 1960s and
early 1970s. Also includes historical information to provide
background on the development of the Anglo-Jewish community.
Mainly focused on communal institutions. The culmination of
the book is the so-called Jacobs affair, which threatened to
tear the community apart in 1969-1970. The affair and all
its ramifications are described objectively by Bermant, who
avoids taking sides. Regardless of the specific issues
involved, Bermant offers a fascinating glimpse into the
inner and outer life of English Jews as well as thumbnail
sketches of the individuals and institutions of Anglo-Jewry.

1141. Brown, M.: "Anglo-Jewish Country Houses from the Resettlement to 1800." TJHSE, v.28 (1981-82): 20-38.

> #62. Cohen, S. and P. Hyman: THE JEWISH FAMILY.

1142. Cowen, Anne and Roger Cowen: VICTORIAN JEWS THROUGH
BRITISH EYES. New York: Oxford Univ. Press for the Littman
Library of Jewish Civilization, 1986. 196 pp., illus.

Thematic study of the attitude of English cartoonists
and reporters toward Jews and Judaism during the early
Victorian period. As such, the book is also an inquiry into
the position of the press in contemporary English society.
Special emphasis is placed on caricatures and satires, for
example, Punch and other popular periodicals. Many of these
were critical of Jews and their mores, some verging on anti-

semitism. In addition to the satirical pieces, serious articles and drawings are included that show the more sympathetic side of the Victorians attitude toward Jews. The persecution of Jews in Russia struck an especially strong chord
in the British press, selections of which show English
indignation with tsarist Russia's governmentally sponsored
barbarism. Introduction by Louis Jacobs.

1143. Diamond, A. S.: "Problems of the London Sephardi
Community, 1720-1733: Philip Carteret Webb's Notebooks."
TJHSE, v.21 (1962/67): 39-63.

1144. Gartner, Lloyd P.: THE JEWISH IMMIGRANT IN ENGLAND,
1870-1914. Detroit: Wayne State Univ. Press, 1960. 320 pp.,
notes, app., gloss., bibliog., index.

Social history of Jewish immigration to England before
World War I. Attempts to place the migration into the
contexts of English and Jewish history. As a result, Gartner
offers some important suggestions relevant to a comparative
history of Jewish migration in modern times. Gartner notes
that a specific image of England led 120,000 Jews to migrate
to her shores in 34 years, proving that migration is not
merely a question of leaving one country, but also reflects
a pull to another. Like the United States, however, England
was ambivalent in regard to Jewish immigration. While no restrictions were placed on Jewish immigration during the last
three decades of the nineteenth century, immigration became
a public issue in the early years of the twentieth. Anti-
alien feeling led to a number of parliamentary studies and
the proposal of restrictive legislation. Neither completely
ended Jewish immigration, although the flow was greatly reduced. The outbreak of World War I stopped immigration altogether, until the pressure of Nazi anti-Jewish policy once
again made England a refuge for Jews.
   While placing immigrant Jews into historic context,
Gartner carefully reconstructs the outlines of immigrant
Jewish life. He covers the economic, social, political, and
religious lives of the new immigrants in separate and detailed chapters. Education also receives prominent attention, as does the process of acculturation to English
society. The position of Anglo-Jewry on immigrants and immigrant aid is also clarified. Altogether, Gartner makes an
important contribution to the study of Jewish migration.

1145. ___: "Notes on the Statistics of Jewish Immigration
to England 1870-1914." JSS, v.22 #2 (Apr., 1960): 97-102.

1146. ___ : "Urban History and the Pattern of Provincial Jewish Settlement in Victorian England." JJoS, v.23 #1 (June, 1981): 37-55.

> #67. Gould, J: JEWISH COMMITMENT.

1147. Gould, J. and S. Esh [eds.]: JEWISH LIFE IN MODERN BRITAIN. London: Routledge and Kegan Paul, 1964. 217 pp., notes, gloss., index.

Anthology on the state of postwar Anglo-Jewry, based on a colloquium held on the subject at The Board of Deputies in 1962. Each of the essays is followed by a discussion, which further develops some of the ideas presented. The book also has historiographical and methodological significance. Especially important essays include Brotman´s "Jewish Communal Organization" and Roth´s "The Anglo-Jewish Community in the Context of World Jewry." Taken together the anthology covers the gamut of Anglo-Jewish life and, as a result, offers an important insight into the largest post-Holocaust European Jewish community.

CONTENTS: A. G. Brotman: Jewish Communal Organization / E. Krausz: The Economic and Social Structure of Anglo-Jewry / N. Cohen: Trends in Anglo-Jewish Religious Life / I. Fishman and H. Levy: Jewish Education in Great Britain / Cecil Roth: The Anglo-Jewish Community in the Context of World Jewry / S. J. Prais: Statistical Research: Needs and Prospects / M. Freedman and Julius Gould: Topics and Methods of Future Research: Sociological / S. Esh and G. Wigoder: Oral History and its Potential Application / V. D. Lipman: Topics and Methods of Future Research in Contemporary Jewish History / J. Gould: Progress and Prospects: a Postscript.

1148. Harris, Isidore: "A Dutch Burial-Ground and its English Connections." TJHSE, v.7 (1911/14): 113-146.

1149. Harris, Sydney: "The Identity of Jews in an English City." JJoS, v.14 #1 (June, 1972): 63-84.

1150. Huttenback, R. A.: "The Patrician Jew and the British Ethos in the Nineteenth and Early Twentieth Centuries." JSS, v.40 #1 (Wint., 1978): 49-62.

1151. Hyamson, Albert M.: HISTORY OF THE JEWS IN ENGLAND. New York: Bloch, 1908. 327 pp., illus., chron., index.

Survey of the Jewish community of England from foundation
to the turn of the century. The book is divided into three
sections, which discuss the history of Anglo-Jewry; Jewish
relations with the surrounding environment; and governmental
interaction with world Jewry. Within these three themes, the
book is evenly focused between social and political history.
The book is primarily descriptive, with relatively less emphasis on analysis. In light of the publication date, the
book is outdated and desperately in need of updating.

1152. Lachs, Phyllis S.: "A Study of a Professional Elite:
Anglo-Jewish Barristers in the Nineteenth Century." JSS,
v.44 #2 (Spr., 1982): 125-134.

1153. Lipman, Sonia and V. D. Lipman [eds.]: JEWISH LIFE
IN BRITAIN, 1962-1977. London: K. G. Sauer, 1980. 203 pp.,
notes, gloss., index.

Sociohistorical inquiry into contemporary British Jewry,
based on a conference held at the University College of
London in March 1977. The book is designed as a follow-up to
JEWISH LIFE IN MODERN TIMES [see #1147]. Though the authors
use a historical approach, the majority of essays are sociological in nature. Methodological generalizations are interwoven with the specific discussion of Anglo-Jewry. Much
attention is paid to religious life, education, and the community. The essays by Kosmin and Williams suggest a new,
local approach to Anglo-Jewish history. Since such an approach has been fruitful when applied to other communities,
in particular, to the United States, it is probably worth
pursuing. Newman's essay is a good overview of the state of
the art on Anglo-Jewish historiography. Also included are
the question-and-answer sessions which broaden the perspectives on specific and sometimes controversial issues.

CONTENTS: S. J. Prais: Polarization or Decline? / E. Krausz:
Concepts and Theoretical Models for Anglo-Jewish Sociology /
I. Jakobovits: An Analysis of Religious versus Secularist
Trends in Anglo-Jewry / D. Marmur: The Challenge of Secu-
larism / P. Feingold: The Counterattack on Secularization /
A. Newman: Recent Research in Anglo-Jewish History / B. A.
Kosmin: The Case for the Local Perspective in the Study of
Contemporary British Jewry / B. Williams: Local Jewish His-
tory: Where Do We Go from Here? / J. Braude: Jewish Educa-
tion in Britain Today / F. Jacobs and V. Prais: Developments
in the Law on State-Aided Schools for Religious Minorities /
M. Rosin: The Jewish Student Scene / G. Paul: The Value of

Controversy in Communal Life / S. Levenberg: The Development
of Anglo-Jewry, 1962-1977 / J. Gould: Grandchildren of the
Ghetto / V. D. Lipman: Postscript.

1154. Lipman, Vivian D.: "The Rise of Jewish suburbia."
TJHSE, v.21 (1962/67): 78-103.

1155. ___: SOCIAL HISTORY OF THE JEWS IN ENGLAND, 1850-
1950. London: Watts, 1954. 200 pp., notes, app., bibliog.,
glossary, index.

Sociological history of English Jewry over the course of
one hundred years. Especially important are Lipman´s sections on immigration and demography. Secondary themes of
great interest are the "Anglicization" of English Jewry
during the period covered - a student of Jewish history can
easily find parallels in the United States and on the Continent - and the development of Anglo-Jewish religious life.
Unfortunately the section on Anglo-Jewry after 1914 is very
weak, while a number of issues, antisemitism and zionism
among them, are almost ignored.

1156. ___: "Survey of Anglo-Jewry in 1851." TJHSE, v.17
(1951/52): 171-188.

1157. ___ [ed.]: THREE CENTURIES OF ANGLO-JEWISH HISTORY.
London: W. Heffer for the Jewish Historical Society, 1961.
201 pp., maps, illus., notes, index.

Anthology of essays based on public addresses at the University College in London, marking the 300th anniversary of
the resettlement of Anglo-Jewry. Covers the period from the
resettlement to the twentieth century, stressing the nineteenth and early twentieth centuries. The essays by Loewe
and Parkes adopt a thematic approach and do not limit themselves chronologically. In the chronological essays stress
is evenly divided between social, religious, and political
history. Surprisingly, the place of Anglo-Jewry in Jewish
history is not addressed directly. Despite this lacuna the
book is an interesting review of the development of the
Jewish community in England.

CONTENTS: C. Roth: The Resettlement of the Jews in England /
E. R. Samuel: The First Fifty Years / R. D. Barnett: Anglo-
Jewry in the Eighteenth Century / V. D. Lipman: The Age of
Emancipation, 1815-1880 / I. Finestein: The New Community,
1880-1918 / R. Loewe: Jewish Scholarship in England / James

Parkes: Jewish-Christian Relations in England / A. Cohen: The Structure of Anglo-Jewry Today.

* 1158. Moonman, J. [ed.]: ANGLO-JEWRY: AN ANALYSIS. London: Joint Israel Appeal, 1980. 64 pp.

1159. Newman, Aubrey: "Anglo-Jewry in the 18th Century: a Presidential Address." TJHSE, v.27 (1978/80): 1-10.

1160. Prais, S. J. and Marlena Schmool: "The Fertility of Jewish Families in Britain, 1971." JJoS, v.15 #2 (Dec., 1973): 189-203.

1161. ___ : "The Size and Structure of the Anglo-Jewish Population 1960-65." JJoS, v.10 #1 (June, 1968): 5-34.

1162. ___ : "The Social-Class Structure of Anglo-Jewry, 1961." JJoS, v.17 #1 (June, 1975): 5-15.

1163. Rollin, A. R.: "Russo-Jewish Immigrants in England before 1881." TJHSE, v.21 (1962/67): 202-213.

1164. Roth, Cecil: ESSAYS AND PORTRAITS IN ANGLO-JEWISH HISTORY. Philadelphia: JPS, 1962. 318 pp., illus., notes.

Collection of essays on Anglo-Jewish history. The subjects covered are as multifaceted as Roth´s talents and interests. Roth´s essay "The Anglo-Jewish Tradition" sets the tone for the book. Roth views Anglo-Jewry as a unique community different from the Jewries of continental Europe and the Americas. The majority of the essays are portraits, thumbnail sketches of individuals, institutions, and events. Roth is at his best with these portraits, for they allow his excellent stylistic expression to shine forth. The other essays cover many issues, for example, English philosemitism, the readmission, and the emancipation of Anglo-Jewry.

1165. ___ : A HISTORY OF THE JEWS IN ENGLAND. 2nd Edition. London: Oxford Univ. Press, 1949. 311 pp., notes, index.

Survey of Anglo-Jewry from the formation of the community until the Emancipation. Broadly social in its approach, the book is focused on communal developments and on relations with the government. This well-documented book provides an in-depth review and analysis of key events in Anglo-Jewish history. Chronological emphasis is on developments in the Middle Ages and after the readmission. Unfortunately, Roth saw fit to end his account with 1858, summarizing the history of post-Emancipation Anglo-Jewry in an all too brief epilogue.

1166. Rubens, Alfred: "Anglo-Jewry in Caricature, 1780-1850." TJHSE, v.23 (1969/70): 96-101.

1167. ___: "Portrait of Anglo-Jewry, 1656-1836." TJHSE, v.19 (1955/59): 13-52.

1168. Rumney, J.: "Anglo-Jewry as seen through Foreign Eyes [1730-1830]." TJHSE, v.13 (1932/35): 323-340.

1169. Schechter, Frank I.: "An Unfamiliar Aspect of Anglo-Jewish History." PAJHS, #25 (1917): 63-74.

> #102. Schmelz, U.: JEWISH POPULATION STUDIES.

1170. Smith, Robert M.: "The London Jews´ Society and Patterns of Jewish Conversion in England, 1801-1859." JSS, v.43 #3/4 (Sum./Fall 1981): 275-290.

1171. Temkin, S. D.: "Three Centuries of Jewish Life in England [1656-1956]." AJYB, v.58 (1957): 3-63.

> #83. Waterman, S. and B. Kosmin: BRITISH JEWRY.

> #90. Wischnitzer, M.: TO DWELL IN SAFETY.

Historiography

1172. Adler, H.: "A Survey of Anglo-Jewish History." TJHSE, v.3 (1896/98): 1-17.

1173. Henriques, H. S. Q.: "Reflections on the History of the Anglo-Jewish Community." TJHSE, v.9 (1918/20): 131-142.

1174. Jacobs, J.: "The Typical Character of Anglo-Jewish History." TJHSE, v.3 (1896/98): 126-143.

1175. Kosmin, Barry A.: "Localism and Pluralism in British Jewry 1900-80." TJHSE, v.28 (1981/82): 111-125.

1176. Levy, S.: "Anglo-Jewish Historiography." TJHSE, v.6 (1908/10): 1-20.

1177. Roth, Cecil: "The Middle Period of Anglo-Jewish History: 1290-1655 Reconsidered." TJHSE, v.19 (1955/59): 1-12.

1178. ___: "Why Anglo-Jewish History?" TJHSE, v.22 (1968/69): 21-29.

1179. Szajkowski, Zosa: "French 17th-18th Century Sources for Anglo-Jewish History." JJoS, v.12 #1/2 (1961): 59-66.

Public Affairs

1180. Adler, Michael: "The Story of British Jewry in the War." AJYB, v.21 (1919/20): 98-119.

1181. Alderman, Geoffrey: THE JEWISH COMMUNITY IN BRITISH POLITICS. New York: Clarendon Press, 1983. 218 pp., charts, tables, notes, index.

Analysis of the Jewish factor in British politics. Attacks the subject both historically and analytically. Argues that English Jews have articulated an independent position on political issues and especially on those which touched on Jewish interests and survival. More simply stated, Alderman is arguing that a Jewish vote exists in England. It must, however, be emphasized that this Jewish vote has not been acknowledged by Anglo-Jewish organizations, which go to great lengths to deny its very existence. Moreover, the grass-roots Jewish political position has not always been represented by the election of Jewish MPs. Interestingly, Alderman also points out that Anglo-Jewish voting patterns, especially the Jewish proclivity to vote Labour, have not always accorded with Jewish interests. One of the strengths of Alderman's account is that it clearly delineates parallels between Anglo-Jewry and other Jewish communities, particularly the United States.

> #1353. Aronsfeld, C. C.: THE GHOSTS OF 1492.

1182. Aronsfeld, C. C.: "Jewish Enemy Aliens in England during the First World War." JSS, v.18 #4 (Oct., 1956): 275-283.

1183. Barnett, R. D.: "Diplomatic Aspects of the Sephardic Influx from Portugal in the Early Eighteenth Century." TJHSE, v.25 (1973/75): 210-221.

1184. Baron, Salo W.: "Great Britain and Damascus Jewry in 1860-61: an Archival Study." JSS, v.2 #2 (Apr., 1940): 179-208.

1185. Baumel, J. T.: "Twice a Refugee: the Jewish Refugee Children in Great Britain during Evacuation 1939-1943." JSS, v.45 #2 (Spr., 1983): 175-184.

1186. Brodie, Israel: "British and Palestinian Jews in World War II." AJYB, v.48 (1946/47): 51-72.

1187. Brotz, Howard: "The Position of the Jews in English Society." JJoS, v.1 #1 (Apr., 1959): 94-113.

1188. Conway, Edward S.: "The Origins of the Jewish Or-phanage." TJHSE, v.22 (1968/69): 53-66.

1189. Fishman, William J.: JEWISH RADICALS 1875-1914: FROM CZARIST STETL TO LONDON GHETTO. New York: Pantheon Books, 1975. 336 pp., illus., notes, apps., bibliog., index.

Studies Jewish Socialist and Anarchist groups in London´s East End between 1881 and 1914. Primarily a social analysis, the book is organized around the activities of the two main advocates of Jewish socialism on the East End: Rudolf Rocker and Aron Lieberman. Although not a Jew, Rocker espoused the cause of the Jewish immigrant workers with passion and dedication. Fishman´s account lacks a specific social background into which the Socialists and anarchists can be placed. Though the framework comparing London´s Jew-ish radicals to New York Jewish radicals is well developed and is of some interest, the book overall does little to explain the development and demise of the Socialists and Anarchists of the Jewish East End.

1190. Gartner, Lloyd P.: "Anglo-Jewry and the Jewish In-ternational Traffic in Prostitution." AJS Review, v.7/8 (1982/83): 129-178.

1191. Gilam, Abraham: "The Burial Grounds Controversy be-tween Anglo-Jewry and the Victorian Board of Health, 1850." JSS, v.45 #2 (Spr., 1983): 147-156.

1192. Kaplan, S.: "The Anglicization of the East European Jewish Immigrant as Seen by the London Jewish Chronicle, 1870-1897." Y/A, v.10 (1955): 267-278.

> #888. Katzburg, N.: HUNGARY AND THE JEWS.

1193. Levy, S.: "John Dury and the English Jewry." TJHSE,
v.4 (1899/1901): 76-82.

1194. Neusner, Jacob: "Anglo-Jewry and the Development of
American Jewish Life 1775-1850." Y/A, v.12 (1958/59): 131-
156.

> #841. Polonsky, A.: "Documents / British Foreign Office."

1195. Ross, J. M.: "Naturalisation of Jews in England."
TJHSE, v.24 (1970/73): 59-72.

1196. Roth, Cecil: "The Court Jews of Edwardian England."
JSS, v.5 #4 (Oct., 1943): 355-366.

1197. ___: "The Jews in the Defence of Britain: Thirteenth
to Nineteenth Centuries." TJHSE, v.15 (1939/1945): 1-28.

> #375. Rubenstein, W.: THE LEFT, THE RIGHT, AND THE JEWS.

1198. Schroeter, D.: "Anglo-Jewry and Essaouira [Mogador],
1860-1900: the Social Implications of Philanthropy." TJHSE,
v.28 (1981/82): 60-88.

1199. Schwab, Walter M.: "Some Aspects of the Relationship
between the German and the Anglo-Jewish Communities." LBIYB,
v.2 (1957): 166-176.

1200. Stiebel, Joan: "The Central British Fund for World
Jewish Relief." TJHSE, v.27 (1978/80): 51-60.

> #392. Szajkowski, Z.: "Conflicts in the A.I.U."

> #476. Wasserstein, B.: BRITAIN AND THE JEWS OF EUROPE.

Readmission

1201. Abrahams, Lionel: "Menasseh Ben Israel´s Mission to
Oliver Cromwell." JQR, v.14 #1 (Oct., 1901): 1-25.

1202. Diamond, A. S.: "The Cemetery of the Resettlement."
TJHSE, v.19 (1955/59): 163-190.

1203. ___ : "The Community of the Resettlement, 1656-1684: a Social Survey." TJHSE, v.24 (1970/73): 134-150.

1204. Gollancz, Hermann: "A Contribution to the History of the Readmission of the Jews." TJHSE, v.6 (1908/10): 189-204.

1205. Henriques, H. S. Q.: THE RETURN OF THE JEWS TO ENGLAND. London: Chatto, 1908. 132 pp., notes, index.

Studies the legal background of the return of Jews to England in 1685. The book was originally serialized in the Jewish Quarterly Review [old series]. At its broadest the book is a review of English law and legal problems that concerned Jews on the individual and community levels. Twenty-one relevant court cases and ninety legal statutes are reviewed. A secondary theme is the sociopolitical background that led to the restoration of English Jewry and to the development of Anglo-Jewish communal status.

1206. Katz, David S.: "English Redemption and Jewish Readmission in 1656." JJS, v.34 #1 (Spr., 1983): 73-91.

1207. ___ : PHILOSEMITISM AND THE READMISSION OF THE JEWS TO ENGLAND, 1603-1655. Oxford: Clarendon Press, 1982. 286 pp., notes, bibliog., index.

Effort at a revisionist history of the readmission of the Jews to England. Though he agrees that the readmission must be placed into the context of the English civil war, Katz argues that elements which could be defined as philosemitic also played a clear role in the readmission. The items that Katz includes are the renewed interest in Hebraism; the search for the ten tribes; the debate on the conditions for the second coming; and the debate on the validity of the Mosaic law. Accordingly, Katz argues that religious and practical reasons both led to the readmission. Surprisingly, Katz argues that love of the Bible was not the main cause for English philosemitism, even though three of his four elements are related to English bibliolatry. An important contribution to the history of the readmission, the book cannot completely replace the sociopolitical explanation of English willingness to readmit Jews.

1208. Osterman, Nathan: "The Controversy Over the Proposed Readmission of the Jews to England [1655]." JSS, v.3 #3 (July, 1941): 301-328.

1209. Patinkin, Don: "Mercantilism and the Readmission of the Jews to England." JSS, v.8 #3 (July, 1946): 161-178.

1210. Rabb, Theodore K.: "The Stirrings of the 1590s and the Return of the Jews to England." TJHSE, v. 26 (1974/78): 26-33.

1211. Roth, Cecil: "New light on the Resettlement." TJHSE, v.11 (1924/27): 112-142.

1212. Wolf, L.: "American Elements in the Resettlement." TJHSE, v.3 (1896/98): 76-100.

1213. ___: "Crypto-Jews Under the Commonwealth." TJHSE, v.1 (1893/94): 55-88.

1214. ___: "The First English Jew." TJHSE, v.2 (1894/95): 14-46.

1215. ___: "The Jewry of the Restoration, 1660-1664." TJHSE, v.5 (1902/05): 5-33.

1216. ___: "Status of the Jews in England After the Re-settlement." TJHSE, v.4 (1899/1901): 177-193.

Emancipation

1217. Abrahams, Lionel: "Sir I. L. Goldsmid and the Admission of the Jews of England to Parliament." TJHSE, v.4 (1899/1901): 116-176.

1218. Endelman, Todd M.: "The Checkered Career of "Jew" King: a Study in Anglo-Jewish Social History." AJS Review, v.7/8 (1982/83): 69-100.

1219. ___: THE JEWS OF GEORGIAN ENGLAND, 1714-1830: TRADITION AND CHANGE IN A LIBERAL SOCIETY. Philadelphia: JPS, 1979. 370 pp., illus., notes, bibliog., index.

Social history of English Jewry during the period just before the Emancipation. Most significant is Endelman's de-emphasis of the intellectual process of haskalah and his focus on social developments. Endelman also approaches the question from a dual perspective: from that of the upper-class Jewish elite, whose views were often analyzed by historians, and from that of the lower Jewish classes, whose

views on haskalah were most often ignored by Jewish historians. One of Endelman's subthemes is the incidence of
crime among lower-class Jews, a highly controversial issue
at the time. Endelman shows that criminal behavior is proof
of the Anglicization of the lower classes, who adopted the
mores of the general society in the same way that the rich
adopted styles appropriate to a more genteel society.

1220. Finestein, I.: "An Aspect of the Jews and English
Marriage Law during the Emancipation." JJoS, v.7 #1 (June,
1965): 3-21.

1221. ___: "Anglo-Jewish Opinion during the Struggle for
Emancipation [1828-1858]." TJHSE, v.20 (1959/61): 113-143.

1222. ___: "A Modern Examination of Macaulay's Case for
the Civil Emancipation of the Jews." TJHSE, v.28 (1981/82):
39-59.

1223. Gilam, A.: THE EMANCIPATION OF THE JEWS IN ENGLAND:
1830-1860. New York: Garland Pub., 1982. 193 pp., notes,
app., bibliog., index.

Political survey of the emancipation of Jews in England.
Focuses primarily on Anglo-Jewish attitudes toward the
struggle for civil rights. Gilam places Jewish grievances
and their sources of support into context. The public debate
on emancipation is also elucidated. The significance of the
Emancipation, according to Gilam, was that it allowed Jews
to attain a full position in English society, a status they
actively sought, but not at the expense of Jewish identity.
The situation on the continent, where emancipation was
granted as a bargain - civil rights in return for assimilation - was thus completely unlike that of England. Gilam
differentiates between the implications of emancipation in
England and in the continent, making an important contribution to European and Jewish history.

1224. Hyamson, Albert M.: "The Jew Bill of 1753." TJHSE,
v.6 (1908/10): 156-188.

> #142. Katz, J.: TOWARD MODERNITY.

1225. Perry, Thomas W.: PUBLIC OPINION, PROPAGANDA AND
POLITICS IN EIGHTEENTH-CENTURY ENGLAND: A STUDY OF THE JEW
BILL OF 1753. Cambridge, MA: Harvard Univ. Press, 1962. 215
pp., illus., notes, bibliog., index.

Study into the Jew Bill of 1753. Primarily emphasizes
the political context into which the bill must be placed.
The book is an attempt to revise the view that there was
little or no ideological politics in England during the
period of Whig domination. As a result Perry is studying
Jewish history to illuminate a chapter in English political
history. The purpose of the bill was to permit the naturalization of individual Jews in a more streamlined way, by
permitting them to petition Parliament directly. The bill
initially passed and then was repealed as a direct result of
a Tory public campaign against the bill. Nevertheless, Perry
argues, with much justification, that the repeal had less to
do with Jews per se than with political alignments on the
migration issue in the mid-eighteenth century.

1226. Pinsker, Polly: "English Opinion and Jewish Emancipation [1830-1860]." JSS, v.14 #1 (Jan., 1952): 51-94.

1227. Reitlinger, Gerald: "The Changed Face of English
Jewry at the End of the Eighteenth Century." TJHSE, v.23
(1969-70): 34-43.

1228. Salbstein, M. C. N.: THE EMANCIPATION OF THE JEWS IN
BRITAIN: THE QUESTION OF THE ADMISSION OF THE JEWS TO PAR-
LIAMENT 1828-1860. Rutherford, NJ: Fairleigh Dickinson Univ.
Press, 1982. 266 pp., notes, bibliog., index.

Investigates the process and result of Jewish emancipation in England. Divides the process into two parts - the
Jewish initiative and the non-Jewish response. Salbstein
primarily focuses on the issue of Jews sitting in Parliament, since by 1828 their exclusion was the most obvious
form of discrimination. Significantly Salbstein seeks to
explain the Emancipation within a specifically British context, although he is also mindful of conditions throughout
the rest of Europe. As a result of unique English conditions, however, it was possible for Jews to argue their own
case publicly and attain civil emancipation while retaining
a full Jewish communal and religious life.

> #131. Scult, M.: "English missions to the Jews."

1229. Shaftesley, John M.: "Jews in English Regular Freemasonry, 1717-1860." TJHSE, v.25 (1973-75): 150-209.

Antisemitism

1230. Goldman, Aaron: "The Resurgence of Antisemitism in Britain during World War II." JSS, v.46 #1 (Wint., 1984): 37-50.

> #333. Hirshfield, C.: "Case Study of Modern Antisemitism."

> #334. Holmes, C.: ANTISEMITISM IN BRITISH SOCIETY.

> #337. Lebzelter, G. G.: POLITICAL ANTISEMITISM IN ENGLAND.

Zionism

1231. Cohen, Stuart A.: "The Conquest of a Community?: the Zionists and the Board of Deputies in 1918." JJoS, v.19 #2 (Dec., 1977): 157-184.

1232. ___ : ENGLISH ZIONISTS AND BRITISH JEWS: THE COMMUNAL POLITICS OF ANGLO-JEWRY, 1895-1925. Princeton, NJ: Princeton Univ. Press, 1982. 349 pp., illus., notes, bibliog., index.

Intensive study of the role zionism played in English communal life from 1895 to 1920. The book is not, however, a recounting of the diplomatic history of the Zionist movement or of the English Zionist Federation [EZF]. Cohen´s interest is communal politics, and his emphasis is on the changes in Anglo-Jewry that brought about the rise of a Zionist movement. Chapters of special interest, therefore, deal primarily with ideology and communal activity, not diplomacy.

Cohen sees British-zionism as pursuing a different communal stategy than continental Zionists. Whereas the latter sought to "conquer" communities and thus tried to provoke communal conflict, the former shied away from conflicts, insofar as it was possible, and preferred a policy of "infiltration." Cohen sees this policy as having both advantages and weaknesses; he in fact seems to emphasize the weaknesses, thereby placing the EZF on the periphery of the Zionist movement.

Interestingly, Cohen does not deal with the role that East European immigrant Jews played in the EZF in any systematic way. Some of his conclusions are, therefore, open to future revision. Nevertheless, the book is a classic of Jewish social history and represents a well-documented addition to the now maturing study of zionism.

1233. ___: "The Reception of Political Zionism in England: Patterns of Alighnment among the Clergy and Rabbinate, 1895-1904." JJoS, v.16 #2 (Dec., 1974): 171-185.

1234. ___: "Selig Brodetsky and the Ascendancy of Zionism in Anglo-Jewry: Another View of his Role and Achievements." JJoS, v.24 #1 (June, 1982): 25-38.

1235. ___: "´The Tactics of Revolt´: the English Zionist Federation and Anglo-Jewry, 1895-1904." JJoS, v.29 #2 (Aut., 1978): 169-185.

> #505. Fraenkel, J.: "The Launching of Political Zionism."

> #551. Friedman, I.: THE QUESTION OF PALESTINE.

> #510. Goodman, P.: ZIONISM IN ENGLAND.

1236. Hyamson, Albert M.: "British Projects for the Restoration of Jews to Palestine." PAJHS, #26 (1918): 127-164.

1237. Jaffe, Benjamin: "The British Press and Zionism in Herzl´s Time [1895-1904]." TJHSE, v.24 (1970-73): 89-100.

> #524. Rose, N. A.: THE GENTILE ZIONISTS.

> #566. Sanders, R.: THE HIGH WALLS OF JERUSALEM.

1238. Shimoni, Gideon: "From Anti-Zionism to Non-Zionism in Anglo Jewry, 1917-1937." JJoS, v.28 #1 (June, 1986): 19-47.

1239. ___: "The Non-Zionists in Anglo-Jewry, 1937-1948." JJoS, v.28 #2 (Dec., 1986): 89-115.

1240. ___: "Poale Zion: a Zionist Transplant in Britain, 1905-1945." SCJ, v.2 (1985): 227-269.

1241. ___: "Selig Brodetsky and the Ascendancy of Zionism in Anglo-Jewry [1939-1945]." JJoS, v.22 #2 (Dec., 1980): 125-161.

> #570. Stein, L.: THE BALFOUR DECLARATION.

> #574. Wilson, H.: THE CHARIOT OF ISRAEL.

Religion

1242. Barnett, Arthur: THE WESTERN SYNAGOGUE THROUGH TWO CENTURIES. London: Vallentine Mitchell, 1961. 310 pp., illus., apps., index.

Communal history of a congregation in West London. The book is a bicentennial commemoration based on the records of the Western Synagogue. Barnett gives a detailed description of the shul, its leading personalities, and the important issues that concerned West End Jewry for over two hundred years. The Western Synagogue originated with the "Hevra Kaddisha" of Westminster, developing into a friendly society and then into a congregation. Barnett views the congregation as a microcosm of London Jewry and of Anglo-Jewry as a whole. Foreword by Cecil Roth.

1243. Bayme, Steven: "Claude Montefiore, Lily Montagu and the Origins of the Jewish Religious Union." TJHSE, v.27 (1978/80): 61-71.

1244. Cohen, Norman: "Non-Religious Factors in the Emergence of the Chief Rabbinate." TJHSE, v.21 (1962/1967): 304-313.

1245. Duschinsky, Charles: THE RABBINATE OF THE GREAT SYNAGOGUE, LONDON, 1756-1842. Franborough: Gregg International, 1971. 305 pp., notes, apps., index.

Idiosyncratic history of the Ashkenazi community of London in the eighteenth and nineteenth centuries. Sections of the book appeared as a series of articles in the JEWISH QUARTERLY REVIEW [o.s.]. Organized around the biographies of the rabbis who ministered at London's Great Synagogue in this period. By reconstructing the lives and literary activity of these eminent rabbis – the rabbinate of the Great Synagogue eventually evolved into the Chief Rabbinate – the development of the Ashkenazi community at the time can be charted as well. Unfortunately, this focus is considerably weakened by Duschinsky's almost exclusively biographical approach. The most interesting sections are on the rabbinate's attempts to cope with communal developments and crises, for example, the development of Reform Judaism in England.

1246. Goulston, Michael: "The Status of the Anglo-Jewish Rabbinate, 1840-1914." JJoS, v.10 #1 (June, 1968): 55-82.

1247. Homa, Bernard: A FORTRESS IN ANGLO-JEWRY: THE STORY
OF THE MACHZIKE HADATH. London: Shapiro, Valentine and Co.,
1953. 224 pp., illus., notes, app., gloss., index.

History of the Machzike Hadath synagogue in London. One
of the most important synagogues of the Edah Haredith,
Machzike Hadath became the center for a more traditional
Orthodox movement among English Jews. The synagogue and its
leaders were very active in spreading observance throughout
all elements of Anglo-Jewry. The book is more a reminiscence of events than a strict historical account, but it
provides an illuminating glimpse into English Orthodox
Jewry.

> #208. ___: ORTHODOXY IN ANGLO-JEWRY.

1248. Kosmin, Barry A. and Caren Levy: "Jewish Circumci-
sions and the Demography of British Jewry, 1965-82." JJoS,
v.27 #1 (June, 1985): 5-11.

1249. ___ and Stanley Waterman: "Recent Trends in Anglo-
Jewish Marriages." JJoS, v.28 #1 (June, 1986): 49-57.

1250. Liberles, Robert: "The Origins of the Reform Movement in England." AJS Review, v.1 (1976): 121-150.

1251. Lipman, Vivian D.: "Synagogal Organization in Anglo-
Jewry." JJoS, v.1 #1 (Apr., 1959): 80-93.

1252. Meirovich, Harvey W.: "Ashkenazic Reactions to the
Conversionists, 1800-1850." TJHSE, v.26 (1974-78): 6-25.

1253. Newman, Aubrey: THE UNITED SYNAGOGUE: 1870-1970.
London: Routledge and Kegan Paul, 1977. 239 pp., illus.,
bibliog., notes, apps., index.

Organizational study of the inner life of the modern
Orthodox synagogues of London and the United Kingdom.
Founded in 1870 the United Synagogue, along with the Office
of the Chief Rabbi, has tended to the needs of religious
Jews in London and its suburbs for more than a century.
Newman, the official historian of the organization, surveys
developments over the course of a key century in Anglo-
Jewish history. He begins by explaining the conditions which
rendered the United Synagogue necessary. The changes that
animated London Jewry are detailed, as are the economic,
religious, political, and social issues that, at times,

became major debates in the committees and subcommittees of the United Synagogue. Despite many problems, both economic and ideological, the United Synagogue has proved to be one of Anglo-Jewry's most important organizations, providing vital services for those Jews who have remained loyal to the traditional style of religious life.

1254. Prais, S. J.: "Synagogue Statistics and the Jewish Population of Great Britain, 1900-70." JJoS, v.14 #2 (Dec., 1972): 215-228.

1255. Roth, Cecil: THE GREAT SYNAGOGUE, LONDON 1690-1940. London: Goldston and Sons, 1950. 311 pp., illus., notes, app., chron., index.

Illustrated history of the Ashkenazi English Orthodox community, surveying the role that the Great Synagogue played in Anglo-Jewish life. Indirectly surveys the means by which Orthodox English Jews were Anglicized, and the methods by which they were able to synthesize Judaism with Anglo-Saxon mores. Especially interesting, in this regard, is Roth's review of the Reform controversy and his discussion of the emergence of the Chief Rabbinate. Inter alia the book is a carefully reconstructed record of Anglo-Jewish religious life over two-and-a-half centuries.

1256. Sharot, Stephen: "Native Jewry and the Religious Anglicization of Immigrants in London: 1870-1905." JJoS, v.16 #1 (June, 1974): 39-56.

Education

1257. Barnett, A.: "Sussex Hall - the First Anglo-Jewish Venture in Popular Education." TJHSE, v.19 (1955/59): 65-79.

1258. Cassell, Curtis E.: "The West Metropolitan Jewish School 1845-1897." TJHSE, v.19 (1955/59): 115-128.

1259. de Kadt, Emanuel J.: "Locating Minority Group Members: Two British Surveys of Jewish University Students." JJoS, v.6 #1 (July, 1964): 30-51.

1260. Goodman, M.: "A Research Note on Jewish Education on Merseyside, 1962." JJoS, v.7 #1 (June, 1965): 30-45.

1261. Levin, Salmond S.: "The Origins of the Jews´ Free School." TJHSE, v.19 (1955/59): 97-114.

1262. Prais, S. J.: "A Sample Survey on Jewish Education in London, 1972-73." JJoS, v.16 #2 (Dec., 1974): 133-154.

1263. Steinberg, B.: "Jewish Education in Great Britain during World War II." JSS, v.29 #1 (Jan., 1967): 27-63.

1264. ___: "Jewish Schooling in Great Britain." JJoS, v.6 #1 (July, 1964): 52-68.

1265. Wasserstein, Bernard: "Jewish Identification among Students at Oxford." JJoS, v.13 #2 (Dec., 1971): 135-152.

Labor and Economics

> #91. Aris, S.: THE JEWS IN BUSINESS.

1266. Elman, Peter: "The Beginnings of the Jewish Trade Union Movement in England." TJHSE, v.17 (1951/52): 53-62.

1267. Giuseppi, J. A.: "Sephardi Jews and the Early Years of The Bank of England." TJHSE, v.19 (1955/59): 53-63.

1268. Lipman, Vivian D.: "Trends in Anglo-Jewish Occupation." JJoS, v.2 #2 (Nov., 1960): 202-218.

1269. Pollins, Harold: ECONOMIC HISTORY OF THE JEWS IN ENGLAND. Rutherford, NJ: Fairleigh Dickinson Univ. Press, 1982. 339 pp., notes, bibliog., gloss., index.

Investigates the place of Anglo-Jewry in the British economy since 1656. Primary focus is on London Jewry, but other Jewish centers in Britain are discussed as well. The role Jews played in the commercial revolution, in the capitalist reorientation of the British economy, and in the Industrial Revolution are assessed. In all three cases, contrary to the predictions of Werner Sombart [see #99], Jewish influence was considerably less than would be expected. Jews made important contributions to some industrial areas of the British economy before 1800, but these contributions were never decisive. On the other hand, Jews made important contributions by financing the entrepreneurial activities of others. After 1880 the Jewish role in the economy changed radically: immigrant Jews comprised a large percentage of the urban working class. Pollins offers both historical and sociological insights, ending his book with a review of the upward mobility of Anglo-Jewry since 1945.

1270. Rollin, A. R.: "The Jewish Contribution to the British Textile Industry: Builders of Bradford." TJHSE, v.17 (1951/52): 54-51.

1271. Rubinstein, Wm. D.: "Jews Among Top British Wealth Holders, 1857-1969: Decline of the Golden Age." JSS, v.34 #1 (Jan., 1972): 73-84.

Communal Histories

1272. Adler, Elkan N.: LONDON. Philadelphia: JPS, 1930. 255 pp., illus., bibliog., chron., index.

Survey of the Jews of London from the settlement [1066] to the twentieth century. Part of the Jewish Publication Society communal history series, and one of the better volumes in that series. In light of London's importance for Anglo-Jewish history the book is, in effect, a history of English Jewry. Most of the chapters deal with distinct eras, organized by the reigning monarch, but a few are thematic. Of special interest are the chapter on Abraham Ibn Ezra's stay in London and the chapter on London's associations with American Jewry. Although generally filial pietistic, Adler also deals with the underside of Anglo-Jewish life. The book is a good example of communal history and has much to offer.

1273. Adler, Michael: "The Jews of Canterbury." TJHSE, v.7 (1911/14): 19-96.

1274. Alderman, Geoffrey: "The Jew as Scapegoat?: the Settlement and Reception of Jews in South Wales before 1914." TJHSE, v.26 (1974/78): 62-70.

> #1242. Barnett, A.: THE WESTERN SYNAGOGUE.

1275. Benas, B. B.: "A Survey of the Jewish Institutional History of Liverpool and District." TJHSE, v.17 (1951/52): 23/37.

1276. Busse, G. W.: "The Herem of Rabenu Tam in Queen Anne's London." TJHSE, v.21 (1962/67): 138-147.

1277. Cromer, Gerald: "Intermarriage and Communal Survival in a London Suburb." JJoS, v.16 #2 (Dec., 1974): 155-169.

1278. Daiches-Dubens, R.: "Eighteenth Century Anglo-Jewry in and around Richmond, Surrey." TJHSE, v.18 (1953/55): 143-169.

> #1245. Dushinsky, C.: RABBINATE OF THE GREAT SYNAGOGUE.

1279. Finberg, Hilda F.: "Jewish Residents in Eighteenth-Century Twickenham." TJHSE, v.16 (1945/51): 129-135.

> #386. Goodman, P.: B´NAI B´RITH.

1280. Grizzard, Nigel and Paula Raisman: "Inner City Jews in Leeds." JJoS, v.22 #1 (June, 1980): 21-33.

1281. Guttentag, G. D.: "The Beginnings of the Newcastle Jewish Community." TJHSE, v.25 (1973/75): 1-24.

> #1247. Homa, B.: A FORTRESS IN ANGLO-JEWRY.

1282. Jacob, Alex M.: "The Jews of Falmouth - 1740-1860." TJHSE, v.17 (1951/52): 63-72.

1283. Joseph, Anthony P.: "Jewry of South-West England and Some of its Australian Connections." TJHSE, v.24 (1970/73): 24-37.

1284. Krausz, Ernest: "An Anglo-Jewish Community: Leeds." JJoS, v.3 #1 (June, 1961): 88-107.

1285. ___ : "The Edgware Survey: Demographic Results." JJoS, v.10 #1 (June, 1968): 83-100.

1286. ___ : "The Edgware Survey: Factors in Jewish Identification." JJoS, v.11 #2 (Dec., 1969): 151-163.

1287. ___ : "The Edgware Survey: Occupation and Social Class." JJoS, v.11 #1 (June, 1969): 75-95.

1288. ___ : LEEDS JEWRY: ITS HISTORY AND SOCIAL STRUCTURE. Cambridge: Heffer for the Jewish Historical Society, 1964. 150 pp., illus., map, notes, bibliog., gloss., index.

Social history of Leeds Jewry from the eighteenth to the twentieth centuries. The book concentrates on the organized

Jewish community; a secondary theme is the place of the individual in the community. The book is based on historical and sociological data, including 200 interviews Krausz conducted with Jews from Leeds and its environs. The data is accurate through the late 1960s, but is by now dated. Even so, Krausz offers many historical insights and has many interesting observations about Anglo-Jewry outside of London. In particular Krausz's comments on the role of zionism as a bolster of Jewish identity in Leeds can be used to compare the effects of zionism in other Jewish cities in England and the United States. Despite the small population, acculturation, and assimilation of Leeds Jewry, Krausz concluded that they were still a viable and cohesive community.

* 1289. Levine, Harry: THE JEWS OF COVENTRY. Coventry: The Jewish Community, 1970. 100 pp., illus.

1290. Levy, A.: "The Origins of Scottish Jewry." TJHSE, v.19 (1955/59): 129-162.

1291. Lipman, Vivian D.: "Social Topography of a London Congrgation: the Bayswater Synagogue, 1863-1963." JJoS, v.6 #1 (July, 1964): 69-74.

1292. Meisels, I. S.: "The Jewish Congregation of Portsmouth [1766-1842]." TJHSE, v.6 (1908/10): 111-127.

1293. Newall, Venetia: "The Jews of Cornwall in Local Tradition." TJHSE, v.26 (1974/78): 119-121.

1294. Newman, Aubrey: "A Note on Recent Research on the Jewish East End of London." JJoS, v.27 #2 (Dec., 1985): 135-138.

1295. ___ : "Provincial Jewry in Victorian Britain: a Report." TJHSE, v.25 (1973/75): 222-229.

1296. Newman, Eugene: "Some New Facts About the Portsmouth Jewish Community." TJHSE, v.17 (1951/52): 251-268.

* 1297. Phillips, A.: A HISTORY OF THE ORIGINS OF THE FIRST JEWISH COMMUNITY IN SCOTLAND: EDINBURGH 1816. Edinburgh: J. Dunald Pub., 1979. 45 pp.

1298. Rosenthal, Erich: "This Was North Lawndale: the Transplantation of a Jewish Community." JJoS, v.22 #2 (Apr., 1960): 67-82.

> #1255. Roth, C.: THE GREAT SYNAGOGUE.

1299. Roth, Cecil: "The Portsmouth Community and its Historical Background." TJHSE, v.13 (1932/35): 157-187.

1300. Samuel, E. R.: "Dr. Meyer Schomberg's Attack on the
Jews of London 1746." TJHSE, v.20 (1959/61): 83-100.

1301. ___: "Portuguese Jews in Jacobean London." TJHSE,
v.18 (1953/55): 171-230.

1302. Samuel, Wilfred S.: "The First London Synagogue of
the Resettlement." TJHSE, v.10 (1921/23): 1-147.

1303. Sharot, S.: "Reform and Liberal Judaism in London:
1840-1940." JSS, v.41 #3/4 (Sum./Fall, 1979): 211-228.

> #1256. ___: "The Religious Anglicization of Immigrants."

1304. ___: "Religious Change in Native Orthodoxy in London
1870-1914: Rabbinate and Clergy." JJoS, v.15 #2 (Dec.,
1973): 167-187.

1305. ___: "Religious Change in Native Orthodoxy in London
1870-1914: the Synagogue Service." JJoS, v.15 #1 (June,
1973): 57-78.

1306. Shepherd, Michael A.: "Cheltenham Jews in the Nineteenth Century." JJoS, v.21 #2 (Dec., 1979): 125-133.

1307. Singer, Steven: "The Anglo-Jewish Ministry in Early
Victorian London." MJ, v.5 #3 (Oct., 1985): 279-299.

1308. ___: "Jewish Religious Observance in Early Victorian
London, 1840-1860." JJoS, v.28 #2 (Dec., 1986): 117-137.

1309. ___: "Jewish Religious Thought in Early Victorian
London." AJS Review, v.10 #2 (Fall, 1985): 181-210.

1310. Spector, David: "The Jews of Brighton, 1770-1900."
TJHSE, v.22 (1968/69): 42-52.

1311. Stein Siegfried: "Some Ashkenazi Charities in London
at the End of the Eighteenth and the Beginning of the Nineteenth Centuries." TJHSE, v.20 (1959/61): 63-81.

1312. Vincent, P.: "Glasgow Jewish Schoolchildren." <u>JJoS</u>, v.6 #2 (Dec., 1964): 220-231.

1313. ___ : "The Measured Intelligence of Glasgow Jewish Schoolchildren." <u>JJoS</u>, v.8 #1 (June, 1966): 92-108.

1314. Williams, Bill: THE MAKING OF MANCHESTER JEWRY 1740-1875. New York: Holmes & Meier, 1976. 454 pp., illus., map, app., notes, bibliog., index.

Surveys the origin and growth of Anglo-Jewry´s second-largest community. Primary emphasis is on social history, although religious issues are also reviewed. The first Jewish settlers were peddlers from London who sought their fortunes in Manchester. Manchester, it might be added, was not a hospitable environment for Jews at that time, and many were literally run out of town. The community was founded around 1740, but did not attain stability until the first decades of the nineteenth century. Much of William´s attention is focused on the workings of the community through its response to internal and external conditions. Manchester Jewry is placed into the context of Anglo-Jewry as a whole, in particular, into the context of the latter´s organizational life. Williams re-creates the conflicts of the mid-nineteenth century in detail but avoids being polemical. Especially interesting is his reconstruction of the conflict between the chief rabbinate, which advocated communal unity, and those who supported local rabbis in their quest for autonomy. Williams ends with 1875, before the influx of East European Jews changed the community again. Moreover, according to Williams, despite shifts in communal focus since 1875, communal structure has remained essentially the same.

1315. Woolf, Maurice: "Eighteenth-century London Jewish Shipowners." <u>TJHSE</u>, v.24 (1970/73): 198-204.

1316. ___ : "Foreign Trade of London Jews in the Seventeenth Century." <u>TJHSE</u>, v.24 (1970/73): 38-58.

1317. Ziderman, A.: "Leisure Activities of Jewish Teenagers in London." <u>JJoS</u>, v.8 #2 (Dec., 1966): 240-264.

HOLLAND/THE NETHERLANDS

1318. Adler, Elkan N.: "The Jews of Amsterdam in 1655." <u>TJHSE</u>, v.4 (1899/1901): 224-229.

1319. Bloom, Herbert I.: THE ECONOMIC ACTIVITIES OF THE JEWS OF AMSTERDAM. Port Washington, NY: Kennikat Press, 1969 [Rep. of 1937 Ed.]. 332 pp., notes, apps., bibliog., index.

Thematic investigation of Jewish economic activity over the course of two centuries. Written to contribute toward a clarification of Werner Sombart´s claim that Jews played a key role in the rise of capitalism [see #99]. Eschewing abstractions and generalizations Bloom sticks to the concrete and the verifiable. Except for a chapter on the settlement in Amsterdam, Bloom does not deal with contexts other than economic history. Three types of Jewish economic activities are reviewed: trade and crafts, colonial and international trade, and finance. Based on his detailed study Bloom concludes that Jews did not invent capitalism, but did adapt to it rapidly and quite successfully.

1320. "Dutch Jewry: a Demographic Analysis." JJoS, v.3 #2 (Dec., 1961): 195-242; v.4 #1 (June, 1962): 47-71.

1321. Fishman, Joel S.: "The Reconstruction of the Dutch Jewish Community and its Implications for the Writings of Contemporary Jewish History." PAAJR, v.45 (1978): 67-101.

1322. Gans, Mozes H.: MEMORBOOK: HISTORY OF DUTCH JEWRY FROM RENAISSANCE TO 1940. Detroit: Wayne State Univ. Press, 1977. 852 pp., illus., bibliog., indexes.

Extensive survey of Jewish life in The Netherlands from the sixteenth through twentieth centuries. The book uses a simple chronological format to deal with the history of one of Europe´s secondary Jewries. Nevertheless, much more is also covered. Including extensive illustration, the book is a virtual encyclopedia of Jewish life in the Low Countries. Important individuals, organizations, and issues are all covered in an amazing amount of detail. Gans liberally quotes from original documents and from previous publications on Dutch Jewry. The volume also includes a briefer, panoramic historical summary.

> #1148. Harris, I.: "A Dutch Burial-Ground."

> #1435. Kaplan, Y.: "Curacao and Amsterdam."

> #142. Katz, J.: TOWARD MODERNITY.

1323. Kuhn, Arthur K.: "Hugo Grotius and the Emancipation of the Jews in Holland." PAJHS, #31 (1928): 173-180.

1324. Michman, Joseph with T. Levine [eds.]: DUTCH JEWISH HISTORY. Jerusalem: Hebrew Univ. Institute for Research on Dutch Jewry, 1984. 568 pp., notes.

Anthology of essays based on a symposium held in Israel in November-December 1982. The essays cover a wide range of historical, literary, and sociological topics. Emphasis is on the sixteenth and seventeenth centuries. The essays are arranged in a rough chronological order, although many gaps are obvious. Although this reduces the anthology's overall value, the essays nevertheless contain many interesting insights for the study of modern European Jewry.

CONTENTS: Joseph Michman: Historiography of the Jews in The Netherlands / J. I. Israel: The Changing Role of the Dutch Sephardim in International Trade, 1515-1715 / Robert J. van Pelt: The ´Instauratio Magna´ and the Jews / Y. Kaplan: The Social Functions of the ´Herem´ in the Portuguese Jewish Community of Amsterdam in the Seventeenth Century / R. H. Popkin: Rabbi Nathan Shapira´s Visit to Amsterdam in 1657 / F. P. Hiegentlich: Reflections on the Relationship between the Dutch Haskalah and the German Haskalah / Henriette Boas: Present-day Interest in Marginal Dutch Jewish Authors / Ivo Schoeffer: Abraham Kuyper and the Jews / S. E. Bloemgarten: Henri Polak: a Jew and a Dutchman Concert of Jewish Liturgy from Amsterdam / J. H. de Vey Mestdagh: A Methodological Approach to the History of Local Jewish Communities in the Province of Groningen / B. W. de Vries: A Corner of Jewish Economic History: Activities of Jews in the Dutch Textile Industry in the 19th Century / J. Arnon: The Jews in the Diamond Industry in Amsterdam / S. Leydesdorff: In Search of the Picture: Jewish Proletarians in Amsterdam between the Two World Wars / J. van Weringh: A Case of Homicide in the Jewish Neighborhood of Amsterdam in 1934 / Luc Dequeker: Jewish Symbolism in the Ghent Altarpiece of Jan van Eyck / C. Boasson: Jewish Problems in Dutch Poetry / Dan Michman: Problems of Religious Life in The Netherlands during the Holocaust / A. J. van Schie: Restitution of Economic Rights after 1945 / J. S. Fishman: The War Orphan Controversy in The Netherlands: Majority-Minority Relations / A. Morgenstern: The Correspondence of Pekidim and Amarcalim of Amsterdam as a Source for the History of Erez Israel / H. Peles: Mizrachi Pioneer Training in The Netherlands between the Two World Wars / M. Eliav: Jacobus Kann as a Zionist

Leader / R. Cohen: Boekman´s Legacy: Historical Demography
of the Jews in The Netherlands / I. Brasz: The Influence of
Economic and Demographic Developments on a Small Jewish
Community between 1870-1930 / Sergio Della Pergola: A Note
on Dutch Jewish Demography.

1325. Moore, B.: "Jewish Refugees in The Netherlands 1933-
1940: the Structure and Pattern of Immigration from Nazi
Germany." LBIYB, v.29 (1984): 73-101.

1326. Van Tijn, Gertrude: "Werkdorp Nieuwesluis." LBIYB,
v.14 (1969): 182-199.

IRELAND

1327. Huehner, Leon: "The Jews of Ireland: an Historical
Sketch." TJHSE, v.5 (1902/05): 226-242.

1328. Hyman, L.: THE JEWS OF IRELAND. Shannon: Irish Univ.
Press, 1972. 403 pp., illus., apps., notes, bibliog., index.

Surveys the history of the Jews in Ireland from the
thirteenth century to 1910. Hyman has uncovered many novel
features of Jewish life on the Emerald Isle, including a
clear Jewish background to the writings of James Joyce.
Deals primarily with social history, but includes a few
forays into literature and religion. Unfortunately, Hyman
does not deal with the interplay between Jewish and Irish
nationalism in twentieth-century Ireland or with the role,
if any, Jews played in modern Eire. Notwithstanding these
lacunae, the book is a very important contribution to the
history of a little-known Jewish community.

1329. Shillman, B.: "The Jewish Cemetery at Ballybough in
Dublin." TJHSE, v.11 (1924/27): 143-167.

1330. ___: SHORT HISTORY OF THE JEWS OF IRELAND. Dublin:
Eason & Son, 1945. 151 pp., bibliog., index.

Brief historical inquiry into Irish Jewry, more like the
foundation for a future history of that community. Almost
exclusively focused on the inner history of the community
and its synagogues. Also contains three postscripts to
Shillman´s essays by Lucien Wolf, Myles Ronan, and Gerald Y.
Goldberg.

1331. Waterman, Stanley: "A Note on the Migration of Jews from Dublin." JJoS, v.27 #1 (June, 1985): 23-27.

ITALY

1332. Bachi, Roberto: "The Demographic Development of Italian Jewry from the Seventeenth Century." JJoS, v.4 #2 (Dec., 1962): 172-192.

1333. Barzilay, Isaac E.: "The Italian and Berlin Haskalah [Parallels and Differences]." PAAJR, v.29 (1960/61): 17-54.

1334. Bato, Y. L.: "Italian Jewry." LBIYB, v.3 (1958): 333-343.

> #212. Cooperman, B.: JEWISH THOUGHT IN THE 16TH CENTURY.

1335. Della Pergola, Sergio: "A Note on Marriage Trends among Jews in Italy." JJoS, v.14 #2 (Dec., 1972): 197-205.

> #135. Duker, A. and M. Ben-Horin: EMANCIPATION.

1336. Dunn, S. P.: "The Roman Jewish Community: a Study in Historical Causation." JJoS, v.2 #2 (Nov., 1960): 185-201.

1337. Friedenwald, Harry: "Jewish Physicians in Italy: Their Relation to the Papal and Italian States." PAJHS, #28 (1922): 133-211.

1338. Grendler, Paul F.: "The Destruction of Hebrew Books in Venice, 1568." PAAJR, v.45 (1978): 103-130.

1339. Hughes, H. Stuart: PRISONERS OF HOPE: THE SILVER AGE OF ITALIAN JEWS. Cambridge, MA: Harvard Univ. Press, 1983. 188 pp., notes, index.

Brief biohistory of Italian Jewry since the rise of fascism. Attempts to evoke the ambiance of Italian Jewry and to peer into Italian Jewish history. The book is, however, limited by its point of view. Dealing with distinct individuals, no matter how typical, does not necessarily reflect upon the community as such. Hughes provides a glimpse into communal life, but this does not constitute a history of Italian Jewry.

* 1340. THE JEWS OF ITALY. Chicago: Anti-Defamation League of B´nai B´rith, 1938. 24 pp., bibliog.

> #142. Katz, J.: TOWARD MODERNITY.

> #338. Ledeen, M. A.: "Italian Fascist Antisemitism."

1341. Milano, Attilio: "The Number of the Jews in Sicily at the Time of Their Expulsion in 1492." JSS, v.15 #1 (Jan., 1953): 25-32.

> #459. Morley, J. F.: VATICAN DIPLOMACY AND THE JEWS.

> #344. Pedatella, R. A.: "Italian Attitudes Toward Jewry."

> #97. Poliakov, L.: JEWISH BANKERS AND THE HOLY SEE.

> #464. ___: "Mussolini and the Extermination of the Jews."

1342. Rossi, Mario: "Emancipation of the Jews in Italy." JSS, v.15 #2 (Apr., 1953): 113-134.

1343. Roth, C.: HISTORY OF THE JEWS IN VENICE. New York: Schocken, 1975. 380 pp., illus., notes, bibliog., index.

Originally part of the JPS series of Jewish communal histories, and the only one to also appear independently. Focuses on the day-to-day life of the community, its social life, and institutions. Venice was a major Jewish community in the sixteenth and seventeenth centuries, and it was Venice that bequeathed the word "ghetto" to the world. Roth surveys the Jews of Venice proper, and Jewish centers in far-flung Venetian territories, from foundation through the era of emancipation. Nevertheless, the book is undocumented and this weakens its overall value.

1344. ___: THE HISTORY OF THE JEWS OF ITALY. Philadelphia: JPS, 1946. 575 pp., illus., index.

Broad survey of Italian Jewish history, with emphasis on social and intellectual currents. Roth operates chronologically, from the Roman Empire until World War II. Although the imperial period is of interest, it is Roth´s weakest section, as sources are lacking and the existing material is laced with legend. The largest part of the book covers the medieval period, from the rise of Christianity. Here Roth is at his best, able to describe very broadly, but in sufficient detail, the ways of life of the Italian Jews. The modern period contains much useful information, but is only an introduction to that era in Italian-Jewish history. One of Roth's best works, the book is unfortunately undocumented and contains only a brief bibliographic note.

> #294. ___: JEWS IN THE RENAISSANCE.

1345. Saperstein, Marc: "Martyrs, Merchants and Rabbis: Jewish Communal Conflict as Reflected in the Responsa on the Boycott of Ancona." _JSS_, v.43 #3/4 (Sum./Fall, 1981): 215-228.

> #102. Schmelz, U.: JEWISH POPULATION STUDIES.

1346. Semi, Emanuela T.: "A Note on the Lubavitch Hassidim in Milan." _JJoS_, v.20 #1 (June, 1978): 39-47.

1347. Shulvas, Moses A.: "Ashkenazic Jewry in Italy." _Y/A_, v.7 (1952): 110-131.

1348. ___: "The Jewish Population in Renaissance Italy." _JSS_, v.13 #1 (Jan., 1951): 3-24.

> #296. ___: JEWS IN THE WORLD OF THE RENAISSANCE.

> #350. Starr, Joshua: "Italy's Antisemites."

1349. ___: "Jewish Life in Crete under the Rule of Venice." _PAAJR_, v.12 (1942): 59-114.

1350. Vogelstein, Hermann: ROME. Trans. from the German by M. Hadas. Philadelphia: JPS, 1940. 421 pp., illus., app., notes, bibliog., index.

History of the Jewish community of Rome from pagan times to the Emancipation. Part of the JPS communities series. Rome has the distinction of having the oldest continuous Jewish community on the European continent, and most but not all of this history is reviewed by the author. Stress is on social history, and most of the material is on the medieval period. The ancient period is discussed adequately, as is life in the ghetto. The modern period is covered to 1870, but nothing after that is included. Much of his attention is focused on Jewish-Christian and Jewish-papal relations. Intellectual history is given proportionately less attention than in other volumes of the series.

> #478. Zucotti, S.: THE ITALIANS AND THE HOLOCAUST.

PORTUGAL

> 1183. Barnett, R. D.: "Sephardic Influx from Portugal."

1351. de Bethencourt, Cardozo: "The Jews in Portugal from 1773 to 1902." JQR, v.15 #2 (Jan., 1903): 251-274.

* 1352. MARRANOS IN PORTUGAL: SURVEY 1926 TO 1938. London: Potuguese Marranos Committee, 1938. 26 pp., illus.

> 1301. Samuel, E. R.: "Portuguese Jews in Jacobean London."

SPAIN

1353. Aronsfeld, C. C.: THE GHOSTS OF 1492: JEWISH ASPECTS OF THE STRUGGLE FOR RELIGIOUS FREEDOM IN SPAIN. New York: Columbia Univ. Press, 1979. 96 pp.

Investigation into the role Jews have played in the search for religious freedom in modern Spain. Aronsfeld begins with the decline and final closing of the Inquisition on July 15, 1834. From that point onward Jews have been in the forefront in the struggle for civil liberties, freedom of worship, and human rights. Of course, it is necesary to note that there were no Jews in Spain at the time; nineteenth-century initiatives on civil rights came from Jews in Germany and England. The latter also called for a Spanish-Jewish reconciliation to be initiated by a reset-tlement of Sephardim. Although these activists did not achieve their goals, they did interest some Spanish public figures in the question of religious freedom. Even so, Spain did not become a haven for East European Jews during the pre-World War I era of mass migration. Only in 1917 was the Jewish community officially reestablished with the opening of a small synagogue in Madrid. More significant, in Aronsfeld´s mind, is the role Franco´s Spain played as a temporary haven for Jews during the Nazi era.

> #425. Avni, H.: SPAIN, THE JEWS, AND FRANCO.

1354. Baer, Yitzhak: A HISTORY OF THE JEWS IN CHRISTIAN SPAIN. Trans. from the Hebrew by Louis Schoffman. 2 vols. Philadelphia: JPS, 1971. 1,000 pp., app., notes, index.

Authoritative study of the Jews of Christian Spain. Baer
begins with the Reconquista and continues through the crisis
years of the fourteenth century, completing his account with
the expulsion in 1492. Special emphasis is placed on conditions within the Jewish community and on Jewish-Christian
relations. Exceedingly well documented; the English edition
is the culmination of many years of research, the results of
which were published in Hebrew and German.

1355. Beinart, Haim: "The Jews in the Canary Islands: a
Re-evaluation." TJHSE, v.25 (1973/75): 48-86.

* 1356. de Madariaga, Salvador: SPAIN AND THE JEWS. London:
Jewish Historical Society of England, 1946. 31 pp.

1357. Gottheil Richard J. H.: "The Jews and the Spanish
Inquisition 1622-1721." JQR, v.15 #2 (Jan., 1903): 182-250.

> #447. Hayes, C.: "Spain, and the Refugee Crisis."

1358. Leshem, Perez: "Rescue Efforts in the Iberian Penin-
sula." LBIYB, v.14 (1969): 231-256.

> #113. Netanyahu, B.: THE MARRANOS OF SPAIN.

1359. Neuman, Abraham A.: THE JEWS IN SPAIN: THEIR SOCIAL,
POLITICAL AND CULTURAL LIFE DURING THE MIDDLE AGES. Philadelphia: JPS, 1942. 685 pp., illus., notes, bibliog., index.

Two volume survey of Spanish Jewry from the tenth century
to 1492. Somewhat arbitrarily, the first volume, A POLI-
TICAL-ECONOMIC STUDY, deals exclusively with political history, and the second, A SOCIAL-CULTURAL STUDY, with social
and cultural history. Nevertheless, it must be emphasized
that the varied subjects of the book are covered intensively. Important chapters, for example, cover the history
of the Spanish kahal and its powers, Jewish courts, taxation, education, domestic life, and the relations between
Jews and non-Jews.

* 1360. Robinson, N.: THE SPAIN OF FRANCO AND ITS POLICIES
TOWARD THE JEWS. New York: IJA/WJC, 1953. 21 pp., notes.

> #115. Roth, C.: A HISTORY OF THE MARRANOS.

> #319. ___: "Marranos and Racial Antisemitism."

14

The Americas

SURVEYS

1361. Adler, Elkan N.: "American Autos." JQR, v.17 #3 (Oct., 1904): 69-77.

> #396. Baron, S. W. and G. Wise: VIOLENCE AND DEFENSE.

1362. Beller, Jacob: JEWS IN LATIN AMERICA. New York: J. David, 1970. 303 pp., index.

Journalistic report on the history and life of South American Jewry. After a brief historical review, Beller surveys his subject on a country by country basis. Three of the chapters cover individual themes: B'nai B'rith, the fight against antisemitism, and the continuing story of Latin American Marranos. Beller sees B'nai B'rith as a unifying force in the Jewish communities. Zionisn also played an important role in maintaining communal cohesion. Israeli diplomatic representatives often became the glue which held marginal Jewries together, even in cases where their missions were unconnected with Jews. Beller concentrates on the interaction of Jews with the non-Jewish environment, including their response to antisemitism. Based on extensive interviews the book offers a glimpse into the inner workings and external relations of Jews from Mexico to the Pampas.

1363. Cohen, Martin A. [ed.]: THE JEWISH EXPERIENCE IN LATIN AMERICA. 2 vols. New York: Ktav for the American Jewish Historical Society, 1971. 873 pp., bibliog., indexes.

Anthology of studies on Latin American Jewry, taken from the PUBLICATIONS OF THE AMERICAN JEWISH HISTORICAL SOCIETY.

Although not a synthetic history, the essays do cover a wide
variety of subjects and are quite interesting. Most of the
essays concentrate on the period before the South American
countries gained independence, and most deal with the early
colonial era. Much attention is focused on the operation of
the Inquisition in the Spanish colonies and on marranism in
colonial Latin America. Other essays deal with social and
intellectual history. The Jewish community of Recife, which
was seized from Spain by the Dutch and then recaptured, is
the subject of four essays. Wiznitzer's essay on the escape
of Dutch Jews from Recife in 1654 and their transfer to New
Amsterdam, provides a bridge between the Jewish communities
of South America and the United States.

CONTENTS: [Volume I]. G. A. Kohut: Jewish Martyrs of the
Inquisition in South America / A. Wiznitzer: Crypto-Jews in
Mexico during the Sixteenth Century; Crypto-Jews during the
Seventeenth Century / G. R. G. Conway: Hernando Alonso, a
Jewish Conquistador with Cortes in Mexico / Martin A. Cohen:
The Autobiography of Luis de Carvajal, the Younger; The
Letters and Last Will and Testament of Luis de Carvajal, the
Younger / C. Adler: Trial of Jorge de Almeida by the Inqui-
ition of Mexico / D. Fergusson: Trial of Gabriel de Granada
by the Inquisition in Mexico 1642-1645.
[Volume II]. Cyrus Adler: Original Unpublished Documents
Relating to Thomas Tremino de Sobremonte / E. N. Adler: The
Inquisition in Peru / G. A. Kohut: The Trial of Francisco
Maldonado de Silva / R. Gottheil: Fray Joseph Diaz Pimienta,
Alias Abraham Diaz Pimienta / M. Zielonka: Francisco Rivas;
A Spanish-American Jewish Periodical / H. L. Bloom: A Study
of Brazilian Jewish History 1623-1654 / A. Wiznitzer: Jewish
Soldiers in Dutch Brazil 1630-1654; The Synagogue and Ceme-
tery of the Jewish Community in Recife, Brazil 1630-1654 /
C. Adler: A Contemporary Memorial Relating to Damages to
Spanish Interests in America Done by Jews of Holland / M.
Kayserling: The Earliest Rabbis and Jewish Writers of
America; Isaac Aboab, the First Jewish Author in America /
A. Wiznitzer: Isaac de Castro, Brazilian Jewish Martyr; The
Members of the Brazilian Jewish Community 1648-1653; The
Minute Book of Congregations Zur Israel of Recife and Magen
Abraham of Mauricia, Brazil; The Exodus from Brazil and
Arrival in New Amsterdam of the Jewish Pilgrim Fathers / L.
Shpall: David Feinberg's Historical Survey of the Coloniza-
tion of the Russian Jews in Argentina.

> #1528. de Bethencourt, C.: "Spanish and Portuguese Jews."

1364. Elkin, Judith L.: "A Demographic Profile of Latin American Jewry." AJA, v.34 #2 (Nov., 1982): 231-248.

1365. ___: JEWS IN THE LATIN AMERICAN REPUBLICS. Chapel Hill: The Univ. of North Carolina Press, 1980. 298 pp., map, illus., notes, bibliog., index.

Broad social history of Latin American Jewry. Extremely useful as both a comparative history and a synthetic work. Although Elkin opens with the colonial era, she stresses the period since the Latin American countries gained independence. Her special emphasis is on the waves of Jewish immigration to Latin America before World War I and the eventual acculturation of the immigrants. Many interesting questions are raised, especially about the meaning of "Americanization" in its southern form. Elkin also makes some important comparative notes on North and South American Jewry in her final chapter.

> #399. Henkin, L.: WORLD POLITICS AND THE JEWISH CONDITION.

> #2039. Herman, D.: "Israel's Latin American Immigrants."

1366. Kohut, Alexander: "Jewish Martyrs of the Inquisition in South America." PAJHS, #4 (1896): 101-187.

1367. Lewin, Boleslao: "The Struggle Against Jewish Immigration into Latin America in Colonial Times." Y/A, v.7 (1952): 212-228.

1368. Liebman, Seymour B.: "Sephardic Ethnicity in the Spanish New World Colonies." JSS, v.37 #2 (Apr., 1975): 141-162.

1369. Sandberg, Harry O.: "The Jews of Latin America." AJYB, v.19 (1917/18): 35-105.

1370. Schers, David and Hadassa Singer: "The Jewish Communities of Latin America: External and Internal Factors in Their Development." JSS, v.39 #3 (Sum., 1977): 241-258.

> #102. Schmelz, U.: JEWISH POPULATION STUDIES.

1371. Sobel, Louis H.: "Jewish Community Life in Latin America." AJYB, v.47 (1945/46): 119-140.

> #1388. Syrquin, M.: "Economic Structure of Jews."

ARGENTINA

1372. Dulfano, Mauricio J.: "Antisemitism in Argentina: Patterns of Jewish Adaptation." JSS, v.31 #2 (Apr., 1969): 122-144.

1373. Elazar, Daniel: "Jewish Frontier Experiences in the Southern Hemisphere: the Cases of Argentina, Australia, and South Africa." MJ, v.3 #2 (May, 1983): 129-146.

1374. ___ and Peter Y. Medding: JEWISH COMMUNITIES IN FRONTIER SOCIETIES. New York: Holmes & Meier, 1983. 357 pp., tables, notes, bibliog., index.

Studies the Jewish political experience in three frontier societies. Intimately linked with Elazar´s other research into Jewish political and communal organization. Each country is studied separately, although a three chapter introduction and an extensive conclusion link the experiences of all three communities. At first glance the choice of Argentina, South Africa, and Australia seems rather odd. Yet the choice could not have been more appropriate. Despite the fact that all three countries are located in the southern hemisphere, all three have developed differently. Even so, all three share common problems as frontier societies. Elazar defines the three countries as "fragment societies," by which he means offshoots of European civilization. Quite usefully Elazar also compares the southern hemispheric Jewish frontier experience to that of the United States. Although arguing strongly for a comparison, Elazar also notes the unique points of each community. Thus, upon further study the communities are shown to have had a similar or at least comparable experience.

1375. Elkin, Judith L.: "The Argentine Jewish Community in Changing Times." JSS, v.48 #2 (Spr., 1986): 175-182.

1376. ___ : "Goodnight, Sweet Gaucho: a Revisionist View of the Jewish Agricultural Experiment in Argentina." AJHQ, v.67 #3 (March, 1978): 208-223.

1377. Horowitz, Irving L.: "The Jewish Community of Buenos Aires." JSS, v.24 #4 (Oct., 1962): 195-222.

1378. Lerner, Natan: "A Note on Argentine Jewry Today." JJoS, v.6 #1 (July, 1964): 75-80.

1379. Liebman, Seymour B.: "Argentine Jews and their Institutions." JSS, v.43 #3/4 (Sum./Fall, 1981): 311-328.

1380. Mirelman, Victor A.: "Attitudes towards Jews in Argentina." JSS, v.37 #3/4 (July/Oct., 1975): 205-220.

1381. ___: "Early Zionist Activities Among Sephardim in Argentina." AJA, v.34 #2 (Nov., 1982): 190-205.

1382. ___: "The Jewish Community Versus Crime: the Case of White Slavery in Buenos Aires." JSS, v.46 #2 (Spr., 1984): 145-168.

1383. ___: "Jewish Life in Buenos Aires before the East European Immigration [1860-1890]." AJHQ, v.67 #3 (March, 1978): 195-207.

1384. ___: "A Note on Jewish Settlement in Argentina 1881-1892." JSS, v.33 #1 (Jan., 1971): 3-12.

1385. ___: "The Semana Trapica of 1919 and the Jews of Argentina." JSS, v.37 #1 (Jan., 1975): 61-73.

1386. Rosenwaike, I.: "The Jewish Population of Argentina: Census and Estimate, 1887-1947." JSS, v.22 #4 (Oct., 1960): 195-214.

> #347. Schwartz, K.: "Antisemitism in Argentine Fiction."

1387. Sofer, Eugene F.: FROM PALE TO PAMPA: A SOCIAL HISTORY OF THE JEWS OF BUENOS AIRES. New York: Holmes & Meier, 1982. 165 pp., notes, bibliog., index.

Social history of the Jews of Buenos Aires, the first systematic study in English on a Latin American community. Covers the development of Buenos Aires Jewry from the 1880s to the 1970s. Special attention is focused on social and economic patterns as they compare to both Argentines in general and Jews in the United States. The Argentine environment is viewed as generally hostile to Jews, although certainly less hostile than tsarist Russia or Nazi Germany. As a result, Argentine Jewry is less assimilated into society than its economic level would suggest. Unfortunately, the position of Argentine Jewry within the society and polity could not be sufficiently reviewed and are worthy of further attention. In light of recent revelations, Sofer's section on antisemitism in contemporary Argentina, and es-

pecially his reliance on Jacobo Timmerman's highly contro-
versial viewpoint, is moot. These caveats notwithstanding,
Sofer's book is an important contribution to the study of
Latin American Jewry.

1388. Syrquin, Moshe: "The Economic Structure of Jews in
Argentina and Other Latin American Countries." JSS, v.47 #2
(Spr., 1985): 115-134.

1389. Weisbrot, Robert: THE JEWS OF ARGENTINA FROM THE
INQUISITION TO PERON. Philadelphia: JPS, 1979. 348 pp.,
illus., bibliog., notes, index.

Thematically organized synthetic history of the world's
fifth largest Jewish community. Argentina was a destination
of Jewish immigration for much of its history. Immigration
and the sociopolitical organization of Argentine Jewry are
the first of Weisbrot's subjects. Argentine Jewish culture
is reviewed in detail. Included in Weisbrot's survey are
zionism, religion, education, and the Argentine Sephardim.
However, the most interesting chapters of the book deal with
the place of the Jewish community in Argentine history. Of
special interest are the chapters on fascism and antisemitism during and after the Peron era. In addition to covering
the main communities, Weisbrot also deals with interior
Jewish centers. Based on archival material, a survey of
Argentine press, and thirty interviews with Jewish communal
leaders.

BOLIVIA

1390. Knudson, Jerry W.: "The Bolivian Immigration Bill of
1942: a Case Study in Latin American Antisemitism." AJA,
v.22 #2 (Nov., 1970): 138-158.

BRAZIL

1391. Bloom, Herbert I.: "A Study of Brazilian Jewish History 1623-1654, Based Chiefly Upon the Findings of the Late
Samuel Oppenheim." PAJHS, #33 (1934): 43-125.

> #1363. Cohen, M.: JEWISH EXPERIENCE IN LATIN AMERICA.

1392. Emmanuel, Isaac S.: "Seventeenth-Century Brazilian
Jewry: a Critical Review." AJA, v.14 #1 (Apr., 1962): 32-68.

1393. Falbel, N.: "Early Zionism in Brazil: the Founding Years, 1913-1922." AJA, v.38 #2 (Nov., 1986): 123-136.

1394. Hirschberg, Alfred: "The Economic Adjustment of Jewish Refugees in Sao Paulo." JSS, v.7 #1 (Jan., 1945): 31-40.

1395. Krausz, Rosa R.: "Some Aspects of Intermarriage in the Jewish Community of Sao Paulo, Brazil." AJA, v.34 #2 (Nov., 1982): 216-230.

1396. Wiznitzer, Arnold: "Jewish Soldiers in Dutch Brazil [1630-1654]." PAJHS, v.46 #1 (Sept., 1956): 40-50.

1397. ___: JEWS IN COLONIAL BRAZIL. New York: Columbia Univ. Press, 1960. 227 pp., notes, bibliog., app., index.

Inquiry into the Jewish community in Brazil during the seventeenth century. The community was initially founded by Portuguese Marranos, but did not grow until the Dutch captured Recife. During the Dutch period, Brazil´s Marrano colonists were permitted to practice Judaism publicly, which many did. Intertwined with the history of Brazilian Jewry at the time is the story of the Inquisition in Brazil and its activities. In addition to social history, Wiznitzer deals with the economic activities of Jews in Dutch Brazil. As is well known, when the Portuguese recaptured Recife the Jewish community was uprooted. Subsequently 23 Recife Jews made their way to Dutch New Amsterdam, thereby establishing the Jewish community in the United States. Only after Brazil became independent, in 1822, did the Inquisition cease to function; thereafter the foundations for a new Jewish community slowly took shape.

1398. ___: "The Jews in the Sugar Industry of Colonial Brazil." JSS, v.18 #3 (July, 1956): 189-198.

1399. ___: "The Members of the Brazilian Jewish Community, 1648-1653." PAJHS, v.42 #4 (June, 1953): 387-395.

1400. ___: "The Minute Book of Congregation Zur Israel of Recife and Magen Abraham of Mauricia, Brazil." PAJHS, v.42 #3 (March, 1953): 217-302.

1401. ___: "The Number of Jews in Dutch Brazil 1630-1654." JSS, v.16 #2 (Apr., 1954): 107-114.

1402. ___: THE RECORDS OF THE EARLIEST JEWISH COMMUNITY IN
THE NEW WORLD. New York: AJHS, 1954. 108 pp., maps, illus.

Inquiry into the minute book of the Recife Jewish community, written as a supplement to Wiznitzer´s history of the
community. Wiznitzer uses the minute book to elucidate
selected topics in the community´s history. The book is organized thematically. An important section reviews finances,
another deals with religious services and minhagim. The bulk
of Wiznitzer´s book is his translation of the record book
from the Portuguese original. Wiznitzer offers an interesting insight into the workings of Recife Jewry, with
special reference to the community´s inner life.

1403. ___: "The Synagogue and Cemetery of the Jewish Community in Recife, Brazil [1630-1954]." PAJHS, v.43 #2 (Dec.,
1953): 127-130.

THE CARIBBEAN

1404. Cohen, Robert: "Early Caribbean Jewry: a Demographic
Perspective." JSS, v.45 #2 (Spr., 1983): 123-134.

1405. Cundall, Frank et al: "Documents Relating to the
History of the Jews in Jamaica and Barbados in the Time of
William III." PAJHS, #23 (1915): 25-29.

1406. Davis, N. Darnell: "Notes on the History of the Jews
in Barbados." PAJHS, #18 (1909): 129-148.

1407. Friedenwald, H.: "Material for the History of the
Jews in the British West Indies." PAJHS, #5 (1897): 45-101.

1408. Hartog, John: "The Honen Daliem Congregation of St.
Eustatius." AJA, v.19 #1 (Apr., 1967): 60-77.

1409. Judah, George F.: "The Jews´ Tribute in Jamaica:
Extracted from the Journals of the House of Assembly of
Jamaica." PAJHS, #18 (1909): 149-177.

1410. Kayserling, M.: "The Jews in Jamaica and Daniel
Israel Lopez Laguna." JQR, v.12 #4 (July, 1900): 708-717.

1411. Loker, Zvi: "Jewish Toponymies in Haiti." JSS, v.40
#3/4 (Sum./Fall, 1978): 287-292.

1412. ___ : "Jews in the Grand´ Anse Colony of Saint-Domingue." AJA, v.34 #1 (Apr., 1982): 89-97.

1413. ___ : "Were There Jewish Communities in St. Domingue, Haiti?" JSS, v.45 #2 (Spr., 1983): 135-146.

1414. Rosenbloom, Joseph R.: "Notes on the Jews´ Tribute in Jamaica." TJHSE, v.20 (1959/61): 247-254.

1415. Samuel, W. S.: "A Review of the Jewish Colonists in Barbados in the Year 1680." TJHSE, v.13 (1932/35): 1-111.

1416. Silverman, Henry P.: "The Hunt´s Bay Jewish Cemetery, Kingston, Jamaica, British West Indies." PAJHS, #37 (1947): 327-344.

1417. Sonne, I.: "Jewish Settlement in the West Indies." PAJHS, #37 (1947): 353-367.

1418. Swetschinski, Daniel M.: "Conflict and Opportunity in ´Europe´s Other Sea´: the Adventure of Caribbean Jewish Settlement." AJHQ, v.72 #2 (Dec., 1982): 212-240.

1419. Wischnitzer, Mark: "The Historical Background of the Settlement of Jewish Refugees in Santo Domingo." JSS, v.4 #1 (Jan., 1942): 45-58.

COLOMBIA

1420. Neumann, G.: "German Jews in Colombia: a Study in Immigrant Adjustment." JSS, v.3 #4 (Oct., 1941): 387-398.

1421. Rosenthal, Celia S.: "The Jews of Barranquilla: a Study of a Jewish Community in South America." JSS, v.18 #4 (Oct., 1956): 262-274.

1422. Smith, John K.: "Jewish Education in Barranquilla: Assimilation Versus Group Survival." JSS, v.35 #3/4 (July/Oct., 1973): 239-254.

CUBA

1423. Sapir, Boris: THE JEWISH COMMUNITY OF CUBA: SETTLEMENT AND GROWTH. Trans. from the Yiddish by Simon Wolin. New York: JTSP Univ. Press, 1948. 94 pp., notes.

History of the Cuban community during the twentieth century. Jews first entered Cuba as a result of increasingly restrictive United States immigration quotas in the 1920s. The book is almost exclusively focused on the community and its relations with both immigrant Jews and Cubans. The Jewish role in the Cuban economy is dealt with in a brief chapter. Cuban policy on Jewish affairs is reviewed indirectly, as relating to immigration and antisemitism. The book is not a comprehensive history of Cuban Jewry, but does lay the groundwork for such a history.

MEXICO

1424. Cohen, Martin A.: THE MARTYR: THE STORY OF A SECRET JEW AND THE MEXICAN INQUISITION IN THE SIXTEENTH CENTURY. Philadelphia: JPS, 1973. 373 pp., illus., app., notes, bibliog., index.

Biographical history of Luis de Carvajal and his family, Marrano martyrs of the Inquisition in Mexico. Cohen dramatically re-creates the turning points in Carvajal´s life. The text is well written, fast paced, and carefully documented. Carvajal was to have become the Spanish governor of Mexico; instead he renounced all political ambitions in order to practice Judaism. Facing the Inquisition, Carvajal met a martyr´s death. Cohen concentrates on Carvajal, but also provides an insight into the lives of the Marranos who sought a haven in the Spanish colonies. In addition, Cohen looks into Carvajal´s literary legacy, especially the letters on Judaism that he wrote while imprisoned and awaiting execution. Included is an appendix listing all pertinent inquisitorial sources.

1425. Hordes, S. M.: "Historiographical Problems in the Study of the Inquisition and the Mexican Crypto-Jews in the Seventeenth Century." AJA, v.34 #2 (Nov., 1982): 138-152.

1426. Lewin, Boleslao: "´Las Confidencias´ of Two Crypto-Jews in the Holy Office Prison of Mexico [1654-1655]." JSS, v.30 #1 (Jan., 1968): 3-22.

* 1427. Liebman, Seymour B.: A GUIDE TO JEWISH REFERENCES IN THE MEXICAN COLONIAL ERA, 1521-1821. Philadelphia: Univ. of Pennsylvania Press, 1964. 134 pp., bibliog., index.

1428. ___: THE JEWS IN NEW SPAIN. Coral Gables, FL: Univ.
of Miami Press, 1970. 381 pp., illus., apps., notes, gloss.,
bibliog., index.

Inquiry into the history of Jews in the Spanish colonies,
primarily Mexico. Liebman's main focus is on the operation
of the Inquisition and its effect in limiting the development of Mexican Jewry. Based on extensive inquisitorial documentation. The book is organized around the various autos-
da-fe. Less attention is paid to the post-Inquisition
period. The era of Mexican independence is discussed
briefly, but in an interesting fashion.

1429. ___: "The Mestizo Jews of Mexico." AJA, v.19 #2
(Nov., 1967): 144-174.

1430. Meisel, Tovye: "The Jews of Mexico." Y/A, v.2/3
(1947/48): 295-312.

1431. Samuels, Shimon: "A Research Note on Jewish Education in Mexico." JJoS, v.20 #2 (Dec., 1978): 143-147.

NETHERLANDS ANTILLES

1432. Cone, G. Herbert: "The Jews of Curacao: According to
Documents from the Archives of the State of New York."
PAJHS, #10 (1902): 141-157.

1433. Emmanuel, Isaac S. and S. A. Emmanuel: A HISTORY OF
THE JEWS OF THE NETHERLANDS ANTILLES. 2 vols. Cincinnati:
American Jewish Archives, 1970. 1,165 pp., illus., gloss.,
notes, bibliog., index.

Detailed history of the Jews of Curacao from the 1650s to
the 1960s. Also reviews the history of Jews in the other
islands of the Dutch West Indies, including Aruba and St.
Martin. The detail with which the Emmanuels reconstructed
the history of Curacao Jewry is impressive. No topic is left
uncovered, although emphasis is on social and religious
history. Internal and external relations, communal politics,
economics, and the fluctuating status of the community as it
passed from Dutch to French, then to English, and finally
back to Dutch rule are all charted. In addition, the book is
richly illustrated throughout, providing a treasure of information on an almost unknown but still vibrant Jewish
community.

Special mention must be made of the appendixes in volume II. Covering a wide selection of documents, they complement the text in volume I at every juncture. Some of the appendixes offer lists, for example, of Jewish shipowners [appendix 3]; others are documents from private, communal, or government archives. The importance of these documents cannot be underestimated – they offer further insight into the life of the community. The book is a model of historical structure and balance, proving what patient research can accomplish even in the case of a small community.

1434. ___: "Jewish Education in Curacao 1692-1802." PAJHS, v.44 #4 (June, 1955): 215-236.

1435. Kaplan Yosef: "The Curacao and Amsterdam Jewish Communities in the 17th and 18th Centuries." AJHQ, v.72 #2 (Dec., 1982): 193-211.

* 1436. Karner, Frances: THE SEPHARDICS OF CURACAO. Assen, Holland: Van Gorcum, 1969. 94 pp., bibliog., index.

1437. Maslin, Simeon J.: "1732 and 1982 in Curacao." AJHQ, v.72 #2 (Dec., 1982): 157-164.

1438. Yerushalmi, Yosef Hayim: "Between Amsterdam and New Amsterdam: the Place of Curacao and the Caribbean in Early Modern Jewish History." AJHQ, v.72 #2 (Dec., 1982): 172-192.

PERU

1439. Adler, Cyrus: "The Inquisition in Peru." PAJHS, #12 (1904): 5-37.

SURINAM

1440. Cohen, Robert: "The Misdated Ketubah: a Note on the Beginnings of the Surinam Jewish Community." AJA, v.36 #1 (Apr., 1984): 13-15.

1441. Felsenthal, B. and Richard Gottheil: "Chronological Sketch of the History of the Jews in Surinam." PAJHS, #4 (1896): 1-8.

1442. Gottheil, Richard: "Contributions to the History of the Jews in Surinam." PAJHS, #9 (1901): 129-142.

1443. Hilfman, P. A.: "Notes on the History of the Jews in Surinam." PAJHS, #18 (1909): 179-207.

1444. ___: "Some Further Notes on the History of the Jews in Surinam." PAJHS, #16 (1907): 7-22.

1445. Hollander, J. H.: "Documents Relating to the Attempted Departure of the Jews from Surinam in 1675." PAJHS, #6 (1898): 9-29.

1446. Oppenheim, S.: "An Early Jewish Colony in Western Guiana, 1658-1666 and Its Relation to the Jews in Surinam, Cayenne and Tobago." PAJHS, #16 (1907): 95-186.

1447. ___: "An Early Jewish Colony in Western Guiana: Supplemental Data." PAJHS, #17 (1908): 53-70.

1448. Roos, J. S.: "Additional Notes on the History of the Jews in Surinam." PAJHS, #13 (1905): 127-136.

VENEZUELA

1449. Aizenberg, Isidoro: "´Die or Leave´: an Anti-Jewish Riot in 19th Century Venezuela." AJHQ, v.69 #4 (June, 1980): 478-487.

1450. ___: "Efforts to Establish a Jewish Cemetery in 19th Century Caracas." AJHQ, v.67 #3 (March, 1978): 224-232.

1451. ___: "The 1855 Expulsion of the Curacoan Jews from Coro, Venezuela." AJHQ, v.72 #4 (June, 1983): 495-507.

* 1452. Emmanuel, Isaac S.: THE JEWS OF CORO, VENEZUELA. Cincinnati: American Jewish Archives, 1973. 63 pp., illus., app., notes.

15

The United States of America
and Canada

UNITED STATES

Historical Overviews

1453. Baum, Bernard: "Fifty Years in America." <u>AJA</u>, v.23 #2 (Nov., 1971): 160-197.

1454. Birmingham, Stephen: THE GRANDEES: AMERICA´S SEPHAR-DIC ELITE. New York: Harper and Row, 1971. 353 pp., illus., geneological chart.

Journalistic biohistory of America´s wealthy Sephardi elite. Starting as a small group, initially with only 23 members, the Sephardim can rightfully claim to have founded American Jewry when they settled in New Amsterdam in 1654. Birmingham covers the history of the Grandees from their origins in Spain to the 1970s. His style is almost exclu-sively descriptive, offering little analysis. Although they played a major role in the foundation of American Jewry, most of the Grandees have assimilated out of the community; conversion and intermarriage consumed a large proportion of their descendants in this century alone. Of themselves the numerous anecdotes that Birmingham relates are interesting, but they are not inserted into a specific historical frame-work and therefore teach little about the origins or development of American Jewry.

1455. Blau, Joseph L. and Salo W. Baron [eds.]: THE JEWS OF THE UNITED STATES, 1790-1840: A DOCUMENTARY HISTORY. 3 vols. New York: Columbia Univ. Press, 1963. 1,034 pp., notes, chronological list of documents, index.

Anthology of American Jewish life. Originally planned as part of a larger series, but none of the other volumes has appeared to date. Covers American Jewry extensively, with chapters on economic, social, and religious affairs. Surveys the role of American Jews in public life. A wide variety of sources are included, most of which were not previously published. Every part and chapter has an introduction, and a general introduction reviews the development of American Jewry at the time.

1456. Feingold, Henry L.: ZION IN AMERICA: THE JEWISH EXPERIENCE FROM COLONIAL TIMES TO THE PRESENT. New York: Hipocrene Books, 1974. 357 pp., notes, bibliog., index.

Thematic and chronological synthetic history of American Jewry from colonial times to the early 1970s. The book is aimed at both the general reader and the college student; it could also be used by advanced high school students. Feingold notes that the American Jewish experience can only be understood in its American and Jewish contexts. Although the pattern of development of American Jewry has paralleled other ethnic groups, it also contains many uniquely Jewish elements and should be examined with this caveat in mind. Important chapters deal with American religious tolerance and with the Holocaust. Although few novel interpretations are included in these chapters, Feingold´s restatement and analysis of the facts is extremely important.

1457. Feldstein, Stanley: THE LAND THAT I SHOW YOU: THREE CENTURIES OF JEWISH LIFE IN AMERICA. Garden City, NY: Anchor Press, 1979. 606 pp., illus., bibliog., index.

Celebration of American Jewish life over three centuries. Begins with the establishment of the earliest Jewish communities and continues through the late 1960s. Interweaves social, economic, political, and religious trends. Attempts to re-create the drama of Jewish life. Feldstein often lets the actors of every period speak for themselves. Based upon extensive research, but breaks no new ground. This is a very important synthetic account.

* 1458. Foner, P. S.: THE JEWS IN AMERICAN HISTORY, 1654-1865. New York: International Publishers, 1945. 96 pp.

1459. Friedman, Lee M.: JEWISH PIONEERS AND PATRIOTS. Philadelphia: JPS, 1948. 434 pp., illus., notes, bibliog., index.

Apologetic history of American Jewry and a companion to
PILGRIMS IN A NEW LAND [see #1531]. This volume is organized
thematically. Once again, however, Friedman is best at
sketching individuals. Tries to prove that Judaism and
Americanism are not incompatible. This is especially clear
from the chapters on the relations between Presidents
Washington, Jefferson, Lincoln and Theodore Roosevelt and
the Jewish community. Preface by A. S. W. Rosenbach.

* 1460. Gartner, Lloyd P.: THE MIDPASSAGE OF AMEIRCAN JEWRY,
1929-1945. Cincinnati: Univ. of Cincinnati Press, 1982. 16
pp., notes.

> #287. Goldberg, J. A.: "Jews in the Medical Profession."

> #290. Kagan, S. R.: JEWISH CONTRIBUTION TO MEDICINE.

1461. Karp, Abraham J.: HAVEN AND HOME: A HISTORY OF THE
JEWS IN AMERICA. New York: Schocken Books, 1986. 401 pp.,
apps., notes, index.

Synthetic history of American Jewry from the 1650s to the
1970s. Argues that in the last fifty years, America has
ceased to be a "haven" and has become a "home," since American Jews have completely adapted to the environment. Deals
with social, religious, economic, and political history, and
is particularly useful in schools. Karp integrates documents
into his text and also provides lengthy excursuses on
sources and important issues for each chapter.

1462. Kisch, Guido: "German Jews in White Labor Servitude
in America." PAJHS, #34 (1937): 11-49.

1463. Korn, Bertram W.: EVENTFUL YEARS AND EXPERIENCES:
STUDIES IN NINETEENTH CENTURY AMERICAN JEWISH HISTORY.
Cincinnati, OH: The American Jewish Archives, 1954. 249 pp.,
notes, index.

Collection of Korn's essays on nineteenth-century American Jewry. Although lacking a single focus, the essays contain interesting comments on aspects of American Jewish history. Included in Korn's analysis are such topics as Jewish
pioneers, the impact of the Civil War, Jews in America's
political life, and Jewish education. Each essay is carefully documented, nicely written, and offers an interesting
insight into the growth of American Jewry during a momentous
century.

1464. Lebeson, Anita L.: PILGRIM PEOPLE: A HISTORY OF THE JEWS IN AMERICA FROM 1492 TO 1974. New York: Minerva Press, 1975. 651 pp., notes, bibliog., index.

Idiosyncratic but fascinating synthetic history of American Jewry. Lebeson attempts to integrate communal history with personal insights, and largely succeeds. In addition, Lebeson attempts to place the American Jew into his environment, both Jewish and American. What emerges is an all-inclusive history which is incisive, perceptive, and very readable. Although novel interpretations are few, Lebeson's use of documents of all types is unmistakable. Her sketches of key individuals are particularly good and Lebeson eschews partisanship. Of special interest is the chapter "American Jews Rescue the Remnant of Israel," which deals with the Holocaust, World War II, and the rise of Israel. Designed more for laypersons, the book is nevertheless also appropriate for classroom use.

1465. St. John, Robert: JEWS, JUSTICE AND JUDAISM: A NARRATIVE OF THE ROLE PLAYED BY THE BIBLE PEOPLE IN SHAPING AMERICAN HISTORY. Garden City, NY: Doubleday, 1969. 390 pp., bibliog., index.

Narrative surveying the place of Jews in the shaping of America and American history. Individual Jews and the Jewish community are both covered, with emphasis on the former. St. John's focus is on the history of the people of the Bible in a land inspired by the Bible. As a result of this interaction, American Jews have played an important role in both American and Jewish history. St. John offers a unique insight into American Jewry, although his orientation is almost theological.

1466. Sarna, J. D. [ed.]: THE AMERICAN JEWISH EXPERIENCE. New York: Holmes & Meier, 1986. 303 pp., apps., bibliog., index.

Anthology of essays covering American Jewry from colonial times to the Holocaust. All of the twenty essays were previously published, either in scholarly periodicals or books. The anthology is organized chronologically. Sarna selected the essays with school use in mind and the book amply serves as a source of information on American Jewry for both students and teachers. Each section concludes with lists of further reading. Sarna's introduction gives a broad and useful summary of the highlights of American Jewish history.

CONTENTS: J. R. Marcus: The American Colonial Jew: a Study in Acculturation / J. D. Sarna: The Impact of the American Revolution on American Jews / M. H. Stern: The 1820s: American Jewry Comes of Age / M. A. Meyer: German-Jewish Identity in Nineteenth-Century America / J. Isaacs: Ulysses S. Grant and the Jews / B. E. Supple: A Business Elite: German-Jewish Financiers in Nineteenth-Century New York / B. Kraut: Reform Judaism and the Unitarian Challenge / D. Dwork: Immigrant Jews on the Lower East Side of New York / Moses Rischin: Germans versus Russians / P. E. Hyman: Immigrant Women and Consumer Protest: the New York City Kosher Meat Boycott of 1902 / A. A. Goren: The Kehillah Vision and the Limits of Community / L. S. Dawidowicz: The Jewishness of the Jewish Labor Movement in the United States / Leo P. Ribuffo: Henry Ford and THE INTERNATIONAL JEW / J. S. Gurock: The Emergence of the American Synagogue / M. I. Urofsky: Zionism: an American Experience / L. P. Gartner: The Midpassage of American Jewry / Henry L. Feingold: Who Shall Bear Guilt for the Holocaust? the Human Dilemma / Deborah D. Moore: At Home in America / R. Alter: The Jew Who Didn´t Get Away: On the Possibility of an American Jewish Culture / S. J. Whitfield: American Jews: Their Story Continues.

1467. Schappes, Morris U. [ed.]: A DOCUMENTARY HISTORY OF THE JEWS IN THE UNITED STATES: 1654-1875. New York: Citadel Press, 1961. 766 pp., notes, index.

Comprehensive anthology on American Jewry in its first 225 years. Contains 159 documents on a variety of topics related to the development of American Jewry during that period. Unfortunately, the documents are not grouped by subject, and therefore many readers will have difficulty following up on some of the issues raised. A brief introduction attempts to place the documents into context, but with only limited success. The notes are very extensive and fill in some of the gaps, again with only mixed results.

1468. Stern-Taeubler, Selma: "American Jewry One Century Ago, 1852: Compilation from the American Jewish Press." AJA, v.4 #2 (June, 1952): 83-87.

* 1469. Suhl, Yuri: AN ALBUM OF THE JEWS IN AMERICA. New York: Franklin Watts, 1972. 86 pp., illus., index.

1470. Teller, Judd L.: STRANGERS AND NATIVES: THE EVOLUTION OF THE AMERICAN JEW FROM 1921 TO THE PRESENT. New York: Delacorte Press, 1968. 308 pp., notes, index.

Journalistic history of American Jewry in the crucial period from 1921 to the Six-Day War. Teller sees this period as one of transformation: the immigrant Jews matured and gave way to the next generation of native sons and daughters. The change was most obvious in the sphere of Jewish communal and institutional leadership. However, institutions do not interest Teller; his subjects are the people who played key roles in American Jewry during this period. Teller also offers insights into his own actions, as both a journalist and activist in Jewish affairs. Many of the biographical sketches are based on close personal observation of the subject. Teller freely expresses his opinion on issues ranging from the trivial to the vital. Of special interest is Teller's chapter on the Holocaust, though some readers may find it one-sided. Teller's view of Black-Jewish relations, expressed in his last chapter, is interesting in light of the gradual deterioration in the Black-Jewish liberal coalition.

Jewish Life in America

> #396. Baron, S. W. and G. Wise: VIOLENCE AND DEFENSE.

* 1471. Bayme, S. and G. Rubin: AMERICAN JEWRY AND JUDAISM IN THE TWENTIETH CENTURY. New York: Hadassah, 1980. 64 pp.

1472. Berger, Graenum: "American Jewish Communal Service, 1776-1976: from Traditional Self-Help to Increasing Dependence on Government Support." JSS, v.38 #3/4 (Sum./Fall, 1976): 225-246.

1473. Bernheimer, Ch. S.: "Jewish Americanization Agencies." AJYB, v.23 (1921/22): 84-111.

> #60. Bubis, G. B.: SERVING THE JEWISH FAMILY.

> #61. Cohen, S. M.: AMERICAN MODERNITY AND JEWISH IDENTITY.

> #62. ___ and P. Hyman: THE JEWISH FAMILY.

1474. Duker, Abraham G.: "Socio-Psychological Trends in the American Jewish Community Since 1900." Y/A, v.9 (1954): 166-178.

1475. Glanz, Rudolf: "The 'Bayer' and the 'Pollack' in America." JSS, v.17 #1 (Jan., 1955): 27-42.

1476. ___: "The Rise of the Jewish Club in America." JSS, v.31 #2 (Apr., 1969): 82-99.

1477. Glazer, Nathan: AMERICAN JUDAISM. Chicago: Univ. of Chicago Press, 1953. 176 pp., apps., notes, key dates, bibliog., index.

Historical sociology of American Jewry. The author adopts a chronological approach, surveying the accommodation and conflict between Jewish tradition and the American ideal. Much of Glazer´s analysis is concerned with developments in the postwar era. His main focus is on the psychological and sociological ramifications of the Americanization of Judaism. The book is especially interesting for its approach, which lends itself to a comparative study with other ethnic and religious groups in the United States.

1478. ___: "Social Characteristics of American Jews, 1654-1954." AJYB, v.56 (1955): 3-41.

> #95. Goldberg, N.: OCCUPATIONAL PATTERNS OF AM. JEWRY.

1479. Goldscheider, Calvin: JEWISH CONTINUITY AND CHANGE: EMERGING PATTERNS IN AMERICA. Bloomington: Indiana Univ. Press, 1986. 195 pp., notes, bibliog., index.

Sociological inquiry into American Jewry. Goldscheider seeks to chart the influence of a changing and dynamic environment on the patterns of Jewish identity and communal cohesiveness. As such, the book is a more detailed follow-up of his THE TRANSFORMATION OF THE JEWS [see #31]. Here Goldscheider hypothesizes that changing patterns of Jewish communal life do not necessarily result in a weakening of Jewish communal cohesion. Basing himself on the Jewish community of Boston, he attempts to verify his hypothesis.
It does appear that Goldscheider has succeeded in proving his main contention, that despite major changes in the organization and modus operandi of Jewish communities in America, they have remained cohesive. Nevertheless, some nagging doubts do exist. First, Goldscheider´s evidence about intermarriage is not clearcut. Although most of those expressing an opinion about intermarriage, did not themselves seem ready to intermarry, a clear majority of certain segments in the sample saw nothing wrong with it. Second, the state of Jewish education in America is not systematically reviewed, and the large-scale lack of basic Jewish education is not taken into account in Goldscheider´s

conclusions. Finally, antisemitism receives very short
shrift. True, this is a book about the Jewish community;
nevertheless, antisemitism is a very real factor in Jewish
communal life and organization. Clearly Goldscheider has an
interesting and possibly fruitful approach, but this is not
the final word on the condition of American Jewry.

1480. Goldstein, Ronald M.: "American Jewish Population
Studies Since World War II." AJA, v.22 #1 (Apr., 1970): 15-
48.

1481. Goldstein, Sidney: "The Changing Socio-Demographic
Structure of an American Jewish Community." JJoS, v.8 #1
(June, 1966): 11-30.

1482. ___: "Population Movement and Redistribution Among
American Jews." JJoS, v.24 #1 (June, 1982): 5-23.

1483. Gordon, Albert J.: JEWS IN SUBURBIA. Westport, CT:
Greenwood Press, 1973 [Rep. of 1959 Ed.]. 264 pp., app.,
notes, index.

Sociological study of 89 suburban Jewish communities.
Gordon sought to chart the result of mobility on Jewish
identity and commitment. The first two chapters offer a
general context of suburban development since World War II.
The impact of suburbanization on Jewish communal life represents the core of Gordon's study. In the cities, Jews
developed a wide variety of communal institutions; these
made for cohesion. The situation in the suburbs, however,
differed drastically. Distances made contact between Jews
more difficult, while the homogenization of individual
tastes and styles made assimilation more desirable. This
process is portrayed by Gordon in chapters on the family,
the synagogue, and ritual. In turn, the process of suburbanization led to serious tensions within the communities, and
between Jews and non-Jews. Gordon also offers a prognosis of
suburban Jewry; in light of recent changes within American
Jewry, it would be interesting to see an update of Gordon's
basic study.

1484. Gould, Julius: "American Jewry: Some Social Trends."
JJoS, v.3 #1 (June, 1961): 55-75.

> #68. Greenberg, M.: "The Jewish Student at Yale."

1485. Janowsky, Oscar I. [ed.]: THE AMERICAN JEW: A COMPO-
SITE PORTRAIT. Freeport, NY: Books for Library Press, 1971
[Rep. of 1942 Ed.]. 322 pp., notes, bibliog., index.

Survey of American Jewry, written for the National Education Committee of Hadassah. The book sets out to survey,
analyze, and interpret American Jewry by providing a composite portrait of the American Jewish community. Written in
1942, the report is by now completely out of date, but is
useful as a historical source. The reader may get a sense of
the priorities in American Jewish communal life during World
War II from a careful reading of the essays. One will also
note that forty or more years later, many of the issues that
concerned Jewish communal activists then - such as education, antisemitism, and identity - are still actively debated within the forums of American Jewry.

CONTENTS: O. I. Janowsky: Historical Background / D. De Sola
Pool: Judaism and the Synagogue / I. B. Berkson: Jewish Edu-
cation - Achievements and Needs / Marie Syrkin: The Cultural
Scene: Literary Expression / A. S. Halkin: Hebrew in Jewish
Culture / A. G. Duker: Structure of the Jewish Community /
N. Reich: Economic Trends / J. J. Weinstein: Antisemitism /
M. Steinberg: Current Philosophies of Jewish Life / Sulamith
Schwartz: Zionism in American Jewish Life / G. N. Shuster:
The Jewish Community and the Outside World / H. M. Kallen:
The National Being and the Jewish Community.

1486. ___ [ed.]: THE AMERICAN JEW: A REAPRAISAL. Philadelphia: JPS, 1964. 468 pp., notes, bibliog., index.

Anthology of studies representing a concerted effort at a
historical and sociological analysis of American Jewry.
Religious, cultural, economic, demographic, and ideological
trends are all summarized. An especially interesting chapter
is Janowsky's analysis of American Jewish education; in view
of recent trends, the analysis was quite perceptive. The essays are brought together in three conclusions dealing with
leadership, culture, and community. Although outdated, the
book is a useful model for a sociological analysis of contemporary Jewry and does contain some interesting insights.

CONTENTS: J. R. Marcus: Background for the History of American Jewry / C. B. Sherman: Demographic and Social Aspects /
N. Reich: Economic Status / M. R. Konvitz: Inter-Group Relations / A. Hertzberg: The American Jew and his Religion /
O. I. Janowsky: Jewish Education / E. Silberschlag: Develop-

ment and Decline of Hebrew Letters / H. Cooperman: Yiddish
Literature / M. Syrkin: Jewish Awareness in American Litera-
ture / A. Werner: Art and the American Jew / J. K.
Eisenstein: Music and the Jew / Ch. S. Levy: Jewish Communal
Services: Health, Welfare, Recreational and Social / J. J.
Schwartz and B. I. Vulcan: Overseas Aid / Judd L. Teller:
Zionism, Israel and American Jewry / Abraham G. Duker: The
Problems of Coordination and Unity / H. Weisberg: Ideologies
of American Jews / E. Wolf: Leadership in the American Jew-
ish Community / J. L. Shapiro: Jewish Culture: Transplanted
and Indigenous / O. I. Janowsky: The Image of the American
Jewish Community.

> #69. Koenig, S.: "Studying Jewish Life in America."

1487. Kohut, Rebekah: "Jewish Women's Organization in the
United States." AJYB, v.33 (1931/32): 165-201.

1488. Kramer, Judith R. and Seymour Leventman: CHILDREN OF
THE GILDED GHETTO: CONFLICT RESOLUTIONS OF THREE GENERATIONS
OF AMERICAN JEWS. New Haven: Yale Univ. Press, 1961. 228
pp., notes, bibliog., index.

Studies the changes that Americanization wrought upon a
small American Jewish community [kept anonymous in the
work]. Kramer and Leventman surveyed three generations and
their responses to the local environment. Although primarily
concerned with sociology, the authors also traced the
historical development of the community to add depth to
their study. Ethnic identity was found to be unusually
strong in the studied city, a result of antisemitism and
other social and economic factors. But pronounced generational patterns, did not necessarily parallel those of
other communities, such as Boston and New York. For example,
synagogue attendance rose over a ten year period, although
commitment to other traditional forms of Jewish behavior,
e.g., kashrut and Sabbath observance, fell. The pattern
typical of other communities, in which the third generation
rediscovers the Jewishness abandoned by the assimilated second generation, was less pronounced in this community. Despite a few deviations from the conventional pattern, the
trends in this community were comparable to those of other
communities. The result is an interesting study, which could
lead to revisions of some of the most cherished ideas about
American Jewry.

> #70. Lehrer, L.: "Psychology of the Jewish Child."

1489. Linfield, H. S.: "Jewish Communities of the United States." <u>AJYB</u>, v.42 (1940/41): 215-266.

1490. Liptzin, Sol: GENERATION OF DECISION: JEWISH REJUVE-NATION IN AMERICA. New York: Bloch, 1958. 307 pp., notes, index.

Survey of American Jewish history, primarily focused on the issue of identity. Liptzin argues, forcefully and correctly, that American Jews have synthesized two identities into a unique way of life. Written as a contribution to Jewish survival in America, Liptzin also gives a review of American Jewry from colonial times to the twentieth century. Changing American perceptions of Jews, and the influence of this view on Jewish perceptions of both Judaism and Americanism, are given systematic coverage. Despite Liptzin's obvious point of view, the text is well documented and nonpolemical. Although readers may disagree with some of his conclusions, the insights Liptzin offers are important.

1491. Martin, Bernard [ed.]: MOVEMENTS AND ISSUES IN AMERICAN JUDAISM: AN ANALYSIS AND SOURCEBOOK OF DEVELOPMENTS SINCE 1945. Westport, CT: Greenwood Press, 1978. 350 pp., notes, bibliog., index.

Anthology providing a portrait of American Jewry since 1945. Every topic in American Jewish affairs is covered, each by a recognized authority. While the book is a useful contribution to the understanding of American Jewry, not all of the contributions are of equal value. The chapters on religious developments are among the best in the book. The chapter on communal organization and philanthropy is adequate, but is limited by its emphasis on the latter. Completely lacking is a chapter on political and lobbying activities, e.g. on behalf of Israel. In light of more recent events, the chapters on antisemitism and Jewish-Christian relations are inadequate, although it is still difficult to discern the precise pattern of American antisemitism since 1945. An especially interesting chapter covers the Canadian Jewish experience which parallels, but also differs from, American Jewry.

CONTENTS: B. Martin: American Jewry Since 1945: an Historical Overview / E. Rosenthal: The Jewish Population of the United States: a Demographic and Sociological Analysis / S. Z. Vincent: Jewish Communal Organization and Philanthropy / S. Spero: Orthodox Judaism / B. Martin: Conservative Judaism

and Reconstructionism / M. A. Meyer: Reform Judaism / David
Polish: Israel and Diaspora Jewry: an American Perspective /
W. I. Ackerman: Jewish Education / David J. Silver: Higher
Jewish Learning / E. L. Friedland: The Synagogue and Litur-
gical Developments / Arnold Forster: Antisemitism / S. A.
Fineberg: Jewish-Christian Relations / E. Rosenthal: Inter-
marriage Among Jewry: a Function of Acculturation, Community
Organization, and Family Structure / W. G. Plaut: Canadian
Experience: the Dynamics of Jewish Life Since 1945.

> #1194. Neusner, J.: "Development of American Jewish Life."

1492. Plesur, Milton: JEWISH LIFE IN TWENTIETH-CENTURY
AMERICA: CHALLENGE AND ACCOMMODATION. Chicago: Nelson-Hall,
1982. 235 pp., bibliog., indexes.

Social history of American Jewry in the twentieth
century. Primarily focused on the need to Americanize the
masses of Jewish immigrants from eastern Europe. Plesur also
covers the cultural and social ideas that East European Jews
brought with them to the United States. America, he notes,
reshaped these new Americans and their ideas in ways that
could not be predicted when they arrived. Antisemitism, particularly in the form of social and economic disrcimination,
is reviewed to help place American Jewry into context. Since
World War II, according to Plesur, American Jewry has
emerged from the periphery of American society to a place at
the center of American social, economic, and political life.
However, the influence has been two-sided; Jews have received much from American society but they have also contributed considerably in every conceivable area of American
life. As a result American Jews have created a unique ethnic
identity.

> #740. Rabinbach, A. and J. D. Zipes: GERMANS AND JEWS.

1493. Rose, Peter I.: "Small-Town Jews and Their Neighbors
in the United States." JJoS, v.3 #2 (Dec., 1961): 174-191.

1494. Roseman, Kenneth D.: "American Jewish Community Institutions in their Historical Context." JJoS, v.16 #1
(June, 1974): 25-38.

1495. Rosen, G. [ed.]: JEWISH LIFE IN AMERICA: HISTORICAL
PERSPECTIVES. New York: Ktav for the Am. Jewish Committee,
1978. 198 pp., notes.

Anthology studying the impact of America on Jewish life and Jewish history. The essays also offer insight into the Jewish contribution to America and the American ideal. Although covering an area potentially fraught with apologetics, the essays are forthright, objective, and judicious in their evaluations. Of particular interest is Gerson D. Cohen's essay "The Meaning of Liberty in the Jewish Tradition," which sets the tone for the anthology. Jewish social and political aspirations are placed into a clearly American context, showing the degree to which American Jews have internalized and judaized American mores.

CONTENTS: G. D. Cohen: The Meaning of Liberty in Jewish Tradition / R. B. Morris: The Role of the Jews in the American Revolution in Historical Perspective / M. B. Konvitz: The Quest for Equality and the Jewish Experience / M. Rischin: The Jews and Pluralism: Toward an American Freedom Symphony / I. Howe: East European Jews and American Culture / E. Ginzberg: Jews in the American Economy: the Dynamics of Opportunity / N. W. Cohen: Responsibilities of Jewish Kinship: Jewish Defense and Philanthropy / N. Podhoretz: The Rise and Fall of the American Jewish Novelist / I. I. Rabi: New Fields to Conquer: the Scientific Adventure on the American Scene / M. Sklare: Jewish Acculturation and American Jewish Identity / R. S. Berman: The American Experience: Some Notes from the Third Generation.

1496. Rosenthal, Erich: "Jewish Fertility in the United States." AJYB, v.62 (1961): 3-27.

1497. Sanua, Victor D.: "Patterns of Identification with the Jewish Community in the U.S.A.." JJoS, v.6 #2 (Dec., 1964): 190-212.

> #102. Schmelz, U.: JEWISH POPULATION STUDIES.

1498. Schwartz, A.: "Intermarriage in the United States." AJYB, v.71 (1970): 101-121.

1499. Sherman, C. B.: THE JEW WITHIN AMERICAN SOCIETY: A STUDY IN ETHNIC INDIVIDUALITY. Detroit: Wayne State Univ. Press, 1961. 260 pp., tables, notes, bibliog., index.

Sociological inquiry into Jewish status and identity in the United States. Taking issue with the "melting-pot" interpretation of American history, Sherman attempts to define Jews' role in American society. Sherman sees assimilation as the "tyranny of the majority" which strips the minority of its unique identity. Surprisingly, Jews have proved more immune to this process, as compared to other ethnic minorities. In Sherman's view, factors unique to the American Jewish community, particularly the existence of the State of Israel, have permitted acculturation without the complete loss of identity. Jews, according to Sherman, are thus assimilated, but in some respects isolated from the mainstream of American society. Jewish immigration is given special attention by Sherman, as are the internal and external causes for communal cohesion. Sherman concludes that Jews have deviated from the pattern of American ethnic minorities, and he offers insightful proof for his position.

1500. Silberman, Charles: A CERTAIN PEOPLE: AMERICAN JEWS AND THEIR LIVES TODAY. New York: Summit Books, 1985. 458 pp., notes, index.

Journalistic account of the state of American Jewry. The book is primarily an argument against the almost legendary American Jewish pessimism. Silberman asserts that conditions of American Jewish life have never been better, nor has any previous Jewish community in any country lived in such a free environment. Silberman marshalls a great deal of evidence in support of three main contentions: [1] religiously and culturally, American Jewry is experiencing a renaissance; [2] fears of numerical decline through intermarriage and assimilation are exaggerated; and [3] antisemitism is declining, although it is far from being completely eradicated. That last assertion is Silberman's weakest, since there is in fact no way to measure antisemitism objectively. Nevertheless, public support for positions that are anti-semitic appears to be waning in most circles.

As interesting as Silberman's account is, the reaction to the book is also interesting - some reviewers felt the book was overly optimistic. Silberman himself notes that some American Jews almost seek disaster, and always expect the worst. Be that as it may, Silberman's argument is of more than passing interest. The account seems accurate, although an objective evaluation is difficult in light of the recent nature of much of the material.

1501. Sklare, Marshall: AMERICA'S JEWS. New York: Random House, 1971. 234 pp., charts, notes, app., index.

Sociological analysis of American Jewry, with primary emphasis on post-World War II developments. Sklare's focus

is on individual and communal identities which have maintained American Jewry. Strong on analysis, the book is not
primarily expository, nor is there much on historical developments. Nevertheless, Sklare does provide a survey of
American Jewry at a single point in time.

1502. ___ [ed.]: THE JEWISH COMMUNITY IN AMERICA. New
York: Behrman, 1974. 388 pp., notes, bibliog., index.

Sociological inquiry into American Jewish communal life.
The book is a complement to THE JEW IN AMERICAN SOCIETY [see
#1503]. Formal and informal communities are reviewed, as is
the religious life of American Jewry. An especially interesting section deals with Jewish education, another with
Jewish-gentile relations. The book is useful in high school
and college courses on American Jewry and was designed for
that purpose from the start. Sklare's introduction attempts
to tie the essays and issues together, but is too brief to
cover both internal and external community affairs successfully. The introductions to the selections help place
them into context. Despite some lacunae, the book offers an
important insight into the American Jewish community.

CONTENTS: H. J. Gans: The Origin of a Jewish Community in
the Suburbs / M. Sklare and J. Greenblum: The Friendship
Pattern of the Lakeville Jew / D. J. Elazar: Decision-Making
in the American Jewish Community / M. Axelrod, F. J. Fowler,
and A. Gurin: The Jewish Community of Boston: Membership in
Synagogues and Jewish Organizations / Ch. S. Liebman: Ortho-
doxy in American Jewish Life / M. Sklare: The Conservative
Movement: Achievements and Problems / L. J. Fein et al:
Reform is a Verb / L. P. Gartner: Jewish Education in the
United States / W. J. Ackerman: The Present Moment in Jewish
Education / L. S. Dawidowicz and L. J. Goldstein: The Ameri-
can Jewish Liberal Tradition / N. Glazer: The New Left and
the Jews / S. M. Lipset: Intergroup Relations: the Changing
Situation of American Jewry / B. B. Ringer: Jewish-Gentile
Relations in Lakeville.

1503. ___ [ed.]: THE JEWS IN AMERICAN SOCIETY. New York:
Behrman, 1974. 404 pp., notes, bibliog., index.

Collection of essays on American Jewish history and sociology. The book is a companion to THE JEWISH COMMUNITY IN
AMERICA [see #1502]. Although the emphasis is on sociology,
many of the essays adopt a historical approach. The book is
especially useful for college or advanced high school

courses on American Jewry, and in fact was planned for that purpose. Sklare´s introduction ties the essays together and also offers some insight into methodology. The introductions to each essay discuss specific issues, placing such items as immigration, demography, and family into context.

CONTENTS: L. P. Gartner: Immigration and the Formation of American Jewry, 1840-1925 / C. B. Sherman: Immigration and Emigration: the Jewish Case / L. S. Dawidowicz: From Past to Past: Jewish East Europe to Jewish East Side / Ben Halpern: America is Different / S. Goldstein: American Jewry, 1970: a Demographic Profile / Z. S. Blau: The Strategy of the Jewish Mother / W. E. Mitchell: Descent Groups Among New York City Jews / S. Goldstein and C. Goldscheider: Jewish Religiosity: Ideological and Ritualistic Dimensions / Ch. S. Liebman: The Religion of American Jews / S. M. Lipset and E. C. Ladd: Jewish Academics in the United States / H. Cohen: Jewish Life and Thought in an Academic Community / A. Schwartz: Intermarriage in the United States / C. Goldscheider: American Aliya: Sociological and Demographic Perspectives.

> #81. ___ and J. Greenbaum: JEWISH IDENTITY.

1504. Sulzberger, David: "Growth of Jewish Population in the United States." PAJHS, #6 (1898): 141-149.

> #104. Vago, B.: JEWISH ASSIMILATION IN MODERN TIMES.

1505. Waxman, Chaim I.: AMERICA´S JEWS IN TRANSITION. Philadelphia: Temple Univ. Press, 1983. 272 pp., tables, maps, bibliog., index.

Sociological history of American Jewry from 1654 to the 1980s. Emphasis is on the contemporary period [since 1880]. Half the chapters cover the subject in chronological order, the remainder cover special topics such as family, religious denominations, education, and communal leadership. Based on numerous empirical studies as well as on purely historical research. Although little new information is uncovered, Waxman´s synthesis presents an important composite picture of American Jewry in the 1980s.

Historiography

1506. Baron, Salo W.: "American Jewish History: Problems and Methods." PAJHS, #39 part 3 (March, 1950): 207-266.

1507. De Sola Pool, David: "Notes on American Jewish History." PAJHS, #22 (1914): 167-175.

1508. ___: "Religious and Cultural Phases of American Jewish History." PAJHS, #39 part 3 (March, 1950): 291-301.

1509. Dublin, Frances: "Jewish Colonial Enterprise in the Light of the Amherst Papers, 1758-1763." PAJHS, #35 (1939): 1-25.

1510. Feingold, H. L.: "American Jewish History and American Jewish Survival." AJHQ, v.71 #4 (June, 1982): 421-431.

1511. ___: "The Condition of American Jewry in Historical Perspective: a Bicentennial Assessment." AJYB, v.76 (1976): 3-39.

1512. Gartner, Lloyd P.: "The History of North American Jewish Communities: a Field for the Jewish Historian." JJoS, v.7 #1 June, 1965): 22-29.

1513. Gittler, Joseph B. [ed.]: JEWISH LIFE IN THE UNITED STATES: PERSPECTIVES FROM THE SOCIAL SCIENCES. New York: New York Univ. Press, 1981. 324 pp., notes, index.

Anthology of historiographical and methodological essays surveying the state of American Jewish studies in the early 1980s. Each essay covers a different field of scholarship. There are few surprises in the essays; the reviews are important for their synthesis of recent scholarly trends. Gittler's introductory essay offers a few broad observations, for example, on who is a Jew, which help tie together the multiplicity of methodologies used in the remaining essays. While the insights in the anthology are more useful for scholars than laypersons, the book is an important contribution to the study of American Jewry.

CONTENTS: J. B. Gittler: Towards a Definition of a Jew and Implications of General Systems Theory for the Study of Jewish Life / S. Goldstein: Jews in the United States: Perspectives from Demography / M. N. Eagle: Jewish Life in the United States: Perspectives from Psychology / E. C. Ladd, Jr.: Jewish Life in the United States: Social and Political Values / S. Z. Klausner: Four Sociologies of American Jewry: Methodological Notes / A. Kahan: Jewish Life in the United States: Perspectives from Economics / H. L. Feingold: Jewish Life in the United States: Perspectives from History / Sol

Tax: Jewish Life in the United States: Perspectives from Anthropology.

1514. Grinstein, Hyman B.: "Communal and Social Aspects of American Jewish History." PAJHS, #39 part 3 (March, 1950): 267-282.

1515. Jonas, Harold J.: "American Jewish History as Reflected in General American History." PAJHS, #39 part 3 (March, 1950): 283-290.

1516. Kaplan, Hyman: "Jewish Social Research in the United States." AJYB, v.22 (1920/21): 31-52.

1517. Kraft, Louis: "The Popularization of American Jewish History." PAJHS, #39 part 3 (March, 1950): 313-317.

1518. Lebeson, Anita L.: "On the Writing of American Jewish History." PAJHS, #39 part 3 (March, 1950): 303-312.

1519. Lederhendler, Eli M.: "Jewish Immigration to America and Revisionist Historiography: a Decade of New Perspectives." Y/A, v.18 (1983): 391-410.

1520. Massarik, Fred: "New Approaches to the Study of the American Jew." JJoS, v.8 #2 (Dec., 1966): 175-191.

1521. Nathan, Gad: "Methodological Problems in Jewish Population Studies in the U.S.A.." JJoS, v.8 #1 (June, 1966): 4-10.

1522. Raphael, Marc Lee: "The Genesis of a Communal History: the Columbus Jewish History Project." AJA, v.29 #1 (Apr., 1977): 53-69.

1523. ___: "The Utilization of Public Local and Federal Sources for Reconstructing American Jewish Local History: the Jews of Columbus, Ohio." AJHQ, v.65 #1 (Sept., 1975): 10-35.

1524. Rosenwaike, Ira: "The Utilization of Census Tract Data in the Study of the American Jewish Population." JSS, v.25 #1 (Jan., 1963): 42-56.

1525. Sklare, Marshall: "The Development and Utilization of Sociological Research: the Case of the American Jewish Community." JJoS, v.5 #2 (Dec., 1963): 167-186.

1526. Whitfield, Stephen J.: "The Presence of the Past: Recent Trends in American Jewish History." AJHQ, v.70 #2 (Dec., 1980): 149-167.

Colonial America

> 1363. Cohen, M.: JEWISH EXPERIENCE IN LATIN AMERICA.

1527. Daniels, Doris G.: "Colonial Jewry: Religion, Domestic and Social Relations." AJHQ, v.66 #3 (March, 1977): 375-400.

1528. de Bethencourt, Cardozo: "Notes on the Spanish and Portuguese Jews in the United States, Guiana, and the Dutch and British West Indies during the Seventeenth and Eighteenth Centuries." PAJHS, #29 (1975): 7-38.

1529. Emmanuel, I. S.: "New Light on Early American Jewry." AJA, v.7 #1 (Jan., 1955): 3-64.

1530. Friedenberg, Albert M.: "The Jews of America, 1654-1787: With Special References to the Revolution." AJYB, v.28 (1926/27): 193-218.

1531. Friedman, Lee M.: PILGRIMS IN A NEW LAND. Philadelphia, JPS, 1948. 471 pp., illus., notes, bibliog., index.

Somewhat apologetic history of early American Jewry. Focused on distinct individuals, rather than on the community. The apologetics enter the book with Friedman's attempt to prove that Jews contributed greatly to Colonial American life. Since few would question the truth of that conclusion, Friedman's emphasis is belabored. Although the portraits Friedman sketches are interesting in themselves, they do not represent a history of early American Jewry per se.

1532. Goodman, Abram V.: AMERICAN OVERTURE. Philadelphia: JPS, 1947. 265 pp., illus., notes, bibliog., index.

Surveys the prehistory of the emancipation of American Jewry. The essence of Goodman's argument is that Jews were accorded civil rights in America as a result of the growing realization that Jews, too, ought to aspire to civil equality. The peculiar developments in American ideology, for example, the popularity of the Bible among the Puritans, led to a willingness to tolerate Jews in a way that was impossible in other countries. Although Goodman concentrates on the colonial period, his analysis is appropriate for the early years of American independence. Emancipation in America occurred without problems: Jews were granted full rights, with few debates, because the right of citizenship could not conceivably be denied to people who helped to build the new nation.

1533. Hollander, J. H.: "The Naturalization of Jews in the American Colonies under the Act of 1740." PAJHS, #5 (1897): 103-117.

1534. Huehner, Leon: "Jews in Connection with the Colleges of the Thirteen Original States Prior to 1800." PAJHS, #19 (1910): 101-124.

1535. ___: "Jews Interested in Privateering in America during the Eighteenth Century." PAJHS, #23 (1915): 163-176.

1536. ___: "Jews in the Legal and Medical Professions in America Prior to 1800." PAJHS, #22 (1914): 147-165.

1537. Kohler, M. J.: "Jewish Activity in American Colonial Commerce." PAJHS, #10 (1902): 47-64.

1538. Marcus, Jacob R. [ed.]: "Jews and the American Revolution: a Bicentennial Documentary." AJA, v.27 #2 (Nov., 1975): 103-257.

1539. Oppenheim, S.: "The Jews and Masonry in the United States Before 1810." PAJHS, #19 (1910): 1-94.

1540. Rosenwaike, Ira: "Estimate and Analysis of the Jewish Population of the United States in 1790." PAJHS, v.50 #1 (Sept., 1960): 23-67.

1541. Roth, Cecil: "Some Jewish Loyalists in the War of American Independence." PAJHS, #38 part 2 (Dec., 1948): 81-107.

1542. Sarna, Jonathan D.: "The Impact of the American Revolution on American Jews." MJ, v.1 #2 (Sept., 1981): 149-160.

1543. Wiznitzer, Arnold: "The Exodus from Brazil and Arrival in New Amsterdam of the Jewish Pilgrim Fathers, 1654." PAJHS, v.44 #2 (Dec., 1954): 80-97.

> #1212. Wolf, L.: "American Elements in the Resettlement."

> #1438. Yerushalmi, Y. H.: "Amsterdam and New Amsterdam."

Waves of Immigration

1544. Angel, Marc D.: "The Sephardim of the United States:
an Exploratory Study." AJYB, v.74 (1973): 77–138.

> #85. Berger, D.: LEGACY OF JEWISH MIGRATION.

1545. De Sola Pool, D.: "The Levantine Jews in the United
States." AJYB, v.15 (1913/14): 207–220.

> #989. Frumkin, J.: RUSSIAN JEWRY 1860–1917.

1546. Glanz, Rudolf: "The German Jewish Mass Emigration:
1820–1880." AJA, v.22 #1 (Apr., 1970): 49–66.

1547. ___ : "Source Materials on the History of Jewish
Immigration to the United States, 1800–1880." Y/A, v.6
(1951): 73–156.

1548. Greenberg, Gershon: "A German–Jewish Immigrant´s
Perception of America 1853–54." AJHQ, v.67 #4 (June, 1978):
307–341.

1549. Grinstein, Hyman B.: "The Efforts of East European
Jewry to Organize Its Own Community in the United States."
PAJHS, v.49 #2 (Dec., 1959): 73–89.

1550. Hermalin, D. M.: "The Roumanian Jews in America."
AJYB, v.3 (1901/02): 88–103.

1551. Hirshler, Eric E. [ed.]: JEWS FROM GERMANY IN THE
UNITED STATES. New York: Farrar, Straus, and Cudahy, 1955.
182 pp., apps., notes, bibliog.

Anthology covering German Jewish immigration to the
United States from colonial times to the Nazi era. The core
of the book is Hirshler´s survey of German Jewish immigration. The essay is organized chronologically; Hirshler
interweaves the immigration experience with the immigrants´
stories and with their accomplishments in the United States.
The other essays are shorter and more analytical, evaluating
the importance of German Jewish immigration for Jewish and

American history. Introduction by Max Gruenwald.

CONTENTS: S. Stern-Taeubler: Problems of American Jewish and German Jewish Historiography / Eric E. Hirshler: Jews from Germany in the United States / B. D. Weinryb: The German Jewish Immigrants to America: a Critical Evaluation / Adolf Kober: Aspects of the Influence of Jews from Germany on American Jewish Spiritual Life of the Nineteenth Century / A. H. Friedlander: Cultural Contributions of the German Jew in America.

1552. Howe, Irving with K. Libo: WORLD OF OUR FATHERS. New York: Harcourt Brace Jovanovich, 1976. 714 pp., illus., notes, gloss., bibliog., index.

Celebration of the East European era of American Jewry. Opens with the society of the shtetl and the mass migration to America. Subsequent chapters deal with the problems of adjustment to America, with primary emphasis on the difficulties of getting a job and of adopting American habits. The process of Americanization is carefully charted, as are the Jewish and American reactions to that process. Yiddish culture in America is treated as a separate topic. The final two chapters cover the maturation of East European Jews in America in the years after World War II.

1553. Kisch, Guido: IN SEARCH OF FREEDOM: A HISTORY OF AMERICAN JEWS FROM CZECHOSLOVAKIA. London: E. Goldston and Son, 1949. 373 pp., apps., notes, bibliog., index.

History of Jewish migration from Czechoslovakia to the United States. Kisch begins by charting Czech Jewry´s earliest awareness of the New World. While some Jews left the Czech lands for America as early as the 1740s, emigration only became significant after the failure of the democratic revolutions of 1848. In addition, Kisch surveys the contributions of Czech Jews to America and American Jewry. Nine documents supplement the text by providing insight into issues related to the history of Jews in Czechoslovakia.

1554. Kober, Adolf: "Jewish Emigration from Wuerttemberg to the United States of America [1848-1855]." PAJHS, v.41 #3 (March, 1951): 225-273.

1555. Kohler, Max J.: "The German-Jewish Migration to America." PAJHS, #9 (1901): 87-105.

1556. Mahler, Raphael: "The Economic Background of Jewish Emigration from Galicia to the United States." Y/A, v.7 (1952): 255-267.

1557. Mandel, Irving A.: "Attitude of the American Jewish Community Toward East-European Immigration as Reflected in the Anglo-Jewish Press, 1880-1890." AJA, V.3 #1 (June, 1950: 11-36.

1558. Price, G. M.: "The Russian Jews in America." PAJHS, v.48 #1 (Sept., 1958): 28-62; #2 (Dec., 1958): 78-133.

1559. Reissner, H. G.: "The German-American Jews [1800-1850]." LBIYB, v.10 (1965): 57-116.

1560. Sanders, Ronald: THE DOWNTOWN JEWS: PORTRAITS OF AN IMMIGRANT GENERATION. New York: Harper & Row, 1969. 477 pp., illus., bibliog.

Journalistic study of the Jews of the Lower East Side, primarily focused on the immigrant experience. Intersperses the wider history with the stories of important individuals, primarily Abraham Cahan. The key theme of the book is the process of accommodation required of the immigrants to American society. Although the book contains no new interpretations, it does offer an interesting and insightful study of the rise of America's East European Jews.

1561. Soyer, D.: "Between Two Worlds: the Jewish Landsman-shaftn and Questions of Immigrant Identity." AJHQ, v.76 #1 (Sept., 1986): 5-24.

1562. Strauss, Herbert A.: "The Immigration and Accultura-tion of the German Jew in the United States of America." LBIYB, v.16 (1971): 63-94.

1563. Szajkowski, Zosa: "The Attitude of American Jews to East European Jewish Immigration [1881-1893]." PAJHS, #40 part 3 (March 1951): 221-280.

> #88. ___: "How the Mass Migration to America Began."

1564. ___: "The Yahudi and the Immigrant: a Reappraisal." AJHQ, v.63 #1 (Sept., 1973): 13-44.

1565. Tcherikower, Elias: "Jewish Immigrants to the United States, 1881-1900." Y/A, v.6 (1951): 157-176.

> #90. Wischnitzer, M.: TO DWELL IN SAFETY.

Jewish Pioneers

1566. Baron, S. W.: "American Jewish Communal Pioneering."
PAJHS, v.43 #3 (March, 1954): 133-150.

1567. Glanz, R.: "The Spread of Jewish Communities Through
America Before the Civil War." Y/A, v.15 (1974): 7-45.

1568. Kohler, Max J.: "Some Jewish Factors in the Settlement of the West." PAJHR, #16 (1907): 23-35.

1569. Korn, Bertram W.: "Jewish 48´ers in America." AJA,
#1 (June, 1949): 3-20.

1570. Libo, Kenneth and Irving Howe: WE LIVED THERE TOO:
IN THEIR OWN WORDS AND PICTURES - PIONEER JEWS AND THE WEST-
WARD MOVEMENT OF AMERICA, 1630-1930. New York: St. Martin´s
Press, 1984. 343 pp., illus.

Illustrated kaleidoscope of the role Jews played in opening and developing the American frontier. Covers the subject
chronologically, beginning with the Dutch Jews. The editors´
definition of "frontier" is vague, identifying the "western
frontier" with virtually all stages of America´s development. Wisely the editors let the participants tell their own
stories, without too much extraneous material. In reading
what the participants felt at the time, the reader is given
a feel for the role individual Jews played in opening the
frontier and in fostering communal development. The book
includes an interpretative essay on "The American Experiment" by Irving Howe.

> #390. Menes, A.: "The Am Oylom Movement."

1571. Rochlin, Harriet and Fred Rochlin: PIONEER JEWS: A
NEW LIFE IN THE FAR WEST. Boston: Houghton Mifflin, 1984.
243 pp., illus., bibliog., index.

Studies the life of American Jewry in the West until
1912. Somewhat oddly, the book begins with a chapter that
covers "western" Jewry before the Gold Rush, although the
individual Jews who resided in the west before the Gold Rush
hardly constituted a community of Jewry. The rest of the

book is basically a collection of anecdotes which illuminate
the ups and downs of the pioneer Jews. Unfortunately, the
Rochlins concentrated on recounting these adventures, rather
than providing specific answers for a number of very useful
questions asked on the last page of the text.

1572. Sharfman I. Harold: JEWS ON THE FRONTIER. Chicago:
Henry Regnery, 1977. 337 pp., illus., notes, index.

Investigation into the often unknown activities of
pioneering American Jews from the colonial era to the period
before the Civil War. Although the book is fully documented,
the style is more that of an adventure story. Proves that
many early American folk heroes, including the pirate Jean
Lafitte, were Jews and that Jews contributed greatly to the
opening of the western frontier.

Public Affairs

1573. Adler, Selig: "The United States and the Holocaust."
AJHQ, v.64 #1 (Sept., 1974): 14-23.

> #379. Agar, H.: THE SAVING REMNANT.

> #367. Berlin, Wm.: ON THE EDGE OF POLITICS.

1574. Bernstein Philip: TO DWELL IN UNITY: THE JEWISH
FEDERATION MOVEMENT IN AMERICA SINCE 1960. Philadelphia:
JPS, 1983. 394 pp., illus., notes, index.

Continuation of the history of the Jewish Federation
movement in the United States [see #1605]. The book is organized thematically and is primarily oriented toward placing
federations and their services into communal context. Emphasis is on domestic services provided by the federations, although international services are not ignored. The chapters
dealing with the way federations function are somewhat dry,
but still contain interesting insights, including some on
finances. Bernstein properly assesses the communal context
of the federations and their importance for Jewish identity.
An especially interesting chapter is on voluntarism. Without volunteers it is doubtful if American Jewry as a whole,
and certainly the federation movement, could survive.
Although limited to the federations, Bernstein´s book also
presents an inside look into the organizational life of
American Jewry during two dramatic decades.

1575. Brody, David: "American Jewry, the Refugees and Immigration Restrictions [1932-1942]." PAJHS, v.45 #4 (June, 1956): 219-247.

1576. Buchler, Joseph: "The Struggle for Unity: Attempts at Union in American Jewish Life: 1654-1868." AJA, v.2 #1 (June, 1949): 21-46.

1577. Chyet, Stanley F.: "The Political Rights of the Jews in the United States 1776-1840." AJA, v.10 #1 (Apr., 1958): 14-75.

1578. Cohen, Henry: "Crisis and Reaction: a Study in Jewish Group Attitudes [1929-1939]." AJA, v.5 #2 (June, 1953): 71-113.

1579. Cohen, N. W.: "The Abrogation of the Russo-American Treaty of 1832." JSS, v.25 #1 (Jan., 1963): 3-41.

> #380. ___: NOT FREE TO DESIST.

1580. ___: "Pioneers of American Jewish Defense." AJA, v.19 #2 (Nov., 1977): 116-150.

1581. Dinnerstein, Leonard: "Jews and the New Deal." AJHQ, v.72 #4 (June, 1983): 461-476.

1582. Elazar, Daniel J.: "American Political Theory and the Political Notions of American Jews: Convergences and Contradictions." JJoS, v.9 #1 (June, 1967): 5-24.

1583. ___: COMMUNITY AND POLITY: THE ORGANIZATIONAL DYNAMICS OF AMERICAN JEWRY. Philadelphia: JPS, 1976. 421 pp., tables, charts, notes, bibliog., index.

Thematic survey concentrating on organized American Jewish communal life. Elazar specifically attempts to prove that American Jewry must be seen as a political body, among many others, and not as a separatist community. As a result, the book is about American Jewish public affairs, and not specifically about American Jewish history. Nevertheless, by positing the dynamic nature of American Jewry, Elazar does clearly delineate a historical development. The work is especially interesting in light of possible comparisons to other Jewries [see #575 and #827]. Also contains four useful appendixes, including a bibliography of communal studies.

> #370. ___: "Place of Jewish Political Studies on Campus."

1584. ___ and Stephen R. Goldstein: "The Legal Status of the American Jewish Community." AJYB, v.73 (1972): 3-94.

> #433. Feingold, H. L.: THE POLITICS OF RESCUE.

> #434. Finger, S.: AMERICAN JEWRY DURING THE HOLOCAUST.

> #909. Fishman, J.: STUDIES ON POLISH JEWRY.

> #1021. Freedman, R.: SOVIET JEWRY IN THE DECISIVE DECADE.

1585. Friedenberg, Albert M.: "The Jews and the American Sunday Laws." PAJHS, #11 (1903): 101-115.

> #382. Fuchs, L.: THE POLITICAL BEHAVIOR OF AMERICAN JEWS.

> #440. Gellman, I. F.: "The St. Louis Tragedy."

> #384. Goldstein, I.: JEWISH JUSTICE AND CONCILIATION.

> #442. Gottlieb, M.: "In the Shadow of War."

> #382. Grusd, E. E.: B´NAI B´RITH.

1586. Handlin, Oscar and Mary F. Handlin: "The Acquisition of Political and Social Rights by the Jews in the United States." AJYB, v.56 (1955): 43-98.

> #399. Henkin, L.: WORLD POLITICS AND THE JEWISH CONDITION.

1587. Hero, Alfred O. Jr.: "Southern Jews, Race Relations, and Foreign Policy." JSS, v.27 #4 (Oct., 1965): 213-235.

1588. Hochbaum, Jerry: "Change and Challenge in Jewish Community Relations in the United States." JJoS, v.12 #2 (Dec., 1970): 181-186.

1589. Huehner, Leon: "Jews in the War of 1812." PAJHS, #26 (1918): 173-200.

1590. ___: "Some Jewish Associates of John Brown." PAJHS, #23 (1915): 55-78.

1591. Hyman, Joseph C.: "Twenty-Five Years of American Aid to Jews Overseas: a Record of the Joint Distribution Committe." AJYB, v.41 (1939/40): 141-179.

1592. Jacobs, Joseph: "The Damascus Affair of 1840 and the Jews of America." PAJHS, #10 (1902): 119-128.

1593. ___: "The Federation Movement in American Jewish Philanthropy." AJYB, v.17 (1915/16): 159-198.

1594. Kagedan, Allan L.: "American Jews and the Soviet Experiment: the Agro-Joint Project, 1924-1937." JSS, v.43 #2 (Spr., 1981): 153-164.

1595. Karpf, Maurice J.: "Jewish Community Organization in the United States." AJYB, v.39 (1937/38): 47-148.

1596. ___: JEWISH COMMUNITY ORGANIZATIONS IN THE UNITED STATES. New York: Arno Press, 1970 [Rep. of 1938 Ed.]. 234 pp., tables, notes, bibliog., index.

Survey of the American Jewish community, with primary emphasis on Jewish communal organization. Karpf begins by assessing Jewish communal issues, including antisemitism, immigrant aid, religious, cultural, and educational requirements, as well as health and welfare. Thereafter, Karpf charts the agencies, either national or local, that are supposed to meet those needs. In addition, agencies whose services embrace Jews in other countries, and social organizations, e.g., Landsmanschaften, are also reviewed. Finally, Karpf offers his conclusions on the state of American Jewish social work as well as on the American Jewish community and its leadership. Originally published in 1938, the book has been superseded [see #1583]. Nevertheless, the book still contains a considerable amount of useful information, especially in its statistical tables. The book is also a useful model for a study on Jewish communal institutions in almost any country, land, and era.

> #888. Katzburg, N.: HUNGARY AND THE JEWS.

1597. Kessler, Lawton et al: "American Jews and the Paris Peace Conference." Y/A, v.2/3 (1947/48): 222-242.

1598. Kohler, Max J.: "The Jews and the American Anti-Slavery Movement." PAJHS, #5 (1897): 125-155; #9 (1901): 45-56.

> #834. ___ and S. Wolf: "Jewish Disabilities."

1599. Korn, Bertram W.: AMERICAN JEWRY AND THE CIVIL WAR.
Philadelphia: JPS, 1951. 331 pp., illus., notes, bibliog.,
apps., index.

Intensive study of the Jewish reaction to the American
Civil War. Primarily focused on the communal rather than the
individual perspective. Korn begins his survey by elucidating the state of American Jewry in both the North and
South up to 1860. Korn´s main theme is the war and how
political and military events affected the community. In
particular, the issue of antisemitism during the war is discussed. Other themes include the Jewish attitude toward
slavery and the problem of providing Jewish chaplains to the
armed forces. Includes a number of key documents in four
appendixes. Introduction by Allan Nevins.

1600. ___ : THE AMERICAN REACTION TO THE MORTARA CASE 1858-
1859. Cincinnati, OH: American Jewish Archives, 1957. 196
pp., illus., notes, note on sources, apps., index.

Surveys the American reaction to the kidnapping of an
Italian Jewish boy by papal police after he had been
secretly baptised. Primarily, though not exclusively focused
on the reaction of Christian Americans and of the American
secular press. Also deals with the reactions of the American
Jewish community and of the Buchanan administration. Korn´s
text basically serves as a link between the various documents cited. The Mortara affair helped galvanize American
Jewry for foreign relief work and was thus something of a
turning point in American Jewish public affairs. Includes an
appendix on Mortara poems, and another comparing the Mortara
affair with the post-Holocaust Finaly case.

1601. ___ : "Jewish Welfare Activities for the Military
during the Spanish-American War." PAJHS, v.41 #4 (June,
1952): 357-380.

1602. Lazin, Frederick A.: "The Non-Centralized Model of
American Jewish Organizations: a Possible Test Case." JSS,
v.44 #3/4 (Sum./Fall, 1982): 299-314.

1603. Leavitt, Julian: "American Jews in the World War."
AJYB, v.21 (1919/20): 141-155.

> #373. Levine, E.: DIASPORA.

1604. Lipstadt, Deborah E.: "The American Press and the Persecution of German Jewry: the Early Years, 1933-1935." LBIYB, v.29 (1984): 27-55.

> #456. ___: BEYOND BELIEF.

> #457. ___: "Pious Sympathies and Sincere Regrets."

1605. Lurie, Harry: A HERITAGE AFFIRMED: THE JEWISH FEDERATION MOVEMENT IN AMERICA. Philadelphia: JPS, 1961. 481 pp., illus., notes, bibliog., index.

History of the Jewish Federation movement in the United States up to 1960 [see #1574]. Primary emphasis is on the Federation as an agency strengthening bonds between Jews and their community. Lurie notes that although most Federations began as philanthropic agencies, a vital function that all still perform, they eventually developed into grass-roots organs of Jewish identification. This holds true most singularly in smaller communities which have high rates of assimilation and intermarriage. Lurie also points out the problems that have faced Jewish Federations, primarily in the years since World War II. His account is fairly balanced between the descriptive and the analytical. It is a history still in the making, since the Federations are growing and display the continued vibrancy of American Jewry.

> #403. Marcus, J. R.: JEWS, JUDAISM, AMERICAN CONSTITUTION.

1606. Markens, Isaac: "Lincoln and the Jews." PAJHS, #17 (1908): 109-165.

1607. Milamed, Susan: "Proskurover Landsmanshaften: a Case Study in Jewish Communal Development." AJHQ, v.76 #1 (Sept., 1986): 40-55.

> #460. Orbach, W.: "Shattering the Shackles."

1608. Osofsky, Gilbert: "The Hebrew Emigrant Aid Society of the United States [1881-1883]." PAJHS, v.49 #3 (March, 1960): 173-187.

> #461. Penkower, M. N.: "American Jewry and the Holocaust."

1609. Pinsky, Edward: "American Jewish Unity During the Holocaust - The Joint Emergency Committee, 1943." AJHQ, v.72 #4 (June, 1983): 477-494.

> #493. Porter, J. N. and P. Dreier: JEWISH RADICALISM.

> #375. Rubenstein, W.: THE LEFT, THE RIGHT AND THE JEWS.

1610. Schoenberg, Philip E.: "The American Reaction to the Kishinev Pogrom of 1903." AJHQ, v.63 #3 (March, 1974): 262-283.

1611. Selekman, B. M.: "The Federation in the Changing American Scene." AJYB, v.36 (1934/35): 65-87.

1612. Shapiro, E. S.: "The Approach to War: Congressional Isolationism and Antisemitism, 1939-1941." AJHQ, v.74 #1 (Sept., 1984): 45-65.

> #468. Spear, S.: "The Persecution of the Jews in Germany."

1613. Stock, Ernest: "In the Absence of Hierarchy: Notes on the Organization of the American Jewish Community." JJoS, v.12 #2 (Dec., 1970): 195-200.

> #822. Strook, S.: "Switzerland and American Jews."

1614. Szajkowski, Z.: "The Alliance Israelite Universelle in the United States, 1860-1949." PAJHS, #39 part 4 (June, 1950): 389-443.

1615. ___: "The Impact of Jewish Overseas Relief on American Jewish and Non-Jewish Philanthropy 1914-1927." AJA, v.22 #1 (Apr., 1970): 67-90.

1616. ___: "´Reconstruction´ vs. ´Palliative Relief´ in American Jewish Overseas Work [1919-1939]." JSS, v.32 #1 (Jan., 1970): 14-42; #2 (Apr., 1970): 111-147.

> #470. ___: "Relief for German Jewry."

1617. Taylor, Maurice: "Jewish Community Organization and Jewish Community Life." Y/A, v.9 (1954): 179-204.

> #846. Vago, B. and G. Mosse: JEWS AND NON-JEWS.

1618. Weiser, Michael R.: A BROTHERHOOD OF MEMORY: JEWISH LANDSMANSHAFTEN IN THE NEW WORLD. New York: Basic Books, 1985. 303 pp., app., notes, index.

History of the American landsmanshaften movement. Lands-

manshaften were societies of Jewish immigrants from a local
region, which joined together for nostalgic, social, and
sometimes self-help reasons. Many landsmanshaften still exist, offering services to second- and third-generation Jews
whose ancestors lived in eastern Europe. The Author adopts a
style he calls the "bube mayse" method, i.e., taking together the tales, stories, and anecdotes, and using their
content and form to establish facts. The method has many
potential pitfalls, but Weisser seems to succeed with it in
this case. To his credit, Weisser has also produced a lively
and readable account, while also contributing to the
understanding of American Jewish ethnicity.

1619. Wolf, S.: "The American Jew as Soldier and Patriot."
PAJHS, #3 (1895): 21-40.

> #394. Woocher, J. S.: SACRED SURVIVAL.

Antisemitism

> #325. Belth, N. C.: A PROMISE TO KEEP.

> #358. Cohen, N. W.: "Antisemitism in the Gilded Age."

> #328. Dobkowski, M. N.: THE TARNISHED DREAM.

> #330. Feingold, H. L.: "Finding a Conceptual Framework."

> #332. Gerber, D. A.: ANTISEMITISM IN AMERICAN HISTORY.

1620. Higham, John: "Social Discrimination Against Jews in
America, 1830-1930." PAJHS, v.47 #1 (Sept., 1957): 1-33.

1621. Lebowich, Joseph: "General Ulysses S. Grant and the
Jews." PAJHS, #17 (1908): 71-79.

> #318. Pollak, O. B.: "Roots of Reverse Discrimination."

Zionism

> #534. Adelson, H. L.: "Ideology and Practice."

> #547. Adler, S.: "Roosevelt Administration and Zionism."

* 1622. Barbarash, Ernest E.: BNAI ZION 75 YEARS: A STELLAR ROLE. New York: Bnai Zion, 1983. 40 pp., illus.

> #502. Cohen, N. W.: AMERICAN JEWS AND THE ZIONIST IDEA.

1623. Cohen, Naomi W.: "The Maccabaean's Message: a Study in American Zionism until World War I." JSS, v.18 #3 (July, 1956): 163-178.

1624. ___: "The Reaction of Reform Judaism in America to Political Zionism." PAJHS, #40 part 4 (June, 1951): 361-394.

1625. Druyan, Nitza: "American Zionist Efforts on Behalf of Yemenite Jews in Eretz Israel 1912-1914." AJHQ, v.69 #1 (Sept., 1979): 92-98.

1626. Feingold, Henry L.: "Assessing an Assessment: the Case for American Zionism." AJHQ, v.75 #2 (Dec., 1985): 165-174.

1627. Fox, Maier B.: "Labor Zionism in America: the Challenge of the 1920s." AJA, v.35 #1 (Apr., 1983): 53-71.

1628. Friesel, Evyatar: "The Influence of American Zionism on the American Jewish Community 1900-1950." AJHQ, v.75 #2 (Dec., 1985): 130-148.

1629. Gal, Allon: "Aspects of the Zionist Movement's Role in the Communal Life of American Jewry [1898-1948]." AJHQ, v.75 #2 (Dec., 1985): 149-164.

1630. ___: "The Mission Motif in American Zionism [1898-1948]." AJHQ, v.75 #4 (June, 1986): 363-385.

> #552. ___: "Zionist Foreign Policy."

> #553. Ganin, Z.: "Limits of Am. Jewish Political Power."

> #554. ___: TRUMAN, AMERICAN JEWRY AND ISRAEL.

> #511. Greenstein, H. R.: TURNING POINT.

> #556. Grose, P.: ISRAEL IN THE MIND OF AMERICA.

> #513. Halperin, S.: POLITICAL WORLD OF AMERICAN ZIONISM.

1631. Kabakoff, Jacob: "Beginnings of Hibbat Zion in America." HYB, v.6 (1964/65): 255-264.

1632. Karp, Abraham J.: "Reaction to Zionism and to the State of Israel in the American Jewish Religious Community." JJoS, v.8 #2 (Dec., 1966): 150-174.

> #559. Kaufman, M.: "The A. J. C. and Jewish Statehood."

> #560. ___: "From Neutrality to Involvement."

1633. Knee, Stuart E.: "From Controversy to Conversion: Liberal Judaism in America and the Zionist Movement, 1917-1941." Y/A, v.17 (1978): 260-289.

> #561. ___: "Jewish Non-Zionism ."

1634. Kohler, Max J.: "Some Early American Zionist Projects." PAJHS, #8 (1900): 75-118.

* 1635. Levinthal, L. E.: THE CREDO OF AN AMERICAN ZIONIST. Washington, DC: ZOA, 1943. 19 pp.

> #562. Neustadt-Noy, I.: "Toward Unity."

1636. Parzen, Herbert: "American Zionism and the Quest for a Jewish State, 1939-43." HYB, v.4 (1961/62): 345-394.

1637. ___: "Conservative Judaism and Zionism [1896-1923]: a Documentary Account." HYB, v.6 (1964/65): 311-368.

1638. Rischin, Moses: "The American Jewish Committee and Zionism 1906-1922." HYB, v.5 (1963): 65-81.

1639. ___: "The Early Attitude of the American Jewish Committee to Zionism 1906-1922." PAJHS, v.49 #3 (March, 1960): 188-201.

> #567. Schechtman, J. B.: U.S. & THE JEWISH STATE MOVEMENT.

1640. Shmidt, S.: "The Parushim: a Secret Episode in American Zionist History." AJHQ, v.65 #2 (Dec., 1975): 121-139.

> #569. Shpiro, D. H.: "Background of Biltmore Resolution."

> #529. Silverberg, R.: IF I FORGET THEE.

> #530. Sternstein, J. P.: "Reform Judaism and Zionism."

1641. Tabachnik, Joseph: "American-Jewish Reaction to the First Zionist Congress." HYB, v.5 (1963): 57-64.

> #531. Urofsky, M. I.: AMERICAN ZIONISM.

> #573, ___: "American Zionists, Partition and Recognition."

> #574. ___: "Rifts in the Movement."

Labor and Economics

1642. Brandes, Joseph: "From Sweatshop to Stability: Jewish Labor between Two World Wars." Y/A, v.16 (1976): 1-149.

1643. David, Henry: "The Jewish Unions and Their Influence Upon the American Labor Movement." PAJHS, v.41 #4 (June, 1952): 339-345.

1644. Davidson, Gabriel: "The Jew in Agriculture in the United States." AJYB, v.37 (1935/36): 99-134.

1645. Epstein, Melech: JEWISH LABOR IN U. S. A.: AN INDUSTRIAL, POLITICAL, AND CULTURAL HISTORY OF THE JEWISH LABOR MOVEMENT, 1882-1952. New York: Ktav, 1969. [Rep. of 1950/53 Ed.]. 2 vols. bound as 1. 922 pp., notes, bibliog., index.

Multifaceted study of the American Jewish trade-union movement from its origins in the 1880s to the 1950s. Emphasis is placed on the Jewish aspects of Jewish labor, although the ethnic labor movement is studied in a general context. Conditions that specifically affected Jews, for example, in nineteenth-century Russia, are explained in detail. Also reviewed are the ideological and political orientations of the laborite parties and organizations. The question of communism and relations with the Soviet Union receives prominent attention. Central to Epstein's study is the International Ladies Garment Workers Union [ILGWU], although that is not the only union studied. In addition to the external history of Jewish labor, Epstein discusses the inner trends within the movement, in particular cultural activities and the role unions played in Americanizing new immigrants. Relations between different segments of the Jewish labor movement are clarified in an objective and nonpolemical way. Epstein does not shy away from contro-

versial topics, and his discussion of the civil war between
the reds of the American Communist Party and the democratic
Socialists deserves careful attention. The new edition
includes an extensive preface which both summarizes the book
and describes the decline of the Jewish labor unions since
World War II.

1646. Frankel, J.: "The Jewish Socialists and the American
Jewish Congress Movement." Y/A, v.16 (1976): 202-341.

1647. Glanz, Rudolf: "Notes on Early Jewish Peddling in
America." JSS, v.7 #2 (Apr., 1945): 119-136.

1648. ___ : "Some Remarks on Jewish Labor and American Public Opinion in the Pre-World War I Era." Y/A, v.16 (1976):
178-201.

1649. Hardman, J. B. S.: "Jewish Workers in the American
Labor Movement." Y/A, v.7 (1952): 229-254.

1650. Herberg, Will: "The Jewish Labor Movement in the
United States." AJYB, v.53 (1952): 3-74.

> #490. Levin, N.: WHILE MESSIAH TARRIED.

> #492. Mendelsohn, E.: "American Jewish Labor Movement."

1651. Mergen, Bernard: "´Another Great Prize´: the Jewish
Labor Movement in the Context of American Labor History."
Y/A, v.16 (1976): 394-423.

1652. Perlman, Selig: "Jewish-American Unionism, Its Birth
Pangs and Contribution to the General American Labor Movement." PAJHS, v.41 #4 (June, 1952): 297-337.

1653. Reich, Nathan: "The Role of the Jews in the American
Economy." Y/A, v.5 (1950): 197-204.

1654. Robinson, Leonard with Morris Loeb: "Agricultural
Activities of the Jews in America." AJYB, v.14 (1912/13):
21-114.

1655. Sorin, Gerald: THE PROPHETIC MINORITY: AMERICAN JEW-
ISH IMMIGRANT RADICALS 1880-1920. Bloomington: Indiana Univ.
Press, 1985. 211 pp., illus., notes, bibliog., index.

Studies the American Jewish radical movement from the

1880s to the   1920s. Sorin focuses on the radicalism of Jewish immigrant workers, primarily in New York. Other key
centers for Jewish radicalism at the time included Boston,
Chicago, and Philadelphia. Sorin attempts to find the roots
of Jewish radicalism in the shtetl culture of the Russian
Pale of Settlement. This is the standard explanation and it
contains a grain of truth. But the cities, not the shtetls,
of Eastern Europe were the source for Jewish radicalism, as
has been proven elsewhere. The weakness of his background
material does not actually affect Sorin´s two hypotheses.
First, that Jewish culture and secularized religious values
gave Jews a predisposition to socialism. Second, that far
from being opposed to Yiddishkeit, Jewish immigrant radicalism was deeply rooted in traditional Jewish values. The
former point is probably correct, the latter point is still
moot and requires clarification. Sorin shows that the ideologues among American Jewish Socialists were ambivalent
about Jewish culture, accepting those ideas which aligned
with their cause and rejecting others. To say that they
upheld Yiddishkeit, when in fact they quoted selectively
from the prophetic works, and explicitly rejected most
Jewish traditions and values, demands clearer definition of
Yiddishkeit than Sorin, at this stage, is able to provide.

1656. Tenenbaum, Shelly: "Immigrants and Capital: Jewish
Loan Societies in the United States, 1880-1945." AJHQ, v.76
#1 (Sept., 1986): 67-77.

1657. Trunk, I.: "The Cultural Dimensions of the American
Jewish Labor Movement." Y/A, v.16 (1976): 342-393.

Religion

1658. Berkowitz, H.: "Notes on the History of the Earliest
German Jewish Congregation in America." PAJHS, #9 (1901):
123-127.

1659. Berman, Jeremiah J.: "The Trend in Jewish Religious
Observance in Mid-Nineteenth-Century America." PAJHS, #37
(1947): 31-53.

> #205. Bernstein, L.: CHALLENGE AND MISSION.

1660. Bernstein, Louis: "Generational Conflict in American
Orthodoxy: the Early Years of the Rabbinical Council of
America." AJHQ, v.69 #2 (Dec., 1979): 226-233.

> #181. Blau, J. L.: REFORM JUDAISM.

1661. Blau, Joseph L.: "The Spiritual Life of American Jewry, 1654-1954." AJYB, v.56 (1955): 99-170.

> #206. Bulka, R. P.: DIMENSIONS OF ORTHODOX JUDAISM.

1662. Carlebach, Alexander: "The German-Jewish Immigration and its Influence on Synagogue Life in the U.S.A. [[1933-1942]." LBIYB, v.9 (1964): 351-372.

1663. Cohen, Arthur A. and Philip Garvin: A PEOPLE APART: HASIDISM IN AMERICA. New York: E. P. Dutton, 1970. 192 pp.

Illustrated study of American hasidism. The photographic coverage is extensive, and every major aspect of hasidic life is included. The text contains Cohen's "An Essay in Praise of Hasidism." While Cohen concentrates on the psychological and social elements of the hasidic community, he also deals with key concepts and practices. The essay is a personal and nostalgic summary, but remains objective and relatively thorough. Although not scholarly, Cohen's essay is a good introduction for Garvin's photographs; together they offer an inside view of hasidism in the United States.

> #192. Davis, M.: THE EMERGENCE OF CONSERVATIVE JUDAISM.

1664. Ehrman, Albert and C. Abraham Fenster: "Conversion and American Orthodox Judaism: a Research Note." JJoS, v.10 #1 (June, 1968): 47-53.

1665. Eisen, Arnold M.: THE CHOSEN PEOPLE IN AMERICA: A STUDY IN JEWISH RELIGIOUS IDEOLOGY. Bloomington: Indiana Univ. Press, 1983. 237 pp., notes, bibliog., index.

Analyzes the impact of America on Jewish religious thought and ideology. Eisen does not deal with theology, but rather with the practical impact of Americanization on the concept of the chosen people. As an introduction Eisen charts the role of the Jewish belief in divine election and its impact on Jewish survival until the Emancipation. Thereafter, Eisen charts the changing definitions of chosenness that have been current among Jewish thinkers in the half-century since 1930. Eisen explains how Reform Judaism modified the idea of chosenness into one of Jewish mission. He also charts the more or less literal affirmation of chosenness by Orthodox and Conservative thinkers. Eisen's chapter

on Mordecai M. Kaplan is a superior summary of Kaplan's
philosophy. Primarily an exercise in intellectual history,
Eisen's work nevertheless tells us a great deal about what
American Jews think of themselves.

1666. Eisenstein, J. D.: "The History of the First Russian
American Jewish Congregation: the Beth Hamedrosh Hagodol."
PAJHS, #9 (1901): 63-74.

1667. Elazar, Daniel J.: "The Development of the American
Synagogue." MJ, v.4 #3 (Oct., 1984): 255-273.

1668. Fox, Steven A.: "On the Road to Unity: The Union of
American Hebrew Congregations and American Jewry 1873-1903."
AJA, v.32 #2 (Nov., 1980): 145-193.

1669. Gordon, M. W.: "Rediscovering Jewish Infrastructure:
the Legacy of U.S. Nineteenth Century American Synagogues."
AJHQ, v.75 #3 (March, 1986): 296-306.

1670. Jick, Leon A. THE AMERICANIZATION OF THE SYNAGOGUE,
1820-1870. Hanover, NH: University Press of New England for
Brandeis Univ., 1976. 247 pp., illus., notes, bibliog.,
index.

Study into the rise of American Reform Judaism. Jick
attempts to revise the standard position, which holds that
Reform in America developed from German roots. In contradistinction, Jick argues that Reform in the United States
developed essentially as a response to American conditions.
Reform was thus not a transplant but a native Jewish phenomenon. Ultimately, according to Jick, American Reform owed
little or nothing to German Reform movements. Clearly, there
were some unique elements to American Reform Judaism; it did
fill a gap that was uniquely American. Nevertheless, almost
all of the early reformers in the United States were immigrants - adjusted immigrants, to be sure - from Germany.
Similarly, almost the entire leadership of the Reform movement before the turn of the twentieth century, was composed
of German immigrant rabbis. Although Jick's revisions do,
therefore, have some merit, so does the standard approach;
most likely, both together provide the best insight into the
rise of American Reform Judaism.

> #201. Kaplan, M. N.: JUDAISM AS A CIVILIZATION.

1671. Liebman, Charles S.: "Orthodoxy in American Jewish Life." AJYB, v.66 (1965): 21-97.

1672. ___: "Reconstructionism in American Jewish Life." AJYB, v.71 (1970): 3-99.

1673. ___: "Religion, Class, and Culture in American Jewish History." JJoS, v.9 #2 (Dec., 1967): 227-241.

1674. Mayer, Egon: "Jewish Orthodoxy in America: Towards the Sociology of a Residual Category." JJoS, v.15 #2 (Dec., 1973): 151-163.

> #194. Parzen, H.: ARCHITECTS OF CONSERVATIVE JUDAISM.

1675. Philipson, David: "The Central Conference of American Rabbis: 1889-1939." AJYB, v.42 (1940/41): 179-214.

> #186. ___: "Progress of the Jewish Reform Movement."

1676. Phillips, N. T.: "The Congregation Shearith Israel: a Historical Review." PAJHS, #6 (1898): 123-140.

> #188. Plaut, W. G.: THE GROWTH OF REFORM JUDAISM.

1677. Raphael, Marc Lee: PROFILES IN AMERICAN JUDAISM: THE REFORM, CONSERVATIVE, ORTHODOX AND RECONSTRUCTIONIST TRADITIONS IN HISTORICAL PERSPECTIVE. San Francisco, CA: Harper & Row, 1984. 238 pp., tables, notes, index.

Comprehensive survey of the development of Judaism in the United States. Each religious denomination is reviewed independently. Raphael´s organization is idiosyncratic, but is also eminently understandable. Correctly, Raphael deals with institutions and ideology as separate issues. Similarly, Raphael notes that the four religious groups developed within different chronological contexts; he does not attempt to force an artificial chronology on the subject. In each case, important thinkers, leaders, and ideologues are integrated into their respective movements. Raphael´s comments are judicious, objective, and well documented. Interested readers will find the book a virtual encyclopedia on the development of Jewish religious movements in the American milieu.

> #283. Riesman, B.: THE CHAVURAH.

> #196. Rosenblum, H.: CONSERVATIVE JUDAISM.

> #161. Rosenthal, G.: FOUR PATHS TO ONE GOD.

> #162. Rudavsky, J.: MODERN JEWISH RELIGIOUS MOVEMENTS.

1678. Schmidt, Nancy J.: "An Orthodox Jewish Community in the United States: a Minority within a Minority." JJoS, v.7 #2 (Dec., 1965): 176-206.

1679. Sklare, Marshall: CONSERVATIVE JUDAISM: AN AMERICAN RELIGIOUS MOVEMENT. New York: Schocken Books, 1972 [Rep. of 1955 Ed.]. 330 pp., notes, index.

Sociological study of American Conservative Judaism. Places Conservatives into context of religion and religious practice. Broadly differentiates between traditionalism [conservatism] and Orthodoxy, but does not systematically view traditionalism in the context of Reform or Reconstructionist Judaism. This is especially surprising, since the Reconstructionist movement grew out of the Conservative milieu. Sklare´s observations on Conservative ideology are most interesting, especially in light of recent events within the movement and around it.

1680. Sussman, Lance J.: "The Suburbanization of American Judaism as Reflected in Synagogue Building and Architecture, 1945-1975." AJHQ, v.75 #1 (Sept., 1985): 31-47.

1681. Temkin, Sefton D.: "A Century of Reform Judaism in America." AJYB, v.74 (1973): 3-75.

> #199. Waxman, M.: TRADITION AND CHANGE.

Education and Culture

> #256. Bomzer, H. W.: KOLEL IN AMERICA.

1682. Chipkin, I. S.: "Twenty-Five Years of Jewish Education in the United States." AJYB, v.38 (1936/37): 27-116.

> #224. Doroshkin, M.: YIDDISH IN AMERICA.

1683. Duker, Abraham G.: "Notes on the Culture of American Jewry." JJoS, v.2 #1 (June, 1960): 98-102.

> #370. Elazar, D. J.: "Place of Jewish political studies."

> #235. Fiedler, L. A.: THE JEW IN THE AMERICAN NOVEL.

> #225. Fishman, J. A.: "Language Maintenance."

1684. Freeman, Samuel D.: "The Adult Programme of the Jewish Community Centre in the United States." JJoS, v.5 #2 (Dec., 1963): 187-198.

1685. Greenstone, J. H.: "Jewish Education in the United States." AJYB, v.16 (1914/15): 90-127.

1686. Honor, Leo L.: "Jewish Elementary Education in the United States, 1901-1950." PAJHS, v.42 #1 (Sept., 1952): 1-42.

1687. Mirsky, David: "Hebrew in the United States." HYB, v.5 (1963): 83-111.

> #244. Opatoshu, J.: "Fifty Years of Yiddish Literature."

> #269. Pate, G.: THE HOLOCAUST IN U.S. TEXT BOOKS.

1688. Rudens, S. P.: "A Half Century of Community Service: the Story of New York Educational Alliance." AJYB, v.46 (1944/45): 73-86.

1689. Sachar, A. L.: "The B´nai B´rith Hillel Foundations in American Universities." AJYB, v.47 (1945/46): 141-152.

1690. Steinberg, Bernard: "Jewish Education in the United States: a Study in Religio-Ethnic Response." JJoS, v.21 #1 (June, 1979): 5-35.

Regional and State Histories

1691. Altfeld, E. Milton: THE JEW´S STRUGGLE FOR RELIGIOUS AND CIVIL LIBERTY IN MARYLAND. New York: Da Capo Press, 1970 [Rep. of 1924 Ed.]. 211 pp., illus., index.

Studies the legislative process of Jewish emancipation in Maryland, which began in 1818 and ended in 1826. Although most of the original thirteen colonies had some restrictions on the rights of non-Christians, i.e., Jews, only Maryland retained these restrictions into the Federalist era. Altfeld deals with the issues in a detailed and nonpolemical way. The pros and cons of Jewish civil rights are also placed into the broader context of American toleration of ethnic and religious minorities. In addition to covering the Jew-Bill that eventually led to emancipation, Altfeld also describes the entry of Jews into colonial and Federalist Maryland.

1692. Berman, Hyman: "Political Antisemitism in Minnesota during the Great Depression." JSS, v.38 #3/4 (Sum./Fall, 1976): 247-264.

1693. Bloom, Jessie S.: "The Jews of Alaska." AJA, v.15 #2 (Nov., 1963): 97-115.

1694. Brandes, Joseph: IMMIGRANTS AND FREEDOM: JEWISH COM-MUNITIES IN RURAL NEW JERSEY SINCE 1882. Philadelphia: Univ. of Pennsylvania Press, 1971. 424 pp., illus., notes, bibliog., index.

History of New Jersey Jewry from 1880 to the 1930s, part of a larger series of histories of local American Jewish communities. Brandes concentrates on rural Jewish communi-ties, with special emphasis on pioneering Jewish farm collectives. Although Jewish, these collectives were neither Socialist nor Zionist in orientation. Some successes were scored, although the failures may be better known. Eventu-ally the communities were united with the Am Olam movement, thereby converting small agricultural settlements into Jew-ish rescue programs that encouraged productive immigration to the United States. Brandes is careful in his evaluation of the farms and uses a wide range of sources. The farms never became major centers of American Jewish communal life, but did contribute an interesting chapter to American Jewish history. Preface by Moshe Davis.

1695. Breck, Allen D.: THE CENTENIAL HISTORY OF THE JEWS OF COLORADO, 1859-1959. Denver, CO: Univ. of Denver Press, 1960. 360 pp., illus., notes, apps., bibliog., index.

History of Jews in Colorado from the 1850s to the 1950s. Divided into three parts. Part I, covering the period 1859-1876, deals with individual Jewish pioneers and details the founding of the community in Denver. Part II, 1876-1918, reviews the expansion of Colorado Jewry after the territory attained statehood. Emphasis is on the expansion of communal organizations and services. An especially interesting chapter details "The Development of Community Leadership." Religious developments, including the creation of a small

but vibrant Orthodox community, are also documented. Part
III, 1918-1959, documents the shifts in the community after
World War I. In particular the suburbanization and the trend
toward greater communal unity are documented. Colorado Jewry
is placed into a broader context of American and world
Jewry. In every section Breck interweaves the history of the
community with brief biographies of important individuals.
Written as a celebration of Colorado Jewry's centennial,
Breck's text is a model of historical objectivity and is
thoroughly documented.

1696. Campbell, Albert A.: "Note on the Jewish Community
of St. Thomas, U.S. Virgin Islands." JSS, v.4 #2 (Apr.,
1942): 166-166.

1697. Cohen, Henry: "Settlement of the Jews in Texas."
PAJHS, #2 (1894): 139-156; #4 (1896): 9-19.

1698. Davidson, G.: "The Palestine Colony in Michigan: an
Adventure in Colonization." PAJHS, #29 (1925): 61-74.

1699. Dembitz, Lewis N.: "Jewish Beginnings in Kentucky."
PAJHS, #1 (1893): 99-101.

1700. Dinnerstein, Leonard and Mary Dale Palsson [eds.]:
JEWS IN THE SOUTH. Baton Rouge, Louisiana State Univ. Press,
1973. 392 pp., bibliog.

Anthology on American Jewry south of the Mason-Dixon
line. The essays were published in a variety of American
scholarly journals, but are here brought together for the
first time. The book is divided into five sections: Jews in
the antebellum and confederate South; Jews in the "new"
South; southern opinion on Jews; Jews in the twentieth
century South; and Jews and desegregation. Many of the
essays are of interest, but the multiplicity of topics and
methodologies do not always fit well together. A broader introduction, covering the warp and woof of Jewish life in the
southern states, probably would have helped. Although the
editors do have an introduction, it is too limited to offer
more than a guideline for further study. As such, the book
is useful and represents a step in the right direction.

CONTENTS: A. V. Goodman: South Carolina from Shaftesbury to
Salvador / Jacob Henry's Speech, 1809 / Ira Rosenwaike:
Further Light on Jacob Henry / L. Huehner: David L. Yulee,
Florida's First Senator / B. Kaplan: Judah Philip Benjamin /

B. W. Korn: Jews and Negro Slavery in the Old South, 1789-1865; American Judaeophobia: Confederate Version / Thomas D. Clark: The Post-Civil War Economy in the South / Leonard Dinnerstein: Atlanta in the Progressive Era: a Dreyfus Affair in Georgia / F. B. Gresham: "The Jew's Daughter": an Example of Ballad Variation / L. L. Knight: The Twentieth Century and the Jews / A. O. Hero, Jr.: Southern Jews / D. and A. Bernstein: Slow Revolution in Richmond, Va.: a New Pattern in the Making / Th. Lowi: Southern Jews: the Two Communities / S. I. Goldstein: Mixed Marriages in the Deep South / L. Reissman: The New Orleans Jewish Community / J. A. Fishman: Southern City / A. Vorspan: The Dilemma of the Southern Jew / M. Friedman: Virginia Jewry in the School Crisis: Antisemitism and Desegregation / Marvin Braiterman: Mississippi Marranos / A. Krause: Rabbis and Negro Rights in the South, 1954-1967.

1701. Dyer, Albion M.: "Points in the First Chapter of New York Jewish History." PAJHS, #3 (1895): 41-60.

1702. Evans, Eli N.: THE PROVINCIALS: A PERSONAL HISTORY OF JEWS IN THE SOUTH. New York: Atheneum, 1973. 368 pp., apps., bibliog., index.

Panoramic but personal history of the Jews in the South. Evans is at ease with his material and can empathize with the Southern Jewish experience. Covers every important issue - Reform Judaism, antisemitism, Jewish-Black relations and zionism. The broad chronological basis of the sections is retained throughout, even though the chapters are thematically organized. Unfortunately, the book is not documented, a result of the journalistic origins of the book.

1703. Fleishaker, Oscar: "Zionism in the Upper Mississippi Valley." HYB, v.5 (1963): 211-219.

1704. Friedenberg, Albert M.: "The Jews of New Jersey from the Earliest Times to 1850." PAJHS, #17 (1908): 33-43.

1705. Friedman, Lee M.: "Early Jewish Residents in Massachusetts." PAJHS, #23 (1915): 79-90.

1706. Gerard, Helene: "Yankees in Yarmulkes: Small Town Jewish Life in Eastern Long Island." AJA, v.38 #1 (Apr., 1986): 23-56.

1707. Glanz, Rudolf: THE JEWS OF CALIFORNIA FROM THE DIS-
COVERY OF GOLD UNTIL 1880. New York: Walden Press, 1960.
188 pp., notes, index.

History of the Jews of California from 1848 to 1880. The
book centers on the interplay between economic activity and
the founding of communities. Thus, although there were Jews
in California before and during the Gold Rush, they did not,
according to Glanz, constitute a community. Only after the
Gold Rush did a relatively large number of Jews begin to
move westward, a migration that resulted in the establishment of small communities in both northern and southern
California. The bulk of Glanz's study details the lifestyles
of Jews in old California. Glanz offers some points of
comparison between Jewish migration to California and to
Australia, both frontier societies at the time of migration.
This subject has been taken up by more recent studies [see
#1374]. Despite the scarcity of available archival material
Glanz did a superb job of piecing together evidence from a
wide range of printed sources.

1708. Heineman, David E.: "Jewish Beginnings in Michigan
before 1850." PAJHS, #13 (1905): 47-70.

1709. Hollander, J. H.: "The Civil Status of the Jews in
Maryland, 1634-1776." PAJHS, #2 (1894): 33-44.

1710. Huehner, Leon: "The Jews of Georgia from the Outbreak of the American Revolution to the Close of the Eighteenth Century." PAJHS, #17 (1908): 89-108.

1711. ___: "The Jews of Georgia in Colonial Times." PAJHS,
#10 (1902): 65-95.

1712. ___: "The Jews of New England [Other than Rhode
Island] Prior to 1800." PAJHS, #11 (1903): 75-99.

1713. ___: "The Jews of North Carolina Prior to 1800."
PAJHS, #29 (1925): 137-148.

1714. ___: "The Jews of South Carolina from the Earliest
Settlement to the End of the American Revolution." PAJHS,
#12 (1904): 39-61.

1715. ___: "The Jews of Virginia from the Earliest Times
to the Close of the Eighteenth Century." PAJHS, #20 (1911):
85-105.

1716. ___ : "The Struggle for Religious Liberty in North Carolina, with Special References to the Jews." PAJHS, #16 (1907): 37-71.

1717. ___ : "Whence Came the First Jewish Settlers of New York?" PAJHS, #9 (1901): 75-85.

1718. Jones, Chas. C., Jr.: "The Settlement of the Jews in Georgia." PAJHS, #1 (1893): 5-12.

1719. Kaplan, Benjamin: THE ETERNAL STRANGER: A STUDY OF JEWISH LIFE IN THE SMALL COMMUNITY. New York: Bookman, 1957. 198 pp., maps, apps., notes, bibliog., index.

Study of the life of small-town American Jewry, exploring the Jewishness of the communities and their relations to the larger society. Primary methodology is sociological, though some history is included as well. The communities studied are from Louisiana and east Florida. Kaplan´s study contains broad analytical insights into Jewish communal life out of the urban environment. Communal life in the towns studied was hampered by the small Jewish population and also by external considerations. Especially problematic was the tendency of young Jews to migrate in order to maintain their Jewishness. Ironically, the very act displaying resistance to assimilation made these communities less cohesive in the long run.

1720. Lowi, Theodor: "Southern Jews: the Two Communities." JJoS, v.6 #1 (July, 1964): 103-117.

1721. Marcus, Jacob R.: EARLY AMERICAN JEWRY: THE JEWS OF NEW YORK, NEW ENGLAND AND CANADA, 1649-1794. Philadelphia: JPS, 1951. 301 pp., illus., notes, index.

Volume I of a comprehensive study of North American Jewry in the colonial and, in the United States, Federalist era. Based on extensive quotes from primary sources, which are interspersed with Marcus´s explanatory comments. Each colony is dealt with separately and chronologically. Most of the material deals with the place of the relatively small Jewish community in the colonial context. A variety of social, economic, and religious issues that animated communal interest are also studied. Of special interest is Marcus´s inclusion of Canadian Jewry which, though also under English rule, developed differently from its American counterpart.

1722. ___: EARLY AMERICAN JEWRY: THE JEWS OF PENNSYLVANIA AND THE SOUTH, 1655-1790. Philadelphia: JPS, 1953. 594 pp., illus., notes, index.

Volume II of Marcus´s encompassing study of American Jewry in the colonial and Federalist eras. Marcus integrates primary sources with explanatory comments. The book is organized by state and by period. Appended is a seven-chapter retrospective on the development of American Jewry during that period. Important issues, including economics, social life, and religious problems, are covered intensively, both in the chapters on individual states and in the overall analysis. Marcus offers some very important insights into American Jewry´s origins and early development.

1723. Philipson, David: "The Jewish Pioneers of the Ohio Valley." PAJHS, #8 (1900): 43-57.

1724. Plaut, W. Gunther: "How Zionism Came to Minnesota." HYB, v.5 (1963): 221-235.

1725. Romanofsky, P.: "An Atmosphere of Success: the Keren Hayesod in Missouri 1921-1922." JSS, v.40 #1 (Wint., 1978): 73-84.

1726. Roseman, Kenneth D.: "Power in a Midwestern Jewish Community." AJA, v.21 #1 (Apr., 1969): 57-83.

1727. Shinedling, Abraham I.: WEST VIRGINIA JEWRY: ORIGINS AND HISTORY, 1850-1959. 3 vols. Philadelphia: JPS, 1961. 1,753 pp., illus., notes, index.

Extensive study of the history of the Jews in West Virginia. The book is organized geographically, although the first two chapters are thematic in their presentation. A good part of the information is presented in raw form, like a lexicon. Offers little insofar as analysis of the data is concerned, although the sheer mass of information is overwhelming. The most interesting part of the book is his introduction where he explains, again in great detail, how he obtained the information. Although weak as a history, the book offers a clue to the kinds of data historians could use in studying Jewish communities around the globe.

1728. Turitz, L. and E. Turitz: JEWS IN EARLY MISSISSIPPI. Jackson: Univ. Press of Mississippi, 1983. 134 pp., illus., bibliog., index.

County by county survey of the founding Jewish communities in Mississippi from 1840 to 1900. Based primarily on photographic evidence, though a number of secondary sources were also consulted. The book may be termed a folk-history and basically comprises a large number of anecdotes about individuals and their experiences. The authors attempt to broaden the context of the discussion in their introduction. To an extent this attempt is successful, although the time-frame in the introduction begins somewhat earlier than that of the photographs, and much earlier than that of the anecdotes. Some anecdotes deal with events after 1900. As a popularized contribution to the history of a little-known Jewish community, the book has some merit, but has little long-term scholarly value.

* 1729. Weiss, Adina and Joseph Aron: THE JEWISH COMMUNITY OF DELAWARE. Philadelphia: The Center for Jewish Community Studies, n. d. 87 pp.

1730. Zweigenhaft, R. L.: "Two Cities in North Carolina: a Comparative Study of Jews in the Upper Class." JSS, v.41 #3/4 (Sum./Fall, 1979): 291-300.

Communal Histories

1731. Adler, Selig and Thomas E. Connolly: FROM ARARAT TO SUBURBIA: THE HISTORY OF THE JEWISH COMMUNITY OF BUFFALO. Philadelphia: JPS, 1960. 498 pp., notes, bibliog., gloss., index.

Communal biography of the Jews in Buffalo from 1814 to the late 1950s. Arranged chronologically. Adler and Connolly based their text on an intensive study undertaken by the United Jewish Federation of Buffalo. Adler oversaw the work of the researchers, and the text was a collaborative effort by the two authors. Of special interest is the section on Mordechai Manuel Noah and his plan to create a Jewish national home - he called it Ararat - in the greater Buffalo area. Although Noah's utopian scheme never materialized, a thriving Jewish community was established in the same area. Adler and Connolly document every stage in the history of the community with great care and patience, and the book is a useful contribution to American Jewish history.

1732. Antonovsky, Aaron: "Aspects of New Haven Jewry: a Sociological Study." Y/A, v.10 (1955): 128-164.

1733. Barron, M. L.: "The Jews of California´s Middletown: Ethnic vs. Secular Social Services." JSS, v.44 #3/4 (Sum./ Fall, 1982): 239-254.

1734. Becker, Sandra H. and Ralph L. Pearson: "The Jewish Community of Hartford, Connecticut, 1880-1929." AJA, v.31 #2 (Nov., 1979): 184-214.

1735. Berman, Jeremiah J.: "Jewish Education in New York City, 1860-1900." Y/A, v.9 (1954): 247-275.

1736. Berman, Myron: RICHMOND´S JEWRY, 1769-1976: SHABBAT IN SHOKOE. Charlottesville: Univ. Press of Virginia, 1979. 438 pp., illus., notes, bibliog., index.

Survey of Jews in Richmond from colonial times to the twentieth century, based on extensive use of archival sources primarily related to the eighteenth and early nineteenth centuries. Berman views the development of Richmond Jewry in light of successive waves of immigration, punctured by periods of significant internal development. His analysis is penetrating and carefully documented. Subthemes include the economic role Jews played in antebellum Richmond, the Civil War, and post-Reconstruction antisemitism. Interestingly, Berman points out that antisemitism has been weakest in Richmond, as compared to the rest of the South. Two important chapters review the changes wrought on the community by World Wars I and II. In particular, the creation of a more structured community and the rise of zionism resulted from the events of our century. On controversial issues Berman is fair but also unafraid to call a spade a spade when drawing his conclusions. Foreword by Jacob Rader Marcus.

1737. Bernstein, Seth: "The Economic Life of the Jews in San Francisco During the 1860s as Reflected in the City Directories." AJA, v.27 #1 (Apr., 1975): 70-77.

1738. Broches, Z.: "A Chapter in the History of the Jews of Boston." Y/A, v.9 (1954): 205-211.

1739. Chyet, Stanley F.: "A Synagogue in Newport." AJA, v.16 #1 (Apr., 1964): 41-50.

1740. Cooper, Ch. I.: "The Jews of Minneapolis and Their Christian Neighbors." JSS, v.8 #1 (Jan., 1946): 31-38.

1741. Decker, P. R.: "Jewish Merchants in San Francisco: Social Mobility on the Urban Frontier." AJHQ, v.68 #4 (June, 1979): 396-407.

1742. De Sola Pool, David and Tamar De Sola Pool: AN OLD FAITH IN THE NEW WORLD: PORTRAIT OF SHEARITH ISRAEL, 1654-1954. New York: Columbia Univ. Press, 1955. 595 pp., illus., apps., notes, bibliog., index.

Communal biography of the Shearith Israel [Spanish and Portuguese] congregation of New York City. The oldest synagogue in the largest Jewish community in the world, Shearith Israel can be seen as a microcosm of American Jewry; it is certainly viewed as such by the authors. In addition to the history of New York´s Jewish community, the De Sola Pools also describe the unique minhagim of the community, and they provide short biographies of the rabbis, hazzanim, and functionaries of Shearith Israel. Other chapters deal with education, hevrot, and financial matters. Based in large part on the minute books of the congregation, the book is an excellent example of what fruits can be brought forth from careful research. Unfortunately, owing to the ravages of the Holocaust, it is unlikely that a similar volume could be written about any other congregation outside of England, the Americas, and Israel.

1743. Dubrovsky, G.: "Farmingdale, New Jersey: a Jewish Farm Community." AJHQ, v.66 #4 (June, 1977): 485-497.

1744. ___: "Growing up in Farmingdale." AJHQ, v.7 #2 (Dec., 1981): 239-255.

1745. Dyer, Albion M.: "Site of the First Synagogue of the Congregation Shearith Israel of New York." PAJHS, #8 (1900): 25-41.

1746. Eliassof, H.: "The Jews of Chicago." PAJHS, #11 (1903): 117-130.

1747. Elovitz, Mark H.: A CENTURY OF JEWISH LIFE IN DIXIE: THE BIRMINGHAM EXPERIENCE. University: The Univ. of Alabama Press, 1974. 258 pp., apps., gloss., notes, bibliog., index.

History of the Jews of Birmingham from the 1870s to the late 1960s. Elovitz attempts to provide a paradigm for the history of the Jews in a southern urban environment. Emphasis is on social history, although religious and political issues are also reviewed. An important subtheme is the role of the Jews in the civil-rights movement in the South. Subsequent to this Jewish civil-rights activism, though by no means a result of it, antisemitism became an important factor in Birmingham's public life. This culminated in the attempted bombing of Temple Beth-El in April 1958. In all, Elovitz offers a fresh and interesting insight into southern Jewry.

1748. Endleman, Judith E.: THE JEWISH COMMUNITY OF INDIANAPOLIS, 1849 TO THE PRESENT. Bloomington: Indiana Univ. Press, 1984. 303 pp., illus., app., notes, index.

Social history of Indianapolis Jewry in the nineteenth and twentieth centuries. Begins with the influx of German Jews and the establishment of the community in the 1840s. Endleman then charts the acculturation of the community, its social and economic role in building Indianapolis, and the interaction of German Jews with the newer immigrants from eastern Europe. Very usefully Endleman continues her account after World War II and, in fact, brings the communal history well into the 1970s. Her willingness to tackle such issues as the response to the Holocaust provide an interesting alternative to the accusatory and polemical accounts dealing with Jewish leaders and organizations; a completely new set of data becomes available when scholars view controversial questions on the grass-roots level. This is a commendable methodological contribution worthy of a follow-up study.

1749. Engelman, Uriah Zevi: "Demographic Note on Jewish Families in Buffalo." JSS, v.3 #4 (Oct., 1941): 399-408.

1750. ___: "Jewish Education in Charleston, South Carolina, during the eighteenth and nineteenth centuries." PAJHS, v.42 #1 (Sept., 1952): 43-70.

1751. ___: "The Jewish Population of Charleston." JSS, v.13 #3 (July, 1951): 195-210.

1752. Ezekiel, Jacob: "The Jews of Richmond." PAJHS, #4 (1896): 21-27.

1753. Fein, Isaac M.: THE MAKING OF AN AMERICAN JEWISH COMMUNITY: THE HISTORY OF BALTIMORE JEWRY FROM 1773 TO 1920. Philadelphia: JPS, 1971. 348 pp., illus., apps., notes, bibliog., index.

History of the Jews of Baltimore from colonial times to
the red scare. Fein interweaves both communal and individual
history. Religious life gets the lion's share of attention,
but the social, political, and economic aspects of the Jewish community are also covered. Half of the book deals with
the "Americanization, and Maturation of Baltimore's East
European Jewish Community." Significantly, Fein was able to
piece together segments of history even though much of the
documentation was unavailable.

1754. Feldman, Egal: "Jews in the Early Growth of New York
City's Men's Clothing Trade." AJA, v.12 #1 (Apr., 1960):
3-14.

1755. Feldman, Jacob S.: "The Pioneers of a Community: Regional Diversity Among the Jews of Pittsburgh, 1845-1861."
AJA, v.32 #2 (Nov., 1980): 119-124.

1756. Felsenthal, B.: "On the History of the Jews of
Chicago." PAJHS, #2 (1894): 21-27.

1757. Frank, Fedora S.: FIVE FAMILIES AND EIGHT YOUNG MEN:
NASHVILLE AND HER JEWRY, 1850-1861. Nashville, TN: Tennessee
Book Company, 1962. 184 pp., illus., notes, bibliog., index.

Brief but intensive investigation into the origins of the
Jews on Nashville. Frank notes that before 1850 there may
have been individual Jews who arrived and perhaps settled in
the city, but only after 1850 were enough Jews present to
constitute a community. Frank also provides an insight into
the history of Nashville and the mass migration of central
Europeans to the United States in the mid-nineteenth century. The book is carefully documented, within the constraints of available documentation. Frank's chapter on
holidays and amusements is fascinating. Simple in style
without being simplistic, the book can be used by younger
readers and is a good introduction to American Jewry.

1758. Frankland, A. E.: "Kronikals of the Times: Memphis,
1862." Ed. by M. Whiteman. AJA, v.9 #2 (Oct., 1957): 83-125.

1759. Friedman, Lee M.: "Boston in American Jewish History." PAJHS, v.42 #4 (June, 1953): 333-340.

1760. Gelfand, Mitchell: "Progress and Prosperity: Jewish
Social Mobility in Los Angeles in the Booming Eighties."
AJHQ, v.68 #4 (June, 1979): 408-433.

1761. Glanz, Rudolf: "German Jews in New York City in the Nineteenth Century." Y/A, v.11 (1956/57): 9-38.

1762. ___: "The History of the Jewish Community in New York." Y/A, v.4 (1949): 34-50.

1763. Glaser, Richard: "The Greek Jews in Baltimore." JSS, v.38 #3/4 (Sum./Fall, 1976): 321-336.

1764. Goldberg, Irving L.: "The Changing Jewish Community of Dallas." AJA, v.11 #1 (Apr., 1959): 82-97.

1765. Goldberg, N.: "Jews in the Police Records of Los Angeles, 1933-1947." Y/A, v.5 (1950): 266-291.

1766. Gorenstein, Arthur: "The Commissioner and the Community: the Beginnings of the New York City Kehillah [1908-1909]." Y/A, v.13 (1965): 187-212.

1767. Grinstein, Hyman B.: THE RISE OF THE JEWISH COMMUNITY OF NEW YORK: 1654-1860. Phaladelphia: Porcupine Press, 1976 [Rep. of 1946 Ed.]. 645 pp., illus., maps, apps., notes, bibliog., index.

Social history of New York Jewry. Primary emphasis is on the inner history that led to the development of the community, mainly in the mid-nineteenth century. Grinstein ends his survey before the mass migrations from eastern Europe, since by the 1880s New York Jewry had already fully developed and become organized. The chapters are arranged thematically. Nine chapters review religious issues, such as leadership, practice, and Reformist trends. An especially interesting section deals with social life, particularly with the tension between Americanization and Jewishness. The last three chapters seek to place New York Jewry into the broader historic contexts of American and world Jewry. Grinstein thus offers both a succint review of the development of America´s largest Jewish community and a model for similar studies of other communities.

1768. Gutstein, Morris A.: THE STORY OF THE JEWS OF NEWPORT: TWO AND A HALF CENTURIES OF JUDAISM, 1658-1908. New York: Bloch, 1936. 393 pp., illus., app., notes, bibliog., index.

Survey of the first 250 years of Newport Jewry, attempting to offer a comprehensive overview of one of North

America's oldest Jewish communities. Based largely on archival material, although Gutstein notes that much material is missing for the earliest periods. Interweaves the communal history with the personal stories of some famous Newport Jews. Newport, it might be noted, was the second Jewish community in the United States, following New York [then New Amsterdam]. As in New York, the first Jews in Newport were Sephardim of Dutch origin. Unlike New York, Newport Jewry rose to prominence and then declined rapidly, only to be revived at the turn of the twentieth century. Gutstein includes information on Kehillat Jeshuat Yisrael, also known as the Touro Synagogue, and on the congregation's main benefactor, Judah Touro. Obviously, the book is not complete and may be considered outdated. Nevertheless Gutstein's work is still a good example of a communal biography.

1769. Hartogensis, Benjamin H.: "The Sephardic Congregation of Baltimore." PAJHS, #23 (1915): 141-146.

1770. Hershkowitz, Leo: "Some Aspects of the New York Jewish Merchant and Community 1654-1820." AJHQ, v.66 #1 (Sept., 1976): 10-34.

1771. Hertzberg, Steven: "Making It in Atlanta: Economic Mobility in a Southern Jewish Community, 1870-1911." Y/A, v.17 (1978): 185-216.

1772. ___ : STRANGERS WITHIN THE GATE CITY: THE JEWS OF ATLANTA 1845-1915. Philadelphia: JPS, 1978. 325 pp., illus., notes, bibliog., index.

Study of the development of Atlanta Jewry from 1845 to World War I. Hertzberg uses Atlanta Jewry as a model for the study of Jews in the South. The book is especially important for its comparison of Jews in the South and the North during a period of rapid change. The book is a classic example of social history; economic, religious, and intellectual trends are given secondary consideration. Hertzberg makes important contributions to the history of Black-Jewish relations and of twentieth-century antisemitism in the South.

1773. Jastrow, Morris: "Notes on the Jews of Philadelphia, from Published Annals." PAJHS, #1 (1893): 49-61.

1774. Kaganoff, Nathan M.: "The Jewish Landsmanshaftn in New York City in the Period Preceding World War I." AJHQ, v.76 #1 (Sept., 1986): 56-66.

1775. Kliger, Hannah: "Traditions of Grass-Roots Organization and Leadership: the Continuity of Landsmanshaftn in New
York." AJHQ, v.76 #1 (Sept., 1986): 25-39.

1776. Kohler, Max J.: "Beginnings of New York Jewish History." PAJHS, #1 (1893): 41-48.

1777. ___: "Civil Status of the Jews in Colonial New
York." PAJHS, #6 (1898): 81-106.

1778. ___: "The Jews in Newport." PAJHS, #6 (1898): 61-80.

1779. ___: "Phases of Jewish Life in New York Before
1800." PAJHS, #2 (1894): 77-100; #3 (1895): 73-86.

1780. Korn, Bertram W.: THE EARLY JEWS OF NEW ORLEANS.
Waltham, MA: American Jewish Historical Society, 1969. 382
pp., illus., notes, bibliog., index.

Biographical history of the Jews of New Orleans from 1718
to 1810. Primary emphasis is on the activity of the Monsanto
family in the founding, refounding, and eventual building up
of the New Orleans Jewish community. The New Orleans Jewish
community was in fact unique; it was the only Jewish community in North America founded under French sovereignty. New
Orleans Jewry was also the only one in North America ever
expelled, which happened when Spain took over the Louisiana
territory in 1763. The community's real development occurred
after the Louisiana Purchase [1803], which gave the city to
the United States. Korn charts the community's developments
to 1810, by which time a normal Jewish community had
developed. Unfortunately, Korn did not broaden his view to
include a comparison with other communities, which would
have made interesting reading at the very least.

1781. Kranzler, George: WILLIAMSBURG - A JEWISH COMMUNITY
IN TRANSITION. New York: Feldheim, 1961. 310 pp., illus.,
maps, notes, bibliog.

Sociological inquiry into the hasidic community of
Williamsburg, Brooklyn. Kranzler divides the community into
different levels, or "phases," based on period and type of
immigration. Native Jews, although not ignored, were not
discussed in as much detail, given the time when he book was
written. Kranzler sees Williamsburg in the 1960s as a community in transition, a condition that he generalized for all
American Jewry.

1782. Krug, Mark M.: "The Yiddish Schools in Chicago." Y/A, v.9 (1954): 276-307.

1783. Kussy, S.: "Reminiscences of Jewish Life in Newark, New Jersey." Y/A, v.6 (1951): 177-186.

1784. Landes, Ruth: "Negro Jews in Harlem." JJoS, v.9 #2 (Dec., 1967): 175-189.

1785. Landesman, Alter: BROWNSVILLE: THE BIRTH, DEVELOP-MENT AND PASSING OF A JEWISH COMMUNITY IN NEW YORK. 2nd Ed. New York: Bloch Pub. 1971. 418 pp., notes, bibliog., index.

Sociological study of the Jews of east central Brooklyn. Landesman covers the birth, maturation, and postwar decline of the Jewish community. Although the book is basically organized in a chronological format, some chapters deal with specific themes, e.g., synagogues, charity, education, and labor. As Brownsville was largely a community of East Euro-pean Jewish immigrants, the development of that community may also be viewed as a model of the Americanization process affecting East European immigrant Jews across the United States. By the 1960s the Jewish community of Browns-ville had largely disappeared; thus Landesman's book is as much a eulogy as a scholarly inquiry.

1786. Lebowich, Joseph: "The Jews in Boston Till 1875." PAJHS, #12 (1904): 101-112.

1787. Leventman, Seymour: "Zionism in Minneapolis." HYB, v.5 (1963): 237-246.

1788. Liebman, Charles S.: "Leadership and Decision-making in a Jewish Federation: The New York Federation of Jewish Philanthropies." AJYB, v.79 (1979): 3-76.

1789. Livingston, J.: "The Industrial Removal Office, the Galveston Project, and the Denver Jewish Community." AJHQ, v.68 #4 (June, 1979): 434-458.

1790. Lowenstein, Steven M.: "The German-Jewish Community of Washington Heights." LBIYB, v.30 (1985): 245-254.

1791. Mayer, Egon: FROM SUBURB TO SHTETL: THE JEWS OF BORO PARK. Philadelphia: Temple Univ. Press, 1979. 196 pp., notes, bibliog., gloss., index.

Sociological analysis of the Jewish community of Boro Park, Brooklyn. Mayer attempts to chart the transformation of the area from a working class suburb to a traditional shtetl and a bastion of American Orthodox Judaism. The transformations have not been one-sided; many tradition-minded Jews have also changed by adopting some mores of the surrounding society. Thus, to a degree, Boro Park Jewry lives in two worlds - the world of religious tradition and the world of secular change. One of Mayer´s subthemes is to explain why the paradoxical relationship between tradition and modernity has led to little religious, psychological, or social deviance among Boro Park Jews. Another subtheme is the transformation and resurgence of American Orthodox Judaism. Although narrowly focused, the book could serve as a model for similar communal biographies.

1792. ___: "Gaps Between Generations of Orthodox Jews in Boro Park, Brooklyn, New York." JSS, v.39 #1/2 (Wint./Spr., 1977): 93-104.

1793. McKelvey, Blake: "The Jews of Rochester: a Contribution to their History during the Nineteenth Century." PAJHS, #40 (Sept., 1950): 57-73.

1794. Meyer, H. J.: "The Economic Structure of the Jewish Community in Detroit." JSS, v.2 #2 (Apr., 1940): 127-148.

1795. Moore, Deborah D.: AT HOME IN AMERICA: SECOND GENER-ATION NEW YORK JEWS. New York: Columbia Univ. Press, 1981. 303 pp., maps, charts, illus., notes, bibliog., index.

Social history of the children of the East Europeam immi-grants. By focusing on New York City, Moore can chart the process of Americanization over the course of a generation, while still maintaining a clear community focus. Her empha-sis is on acculturation and assimilation; Moore´s primary theme is the distinctive Jewish identity that second-generation American Jews maintained. Significantly, the second generation established the New York community that has become the largest, richest, and best-organized Jewish community in history. Insofar as they relate to the social history, political and religious development are also discussed.

1796. ___: "From Kehillah to Federation: the Communal Functions of Federated Philanthropy in New York City, 1917-1933." AJHQ, v.68 #2 (Dec., 1978): 131-146.

1797. ___: "Jewish Ethnicity and Acculturation in the 1920s: Public Education in New York City." JJoS, v.18 #2 (Dec., 1976): 96-104.

1798. Mopsik, Samuel: "The Jewish Population of Worcester, 1942." JSS, v.7 #1 (Jan., 1945): 41-62.

1799. Morais, Sabato: "Mickve Israel Congregation of Philadelphia." PAJHS, #1 (1893): 13-24.

1800. Moses, Alfred G.: "A History of the Jews of Mobile." PAJHS, #12 (1904): 113-125.

1801. ___: "The History of the Jews of Montgomery." PAJHS, #13 (1905): 83-88.

1802. Mostov, Stephen G.: "Dun and Bradstreet Reports as a Source of Jewish Economic History: Cincinnati, 1840-1875." AJHQ, v.72 #3 (March, 1983): 333-353.

1803. ___: "A Sociological Portrait of German Jewish Immigrants in Boston: 1845-1861." AJS Review, v.3 (1978): 121-152.

1804. Necarsulmer, Henry: "The Early Jewish Settlement at Lancaster, Pennsylvania." PAJHS, #9 (1901): 29-44.

1805. Neusner, Jacob: "The Impact of Immigration and Philanthropy Upon the Boston Jewish Community [1880-1914]." PAJHS, v.46 #2 (Dec., 1956): 71-85.

1806. Olitzky, Kerry M.: "Sundays at Chicago Sinai Congregation: Paradigm for a Movement." AJHQ, v.74 #4 (June, 1985): 356-368.

1807. Oppenheim, Samuel: "The Early History of the Jews in New York, 1654-1664: Some New Matter on the Subject." PAJHS, #18 (1909): 1-91.

1808. ___: "The First Settlement of the Jews in Newport: Some New Matter on the Subject." PAJHS, #34 (1937): 1-10.

1809. ___: "The Jewish Burial Ground on New Bowery, New York, Acquired in 1682, not 1656." PAJHS, #31 (1928): 77-103.

1810. ___: "The Question of the Kosher Meat Supply in New York in 1813: With a Sketch of Earlier Conditions." PAJHS, #25 (1917): 21-62.

1811. Perlmann, Joel: "Beyond New York: the Occupation of Russian Jewish Immigrants in Providence, R. I. and in Other Small Jewish Communities, 1900-1915." AJHQ, v.72 #3 (March, 1983): 369-394.

1812. Petrusak, Frank and Steven Steinert: "The Jews of Charleston: Some Old Wine in New Bottles." JSS, v.38 #3/4 (Sum./Fall, 1976): 337-346.

1813. Philipson, D.: "The Cincinnati Community in 1825." PAJHS, #10 (1902): 97-99.

1814. Phillips, N. Taylor: "Items Relating to the History of the Jews of New York." PAJHS, #11 (1903): 149-161.

1815. Pierce, L. E.: "The Jewish Settlement on St. Paul´s Lower West Side." AJA, v.28 #2 (Nov., 1976): 143-161.

1816. Poll, Solomon: THE HASIDIC COMMUNITY OF WILLIAMS- BURG: A STUDY IN THE SOCIOLOGY OF RELIGION. New York: Schocken Books, 1962. 308 pp., notes, app., gloss., bib- liog., index.

Sociological inquiry into the hasidic Jews of Brooklyn. Primary emphasis is on the Satmar hasidim, although other groups, e.g. the Skvirer, are also reviewed. All the groups studied shared a common belief in the need to isolate themselves from other Jews as well as non-Jews in order to re-create their traditional societies. Poll concludes that, as of the time of writing, the hasidim were successful in their search for isolation. He does, however, question how long such isolation can be maintained under present cir- cumstances. Poll´s analysis of the issue of isolation becomes especially meaningful in light of the economic structure of Williamsburg Jewry. Changes in economic activities that have taken place since the early 1960s seem to bear out Poll´s conclusions and do point to some changes in the orientation of many hasidic groups.

1817. Porter, Jack: "Differentiating Features of Orthodox, Conservative, and Reform Jewish Groups in Metropolitan Philadelphia." JSS, v.25 #3 (July, 1963): 186-194.

1818. Reznikoff, Charles and Uriah Zevi Engelman: THE JEWS OF CHARLESTON: A HISTORY OF AN AMERICAN JEWISH COMMUNITY. Philadelphia: JPS, 1950. 343 pp., illus., notes, index.

Communal biography of Charleston Jewry. Primary emphasis is on describing the key figures and events in the community's history. As the book was written in 1950, the coverage is intensive only until the turn of the century. Then too, many issues, e.g., antisemitism, are not dealt with per se. As with its companion volumes, the books do not represent real histories, but are useful as sources of information and statistics on American Jewry. Foreword by Salo W. Baron.

1819. Rischin, Moses: THE PROMISED CITY: NEW YORK'S JEWS, 1870-1914. New York: Corinth Books, 1964. 342 pp., maps, illus., app., notes, bibliog., index.

Sketches Jewish life on the Lower East Side of New York at the turn of the century. The book is a model of urban social history focused on Jews. The work concentrates on the Jews' quest for community and continuity in light of the profound changes in lifestyle brought about by migration to America. Relations between "downtown" and "uptown" Jews are charted, as are efforts at improving the lot of the tenement and slum dwellers. The book sheds a good deal of light on both urban and Jewish history, providing a useful methodological guide for other local histories.

1820. Robison, Sophia M.: "Some Characteristics of Trenton and Passaic Jews." JSS, v.2 #3 (July, 1940): 249-254.

1821. Rockaway, R. A.: "Antisemitism in an American City: Detroit 1850-1914." AJHQ, v.64 #1 (Sept., 1974): 42-54.

1822. ___: "The Eastern European Jewish Community of Detroit, 1881-1914." Y/A, v.15 (1974): 82-105.

1823. ___: THE JEWS OF DETROIT FROM THE BEGINNING: 1762-1914. Detroit, MI: Wayne State Univ. Press, 1970. 162 pp., illus., maps, notes, apps., bibliog., index.

Communal biography of Detroit Jewry over 150 years. Although scholarly in approach, the book is written in a popular style. Rockaway concentrates on social history, integrating the lives of the community's key members into the overall story. Different waves of immigration, Jewish eco-

nomic activities, and religious developments are all reviewed. Based on extensive documentary material, as well as
on other primary and secondary sources. Rockaway has written
an important and readable history of a midwestern Jewish
community.

1824. Rosenbach, Abraham S. Wolf: "Notes on the First Settlement of Jews in Pennsylvania, 1655-1703." PAJHS, #5
(1897): 191-198.

1825. Rosenwaike, Ira: "The Founding of Baltimore´s First
Jewish Congregation: Fact vs. Fiction." AJA, v.28 #2 (Nov.,
1976): 119-125.

1826. ___: "The Jews of Baltimore to 1810." AJHQ, v.64 #4
(June, 1975): 291-320.

1827. ___: "The Jews of Baltimore: 1810 to 1820." AJHQ,
v.67 #2 (Dec., 1977): 101-124.

1828. ___: "The Jews of Baltimore: 1820 to 1830." AJHQ,
v.67 #3 (March, 1978): 246-259.

1829. Rubin, Israel: SATMAR - AN ISLAND IN THE CITY. New
York: Quadrangle, 1972. 272 pp., charts, notes, index.

Sociological study of the ultra-Orthodox Satmar group in
Brooklyn. The historical background is somewhat weak, but is
nonetheless useful for the general reader. Rubin paints a
picture of the Satmar community in all its manifestations.
Two themes emerge from the text. First, the ability of an
insular community to withstand the pressure to Americanize;
second, the vitally important role that the Rebbe plays
within the community. It should be noted that in all hasidic
communities, the Rebbe or zaddik plays a similar role, which
differs only in degree from one hasidic community to
another. Satmar´s controversial role in Jewish affairs is
only touched upon, as it is not central to Rubin´s analysis.

1830. Ruxin, Robert H.: "The Jewish Farmer and the Small-
Town Jewish Community: Schoharie County, New York." AJA,
v.29 #1 (Apr., 1977): 3-21.

1831. Sanua, Victor D.: "A Study of the Adjustment of Sephardi Jews in the New York Metropolitan Area." JJoS, v.9 #1
(June, 1967): 25-33.

1832. Schmier, Louis: "Notes and Documents on the 1862 Ex-pulsion of Jews from Thomasville, Georgia." AJA, v.32 #1 (Apr., 1980): 9-22.

1833. Schultz, Joseph P. [ed.]: MID-AMERICA'S PROMISE: A PROFILE OF KANSAS CITY JEWRY. Waltham, MA: American Jewish Historical Society for the Jewish Community Foundation of Greater Kansas City, 1982. 405 pp., illus., notes, index.

Anthology illuminating the history of the Jews of Kansas City. Main emphasis is on social history, but political and cultural history are also covered. Antisemitism is not dealt with systematically, but is reviewed within the contexts of community relations, zionism, and Jewish self-government. Although not organized chronologically, the thematic order of presentation has some merit. The book particularly suggests the possibility of a comparative history on any one of a number of topics. All of the essays are well written and documented.

CONTENTS: Judith M. Firestone: Jewish Journalism in Kansas City / A. C. Heiligman: The Demographic Perspective / David M. Katzman: Jewish Self-Government in Kansas City: the Origins and Ascendancy of the Federation, 1933-1946 / Carla E. Klausner: The Zionist Spectrum / Sharon Lowenstein: New Beginnings in the Heart of America: Organized Resettlement in Kansas City / H. F. Sachs: Seeking the Welfare of the City: a Survey of Public Relations, Economics, and Social and Civic Activity / B. E. Schultz: The Highest Degree to Tzedakah: Jewish Philanthropy in Kansas City, 1870-1933; Transmitting the Heritage: Jewish Education in Kansas City / Joseph P. Schultz: The Consensus of "Civil Judaism": the Religious Life of Kansas City Jewry.

1834. ___ And Carla L. Klausner: "Rabbi Simon Glazer and the Quest for Jewish Community in Kansas City, 1920-1923." AJA, v.35 #1 (Apr., 1983): 13-26.

1835. Selavan, Ida Cohen: "The Education of Jewish Immi-grants in Pittsburgh, 1862-1932." Y/A, v.15 (1974): 126-144.

1836. Shankman, Arnold: "Atlanta Jewry: 1900-1930." AJA, v.25 #2 (Nov., 1973): 131-155.

1837. ___: "Happyville, the Forgotten Colony." AJA, v.30 #1 (Apr., 1978): 3-19.

1838. Silver, Louis: "The Jews in Albany, New York [1655-1914]." Y/A, v.9 (1954): 212-246.

1839. Sulzberger, David: "The Beginning of Russo-Jewish Immigration to Philadelphia." PAJHS, #19 (1910): 125-150.

1840. Sutton, Joseph A.: MAGIC CARPET: ALEPPO IN FLATBUSH. THE STORY OF A UNIQUE ETHNIC JEWISH COMMUNITY. New York: Thayer-Jacoby, 1979. 304 pp., illus., apps., notes, gloss., bibliog., index.

Portrait of America's Syrian Jewish community, the book is both a historical review and sociological analysis. Three chapters deal with the history of the Jews of Syria, although inexplicably these are the last three chapters of the book. The remaining ten chapters cover the transferred community and its reconstruction in New York City. Economic, religious, and social life are all reviewed. Although most of Sutton's attention is focused on Jews from Aleppo, a chapter is devoted to Damascus Jews in the United States. The sociological analysis makes for interesting comparisons. The cohesion of the Syrian community is remarkable. Seven appendixes add further information, including a fully annotated questionnaire that shows what kind of information was sought and collected for the book. Foreword by Shlomo D. Goitein.

1841. Swichkow, L. J.: "The Jewish Community of Milwaukee, Wisconsin, 1860-1870." PAJHS, v.47 #1 (Sept., 1957): 34-58.

1842. ___ and Lloyd P. Gartner: THE HISTORY OF THE JEWS OF MILWAUKEE. Philadelphia: JPS, 1963. 533 pp., illus., maps, apps., notes, bibliog., index.

Communal biography of Milwaukee Jewry, part of a planned series of Jewish communal histories undertaken by the American History Center of the Jewish Theological Seminary. The book is divided into three sections, organized chronologically. The first covers the pioneering period and basically deals with the German Jews who founded and organized the community. The second [1870-1925] covers the maturation period of Milwaukee Jewry, and special attention is given to the immigration and accommodation of East European Jews. The last section reviews the period of crisis that arose after World War I, dealing with communal tension during the interwar era and the post-Holocaust consolidation of Milwaukee Jewry. An argument could be made for using a similar organization for the study of American Jewish history in general, although the more conventional division is based on waves of Jewish immigration. The survey is thorough, covering all important topics and issues. Emphasis is on social history, and the role Jews played in building up Milwaukee is given special attention.

1843. Toll, William: "American Jewish Families: the Occupational Basis of Adaptability in Portland, Oregon." JJoS, v.19 #1 (June, 1977): 33-47.

1844. ___: "Mobility, Fraternalism and Jewish Cultural Change: Portland, 1910-1930." AJHQ, v.68 #4 (June, 1979): 459-491.

1845. Varady, David P.: "Migration and Mobility Patterns of the Jewish Population of Cincinnati." AJA, v.32 #1 (Apr., 1980): 78-88.

1846. Vorspan, Max and L. P. Gartner: HISTORY OF THE JEWS OF LOS ANGELES. Philadelphia: JPS, 1970. 312 pp., illus., apps., notes, index.

Character study or communal biography spanning a century of Jewish life in Los Angeles [1850s-1960s]. Integrates both communal and individual history. The book is divided into two sections, the first covering the nineteenth century and the second dealing with the twentieth century. Although the former contains much new material, it is the latter, with its analysis of how Los Angeles Jewry grew and matured, that provides an interesting insight into the dynamics of American Jewish communal life.

1847. Wieder, Arnold A.: THE EARLY JEWISH COMMUNITY OF BOSTON´S NORTH END. Waltham, MA: Brandeis Univ. Press, 1962. 100 pp., illus., notes, gloss., apps.

Brief sociological inquiry into the Jewish community of North Boston. The main focus of the study is on the social adaptation and religiocultural attitudes of Jewish immigrants in Boston between 1870-1900. The study is based almost entirely on interviews conducted with Jewish residents of the area. While the study is somewhat weak methodologically - a fact admitted by its author - Wieder´s conclusions seem reasonable and generally accord with what is known from other communities. The book is thus of some use as an introductory study and has potential comparative applications.

1848. Wolf, Edwin and Maxwell Whiteman: THE HISTORY OF THE
JEWS OF PHILADELPHIA FROM COLONIAL TIMES TO THE AGE OF
JACKSON. Philadelphia: JPS, 1957. 534 pp., illus., notes,
bibliog., index.

Communal history of early Philadelphia Jewry. The book is
organized thematically within a chronological framework. The
first chapter sets out the background of Philadelphia's
history and the migration of Jews to America. The history
of the Philadelphia Jewish community begins in the second
chapter. Key individuals, for example, Isaac Leeser or the
Gratz family, are interwoven into the picture. A wide variety of issues are reviewed by the authors. Although the
tenor of the writing may strike the reader as pretentious,
the book is an important storehouse of vital information
about the earliest development of American Jewry.

CANADA

Surveys

1849. Belkin, Simon: THROUGH NARROW GATES: A REVIEW OF
JEWISH IMMIGRATION, COLONIZATION AND IMMIGRANT AID WORK IN
CANADA, 1840-1940. Montreal: Canadian Jewish Congress, 1966.
235 pp., notes, apps., bibliog., gloss., index.

History of Jewish immigration to Canada. Divides the
subject into two periods: before World War I, when the
Canadian government encouraged Jewish immigration and
colonization, and after World War I, when the government
became increasingly restrictive. A major subtheme is that of
Jewish agricultural colonization, under the auspices of the
Jewish Colonization Association and the Am Olam Society.
Another subtheme is the social services offered by Canadian
Jewish organizations to new immigrants. Belkin's approach
is particularly useful when he compares contemporary events
in Canada and the United States, especially in regard to
immigration policy. Belkin is quite blunt when he analyzes
Canadian apathy toward Jewish refugees during the Nazi
period. A brief conclusion details the situation of Jewish
immigration to Canada from 1941 to 1951.

1850. Benjamin, L. M.: "A Bird's Eye View of Canadian Jewish History." CJYB, v.1 (1939/40): 67-81.

1851. Bercuson, David: CANADA AND THE BIRTH OF ISRAEL: A STUDY OF CANADIAN FOREIGN POLICY. Toronto: Univ. of Toronto Press, 1985. 291 pp., notes, bibliog., index.

Intensive investigation of Canadian governmental policy on the Palestine question. Bercuson tries to avoid over-simplification in his review of both pro- and anti-Zionist standpoints. Although Canada was and is still widely perceived as supportive of Jewish goals, Bercuson notes that the situation was much more complicated. Canadian sympathy for Jewish aspirations was only granted grudgingly, despite intense propaganda by Canadian Zionists. Canadian policy on the Middle East has always been formulated, according to Bercuson, on the basis of self-interest and not on moral or ideological grounds. Furthermore, Canada's Middle East policy must be viewed in the context of British and United States policy. Well documented, the book is an important contribution to the study of Zionist politics in the Anglo-American sphere.

1852. Brown, Michael: "The American Connection of Canadian Jews: 1759-1914." AJS Review, v.3 (1978): 21-77.

1853. ___: "The Beginnings of Reform Judaism in Canada." JSS, v.34 #4 (Oct., 1972): 322-342.

1854. Fathi, Asghar: "Some Aspects of Changing Ethnic Identity of Canadian Jewish Youth." JSS, v.34 #1 (Jan., 1972): 23-30.

1855. Hayes, Saul: "Jewish Refugees in Canada." CJYB, v.2 (1940/41): 40-55.

1856. Joseph, A. C.: "The Settlement of Jews in Canada." PAJHS, #1 (1893): 117-120.

1857. Kay, Zachariah: "A Note on Canada and the Formation of the Jewish Legion." JSS, v.29 #3 (July, 1967): 171-177.

1858. Lazar, Morty M.: "The Role of Women in Synagogue Ritual in Canadian Conservative Congregations." JJoS, v.20 #2 (Dec., 1978): 165-171.

> #1721. Marcus, J. R.: EARLY AMERICAN JEWRY.

1859. Rosenberg, Louis: "The Demography of the Jewish Community in Canada." JJoS, v.1 #2 (Dec., 1959): 217-233.

1860. ___ : "Jewish Agriculture in Canada." Y/A, v.5 (1950): 205-215.

1861. ___ : "The Jewish Population of Canada: a Statistical Summary from 1850 to 1943." AJYB, v.48 (1946/47): 19-50.

1862. ___ : "Some Aspects of the Historical Development of the Canadian Jewish Community." PAJHS, v.50 #2 (Dec., 1960): 121-142.

1863. ___ : "Two Centuries of Jewish Life in Canada, 1760-1960." AJYB, v.62 (1961): 28-49.

1864. Rosenberg, Stuart: THE JEWISH COMMUNITY IN CANADA. 2 vols. Toronto: McClelland & Stewart, 1970. 464 pp., illus., notes, apps., bibliog. index.

Two volume history and guide to Jewish life in Canada. Volume I, A HISTORY, is a chronologically organized history of Canadian Jewry, from the earliest settlers to the 1960s. Rosenberg notes that the date of the first settlement of Jews in Canada is open to conjecture. Only with the conquest of Canada by the British was a community actually founded. The Canadian community developed very slowly, growing only as a result of the migration of East European Jews. In addition to purely chronological chapters, Rosenberg includes some of a thematic nature, dealing, for example, with education and emancipation. Volume II, IN THE MIDST OF FREEDOM, is a thematically arranged study with a dual focus: the organized community as it exists today and the role of Jews in Canada's history. An interesting section deals with the "Americanization" of Canadian Jewry. Although somewhat filial pietistic, Rosenberg's work is nevertheless an interesting and useful contribution to Canadian Jewish history.

1865. Sack, Benjamin G.: HISTORY OF THE JEWS IN CANADA. Trans. from the Yiddish by Ralph Novek. Montreal: Harvest House, 1965 [Rep. of 1945 Ed.]. 299 pp., notes, apps., bibliog., index.

Synthetic history of Canadian Jews up to the twentieth century. Unlike other authors, Sack believes that there is strong evidence pointing to a Jewish or quasi-Jewish presence in French Canada. Sack's reconstruction of the development of the community under British rule rests on more solid ground. Interestingly, Sack follows American Jewish historians in their division of Jewish communal life into waves

of immigration - Sephardic, German, and East European. Although the dating of each wave differs, the logic behind
such a division seems appropriate. An especially interesting
chapter details the emancipation of Canadian Jewry. In each
generation the inner life of the community is interwoven
with external relations. Efforts at Jewish colonization
receive special attention, even though most were abortive
and, in Sack's eyes, naive. Ending with the turn of the
century, the book is outdated but still a source of much
interesting information.

1866. Sarna, Jonathan D.: "Jewish Immigration to North
America: the Canadian Experience [1870-1900]." JJoS, v.18 #1
(June, 1976): 31-41.

1867. Wolff, Martin: "The Jews of Canada." AJYB, v.27
(1925/26): 154-229.

Communal Histories

1868. Arnoni, M.: "The First Jewish Settlers of Ottawa."
CJYB, v.2 (1940/41): 115-120.

1869. Blaustein, Esther I. et al: "Spanish and Portuguese
Synagogue [Shearith Israel] Montreal, 1768-1968." TJHSE,
v.23 (1969/70): 111-142.

1870. Chiel, Arthur: THE JEWS IN MANITOBA: A SOCIAL HIS-
TORY. Toronto: Univ. of Toronto Press, 1961. 203 pp., notes,
apps., index.

History of the Jews in northern Canada, with special emphasis on Jewish immigration and pioneering. Jews first settled in Manitoba in the 1850s, although the community as
such did not develop until after the influx of Russian Jews
in the 1880s. The most important community was, and still
is, in Winnipeg. Chiel covers the social and religious life
of the new immigrants and their economic adjustment to
Canada. A systematic effort to retrain new immigrants for
agricultural work was undertaken by the government in
collaboration with a number of Jewish organizations. However, the scheme fell through and by the early twentieth
century was abandoned. Chiel's chapters on the inner life of
Jews in Winnipeg are interesting and provide an insight into
a dynamic and vibrant Jewish community.

1871. Gutwirth, Jacques: "The Structure of a Hasidic Community in Montreal." JJoS, v.14 #1 (June, 1972): 43-62.

1872. Kalter, Bella B.: "A Jewish Community That Was - Ansonville, Ontario, Canada." AJA, v.30 #2 (Nov., 1978): 107-125.

1873. Rome, David: "Jews in the Far Northwest." CJYB, v.1 (1939/40): 82-102.

1874. Shaffir, Wm.: "Hasidic Jews and Quebec Politics." JJoS, v.25 #2 (Dec., 1983): 105-118.

1875. Speisman, Stephen A.: THE JEWS OF TORONTO: A HISTORY TO 1937. Toronto: McClelland and Stewart, 1979. 380 pp., illus., notes, index.

Covers a century of social history of Toronto Jewry from the 1830s to the 1930s. Jews established themselves in Toronto in the 1830s, but communal development was slow until the turn of the century. According to Speisman, Toronto was rarely a destination of choice for East European Jews despite governmental inducements and organizational assistance. Nevertheless, it was East European immigration that established the community. Speisman´s main theme is the entry of new immigrants into the community and their acculturation. Much attention is focused on the community and its institutions. Despite many divisive forces, Toronto Jewry developed into a unified - though not monolithic - community. Although he concentrates mainly on social issues, Speisman also reviews Canadian Jewish public affairs in four especially important chapters on the twentieth century. In addition, Speisman surveys the changes that acculturation wrought on Toronto Jews, for example, in the area of religious practice. At every turn Toronto Jewry is placed into context. Speisman also draws some useful comparisons between Jews in Canada and the United States.

1876. Weinfeld, Morton: "The Jews of Quebec: Perceived Antisemitism, Segregation, and Emigration." JJoS, v.22 #1 (June, 1980): 5-20.

* 1877. ____ and William W. Eaton: THE JEWISH COMMUNITY OF MONTREAL: SURVEY REPORT. Montreal: Jewish Community Research Institute, 1979. 86 pp.

16

The Middle East

SURVEYS

1878. Angel, Marc D.: THE JEWS OF RHODES: THE HISTORY OF A
SEPHARDIC COMMUNITY. New York: Sepher-Hermon Press, 1978.
199 pp., illus., notes, bibliog., index.

Social history of Rhodes Jewry from the sixteenth to the
twentieth centuries. Founded in 1523, the Rhodes Jewish community was almost completely composed of Sephardim fleeing
Spain. Internal and external history are both reviewed, with
emphasis on the former. The balance between social, economic, and intellectual history is good. Jewish relations
with the environment are charted in a separate chapter.
Unfortunately, the events of the twentieth century are
discussed in only a cursory fashion. An Ottoman territory,
Rhodes was seized by the Italians in 1918. In 1939 Rhodes
became a center of wartime attention, although the community
had been faced with severe restrictions since the mid-1930s.
In the summer of 1943 Rhodes was occupied by the Nazis and
the Jews were systematically deported, first to Athens and
then to Auschwitz. Despite certain omissions, the work is an
important contribution to the history of Sephardic and
Middle Eastern Jewry.

> #396. Baron, S. W. and G. Wise: VIOLENCE AND DEFENSE.

1879. Bat Ye'or: DHIMMI: JEWS AND CHRISTIANS UNDER ISLAM.
Trans. from the French by D. Maisel. Cranbury, NJ: Fairleigh
Dickinson Univ. Press, 1985. 444 pp., illus., notes, bib-
liog., indexes.

Studies the treatment accorded to non-Muslim minorities

in the Arab world. Basically attempts to revise the widely
held notion that religious minorities, especially Jews, were
unequivocally tolerated in the Muslim world. The central
thrust of her analysis is the status accorded to the Dhimmi,
protected and tolerated minorities whose members accepted
monotheism and the Scriptures that Muslims considered a precursor to the Koran. In attempting to demythologize Muslim-
Jewish relations Bat Ye´or may, perhaps, go too far in
emphasizing the negative elements in the Dhimmi status.
While Dhimmi were not treated royally and were always
considered second-class citizens, possessing a lower form of
religious truth, they were permitted life and freedom to
worship in their own way. Even so, as a corrective, especially to refute allegations that the creation of modern
Israel is the cause of Muslim-Jewish enmity, the book is
extremely useful. Over 100 documents, most of which never
appeared in English before, are included in this work.

1880. Ben-Zvi, Itzhak: THE EXILED AND THE REDEEMED. Trans.
from the Hebrew by Isaac A. Abbady. Philadelphia: JPS, 1961.
285 pp., notes, index.

Kaleidoscopic view of Middle Eastern Jewish communities
by Israel´s second president. Also discusses the Samaritans
and other quasi- or crypto-Jewish tribes. An especially
interesting section deals with the rise and fall of small
independent Jewish states in the East during the Middle
Ages. Folklore, both Jewish and Arab, plays an important
role in Ben-Zvi´s analysis, although statistical and other
sociological data are not ignored. Ben-Zvi´s descriptions
of tribal lifestyles and folklore make the book both interesting and fascinating. Ben-Zvi´s life-work on Jewish sects
was but one reflection of a life dedicated to Klal Yisrael.

1881. Chouraqui, Andre N.: BETWEEN EAST AND WEST: A HIS-
TORY OF THE JEWS OF NORTH AFRICA. Trans. from the French by
Michael M. Bernet. New York: Atheneum, 1973. 376 pp., notes,
apps., bibliog., index.

Synthetic history of North African Jewry from the
earliest traces of Jewish settlement [ca 813 B.C.E.] to
1948. The book is organized chronologically and is based on
the dominant groups that ruled North Africa in any era. The
Jewish communities are reviewed and placed into the dual
contexts of internal organization and the policy of various
ruling powers towards Jews. It is interesting to note the
differing fate of North African Jewry under the Romans,

Byzantines, Vandals, Muslims, French, and modern Arab states. Political factors are integrated with social and intellectual trends. The book ends with the transfer of Maghrebian Jewry to the State of Israel in 1948.

1882. ___ : "North African Jewry Today." JJoS, v.1 #1 (Apr., 1959): 58-68.

> #94. Fischel, W.: JEWS IN THE ECONOMIC AND POLITICAL LIFE.

> #226. Fishman, J.: THE SOCIOLOGY OF JEWISH LANGUAGES.

1883. Goitein, Shlomo Dov: JEWS AND ARABS: THEIR CONTACTS THROUGH THE AGES. New York: Schocken Books, 1955. 263 pp., bibliog., chronological table, index.

Synthetic history of Jewish-Arab relations in good and bad times over the course of 1300 years. Attempts to assess the reciprocal influences that each group has had on the other. The book also represents an effort at integrating Jewish and Arab history. In addition to dealing with the positive elements, twentieth-century enmity and conflict between Jews and Arabs is also analyzed. Especially important is Goitein's chapter on "Why Has the History of the Two Peoples Taken Such Different Courses."

1884. Goldberg, Harvey: "Patronymic Groups in a Tripoli-tanian Jewish Village: Reconstruction and Interpretation." JJoS, v.9 #2 (Dec., 1967): 208-225.

1885. Hacohen, Devorah and Menachem Hacohen: ONE PEOPLE - THE STORY OF THE EASTERN JEWS. Revised Edition. New York: Adama Books, 1986. 195 pp., illus., bibliog.

Popular anthology surveying the lifestyles and customs of the Oriental Jewish communities. Although differing in many of their customs, these communities prove that Jews are indeed one people, irrespective of idiosyncratic minhagim. The Hacohens also offer an interesting comparative insight into Jewish ways of life in Mediteranean countries. Written for the layperson, the book is fully illustrated. The Oriental Jewish communities virtually ceased to exist in 1948, when almost all their members relocated to Israel.

1886. Haddad, Heskel M.: JEWS OF ARAB AND ISLAMIC COUNT-RIES: HISTORY, PROBLEMS, SOLUTIONS. New York: Shengold Pub., 1984. 167 pp., Charts, tables, chron., bibliog., index.

Thematic history of Jews from Arab countries, interweaved
with the history of Sephardi Jewry and of Jews in non-Arab
Muslim lands. Also includes a detailed analysis of Sephardi-
Ashkenazi relations, with primary emphasis on the problem of
Ashkenazim and Sephardim in Israel. Although ethnic tension
seems to be the core of what Haddad wanted to write about,
it is the historical, sociological, and demographic material
that is the most interesting.

1887. Hirschberg, H. Z.: A HISTORY OF THE JEWS IN NORTH
AFRICA. Leiden: E. J. Brill, 1974. 2 vols. 869 pp., notes,
apps., bibliog., indexes.

Detailed social history of the Jews in North Africa from
late antiquity to modern times. Published in two volumes,
which are arranged chronologically. Volume I covers the
period from the Greeks to the sixteenth century and is organized thematically. Volume II, from the sixteenth century
to modern times, is organized geographically. In both volumes stress is on the development of the Jewish community
and the manifestations of Jewish life in North Africa.
Spiritual and economic activities are also discussed. Volume
II appears incomplete; the chapter on Algeria ends with the
French conquest [1830-31], while the chapters on Libya,
Tunisia, and Morocco cover the history of those communities
through the 1940s. Although not definitive, Hirschberg's
text is well documented and offers keen insight into the
lives of North Africa's Jews in addition to assessing the
importance of the North African Jewish communities.

* 1888. Landshut, S.: JEWISH COMMUNITIES IN THE MUSLIM COUN-
TRIES OF THE MIDDLE EAST. London: Jewish Chronicle, 1950.
102 pp., bibliog.

1889. Laskier, Michael M.: "Aspects of the Activities of
the Alliance Israelite Universelle in the Jewish Communities
of the Middle East and North Africa: 1860-1918." MJ, v.3 #2
(May, 1983): 147-171.

1890. Lewis, Bernard: THE JEWS OF ISLAM. Princeton, NJ:
Princeton Univ. Press, 1984. 245 pp., illus., notes, index.

Attempts to revise recent historiography on Arab-Jewish
relations. Lewis probes the Muslim attitude toward Jews and
Judaism with a view to establishing the parameters of the
Judaeo-Islamic tradition. Lewis notes that this tradition
had both positive and negative elements. Jews, it is clear,

were treated better in Muslim lands during the High Middle
Ages [ca. 800-1100] than in Christian countries in the same
period. Nevertheless, Jews were always second-class citizens
and their lives were hardly utopias. Muslims, like Christians, viewed Judaism as an obsolete religion and a lower
form of truth, but permitted it to survive and, at times,
thrive. Important for Jewish survival was the acceptance by
Muslims of the premise that Judaism did contain an element
of truth. Lewis´s discussion of the decline of the Judaeo-
Islamic tradition is a classic example of scholarly objectivity; he is unwilling to issue broad condemnations of
Arabs. In particular, Lewis does not readily resort to the
term antisemitism, although he understands that pure hatred
is also a factor in contemporary Arab-Jewish relations.

> #340. Ma´oz, M.: THE IMAGE OF THE JEW.

1891. Raphael, Chaim: THE ROAD FROM BABYLON: THE STORY OF
SEPHARDI AND ORIENTAL JEWS. New York: Bessie / Harper & Row,
1985. 294 pp., illus., maps, notes, bibliog., index.

    History of the Sephardim and of the Jews of the Middle
East. The book is organized chronologically. Each community
is covered individually, although the Spanish Jews get the
lion´s share of Raphael´s attention. He sees two pivotal
eras in the history of Sephardic Jewry: [1] the expulsion
from Spain in 1492 and [2] World War II and the years imme-
diately following, which led to the uprooting of Middle
Eastern Jews and their resettlement in the State of Israel.
Primary emphasis is on social history, but folkways are a
major subtheme. A very useful section deals with the integration of the Sephardim in Israel since 1948, written in
very clear, honest, and nonpolemical terms. Uncovering few
new facts, the book is primarily useful as a synthetic history of an oft-ignored Jewish community.

> #981. Starr, J.: ROMANIA.

1892. Stillman, Norman A.: THE JEWS OF ARAB LANDS: A HIS-
TORY AND SOURCE BOOK. Philadelphia: JPS, 1979. 473 pp.,
illus., notes, bibliog., index.

    Historical survey and anthology covering the history of
Jews in Muslim lands from the founding of Islam to the nineteenth century. Primary focus in both sections of the book
is on Muslim-Jewish relations. The documents, which represent about two-thirds of the book, flow with the text, thus

allowing those involved in the events to speak for themselves. The book is especially useful as a text for college
courses on the history of Middle Eastern Jewry.

1893. ___: "The Sefrou Remnant." JSS, v.35 #3/4 (July/
Oct., 1973): 255-263.

1894. Strizower, Shifra: EXOTIC JEWISH COMMUNITIES. New
York: Thomas Yoseloff, 1962. 157 pp., notes.

History of five Jewish sects that have existed on the
fringes of Jewish life. The first of these, Yemenite Jewry,
remained the most clearly "Jewish," despite their idiosyncratic customs. The others have led to more problematic
definitions of what constitutes Jewishness. The Samaritans,
considered Jewish by the government of Israel but not by the
Jewish religious establishment, are the most problematic in
this regard. The Bene Israel, the Cochin Jews, and the
Karaites fall somewhere in between, although few today deny
their Jewishness.

AFGHANISTAN

1895. Brauer, Erich: "The Jews of Afghanistan: an Anthropological Report." JSS, v.4 #2 (Apr., 1942): 121-138.

* 1896. Robinson, Nehemiah: PERSIA AND AFGHANISTAN AND THEIR
JEWISH COMMUNITIES. New York: IJA, 1953. 31 pp.

ALGERIA

> #1107. Benguigni, G.: ASPECTS OF FRENCH JEWRY.

> #1887. Hirschberg, H. Z.: THE JEWS OF NORTH AFRICA.

1897. Rosenstock, Morton: "The Establishment of the Con-
sistorial System in Algeria." JSS, v.18 #1 (Jan., 1956):
41-54.

1898. ___: "The House of Bacri and Busnach: a Chapter from
Algeria´s Commercial History." JSS, v.14 #4 (Oct., 1952):
343-364.

> #351. Szajkowski, Z.: "Socialists and Radicals."

CYPRUS

1899. Arbel, B.: "The Jews in Cyprus: New Evidence fron the Venetian Period." JSS, v.41 #1 (Wint., 1979): 23-40.

1900. Shaftesley, John M.: "Jewish Colonies in Cyprus - Further Information." TJHSE, v.24 (1970/73): 183-190.

1901. ___: "Nineteenth-Century Jewish Colonies in Cyprus." TJHSE, v.22 (1968/69): 88-107.

EGYPT

1902. Goitein, Shelomo D.: "The Local Jewish Community in the Light of the Cairo Geniza Records." JJS, v.12 #3/4 (1961): 133-158.

1903. ___: "The Social Services of the Jewish Community as Reflected in the Cairo Geniza Records." JSS, v.26 #1 (Jan., 1964): 3-22; #2 (Apr., 1964): 67-86.

1904. Landau, Jacob M.: JEWS IN NINETEENTH-CENTURY EGYPT. New York: New York Univ. Press, 1969. 354 pp., notes, documents, illus., bibliog., index.

Provides an in-depth scholarly account of Jewish life in nineteenth-century Egypt. Primarily focused on the communities and their institutions. Concentrating on social history, Landau also surveys religious and intellectual trends. A wide variety of sources were used, including diplomatic papers from England, France, Italy, and Israel. Personal papers, rabbinic documents, and travelogues were utilized as well. Also included is an analysis of Egyptian zionism to World War I. 120 documents are cited, although not all are provided in English translation.

1905. Laskier, Michael M.: "From War to War: the Jews of Egypt from 1948 to 1970." SiZ, v.7 #1 (Spr., 1986): 111-147.

IRAN/PERSIA

1906. Cohen, A.: "Iranian Jewry and the Educational Endeavors of the Alliance Israelite Universelle." JSS, v.48 #1 (Wint., 1986): 15-44.

1907. Fischel, Walter J.: "The Jews of Persia, 1795-1940."
JSS, v.12 #2 (Apr., 1950): 119-160.

1908. Loeb, Laurence D.: OUTCASTE: JEWISH LIFE IN SOUTHERN
IRAN. New York: Gordon and Breach, 1977. 328 pp., illus.,
apps., gloss., bibliog., indexes.

Anthropological and sociological study of Shiraz Jewry.
Although Loeb includes historical data, that is not his primary focus. The book concentrates on two objectives. First,
to detail the social interactions between Iranian Jews and
the Shiite majority. Second, Loeb attempts to depict the
adaptation of Iranian Jews to the hostile sociopolitical
environment. Much of the book´s introduction is taken up
with methodology, which can provide an insight into current
anthropological thinking. In its use of an alternative methodology, Loeb´s discussion may be of interest to historians
and social scientists alike. In particular Loeb´s care with
terminology, especially his very narrow use of the concept
of pariah, should be followed by other authors on Jewish
affairs. Of special interest is Loeb´s chapter on Shi´a
intolerance, which should be read by all interested in the
role of religion and religious hatred in the contemporary
Middle East.

1909. Magnarella, Paul J.: "A Note on Aspects of Social
Life Among the Jewish Kurds of Sanandaj, Iran." JJoS, v.11
#1 (June, 1969): 51-58.

> #1896. Robinson, N.: PERSIA AND AFGHANISTAN.

IRAQ

1910. Cohen, Hayyim J.: "The Anti-Jewish Farhud in Baghdad
1941." MES, v.3 #1 (Oct., 1966): 2-17.

1911. ___: "A Note on Social Change Among Iraqi Jews,
1917-1951." JJoS, v.8 #2 (Dec., 1966): 204-208.

1912. ___: "University Education Among Iraqi-Born Jews."
JJoS, v.11 #1 (June, 1969): 59-66.

1913. Feitelson, Dina: "Aspects of the Social Life of
Kurdish Jews." JJoS, v.1 #2 (Dec., 1959): 201-216.

1914. Fischel, Walter J.: "The Jews of Kurdistan a Hundred
Years Ago: a Traveler's Record." JSS, v.6 #3 (July, 1944):
195-226.

1915. Haim, Sylvia G.: "Aspects of Jewish Life in Baghdad
under the Monarchy." MES, v.12 #2 (May, 1976): 188-208.

1916. Schechtman, Joseph B.: "The Repatriation of Iraq
Jewry." JSS, v.15 #2 (Apr., 1953): 151-172.

LIBYA

1917. De Felice, Renzo: JEWS IN AN ARAB LAND: LIBYA, 1835-
1970. Austin: The Univ. of Texas Press, 1985. 406 pp.,
illus., maps, notes, index.

Sociopolitical study of Jews in Libya during the nine-
eenth and twentieth centuries. Although emphasis is on the
Jewish community and its interactions with the various external and internal powers who have ruled Libya, the religious, cultural, and intellectual life of Libyan Jewry is
also reviewed. The book is organized chronologically, beginning with the decline of Ottoman rule in Libya. The attitude
of Libyan Jewry to Libyan nationalism, long before the
Qaddafi era, is covered in an important chapter on "The Arab
Revolt and Italian Reconquest." The book is based almost exclusively on archival sources from Italy, France, Israel,
and England. De Felice has provided the first comprehensive
study of Libyan Jewry. He also offers significant insights
into Muslim-Jewish relations in the twentieth century.

MALTA

1918. Davis, D.: "The Jewish Cemetery at Kalkara, Malta."
TJHSE, v.28 (1981/82): 145-170.

1919. Roth, Cecil: "The Jews of Malta." TJHSE, v.12 (1928/
1931): 187-251.

MOROCCO

* 1920. Chouraqui, Andre: THE SOCIAL AND LEGAL STATUS OF THE
JEWS OF FRENCH MOROCCO. New York: The American Jewish Committee, 1952. 42 pp.

1921. Israel, Jonathan: "The Jews of Spanish North Africa, 1600-1669." TJHSE, v.26 (1974/78): 71-86.

1922. Laskier, M. M.: THE ALLIANCE ISRAELITE UNIVERSELLE AND THE JEWISH COMMUNITIES OF MOROCCO 1862-1962. Albany, NY: SUNY Press, 1983. 372 pp., illus., notes, bibliog., index.

Extensive study of the history of the Alliance, as well as a communal history of Moroccan Jewry. The book covers the issues chronologically. Showing deep erudition of both Moroccan-Jewish history and the organizational dynamics of the Alliance Israelite Universelle, Laskier nevertheless, seems to be taking on too much at one time. Thus, the chapters on zionism and the Moroccan Jewish community and on Muslim-Jewish relations are of interest, but do not fit well into the topic of the Alliance and Moroccan Jewry. To be sure, the Alliance had an official opinion on zionism, but that opinion was not a function of specifically Moroccan conditions. That Laskier is able to limit himself solely to Morocco is a credit to his scholarship, although the tension between communal and organizational history is apparent.

1923. ___: "Zionism and the Jewish Communities of Morocco: 1956-1962." SiZ, v.6 #1 (Spr., 1985): 119-138.

1924. Meakin, J. E. Budgett: "The Jews of Morocco." JQR, v.4 #3 (Apr., 1892): 369-396.

1925. Minkovitz, Moshe: "Old Conflicts in a New Environment: a Study of a Moroccan Atlas Mountain Community Transplanted to Israel." JJoS, v.9 #2 (Dec., 1967): 191-208.

1926. Rosenbloom, Joseph R.: "A Note on the Size of the Jewish Communities in the South of Morocco." JJoS, v.8 #2 (Dec., 1966): 209-212.

1927. Willner, Dorothy and Margot Kohls: "Jews in the High Atlas Mountains of Morocco: a Partial Reconstruction." JJoS, v.4 #2 (Dec., 1962): 207-241.

1928. Yehuda, Z.: "The Place of Aliyah in Moroccan Jewry's Conception of Zionism." SiZ, v.6 #2 (Aut., 1985): 199-210.

SYRIA

> #1184. Baron, S. W.: "Great Britain and Damascus Jewry."

1929. Baron, Salo W.: "The Jews and the Syrian Massacres of 1860." PAAJR, v.4 (1933): 3-31.

1930. Hyamson, Albert M.: "The Damascus Affair - 1840." TJHSE, v.16 (1945/51): 47-71.

> #1592. Jacobs, J.: "The Damascus Affair of 1840."

1931. Philipp, Thomas: "The Farhi Family and the Changing Position of the Jews in Syria, 1750-1860." MES, v.20 #4 (Oct., 1984): 37-52.

> #1840. Sutton, J.: MAGIC CARPET.

1932. Zenner, Walter P.: "Syrian Jews in Three Social Settings." JJoS, v.10 #1 (June, 1968): 101-120.

TUNISIA

1933. Attal, R.: "Tunisian Jewry During the Last Twenty Years." JJoS, v.2 #1 (June, 1960): 3-15.

TURKEY

> #827. Elazar, D. J. et al: BALKAN JEWISH COMMUNITIES.

1934. Feldman, Eliyahu: "The Question of Jewish Emancipation in the Ottoman Empire and the Danubian Principalities after the Crimean War." JSS, v.41 #1 (Wint., 1979): 41-74.

1935. Nathan, Naphtali: "Notes on the Jews of Turkey." JJoS, v.6 #2 (Dec., 1964): 172-189.

> #522. Oke, M. K.: "Young Turks, Freemasons, Jews."

1936. Olson, Robert W.: "Jews in the Ottoman Empire in Light of New Documents." JSS, v.41 #1 (Wint., 1979): 75-88.

YEMEN

1937. Ahroni, Reuben: YEMENITE JEWRY: ORIGINS, CULTURE, AND LITERATURE. Bloomington: Indiana Univ. Press, 1986. 227 pp., illus., map, notes, bibliog., index.

Synthetic history of the Jews of South Arabia, ending with the fall of the Ottoman Empire. Using a wide variety of sources, Ahroni has put together the first comprehensive history of the Yemenite community in English. Emphasis is on social and cultural history, and intellectual history is a major subtheme. Of special interest to Ahroni is the question of the antiquity of Yemenite Jewry. Ahroni´s discussion is based on the evaluation of numerous sources and may be considered authoritative, although by no means definitive. A particularly informative chapter deals with Yemenite Jewish literature, a little known subject. Unfortunately Ahroni´s discussion of contemporary Yemenite Jews and their transfer to Israel, is linked to a brief epilogue.

1938. Goitein, Shelomo D.: "Portrait of a Yemenite Weavers Village." JSS, v.17 #1 (Jan., 1955): 3-26.

> #243. Neubauer, A.: "The Literature of the Jews in Yemen."

* 1939. Ozeri, Zion M.: YEMENITE JEWS: A PHOTOGRAPHIC ESSAY New York: Schocken Books, 1985. 78 pp., illus.

1940. Schechtman, Joseph B.: "The Jews of Aden." JSS, v.13 #2 (Apr., 1951): 133-148.

1941. ___: "The Repatriation of Yemenite Jewry." JSS, v.14 #3 (July, 1952): 209-224.

17

The Land of Israel

PRE-STATE PALESTINE

Surveys

1942. Avi-Yonah, Michael [ed.]: A HISTORY OF THE HOLY LAND. Trans. by Ch. Weiss and P. Fitton. Toronto: Macmillan, 1969. 323 pp., illus., index.

Anthology covering the history of the Land of Israel from prehistoric times to 1968. In each essay special emphasis is placed on the close connection between Jews and the Holy Land. Even during the long period of exile, Jews continued to see the land as their land of destiny. The text is complemented throughout by numerous stunning photographs. Written by reputable scholars, the book is primarily oriented to a lay readership.

CONTENTS: E. Anati: The Prehistory of the Holy Land until 3200 BCE / Hanoch Reviv: The Canaanite and Israelite Periods [3200-332 BCE] / M. Avi-Yonah: The Second Temple [332 BCE-70 CE]; Jews, Romans and Byzantines [70-640] / Moshe Sharon: The History of Palestine from the Arab Conquest until the Crusades [633-1099] / Emmanuel Sivan: Palestine during the Crusades [1099-1291] / Moshe Sharon: Palestine under the Mameluks and the Ottoman Empire [1291-1918]/ A. Lourie: The Birth of Israel - Epilogue [1918-1968].

* 1943. Bahat, Dan: TWENTY CENTURIES OF JEWISH LIFE IN THE HOLY LAND. Jerusalem: The Israel Economist, 1975. 68 pp., maps, illus., notes, bibliog.

> #396. Baron, S. W. and G. Wise: VIOLENCE AND DEFENSE.

1944. Ben-Gurion, David [ed.]: THE JEWS IN THEIR LAND. Trans. from the Hebrew by M. Nurock and M. Louvish. Garden City, NY: Doubleday, 1966. 392 pp., illus., maps, gloss., index.

Illustrated anthology covering the connection between Jews and the Land of Israel. Conceived by David Ben-Gurion, Israel's first prime minister, the book is somewhat limited in its focus. The history of the diaspora is not dealt with systematically, even though the Zionist movement came into being there. The text is arranged chronologically. Despite the essay on prophecy, the main focus of the anthology is political history. Foreword by Zalman Shazar.

CONTENTS: Y. Aharoni: Entry to Exile / E. Auerbach: The Prophets / Y. Guttman and M. Stern: From the Babylonian Exile to the Bar-Kochba Revolt / B. Dinur: From Bar Kochba's Revolt to the Turkish Conquest / I. Ben-Zvi: Under Ottoman Rule / D. Ben-Gurion: From the Founding of Petah-Tikva to the Present Day.

1945. Eban, Abba: MY COUNTRY: THE STORY OF MODERN ISRAEL. New York: Random House, 1972. 304 pp., maps, illus., index.

Popularized history of Israel and a continuation of MY PEOPLE [see #9]. Written to mark the twenty-fifth anniversary of the Jewish state. The political and military history of Israel are Eban's main focus, with the development of Israeli society and culture being major secondary themes. Despite his Labor party affiliations, Eban is objective, although the book is by no means a scholarly study.

> #226. Fishman, J.: THE SOCIOLOGY OF JEWISH LANGUAGES.

> #555. Gilbert, M.: EXILE AND RETURN.

* 1946. Guiladi, Yael: ONE JERUSALEM. Jerusalem: Keter Pub., 1983. 75 pp., map, illus., chron., bibliog.

1947. O'Brien, Conor C.: THE SIEGE: THE SAGA OF ISRAEL AND ZIONISM. New York: Simon & Schuster, 1986. 798 pp., illus., notes, gloss., chron., bibliog., index.

Sensitive and sympathetic history of zionism and Israel by a noted Irish politician and journalist. O'Brien's thesis is that the reality of siege - of being surrounded by hostile enemies - is the key to understanding Israel's psyche.

The book contains a rather detailed analysis of the rise of Israel and its history since 1948. Though some readers may quibble with some of O´Brien´s conclusions, the book is thought-provoking and nicely written. A particularly interesting chapter compares the history and fate of Jewish and Irish nationalism.

> #563. Peters, J.: FROM TIME IMMEMORIAL.

> #543. Schweid, E.: THE LAND OF ISRAEL.

1948. Soshuk, Levi and Azriel Eisenberg [eds.]: MOMENTOUS CENTURY: PERSONAL AND EYEWITNESS ACCOUNTS OF THE RISE OF THE JEWISH HOMELAND AND STATE, 1875-1978. Hew York: Herzl Press, 1984. 471 pp., illus., notes, bibliog.

Anthology of sources on the rise of modern Israel. the book is arranged chronologically, although some of the citations break the strict order. Most of the documents have appeared before, although almost none were originally available in English. The importance of the anthology lies in the personal viewpoints cited. The key events of each period before statehood and since the rise of Israel are viewed from the perspective of the participants and witnesses. The reader is thus drawn into the events, viewing them from the inside, and thereby gaining a better understanding of what the participants felt and thought at the time.

* 1949. Werblowsky, R. J. Zvi: THE MEANING OF JERUSALEM TO JEWS, CHRISTIANS AND MUSLIMS. Jerusalem: Israel Univ., Study Group, 1977. 15 pp., notes.

Immigration and Settlement

1950. Avneri, Arieh L.: THE CLAIM OF DISPOSSESSION: JEWISH LAND SETTLEMENT AND THE ARABS, 1878-1948. Trans. from the Hebrew by the Kfar-Blum Translation Group. New York: Herzl Press, 1984. 303 pp., maps, notes, bibliog.

Important and careful study of the issue of Jewish settlement in Eretz Israel from 1878 to 1948. Avneri attempts to chart the effects of the renewed Jewish settlement of Eretz Israel on the local Arab population. To place the events into context, Avneri describes the state of the Arabs in the land before the mass Jewish influx. After careful research into the areas Jews settled, especially during the

British Mandate, Avneri came to startling conclusions: Far from uprooting the Arabs, Jewish settlements so bolstered Palestine´s economy that many Arabs immigrated to the country between 1920 and 1936. Moreover, Avneri emphasizes that many Arab immigrants entered the country illegally. Those Arabs who chose to leave in 1948 and became refugees did so of their own volition. Avneri maintains that neither Jews nor Arab governments wanted them to leave Israel. His book is a noteworthy attempt to revise current myths regarding the Arab-Israeli conflict.

1951. Eliav, Mordehai: "German Jews´ Share in the Building of the National Home in Palestine and the State of Israel." LBIYB, v.30 (1985): 255-263.

1952. Gerber, Haim: "Modernization in Nineteenth-Century Palestine - the Role of Foreign Trade." MES, v.18 #3 (July, 1982): 250-264.

1953. Kark, Ruth: "The Agricultural Character of Jewish Settlement in the Negev: 1939-1947." JSS, v.45 #2 (Spr., 1983): 157-174.

1954. ___: "Jewish Frontier Settlement in the Negev, 1880-1948: Perception and Realization." MES, v.17 #3 (July, 1981): 334-356.

1955. Marmorstein, Emile: "European Jews in Muslim Palestine." MES, v.11 #1 (Jan., 1975): 74-87.

1956. Patterson, D.: "The First Fifty Years of Collective Settlement in Israel." JJoS, v.2 #1 (June, 1960): 43-55.

1957. Reinharz, Jehuda: "The Esra Verein and Jewish Colonisation in Palestine." LBIYB, v.24 (1979): 261-289.

> #526. Schama, S.: TWO ROTHSCHILDS AND THE LAND OF ISRAEL.

1958. Sheffer, G.: "Political Considerations in British Policy-Making on Immigration to Palestine." SiZ, v.4 (Aut., 1981): 237-274.

1959. Shulman, Abraham: COMING HOME TO ZION: A PICTORIAL HISTORY OF PRE-ISRAEL PALESTINE. Garden City, NY: Doubleday, 1979. 236 pp., illus., chron.

Photographic history of pre-state Eretz Israel. The text

describes the scenery - human, geographic, and historical - that provides the background for the photos. The pictures are stunning, and most were never previously published. The book is an excellent summary of the reality behind Zionist ideology and is a colorful review of the early history of the modern Yishuv. Introduction by Golda Meir.

1960. Szold, Henrietta: "Recent Jewish Progress in Palestine." AJYB, v.17 (1915/16): 24-158.

> #90. Wischnitzer, M.: TO DWELL IN SAFETY.

Social and Economic Life

1961. Ackerman, Walter A.: "Religion in the Schools of Eretz-Yisrael, 1904-1914." SiZ, v.6 #1 (Spr., 1985): 1-13.

1962. Aisenstadt, S. N.: "The Sociological Structure of the Jewish Community in Palestine." JSS, v.10 #1 (Jan., 1948): 3-18.

* 1963. Aumann, Moshe: LAND OWNERSHIP IN PALESTINE, 1880-1948. Jerusalem: Israel Academic Committee, 1976. 24 pp.

1964. Biger, Gideon: "Urban Planning and the Garden Suburbs of Jerusalem 1918-1925." SiZ, v.7 #1 (Spr., 1986): 1-9.

1965. Blumberg, Arnold: ZION BEFORE ZIONISM, 1838-1880. Syracuse, NY: Syracuse Univ. Press, 1985. 235 pp., illus., notes, gloss., bibliog., index.

Study of the social and political situation in Palestine during the mid-nineteenth century. Blumberg's main focus is the interaction between the Turks, various foreign consuls, and the local population. The latter includes both Jews and Arabs. Blumberg ends his account before the massive Jewish immigration beginning in 1881, although he details Turkish efforts at Muslim colonization. Fully documented, the book is nevertheless written with the layperson in mind. Blumberg provides the necessary background for the understanding of developments in the Middle East since 1881.

1966. Cordova, Abraham and Hanna Herzog: "The Cultural Endeavor of the Labor Movement in Palestine: a Study of the Relationship Between Intelligentsia and Intellectuals." Y/A, v.17 (1978): 238-259.

> #1625. Druyan, N.: "American Zionist Efforts."

1967. Fischer, Eric: "The Mikveh Israel School during the War Years, 1914-1918." JSS, v.4 #3 (July, 1942): 269-274.

1968. Friedman, Saul S.: LAND OF DUST: PALESTINE AT THE TURN OF THE CENTURY. Washington, DC: Univ. Press of America, 1982. 240 pp., illus., maps, notes.

Investigates the myth of the Zionist uprooting of the Arab population of Palestine over the course of the nine-teenth and twentieth centuries. Friedman demolishes the myth, which unfortunately has become widely accepted in Arab and Western countries, by describing the condition of the land and the standard of living of the indigenous population before 1881. Referring to Ottoman census figures of 1905, Friedman discovered that nearly half the population of Palestine was Jewish. Although not a clear majority, the Jews were hardly the inconsiderable minority that Arab apologists attempt to portray. Similarly, when looking at the Arab economy and standard of living, Friedman finds that the land was more neglected than worked by its Arab inhabitants. Although problems may arise from Friedman´s combative style, the book offers an important revision of a politically motivated and malicious myth.

1969. Gilbert, Martin: JERUSALEM: REBIRTH OF A CITY. New York: Viking Press, 1985. 238 pp., illus., bibliog., index.

Historical investigation into the rebirth and expansion of the city of Jerusalem during the last half of the nine-teenth century. Ends with 1898, by which time the old sec-tions of Jerusalem were rebuilt. The fact that the period covered is both the first major era in the development of the new Yishuv and also part of the First Aliyah [1881-1903] is not, to Gilbert´s mind, coincidental. Jewish rejuvenation of Eretz Israel led naturally to a rebirth of the whole land and to increased immigration. Profusely illustrated, the book is also based on extensive research and, most notably, uses many travelogues about nineteenth-century Jerusalem.

1970. Gottheil, Fred M.: "The Population of Palestine, Circa 1875." MES, v.15 #3 (Oct., 1979): 310-321.

1971. Halevi, Nadav: "The Political Economy of Absorptive Capacity: Growth and Cycles in Jewish Palestine Under the British Mandate." MES, v.19 #4 (Oct., 1983): 456-469.

1972. Schmelz, O.: "Development of the Jewish Population of Jerusalem During the Last Hundred Years." JJoS, v.2 #1 (June, 1960): 56-73.

1973. ___: "The Jewish Population of Jerusalem." JJoS, v.6 #2 (Dec., 1964): 243-263.

1974. Stein, Kenneth W.: THE LAND QUESTION IN PALESTINE, 1917-1939. Chapel Hill: The Univ. of North Carolina Press, 1984. 314 pp., maps, illus., notes, apps., bibliog., index.

Investigation into the social and economic history of Mandatory Palestine. Stein concentrates on the issue of land control and ownership. Buying land was a cornerstone of Zionist policy, became a major cause of conflict between Jew and Arab, and developed into one of the most serious failures of the Mandatory administration. According to Stein, neither British regulation nor Arab opposition actually forestalled Zionist land acquisition. In fact, some of the most vocal Arab opponents of zionism and Jewish immigration were willing to sell parcels to the Zionists and dislocate their Arab tenants. Stein correctly concludes that land acquisition set the stage for the eventual Jewish state, but exaggerates the suffering of Arab fellahin who lost their tenancy. As Stein himself shows, in 1939 Jews owned less than ten percent of all land in Palestine; much of it was swampland and was hardly worth the exorbitant prices Jews paid for it.

1975. Weinryb, Bernard: "Occupational Shifts of Workers in Palestine." JSS, v.2 #2 (Apr., 1940): 149-156.

1976. ___: "The Occupational Structure of the Second Generation of Jews in Palestine." JSS, v.2 #3 (July, 1940): 279-294; #4 (Oct., 1940): 435-480.

Mandatory Palestine

1977. Bauer, Yehuda: "From Cooperation to Resistance: the Haganah 1938-1946." MES, v.2 #3 (Apr., 1966): 182-210.

> #550. ___: FROM DIPLOMACY TO RESISTANCE.

1978. Brenner, Y. S.: "The Stern Gang, 1940-48." MES, v.2 #1 (Oct., 1965): 2-30.

> 1186. Brodie, I.: "Palestinian Jews in World War II."

1979. Caplan, Neil: PALESTINE JEWRY AND THE ARAB QUESTION, 1917-1925. Leiden: E. J. Brill, 1978. 268 pp., notes, bibliog., index.

Important revisionist history of Arab-Jewish relations from the Balfour Declaration to 1925. Caplan's primary theme is that, contrary to popular belief, the Zionists were not unaware of the existence of a large Arab population in Palestine; nor did they, in fact, hope that merely by improving the economy the Arabs could be induced to accept the Jewish national home. Rather, Caplan believes that Zionist policy was based on the confluence of four forms of activity: economic development, firm British administration, Jewish self-defense, and astute diplomacy. Caplan's arguments are convincing and his book is a useful study of the origins of the Arab-Jewish conflict.

1980. Cohen, Michael J.: "Direction of Policy in Palestine 1936-45." MES, v.11 #3 (Oct., 1975): 237-261.

> #536. Cohen, Mitchell: ZION AND STATE.

1981. Eliash, Shulamit: "The Political Role of the Chief Rabbinate of Palestine During the Mandate: Its Character and Nature." JSS, v.47 #1 (Wint., 1985): 33-50.

1982. Friedman, Isaiah: "German Intervention on Behalf of the Yishuv, 1917." JSS, v.33 #1 (Jan., 1971): 23-43.

1983. ___ : "Lord Palmerston and the Protection of Jews in Palestine 1839-1851." JSS, v.30 #1 (Jan., 1968): 23-41.

> #439. Gelber, Y.: "Jewish Parachutists from Palestine."

1984. Gillon, D. Z.: "The Antecedents of the Balfour Declaration." MES, v.5 #2 (May, 1969): 131-150.

1985. Gilner, Elias: WAR AND HOPE: A HISTORY OF THE JEWISH LEGION. New York: Herzl Press, 1969. 466 pp.

History of the Jewish Legion during World War I. The book is organized in chronological order and follows the idea of the Legion from its inception in 1914, through its fulfillment in 1916 and its decline during the first years of the Mandate. The men of the Legion, along with Jabotinsky and

Trumpeldor, are clearly the heroes of the book. However, Gilner's criticism of Viscount Herbert Samuel's relations with the Legion, and especially his version of the events leading to its demobilization, seem to be one-sided. More important, Gilner's book is outdated, since most of the currently available archival material was still classified when the book was written.

1986. Habas, Bracha: THE GATE BREAKERS. New York: Herzl Press, 1963. 407 pp., illus.

Saga of Jewish immigration to Palestine in defiance of immigrant quotas imposed by Britain. Nominally illegal, this immigration was to prove one of the major causes for the collapse of the British administration in Palestine after World War II. Concentrates almost exclusively on the activities of the Mossad le'Aliyah Bet, but hardly mentions the activities of the Revisionist Zionists for haapalah. Given these limitations, Habas is quite objective in dealing with both the successes and failures of the Mossad, especially during the war period. Although the discussion of illegal immigration centers on the "death ships," much immigration occurred overland, and Habas covers this aspect of haapalah extensively.

1987. Haron, Miriam J.: "Palestine and the Anglo-American Connection." MJ, v.2 #2 (May, 1982): 199-211.

1988. Hattis, Susan Lee: "Jabotinsky's Parity Plan for Palestine." MES, v.13 #1 (Jan., 1977): 90-96.

1989. Hirszowicz, Lukasz: "Nazi Germany and the Palestine Partition Plan." MES, v.1 #1 (Oct., 1964): 40-65.

1990. Horowitz, Dan and M. Lissak: ORIGINS OF THE ISRAELI POLITY: PALESTINE UNDER THE MANDATE. Trans. from the Hebrew by Charles Hoffman. Chicago: Univ. of Chicago Press, 1978. 292 pp., notes, gloss., index.

Social and political inquiry into the Yishuv during the British Mandate. According to Horowitz and Lissak, the roots of Israel were planted by the autonomous Jewish organizations established under the terms of The League of Nations Mandate for Palestine. Although these autonomous agencies were not sovereign and exercised no form of legal sanctions, they nevertheless commanded almost complete authority within the Yishuv. The book is oriented toward political sociology

and presents an alternative model for the study of autonomous political structures within a dual national context. In
this respect the authors offer insight into both the rise of
Israel and into methodological issues related to the study
of developing societies.

> #558. Hurewitz, J. C.: THE STRUGGLE FOR PALESTINE.

1991. Kedouri, Elie: "Sir Herbert Samuel and the Government of Palestine." MES, v.5 #1 (Jan., 1969): 44-68.

1992. Mandel, Neville J.: "Ottoman Policy and Restrictions
on Jewish Settlement in Palestine: 1881-1908 [I]." MES, v.10
#3 (Oct., 1974): 312-332.

1993. ___ : "Ottoman Practice as regards Jewish Settlement
in Palestine: 1881-1908 [II]." MES, v.11 #1 (Jan., 1975):
33-46.

1994. Melka, R.: "Nazi Germany and the Palestine Question." MES, v.5 #3 (Oct., 1969): 221-233.

1995. Neumann, Joshua H.: "The Jewish Battalions and the
Palestine Campaign." AJYB, v.21 (1919/20): 120-140.

1996. Parzen, Herbert: "A Chapter in Arab-Jewish Relations
During the Mandate Era." JSS, v.29 #4 (Oct., 1967): 203-233.

1997. ___ : "The Enlargement of the Jewish Agency for
Palestine: 1923-1929 a Hope - Hamstrung." JSS, v.39 #1/2
(Wint./Spr., 1977): 129-158.

1998. Postal, B. and H. W. Levy: AND THE HILLS SHOUTED FOR
JOY. New York: David McKay, 1973. 430 pp., illus., apps.,
bibliog., index.

History of the emergence of Israel, primarily focused on
the last days of the Mandate. Writing in a journalistic
style, the authors use flashbacks to review the history of
zionism up to 1948. The War of Independence and Zionist
political activities in the United States and Europe round
out the book´s other subthemes. Written to mark the twenty-
fifth anniversary of Israel, the volume is an interesting
attempt to capture the spirit of the time and to recall the
events that led to the establishment of Israel.

1999. Shapira, A.: "The Concept of Time in the Partition Controversy of 1937." SiZ, v.6 #2 (Aut., 1985): 211-228.

> #467. ___: "Yishuv and the Survivors of the Holocaust."

2000. Sheffer, G.: "British Colonial Policy-Making towards Palestine 1929-1939." MES, v. 14 # 3 (Oct., 1978): 307-322.

2001. Sykes, Ch.: CROSS ROADS TO ISRAEL. London: Collins, 1965. 479 pp., illus., notes, app., bibliog., index.

Useful, though at times tendentious, account of the British Mandate and the rise of Israel, written from the British perspective. The earlier chapters of the book tend to be better written and are generally well balanced; this does not always hold true for the later chapters. The book does, however, have some usefulness, especially for scholars of the period.

2002. Tartakower, Arieh: "The Making of Jewish Statehood in Palestine." JSS, v.10 #3 (July, 1948): 207-222.

2003. Weissbrod, Lilly: "Economic Factors and Political Strategies: the Defeat of the Revisionists in Mandatory Palestine." MES, v.19 #3 (July, 1983): 326-344.

THE STATE OF ISRAEL

Political History

2004. Arian, Asher: POLITICS IN ISRAEL: THE SECOND GENERA-TION. Chatham, NJ: Chatham House Pub., 1985. 290 pp., notes, gloss., index.

Inquiry into Israeli political life, using the techniques of sociology and political science. Arian sees the change in the orientation of the Israeli polity as resulting from the rise of what he terms the second generation - Sabra politicians - and their entry into the forefront of public affairs. For example, Arian pays considerable attention to the rise and maturation of the Sephardi community, as exemplified by the election of Yitzhak Navon, Israel´s first Sephardi president. Arian sees this as a sign of the maturation of Israel; his main goals are to explain the issues of second-generation politics as they relate to the polity as a whole. A secondary theme is to view Israeli

politics in the broader context of the few developing
nations that have remained democracies. Arian concludes that
Israeli political life in the near future will be based on
the paradoxical relationship between the Sabra's self-
assured individualism and the need and desire for a more
stable and orderly society. The book is thus an important
contribution to the study of Israel and an inquiry into the
present state of the Israeli polity.

2005. Ben-Gurion, David: ISRAEL: A PERSONAL HISTORY. New
York: Funk and Wagnals / Tel Aviv: Sabra Books, 1971. 862
pp., chron., illus., index.

Intensely personal history and memoir of the State of
Israel by the man who, more than any other individual,
forged the new state. Takes the study of the state from
founding to 1967, although the emphasis is on the period
when Ben-Gurion was prime minister. Deals with both internal
and external issues. Quotes liberally from his political
diary as well as from numerous state papers. These citations
are clearly the most interesting and enlightening part of
this very useful book.

> #1851. Bercuson, D.: CANADA AND THE BIRTH OF ISRAEL.

2006. Bialer, Uri: "The Road to the Capital: the Establishment of Jerusalem as the Official Seat of the Israeli
Government in 1949." SiZ, v.5 #2 (Aut., 1984): 273-296.

> #381. Etzioni-Halevi, E.: POLITICAL CULTURE.

2007. Eytan, Walter: THE FIRST TEN YEARS: A DIPLOMATIC
HISTORY OF ISRAEL. New York: Simon & Schuster, 1958. 293 pp.

Survey of Israel's foreign relations from 1948 to 1958,
arranged thematically. A career diplomat in Israel's foreign
service, Eytan draws on his own experiences as well as on
documents that are only now becoming available to scholars.
Since the state papers of Israel are declassified only to
1949 [as of this writing], Eytan's information on foreign
relations is important. An especially interesting chapter
reviews the involvement of the great powers in the Middle
East; in view of the involvement of America and Russia in
the region, in both war and peace, this chapter is of continuing importance to both scholars and interested laypersons. The difficulty of making peace is described in
Eytan's early chapters and is presented from an Israeli per-

spective. Making no pretense to complete objectivity, Eytan is still an important source of information on the development of Israel´s foreign policy in the early years of the state.

2008. Frankel, William: ISRAEL OBSERVED: AN ANATOMY OF THE STATE. London: Thames and Hudson, 1980. 288 pp., bibliog., index.

Journalistic account of the State of Israel. Chapters are organized thematically and cover a wide range of topics. Interspersed with contemporary observations are sections providing historical and political background. Frankel´s starting point is the parliamentary elections of 1977 and the defeat of the Labor party by the Likud. The text is written in a chatty and personal style, allowing Frankel to observe and comment on almost every feature of Israeli life without the need to document his impressions. Events in Israel since 1977, including the peace treaty with Egypt and the war in Lebanon, have rendered some chapters obsolete.

2009. Freedman, Robert O. [ed.]: ISRAEL IN THE BEGIN ERA. New York: Praeger Special Studies, 1982. 280 pp., notes, apps., bibliog., index.

Anthology reviewing the changes in the Israeli government between the rise of the Likud in 1977 and the elections of 1981. Based on a conference held in Hebrew College in Baltimore on April 8, 1979. Covers Begin´s impact on the Israeli political system from both domestic and foreign-policy perspectives. Bringing together Israeli and American political scientists, the book also offers insight into recent changes in the orientation of the Israeli polity. The Israeli-Egyptian peace negotiations play an important role in the analysis, but surprisingly are not analyzed separately. The introduction ties the essays together, providing a chronolgical history of the first Begin government. Four appendixes cite important documents mentioned in the essays. Taken together the anthology offers a detailed, objective, and interesting look at Israel today.

CONTENTS: E. Torgovnik: Likud 1977-81: the Consolidation of Power / D. Pollock: Likud in Power: Divided We Stand / Ira Sharkansky and A. Radian: Changing Domestic Policy 1977-81 / M. J. Aronoff: The Labor Party in Opposition / D. J. Elazar: Religious Parties and Politics in the Begin Era / Robert O. Freedman: Moscow, Jerusalem, and Washington in the Begin

Era / R. O. Friedlander: Autonomy, the Palestinians, and
International Law: the Begin Legacy.

2010. Haron, Miriam: "Britain and Israel, 1948-1950." MJ,
v.3 #2 (May, 1983): 217-223.

> #399. Henkin, L.: WORLD POLITICS AND THE JEWISH CONDITION.

> #516. Karpman, I.: GENERAL ZIONISM IN ERETZ-ISRAEL.

* 2011. Liebman, Ch. S.: THE RELIGIOUS COMPONENT IN ISRAELI
ULTRA-NATIONALISM. Cincinnati: Univ. of Cincinnati Press,
1985. 21 pp., notes, bibliog.

2012. Medding, Peter Y.: MAPAI IN ISRAEL: POLITICAL ORGAN-
IZATION AND GOVERNMENT IN A NEW SOCIETY.   Cambridge: At the
Univ. Press, 1972. 326 pp., notes, bibliog., index.

Political and social investigation of the Israel Labor
Party [Mapai]. As Mapai was the core of Israel´s governing
coalition from 1948 to 1977, Medding is also studying the
relations between party and government in a developing country. Mapai is placed into three contexts: internal organization, relations with society as a whole, and relations with
the government. According to Medding, the party performs the
function of linking diverse elements in the society to the
state, giving them a role to play in the building of the
Jewish nation. At the same time, however, ideological rifts
split Mapai into different and often feuding factions.
According to Medding, these splits had personal as well as
ideological overtones. He concludes that for a political
party to succeed in a democracy, it must continue to offer
voters an acceptable vision of the state and its people,
while remaining flexible to changing conditions within and
outside that society.

2013. Meyer, Lawrence: ISRAEL NOW: PORTRAIT OF A TROUBLED
LAND. New York: Delacorte Press, 1982. 404 pp., maps, bibliog., index.

Journalistic portrait of conditions in Israel. Using a
number of sources, both official and anecdotal, Meyer
fashioned a sympathetic but objective picture of Israel´s
successes and problems. Meyer is unafraid to tackle thorny
problems, especially those relating to defense and foreign
affairs. He especially underscores the weakness of Israel´s
economy. Ultimately, Meyer concludes, although Israel is a

troubled nation today, the country will survive and, most likely, thrive.

2014. Nyrop, R. F.: ISRAEL: A COUNTRY STUDY. Washington, DC: U. S. Government Printing Office, 1979. 412 pp., illus., maps, tables, apps., bibliog., index.

Study of the State of Israel, part of a series of similar studies of foreign countries. Designed for use by foreign service and other interested parties. Giving extensive historical background the book is a virtual encyclopedia about Israel. Extensive statistical material, key documents, and illustrations round out this useful survey.

2015. Peleg, Ilan: BEGIN´S FOREIGN POLICY, 1977-1983: ISRAEL´S MOVE TO THE RIGHT. Westport, CT: Greenwood Press, 1987. 227 pp., notes, bibliog., index.

Study of the foreign policy pursued by Prime Minister Menachem Begin, from his election in 1977 to his retirement in 1983. Peleg assumes that Begin´s foreign policy was determined largely by a neo-Revisionist Zionist ideology, and he attempts to verify his assumption by analyzing key events that occurred during the six years in question. In order to chart Israel´s turn to the right, Peleg traces the background of Revisionist Zionist ideology from Ze´ev Jabotinsky to Begin. Emphasis is placed on the practical outcome of what Peleg sees as a negation of the world, resulting from Begin´s experience during the Holocaust. Begin´s neo-revisionism is placed into political, diplomatic, and military contexts in a series of case studies that include the war in Lebanon, the annexation of the Golan Heights, and the destruction of the Osiraq nuclear reactor. Unfortunately, Peleg does not explain how the peace talks with Egypt fit into Begin´s neo-revisionism. As a result, many readers will find Peleg´s analysis too one-sided. Given the recent nature of the events described, Peleg´s conclusions must be considered tentative.

2016. Perlmutter, Amos: ISRAEL THE PARTITIONED STATE: A POLITICAL HISTORY SINCE 1900. New York: Charles Scribner´s Sons, 1985. 398 pp., illus., notes, bibliog., gloss., index.

Comprehensive political history of modern Israel. The author focuses on the influence of the concept of partition on the development of the Zionist idea. Perlmutter also places partition into the context of Zionist ideology and

Israel's forty-year search for security. His analysis is comprehensive and non-polemical. Unlike many other analysts, Perlmutter voices a moderate position; he neither advocates nor rejects partition, but seeks to analyze the current implications of a potential future partition for Israel. The breadth of his analysis makes the book an important contribution to the history of Israel.

2017. ___: MILITARY AND POLITICS IN ISRAEL: NATION BUILD-ING AND ROLE EXPANSION. New York: Praeger, 1969. 161 pp., charts, tables, notes, bibliog., index.

Studies the role the military has played in Israel's political life. Concentrates on civil-military relations and on the role the IDF has played in the creation of an Israeli ethos. In light of the IDF'S expanded influence in such fields as education and social reform, it is to Israel's everlasting credit that although militarized, as any garrison state must be, it is not militaristic. This important distinction between Israel and most other third-world states is highlighted in Perlmutter's analysis. He sees success in this area as developing from the early creation of effective civilian control over the military and the commitment of all elements of Israel's society to both security and democracy. Exemplifying all these trends, for Perlmutter, is the fact that Moshe Dayan sought a political career only after his retirement from active duty, a precedent followed by all major military figures in Israel who later became involved in politics.

2018. Preuss, Walter: THE LABOUR MOVEMENT IN ISRAEL. 3rd Edition. Jerusalem: R. Mass, 1965. 239 pp.

Outdated but still important history of Socialist zionism from the Second Aliyah [1903-1914] to 1965. The Histadrut is the center of Preuss's attention; its numerous activities, particularly in the Mandatory period, are described in detail. The latter chapters deal with the economic, social, and political activities of the Israeli labor movement and also review the problems which needed solving as of 1965. Surveying sixty years of history, Preuss's work may be considered an authoritative, though undocumented, source on Israel's Labor party and movement. The first edition has a preface by David Ben-Gurion.

2019. Rabinovich, Itamar and J. Reinharz [eds.]: ISRAEL IN THE MIDDLE EAST: DOCUMENTS AND READINGS ON SOCIETY, POLITICS

AND FOREIGN RELATIONS. New York: Oxford Univ. Press, 1984. 407 pp., app., index.

Anthology of documents on the history of the State of Israel since 1948. The book is organized chronologically and subdivided into foreign and domestic issues. Unfortunately, the distinction between the two is not always clear. Furthermore, most of the sources appeared in English before and are thus by no means unavailable. The book does have some use, in that it broadens the study of Israel´s history to include society and culture in addition to diplomacy and politics.

2020. Rosenne, Shabtai: "Israel and the United Nations: Changed Perspectives, 1945-1976." AJYB, v.78 (1978): 3-59.

2021. Sachar, Howard M.: THE HISTORY OF ISRAEL: FROM THE AFTERMATH OF THE YOM KIPPUR WAR. New York: Oxford Univ. Press, 1987. 319 pp., maps, bibliog., index.

Follow-up volume to his A HISTORY OF ISRAEL [see #525]. Covers the period from the Yom Kippur War through the post-Lebanon trauma and the transition from the Begin era. As with the first volume, the key is Sachar´s synthesis of widely scattered research. Primary focus is on political history, although the development of Israeli culture is also reviewed. Sachar strikes a fair balance between the descriptive and the analytical, although obviously most of his conclusions are tentative.

2022. Safran, N.: ISRAEL: THE EMBATTLED ALLY. Cambridge, MA: The Belknap Press of Harvard Univ., 1981. 655 pp., bibliog., index.

Investigation of the evolution of Israeli-American relations. The book is also a history of Israel from the rise of zionism to the Camp David accords. Considerable attention is focused on political life in Israel. The role of the United States in the birth of Israel and relations between the two countries since the establishment of the state provide the core of Safran´s analysis. Safran´s discussion of the military aspects of Israel´s history, including America´s role in Israel´s defense, and of Israel´s foreign relations is detailed and can be considered authoritative. Safran was one of the first to view relations between the two countries as a tacit alliance. The second edition includes a new preface and postscript which review the peace negotiations between

Israel and Egypt and their implications for American-Israeli relations.

2023. Sager, Samuel: "Israel´s Provisional State Council and Government." MES, v.14 #1 (Jan., 1978): 91-101.

2024. Segev, Tom: 1949: THE FIRST ISRAELIS. New York: The Free Press, 1986. 379 pp., illus., notes, bibliog., index.

Revisionist history of Israel´s first year. Segev attempts to expose many of the myths about the birth of Israel and the Arab-Israeli conflict. The book is based on extensive documentation. Many of Segev´s points are important and help explain some of Israel´s current social and political problems. Nevertheless, in a few cases Segev goes much too far in his zeal for revising supposed myths, while some of his insights are open to other interpretations. As an anti-nostalgic book, Segev´s work is important, but as a history the book is far from authoritative.

2025. Seliktar, Ofira: NEW ZIONISM AND THE FOREIGN POLICY SYSTEM OF ISRAEL. Carbondale: Southern Illinois Univ. Press, 1986. 308 pp., notes, apps., bibliog., index.

Psychopolitical investigation into the changes wrought upon Israeli foreign policy by the election of Menachem Begin in 1977. The book´s prime importance is its investigation of a new model for political-science research: the impact of psychology on ideology. She identifies Begin´s foreign policy with a "new zionism" that arose in the aftermath of the Six-Day War and which led to a transvaluation of Israel´s political culture. Seliktar´s background sections are weak; this is especially true of her analysis of the religious, or quasi-religious, component in the "new zionism." Moreover, in light of the recent nature of the issues involved, and in view of the fact that Seliktar began her research before Begin´s retirement in 1983, her conclusions are only tentative.

2026. Shimshoni, Daniel: ISRAELI DEMOCRACY: THE MIDDLE OF THE JOURNEY. New York: The Free Press, 1982. 543 pp., maps, notes, apps., indexes.

Political inquiry into the operation of the Israeli government from 1948 to 1977. Both domestic and foreign affairs are reviewed, although emphasis is on the former. An especially interesting chapter deals with the bases of the

Israeli government during the Mandatory period. Shimshoni´s chapters on public policy are thematic and include such issues as defense, the economy, education, social welfare, and the protection of the environment. In each case political and social issues are placed into historical context. In charting how certain problems were handled in various periods, from the Yishuv into the early state and down to the mid-1970s, Shimshoni has adopted an interesting and fruitful approach which enables him to judge the effectiveness of Israeli democracy. He also offers some insights into events after the Likud victory of 1977 and the political implications of peace with Egypt. Six appendixes covering governmental and quasi-governmental organization round out this useful book.

Military Histories

2027. Allon, Yigal: THE MAKING OF ISRAEL´S ARMY. London: Sphere Books, 1971. 270 pp., maps, notes.

Insider history of the Israel Defense Foeces [IDF] by one of its founders and early leaders. Allon commanded the elite Palmach during the War of Independence. Part I comprises Allon´s historical review of the Haganah and IDF until 1967. Part II contains documents illustrating many of the points that Allon makes regarding the nature of the IDF. The book concentrates on the pre-independence period and the War of Independence. Allon´s review contains a number of insights into Israel´s position: military, political, and social.

2028. Bercuson, David J.: THE SECRET ARMY. New York: Stein and Day, 1984. 278 pp., illus., notes, bibliog., index.

Historical study of the MAHAL, the foreign volunteers who helped create Israel´s army. Assesses the role of the volunteers, many of them combat veterans of World War II, in Israel´s victory. Interestingly many volunteers, perhaps a majority, were not Jews. Bercuson tends to deemphasize the role of the volunteers - noting that most fought as individuals. Nevertheless, the book is an important contribution to Israel´s early history, to the understanding of the development of the IDF, and is a worthy memorial to the volunteers, Jews and Gentiles, men and women, who fought for the Jewish state.

2029. Heckelman, A. J.: AMERICAN VOLUNTEERS AND ISRAEL'S WAR OF INDEPENDENCE. New York: Ktav, 1974. 304 pp., apps., bibliog., notes, index.

Idiosyncratic history of the role American volunteers played in the rise of Israel. The book is organized into four parts. Part I contains a series of studies on the history of the War of Independence. Part II assesses the role of the American volunteers in particular military fields. Part III evaluates the historical significance of MAHAL, as the volunteers were called. Part IV contains a series of appendixes covering a number of related issues. Heckelman concludes that without the volunteers Israel might not have come into existence. While probably correct, the material is so diffuse that it is difficult to follow his argument.

2030. Herzog, Chaim: THE ARAB-ISRAELI WARS: WAR AND PEACE IN THE MIDDLE EAST. New York: Random House, 1982. 392 pp., illus., maps, bibliog., index.

An insightful and authoritative review of Israel's military history by Israel's sixth president. President Herzog has been intimately involved with every aspect of Israel's defense: as a chief of military intelligence, ambassador to the United Nations, military analyst, and member of Knesset. He is thus in a unique position to analyze - sympathetically but objectively - Israel's daily battle for survival.

2031. ___ : THE WAR OF ATONEMENT: OCTOBER, 1973. Boston: Little, Brown, 1975. 300 pp., maps, illus., index.

Early but still authoritative account of the Yom Kippur War. Primarily a work of military history, but also includes the political background of the war. Covers the war dispassionately, assigning praise and blame where necessary. Most of the book deals with the war on the ground, although the air and naval battles are reviewed briefly. After a decade it is clear that Herzog's most important chapter is the one dealing with the tactical implications of the war. There he argues against drawing overly hasty conclusions about the military results of the war, especially in terms of the impact of technology on Israel's defenses. Since 1975 the IDF has undergone an extensive program of modernization and reorganization, which has led to the eradication of most of the defects in the structure and tactics underscored by Herzog and other military analysts.

2032. Lorch, Nathanel: THE EDGE OF THE SWORD: ISRAEL'S WAR
OF INDEPENDENCE, 1947-1949. New York: Putnam, 1961. 580 pp.,
illus., maps, apps., index.

Authoritative account of Israel's War of Independence.
Focused on military history, although Lorch covers political
factors as well. His review of battles and campaigns is
objective. Lorch begins by sketching the strengths and weaknesses of the various forces involved. The main emphasis is
on the ground battles, since neither side made extensive use
Of air or sea forces in 1948.

2033. ___: ONE LONG WAR: ARAB VERSUS JEW SINCE 1920. Jerusalem: Keter, 1976. 254 pp., illus., gloss., bibliog.

Brief survey of Israel's military history from 1920 to
1973. Israel's defense problems are covered chronologically,
beginning with the birth of the Haganah. Most attention is
given to military operations in the period since 1949. The
analysis is brief, but to the point. Includes an interesting
chapter comparing Israel's wars in terms of Arab and Israeli
objectives, results, and losses.

> #2017. Perlmutter, A.: MILITARY AND POLITICS IN ISRAEL.

Immigration

2034. Antonovsky, Aaron and David Katz: "Factors in the
Adjustment to Israeli Life of American and Canadian Immigrants." JJoS, v.12 #1 (June, 1970): 77-87.

* 2035. Bahral, Uri: THE EFFECT OF MASS IMMIGRATION ON WAGES
IN ISRAEL. Jerusalem: Falk Project for Economic Research in
Israel, 1965. 81 pp., bibliog.

2036. Barer, Shlomo: THE MAGIC CARPET. New York: Harper &
Brothers, 1952. 243 pp., illus.

Dated but nevertheless still interesting journalistic
account of the airlift which rescued the Jews of Yemen.
Interspersed with Barer's after-the-events account are pages
from his diary, written while the author was in Aden as a
representative of Kol Israel, the Israeli radio network.
Also includes flashbacks on the history of Yemenite Jewry.

2037. Della Pergola, Sergio: "On the Differential Frequency of Western Migration to Israel." SCJ, v.1 (1984): 292-315.

> #829. Elazar, D.: THE BALKAN JEWISH COMMUNITIES.

2038. Engel, Gerald: "North American Settlers in Israel." AJYB, v.71 (1970): 161-187.

2039. Farago, Uri: "Changes in the Ethnic Identity of Russian Immigrant Students in Israel [1973-75]." JJoS, v.21 #1 (June, 1979): 37-52.

> #1021. Freedman, R.: SOVIET JEWRY IN THE DECISIVE DECADE.

2040. Herman, D. L.: "Israel's Latin American Immigrants." AJA, v.36 #1 (Apr., 1984): 16-49.

* 2041. Martin, Edward T.: I FLEW THEM HOME: A PILOT'S STORY OF THE YEMENITE AIRLIFT. New York: Theodor Herzl Institute, 1958. 63 pp., map.

2042. Samuel, Herbert: "Where Did Israel put its Million Jewish Immigrants?" JJoS, v.8 #1 (June, 1966): 81-91.

> #1916. Schechtman, J. B.: "Repatriation of Iraq Jewry."

> #1941. ___: "Repatriation of Yemenite Jewry."

2043. Snarey, John R.: "Becoming a Kibbutz Founder: an Ethnographic Study of the First All-American Kibbutz in Israel." JSS, v.46 #2 (Spr., 1984): 103-130.

2044. Weintraub, D. and M. Lissak: "The Absorption of North African Immigrants in Agricultural Settlements in Israel." JJoS, v.3 #1 (June, 1961): 29-54.

2045. Wormann, Curt D.: "German Jews in Israel: Their Cultural Situation since 1933." LBIYB, v.15 (1970): 73-103.

Sociology

2046. Arian, Asher: "Consensus and Community in Israel." JJoS, v.12 #1 (June, 1970): 39-53.

2047. Aronoff, Myron J.: "Communal Cohesion Through Political Strife in an Israeli New Town." JJoS, v.15 #1 (June,
1973): 79-105.

2048. Blackstone, T.: "Education and the Under-Privileged
in Israel." JJoS, v.13 #2 (Dec., 1971): 173-187.

> #62. Cohen, S. and P. Hyman: THE JEWISH FAMILY.

2049. Eisenstadt, S. N.: ISRAELI SOCIETY. New York: Basic
Books, 1967. 451 pp., notes, bibliog., index.

Synthetic sociological survey of Israel, divided into two
parts. In Part I, Eisenstadt surveys the historical process
by which the Yishuv was transformed into the State of
Israel. This section provides an interesting insight into
the development of the Yishuv, and includes an important
chapter on its institutional history. Special attention is
rightfully given to the development of the Jewish Agency and
the Histadrut. Part II is a study of the emerging social
structure of the state. Eisenstadt reviews economic, social,
and political trends and the cultural values that Israel
represents. The difficulties in molding a united society out
of the multiplicity of cultural backgrounds is clearly
charted, as is the social stratification between Ashkenazim
and Sephardim. An interesting chapter deals with the status
of non-Jewish minorities in Israel. Eisenstadt´s final
chapter contains some insights into the continuing problems
of Israeli society and a prognosis of Israel´s future.

2050. Elazar, Daniel J.: ISRAEL: BUILDING A NEW SOCIETY.
Bloomington: Indiana Univ. Press, 1986. 287 pp., notes,
index.

Inquiry into the development of Israeli society and politics. Elazar sees Israel on the threshold of a new era as it
changes from an ideological to a territorial entity. However, he notes that Israel is a unique polity which cannot
be assessed in terms of traditional political-and social-
science concepts. Thus, Israel must be viewed as both a
European and Middle Eastern nation, and as an amalgam of
secular and religious beliefs. Elazar also argues that
Israel be viewed as a frontier society.
Elazar´s analysis stresses the maturation of Israeli
political perceptions. The emergence and maturation of the
territorial entity can be seen in his analyses of local politics in Israel and the civil service, both of which receive

scant attention in most works on Israeli politics. Elazar´s
analysis of the Sephardi-Ashkenazi situation will not be
acceptable to those who view Israeli politics with ideologically fixed blinders, or to those who wish to see a schism
in the Israeli polity; yet his analysis rings true in most
cases. The same can be said for his analysis of the role of
religion in a modern, secular state. This in no way implies
that the book is perfect. As befits a still evolving polity,
Elazar´s book offers only tentative conclusions. The research done for the book is still continuing, and there are
some gaps. Notably, the role of the IDF in Israeli society
was not systematically addressed by Elazar. Even so, as a
first analysis the book is worthy of serious attention.

2051. Katz, Elihu: "Culture and Communication in Israel:
the Transformation of Tradition." JJoS, v.15 #1 (June,
1973): 5-21.

2052. Lazar, David: "Israel´s Political Structure and Social issues." JJoS, v.15 #1 (June, 1973): 23-43.

2053. Lissak, Moshe: "Patterns of Change in Ideology and
Class Structure in Israel." JJoS, v.7 #1 (June, 1965):
46-62.

2054. Rothman, R. C.: "Education and Participation in the
Israeli Defense Forces." JSS, v.34 #2 (Apr., 1972): 155-172.

2055. Sabatello, Eitan F.: "Patterns of Illegitimacy in
Israel." JJoS, v.21 #1 (June, 1979): 53-65.

2056. Swirski, Shlomo: "Community and the Meaning of the
Modern State: the Case of Israel." JJoS, v.18 #2 (Dec.,
1976): 123-140.

2057. Weiner, Eugene C. at all: "Adult Evaluation of the
Young: the Case of Israel´s Victorious Youth in the Six-Day
War." JJoS, v.15 #1 (June, 1973): 107-117.

2058. Weingrod, Alex and Michael Gurevitch: "Who are the
Israeli Elites?" JJoS, v.19 #1 (June, 1977): 67-77.

> #84. Weller, L.: SOCIOLOGY IN ISRAEL.

2059. Wershow, Harold J.: "Aging in the Israeli Kibbutz:
Growing Old in a Mini-Socialist Society." JSS, v.35 #2
(Apr., 1973): 141-148.

2060. Yishai, Yael: "Israel´s Right-Wing Jewish Proletariat." JJoS, v.24 #2 (Dec., 1982): 87-98.

The Kibbutz

2061. Krausz, Ernest [ed.]: THE SOCIOLOGY OF THE KIBBUTZ. New Brunswick, NJ: Transaction Books, 1983. 429 pp., notes, bibliog., index.

Sociological anthology on the subject of the kibbutz. The object of the book is to identify the social function the kibbutz plays in Israeli society. Four areas of collective life are explored: the concept of the kibbutz; social stratification; the role of the family; and work and productivity. As such, the anthology is also a contribution to the study of Israeli society. Most of the essays were previously published in scholarly books and periodicals. Two essays written for the anthology summarize the current state of research on the kibbutz and offer an introduction to the book. The gist of the anthology is that the kibbutz has been a successful experiment in social organization. Success was achieved because of the ability of the kibbutz to adapt its structure to new conditions while maintaining essential values.

CONTENTS: M. E. Spiro: Thirty Years of Kibbutz Research / M. Rosner: Social Research, Change, and the Kibbutz / M. Buber: An Experiment That Did Not Fail / J. Ben-David: The Kibbutz and the Moshav / D. Katz and N. Golomb: Integration, Effectiveness, and Adaptation in Social Systems: a Comparative Analysis of Kibbutzim Communities / E. Cohen: The Structural Transformation of the Kibbutz / A. Fishman: The Religious Kibbutz: Religion, Nationalism, and Socialism in a Communal Framework / M. Saltman: Legality and Ideology in the Kibbutz Movement / S. N. Eisenstadt: Some Observations on Historical Changes in the Structure of Kibbutzim / E. Rosenfeld: Social Stratification in a "Classless" Society / A. Etzioni: The Functional Differentiation of Elites in the Kibbutz / E. Yuchtman: Reward Distribution and Work-role Attractiveness in the Kibbutz: Reflections on Equity Theory / Eliezer Ben-Rafael: Dynamics of Social Stratification in Kibbutzim / M. Rosner and N. Cohen: Is Direct Democracy Feasible in Modern Society? the Lesson of the Kibbutz Experience / M. E. Spiro: Is the Family Universal? - the Israeli Case / Yonina Talmon-Garber: The Family in a Revolutionary Movement: the Case of the Kibbutz in Israel / J. Shepher and L. Tiger: Kibbutz and

Parental Investment / Erik Cohen and M. Rosner: Relations between Generations in the Israeli Kibbutz / E. C. Devereux et al: Socialization Practices of Parents, Teachers, and Peers in Israel: the Kibbutz Versus the City / R. Kahane: The Committed: Preliminary Reflections on the Impact of the Kibbutz Socialization Pattern on Adolescents / I. Vallier: Structural Differentiation, Production Imperatives, and Communal Norms: the Kibbutz in Crisis / David Barkin and J. W. Bennet: Kibbutz and Colony: Collective Economies and the Outside World / Y. Don: Industrialization in Advanced Rural Communities: the Israeli Kibbutz / U. Leviatan: Organizational Effects of Managerial Turnover in Kibbutz Production Branches / E. Orchan: Statistical Appendix / S. Shur and D. Glanz: The Kibbutz: Selected Bibliography.

2062. Lilker, Shalom: KIBBUTZ JUDAISM: A NEW TRADITION IN THE MAKING. New York: Herzl Press, 1982. 264 pp., notes, gloss., bibliog., index.

Social and religious investigation of the kibbutz. Lilker specifically hopes to explain the mutual relations between religious Judaism and the socialistic commune. In order to be true to both Jewish tradition and socialism, the kibbutz has been the center of an experiment in establishing new Jewish traditions. Lilker also notes the rejection of Judaism by the early halutzim, explaining that over the years the dogmatic secularist attitude has changed considerably. Rituals, holidays, and Jewish rights of passage are now celebrated in a style unique to kibbutzim. Unfortunately, Lilker completely ignores the religious kibbutz movement, where both old and new elements are synthesized in a traditional Jewish environment.

2063. Spiro, Melford E.: KIBBUTZ: VENTURE IN UTOPIA. Augmented Edition. New York: Schocken Books, 1970. 307 pp., gloss., notes, bibliog., index.

Classic socioanthropological study of the kibbutz. Based on an intensive study of one kibbutz, which Spiro calls Kiryat Yedidim. Spiro undertook close and careful study of kibbutz lifestyles, with special emphasis on the communal setting of the kibbutz. He views the kibbutz as a utopian experiment based on unique and original social postulates. The augmented edition updates the original text and is based on research of the early 1950s, bringing the story of Kiryat Yedidim into the early 1960s. The revised text adds a further epilogue on the changes in the kibbutz after the Six-

Day War. Spiro shows that changes in the environment have
led to relatively minor changes in kibbutz organization;
despite these changes, Spiro maintains that most kibbutzim
have remained essentially as they were.

Ethnic Groups

2064. Cohen, E.: "The Black Panthers and Israeli Society."
JJoS, v.14 #1 (June, 1972): 93-109.

2065. Eisenstadt, S. N.: "The Oriental Jews in Israel [a
Report on a Preliminary Study in Culture-Contacts]." JSS,
v.12 #3 (July, 1950): 199-222.

2066. Gordon, L.: "Reflections on Inter-and Intragroup Relations in Israeli Society." JSS, v.36 #3/4 (July/Oct.,
1974): 262-270.

> #1886. Haddad, H.: JEWS OF ARAB AND ISLAMIC COUNTRIES.

2067. Krausz, Ernest: "Edah and ´Ethnic Group´ in Israel."
JJoS, v.28 #1 (June, 1986): 5-18.

2068. Lewis, Herbert S.: "Yemenite Ethnicity in Israel."
JJoS, v.26 #1 (June, 1984): 5-24.

2069. Lustick, Ian: "Zionism and the State of Israel: Regime Objectives and the Arab Minority in the First Years of
Statehood." MES, v.16 #1 (Jan., 1980): 127-146.

* 2070. Poll, S. and Ernest Krausz: ON ETHNIC AND RELIGIOUS
DIVERSITY IN ISRAEL. Ramat-Gan: Bar Ilan Univ. Press, 1975.
125 pp.

2071. Strizower, Schifra: "The ´Bene Israel´ in Israel."
MES, v.2 #2 (Jan., 1966): 123-143.

2072. Zenner, W.: "Ambivalence and Self-Image among Oriental Jews in Israel." JJoS, v.5 #2 (Dec., 1963): 214-223.

Religion and Culture

2073. Abramov, S. Z.: PERPETUAL DILEMMA: JEWISH RELIGION
IN THE JEWISH STATE. Jerusalem: World Union of Progressive
Judaism, 1976. 459 pp., notes, gloss., bibliog., index.

Studies the problematics of Judaism in the modern world
and the State of Israel. Abramov adopts a historical and
constitutional perspective on the issues raised by the
status of Judaism in the Jewish state. The historical chapters are a good review of the development of the religious
element in zionism and the relations between religious and
secular Jews in the Yishuv. Unfortunately, when dealing with
constitutional issues Abramov becomes polemical and tendentious. His position is not only non-religious, but anti-
religious. This leads him to misconstrue the positions of
many Orthodox leaders and to virtually ignore the ideology
of religious zionism. There is much to be said for an objective analysis of the position of religion in the State of
Israel, but Abramov's analysis falls short of that goal.

2074. Aran, Gideon: "From Religious Zionism to Zionist Religion: the Roots of Gush Emunim." SCJ, v.2 (1985): 116-143.

2075. Ben-Dov, Meir et al: THE WESTERN WALL. Trans. from
the Hebrew by Raphael Posner. New York: Adama Books, 1983.
345 pp., illus., notes, bibliog.

History of the Western Wall from the period of the First
Temple until the 1980s. In addition, the authors deal with
the place of the Wall in Jewish belief and folklore, as well
as its influence on arts and crafts. Integrating the
scholarly with the popular, the book presents a kaleidoscopic review of the Wall, the city of Jerusalem, and the
experience - individual and collective - of the Kotel.

CONTENTS: M. Ben-Dov: From the Temple to the Western Wall;
Architecture and Archaeology / M. Naor: The Wall in Accounts
of Travellers and Visitors / M. Ha'cohen: Sanctity, Law and
Customs / Dov Noy: Folk Tales about the Western Wall / Zeev
Aner: The Struggle for the Wall / M. Naor: The Wall in the
Six-Day War / M. Ben-Dov: Planning the Piazza at the Western
Wall / Z. Aner: The Wall in Art and in Crafts / Y. Feliks:
Flora and Fauna at the Wall / M. Ben-Dov: Four Stones / The
Wall has a Thousand Faces.

2076. Don-Yehiya, Eliezer: "Religious Leaders in the Political Arena: the Case of Israel." MES, v.20 #2 (Apr.,
1984): 154-171.

2077. Edelman, M.: "The Rabbinical Courts in the Evolving
Political Culture of Israel." MES, v.16 #3 (Oct., 1980):
145-166.

2078. Fishman, Aryei: "The Religious Kibbutz Movement: the Pursuit of a Complete Life within an Orthodox Framework." SCJ, v.2 (1985): 97-115.

> #153. Horowitz, G.: THE SPIRIT OF JEWISH LAW.

> #389. Kahana, K.: THE CASE FOR JEWISH CIVIL LAW.

* 2079. Korn, Itzhak and Shlomo Derekh: BETWEEN THE STATE OF ISRAEL AND THE DIASPORA. Tel Aviv: World Labour Zionist Movement, 1973. 59 pp.

2080. Kraines, Oscar: THE IMPOSSIBLE DILEMMA: WHO IS A JEW IN THE STATE OF ISRAEL. New York: Bloch Pub., 1976. 156 pp., apps., notes, bibliog., gloss., index.

Legal and judicial investigation into the "who is a Jew" question that has plagued the State of Israel since 1948. Legal issues as well as key cases are set out clearly and without polemic. Kraines places the problem into the broader contexts of the status of civil law and religion in Israel. Under present conditions, the dilemma of who is a Jew has still not been solved to the satisfaction of all parties, religious and secular. Given the inflexible positions of the opposing factions, it may be impossible to solve.

2081. Krausz, E. and M. Bar-Lev: "Varieties of Orthodox Religious Behaviour: a Case Study of Yeshiva High School Graduates in Israel." JJoS, v.20 #1 (June, 1978): 59-74.

> #373. Levine, E.: DIASPORA.

> #374. Lewittes, M.: RELIGIOUS FOUNDATIONS.

2082. Liebman, Charles S.: "Religion and Political Integration in Israel." JJoS, v.17 #1 (June, 1975): 17-27.

2083. Rabinowicz, Harry: HASIDISM AND THE STATE OF ISRAEL. Rutherford, NJ: Fairleigh Dickinson Univ. Press, 1982. 346 pp., table, gloss., notes, bibliog., index.

Surveys the interaction of hasidism with the land of Israel over two centuries. Part I deals with the hasidic position before the establishment of the State of Israel, Part II with hasidism in Israel since 1948. Unfortunately the position of the hasidic leadership to zionism is not adequately reviewed: Zaddikim were not merely passive or

silent on the virtues of a Zionist return to Eretz Israel,
as may be inferred from his review, but many were actively
opposed to what they considered a false messianism. Although
many hasidic groups have found some modus vivendi with the
State of Israel, not all have done so and some, e.g.,
Satmar, are still vocal in their condemnation of zionism and
Zionists. Although one of only a few studies on contemporary
hasidism, Rabinowicz's book is by no means authoritative.

2084. Roshwald, Mordecai: "Who is a Jew in Israel?" JJoS,
v.12 #2 (Dec., 1970): 233-266.

> #273. Shomsky, A.: CLASH OF CULTURES IN ISRAEL.

2085. Yaron, Z.: "Religion in Israel." AJYB, v.76 (1976):
41-90.

18

Africa, Asia, and the Pacific

SURVEYS

2086. Kohut, A.: "Jewish Heretics in the Philippines in the Sixteenth and Seventeenth Century." PAJHS, #12 (1904): 149-156.

2087. Kosmin, B. A.: "A Note on Southern Rhodesian Jewry." JJoS, v.15 #2 (Dec., 1973): 205-212.

2088. Lord, James H.: THE JEWS IN INDIA AND THE FAR EAST. Westport, CT: Greenwood Press, 1976 [Rep. of 1907 Ed.]. 137 pp., apps., notes.

First published in 1907 from a series of essays in Church and Synagogue, this volume has now been largely superseded. At the time it was written, however, it represented one of very few studies on the Jews of the Far East. Most of the book is a description of the Bene-Israel and their customs, although Lord also hypothesizes on how Jews first came to India and other parts of the Far East. Relatively less information is provided on Jews in other parts of Asia. More interesting, from the perspective of the eighty years since the book was originally published, are Lord´s appendixes which deal with statistical, social, and documentary issues.

> #484. Weisbord, R.: AFRICAN ZION.

2089. Wolf, Lucien: "Crypto-Jews in the Canaries." TJHSE, v.7 (1911/14): 97-112.

AUSTRALIA

2090. Blakeney, Michael: "Australia and the Jewish Refugees from Central Europe: Government Policy, 1933-1939."
LBIYB, v.29 (1984): 103-133.

2091. Buckley, B. and Sol Encel: "The Demographic History
of the New South Wales Jewish Community, 1933-1966." JSS,
v.34 #2 (Apr., 1972): 140-154.

2092. Crown, A. D.: "The Initiatives and Influences in the
Development of Australian Zionism, 1850-1948." JSS, v.39 #4
(Fall, 1977): 299-322.

> #1373. Elazar, D. J.: "Jewish Frontier Experiences."

> #1374. ___ and P. Y. Medding: JEWISH COMMUNITIES.

> #1283. Joseph, A. P.: "Jewry of South-West England."

2093. Klarberg, F.: "Yiddish in Melbourne." JJoS, v.12 #1
(June, 1970): 59-76.

2094. Lippmann, Walter M.: "Australian Jewry in 1966."
JJoS, v.11 #1 (June, 1969): 67-73.

2095. ___: "The Demography of Australian Jewry." JJoS, v.8
#2 (Dec., 1966): 213-239.

2096. Medding, Peter Y.: FROM ASSIMILATION TO GROUP SUR-
VIVAL: A POLITICAL AND SOCIOLOGICAL STUDY OF THE AUSTRALIAN
JEWISH COMMUNITY. New York: Hart, 1969. 309 pp., notes,
bibliog., app., index.

Sociological and political history of Australian Jewry.
Primary focus is on the Jews of Melbourne, and the work
analyzes the community as well as distinct individuals. The
book might be subtitled the decline and rise of Melbourne
Jewry, as the author sees the Australian Jewish community
turning to a policy of survival rather than assimilation.
According to Medding, two phenomena changed the community's
attitude: zionism and large scale immigration of Jews from
eastern and central Europe. His conclusion is sound, not
only for Australia but for other Jewries as well. The book
easily lends itself to a comparative study.

2097. ___: "The Persistence of Ethnic Political Preferences: Factors Influencing the Voting Behavior of Jews in
Australia." JJoS, v.13 #1 (June, 1971): 17-39.

2098. ___ [ed.]: JEWS IN AUSTRALIAN SOCIETY. Melbourne:
Macmillan for Monash Univ., 1973. 299 pp., apps., index.

Anthology based on the Jewish communal survey of 1967.
The survey, in turn, was the basis for a conference held at
Monash University on August 24-25, 1969. Some of the essays
have also appeared in a number of scholarly journals. The
theme of the anthology is Jewishness in the Australian
environment. Primary focus is sociological, with political,
economic, and religious factors also reviewed. Medding's
introduction contains the book's only historical insight and
emphasizes the treatment of ethnic minorities in Australia.
Taft's essay on the impact of the Six-day War and Liffman's
on antisemitism shed light on communal self-perceptions as
well as relations with the non-Jewish environment. The
questionnaire which formed the basis for the study is
included as an appendix; the two other appendixes detail
methodology used in the study. Overall, the findings of the
study coincide with data about other communities, including
the United States. Although some forms of Jewish practice
are shown to have declined, Jewish identification is still
quite high, reinforced by the role Israel plays in maintaining contact between Jews worldwide. Now dated, the data are
still of interest and help broaden the understanding of
postwar Jewish communal life.

CONTENTS: P. Y. Medding: Ethnic Minorities and Australian
Society / W. Lippmann: Melbourne Jewry: a Profile / L. S.
Sharpe: A Study of Poverty among Jews in Melbourne / P. Y.
Medding: Orthodoxy, Liberalism and Secularism in Melbourne
Jewry / R. Taft: Jewish Identification of Melbourne Jewry /
M. Klarberg: Yiddish in Melbourne / R. Taft: The Impact of
the Middle East Crisis of June 1967 on Jews in Melbourne /
M. Lifman: The Perception of Discrimination / P. Y. Medding:
Factors Influencing the Voting Behaviour of Melbourne Jews /
J. Goldlust: Party Preferences of Jewish Adolescents in
Melbourne / G. Solomon: Jewish Education in Australia / J.
Goldlust: The Impact of Jewish Education on Adolescents / R.
Taft: Beyond the Third Generation: the Ethnic Identification
of Jewish Youth / D. Altman et al: The Personal Experiences
and Views of Young Jewish Intellectuals / P. Y. Medding:
Jews in Australia - Continuity and Adaptation.

* 2099. Platz, Ernest: NEW AUSTRALIANS. Melbourne: Jewish Council to Combat Fascism and Antisemitism, 1948. 28 pp.

2100. Price, Ch.: "Chain Migration and Immigrant Groups, with Special Reference to Australian Jewry." JJoS, v.6 #2 (Dec., 1964): 157-171.

* 2101. ___ with L. Wilson and E. Tyler: JEWISH SETTLERS IN AUSTRALIA. Canberra: Australian National Univ., 1964. 102 pp., notes, apps.

> #375. Rubenstein, W.: THE LEFT, THE RIGHT AND THE JEWS.

> #102. Schmeltz, U.: JEWISH POPULATION STUDIES.

2102. Staedter, Joseph and Hans Kimmel [eds.]: SYDNEY´S JEWISH COMMUNITY: MATERIALS FOR A POST-WAR [II] HISTORY. 2 vols. Pennant Hills, N.S.W.: Australian Jewish Communities Series, 1953. 671 pp., illus., index.

Compilation of materials for a history of the Jewish community of Australia. Volume I covers 1948-1950 and part of 1952, while Volume II covers 1951-1953. Most selections were culled from the Sydney Jewish press, with a number of items selected from other sources. Issues that animated communal conflict, both internal and external, are included. Unfortunately the documents are not clearly designated and tend to be lost in the context of the press articles. Volume II includes a selection of "Historical and Biographical Notes" and "Specimens of Writings by Australian Jewish Authors." Both volumes are profusely illustrated and offer a glimpse into the life of Sydney Jewry.

2103. Taft, Ronald: "The Impact of the Middle East Crisis of June 1967 on Melbourne Jewry: an Empirical Study." JJoS, v.9 #2 (Dec., 1967): 243-262.

2104. ___ And G. Solomon: "The Melbourne Jewish Community and the Middle East War of 1973." JJoS, v.16 #1 (June, 1974): 57-73.

2105. Wright, I. M.: "The Jews of Australia." CJYB, v.3 (1941/42): 160-166.

CHINA

2106. Adler, M. N.: "Chinese Jews." JQR, v.13 #1 (Oct., 1900): 18-41.

2107. Gruenberger, Felix: "Jewish Refugees in Shanghai." JSS, v.12 #4 (Oct., 1950): 329-348.

2108. Kramer, L. I.: "The K´aifeng Jews: a Disappearing Community." JSS, v.18 #2 (Apr., 1956): 125-144.

2109. Kranzler, David: "Restrictions Against German-Jewish Refugee Immigration to Shanghai in 1939." JSS, v.36 #1 (Jan., 1974): 40-60.

2110. Leslie, Donald D.: "The Kaifeng Jewish Community: a Summary." JJoS, v.11 #2 (Dec., 1969): 175-185.

2111. Loewe, Michael: "Jews in China." JJS, v.19 #1/4 (1968): 75-80.

2112. Mars, Alvin: "A Note on the Jewish Refugees in Shanghai." JSS, v.31 #4 (Oct., 1969): 286-291.

2113. Neubauer, A.: "Jews in China." JQR, v.8 #1 (Oct., 1895): 123-193.

2114. Pollak, Michael: MANDARINS, JEWS, AND MISSIONARIES: THE JEWISH EXPERIENCE IN THE CHINESE EMPIRE. Philadelphia: JPS, 1980. 436 pp., illus., app., notes, bibliog., index.

Two-part investigation into the rise and fall of the Jewish community of Kaifeng. Part I deals with the interest expressed about Chinese Jews by Westerners, missionaries, and scholars. Part II details the inner life of the community. The book is organized thematically. Pollack maintains a degree of scholarly scepticism, setting out to divide fact from fiction. Unwilling to accept the implausible, he largely succeeds in steering clear of mythology and provides an incisive study on the Chinese Jews.

2115. Shapiro, Sidney [ed.]: JEWS IN OLD CHINA: STUDIES BY CHINESE SCHOLARS. Trans. from the Chinese by the Editor. New York: Hippocrene Books, 1984. 204 pp., illus., notes, bibliog., index.

Collection of opinions by Chinese scholars on the history

of the Jews in China. The book is more a loose compilation
of scholarly positions, tied together by Shapiro´s remarks,
than a collection of essays. The format and tendentious
nature of some of the articles reduces the scholarly value
of the book. On the other hand Shapiro´s prologue offers a
good summary of Western scholarship on this somewhat arcane
but intersting subject.

CONTENTS: Hong Jun: A Survey of the Various Religious Sects
During the Yuan Dynasty / Zhang Xinglang: Contacts Between
Ancient China and the Jews / W. Tu-Chien: A Study of Wotuo /
Chen Yuan: A Study of the Israelite Religion in Kaifeng / P.
Guandan: Jews in Ancient China - a Historical Survey / Jiang
Qingxiang and Xiao Guoliang: Glimpses of the Urban Economy
of Bianjing, Capital of the Northern Song Dynasty / Gao
Wangzhi: Concerning Chinese Jews / Li Jixian: An San An
Cheng / Chen Changqi: Buddhist Monk or Jewish Rabbi? / Zhu
Jiang: Jewish Traces in Yangzhou / Xu Zonghe: Some Observa-
tions on the Jews of Kaifeng / Wu Zelin: An Ethnic Historian
Looks at China´s Jews / Wang Yisha: The Descendants of the
Kaifeng Jews.

2116. White, Wm. C.: CHINESE JEWS. 2nd Edition. New York:
Paragon Books, 1966 [Rep. of 1942 Ed.]. 625 pp., illus.,
indexes.

Compilation of materials relating to the Jews of Kaifeng.
The original edition was published in three volumes, which
were organized thematically. The Paragon edition is bound as
one volume, but retains White´s original organization. The
revised edition is suplemented by Cecil Roth´s introduction
and includes an essay by Roth on a Chinese manuscript of
Megillat Esther. The book´s three parts cover historical,
inscriptional, and genealogical materials from a wide
variety of sources. All materials are cited in the Chinese
original as well as in English translation. The book is
clearly an indispensable tool for scholars and students interested in Chinese Jewry.

ETHIOPIA

2117. Faitlovitch, Jacques: "The Falashas." AJYB, v.22
(1920/21): 80-100.

2118. Leslau, Wolf: "A Falasha Religious Dispute." PAAJR,
v.16 (1946/47): 71-95.

2119. Rapoport, Louis: THE LOST JEWS: LAST OF THE ETHIO-
PIAN FALASHAS. Briarcliff Manor, NY: Stein & Day/Scarborough
House, 1980. 264 pp., maps, illus., notes, bibliog., index.

Journalistic history of the Falashas. Deals primarily
with the contemporary plight of the Falashas, although historical data about their origins are also included. The role
Falashas have played in the State of Israel is discussed in
detail. Falasha lifestyles and customs are also described.
The appalling conditions faced by the community after the
fall of Haile Selassie and the need to mount a rescue
operation provide Rapoport with his passion, and result in
his stirring prose. The implied criticism of the government
of Israel for its supposed inaction has, of course, been
given the lie by Operation Moses. Nevertheless, Rapoport´s
book is a good introduction to the subject of this unique
Jewish tribe. Foreword by Meyer Levin.

2120. ___: REDEMPTION SONG: THE STORY OF OPERATION MOSES.
New York: Harcourt, Brace Jovanovich, 1986. 234 pp., illus.,
bibliog., index.

Journalistic account of the rescue and transfer of 10,000
Falashas from Ethiopia to Israel. The book is a follow-up to
THE LOST JEWS [see #2119]. Includes insights into Falasha
lifestyles and details the sources of their Judaism.
Rapoport is forthright in his reconstruction of the operation, assigning both praise and blame where they belong. He
is, however, too critical of what he sees as Israel´s slow
reaction to the Falasha crisis. Similarly his rejection of
the position of those Israeli religious leaders who are not
enthusiastic supporters of the Falashas is cavalier and, at
times, unfair. That the Falashas are Jews is no longer
doubted by most scholars. Nevertheless, those who disagreed
with this analysis were neither malicious nor insincere.
Rapoport has provided an important first look at the subject, but not a definitive account.

2121. Semi, E. Trevisan: "The Beta Israel [Falashas]: from
Purity to Impurity." JJoS, v.27 #2 (Dec., 1985): 103-114.

INDIA

2122. Barber, Ezekiel: THE BENE-ISRAEL OF INDIA: IMAGES
AND REALITY. Lanham, MD: Univ. Press of America, 1981. 155
pp., illus., notes, bibliog., index.

Anthropological inquiry into the history, lifestyles, and customs of the Bene-Israel. Barber also charts cultural influences on the community, Jewish and non-Jewish, Indian and foreign. A particularly interesting chapter attempts to uncover the date of the Jews´ migration to India. Barber briefly describes the lives of the Cochin Jews, rounding out the history of Jews in the subcontinent. Barber correctly notes that it is impossible to completely reconstruct the history of the Bene-Israel. For a variety of reasons communal records were not preserved until relatively recently. As a result, our knowledge of the Bene-Israel is and will likely remain incomplete. Even so, Barber offers an interesting and important insight into the history of a little known community.

2123. Elias, Flower and J. Cooper: THE JEWS OF CALCUTTA: THE AUTOBIOGRAPHY OF A COMMUNITY 1798-1972. Calcutta: Jewish Association of Calcutta, 1974. 243 pp., illus.

Studies Jews from Calcutta who have resettled in England. Primarily discusses Calcutta Jewish identity, although the authors also provide a history of the Jewish community. The book might more properly be described as a communal biography. Chapters are thematic and deal with social and religious life. Unique customs are also described. The most interesting chapter details the difficulties Jews from Calcutta have faced in maintaining their unique communal identity. Assimilation and intermarriage have taken a massive toll on the Calcutta Jews, although the existence of Israel has helped bolster the community. In light of their origins in India, it is interesting to see how many of the Calcutta Jews refer to the Holocaust; typically the lesson Calcutta Jews learned from the suffering of their European brethren was the need for a strong and secure state of Israel. The authors point out some differences between older and younger generations. The book offers a unique and interesting review of a distinct Jewish subcommunity.

2124. Fischel, Walter J.: "Bombay in Jewish History in the Light of New Documents from the Indian Archives." PAAJR, v.38/39 (1970/71): 119-144.

2125. ___: "Early Zionism in India." HYB, v.4 (1961/62): 309-328.

2126. ___: "The Immigration of ´Arabian´ Jews to India in the Eighteenth Century." PAAJR, v.33 (1965): 1-20.

2127. Mandelbaum, David G.: "The Jewish Way of Life in Cochin." JSS, v.1 #4 (Oct., 1939): 423-460.

2128. ___ : "Social Stratification among the Jews of Cochin in India and in Israel." JJoS, v.17 #2 (Dec., 1975): 165-210.

2129. Reissner, H. G.: "Indian-Jewish Statistics [1837-1941]." JSS, v.12 #4 (Oct., 1950): 349-366.

2130. Roland, J. G.: "The Jews of India: Communal Survival or the End of a Sojourn?" JSS, v.42 #1 (Wint., 1980): 75-90.

> #2070. Strizower, S.: "The Bene-Israel in Israel."

2131. Strizower, Schifra: THE BENE ISRAEL OF BOMBAY: A STUDY OF A JEWISH COMMUNITY. New York: Schocken Books, 1971. 176 pp., notes, bibliog., index.

Synthetic history of the native Jewish community of Bombay, with primary focus on sociology and anthropology. The book is also a eulogy for a community in decline, since the Indian Jewish community has been markedly decreasing in size as of the late 1940s. The book offers an in-depth analysis of the lifestyle of the Bene-Israel and their role in Indian national life and history. The place of the Bene-Israel within the broader parameters of Jewish history is not sufficiently reviewed. Of particular interest is her study into the myths surrounding the origins of the Bene-Israel and their possible links to the ten lost tribes.

2132. ___ : "Jews as an Indian Caste." JJoS, v.1 #1 (Apr., 1959): 43-57.

NEW ZEALAND

2133. Goldman, Lazarus M.: THE HISTORY OF THE JEWS IN NEW ZEALAND. Wellington: A. H. and A. W. Reed, 1958 / New York: Heineman, 1960. 272 pp., illus., gloss., bibliog., index.

Synthetic history of New Zealand Jewry from the 1830s to the 1950s. Although obviously sympathetic to the Jewish community, Goldman is also keenly aware of the problems that have beset Jews in New Zealand, for example, a high intermarriage rate and antisemitism. Anti-Jewish sentiments in the New Zealand government are dealt with in a forthright

manner. Unfortunately, scant information is given on Jewish
responses to antisemitism; such data might have been used to
compare reactions to antisemitism in New Zealand to those of
other Jewish communities. Considerable attention is paid to
social topics, e.g., education. Overall, the book takes a
fresh approach to Jewish history in an Anglo-Saxon country.

SINGAPORE

2134. Nathan, Eze: THE HISTORY OF JEWS IN SINGAPORE: 1830-
1945. Singapore: Herbilu Editorial and Marketing Services,
1986. 212 pp., illus., bibliog., apps.

History of Singapore Jewry from the first settlement in
1830 to the exodus of the last Jews in the late 1940s.
Nathan interweaves biographical and historical data in every
chapter. Though always a small and largely peripheral
center, Singapore can be seen as a case study in the
development of a Jewish community under British colonial
rule. The earliest settlers were merchants; trade within
Malaysia and the world continued to play a key role in
Jewish economic activity until the Japanese occupation of
1942. The community was composed mainly of Sephardic Jews
and a strong component of Middle Easterners, and some
Ashkenazim. Most of the communal records were destroyed
during the Japanese occupation, and as a result some of
Nathan´s chapters are only outlines lacking details. Still,
the book explores an almost unknown Jewish community which
developed in a frontier setting.

SOUTH AFRICA

2135. Arkin, Marcus [ed.]: SOUTH AFRICAN JEWRY: A CONTEM-
PORARY SURVEY. Cape Town: Oxford Univ. Press, 1984. 212 pp.,
notes, bibliog., index.

Surveys the changes that have occurred in South African
Jewry since World War II. Most of the chapters also provide
background information extending the survey back to the
1880s. The coverage is extensive, offering a good picture of
South African Jewry. An especially interesting chapter
covers "Political Attitude and Inter-Action." The Jewish
community numbers about 120,000, a small minority in a
nation whose ruling white polity is itself a minority. South
African Jewry´s political attitudes thus help to place the

community into a broad and important context. South African
Jewry´s   approach to society and politics differs from that
of American, English, or West European Jewry. For example,
the Jewish immigrant experience in South Africa differed
greatly from that of Jews in the United States, England, or
Palestine. Arkin´s book provides the raw data for comparative studies of the immigrant experience and of other facets
of Jewish life worldwide.

CONTENTS: S. Cohen: The Historical Background / Allie Dubb:
Demographic Picture / A. Goldberg: Communal Infrastructure /
A. Arkin: Economic Activities / Marcus Arkin: The Zionist
Dimension / Jocelyn Hellig: Religious Expression / R. Mink:
Education / Harry Schwarz: Political Attitudes and Inter-
action / L. Abrahams et al: Cultural Life / Arthur Goldman:
The World of Sport.

2136. Aschheim, Steven E.: "The Communal Organization of
South African Jewry." JJoS, v.12 #2 (Dec., 1970): 201-231.

2137. Bentwich, N.: "Jewish Life in British South Africa."
JSS, v.4 #1 (Jan., 1942): 73-84.

2138. Dubb, A. A.: "Changes in Ethnic Attitudes of Jewish
Youth in Johannesburg." JSS, v.34 #1 (Jan., 1972): 58-72.

> #1373. Elazar, D. J.: "Jewish Frontier Experiences."

> #1374. ___ and P. Y. Medding: JEWISH COMMUNITIES.

2139. Herrman, L.: A HISTORY OF THE JEWS IN SOUTH AFRICA
FROM THE EARLIEST TIMES TO 1895. London: V. Gollancz, 1930.
287 pp., illus., bibliographic appendix, index.

Inquiry into the Jews of South Africa before the Boer
War. The book can be divided into two sections. The first
deals with prominent individuals, the second deals with the
Jewish community as a whole. In both style and sources the
book is outdated, but nevertheless contains very useful
information on a little-studied community. Of particular interest are the chapters dealing with the role of Portuguese
Marranos in the discovery and early exploration of the Cape
region and of southern Africa in general.

> #361. Herman, S. N.: THE REACTION OF JEWS TO ANTISEMITISM.

2140. Lever, H. and O. J. M. Wagner: "Ethnic Preferences of Jewish Youth in Johannesburg." JJoS, v.9 #1 (June, 1967): 34-48.

2141. Levy, Ephraim M.: "The Jews of South Africa." CJYB, v.3 (1941/42): 138-159.

2142. Mendelssohn, S.: "Jewish Pioneers of South Africa." TJHSE, v.7 (1911/1914): 180-205.

* 2143. Saron, G.: COMBATING ANTISEMITISM IN SOUTH AFRICA. Johannesburg: South African Jewish Board of Deputies, 1945. 21 pp.

2144. ___ and L. Hotz [eds.]: THE JEWS IN SOUTH AFRICA. London: Oxford Univ. Press, 1955. 422 pp., map, bibliog., index.

Survey of South African Jewish history from 1800 to 1910. The work is actually a collective report written by sixteen authors and edited by Saron and Hotz for the South African Jewish Sociological and Historical Society. The authors chose to end with 1910, the year of the unification of the four colonial entities into the Union of South Africa. Primary emphasis is on social and economic developments, and special emphasis is placed on Jewish migration patterns. Topics discussed include the unification of the community after the Boer War, South African zionism, and the development of the South African chief rabbinate. As one of only a few major works dealing with one of the "second string" Jewries, the book is a useful contribution to both South African and Jewish history.

CONTENTS: L. Herrman: Cape Jewry before 1870 / I. Abrahams: Western Province Jewry, 1870-1902 / Max Geffen: Cape Town Jewry, 1902-1910 / C. Gershater: From Lithuania to South Africa / Gustav Saron: Jewish Immigration, 1880-1913 / Eric Rosenthal: On the Diamond Fields / G. Aschman: Oudtshoorn in the Early Days / S. A. Rochlin: The Early Gold-fields / Dora L. Sowden: In the Transvaal till 1899 / Louis I. Rabinowitz: The Transvaal Congregations / G. Saron: Boers, Uitlanders, Jews / D. L. Sowden: Transvaal Jewry, 1902-10 / G. Saron: The Long Road to Unity / Jack Alexander: South African Zionism / S. Rappaport: J. L. Landau - Thinker and Writer / A. Addleson: In the Eastern Province / M. Pencharz and D. L. Sowden: In the Orange Free State / D. Abelson: In Natal / L. Hotz: Contributions to Economic Development.

2145. Shain, Milton: "From Pariah to Parvenu: the Anti-Jewish Stereotype in South Africa, 1880-1910." JJoS, v.26 #2 (Dec., 1984): 111-127.

2146. Shimoni, Gideon: "Jan Christiaan Smuts and Zionism." JSS, v.39 #4 (Fall, 1977): 269-298.

2147. ___ : JEWS AND ZIONISM: THE SOUTH AFRICAN EXPERIENCE [1910-1967]. Cape Town: Oxford Univ. Press, 1980. 428 pp., illus., notes, index.

Well documented history of the Zionist experience in South Africa. By focusing on one community, Shimoni seeks to explore the role that nationalism has played in Jewish relations with non-Jews. The South African case is an interesting one. Since Jews were not the only prominent minority group, their place in South African society has not paralleled Jewish experiences elsewhere. Surprisingly, the problem of dual loyalty nevertheless plagued South African Zionists in the period between 1948 and 1967. The key reason for South African Jewry's dual-loyalty problem is the paradox brought about by apartheid: while South African Jews have always been considered part of the privileged white race, Israel's African policy led to very strong condemnation of South Africa's racial system. Thus South African Zionists were caught in a dilemma: loyalists to the Zionist cause were opponents of South Africa; loyalists to apartheid could not, it seemed to some, be good Zionists or good Jews. Shimoni's analysis opens a completely new vista in Jewish community studies, especially in the Southern Hemisphere.

2148. Strelitz, Ziona: "Jewish Identity in Cape Town, with Special Reference to Out-Marriage." JJoS, v.13 #1 (June, 1971): 73-93.

19

Bibliographies and Guides

2149. Alexander, Yonah et al [comps.]: A BIBLIOGRAPHY OF ISRAEL. New York: Herzl Press, 1982. 263 pp.

2150. Braham, R. L. [ed.]: JEWS IN THE COMMUNIST WORLD: A BIBLIOGRAPHY, 1945-1960. New York: Twayne, 1961. 64 pp.

2151. Brickman, William W. [ed.]: THE JEWISH COMMUNITY IN AMERICA: AN ANNOTATED AND CLASSIFIED BIBLIOGRAPHIC GUIDE. New York: B. Franklin, 1977. 396 pp.

2152. Cutter, Ch. and M. F. Oppenheim [eds.]: JEWISH REFERENCE SOURCES: A SELECTIVE, ANNOTATED BIBLIOGRAPHIC GUIDE. New York: Garland Pub., 1982. 180 pp.

2153. Edelheit, Abraham J. and Hershel Edelheit [eds.]: BIBLIOGRAPHY ON HOLOCAUST LITERATURE. Boulder, CO: Westview Press, 1986. 842 pp.

2154. ENCYCLOPAEDIA JUDAICA. 16 vols. + 3 Yearbooks. + Decennial volume. Jerusalem: Keter, 1972-1982.

2155. Engelman, Uriah Z. [ed.]: JEWISH EDUCATION IN EUROPE 1914-1962: ANNOTATED BIBLIOGRAPHY. Jerusalem: Hebrew Univ. Institute of Contemporary Jewry, 1966. 430 pp.

2156. Fraenkel, Josef: GUIDE TO THE JEWISH LIBRARIES OF THE WORLD. London: World Jewish Congress, 1959. 64 pp.

2157. ___: THE JEWISH PRESS OF THE WORLD. London: World Jewish Congress, 1972. 128 pp.

2158. Gilbert, Martin: JEWISH HISTORY ATLAS. Rev. Edition. New York: Macmillan, 1976. 121 pp.

2159. Gurock, Jeffrey: AMERICAN JEWISH HISTORY: A BIBLIO-GRAPHICAL GUIDE. New York: ADL, 1983. 195 pp.

2160. Kaplan, Jonathan [ed.]: INTERNATIONAL BIBLIOGRAPHY OF JEWISH HISTORY AND THOUGHT. Jerusalem: Magnes Press / Munchen: K. G. Saur, 1984. 483 pp.

2161. Lehmann, Ruth P.: NOVA BIBLIOTHECA ANGLO-JUDAICA, 1937-1960. London: Jewish Historical Society of England, 1961. 232 pp.

2162. Mason, Philip P.: DIRECTORY OF JEWISH ARCHIVAL IN-STITUTIONS. Detroit: Wayne State Univ. Press, 1975. 72 pp.

2163. Mendelsohn, Ezra [ed.]: THE JEWS OF EAST-CENTRAL EUROPE BETWEEN THE TWO WORLD WARS: A SELECTED BIBLIOGRAPHY. Jerusalem: The Zalman Shazar Institute, 1978. 62 pp.

2164. Orenstein, Sylvia [comp.]: SOURCE BOOK ON SOVIET JEWRY: AN ANNOTATED BIBLIOGRAPHY. New York: American Jewish Committee, 1981. 116 pp.

2165. Robinson, Nehemiah [ed.]: DICTIONARY OF JEWISH PUB-LIC AFFAIRS AND RELATED MATTERS. New York: Institute of Jewish Affairs, 1958. 232 pp.

2166. Roth, Cecil [ed.]: MAGNA BIBLIOTHECA ANGLO-JUDAICA: A BIBLIOGRAPHICAL GUIDE TO ANGLO-JEWISH HISTORY. London: Jewish Historical Society of England, Univ. College, 1937. 464 pp.

2167. Sable, M. H. [ed.]: LATIN AMERICAN JEWRY: A RESEARCH GUIDE. Cincinnati: Hebrew Union College Press, 1978. 633 pp.

2168. Segall, Aryeh [ed.]: GUIDE TO JEWISH ARCHIVES. Jerusalem: World Council on Jewish Archives, 1981. 90 pp.

2169. Singerman, R. [ed.]: ANTISEMITIC PROPAGANDA: AN AN-NOTATED BIBLIOGRAPHY AND RESEARCH GUIDE. New York: Garland Pub., 1982. 448 pp.

2170. ___ [ed.]: THE JEWS IN SPAIN AND PORTUGAL: A BIBLI-OGRAPHY. New York: Garland Pub., 1975. 364 pp.

Glossary

AGUDAS YISROEL: Non-Zionist religious party founded in Germany in 1912.

ALIYAH: Immigration of Jews to Eretz Israel.

ALLIANCE ISRAELITE UNIVERSELLE: French based, world Jewish philanthropic organization founded May 1860.

ANSCHLUSS: The forcible reunification of Germany and Austria, March 13, 1938.

AREVUT: Mutual responsibility.

ARMEE JUIVE: Jewish anti-Nazi underground movement in France founded in 1940.

ASHKENAZI/ASHKENAZIM: Jews living in and originating from northern Europe.

AUSMERZUNG: Total anihilation.

AUTONOMISM: The belief in Jewish spiritual nationalism, popular between the two world wars, which called for the granting of autonomy to diaspora Jewish communities.

AVODAH: Worship services.

BAR-MITZVAH: The coming of age ceremony for 13 year-old Jewish boys.

BETH DIN/BATEI DIN: Rabbinical court[s].

BETH MIDRASH: House of study.

BILDUNGSBUERGERTUM: Cultural citizenship in the "Germanic" nation.

B´NAI B´RITH: World-wide Jewish social organization founded in the United States, November 1, 1843.

BUND: The General Jewish Workers Union of Lithuania, Poland, and Russia, the Jewish Marxist nationalist party founded October 7, 1897.

CENTRALVEREIN: Central organization of German citizens of the Jewish faith founded in 1893.

CPSU: Communist Party of the Soviet Union.

DEUTSCHTUM: Germanness.

DHIMMI: Protected minorities in the Muslim world, primarily Jews and Christians.

DINA DE-MALKHUTA DINA: Jewish legal principle which stipulates that the law of the land has validity in Jewish law.

EDAH HAREDIT: Ultra-Orthodox non-hasidic Jewish communities in the United States, Israel, and western Europe.

ERETZ ISRAEL: The Land of Israel.

FARAYNIKTE PARTIZANER ORGANIZACIE: United Partisan Organization, the Jewish underground of the Vilna ghetto.

GALUT: Diaspora, exile.

GENIZAH: Storage room for disused sacred items.

GEZEROT TAH-VE-TAT: Jewish term for the Chmielnicki massacres during the Cossak uprising in Poland, 1648-1649.

GOLAH: Dispersion, the Jewish communities outside Eretz Israel.

HA´APALAH: Jewish immigration in opposition to the British blockade during the Mandate.

HABAD: Lubavitcher world movement.

HAGANAH: Defense, Jewish underground movement in pre-state Palestine founded in 1920 and the core of the IDF.

HALAKHAH: The traditional Jewish law.

HALAKHISTS: Interpretors of the law.

HALUTZ/HALUTZIM: Pioneer[s].

HASIDEI UMOT HA´OLAM: Righteous gentiles.

HASIDISM/HASIDIM: Jewish mystical-pietistic religious movement arising in eighteenth century eastern Europe.

HASKALAH: Movement for Jewish enlightenment originating in Germany during the eighteenth century.

HAUSFRAU: Housewife.

HAVURA: Group of individuals with similar interests, usually associated with a synagogue.

HAZAKAH: Talmudic principle for the establishment of claims of possession and occupation.

HAZZAN/HAZZANIM: Cantor[s], leader of synagogue services.

HEIKHAL SHELOMO: The seat of the Chief Rabbinate of Israel.

HEKDESH: Poor-house.

HEVRA KADDISHA: Burial society.

HEVROT/HEVRAH: Friendly societies within the Jewish community.

HIBAT ZION: Love of Zion, Zionist organization founded by Leon Pinsker in Russia in 1882.

HISTADRUT: General workers union of Israel founded in 1920.

HITLAHAVUT: The hasidic doctrine calling for enthusiastic performance of Jewish rituals.

HOFJUDEN: Court Jews.

IRGUN ZEVAI LEUMI: National military organization, one of the underground movements in pre-state Palestine.

JUDENAELTESTE: Elder of the Jews, head of a Judenrat.
JUDENFREUNDSCHAFT: Friendship with Jews.
JUDENRAT/JUDENRAETE: Nazi-imposed Jewish governing bodies.
JUDENTUM: Jewishness.
JUDENWAHLEN: "Jew elections."
JUDENZAEHLUNG: Jewish census.
KABBALAH: Jewish mysticism.
KAHAL/KEHILLAH: The organized Jewish community, or the
  council running the community.
KAISERJUDEN: The King´s Jews.
KASHRUT: Jewish dietary laws.
KAVANAH: Concentration in prayer.
KETUBAH: Jewish marriage contract.
KHEYDER: One room shtetl school.
KIBBUTZ: Zionist communal settlement in Eretz Israel.
KIDDUSH HA´SHEM: Martyrdom; sanctification of the Divine
  Name.
KLAL YISRAEL: The universal community of all Jews.
KOLEL: Post-graduate rabbinic study center.
LANDSMANSCHAFTEN: Immigrant societies of Jews from a town,
  city, or district in eastern Europe.
LIKKUD: Israel´s center-right party, founded by Menachem
  Begin in 1973.
LOHAMEI HERUT ISRAEL: Fighters for the freedom of Israel,
  the "Stern Gang."
MAGYAR: Hungarian.
MAHAL: Abbreviation for Foreign Volunteers who served with
  the fledgeling Israel Defense Forces [IDF] in 1948.
MAPAI: The Israel Labor Party, founded in 1930.
MARRANO/MARRANOS: Lit. pigs. The popular name for Spanish
  Jews who, under duress, converted to Christianity during
  the late Middle Ages.
MASKILIM: see Haskalah.
MASORATI: Traditional.
MEGILLAT TAANIT: First century Jewish historical text.
MISHPAT IVRI: Jewish civil law.
MITNAGDIM: Opponents of hasidism.
MOSSAD LE´ALIYAH BET: Agency for "illegal" immigration in
  Mandatory Palestine.
MUSAR: Ethics.
NUSAH/NUSHAOT: Variations on the order of the daily prayers.
RASHI: Acronyn of Rabbi Solomon ben Israel, northern French
  scholar and exegete [1040-1105].
REBBE: see Zaddik.
RECONQUISTA: The Christian reconquest of Spain [eleventh to
  fifteenth centuries].

REICHSVERTERTUNG: State representation, German Jewish communal organization founded in 1933.

SAMIZDAT: Underground publishing and distribution of ideas banned by the Communist government in Russia.

SANHEDRIN: Assembly of seventy-one scholars which functioned as both court and legislature in ancient Israel. The Paris Sanhedrin was called in 1806 by Napoleon Bonaparte to deal with the modernization of French Jewry.

SEPHARDI/SEPHARDIM: Jews living in or originating from Spain.

SERVI CAMERAE: Serfs or slaves of the chamber.

SHABBAT: The Sabbath

SHEMA: Jewish prayer asserting God's oneness.

SHEMONEH ESREI: The eighteen benedictions of Jewish daily prayer.

SHIFLUT: Humility.

SHTETL: Small Jewish community of eastern Europe.

SIDDUR: Prayer book.

SZLACHTA: Landed-gentry, Assembly of Nobles in early modern Poland.

TALMUD: Rabbinic commentaries on the Mishna, compiled between 300-500 C. E.

TARBUT: Zionist school organization in interwar Poland.

TIKKUN: To repair and transform the world.

TORAH: The Five Books of Moses; the Written and Oral Law.

TZEDAKAH: Charity.

VA´AD ARBA ARATZOT: Lit. Council of the Four Lands; the governing body of Polish-Lithuanian Jewry before the eighteenth century.

VA´AD LEUMI: The representative body of Palestinian Jewry under the British Mandate, established in October 1920.

YAD VASHEM: The Israeli Holocaust memorial and research institution in Jerusalem.

YARHEI KALLAH: Bi-annual public Torah-study sessions.

YARMULKE[S]: Skull cap.

YESHIVA/ YESHIVOT: Academy for the intensive study of Talmud and rabbinic lore.

YEVSEKTSIA: Jewish sections of the Russian Communist party.

YIDDISHKEIT: Jewishness.

YISHUV: The Jewish settlement in Eretz Israel.

YIVO: Yiddish Scientific Institute.

YOM KIPPUR: The Day of Atonement.

ZADDIK: A hasidic master.

ZAKHOR: [Biblical injunction] to remember.

Author Index

Title Index

A

482

C

G

H

S

Subject Index

Acculturation, 1, 4-40, 51, 61, 63, 66-68, 75, 80-83, 85,
104, 118-121, 123, 125, 135-142, 145, 150, 162, 211-215,
229, 233, 238, 292-297, 365, 396, 575-576, 591-592, 601-
603, 606-608, 612, 639-640, 654, 659-661, 663, 666, 751-
755, 760, 812, 832, 838-840, 863, 873, 877-878, 880-881,
908-909, 911, 953, 984, 986-987, 1011, 1013-1016, 1018-
1020, 1024, 1052, 1081, 1085-1087, 1089, 1095, 1107-1109,
1137, 1144, 1155, 1219, 1227, 1229, 1322, 1324, 1333, 1339,
1362, 1365, 1370, 1374, 1454, 1456-1457, 1460-1461, 1464-
1467, 1470-1471, 1473, 1477-1479, 1483, 1485-1486, 1488,
1490-1493, 1495, 1499-1503, 1505, 1513, 1552, 1560-1562,
1583, 1665, 1679, 1683, 1695, 1700, 1702, 1719, 1731-
1734, 1736, 1747-1748, 1753, 1772, 1789, 1795, 1797, 1818-
1819, 1823, 1826-1829, 1831, 1833, 1842, 1844, 1846, 1864,
1870, 1875, 1883, 1890, 1892, 2096-2098, 2133-2135, 2137,
2144, 2147.

Afghanistan, Jews of, 1, 75, 303, 555, 1880, 1895-1896.

Agriculture, Jews in, 1-4, 7-13, 15-16, 18-21, 23, 27, 29,
31, 34-39, 90, 121, 192, 293, 297, 390-391, 396, 433, 481,
525-526, 566, 615, 826, 832, 838, 846, 909, 912, 957, 986,
992, 1019, 1024-1025, 1027, 1035, 1059, 1095, 1098, 1374,
1376, 1456-1457, 1461, 1464-1465, 1467, 1531, 1644, 1654,
1694, 1819, 1860, 1864, 1883, 1908, 1942-1945, 1950, 1953-
1954, 1959, 1968, 1974, 2005, 2018, 2022, 2024, 2050, 2135.

Agudath Yisroel, 1, 4, 7, 10, 12-13, 23, 27-29, 31, 33, 40,
145, 161, 205-207, 217, 366, 368, 371, 374, 381, 394, 408-
409, 434, 462, 474, 513, 518, 531, 580, 603, 606, 617, 624,
668, 744, 748, 754, 825-826, 832, 838, 840, 846, 863, 900-
912, 924, 929, 933-936, 953, 1024, 1181, 1232-1233, 1461,

Antisemitism [cont.], 1865, 1870, 1875, 1878-1883, 1886-
1887, 1889-1892, 1904-1905, 1908, 1910, 1917, 1922, 1929-
1933, 1941, 1944, 1947, 2001, 2025, 2050, 2063, 2090, 2096-
2099, 2102, 2119-2120, 2122-2123, 2133-2135, 2143-2147.

Arab-Israeli conflict, the, 1, 4, 8-9, 12, 14, 16, 20, 23,
28, 31, 39, 303, 311-312, 339, 375, 381, 396, 399, 514,
525, 529, 558, 562, 564-565, 574, 1456-1457, 1461, 1470,
1500, 1502, 1583, 1851, 1879, 1883, 1890, 1892, 1942, 1944-
1945, 1947-1948, 1950, 1968, 1974, 1977-1979, 1985, 1988,
1996, 1998, 2001, 2005, 2007-2009, 2015-2017, 2019, 2021-
2022, 2024-2033, 2050, 2098, 2103-2104.

Arabs, Jews and, 1-5, 7, 10-13, 15, 19, 21, 24, 38-40, 45,
50, 84, 94, 112, 150-151, 217, 253, 255, 303, 309, 312,
396, 515, 526, 531, 826, 1878-1879, 1883, 1886-1888, 1890-
1893, 1904, 1917, 1920, 2001, 2005.

Argentina, Jews of, 1, 4, 6, 12, 20, 22-23, 29, 34, 39-40,
90, 102, 302, 347, 380, 384, 396, 433, 476, 481, 532, 535,
555, 826, 1362, 1372-1389.

Ashkenazim, 1-40, 59, 61-62, 75, 84, 87, 105-112, 116, 121,
142, 175, 192, 212, 214, 217, 221, 226, 236, 253-255, 273,
281, 309, 339, 379, 413, 425, 531, 664, 827, 838, 842, 848,
923, 984-985, 1034, 1093, 1098, 1107, 1109, 1127, 1245,
1252, 1255, 1311, 1374, 1454, 1456-1457, 1461, 1464-1466,
1477, 1485-1486, 1508, 1532, 1560, 1570, 1583, 1721-1722,
1753, 1767, 1818, 1829, 1848, 1865, 1880, 1890-1892, 1908,
1944, 1947, 1955, 2004, 2008-2009, 2013, 2015-2016, 2022,
2025, 2049-2050, 2070, 2134.

Assimilation, 1-7, 12, 21, 35-37, 45, 51, 53, 59, 61, 67-68,
79-81, 83, 101-104, 121, 135, 141, 145, 150, 182, 201, 218,
306, 309, 332, 336-337, 339, 368, 380, 396, 471, 496, 508-
509, 513, 518, 531-532, 576, 589, 591-592, 603, 637, 639,
644, 666, 751-752, 754-756, 820, 825-826, 838, 846, 857,
862-863, 878, 888, 908-909, 911-912, 953, 957, 984, 990,
992, 1023-1024, 1027, 1034-1035, 1085, 1090, 1107, 1109,
1138, 1147, 1155, 1219, 1265, 1288, 1339, 1387, 1422, 1456-
1457, 1465-1477, 1488, 1497-1500, 1503, 1531, 1596, 1679,
1767, 1781, 1795-1797, 1864, 2096-2098, 2123, 2135.

Auschwitz, 1, 4, 8-10, 16, 23, 25-28, 31, 33, 39, 90, 150,
302, 307, 311-312, 332, 339, 379, 396, 408-416, 419-420,
422-423, 425-426, 428-429, 433-434, 436, 441, 446, 450-452,
455-456, 458-460, 462, 465, 471, 473-474, 476-478, 508,